Introduction to Human Management

A Guide to HR in Practice

2nd edition

Charles Leatherbarrow
Janet Fletcher
Donald Currie

The Chartered Institute of Personnel and Development is the leading publisher of books and reports for personnel and training professionals, students, and all those concerned with the effective management and development of people at work. For details of all our titles, please contact the publishing department:

tel: 020 8612 6204

e-mail: publish@cipd.co.uk

The catalogue of all CIPD titles can be viewed on the CIPD website:

www.cipd.co.uk/bookstore

Introduction to Human Resource Management
A Guide to HR in Practice

2nd edition

Charles Leatherbarrow is a Senior Lecturer in HRM at the University of Wolverhampton.

Janet Fletcher is a Senior Lecturer at Staffordshire University.

The late **Donald Currie** worked as a personnel officer for over 15 years before joining Southampton Solent University as a lecturer in personnel management.

Chartered Institute of Personnel and Development.

Published by the Chartered Institute of Personnel and Development,
151, The Broadway, London, SW19 1JQ
First edition published 2006
Reprinted 2007, 2008, 2009

This edition first published 2010

© Chartered Institute of Personnel and Development, 2010

Typeset by Fakenham Photosetting Ltd, Norfolk
Printed in Spain by GraphyCems

British Library Cataloguing in Publication Data
A catalogue of this publication is available from the British Library

ISBN 978 1 84398 258 6

The views expressed in this publication are the authors' own and may not necessarily reflect those of the CIPD.

Chartered Institute of Personnel and Development, CIPD House,
151 The Broadway, London, SW19 1JQ

Tel: 020 8612 6200
E-mail: cipd@cipd.co.uk
Website: www.cipd.co.uk
Incorporated by Royal Charter
Registered Charity No. 1079797

Contents

Preface   vi
Overview of the book   vii
Walkthrough of textbook features and online resources   xiii

Chapter 1   Organisations   1

Chapter 2   Aspects of Organisational Culture   22

Chapter 3   Human Resource Management (HRM)   44

Chapter 4   The Role of the HR Practitioner   71

Chapter 5   Human Resource Planning   87

Chapter 6   Recruitment   119

Chapter 7   Selection   137

Chapter 8   Induction and Retention   158

Chapter 9   Learning   182

Chapter 10   Human Resource Development   200

Chapter 11   Performance Management   223

Chapter 12   Employee Reward   247

Chapter 13   The Employment Relationship and Work–life Balance   274

Chapter 14   Health, Safety and Well-being   310

Chapter 15   Diversity and Equality   337

Chapter 16   Understanding Employment Law   358

Chapter 17   Ending the Employment Relationship   396

Chapter 18   Change Management   409

Chapter 19   Handling and Managing Information   432

References   451
Index   471

Preface

The aim of this book is to cover both the theory and the practice of the employment cycle.

The book is aimed at students on the new CIPD Certificate in HR Practice (CHRP) course, but also for those taking higher-level studies – undergraduate or CIPD qualifications. Mapping of the chapters to the CHRP qualification is given at the end of the overview, on page xii.

The book will offer the opportunity for lecturers to give a focus to learning from both an academic perspective and also for those interested in developing practical student skills.

We have updated the first edition of the text to include the latest thinking and practice in HR. There are new chapters in this edition, covering 'Organisational Change', 'Understanding Employment Law' and 'Ending the Employment Relationship'. There is also a chapter on 'Handling and Managing Information' to fit in with the new CHRP qualification.

We hope you will enjoy studying human resource management and that you find the book useful.

Good luck.

Charles Leatherbarrow and Janet Fletcher

Lichfield, April 2010

Overview of the book

Chapter 1: Organisations

This chapter addresses the classification of organisations, HR's role, corporate strategy, policy and objectives, how organisations are structured and concepts such as span of control. The chapter further discusses how organisations are characterised in terms of staff numbers but also in terms of their role in business and society and how organisations interact with their business environment. Discussion addresses the role of corporate strategy in business development and the use of tools such as SWOT and PESTLE (STEEPLE), which can be used to assess the business environment.

Chapter 2: Aspects of Organisational Culture

The aim of this chapter is to introduce and provide an understanding of the importance of organisation culture. It links into other chapters in the book, specifically the chapters that address induction, reward, and health and safety. An attempt is made to demonstrate that culture forms the weave and weft of the fabric that identifies and distinguishes one, outwardly similar, organisation from the other, although both may be perceived by the external and casual observer to be very similar.

Chapter 3: Human Resource Management

Chapter 3 offers an explanation and discussion of HRM, its theoretical underpinning, the nature of HRM and the differences between HRM and personnel management. Reference is made to early theories of motivation management, Weber and bureaucracy, Maslow, Herzberg, and so on, the work of Trist and Bamforth in the context of the socio-technical theories of the organisation and how they impact upon the management of people.

The chapter also addresses the concepts of the 'hard' and 'soft' models of HRM, and the idea of the unitarist and pluralist approaches to the (theoretical) management of people. Consideration is also given to the contributions of Guest, Storey and Ulrich to the understanding of HRM and how it is set in an organisational environment.

Strategic HRM is also considered, in a limited manner, with discussion of three models of strategic HRM: the best-fit, the best practice and the resource-based view.

In the current climate of the 'customer is king', this chapter also addresses the link between HRM and customer service.

Chapter 4: The Role of the HR Practitioner

This chapter covers the roles and responsibilities of HR, seeing how the role of the HR practitioner operates within an organisational context, how the HR department functions and interrelates with the rest of the organisation as a source for advice and how it can give support to the line departments. The chapter also discusses HR information systems. It concludes with a look at the CIPD HR Profession Map and the expected behaviours of an HR professional.

Chapter 5: Human Resource Planning

The chapter begins with an explanation of the historical context of human resource planning (HRP) and then proceeds to show how it has changed over time from a role that gave focus to numbers, that of 'manpower planning' which concentrated on 'headcount' of staff present in an organisation, to one that gives concern and deliberate focus to the 'softer' developmental issues of people management and how these can be addressed when planning for the future, that is, moving from 'manpower', to 'human resource planning'. The core mechanisms for human resource planning are addressed:

- forecasting HR demand
- identifying sources of HR supply (internal to, and external from the organisation)
- producing the HR plan
- activating and maintaining the plan.

Key issues associated with the induction and retention of staff are discussed and details of the way that staff turnover can be calculated and how these figures can be usefully employed are included in the chapter.

HRP in its very broadest sense is discussed, addressing the idea of how HRP is impacted upon by HR supply plans, organisation and structure plans, employee utilisation plans, reward plans and so on.

Chapter 6: Recruitment

This chapter is about recruiting talent and follows the systematic recruitment cycle approach. The main objectives are to explain the purposes and the processes of recruitment. It looks at job analysis, writing job descriptions and person specifications, as well as advertising for the post. The legal aspects are addressed but a new section in the book addresses the legal requirements more fully.

Chapter 7: Selection

A natural progression from recruitment, this chapter covers the process of screening applications, shortlisting candidates and associated administration that surrounds the role. Various selection methods are discussed with particular attention paid to interviewing. As in Chapter 6, the legal aspects are addressed but additional detail can be found in Chapter 16, 'Understanding Employment Law'.

Chapter 8: Induction and Retention

The purpose of this chapter is to explore the importance and relevance of good induction processes. The questions of why, relating to purpose, and what, relating to content, are addressed in the course of this chapter. The notion of, and discussion around, the concept of the 'induction crisis' is also addressed and discussed.

Chapter 9: Learning

Learning is the foundation of training, development and performance in an organisation. The chapter explores the strategic nature of learning in an organisation, touching on the concept of human capital and generally lays the foundation of human resource development and performance management. Learning theories are considered together with learning styles and the links to career choice.

Chapter 10: Human Resource Development

This chapter starts by exploring the relationship between learning, training and development. It follows the systematic training cycle including training needs analysis, planning and delivering training, assessment and evaluation. The wider role of government and government initiatives are addressed in the course of the chapter.

Chapter 11: Performance Management

The chapter defines and describes performance management and its role in the workplace and looks at performance appraisal in particular. A range of motivation theories are explored and discussed. Different approaches to performance management are considered, such as the use of rating scales, 360-degree feedback, and so on. The concept of personal development plans (PDPs) is introduced.

Chapter 12: Employee Reward

This chapter explains the concept of reward, including payment and non-cash rewards. The discussion also distinguishes between different types of payment system, and a variety of approaches to job evaluation, performance-related pay (PRP) and profit-related pay. It also presents discussion on traditional and HRM approaches to reward (new pay as opposed to old pay), reward strategy and benefits.

Chapter 13: The Employment Relationship and Work–life Balance

Discussion centres on employee relations perspectives and policies, and managerial and employee attitudes and the notion and impact of the psychological contract. Contracts of employment are addressed but these are dealt with in greater detail within Chapter 16, 'Understanding Employment Law'. The theoretical perspectives of the unitary and pluralist views of the employment relationship are considered in the context of people management. The pluralist perspective is further expanded by considering, in some detail, the parties in the employment relationship. The chapter also addresses recent initiatives in workplace learning by the TUC and British-based unions.

Work–life balance is an important issue because of its relatively new place in business life. The chapter addresses the issue from two perspectives. From the employee perspective: how the tension between work and family can in itself bring about stress that can and does expand into the employee's ability to do their nine-to-five work-day role. In a similar vein, the work–life balance issue is addressed from the legal and employer perspective in terms of how the employer needs to respond to requests from employees, for example for flexible or part-time working.

Chapter 14: Health, Safety and Well-being

Although not part of the CIPD standards, this chapter is an integral part of the role of any business professional and no less so for the HR specialist. Discussion is made of the legal framework, the role of Health and Safety Executive (HSE) and the link between a positive organisational culture and a healthy workplace. Clear guidance of what employers must do in the context of health and safety management is offered to readers. The chapter addresses managing stress, the issue of stress in the workplace, including employee assistance programmes, relevant law and the idea and practice of risk assessment as well as employee well-being.

Chapter 15: Diversity and Equality

This chapter considers diversity and equality issues in the workplace. It addresses equality from both a legal point of view and a 'business case' perspective. Discrimination on the grounds of sex, race, disability, age, sexual orientation, religion or belief is discussed and the concepts of stereotyping, direct and indirect discrimination and institutional discrimination are all covered. The related issues of bullying and harassment are also discussed.

Chapter 16: Understanding Employment Law

The chapter addresses the employment contract, its nature and the obligations it places on the two parties, and how this impacts upon the employment relationship. This chapter links with Chapter 13 on the employment relationship and work–life balance.

Specifically the chapter considers the essence of a contract and the differences between the various types of contract that are in the employment relationship, the main terms and conditions of employment, employee rights and where information, within the statutes of law, can be found.

The chapter specifically explores the legislation that supports family-friendly policies and rights and employee well-being, such as the right to request flexible working and to whom the right extends. A chapter on employment law cannot be complete without discussion of equal rights legislation, with some discussion about privacy and the need to control information, and the issue of data protection.

Discussion of and about grievance and disciplinary procedures and how to manage them within the law is addressed with some guidance on the type of disciplinary rules organisations could adopt.

Chapter 17: Ending the Employment Relationship

This chapter discusses why and how the employment relationship can be ended, the issues around fair and unfair dismissal and how the types of dismissal can affect both the employee who is about to leave the company, as well as those existing employees who remain, particularly in the case of redundancy.

Discussion is held on what is fair and unfair dismissal (for example constructive dismissal) and the relevant legislation and guidance that surrounds these issues. As a specific case the chapter addresses how a redundancy situation should be handled from an HR perspective, for example how to select for redundancy, together with the relevant legislation that impacts upon this form of fair dismissal. Ways of avoiding redundancy are discussed with a final section of how to manage the survivors of the redundancy process.

Chapter 18: Change Management

This chapter specifically addresses the need for change, the drivers (triggers) and the types of resistors to change. The organisational development and emergent approaches to change are specifically discussed, showing that different approaches are needed to manage the change process. Included are some tools to help analyse and thus to manage the change process. Discussion of how changes impact upon employees and how this can be managed and the role of HR in the change management process are addressed.

Chapter 19: Handling and Managing Information

This chapter relates particularly to the CIPD unit 'Recording, Analysing and Using Human Resources Information' and discusses how information can be identified and used for the benefit of organisations. The chapter is based around a case study of a fictitious organisation that has recruitment and retention problems. The reader is taken through, step by step, the process of collating, presenting and analysing data to identify problem areas and develop solutions. There is an introduction to data management techniques and ways of presenting information.

The content of the CIPD Certificates in HR Practice and Learning and Development Practice are covered as follows:

Unit code	Unit title	Relevant chapter
4DEP	Developing Yourself as an Effective Human Resources or Learning and Development Practitioner	Ch 1, 3, 4, 9, 10, 11
3HRC	Understanding Organisations and the Role of Human Resources	Ch 1, 2, 3, 4
3RAI	Recording, Analysing and Using Human Resources Information	Ch 4, 5, 8, 10, 15, 16, 19
3RTO	Resourcing Talent	Ch 6, 7, 8, 10, 11, 16
3CJA	Contributing to the Process of Job Analysis	Ch 5, 6
3PRM	Supporting Good Practice in Performance and Reward Management	Ch 11, 12
3SCO	Supporting Change within Organisations	Ch 2, 18
3MER	Supporting Good Practice in Managing Employment Relations	Ch 11, 13, 15, 16, 17
3DLA	Delivering Learning and Development Activities	Ch 9, 10, 11
3LNA	Undertaking a Learning Needs Analysis	Ch 9, 10, 11
3PDL	Preparing and Designing Learning and Development Activities	Ch 9, 10, 11
3ELA	Evaluating Learning and Development Activities	Ch 9, 10, 11
3DCS	Developing Coaching Skills for the Workplace	Ch 9, 10, 11
3DMS	Developing Mentoring Skills for the Workplace	Ch 9, 10, 11

Walkthrough of textbook features and online resources

LEARNING OBJECTIVES

After studying this chapter you should understand:

- organisations: what they are for and how they are classified
- why organisations are designed in the way they are
- corporate strategy, policy and objectives
- SWOT and PESTLE (STEEPLE) analysis
- the flexible firm.

LEARNING OBJECTIVES

At the beginning of each chapter a bulleted set of learning objectives summarises what you can expect to learn from the chapter, helping you to track your learning.

ACTIVITY 11.3

In your organisation, or one with which you are familiar, analyse the performance appraisal system with a view to updating and improving it. Prepare yourself to answer questions on why your proposed changes would improve the system.

ACTIVITIES

Questions and activities throughout the text encourage you to reflect on what you have learnt and to apply your knowledge and skills in practice.

CASE EXAMPLE

SHAREHOLDER POWER AT ROYAL DUTCH SHELL

Reported in the *Financial Times* by Kate Burgess and Michael Steen on 20 May 2009, *Shell's executive pay plan voted down in shareholder rebellion*.

Shareholders voted down by a majority 'no' vote the proposal on executive pay. Shareholders were concerned because Royal Dutch Shell had not met its performance targets for the year, yet the board still wished to pay its executives significant bonuses.

This was just one of several similar events where shareholders had rebelled against proposals for senior staff pay awards in other companies in the UK.

CASE EXAMPLES

A number of case studies from different sectors will help you to place the concepts discussed into a real-life context.

PAUSE FOR THOUGHT

Is money a motivator? Consider your own situation. Would you still go to work if you were paid less? Does money actually make you work harder? What about voluntary work? What makes people work in that situation – where they are not paid?

PAUSE FOR THOUGHT

Boxes provide questions or facts to keep you thinking about the key themes of the chapter.

KEY CONCEPT: CORPORATE STRATEGY

Corporate strategy is a decision-making process by which the organisation attempts to meet its objectives. It is the way in which the organisation plans its long-term future.

DEFINITIONS AND KEY CONCEPTS

Boxes give explanations of key terms and concepts in the book.

REVIEW QUESTIONS

1 How would you define the basic concept of unlawful discrimination?

2 What do people mean when they talk or write about diversity in the organisation?

3 How would you distinguish between the 'business case' and the 'social justice' case for recognising and respecting diversity?

4 What factors in an individual or group might arouse a person's prejudices?

5 Name the main Acts that legislate against unfair discrimination in the UK.

6 Under the Disability Discrimination Act, what do you understand by the term 'reasonable adjustment'?

7 It has been suggested that we should examine to what extent our impressions of others are based upon stereotyping. What are the dangers of doing this?

8 How do we distinguish 'direct' from 'indirect' discrimination?

9 What might constitute a 'genuine occupational requirement'?

10 What should a policy on bullying and harassment include?

REVIEW QUESTIONS

These review questions are aimed at reinforcing what you have learnt in the chapter.

EXPLORE FURTHER

BOOKS

DANIELS, K. and MACDONALD, L. (2005) *Equality, diversity and discrimination.* **London: CIPD.**

This text is recommended for those who wish to take a special and detailed interest in this subject.

WEB LINKS

Acas (age discrimination): www.acas.org.uk/index.aspx?articleid=1841

Acas (bullying and harassment): www.acas.org.uk/index.aspx?articleid=797

Directgov (disabled people, employment rights): www.direct.gov.uk/en/DisabledPeople/index.htm

Equality and Human Rights: www.equalityhumanrights.com/

Gender Identity Research and Education Society: www.gires.org.uk/grp.php

EXPLORE FURTHER

Explore further boxes contain suggestions for further reading and useful websites, encouraging you to delve further into areas of particular interest.

ONLINE RESOURCES FOR TUTORS

Visit **www.cipd.co.uk/tss**

· LECTURER'S GUIDE – practical advice on teaching an introductory HRM module using this text

· POWERPOINT SLIDES – build and deliver your course around these ready-made lectures, ensuring complete coverage of the module

ONLINE RESOURCES FOR STUDENTS

Visit **www.cipd.co.uk/sss**

· WEB LINKS

Organisations

INTRODUCTION

The organisation provides the background within which the HR function works, so if you are studying HR for the first time, you need to develop a clear understanding of the context in which it is set. In other words, you need to have a sound understanding of organisations because the nature of the organisation impacts upon how we manage people. The purpose of this chapter, therefore, is to help you to develop that understanding so that you can operate efficiently and effectively.

USING THIS CHAPTER

This is a chapter that (we hope) you will find yourself dipping into from time to time for information about organisations. Different categories of organisation are explained as well as how their purposes vary from one to another. The explanations of corporate strategy, policy formulation and objective-setting will help you to understand how the organisation assesses and reviews its past performance, how it plans its long-term future and operates in the day-to-day context.

ORGANISATIONS

WHY ORGANISATIONS EXIST

We live in a society that is dominated by organisations. All of the major factors of our lives – our birth, health, education, marriage, employment, even our death – are influenced or handled by one kind of organisation or another. So why do we create organisations? The fundamental answer is that we do so in order to survive. Unlike other living creatures, human beings are rational and are therefore able to reflect upon their past, assess their current situation and make plans for the future. Since we are aware of our survival needs of the future, we create organisations to ensure that those needs will be met. The interdependency of human life makes the need for an organisation an imperative.

Organisations allow us to manage a range of complex activities that result in the provision of a product or service to a customer.

There are therefore vast industries involved in producing our basic needs, such as those for food, drink, shelter, security and a host of essential services; and on the lighter side, there are travel and entertainment companies. In fact, organisations are set up to serve us, not solely in order to survive, but to survive for longer, in greater comfort, and so that we may lead an interesting and pleasurable life. Organisations are the infrastructure of modern civilised societies.

PUBLIC SECTOR ORGANISATIONS

The UK has a *mixed economy*, which means that some organisations are managed by central government. For example, government departments and local authorities provide us with essential services such as those for health, education, highways, policing, social services and dealing with emergencies. These organisations are said to be in the *public sector*. The provision of such services as drinking water, drainage, gas, electricity and public transport used to be in the public sector, but privatisation towards the end of the twentieth century transferred them to what we call the *private sector* (see below).

Ultimately, all public sector organisations are responsible to central government; and those who run them, the politicians, are accountable to the public. They derive their authority to make decisions and take actions on our behalf from what we call *public trust*. If the public is not satisfied with the way the politicians are managing, they can replace them at the next election through the voting system. Usually, politicians are amateurs in terms of the specific responsibilities they are given, and the policy decisions they make are based upon advice from employed experts, who also have the decisions implemented. These experts, who are senior civil servants, remain in their positions regardless of any political changes that the electorate makes, hence the term *permanent secretary*.

PRIVATE SECTOR ORGANISATIONS

The *private sector* is made up of industrial and commercial companies that have evolved to respond to the stable and changing demands of the market. Each company exists to make a profit and is owned by its *shareholders*, who are the prime beneficiaries. The members of the *board of directors*, who are responsible for managing the company, are elected to their positions by the shareholders. In the private sector, therefore, it is said that directors' authority to make decisions and take actions is derived from the *ownership* of the organisation.

The directors on the board are employed experts who formulate and implement policy. If the shareholders do not approve of the way the organisation is being managed, they can vote for changes in particular decisions, and when they think it is necessary, they may vote directors out of office. The shareholders' opportunity to vote arises at the organisation's *annual general meeting (AGM)*, where the directors report on the past year's performance, particularly the financial performance, and state their plans for the future. In reality, shareholding has become scattered widely among individuals and institutions, and many shareholders never attend AGMs.

DEFINITIONS OF ORGANISATIONS

There have been many definitions of organisations, mostly drafted by academics. How an academic defines an organisation is usually determined by why they are defining it in the first place. Economists, management scientists, social scientists and organisational psychologists have produced new and different ways of looking at organisations, while other definitions have been produced by working managers.

 CASE EXAMPLE

SHAREHOLDER POWER AT ROYAL DUTCH SHELL

Reported in the *Financial Times* by Kate Burgess and Michael Steen on 20 May 2009, *Shell's executive pay plan voted down in shareholder rebellion*.

Shareholders voted down by a majority 'no' vote the proposal on executive pay. Shareholders were concerned because Royal Dutch Shell had not met its

performance targets for the year, yet the board still wished to pay its executives significant bonuses.

This was just one of several similar events where shareholders had rebelled against proposals for senior staff pay awards in other companies in the UK.

Theorists study organisations through the framework of their own particular science; each will study different aspects and, not surprisingly, they all define them differently. Academics and practising managers have been studying organisations and how they should be managed for more than 100 years, and some of them say that the study of organisations and the study of 'management as an organisational process' are inextricably linked. Indeed, E.F.L. Brech (1965), a management theorist, defines organisations as 'the framework of the management process'.

Schein (1980) defines the organisation as:

> the planned coordination of the activities of a number of people for the achievement of some common, explicit purpose or goal, through division of labour and function, and through a hierarchy of authority and responsibility.

 ACTIVITY 1.1

Using Edgar Schein's definition of an organisation, do you think it adequately describes the activities of:

- the Royal Society for the Prevention of Cruelty to Animals (RSPCA)
- a hiking club
- British Petroleum (BP).

As well as defining organisations, theorists also classify them. Above we described organisations as *public* and *private* sector undertakings. In 1966, Blau and Scott classified them in terms of who are the prime beneficiaries of the organisation. They proposed four types:

- **Mutual benefit organisations**, in which the members are the prime beneficiaries. A trade union is one obvious example. Others include sports and social clubs, some building societies and professional institutions, such as the Chartered Institute of Personnel and Development (CIPD).

- **Business concerns**, in which the shareholders are the prime beneficiaries. These are commercial and industrial profit-oriented organisations. Examples are motor car manufacturers and supermarkets.

- **Service organisations**, in which the prime beneficiaries are the users, such as customers and clients. Examples of such organisations are health and educational institutions.

- **Commonweal organisations**, in which the public are the prime beneficiaries. Examples are the armed services, central and local government and the United Nations Organization (Blau and Scott 1966).

Charitable organisations in the UK have grown considerably since Blau and Scott proposed their classification. It was claimed then that any organisation would fit into one of their four categories, but it is difficult to see how any of them could accommodate a charitable organisation; perhaps there is room for a fifth category.

Further work by Maltby (2003), cited in Kew and Stredwick (2008, p123) suggests that the typology defined by Blau and Scott (1966) is perhaps too simplistic and dated. It is suggested that a continuum of types, ranging from nationalised to private companies, is probably more realistic:

- nationalised industries

- public PLCs, where a company operates as though it is in the private sector (the Post Office)

- public interest companies (Kew and Stredwick quote Network Rail as an example of this type of company)

- public–private partnerships, including privately funded institution (PFI) contracts

- regulated private companies – these are typically privatised institutions such as the water and gas boards

- private companies.

 ACTIVITY 1.2

Think about the organisation for which you work or one with which you are familiar. Where does it fit into Blau and Scott's or Maltby's typology? What kind of organisation is it? Who are the prime beneficiaries?

MECHANISTIC AND ORGANIC ORGANISATIONS

Burns and Stalker (1966), after extensive research into organisations, defined them according to the degree to which they were mechanistic or organic. The research was related to the marketing function and market forces.

Mechanistic organisations

The researchers said that mechanistic organisations are those that have been serving a stable market for many years, that is to say that the demand for their products has consolidated, the assumption is made that things will not change significantly, and therefore the product demand, in terms of quantity and quality, can be predicted with a reasonable degree of accuracy. Internally, the result is a highly structured organisation with centralised policies, rigid hierarchical ranks, a strong emphasis on administration and tightly drawn boundaries between the departments and functions.

Organic organisations

Conversely, where customer demands are ever-changing, a mechanistic approach would seriously inhibit the organisation's ability to remain in the market. This kind of market situation, say the researchers, demands a flattened structure, *colleague*, rather than *command and control relationships* as the predominant mode, short-lived and flexible administrative systems and fuzzy departmental boundaries.

This is not to imply that industry is a dichotomy in which some organisations are totally mechanistic while others are totally organic. Organisations may be more or less mechanistic or more or less organic, which is best thought of as a dimension, ranging from mechanistic through to organic:

Mechanistic ←→ movement ←→ *Organic*

All organisations can be found somewhere on this dimension. Also, as market demands change and new products are developed, organisations are seen to shift to the left or right as they become more organic or more mechanistic.

SIZES OF ORGANISATION

Finally, organisations may be classified by their size. They may range from the sole proprietor type of business to vast international and multinational undertakings employing hundreds of thousands of people. Curran and Stanworth (1988) identify three categories of size:

1 **Small to medium-sized enterprises (SMEs)**, which are subdivided by the European Commission into:

   i.   micro-enterprises, with fewer than 10 employees

   ii. small enterprises, with between 10 and 99 employees

   iii. medium-sized enterprises, with 100–499 employees.

2 **Large commercial enterprises** with over 500 employees.

3 **Public sector organisations**, such as those described earlier in this chapter.

Within this wide variety of sizes, the way in which HR is managed varies in style and sophistication. In micro-enterprises, for example, HR is dealt with by the owner(s), as are all of the management functions. Inevitably, in some cases, professional standards and legal requirements and compliance with employment legislation may be questionable, yet the employee relationship can be positive. The larger organisations, on the other hand, use systems and procedures that are based on sophisticated strategies and policies and they usually employ an HR professional to manage the complex personnel-related policies.

Small to medium-sized enterprises

There has been considerable growth in SMEs in recent years, and their importance to the economy has grown commensurately, employing collectively large numbers of people. The owners of such enterprises are usually busy people and are reluctant to allocate time to academics who wish to carry out research. Price (1997), however, says that smaller companies should be fruitful subjects for study because many conduct people management in the direct fashion advocated by HRM models.

Future growth

SMEs are a dynamic force in any country's economy; they are tomorrow's large organisations. They tend to start up on the basis of a single idea, and those that succeed go on to diversify and grow further. While it is clear that they do not all succeed and grow, many do, which is when they introduce the professional element into their internal systems, such as marketing, management and HR.

THE PURPOSES OF ORGANISATIONS

The main purposes of all organisations are to provide: a service or financial return for those that they serve, to survive and to develop. To survive, the organisation must continue to provide the kinds of goods and services demanded by its customers and clients, bearing in mind, of course, that such demands change. Organisations also stimulate demand by creating and marketing new products and by modifying existing ones. The mobile telephone is an example of continuous modification.

CORPORATE STRATEGY

Everyone wants the organisation to succeed and achieve its purposes of survival and development, and it is the responsibility of those at the very top, the board of directors, to ensure that this happens. Someone has to be at the steering wheel making decisions about the direction that the organisation should take; such decision-making is complex and sometimes involves considerable risk. The people at the wheel, making the decisions that shape the future direction of the organisation, are engaged in *strategy*. We discuss strategy in greater depth later in this chapter. Suffice to point out at this stage that strategy exists at corporate and operational/functional levels.

 KEY CONCEPT: CORPORATE STRATEGY

Corporate strategy is a decision-making process by which the organisation attempts to meet its objectives. It is the way in which the organisation plans its long-term future.

OBJECTIVES AND POLICIES

For the organisation to reach its strategic goals, *objectives* are set, which are targets that need to be achieved by pre-specified dates. The achievement of objectives is a critically important factor in which appropriate timing is vital. The work that leads to the achievement of objectives has to be carried out within the limits of the organisation's *policies*. Policies are statements of intent about how the organisation proposes to conduct its business and achieve its strategic objectives. The organisation's specialists draft procedures that describe how policy decisions are to be carried out.

 ACTIVITY 1.3

Find a copy of your organisation's policy on matters of health and safety at work. You should also find that there are procedures that describe how the policy is to be implemented.

When the organisation knows where it is going (it has a *strategy*), what it has to do to get there (it has *objectives*) and how and when it is going to achieve those objectives (it has *policies and procedures*), attention may be turned to *resources*. The organisation needs resources in the form of money, materials, machinery and, of course, the human resource.

SURVIVAL AND DEVELOPMENT

As we have seen, the main purposes of any organisation are to survive and develop (and to give returns to its shareholders in the case of a company), and to do this it has to continue to supply the types of goods and services demanded by its customers and clients. It is vital for a business to keep a keen eye on the activities of its competitors, changing market demands and the nature of internal and external pressures. The senior managers and specialists, therefore, carry out an annual review of the organisation's performance, and at the review, questions are asked about the internal and external situations. In today's fiercely competitive markets and rapidly developing innovation, such monitoring is a continuous, day-to-day process, since the rate of change in today's businesses is greater than ever before. Annual reviews are still held, especially in public limited companies (PLCs), but what is discussed there now is the cumulative product of continuous monitoring. The organisation's current situation is discussed and strategic decisions are made about the future. In short, the process appraises the organisation's past performance and makes plans for the future.

CASE EXAMPLE

When the Corporate Strategy Section of J.K. Jones Ltd was conducting its annual review of the company's performance, it came to light that while the objectives it had set in the last period had been achieved in principle, there was room for improvement in certain areas. Productivity, for example, had experienced difficulty in keeping pace with sales, so the meeting decided to have the problem investigated with a view to improving productivity for the forthcoming year. The investigative report, which took into account how their competitors had changed their business, showed that investment in new technology would facilitate increased productivity and thereby solve the problem.

STRATEGIC PLANNING TECHNIQUES

Two main techniques have been developed to provide a structure to the strategic planning process, and it is vital for the aspiring HR practitioner to understand and be able to use these techniques.

The first was developed by Ansoff (1987). It focuses on an organisation's *strengths, weaknesses, opportunities* and *threats* and is usually referred to by the acronym SWOT. The second technique focuses on the internal and external pressures that impinge upon an organisation and these include such factors as political, economic, social, technological, legal-related and environmental pressures. The acronym PESTLE is used to refer to this technique; this has been modified and extended and is sometimes called a STEEPLE analysis (see below).

SWOT analysis

Of the two techniques, this is the most well known. What follows is an analysis of the process that demonstrates the extent of the detail that goes into its application.

Strengths are the valuable and successful aspects of the organisation, such as having ample resources, highly skilled people and appropriate technology for achieving the objectives. Being good at product design, quality assurance and customer care are also examples of strengths, since they help to sustain and improve the organisation's position in the market. The organisation may also be doing well in some particular functions of the business, for example the engineering or finance function; it is a good idea to analyse this to see if lessons may be learned for other functions.

Weaknesses are the organisation's negative features, such as financial or skill deficiencies, out-of-date work systems or poor employee relations. The identification of weaknesses is essential since areas for improvement have to be addressed urgently.

Opportunities are events or openings that may arise from the market or other areas of the business environment. Perhaps the need for a new or modified product is identified, or it may be that the organisation's unique skills can be applied to a new venture or diversification.

Threats can arise from the business environment. For example, an aspiring competitor may be about to invade the market and endanger the business. Competitors are also a threat when they modify standard products to achieve a market advantage. In this analysis, threats are usually thought to be external, but of course, threats may also arise from poor internal relations; it could be that employees are dissatisfied with the terms and conditions of employment and are threatening to interrupt business progress by taking industrial action.

 ACTIVITY 1.4

Examine your own organisation and assess how it would stand up to a SWOT analysis. Make a list of what you regard as:

(i) its strengths and (ii) its weaknesses and think about how they might be capitalised upon and improved respectively.

PESTLE or STEEPLE analysis

Organisations have to keep abreast of, and respond to, the internal and external pressures that impinge upon them.

Political interventions are pressures that appear in the form of new legislation, particularly on business practices, employment, health and safety, taxation and many other factors. In today's global market, however, pressures may also relate to overseas trading, for example, in the form of European policies on agriculture and regulations relating to commercial fishing. New employment legislation carries implications for the organisation, and these are discussed in Chapter 16, 'Understanding Employment Law'. In the wider overseas trading context, internationally agreed sanctions may curtail, or even outlaw, our trading with particular countries that, for example, may be involved in terrorism or human rights abuses.

Economic changes – the influence of regional, national and international economic conditions plays a large part in the fortunes of organisations. Sometimes the economy is buoyant and in a state of boom and plenty, unemployment is low, industrial and high-street spending is high and property values soar. At other times the economy dips and the 'highs' that are mentioned above go into reverse. These are exactly the 'bust' conditions of an economic recession as caused by the banking crisis that occurred from 2008 and into 2009 in the UK. Organisations have to adjust to the alternate peaking and dipping of the economy and, internally, they must prepare themselves accordingly; sometimes though it is difficult to prepare, especially if the downturn has been caused by an unforeseen crisis, as mentioned. In a global economy, competition is very fierce, and organisations take steps to ensure that they remain competitive. HR specialists keep an eye on the changing economy, since in a good economy when the organisation is expanding, there are usually staff shortages, especially of rare technical skills, but when it is bad and the organisation has to contract, redundancies may have to be made.

Social trends, in which market demands change according to changes in cultures, values, fashion, and even mere whim. The rate at which social preferences change can limit or extend product lifecycles and, internally, the need to keep pace will create the need for more frequent changes to be made. For example the concern for climate change has caused people to think about ecology and ecological issues, which has caused large and small organisations alike to consider how they should respond to reduce their 'carbon footprint' and so become more environmentally friendly.

Technological innovation occurs on two broad fronts. The first is in terms of process innovation, which includes modifying or replacing machinery and the production and administrative systems, because new and better systems have been developed, giving greater productivity, cost-efficiency and effectiveness. The second is in terms of product innovation, in which new products and services are developed and/or modifications to existing ones made. Organisations tend to develop their own product innovation. So far as process innovation is concerned, organisations are largely 'users' of technology that has been developed by manufacturers of capital equipment and computer software.

Legal-related pressures derive from competition law, government and EU policy, and, in a broader sense, safety issues such as the recent law on corporate manslaughter. Employment legislation is continually being added to, which makes the life of the HR professional that much more complex, yet interesting. Over the past several years much legislation has been associated with welfare at work, for example the Working Time Directive and the Work and Families Act (2006), which provides rights for a parent of a child under 16 (18 if disabled) to *apply* for a change in working arrangements. Rights extended in 2007 to employees caring for adults.

Environmental factors – people are now extremely concerned about the effect that industrial activity is having on the environment, and pressure groups monitor and frequently demonstrate against particular business and scientific activities. Pressure groups such as Greenpeace monitor oil spills, deforestation and a host of other effects upon nature. Animal rights activists apply considerable pressure to organisations that carry out biological and cosmetic tests on living creatures, and sometimes even make physically violent attacks on the premises of such organisations and on the people who work within them.

A more recent approach is to turn the anagram around, add an 'E' and call it STEEPLE. The extra 'E' stands for ethical considerations (Kew and Stredwick 2005, p3).

USING SWOT AND PESTLE (STEEPLE) ANALYSES

The information that is derived from carrying out SWOT and PESTLE (STEEPLE) analyses, including the facts that have accumulated as a result of continuous monitoring, provides a basis for the decisions that are made about the organisation's future. Where problems have come to light, the strategists look for causes with a view to resolving the problems, and where strengths are identified, they examine the possibilities of improving on those strengths in the future. This results in organisations formulating new policies to respond to the influences of legislation and other pressures.

 ACTIVITY 1.5

It has been noticed that some students confuse these two analytical techniques. Consider your own organisation in the light of both, and note the different answers that emerge from your analysis. While both are used to assist the strategic planning process, they should be kept apart conceptually because they serve different purposes. SWOT analysis is a reality check on the organisation's internal and external situations and its past performance, while PESTLE analysis focuses on the internal and external pressures that impinge upon the organisation. Looking at your own organisation in this way will enable you to remember which is which.

ORGANISATIONAL STRUCTURES

Most of us are familiar with the conventional shape of an organisation's structure. It has a hierarchical design with descending levels of authority. Viewed vertically, we can see how the various departments and specialisms are separated, while laterally, we can see the layers that indicate levels of authority and responsibility.

 KEY CONCEPT: CORPORATE STRUCTURE

Commonly referred to as the 'organisational chart', the corporate structure is a hierarchical design (like a family tree), which may be 'tall', meaning that there are many layers of authority and responsibility, or 'flat', meaning that there are fewer layers. Tall structures are generally bureaucratically managed, while with flatter structures managers and employees usually work together in a 'colleague' type of relationship, in which communication is eased and more direct.

The structure shows the relationships that exist between the employees at *vertical* and *horizontal* levels, which are referred to as *vertical* and *horizontal integration*. The structure also outlines what we call *vertical* and *horizontal differentiation*. Vertical differentiation can be seen in the different roles of people within a department or function, such as in the role of the HR director who has reporting to them the resourcing manager, who has, in turn, administrative staff reporting to them. The structure not only shows the chain of command but also, in a similar way, the vertical hierarchy of how roles are differentiated. On the other hand, horizontal differentiation can be seen in the way that functional managers take responsibility for separate departments, such as the roles of the marketing manager, finance manager, the production manager and so on. (You will find that some writers use the word *lateral* instead of *horizontal*.)

 SOMETHING AFOOT

CASE EXAMPLE

Jane Firmstone is a regional sales manager for Something Afoot, a company providing tough footwear for agricultural workers, climbers, and so on. Jane has divided the region into three districts and John Glass, Jim Ford and Masha Veretov are her district representatives. Before leaving home, John telephoned Jane to say that he would be calling in to the regional sales office on his way home to let her have a detailed breakdown of his sales figures for last month. This pleased Jane because she is about to compile the regional sales report for that month and she is anxious that her figures stand up well in the light of those from other regions with which her

figures will be compared. The sales figures and current profit and loss accounts are provided by the senior accountant, Jatinder Sandhu, who reports directly to Jane. In terms of the organisation's structure Jatinder is on a similar level as the three district sales representatives.

Just before ringing off, Jane wished John luck with Grays, an awkward client that she knew he was seeing that day, 'and don't go giving them discounts above the company norm, you know it annoys them at head office'. John is worried about his call on Grays. It is his district's largest shoe store and at one time was Something Afoot's biggest retail outlet. Over the past year, however, Grays has stocked fewer and fewer of Something Afoot's products and replaced them with imports from Poland. John believes that the problem lay in his company's introduction of a standard discount policy a year ago. Previously, the sales staff had been free to determine the discounts they offered, and major clients were able to obtain larger discounts than are possible under the company's new standard discounts policy.

John cheered up as he thought of lunch. He had arranged to eat with Masha Veretov. She had promised to bring samples of some of the company's latest designs that John thought would be of particular interest to Grays, whose customers are particularly fashion-conscious. John reflected that working with the sales team was not so bad. They really are a team and their monthly meetings are one of the best parts of the job.

 ## ACTIVITY 1.6

Read the above case example and list all of the examples you can find of:

- horizontal differentiation
- vertical differentiation
- horizontal integration
- vertical integration.

DESIGNING THE STRUCTURE

Designing a structure is not a simple task. Before embarking upon such a project, the needs of the organisation have to be identified. Child (1988) says that most of the information one needs can be found in the answers to five key questions:

1 Should jobs be broken down into narrow areas of work and responsibility so as to secure the benefits of specialisation, or should the degree of specialisation be kept to a minimum to simplify communication and to offer members of the organisation greater scope and responsibility in their work?

2 Should the overall structure of an organisation be 'tall' rather than 'flat' in terms of its levels and spans of control? What are the implications for communication, motivation and overhead costs of moving towards one of these alternatives rather than the other?

3 Should jobs and departments be grouped together in a 'functional' way according to the specialist expertise and interests that they share? Or should they be grouped according to the different services and products that are being offered, or the different geographical areas being served, or according to yet another criterion?

4 Is it appropriate to aim for an intensive form of integration between the different segments of the organisation, or not? What kind of integrative mechanisms are there to choose from?

5 What approach should management take towards maintaining adequate control over work done? Should it centralise or delegate decisions? Should

a policy of extensive formalisation be adopted in which standing orders and written records are used for control purposes? Should work be subject to close supervision?

If we examine these questions, we see that Child presents us with alternatives, implying that each organisation has its own specific structural needs. The questions have very strong human resource implications in terms of 'greater scope and responsibility' (question 1), 'communication and motivation' (question 2) and 'sharing specialist expertise and interests' (question 3). According to the principles of HRM, these advantages are best achieved by introducing a flattened rather than a tall structure, so that managers and employees can work closely together, and the integrity of formal, vertical communication is improved, since it passes through fewer hierarchical levels.

Organisational structures are designed to reflect the roles and relationships of the various positions and employees. The structure should show the logic underlying the division of the organisation's expertise and how functions are placed to work in a co-ordinated way.

Brooks (2009, p191) writes of the traditional view of organisational structure: 'It describes the way an organisation is configured into work groups and the reporting and authority relationships that connect individuals and groups together.'

Restructuring may be seen as a reflection of the need to make internal changes to continue to complement external changes. In the early twentieth century, academics and practising managers produced theories that have come to be known as classical approaches to management, which were succeeded by the human relations approach, management by objectives, system and contingency theories and, more recently, human resource management.

While some of these ideas remain relevant for particular organisations, the adoption of the principles and techniques of human resource management (HRM) has significant implications for structures.

SPAN OF CONTROL

This term relates to the number of employees that fall directly under the control of one manager. Given that the organisation has a particular number of employees, the number of layers in the overall structure will be determined by the sizes of the spans of control within it. Organisations with tall spans of control will have many layers (as in Figure 1.1), and those with flattened ones will have fewer layers. Structures are referred to as 'tall' or 'flat' and the advent of HRM in the 1980s brought with it a tendency for organisations to flatten their structures (see Figure 1.2).

One of the effects of the trend towards flattened structures was to reduce the number of managers and increase the number of employees reporting to each manager. This changed employees' working situations in that in addition to

Figure 1.1 A conventional organisational structure (tall structure showing 55 jobs on 5 levels)

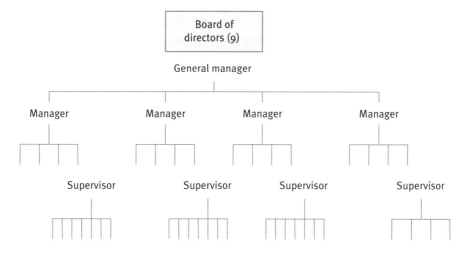

Figure 1.2 Span of control influencing structure (flat structure showing 54 jobs on 4 levels)

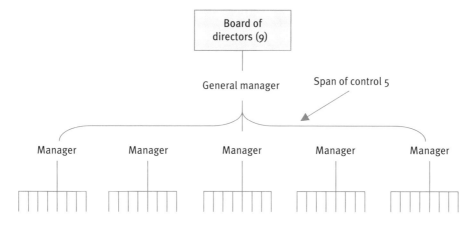

having to adapt to changes in the work itself, they found themselves reporting to different managers and working with different colleagues.

MATRIX ORGANISATIONS

This form of structure may be introduced in organisations in which there is a need for teams to work on projects, such as those in the construction industry, civil engineering and other types of commissioning firms. Matrix structures may also be found in an enterprise in which there is a need to set up a temporary unit to carry out a specific project. Managers and specialists are seconded from different parts of the organisation for the duration of the project. On completion, the team may be disbanded and reintegrated into the main structure, or may move on to another new project; an organisation may have several projects running concurrently. A civil engineering concern, for example, may, *inter alia*, be carrying out such projects as building a bridge in the Midlands, a tunnel in Scotland, a high-rise building in Belfast and a road in East Anglia.

A matrix design is typified by a grid that depicts a two-dimensional track of authority and responsibility. Authority and responsibility in the functional departments track downwards, while from the project manager, authority and responsibility track laterally across the main structure. In this way, project managers may look across the organisation to access its resources, a concept that produces economic as well as practical advantages (see Figure 1.3).

Matrix structures have drawn criticism from employees. They say they become frustrated as a result of working for two bosses: first, the functional heads to whom they report, and second, the project managers who make demands on their services. Such frustrations usually arise from conflicting time constraints and priorities.

Figure 1.3 How a matrix organisation works

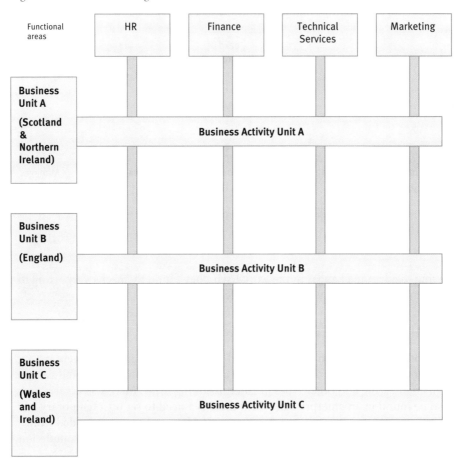

In the example in Figure 1.3, the company is split into three business units based on a geographical split of responsibilities. Each business can call on the services of HR, Finance, Technical and Marketing as they require. The advantage for the business unit is that they can control their costs and create a sense of competition because it is clear, in the matrix organisation, that HR, Finance, Technical and Marketing are service functions. One could imagine the scenario if it was considered that the finance function, for example, were deemed not to be providing an efficient service to Business Unit A, then that business unit could go outside the larger organisation and 'buy in' financial services.

THE FLEXIBLE ORGANISATION

The need for senior managers to focus on survival and development while remaining competitive in a fierce global market has caused them to review their attitudes towards employment, and *flexible working* (not to be confused with 'flexi-time') is one of the ideas that has emerged. Flexible working was first introduced in the early 1970s, when it was referred to as *core staff theory*, but did not become widespread until the 1980s and popularised through the work of Atkinson (1984). Within this concept, the notion that the organisation needs to access particular skills no longer implies that it has to offer a conventional full-time contract of employment. The nature of the contract offered to the person is determined by the rarity and availability of their skills and the amount of time for which those skills are needed. For these reasons, the terms and conditions of employment vary from one category of employee to another. Organisations distinguish between *core* and *peripheral* workers (see Figure 1.4).

CORE AND PERIPHERAL WORKERS

Referring to Figure 1.4, the core workers are those who are regarded as critically important to the organisation and who are, therefore, encouraged to stay by virtue of attractive prospects, rewards and usually good terms and conditions of service. Core staff are recognised as highly skilled and motivated technical, scientific or professional people without whom the organisation cannot optimise performance. They also tend to have a range of skills (functional flexibility) and significant discretion as to how they go about their work. Positive retention planning, therefore, has become an integral part of HR strategy.

Peripheral workers, on the other hand, are not treated so generously and have little scope for discretion as to how they can do their work. In some cases they would not be discouraged in seeking employment elsewhere; they are more expendable. In a similar manner, if extra staff are required in this group then they can be readily recruited. Peripheral groups 1 and 2 sit within the confines of the organisation and members of these groups would be paid directly from the payroll. Specifically, peripheral group 1, in Figure 1.4, would be those types of worker who would be doing repetitive jobs such as accounts payable or production work. In the context of Atkinson's model, this group would be

Figure 1.4 Flexibility in organisations (adapted from Atkinson 1984)

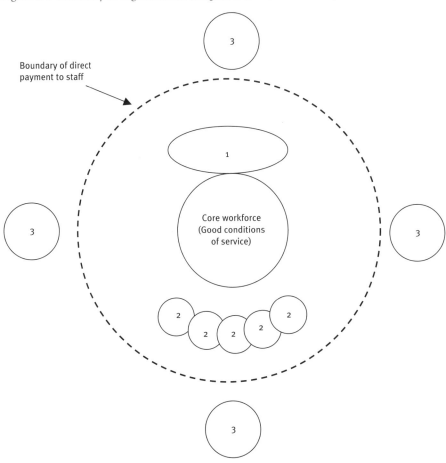

ascribed as 'numerical flexibility'. Their contracts of work, in respect to working hours and types of hourly contract, can be varied.

The second peripheral group would not be a homogeneous group, *per se*, but the grouping is associated with how work is managed. For example, this group could be job-share people, part-time workers; it could even include delayed recruitment or short-term contracts to cover absences or peaks in workload, or work that is of a repetitive nature. This secondary group could also include apprentices, some of whom could, at some time later depending upon individual competence, transfer to the core group of employees and so be part of the 'talent pipeline'.

Finally the flexible firm includes those who are not directly employed by the organisation, the third or tertiary peripheral group. This group would include the self-employed, contractors, temporary workers and of course outsourced activities.

The idea of having workers who are in receipt of different terms and conditions of service can, of course, create issues between those who have the better conditions of service and those who have not. Interestingly the Government intends to introduce a bill that will harmonise the pay and some conditions of agency workers, called the 'Agency Workers' Directive'; this was initially proposed for introduction in 2009 but has been postponed until 2011.

The organisation's attitude towards different categories of worker is reflected in the *reward management* structure. The development of the ideas behind the flexible firm has grown in popularity for several reasons:

- operation of new technology that demands higher skills
- need for greater economic efficiency
- need to improve upon and sustain the quality of the organisation's product
- need for a more flexible and speedy response to external demands
- need for a greater degree of involvement and, thereby, satisfaction on the part of valued employees.

THE VIRTUAL ORGANISATION

A futuristic example of the flexible organisation is summarised by Robbins and Judge (2009, p564), in which they describe the 'virtual organisation' as 'a small, core organization that outsources major business functions'. They describe the American 'motion picture' (film) industry as a prime example of this type of organisation. Many hundreds of specialists, ranging from electrical technicians to camera operatives to catering companies, all come together to create a picture then disperse before being called together once again to make another picture at a different location under a different production company.

SUMMARY

In this chapter we learned why organisations exist: to provide goods or services to a consumer. We also learned how to classify organisations, whether they are public or private sector and also how they are structured. Organisations can be classified as:

- mutual benefit
- business concerns
- service organisations
- commonweal organisations.

This classification was later modified by Maltby (2003):

- nationalised industries
- public PLCs
- public interest companies
- public–private partnerships, including privately funded institution (PFI) contracts

- regulated private companies
- private companies.

As well as classifying organisations by the type of service they offer we also saw that they can be classified as to whether they are mechanistic or organic, and also in terms of their size, ranging from micro to small, medium and large, rather like clothes.

As well as being able to describe organisations, as above, we also considered how to, in a systematic way, consider the internal weaknesses and strengths of an organisation using the SWOT analysis technique and to identify, looking outwards from the organisation, the immediate issues that the business environment offered or threatened using a PESTLE (STEEPLE) analysis.

Work was discussed in the context of horizontal and vertical integration, and terminology such as 'span of control' was introduced to further extend our understanding of how business is discussed.

Finally, the chapter addressed how organisations can structure themselves, from a strategic perspective, in the form of the 'flexible firm', a concept that was first attributed to Atkinson in 1984.

REVIEW QUESTIONS

1 What are the main purposes of all organisations?

2 Name the four categories into which Blau and Scott classified organisations.

3 From where do those who manage public and private sector organisations derive their authority to make decisions and take actions?

4 What are the main differences between the two main techniques (SWOT and PESTLE [STEEPLE]) that senior managers use to assist the strategic planning process?

5 What HR implications arise from the five questions posed by Child (1988) when considering the design of an organisation's structure?

6 What do you understand by the following organisation forms:
- nationalised industries
- public PLCs
- public interest companies
- public–private partnerships, including privately funded institution (PFI) contracts

- regulated private companies
- private companies.

7 In the above example, where would a charity and a university be placed?

8 What do we mean by 'flexible working'?

9 Has your organisation adopted any flexible working practices? Do you see any real advantages in what management have done? Do you think there are opportunities to introduce flexible working practices?

10 What do you understand by the term the 'flexible firm'?

11 In the context of the flexible firm, in terms of the peripheral groups, where would those working annualised hours fit?

12 What is outsourcing?

13 Why does the first peripheral group in the flexible firm have poorer conditions of service than the 'core' group? Is this unfair? How does HR manage the tensions generated?

EXPLORE FURTHER

BOOKS

KEW, J. and STREDWICK, J. (2008) *Business environment: managing in a strategic context.* **(2ⁿᵈ ed.) London: CIPD.**

Although Kew and Stredwick's book is written for a postgraduate CIPD course, it is very accessible and opens up a broader understanding of the business context, including discussion of the role of government, the European Union and the impact of demographic change.

MULLINS, L.J. (2009) *Management and organisational behaviour.* **(8ᵗʰ ed). Harlow: Pearson Education.**

A good all-round text on organisational behaviour (OB) and management, Mullins is suitable for both undergraduate and postgraduate students who are studying organisations for the first time. In the context of this chapter on the organisation, the Mullins text offers further insight into organisational setting, the structures of organisations, the nature of management and organisation management.

WEB LINKS

SWOT analysis (giving an explanation of what SWOT covers):

Institute for Manufacturing, University of Cambridge: www.ifm.eng.cam.ac.uk/dstools/paradigm/swot.html

CIPD factsheet on SWOT analysis: www.cipd.co.uk/subjects/corpstrtgy/general/swot-analysis.htm?IsSrchRes=1

PESTLE analysis:

CIPD factsheet on PESTLE analysis: www.cipd.co.uk/subjects/corpstrtgy/general/pestle-analysis.htm

CHAPTER 2

Aspects of Organisational Culture

LEARNING OBJECTIVES

After studying this chapter you should:

- understand the concept of culture, its values and norms
- understand and take account of your organisation's culture in your role as an HR practitioner
- understand the importance of culture as a determinant of workplace behaviour
- be able to demonstrate an understanding of how history, corporate climate, managerial style and other factors contribute to the make-up of culture.

INTRODUCTION

The aim of this chapter is to provide an insight into societal culture and an understanding of organisational culture: what it is, how it develops and its importance as the organisation's most powerful determinant of behaviour. In order for you to develop a complete understanding of what is meant by organisational culture, it will be helpful to provide first an account of how culture is perceived in the societal context. Reading about culture in extra-organisational contexts should help you to understand behaviour that occurs in a diverse workforce.

WHAT IS CULTURE?

As far back as 1871, the anthropologist Edward Tylor defined culture as 'knowledge, belief, art, morals, law, custom and any other capabilities and habits acquired through membership of society'. In a narrower sense the term is used to describe the differences between one society and another. In this context, according to Giddens:

> ... a culture is an all-pervasive system of beliefs and behaviours transmitted socially. Specifically, it consists of the sets of values and norms or rules held by a society, together with its material expressions. (Giddens 1989, p30)

Values are internalised by young people as they learn what is good and what is desirable. They define for us what is important and worth striving for. Values represent the basic conviction that in a personal or social context, a specific mode of conduct is preferable to any other.

 ### KEY CONCEPT: VALUES

A *value* is an ideal to which an individual subscribes; it is something that we would like to be true (Rollinson 2008, p130). People's values are learned during the socialisation process; individuals adopt them from the values of the society to which they belong; values have an influence on behaviour.

'In a Western society, for example, young people learn that achievement and wealth are important and indeed, the measure of an individual's achievement is usually indicated by the quality and quantity of his or her material possessions' (Haralambos 1986).

 ### KEY CONCEPT: NORMS

A *norm* is a tacit guideline that determines an individual's (or group's) behaviour in particular situations. For example, as a member of a group or team, or of a student group, you learn that there are particular behaviours that conform to the group's expectations, and behaviours that do not. If you breach the code of behaviour, the group will demonstrate its disapproval, usually by applying formal or informal sanctions.

If a norm is breached in a serious way, the sanctions will be more severe. The sanctions are designed to elicit conformity and are a significant feature of controlling overall behaviour and the maintenance of order in a society. Indeed, certain norms are incorporated into law and conformity is enforced through punishment.

THE POWER OF VALUES AND NORMS

The relationship between values and norms becomes clear when a breach of norms defies the group's values; the establishment of behavioural norms reflects its values. This concept extends beyond the group, into larger groups, and out into the whole of society itself: for example, the way people address each other, their table manners and how they conduct themselves in public. People dress according to what is expected of them on special occasions, such as a formal ball, a funeral, an evening at the theatre or visiting a friend in hospital. All such situations demand certain attire and particular ways of behaving.

So, examined through its systems of norms and values, 'The culture of a society is the way of life of its members; the collection of ideas and habits which they learn, share and transmit from generation to generation' (Linton 1945). At birth, children are totally helpless and dependent on others to provide for their needs. To survive in the longer term, however, children must develop knowledge and skills, and must learn how those around them survive. In other words, children must learn the culture of the society into which they were born.

Culture therefore has to be learned, and for a society to operate effectively, its 'guidelines' must be shared by its members through their behaviour. Learning and sharing a culture is achieved largely without conscious control. It just happens as people develop and become socialised, and even though it directs their actions and thinking, and establishes their outlook on life, most members of a society take their culture for granted. People are hardly aware of their culture, even though their adoption of its values and conformity to its norms demonstrate a mutual understanding of what is and is not acceptable.

DEFINITIONS OF CULTURE

It is difficult to define overall culture since it is an elusive concept. Culture is a dichotomy in the sense that it constitutes, first, visible and tangible factors, and second, abstract and intangible characteristics. For example, it was noted earlier that Giddens summarises culture as consisting of the sets of *values* and *norms* or rules held by a society, together with its material expressions. The term 'material expressions' refers to features of the environment that were put in place by people; this includes such tangible items as bridges, buildings, roads, tools, machinery and equipment. Values and norms, however, are among the abstract and intangible psychological characteristics of individuals and groups.

Herskovits (1948) defined culture as 'the man-made part of the human environment'. Triandis *et al* (1972) qualified this by pointing out that:

> ... this includes both physical objects, such as roads, buildings and tools, which constitute *physical culture*, and subjective responses to what is 'man-made', such as myths, roles, values and attitudes, which constitute *subjective culture*.

Later, however, Triandis further qualified this, saying that 'cultures are human creations but, unlike bridges, buildings, roads and other material objects of our making, cultures are subjective' (Triandis 1990, p36).

Undoubtedly there is a strong relationship between physical and subjective cultures. Subjective perceptions of how things are, how they should be and how they should look do vary from one society to another. For example, the architecture of buildings and the design of particular artefacts are determined by what, within a culture, is regarded subjectively as generally acceptable and right. This is reflected by the obvious differences in the appearance of buildings in different parts of the world. Even cooking utensils are specifically designed to meet idiosyncratic culinary needs, since what people eat and how their food is prepared vary from one culture to another.

It is in these and many other ways that cultures vary from one society to another, and since culture defines what is acceptable and what is not, frequent misunderstandings occur.

KEY CONCEPT: PHYSICAL AND SUBJECTIVE CULTURE

It seems that the physical culture, which is created by people, may be separated from the subjective culture, which is apparent through the values and norms of societies. It is certainly true that academics who have produced *non*-organisational definitions of culture all include the physical culture. As we shall see later, however, those who define organisational culture tend to exclude the physical aspects between members of different societies, as illustrated in the following example by Edward T. Hall (1973).

 SPACE INVADERS

CASE EXAMPLE

Two men, one from North America and one from South America, are chatting in a hall that is 40 feet long. They begin at one end of the hall and finish at the other end, the North American steadily retreating and the South American steadily advancing. Each is trying to establish the 'customary conversation distance' as defined by his culture. To the North American, his South American counterpart comes too close for comfort, whereas the South American feels uneasy conversing at the distance his partner demands. Sometimes it takes meetings such as this to reveal the pervasive nature of culturally determined behaviour. It is by understanding these types of cultural differences that people can eventually work with those from different societal cultures.

IDENTIFYING CULTURES

Misunderstanding may occur if cultures are treated as discrete entities. Just as there is diversity within indigenous populations, there is also *intra-cultural diversity* created by individual and small-group differences. Within a culture, groups (subcultures) look across at each other and do not always approve of what they see and hear.

ETHNOCENTRISM AND 'IN-GROUPS'

According to Price (1997, p125), we look at people from other cultures, see that their ways are different and often dislike these ways. Triandis (1990, p34) supports this view, saying that we use our own culture as the standard and judge other cultures by the extent to which they meet our standard. This is referred to as *ethnocentrism* and is similar to the *in-group* concept, the people with whom we identify.

Studies of ethnocentrism show that everyone tends to:

- define their own culture as 'natural' and 'correct' and other cultures as 'unnatural' and 'incorrect'
- perceive in-group customs as universally valid – what is good for us is good for everybody
- think that in-group norms, rules and values are obviously correct
- consider it natural to help and co-operate with members of one's in-group

- act in ways which favour the in-group
- feel proud of the in-group
- feel hostility towards out-groups (based on the work of Campbell et al, cited in Triandis (1990, p35) and Price (1997, p125)).

PAUSE FOR THOUGHT

If you were born and raised in, say, the United Kingdom, but felt in need of a change and wanted to abandon your roots to live elsewhere in the world, in what kind of society would you choose to live: a small tribal island in the Pacific Ocean? a Middle Eastern country? central Africa? Spain? Could you survive in another culture? Would you try to continue living like as a UK citizen or would you try to adopt the culture into which you had moved? Do you think it would take courage to make such a move? Do you know anyone from an entirely different culture who has moved to the UK? What sort of problems do they face?

WHERE DO WE FIND CULTURE?

When people speak and write about the 'English culture' or the 'Spanish culture', we somehow know what they mean. We take it that they are referring to particular idiosyncratic features that may be found only in England, and others that may be found only in Spain, but these might be thought of as *national differences*, as well as cultural differences. All countries have their own particular characteristics, and members of indigenous populations share dominant common values and conform to the accepted norms of their society.

While culture is not nationality, because there can be a range of people who have different ethnic backgrounds within one nation, the two do interact. Within any country, there are groups whose members share additional values, or perceive one of the common values as more important than any of the others, as the following example shows.

Animal rights

CASE EXAMPLE

One of the values that most people in the UK share is their disapproval of cruelty to animals, which is a value that is not held in all countries. For example, groups of animal rights activists regard the cessation of animal experiments as highly important, to the extent that they seek out those that they think are responsible and apply sanctions, sometimes including violence and other forms of intimidation. There are other, more moderate, animal rights groups who share the same singular value as the activists, but prefer to show their disapproval by staging peaceful demonstrations. These groups place one of the national values at the top of their agenda. Examples of other national values that receive the attention of particular groups include concerns about health and the environment.

DIFFERENCES WITHIN A CULTURE

Sometimes it is useful to regard culture as the personality of the group. In the case of individuals, it is their personality characteristics such as attitudes, values and beliefs that direct their behaviour, and it is not difficult to read this across and into group culture. The relationship between the group and a 'strong-minded' individual member can be quite complex. Sometimes such a member attains the leadership position, and therefore has an element of control over the group's behaviour, but if this does not happen, there might be costs to the individual in the form of reduced freedom of action. William Foote Whyte (1955, p331) wrote that:

> The group is a jealous master. It encourages participation, indeed it demands it, but it demands one kind of participation – its own kind and the better integrated with it a member becomes the less free he is to express himself in other ways.

PAUSE FOR THOUGHT

The individual and the group

At this point it is important to note that people's group behaviour is different from their individual behaviour. As we have seen, groups have values and norms to which their members adhere, but such conformity can be misleading. People place a high value on being accepted as group members, and when the situation demands it, they may suspend their values and conform to the group norms in order to sustain their group membership. Conversely, the value in question might be so deeply felt that they might decide not to conform to the norm and to leave the group rather than surrender that particular value.

THE BOUNDARIES OF CULTURE

Cross-cultural studies involve making comparisons between one culture and another. Naroll, who was involved in cross-cultural studies, devised the term *cultunit* to describe people who are domestic speakers of a common district dialect of a language, and who belong to either the same state or the same 'contact group' (Naroll 1970). Some cross-cultural psychologists study cultunits (which are small cultures); others study larger units, including states. From their studies, it is clear that the attitudes and values that determine behaviour in the individual, group and state change with time.

The boundaries of the cultunit, therefore, are time, place and language: *time*, because cultures change across time as old values and beliefs replace new ones; *place*, because we emphasise interpersonal contact within the location of the culture; and *language*, because it defines cultures by directing thinking and enables us to distinguish one culture from another. Consider the following example.

CASE EXAMPLE

Time, place and language

St Cyril, the ninth-century Greek missionary, travelled north out of Greece to preach Christianity. On his travels he encountered several tribes, each of which had its own encampment. Each was a discrete cultunit having its own location, language, values and rituals. The inter-group language barrier prevented communication between the tribes, who as a result were fearful and suspicious of each other.

St Cyril was unable to communicate with them and returned to Greece to consult his brother, St Methodius, and together they developed a new language. St Cyril returned to the tribes, taught them the new language and was then able to spread the Christian word. This also enabled the tribes to interact and integrate by forming themselves into larger units. The language had its roots in Greek, but since the ninth century it has become known as the Cyrillic language. Originally the Cyrillic alphabet

had 43 characters, but continuously changing versions have reduced this to about 30. Eventually the language became widespread among many tribes.

The modern Cyrillic language is spoken in about ten countries, including Russia, Belarus, Ukraine, Bulgaria, Serbia and other countries that were once part of the Soviet Union.

While this is an ancient example that demonstrates the linguistic ingenuity of the two Greek brothers, it also points to the effect that change can have upon cultures. The language, for example, removed the barriers between the tribes, extended the boundaries and helped to dispense with the fears and suspicions that they held about each other. Clearly, the tribes had integrated and shared the same, larger location.

PAUSE FOR THOUGHT

Although St Cyril used language to communicate and to spread, effectively, the Christian message and eventually the Cyrillic language became common across many countries, why do you think that the Russian language, which became compulsory across the Soviet Union after the 1918 Revolution, has been shunned in favour of the native languages of the countries that have split away from the Soviet Union – for example, Poland, Kazakhstan, Romania, Bulgaria – since the fall of the 'Iron Curtain' in 1989?

SUMMARY OF CULTURE (SOCIETAL CULTURE)

Culture may be perceived as *physical*, in the form of bridges, roads, machinery, tools, and so on, and as *subjective,* such as attitudes, beliefs, values and tacit norms. While culture is not religion, sex, race or nationality, they all do interact. History shows that the physical and the subjective elements of a culture change across time as scientific innovation and intellectual advancements replace old structural designs, attitudes, values and beliefs. Cultures relocate themselves and their languages become more complex; they are therefore continuously evolving.

ORGANISATIONAL CULTURE

Having studied the foregoing section, you should now have a sound understanding of the elements of societal culture. In this section, we examine the degree to which those elements can be read across into the organisational situation. First, however, the following definitions will clarify the concept of organisational culture.

KEY CONCEPT: ORGANISATIONAL CULTURE

Organisational or corporate culture is the pattern of values, norms, beliefs, attitudes and assumptions that may not have been articulated but shape the ways in which people behave and get things done. (Armstrong 2006, p304)

Other definitions are offered by Robbins and the CIPD:

Organisational culture refers to a system of shared meaning held by members that distinguish the organisation from other organisations. This system of shared meaning is ... a set of key characteristics that the organisation values. (Robbins and Judge 2009, p585)

The CIPD defines culture as:

a system of shared values and beliefs about what is important, what behaviours are appropriate and about feelings and relationships internally and externally. Values and cultures need to be unique to the organisation, widely shared and reflected in daily practice and relevant to the company purpose and strategy. But there is no single best culture. (Purcell et al 2004)

Many texts on business use the notion that organisational culture is the collection of relatively uniform and enduring values, beliefs, customs, traditions and practices that are shared by an organisation's members. These values, beliefs, and so on, are learned by new recruits, and so they are passed from one generation of employees to the next.

You may have noticed that the above definitions of organisational culture include only the subjective culture, those things that are intangible, untouchable, even though organisations do contain a physical culture, such as uniforms, buildings, equipment, machinery and tools. The physical culture is determined by the organisation's location and the nature of its technology. If, for example, you studied the culture in a Ford manufacturing plant, and then did the same in a Vauxhall plant, you would find strong similarities. This is because of the similarity of the design of the buildings, the machinery, the noises and the work systems; the technology determines the activities that employees have to perform to do their work. You would find, however, that while there are similarities in the subjective culture, they do not match exactly.

INDUSTRIAL CULTURE

Motor car manufacturing companies all have very similar technology, including their capital equipment and workshop layouts. An employee who has moved from one firm to another would recognise the physical culture and very quickly adapt to the subjective culture.

ACTIVITY 2.1

1   Do you think that what is said above is true of a variety of industries? Try to list similarities between large-scale firms in the retail business, for example the big supermarkets.

2   How would you identify the organisational culture of the firm you work for? What are its characteristics? Is it hierarchical? Do you have rituals (such as cakes or samosas on a Friday)? Is the boss approachable?

3   Compare and contrast the organisation culture of your firm with that of a colleague in your class.

The influence of the physical culture is demonstrated in the following case example, which is drawn from the industrial history of the UK.

CASE EXAMPLE

The Luddites

In the Lancashire cotton mills before the end of the eighteenth century, the cotton thread was spun by handicraftsmen and women. In the 1770s Arkwright, Crompton and Hargreaves invented labour-saving spinning machines that were capable of producing material of a higher quality and at a greater speed than was previously possible. In 1811, the craft spinners saw the machines as a threat to their livelihood, and, led by Ned Ludd, they vandalised the machines. The factory owners persisted with the machines, which, in modified form, were used until the twentieth century.

One of the features of the machines that was disliked intensely by the workers was the very loud noise they made. Previously, there was a strong social culture in the workrooms, but with the 'new' machines, they could not hear each other speak. They added lip-reading to their repertoire of skills, but to use their words, 'this place will never be the same again'. The change to the physical culture had altered the subjective culture, showing that they are interrelated.

The position then is that while the physical culture does have a strong influence on the overall culture of the organisation, it is the subjective culture that principally interests managers and HR practitioners. Robbins (2001, p53) supports this, saying that:

> … the physical properties of organisations tend to obscure the fact that organisations are really nothing other than an aggregate of individuals. Individuals, therefore, provide the foundation of the organisation; they bring it to life, and to understand why the organisation is what it is and why people behave in the way they do, you have to focus upon the individuals.

However, to moderate this view one must consider how individuals behave as groups when they are impacted by strong group norms and strong, either positive or negative, organisation cultures.

ORGANISATIONAL SUBCULTURES

The interested parties – managers and academics – tend to talk and write about any single organisational culture as if it is a uniform phenomenon, while in fact organisations are made up of subcultures that represent different professions, locations, functions and levels (Hampden-Turner 1990). This reduces the number of attitudes and core values that are shared across the whole organisation.

 KEY CONCEPT: SUBCULTURES

it seems, therefore, that from this one may deduce that the subculture on the workshop floor at, say, location A, will be different from that of the marketing department at location B. Furthermore, organisations may have a boardroom subculture, a middle management subculture, a staff subculture and a shop-floor subculture.

THE INFLUENCE OF SUBCULTURES

Furnham and Gunter (1993) describe the possible effects of the existence of subcultures at different levels and functions:

These sub-cultures can assume varying degrees of significance within the organisation, and can be beneficial if they adopt a common sense of purpose, but problems arise where they have different priorities and agendas. Then sub-cultures can clash with each other or with the overall corporate culture, impeding organisational functioning and performance.

CLASSIFYING CULTURAL THOUGHT

Clegg et al (2008) suggest that different perspectives can be taken on culture in respect of how they have been researched and are therefore viewed. They define three different perspectives:

- integration perspective
- differentiation perspective
- fragmentation perspective.

The *integration* perspective is a *managerialist* view of culture as opposed to a *social scientific* view of culture. The integration perspective assumes that management can mould and change culture and develop ways of working that, as Clegg et al (2008, p239) argue, '... promise the dissolution of all that friction and resistance that managers know they often produce routinely. ... In place of conflict is offered integration.' In this way the predominant ways of thinking and doing permeate throughout the organisation; there is a predominant culture that everyone understands. The idea is that an organisation *'has'* a culture that management can manipulate.

The *differentiation* perspective is based upon the view that the organisation is made up of a number of subcultures, which both have their own peculiarities and characteristics and will, in all probability, be different from each other (Huczynski and Buchanan 2007). In this sense the culture of an organisation cannot be defined in one way but is dispersed, having been built by groups or groupings that have different interests. As Huczynski and Buchanan (2007, p636) write, there is a 'cultural pluralism'. The idea of the *differentiation* perspective is that taken by the social scientist and so culture *'is'* and is defined by the subcultural groups and so is difficult to change, it being embedded into the deep-seated understanding of how a part of the organisation works.

The *fragmentation* perspective '… shares very little with the normative integration theorists …' (Clegg et al 2008, p242). It is a theory of the social scientific community, who argue that there is no consensus, even at a subcultural level, as to what a culture can be defined as, since cultural norms may be short-lived. That culture is only constructed because certain methods have been constructed with which to investigate it. In essence the argument centres on how culture is investigated. This does not mean to say that there is not a reality in what is described as a fragmented culture. The fragmentation can be caused by the fact that cultures are confused. One can imagine in an organisation, take a typical school, that there are cultural groupings made up of the functional sections – mathematics, languages, the arts, and so on – that are unique. Within these functional groups there are heads of department (HoDs) who together form a clique or grouping that report into a deputy head. The strength of the bindings will depend upon which 'cultural group' is the stronger. Is the departmental head grouping stronger, in terms of allegiance, or could the allegiance be to the functional group, of which the HoD is leader and a member? This duality could cause a fragmentation between allegiances.

WHY STUDY ORGANISATIONAL CULTURE?

As a subject of concern for managers and of study for academics working in the field of organisational behaviour, organisational culture emerged in the 1980s. It was always there, hidden in the general atmosphere of the place, and since it was finally teased out and studied, it has achieved an importance that ranks it alongside other principal aspects of management and organisational studies. Understanding culture enables HR practitioners, managers and consultants to understand why people in organisations behave as they do, and enables them to alter the culture to make it more conducive to the achievement of sectional and overall objectives.

According to Moorhead and Griffin (1992), organisational culture probably exerts the greatest influence on individual behaviour when it is taken for granted. One of the major reasons that organisational culture is such a powerful influence on employees in an organisation is that it is not explicit. Instead, it is an implicit – meaning it is not written down – part of the employees' values and beliefs. It is for these reasons that managers and academics study organisational culture.

INDIVIDUAL DIFFERENCES WITHIN CULTURES

When you ask people about where they work, they tend to tell you something of the nature of the business, and perhaps its size and location. Then when you go to visit the organisation you see its buildings, the machinery and equipment. None of this tells you what it is like to work there; only the people can tell you that. If you were to ask them, however, you would get a different account from each of them, since they are a diverse group and each will have their own unique interpretation of the place and of its culture. As an outsider, it is only from this combination of perceptions that you begin to get an idea of the kind of culture in which they work.

ORGANISATIONAL VALUES

The values and norms that make up the culture of the organisation are taken for granted by the employees ('the way things are around here') and there seems to be a degree of passive acceptance about this.

> They – the organisational values and norms – are basic assumptions made by employees, do not necessarily appear in a document and are not transmitted in a training programme, although they can be expressed in written form. (McKenna 1994)

If, however, you undertook to analyse the culture of an organisation to identify and describe it, you would find significant indications of its values in the:

- structure, which demonstrates the lateral layers of authority and decision-making and the vertical patterns of expertise
- documentation, particularly including HR policies such as the systems of performance and reward management
- managerial style, including the formal and informal modes of communication between managers and employees
- condition of the employee relationship, including agreements reached, the absence and staff turnover rates
- nature of the business.

IDENTIFYING ORGANISATIONAL CULTURE

In the 1970s and 1980s several academics attempted, through analysis, to identify and classify organisational cultures with a view to develop the ability of altering their nature to make them more conducive to the achievement of objectives. As you will see, the names of the classifications indicate the predominant characteristic of each type of culture. There are strong similarities between some of these classifications; the following describes two that are somewhat different from each other.

Handy (1976) proposed four types of culture as follows:

- **Power culture** is one with a central power source that exercises control. There are few rules or procedures and the atmosphere is competitive, power-oriented and political. It is useful for rapid response where power and control are important.

- **Role culture** is one in which work is controlled by procedures and rules, and the role, or job description, is more important than the person who fills it. Power is associated with positions, not people. It is useful where repetitive tasks are done and structures and procedures are important.

- **Task culture** is one in which the aim is to bring together the right people and let them get on with it. Influence is based more on expert power than on position or personal power. The culture is adaptable and teamwork is important.

- **Person culture** is one in which the individual is the central point. The organisation exists only to serve and assist the individuals in it. This can be effective in an innovative, entrepreneurial enterprise.

CASE EXAMPLE

Scott, A. (2008) Clashes mar mergers and acquisitions. *People Management*. 1 October.

Firms involved in mergers and acquisitions (M&As) are losing millions of pounds as a result of cultural integration issues, a survey has found. More than half of the 119 organisations across the Americas and Europe surveyed by consultants Mercer reported that the success of M&A transactions was marred by unsuccessful cultural integration.

Asked to estimate losses to their company in recent M&A transactions, 44% of America's firms said that between $1 million (£550,000) and $5 million (£2.8 million) was lost or not realised. Of the European firms, 43% suggested losses of between €1 million (£800,000) and €5 million (£4 million).

Elisa Hukins, leader for cultural integration at Mercer, said organisations that had invested in structured cultural integration processes and programmes from as early as the due diligence phase were reporting a more positive impact. She said: 'Organisations are starting to turn this tide by developing processes, tools and capabilities aimed at reducing the risks and taking advantage of the opportunities presented by organisation culture before, during and after a deal closes.' Bob Bundy, Mercer's M&A Global Leader, added that companies should start assessing cultural differences that would affect deal value as early as possible during the initial consideration of a deal. 'It is remarkable just how much information we are able to gather and analyse even without "touching" the target,' he said. 'We are able to inform senior teams about how differently the two organisations operate and behave, and identify potential challenges and risks to deal success.'

But the survey also highlighted the fact

that many organisations were not well prepared to manage cultural integration issues effectively. While nearly a quarter of companies are moving towards developing a more formal cultural integration process, 68% still do not regularly use a systematic approach to identify gaps between organisational cultures.

The survey was conducted by Mercer, whose website can be found at: www.mercer.com. At the time of writing this book (2009) a copy of their survey could be obtained by emailing: GlobalM&A@mercer.com

 ## ACTIVITY 2.2

With the above case example in mind, why do you think that different cultures can bring about the failure of two firms that have come together in what appears to be a harmonious and mutually beneficial relation? Explore this idea by investigating, using the Internet, how the merger of AOL and Time Warner became the most expensive failure in corporate history, costing $183 billion. Do you think that the barriers caused by incompatible cultures can be overcome?

You can obtain further help by reviewing in the CIPD's 'How to' documents on mergers and acquisitions. The most recent was published in *People Management*: Henri, C. (2008) How to … lend HR expertise to mergers. *People Management*, Vol 14, No 4. pp42–43.

Schein (1985) also proposed four types of culture:

- **Power culture** is one in which leadership resides in a few and rests on their ability, which tends to be entrepreneurial.
- **Role culture** is one in which power is balanced between the leader and the bureaucratic structure. The environment is likely to be stable, and roles and rules are clearly defined.
- **Achievement culture** is one in which personal motivation and commitment are stressed and action, excitement and impact are valued.
- **Support culture** is one in which people contribute out of a sense of commitment and solidarity. Relationships are characterised by mutuality and trust.

Typologies such as these provide indications of what happens in organisations according to the ideologies of the top managers and the type of organisation. One could, for example, draw parallels between what is said about *power culture* and what other writers have said about the *unitary perspective* (for example Fox 1966) (refer to Chapter 13); what is said about *role culture* and what writers have said about *bureaucracy* (for example Weber 1964); what is said about support culture and aspects of human resource management, such as commitment, solidarity, mutuality and trust.

This might be confusing to the student who is new to the study of culture, since the typologies say little about values and norms, which are two of the main components of culture. Particular attitudes and beliefs are implied by some of the qualifying descriptions; for example, 'strive to maintain absolute control over subordinates' and 'the role, or job description, is more important than the person who fills it'. If, on the other hand, we examine a perception that describes the dimensions of a single culture, we see it from a different perspective.

Trice and Beyer (1984) proposed an organisational culture consisting of four major dimensions: (1) company practices; (2) company communications; (3) physical cultural forms; and (4) common language:

1 **Company practices** consist of events and ceremonies that help employees to identify with the organisation and its successes. These might include employees attending an extended induction period, attending the ceremonial launching of a new product, or the opportunity to socialise informally at the annual ball or a sports event.

2 **Company communications** consist, *inter alia*, of informal chats such as when long-serving employees tell newcomers about past events and relate the myths and legends that are associated with the organisation. There are also signs and symbols designed to convey positive messages about the organisation, such as the company slogan, its logo, messages contained in the mission statement and in the marketing information.

3 **Physical cultural forms** include the design of the buildings and the nature of the capital equipment, which convey something distinctive about the organisation. It also includes the décor and the layout of the offices and workshops, including the posters, cartoons and even the screensavers that employees choose.

4 **Common language** is probably the most significant indication of overall organisational culture and the nature of the subcultures within it. In any organisation there is a secondary language that is not understood by outsiders. It is based on technical vocabularies and the 'in' jargon of the place.

As you can see, the work of Trice and Beyer (1984) resembles more closely the accounts of culture that are given in the first half of this chapter. References to signs and symbols, myths and legends, and the sharing of a common language indicate that the components and boundaries of ethnic culture can be detected within, and read into, organisational culture.

PUBLIC SECTOR CULTURE

Consider Lawton and Rose's (1994) work, cited in Kew and Stredwick (2008, p49), which argues that in the public sector there are four different cultures that are prevalent: (1) political culture, (2) legal culture, (3) administrative culture, and (4) market culture. To explain the meaning of these one can consider that the *political culture* is defined by the way local government officials have to engage with politicians. The *legal culture* is defined by how the work of many central and local government offices is controlled by a strong legal framework and there is a requirement to comply. The *administrative culture* is a function of how rules and procedures have been passed down from the time, pre-1980s, when bureaucratic processes were seen as important and finally, since Margaret Thatcher's Government of the late 1970s and into the 1980s, followed by the Labour Government of the late 1990s and into the twenty-first century, there has been a move to introduce market forces and commercial ways of thinking into how public services go about their work, especially in the context of meeting centrally set targets of performance.

Lawton and Rose's typology differs from that of Trice and Beyer in as much as they, Lawton and Rose, define culture by the way the public sector carries out work rather than considering the constructs of communication and the organisation's symbols that, as mentioned, have strong links with how societal culture is defined and that identifies Trice and Beyer's approach.

 ACTIVITY 2.3

Draw up a list of 15 words and terms that are taken for granted and used regularly by employees in your organisation (or an organisation with which you are familiar) but would not be understood if you used them at home or elsewhere.

For example in the process control industry they use the term **SCADA,** meaning a control system that gives: **S**upervisory **C**ontrol **A**nd **D**ata **A**cquisition.

THE IMPORTANCE OF PLACE

Earlier in this chapter it was noted that the boundaries of a cultunit are time, place and language. What follows is an explanation and discussion of the importance of *place* in relation to organisational cultures and subcultures. The discussion centres on the influence of the national differences between the geographical locations of organisations that have installations in several countries, and the subcultures that exist within UK national organisations that have installations in several areas of the country.

ETHNIC OR SOCIETAL CULTURE VERSUS ORGANISATIONAL CULTURE

There is always an element of ethnic culture in the organisational culture, and it is important to take this into account if we wish to prescribe a culture that matches the organisation's core values. Additionally, it is important to understand whether ethnic or organisational culture is the stronger in the organisation. Which culture would predominate in particular situations? Research supports the view that ethnic culture, rather than the organisation's culture, is more influential over employee behaviour (Adler 1997, pp61–3). Muslim workers in the UK, for example, will be influenced more strongly by their ethnic culture than by that of the employing organisation.

Organisations that have installations in different parts of the world have to be able to predict, with a reasonable degree of accuracy, the behaviour of their overseas employees. It was noted earlier that culture is the greatest determinant of employee behaviour, but in situations in which the two cultures clash, the ethnic culture will predominate.

CULTURAL FIT

One situation in which the task is that of predicting behaviour is the selection process. What one might call *cultural fit* is the degree to which a prospective employee's attitudes, beliefs, values and customary norms match those of the organisation. Is this something that should be assessed? According to Robbins (2001):

> We should expect ... that the employee selection process will be used by multinationals to find and hire job applicants who are a good fit with their organisation's dominant culture, even if such applicants are somewhat atypical for members of their country.

PAUSE FOR THOUGHT

From what is said in the above quote, do you think that multinational companies could risk rejecting the right person for the job by focusing on their culture rather than on a prospective employee's suitability in terms of knowledge and skills? Could this develop into a discriminatory policy? How could the 'fit' between employee and employer be improved?

CULTURE SHIFT

Human beings are the most adaptable creatures on Earth. They quickly acclimatise to unaccustomed conditions, and can move through a variety of different situations dealing with them as they go. People live their lives in stages, and they adopt roles as they move from one stage to the next; through infancy, teens, adulthood, and then middle age to old age. There are also stages in each day: the breakfast scene, the trip to work, the work situation, the trip home, the home scene.

 ACTIVITY 2.4

Go through the above paragraph and think about how you behave in each of the stages and in each of the daily situations. Are you aware that your behaviour changes gradually during your life and frequently during each day? Do you speak and treat people differently at home, at work, at study or where you spend your leisure hours?

One of the most important changes is the one that takes place as you enter the workplace. As you go through those doors, you put aside much of your ethnic culture and slip into the *place* where you spend *time* and where the *language* is different. By doing this, you and your workplace colleagues become part of a different culture. Without having to make a conscious effort, you adopt the workplace values and observe the norms. Furthermore, if you are a team member, you adapt again.

PAUSE FOR THOUGHT

How many different ethnic backgrounds are there in your team or classroom? Is there mutual understanding about what you have to do? How well do you work together? Is there a bond with your work group or team?

The point that is being made here is that people from a variety of ethnic cultures join together to form a new culture to achieve particular objectives by working harmoniously together. This is not a description of an idealistic situation; it happens for real in all kinds of organisations every day. Indeed, there are times when team members have to close ranks in order to defend their position.

INTEGRATION OF DIVERSE ELEMENTS

The organisation is an ideal venue for integration. It is more disciplined than the external environment and is a space in which the organisation's own values and beliefs can be learned by all, regardless of their backgrounds.

THE PROCESS OF 'ENCULTURISATION' – OR HOW WE INDUCT A NEW MEMBER INTO THE ORGANISATION

As described in Chapter 8, the induction process is vital to socialising the new starter into the organisation because it is through this process that the individual learns what is acceptable and what is not acceptable behaviour and, with a mentor or through co-workers, quickly learns the norms of the organisation's culture. If one thinks about this, the process of induction, then what we are doing is starting the process of familiarising the person into how the organisation works, in short the process of 'enculturisation'. We select the individual against a set of standards that managers have agreed. These standards effectively identify those who will 'fit' with the organisation's culture; there is in effect some pre-selection going on. This process of socialisation continues with how senior managers and other key cultural carriers (Robbins and Judge 2005), such as the HR department's staff, engage with the new starter. After a while the new member learns how to behave and starts to adopt the acceptable ways, the norms, of how to do things.

The policies and procedures that the HR department has developed further reinforce the culture of the organisation. The policies and procedures, and how they are enforced, say a lot about the running of the organisation, and thus its culture.

CHANGING ORGANISATION CULTURE

Over time both the work practices and the competitive environment in which companies operate changes. How things are done at work can become ritualised and if there has been no major catastrophic event to create the need to drastically change work practices then business can tend to 'roll on as normal'. The stock market collapse of 2008 impacted upon the premium rate air passenger travel business between the United Kingdom and the United States of America. The significant fall in business-class travel affected British Airways and it had to put in place plans to cope with the fall in its revenues.

Business needs to revitalise itself from time to time; change is inevitable and sometimes, as with British Airways, culture change is also important. British Airways had to work towards changing its work practices to compete with the low-cost airlines.

Bringing about a culture change is not impossible but, because it deals with the 'soft' people issues of attitudes and motivations, it is not easy to bring about. Changing organisational culture is dealt with in some depth in Chapter 18.

DISSECTING ORGANISATIONAL CULTURE

Johnson and Scholes (2002) offer a way of analysing organisational culture, which is useful from two perspectives: first, to be able to understand the culture of an organisation and, second, once understood, one can think how and what to change in a culture to bring about better performance or service.

Johnson and Scholes picture culture as a central *paradigm* (a pattern or model of how it works) surrounded by: the *symbols* of the culture, the *power structure*, the *organisational structures*, the *control systems*, the *rituals and routines* and the *stories*:

- The *paradigm* explains, as indicated above, how the organisation is seen to operate. It is about expected and observed behaviours and reflects the organisation's reality to those within and those outside who have some first-hand knowledge of the organisation. It is an expression of the intended and real values of the organisation.

- *Routines* are the way members behave towards each other and make up, 'the way things are done around here'.

- The *stories* are perhaps of significant events that help to fix the culture in time and place and give meaning to how the organisation sees itself.

- The *symbols* are the artefacts, logos, the titles of how people within the organisation address each other. They are, as Johnson and Scholes write (2002, p231), '… shorthand representation of the nature of the organisation'. They could be reserved car parking spaces, preferential office sites, dress codes for managers, and so on.

- *Power structures* are associated with the effective power in organisations. In a car sales operation power is likely to be with the sales department rather than any of the service functions, such as financial services, HR or maintenance.

- *Organisation structures* reflect how power is devolved within an organisation. A bureaucratic organisation of many layers may see process to be important and that order and discipline, in terms of following procedure, to be key to how it works. This may be relevant and important where quality and safety is wholly dependent on how, for example, a large piece of equipment is put together, such as a jet engine.

- *Control systems* are how the workings of the organisation are focused. The operation of an emergency service control room is controlled by procedure, as is how a pilot flies a commercial airliner. To incentivise either of these activities with bonus payments, for example for the rate of handling calls or time to destination for the pilot, may cause the 'actors in the process' to move away from procedure with disastrous effect.

(adapted from Johnson and Scholes 2002, pp230–1)

SUMMARY – CULTURE

Culture can be considered in two ways. It can be considered as ethnic or societal culture or it can be viewed from the perspective of the organisation as the culture that an organisation has. Organisation culture, according to Clegg et al (2008) can be considered from an integration perspective, differentiation perspective or a fragmentation perspective.

Physical culture is created by people and is the cars, roads and bridges of our physical society. We also have the subjective culture, which is apparent through the norms and values of society and is influenced by our upbringing, religion, schooling and so on. The two are very closely tied because both place and time are important; for example, places of religious worship have significance in our cultural understanding and being. The physical culture is closely linked to and defined by our societal culture. We tend to view other cultures through a lens that is shaped by our own cultural norms and values; we take an ethnocentric view of other cultures and measure and judge others against our own standards, our own 'in' group.

Organisation culture is different from ethnic/societal culture because the focus is on how organisations can be viewed from a cultural perspective; remembering, of course, that organisations operate within different societies. Schein, Handy, Trice and Beyer, Lawton and Rose, and Johnson and Scholes (and many others) all offer a view on how to dissect culture.

From the above discussion one can see that the debate of and about culture is far-reaching and can be viewed from a number of perspectives. Picking up on the writings of Clegg et al (2008), it is convenient to take a managerialist perspective if one is in business, because this assumes an organisation 'has' a culture that can be moulded and changed, and therefore improved. If, however, one takes the social scientist's perspective – that the culture of an organisation 'is' – this implies that it is fixed in time and space and has been developed organically over time and so cannot be changed by managerial processes.

If one considers that an organisation 'has' a culture, then of course it can be changed, which is part of the discussion that Chapter 18 addresses. The work of Johnson and Scholes is useful as a tool in respect of how to dissect culture.

REVIEW QUESTIONS

1 How would you define organisational culture?

2 What is the relationship between values and norms?

3 Why is culture said to be a powerful determinant of behaviour?

4 How would you distinguish between the physical culture and the subjective culture? How do they influence each other?

5 What is ethnocentrism and why is it important in organisational culture?

6 What are the boundaries of culture?

7 In what circumstances do members of different ethnic cultures join forces to create a distinctive subculture?

8 What value is there in defining different types of organisational culture?

9 What is meant if one accepts that an organisation 'has' a culture compared with the view that the culture of an organisation 'is'?

10 How does a differentiated culture differ from an integrated culture?

11 Is it useful, when trying to describe cultures, to think of them as Handy or Schein describes them?

12 What role does personnel (HR) play in the introduction of the individual to the organisation's culture?

13 Write down four levels of organisational subculture.

14 What are the positive and negative influences of organisational subcultures?

15 What are the possible consequences of allowing an out-of-date culture to persist at a time of significant external change?

EXPLORE FURTHER

BOOKS

FRENCH, R., RAYNER, C., REES, G. and RUMBLES, S. (2008) *Organizational behaviour.* **Chichester: John Wiley and Sons.**

French et al's book, *Organizational Behaviour,* offers a very refreshing read on a number of topics, including organisational culture. As they say in their conclusion to the chapter on organisational culture, '[Organisational culture] is concerned with the ways its members interpret the everyday realities of organizational life' (p405). The text examines culture from a number of perspectives and introduces a number of models that help the reader obtain a fuller picture of the meaning and impact of organisational culture.

GREENBERG, J. and BARON, R.A. (2010) *Behaviour in organizations.* **New Jersey: Pearson Education Ltd.**

Greenberg and Baron's text views organisational as well as ethnic/national culture from a number of differing perspectives: its impact upon creativity, decision-making, communication and so on. Their work on culture is not limited to one chapter but is dealt with across the spectrum of organisational behaviour in the way, for example, it impacts upon communication and negotiating across cultures. An easy-to-read and well-illustrated text.

HOFSTEDE, G. (1997) *Cultures and organizations: software of the mind.* **New York: McGraw Hill.**

Geret Hofstede's text is dated but nevertheless his work is revisited and repeated in many discussions on and about organisational culture. It is worth dipping into this book to understand how he was able to categorise national cultural attributes, values and meanings to cultural ethnic identity.

CHAPTER 3

Human Resource Management (HRM)

LEARNING OBJECTIVES

After studying this chapter you should understand:

- human resource management
- the difference between modern HRM and personnel management
- the various approaches to HRM
- strategic HRM and the best-fit, best practice and resource-based view of strategic human resource management (SHRM)
- the impact HRM has had upon organisations' approach to management since the 1980s
- the influence of HRM on the management of people.

INTRODUCTION

There is a wide variety of views about HRM. The concept has been variously interpreted, and the style with which its principles and practices are applied varies among academics, practitioners and, indeed, from one country to another. There is neither the space nor the need in a book of this size and level to venture deeply into a discussion of the philosophical pronouncements about HRM, but it is necessary to provide an understanding of how it has influenced not only the management of the employment relationship, but the management of the whole organisation.

This chapter offers some of the insights of academics and practitioners, and we hope you will attain an understanding of HRM that you will be able to take further in your later studies. If, however, you wish to look into the concept more deeply at this stage, the references that are cited here will lead you to a comprehensive account of the HRM debate: the philosophies underlying the various interpretations and how the principles and practices upon which HRM is founded are applied.

In addition to developing a sound understanding of HRM, you also need to be aware of the management systems that emerged earlier in the twentieth century. This is because many organisations have not fully adopted HRM and still adhere to the traditional practices of personnel management.

WHAT EXACTLY IS HRM?

The history of management thought, which began in earnest in the early twentieth century, produced theories that contain allusions to what we now regard as HRM principles and practices (Taylor 1947; Burns and Stalker 1966), but they were not introduced into British organisations, as a totally new management system, until the 1980s. At the time, people became confused about what the term meant, and this was understandable since the words 'human resource' caused people to think of personnel. Sisson (1995) says that in the late 1980s, there was much debate among practitioners and academics alike about the implications of HRM for the personnel function. He said that even if some found it difficult to understand what the fuss was about (HRM looked very much like the personnel management they thought they were practising), many practitioners welcomed the new paradigm (Armstrong 1987; Fowler 1987).

IDEAL TYPE OF ORGANISATION

The main question became, what is the difference between HRM and personnel management? Indeed, is there a difference or was it just that the term personnel management had lost credibility and needed a new label? A second question that required an answer was, how, in such a dramatic manner, is it possible to introduce a new way of managing employment without affecting the ways in which the whole organisation is managed? On the basis of studying organisations in a series of case studies, Storey (1992) created an 'ideal type' of organisation in order to clarify and simplify the essential features that distinguish HRM from other forms of people management. His classification shows 27 points of differences in practice between personnel and industrial relations and HRM practice (see Table 3.1).

It has to be understood that the comparative model illustrated in Table 3.1 is purely theoretical and that no single organisation conforms to all of the conditions within it. However, it does give some concrete examples of where 'personnel management' and 'human resource management' differ.

What can be seen from the model is that those who have adopted the principles and practices of HRM have shifted from what was regarded as standard practice in personnel and industrial relations terms (the middle column in Table 3.1), to the generally more flexible, open and mutually co-operative standard of HRM (the right-hand column of Table 3.1).

Research shows that HRM has been *more* or *less* adopted by organisations. Beardwell et al (2004, p24) and Beardwell and Claydon (2007, p22) point out, '... in the 1998 Workplace Employee Relations Survey, WERS 98, Cully et al, (1999) investigated sixteen practices commonly associated with HRM, including team working, employee involvement ... The survey found evidence of each of the sixteen practices ....' This implied that there was a take-up of HRM practices and that they '... are well entrenched in many British workplaces'. British managers, however, have a record of reluctance to adopt new ideas in the comprehensive sense; they are very financially orientated and change, which is always a costly process, is usually carried out in a cautious and piecemeal fashion.

Sisson (2001, pp80–1) identifies two main explanations for this cautious reluctance. First, he says that they are inclined to 'try one or two elements and assess their impact before going further, even though this means forgoing the benefits of the integration associated with bundles of complementary practices'. The second, and in Sisson's words 'less comfortable', explanation is that 'HRM is not the only means of achieving competitive advantage and other methods, adopted by organisations … do not involve a change in the way that people are managed'. 'Other methods' refers to adaptations of the tried and tested management systems of the twentieth century. In many cases, this involves the use of an eclectic mix of the elements of earlier theories.

One can draw a distinction between personnel management and HRM by reflecting on the Storey model. Personnel management can be seen to have a focus on the personnel, with the personnel department being the 'hand-maiden' of the line department, providing a monitoring and largely service function. On the other hand, the human resource management function considers people as a strategic asset that can impact upon the bottom line and, at the same time, grow in value. As Francis and Keegan say (2006, p231), '… research in HRM has focused on the take-up and impact of commitment seeking "high performance" HR practices that are argued to lead to improved employee and organisational performance'. And Martin, cited in Francis and Keegan (2006, p231) argues that, 'More recently, attention has been drawn to the potential of "e-enabled HRM" to reduce costs of HR services and to "liberate" HR practitioners from routine administration so they can focus on strategic and change management issues.'

A large number of organisations, however, do use HRM terminology. Gradually, since the 1980s, 'personnel departments' have become 'HR departments' and the same staff working in those departments have become 'HR specialists', 'HR advisers' or 'HR business partners' regardless, it seems, as to whether or not the organisation has formally adopted the principles and practices of HRM itself. Some of course have hung on to the old title of 'personnel department'.

 ACTIVITY 3.1

Storey's '27 points of difference'

Study Table 3.1 and identify the degree to which your organisation conforms (1) to the criteria that typify traditional personnel and industrial relations (IR), and (2), to the HRM criteria.

An important point that should be made here is that the personnel and industrial relations activities that indicated good practice before the 1980s are still practised today using the same methods and techniques, but within HRM a new style of thinking underlies the practices and affects the degree to which the outcomes serve the purposes of overall corporate strategy.

HRM AND TRADITIONAL MANAGEMENT

So far in this chapter the discussion has been about the history, principles and practices of HRM, without significant reference to the theories of management that were widespread before 1980. Academics and practitioners have been studying organisational management for more than 100 years, resulting in several generations of different approaches (see Table 3.2).

The *human relations* approach emerged in the 1930s. While the classical theorists were concerned with structures, physical working conditions, work methods, measurement and proposing formal 'rules' of management, it became evident in the late 1920s that attention should be paid to the social aspects of workplace life. It was the study of employees' social interactions, their attitudes and values that gave rise to the human relations approach. One study in particular that stimulated academic and practitioner interest in the motivations of people at work is the Hawthorne study, which took place between 1924 and 1936 at the Hawthorne Plant of the Western Electric Company in Chicago. This was when the importance of people's motivations, in the social as well as the technical aspects of being at work, became evident.

BUREAUCRACY

The main theorist that followed these early researchers was the sociologist Max Weber (1964), whose most well-known work, *The Theory of Social and Economic Organisation*, was the result of his study of the German civil service. In that book he first used the term *bureaucracy* and said that to some extent, bureaucracy existed in all organisations, in the private as well as the public sector. Weber drew distinctions between three types of organisation in terms of the kinds of authority that existed within them, which he described as *traditional, charismatic* and *legal-rational*. Bureaucracy is a frequently found form of organisation. Many writers believe that to some degree, all organisations are bureaucratised.

Table 3.1 27 points of difference

Dimension		Personnel and IR	HRM
Beliefs and assumptions			
1	Contract	Careful delineation of written contracts	Aim to go 'beyond contract'
2	Rules	Importance of devising clear rules/mutuality	'Can do' outlook; impatience with 'rule'
3	Guide to management action	Procedures	'Business need'
4	Behaviour referent	Norms/custom and practice	Values/mission
5	Managerial task *vis-à-vis* labour	Monitoring	Nurturing
6	Nature of relations	Pluralist	Unitarist
7	Conflict	Institutionalised	De-emphasised
Strategic aspects			
8	Key relations	Labour management	Customer
9	Initiatives	Piecemeal	Integrated
10	Corporate plan	Marginal to	Central to
11	Speed of decision	Slow	Fast
Line management			
12	Management role	Transactional	Transformational leadership
13	Key managers	Personnel/IR specialists	General/business/line managers
14	Communication	Indirect	Direct
15	Standardisation	High (for example 'parity' an issue)	Low (for example 'parity' not seen as relevant)
16	Prized managerial skills	Negotiation	Facilitation
Key levers			
17	Selection	Separate, marginal task	Integrated, key task
18	Pay	Job evaluation (fixed grades)	Performance-related
19	Conditions	Separately negotiated	Harmonisation
20	Labour management	Collective bargaining contracts	Towards individual contracts

21	Thrust of relations with stewards	Regularised through facilities and training	Marginalised (with exception of some bargaining for change models)
22	Jobs categories and grades	Many	Few
23	Communication	Restricted flow	Increased flow
24	Job design	Division of labour	Teamwork
25	Conflict-handling	Reach temporary truces	Manage climate and culture
26	Training and development	Controlled access to courses	Learning companies
27	Foci of attention for interventions	Personnel procedures	Wide-ranging cultural, structural and personnel strategies

Adapted from Storey (1992, p38). Reproduced by kind permission of Wiley-Blackwell Publishers

Table 3.2 Early management theories and theorists

Classical theorists			Classical theories
H. Fayol 1949	}	Management practitioners	General principles of management
F.W. Taylor 1947			Scientific management
F. and L. Gilbreth 1917	}	Academics	The science of management
M.P. Follett 1941			Democratic management, democratic use of power
E.F.L. Brech 1965			The framework of management

Table 3.3 Twentieth-century theories and theorists

Human relations approach	Systems and contingency approaches
Elton Mayo and the Hawthorne studies (1930s)	Trist et al (1963) Organisational choice
A.H. Maslow (1954–72) Motivation and personality	Burns and Stalker (1966) The management of innovation
F.W. Herzberg et al (1957) Work and the nature of man	Joan Woodward (1980) Industrial organisation
D. McGregor (1960) The human side of enterprise	

The theories and theorists outlined in Tables 3.2 and 3.3 were all different approaches to managing, and they were based on academic research (for example McGregor 1960; Weber 1964) and the experience of practising managers (for example Taylor 1911; Fayol 1949). Throughout the classical and mid-twentieth-century studies of management the accepted managerial skills were described as planning, organising, directing and controlling; the four functions were linked together through co-ordination (Fayol 1949).

1 **Planning**. This includes setting objectives and making decisions about how objectives are to be achieved.

2 **Organising**. In this context, organising means developing a structure through which the work may be carried out, allocating the work to various staff members, delegating tasks and giving people commensurate authority to have them carried out.

3 **Directing**. Within this function, the manager 'gets things done' through people; it means actually directing, or 'showing the way' (Taylor 1947 and Weber, cited in Clegg et al 2008, p489). Directing therefore includes the use of such skills as leadership, motivation, communication, coaching and counselling employees.

4 **Controlling**. The manager monitors and assesses the degree to which predetermined objectives have been met. This involves identifying any shortfalls between the work that was planned and the work that was actually carried out. Decisions then have to be made about how to head off those shortfalls in the future.

CONTROL AND COMPLIANCE

Clearly, from the use of the word 'control' we can see that, before HRM, work was carried out because managers 'controlled' everything and issued orders while employees complied by applying their knowledge and skills to the tasks. As far as history shows, it was not until the Hawthorne study that employees were consulted about their physical working conditions and their attitudes towards their supervisors. Even after that, control and compliance still prevailed.

THE SOCIO-TECHNICAL SYSTEM

An important discovery made by Elton Mayo at the Hawthorne plant was that employees made decisions and took actions that were not planned or in any way determined by the managers. Previously, it had been assumed that productivity levels were the result of managerial exhortation and the fact that the employees were skilled enough to do the jobs. Now, however, it was apparent that organisations have a social as well as a technical side. It had become clear to Mayo that the work groups, which had been put together for technical reasons, had developed socially. It had been thought that variations in productivity at the plant were attributable to problems with the physical working conditions, but Mayo realised that the groups, in the social role, were making productivity decisions that were different from those demanded by the managers. This was a second source of power in the organisation, and the question of what to do about it became important (Mayo 1933).

What became known as the socio-technical system (the organisation has a social as well as a technical side) was taken a step further by Trist and other researchers (Bamforth) at the Tavistock Institute of Human Relations in London in 1963 by bringing into fuller realisation the interaction between a work group and the task it has to perform. Their research was into the long wall mining techniques introduced into the County Durham coal fields of the 1940s. Transforming the 'narrow face' mining techniques into 'long wall' faces, and at the same time introducing new, larger and more efficient equipment 'upset' the social balance previously experienced by the miners. Morale suffered and absenteeism increased. Tightly knit social groups had been split up, the new ways of working made communication difficult and differential bonus systems exasperated matters. The organisation was really a social system and a technical system; the two systems interacted and this had to be taken into account since it was realised that there would always be an interaction between the methods of work, technology and social relationships. Earlier approaches to change had concentrated on either technical aspects (for example scientific management), or the social aspects (for example the human relations approach) (see Tables 3.2 and 3.3).

HUMAN RESOURCE MANAGEMENT

Few would argue with the notion that it was the success of Asian industry in the 1970s and 1980s that gave rise to the development of HRM; it was one of the reactions of the West to the Asian invasion of European and US markets. Indeed, according to Goss (1996), it was a little more than that:

> The development of HRM as a body of management thought in the 1980s can be linked to a conjunction of socio-economic factors – in particular, changes in international competition, the restructuring of industrial sectors and organizations, and a rise of a new confidence in the power of managers to manage.

Undoubtedly, the Thatcher years restored managers' confidence, and this was achieved in part by waging war upon the militant trade unions in the automobile and mining industries, particularly, which were considerably weakened in the 1980s.

A NEW PERSPECTIVE

At the time, most managers had 'cherry-picked' past theories and were managing through an eclectic mixture of ideas drawn from past theories, ideas and concepts. Indeed, some are still doing that today. But there was an urgent need to reorient industry's focus away from the traditional view of management and towards a new perspective. The nature of business was changing rapidly, new technology had increased the speed at which business was carried out and competition had already become fierce in the global context.

> ⚷ **KEY CONCEPT**
>
> David Goss (1996) treats HRM as:
>
> a diverse body of thought and practice, loosely unified by a concern to integrate the management of personnel more closely with the core management activity of organisations.
>
> Armstrong (1999) defines HRM as:
>
> a strategic and coherent approach to the management of an organisation's most valued assets – the people working there who individually and collectively contribute to the achievement of its goal.
>
> According to Storey (1995):
>
> Human resource management is a distinctive approach to employment management which seeks to obtain competitive advantage through the strategic deployment of a highly committed and skilled workforce, using an array of cultural, structural and personnel techniques.

While it is clear that these three definitions have similarities in that they all refer to the importance of people, the emphases are different. Goss emphasises the need to integrate people management more closely with the core management activity of the organisation. Armstrong, on the other hand, says that it is an approach to the management of people, whereas Storey says that it is an approach that seeks to obtain a competitive advantage. Armstrong says what the employees do (they contribute to the achievement of goals), while Storey says what HRM does with the people (it strategically deploys a highly committed and skilled workforce). Storey (1992) says that HRM can be regarded as a 'set of interrelated principles with an ideological and philosophical underpinning'. It is concerned with the employment, development and reward of people in organisations and the conduct of relationships between management and the workforce. It involves all line managers and team leaders, but HR specialists exist to make important contributions to the processes involved.

Krulis-Randa (1990, p136) says that in contrast to the 'control and compliance' models (see above), HRM is typified by the following characteristics:

- A focus on horizontal authority and reduced hierarchy; a blurring of the rigid distinction between management and non-management.

- Wherever possible, responsibility for people management is devolved to line managers; the role of personnel professionals is to support and facilitate line management in this task, not to control it.

- Human resource planning is proactive and fused with corporate-level planning; human resource issues are treated strategically in an integrated manner.

- Employees are viewed as subjects with the potential for growth and development; the purpose of human resource management is to identify this potential and develop it in line with the adaptive needs of the organisation.

- HRM suggests that management and non-management have a common interest in the success of the organisation. Its purpose is to ensure that all employees are aware of this and committed to common goals.

With regard to the second point, it is not difficult to criticise the notion that devolving responsibility for managing people to the line managers is 'something new'. For example, line managers have been responsible for people management since industry's earliest days, certainly long before personnel management was conceived as a discrete function.

David Guest (1989) defined HRM in a different manner. Guest defines a set of four propositions that he suggests combine to create more effective organisations (refer to Beardwell and Claydon 2007, p9, for a more detailed discussion):

1 **Strategic integration:** the way an organisation integrates HRM issues into a strategic plan.

Integration is the operative word because there is a need to link with how line management operates, how remuneration policies are developed, and so on, so the individual parts become a holistic whole.

2 **High commitment:** is as much about attitude as the delivering of goals. In terms of the psychological contract the desired outcome would be for staff to work beyond contract.

3 **High quality:** this considers how management behaves and would include management of employees and investment in high-quality employees, which implies high-quality recruitment and selection techniques.

4 **Flexibility** for Guest is primarily concerned with *functional flexibility*.

The Guest and Storey models are particularly important because it was they who took the American concepts of HRM, the Michigan (University) and the Harvard (University) models, and sold them to the British market.

However one defines HRM as a concept, it does not have a scientific underpinning but rather it is a belief. There has been much work done over the years to try to demonstrate its effectiveness and contribution to the bottom line but the inescapable fact is it is no more than a concept, but a well-refined concept.

Personnel management as a profession that offers expert advice and assistance to line managers is an early twentieth-century phenomenon. What is now the CIPD began life in 1913 as the Industrial Welfare Society. In fact, HRM, along with legislative changes, has added to rather than conferred people responsibilities upon line managers.

PAUSE FOR THOUGHT

Who assesses your performance? Who talks to you about training? If you are given a task that you have never carried out before, who shows you how to do it? Does the HR/personnel department get involved? What is their role in the process?

Two further HRM principles are:

- a recognition of the strength of the relationship between human performance and organisational success, producing the need to develop people to their ultimate potential as contributors to the realisation of the business plans

- the notion that there is a mutuality of interest between the organisation and its managers and employees in the survival and development of the organisation – this is the unitarist perspective.

Doubts may surround the second point, which calls for the need for employees to be committed to, and involved in, the success of the organisation. Undoubtedly, there is a 'feel good factor' that typifies employees' experiences of their organisation's successes and, clearly, this has a visible, positive effect on them. However, one would suggest that this is far more frequently due to the enhanced feelings of job security that are produced when employees learn of the organisation's successes and perhaps feelings of personal achievement, rather than to feelings of personal involvement that might include, say, endorsement of the nature of the organisation's goals *per se*, or perhaps that for the enterprise to have achieved its objectives is seen as a 'good thing'.

HARD AND SOFT HRM

An analysis of HRM in terms of the style with which it is employed may be regarded in two ways: as hard or soft. According to Clegg et al (2008, p176):

- **Hard HRM**: It is assumed that people do not want empowerment, they simply want to be told what is required of them, [and] given the resources and training to achieve these requirements, and be remunerated if they go beyond these requirements. People will be attracted by good pay, clear objectives and unambiguous job duties.

  Further to the definition given above the consideration is that there is a clear 'fit' between the corporate strategy and goals and the operational/functional objectives of the HRM department. The above approach would sit within the concept of *utilitarian instrumentalism* (see the following discussion of Legge) and has strong links to McGregor's Theory X.

CASE EXAMPLE

During the October 2009 postal workers' strike all of the emphasis in the politicians', trade union leaders' and management pronouncements was on securing continued employment for the postal workers, modernising the business to secure its future against competition and providing a service for its customers. Nobody mentioned commitment or involvement.

- **Soft HRM**: It is assumed that work is an integral part of life and should provide a fulfilling, empowering and positive experience for people. People will be attracted to jobs that provide opportunity for growth and advancement; they will stay in jobs that invest in them as valued assets.

  The above approach would sit within the concept of *developmental humanism* (also see the following discussion of Legge) and has strong links to McGregor's Theory Y.

However, Legge (1995, pp66–7) points out that the two are not mutually exclusive. Hard HRM is sometimes defined in terms of the particular policies that stress a cost-minimisation strategy with an emphasis on leanness in production, the use of labour as a resource and what Legge calls a 'utilitarian instrumentalism' in the employment relationship. At other times, hard HRM is defined in terms of the tightness of fit between organisational goals and strategic objectives on the one hand and HRM policies on the other. By contrast, soft HRM is sometimes viewed as 'developmental humanism' (Legge 1995) in which the individual is integrated into a work process that values trust, commitment and communication.

Allusions to these two features of how HRM may be interpreted and applied may be found in the theoretically diverse approaches to management that were expressed earlier in the twentieth century. For example, John Bramham's 1988 version of *Manpower Planning* adopts an approach that may be regarded as hard HRM because the demand and supply of human resources is calculated using statistics, employee numbers and costs, while the ideas of the human relations school (Mayo 1933; Maslow 1954; McGregor 1960) may be regarded as soft HRM because they take the human factor into account.

From the employee's point of view, HRM has its disadvantages as well as advantages. Obviously flattened structures, which produce a greater number of employees reporting to each manager, restrict the scope for promotion since each worker has a longer line of competitors for the next job up the short ladder of promotion. To some extent, therefore, the message that is communicated to ambitious, career-minded employees has shifted from aspiration to inspiration, and the importance of their performance in their current positions. It all throws a challenge to the employer as to how they can motivate staff who have little promotional opportunity.

PAUSE FOR THOUGHT

Assume the role of a manager in an organisation in which there is little upward opportunity for promotion, that is, your organisation has a very flat structure. How could you reward and motivate staff who work for you to maintain a good morale?

Also, there is at least as much evidence of hard as there is of soft HRM. The culture that is found in some companies is far from benign. UK employees work the longest hours in Europe and workplace stress is more widespread than ever before. The nature of employment contracts has changed; one managing director was heard to say, 'just because you need to access someone's skills doesn't mean you have to offer a contract of employment in the conventional sense' (refer to Chapter 13, which deals with the employment relationship). This idea is a 'throw back' to the days of scientific management at the turn of the nineteenth to the twentieth century when internal contracting was rife and there was a downward pressure on wages.

On the positive side, HRM has actually achieved the integration of HR strategy and corporate strategy, and perversely, in terms of its unitary perspective, has managed to replace the *command–compliance* type of manager–worker relationship with a more colleague type of relationship, meaning that the employee works with, rather than for, the manager.

STRATEGY AND OPERATIONS

The hierarchical nature of the traditional organisational structure may be used to demonstrate the difference between strategy and operations. To the traditionalist, management is strictly a top–down function in which the strategic decisions about the future of the organisation – what needs to be done in order to survive and develop – are made by those at the top. This implies that an understanding of the purpose of a strategy need be known only to those at the top, and the workforce is there to carry out the operational tasks that lead to the success of the strategy.

STRATEGIC HUMAN RESOURCE MANAGEMENT

Strategic human resource management, on the other hand, integrates rather than separates strategy and operations. In this chapter we have seen that the nature of strategic decision-making has changed in order to remain competitive, with a new and greater emphasis on:

- the importance of having a structure that is flexible enough to respond adequately in a variety of circumstances
- the price and quality of goods and services
- the organisation's speed of response to customer demands.

In fact today, all of the functions within the organisation have to be able to show how well they contribute to the success of the organisation; and this, of course, includes the functioning of the HR department.

The notion that the organisation's activities are contingent upon the strategy, however, is not new. If you read the earlier texts on 'management', you could be forgiven for concluding that the functional heads of an organisation were sitting around strumming their fingers, waiting for Moses to come down the mountain bearing the tablets so that they could then get on with drafting their own plans. One of the CIPD national examination questions that was asked in the 1980s read, 'Is it possible to develop a manpower plan in the absence of a corporate plan?' Thankfully, things are different today. Strategic human resource management (SHRM) advocates say that HR planning should be integrated with corporate strategy which, simply as a concept, makes more sense, and many organisations now do that. Indeed, academics and personnel practitioners had been campaigning for such integration for decades.

In terms of the management of HR and employment relations, SHRM blurs the distinction between strategy and operations. There is a 'wave of strategic human resource management literature focusing on the link or *vertical integration* [see Chapter 1] between human resource practices and organisations' business strategy in order to enhance performance' (Golding 2004). We saw in Chapter 1 that the organisation's strategy is described in its plans, and that all of the activities or operations that are carried out internally and externally by the employees of the organisation are designed to contribute to the success of the strategy. It is, therefore, essential for those at the operational level to understand the strategy. It has long been known that employees derive a great deal of satisfaction from understanding how their work contributes to the achievement of corporate objectives.

ACHIEVING A COMPETITIVE ADVANTAGE

BEST-FIT MODEL OF STRATEGIC HRM

We saw above that Golding (2004) refers to vertical integration as a means of enhancing performance, but what actually happens? One view of strategic human resource management (SHRM) that is taken by some academics and practitioners is generally referred to as the 'best-fit school of SHRM', which assesses the degree to which there actually is vertical integration between business strategy, policies and practices and activities. This implies 'the notion of a link between business strategy and the performance of every individual in the organisation' (Golding 2004).

Vertical integration therefore ensures an explicit link or relationship between internal people processes and policies and the external market or business strategy, and thereby ensures that competences are created which have a potential to be a key source of competitive advantage (Wright et al 1994).

Figure 3.1 shows the classical *top–down* approach to developing an organisation's strategies: corporate, business and operational.

Figure 3.1 Classical (top–down) model of an organisation's strategy

Corporate strategy

Business strategy

Operational or functional strategy

In Figure 3.1, the corporate strategy deals with the size, shape (that is, its structural configuration, for example hierarchical, flat, and so on) and scope of the organisation and the financing plans of a company. A good example of the finance plans would be the strategic decision to borrow money from banks to finance expansion plans or, alternatively, finance the expansion from its own 'pocket'.

The next layer below the corporate strategy is the business strategy. This deals with competitive strategy of the business and how it would, for example, manage its customer relations. The business strategy would also address developing its new products.

The final layer in the strategic model is the layer that deals with operational strategy. This would be the level where the various functions that make up the business – HR, production, logistics, finance, marketing and so on – all make their contribution to the organisational goals.

 ACTIVITY 3.2

A good example of differentiation in the marketplace is to consider how the main supermarkets compete. Some clearly compete on quality and some on cost. Discuss which ones you consider compete on cost and which compete on quality, and consider how this strategy bears on customer relations and perhaps on how it manifests in how the different supermarkets may engage with their staff.

Clearly, the lower down the chain the more thought has to go into how strategy melds with the one above or the one above that. For HR the strategy should not only blend with and support those strategies in the chain above but also it should support the strategies developed by other functions that lie in a horizontal line. For example, if the production department aims to develop teamworking or to develop autonomous working groups as a key way of going about its business, then the HR strategy must support this initiative by working through its strategies, policies and procedures to ensure they either support teamworking or do not hinder it. The HR reward strategy should, in this case, be structured to give focus to team achievement and reward and not to the reward of individuals.

ACTIVITY 3.3

1   Can you think of where the HR strategy, policies and procedures may help or hinder the strategic intent of other departments?

2   Think about the tasks you carry out on a day-to-day basis. Do you know why your job exists and how it fits into the grand scheme of things? How does your section or department contribute to the achievement of objectives? Was it clear to you how your objectives were developed?

THE BEST PRACTICE MODEL OF SHRM

The best practice model was originally researched by Jeffery Pfeffer (1998). Here the business takes, as Marchington and Grugulis state (2000, p1106), 'the particular brand of HRM that … relies on employers adopting high-cost, high-skill employment policies'. Particularly this implies:

- employment security
- selective hiring
- self-managed teams/teamworking
- high compensation contingent upon organisational performance
- extensive training
- reduction of status differences
- sharing information.

The emphasis is either incorporating all of the above processes into the human resource strategy (HRS) or bundles of say three, four or five of these processes. In this way specific outcomes – say in the development of commitment because the firm will do all in its power to avoid redundancies – would be supported by carefully selecting the *type* of people who are employed and how they are trained.

The question of course that must be asked is how many companies can adopt this model of SHRM and, if they do, would they do so for all their workforce and which practices are best suited for individual companies? Pfeffer and Sutton (2006) argue that business should take a research-based approach to the introduction of people management practices and not rely on the fact that because an approach to, for example, rewarding people has worked in one company then it should work in another company.

There have been many claims that these high-performance (best practice) approaches to HRM have indeed contributed more to company profitability than, say, research and development, strategy and quality (Marchington and Grugulis 2000). However appealing these claims are, there is still a problem to prove, in absolute terms, that introducing these practices into a business directly contributes – proportionally when compared with other factors that impact upon profit, such as business climate and product – to bottom-line profits. The difficulty is in determining, in a foolproof manner, the linkage between how the management of someone working in the, for example, 'back office' finance suite of a car sales company impacts upon the bottom line simply because of the prevalent 'best practice' HRM strategy, that is, in effect how the person has been managed. Nevertheless there are companies, particularly public sector organisations, that take this approach to managing their people.

PAUSE FOR THOUGHT

Consider the work practices in the company you work for or of a company you know. Do you think that they take a best practice human resource strategy to managing their people? Does the company employ all of the seven practices bullet pointed above or a limited number, a *bundle,* of them? Would it be reasonable or practicable in all circumstances for an organisation to engage all seven practices from the list?

THE RESOURCE-BASED VIEW (RBV) OF THE ORGANISATION

Unlike the *best-fit* approach to SHRM, which is a top–down approach, the *resource-based view* of strategy is bottom–up. How can this be so? A bottom-up approach implies that it is the HRM strategy that informs, for example, the corporate strategy. This is exactly what happens. There are, though, a number of factors that have to be in place for this set of circumstances to become practice.

In this scenario it is the human resource strategy that is informed by the type of people involved with the business. For a business to hope to have a sustained competitive advantage, it '... must have four attributes: (a) it must be valuable in the sense that it exploits opportunities or neutralizes threats ..., (b) it must be rare amongst a firm's current and potential competition, (c) it must be imperfectly imitable, (d) there cannot be strategically equivalent substitutes for this resource that are valuable but neither rare nor imperfectly imitable ...' (Barney 1991, p105). In short, skills have to be rare and not easily imitated or duplicated, nor is there a clear alternative in the marketplace. With these caveats in place then the organisation has a fair chance of being able to develop business and corporate strategies around its workforce. With staff who have rare skills, then there is a need to nurture these talents, for without them the business does not have a future. In practical terms one could imagine a research and development (R&D) organisation having the knowledge and skills around which its higher-level strategies can be formed. Arguably this is what happened when the Ministry of Defence sold off into the private sector its weapons research establishment and which has metamorphosed into the privately owned military research company QinetiQ, which now has assets (2009) of £267 million. The value of the company, should it be sold on the stock market, would be much greater than this because of the value of its patents, current research and human resources.

STRUCTURING HUMAN RESOURCES IN THE ORGANISATION

The structuring of HR in the organisation, according to Ulrich (refer to Arkin 2007), is in the form of a three-legged stool, as below:

1 shared services

2 centres of excellence

3 HR business partners.

Companies have adopted this model in various guises in the past, but as Arkin (2007, p28) says, the model initially proposed by Ulrich has been transformed: '… that to deliver value, the HR function in large organisations needs to consist of the following streams of work:

- Transactional HR…

- Embedded HR…

- Centres of expertise…

- Corporate HR…'

THE ROLE OF THE HR PROFESSIONAL IN THE ORGANISATION

Ulrich and Brockbank (2005) propose a model of how HRM is put into practice premised upon five interdependent roles of the HR professional (performance-specific roles):

- HR leader

- employee advocate

- human capital developer

- strategic partner

- functional expert.

The way that Ulrich and Brockbank arrange the model is as a central circle, representing the HR leader, with the other four roles sited around the periphery. The HR leader is seen as *core* to the five roles because, as leader, the HR professional provides '… leadership to those in the business as well as those in the function' (Ulrich and Brockbank 2005, p24) – emphasising the business role of the HR professional or, as the CIPD calls them, the HR business partner.

The remaining four peripheral roles define the task of the HR business partner. *Human capital developer* takes on the mantle of preparing the workforce for the future (Ulrich and Brockbank 2005, pp24–5), '… often [developing] one employee at a time, developing plans that offer each employee opportunities to develop future abilities, matching desires with opportunities …'. As *strategic partner*, 'they partner with line managers to help them reach their goals through strategy formulation and execution'. As *functional experts* the HR business partner has knowledge of the business, they offer expertise in the main HR processes of recruitment, selection, promotions, training development, outplacement and so on, as well as work process design and organisational structures. The role of *employee advocate* is somewhat different because this role requires the HR professional to understand all their customers, including the employee, to be able to see the world through their eyes to best be able to express their views and, '... when the management team discusses the strategy closing a plant ... your job is to represent employees'. It gives employees a voice at the top table. This does not mean of course that the employees' views are paramount but what it does allow is discussion of the issues and perhaps judgements to be made on the best ways to proceed.

RESTRUCTURING THE ORGANISATION

One of the most visible features of the introduction of HRM in Britain resulted from the depression of the 1980s. To compete effectively in a global market, organisations had to become more flexible and responsive, and one of the approaches to achieving these qualities was the restructuring of the organisation. The objective was to create a 'leaner and fitter' organisation that could achieve similar or even greater productivity using a smaller number of employees. 'Increasingly, organisations have sought to cut costs by reducing the number of employees who are not contributing directly to production or service delivery' (Claydon 2004, p138). The restructuring techniques that are used to achieve the leaner and fitter organisation are as follows:

- **Downsizing**, also referred to as *rightsizing*. This means reducing the number of employees at operational levels and reorganising the work system to attain greater productivity.

- **De-layering**. This means reducing the number of staff at managerial levels, including middle managers and supervisors, to reduce costs. The result of this is a flattened structure in which a greater number of employees report to one manager. By doing this, the structure of a small production team might move from that shown in Figure 3.2 to one similar to Figure 3.3.

The structure in Figure 3.3 has only nine employees since downsizing would also have reduced the number reporting upwards.

Clearly, if such a change is made, communication between the workers and their supervisor would flow more freely but the same types of tasks would have to be carried out, which implies that a training programme would be necessary to ensure that the employees possessed all of the necessary interpersonal skills to relate to each other in the new structure. In a larger and/or more complex situation a programme of multiskilling would have to be introduced; also, the work methods would have to be changed to accommodate this.

- **Externalisation** – often referred to as *outsourcing* or *contracting out* – refers to activities that the organisation needs to have carried out but are not at the core of the main functions. Outsourcing is a means of reducing employee numbers by having selected activities carried out by external specialist organisations, thus saving on employment costs and work space. The most frequently found examples of 'contracting out' are catering, cleaning, transport and security. Increasingly, some of the organisation's administrative tasks, such as computer maintenance and payroll, are now being contracted out.

Figure 3.2 Tall or 'house of cards' structure with 12 employees reporting upwards

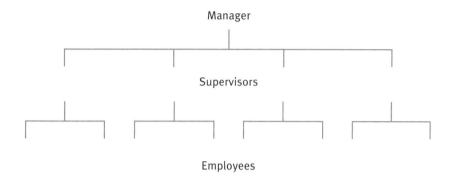

Figure 3.3 Flattened or 'garden rake' structure with nine employees reporting upwards

Significant changes such as those discussed above have further implications in terms of employment. A variety of the techniques for creating a flexible workforce, for example, have to be applied when the market is volatile. The instability (ups and downs) of the market means that the organisation has to be flexible enough to vary the size and skills of its workforce according to demand. We discuss this in more detail in the Chapters 5, 7, 8 and 10, which deal with HR Planning selection, and human resource development.

HRM AND CUSTOMER SERVICE

When we contact our bank with a query on its online banking system or take faulty goods back to a retail store we always expect good customer service. If we turn this around we can see that, by offering a quality customer experience during these times, potential exists to differentiate our product from other providers in the marketplace. In general, according to Schneider (2004), higher levels of service quality produce higher levels of customer satisfaction, which leads to increased customer loyalty and increased sales.

The key to Schneider's hypothesis is that it is the employee experience of a climate of service that is a predictor of good customer satisfaction. The question is what constitutes a 'service climate'? The basic ideas that Schneider works from are that:

1 Good general management practices (supportive supervision, appropriate training, necessary equipment) provide a foundation on which a service climate can be built;

2 Service climate emerges by management focusing on service quality in all that it does (rewards focus on service quality, planning and goal-setting focus on service quality, measurement focuses on service quality, employee competencies for delivering service quality are emphasised);

3 Those who deliver service to customers must in turn be served well by those whom they depend. (Schneider 2004, p146)

Point 3 above leads to the notion of customers that can either be internal or external to the organisation.

 ACTIVITY 3.4

Customer care

In either your organisation or one that you know:

● What internal customers does the organisation have?

● Think of how HR practices can improve the service that the organisation provides, which can impact upon:

– its internal customers

– its external customers.

Where does management fit into the whole concept of the service organisation? In the context of providing a 'climate of service', as espoused by Schneider (2004) above, he suggests that it is what management does that has a key impact upon service quality. This is supported by the work of Purcell (2003), who identified that the role of the line manager was key in the delivery of HR outcomes and the improvement in the bottom-line performance.

Schneider's work offers a further set of variables that need to be in place for good customer satisfaction to be experienced. This occurs when contact between customers and employees is high and there is high interdependence between service deliverers, that is, the need to produce service as part of an integrated team – as does a 'crash team' at an emergency and accident department of a hospital; where speed and reliance on others is critical this tends to produce good customer service to keep a critically ill patient alive. This of course works if management is supporting these activities with sufficient levels of commitment. The measurement tools for assessing the 'customer experience' also need to be appropriate. The overweighting on government targets within NHS trust hospitals arguably led some trusts' management to focus on issues such as waiting time and not give due consideration to the quality of patient care, clean wards with available and attentive staff. The metrics against which customer care are measured will cause employees to amend their behaviours and to give focus to these measures, especially if appraisal results are to be assessed against these metrics.

Schneider (2004, p148) offers some measures against which customer satisfaction can be measured; not all are relevant to all organisations but the following gives some examples: total in the customer base, customers who have increased or deepened their relationship, proportion of customers who have rated the service quality as excellent or outstanding, and so on. On the other hand there should be some measure of employee effectiveness, over which HR has control. These could be: 'immediacy with which customer contact jobs are filled when they become vacant, the proportion of employees placed in jobs who are fully trained prior to replacement, results from monitoring customer-contact behaviour of employees (eg "mystery shopper" programs), employee absenteeism and turnover (which is directly linked to customer account turnover), and survey data with regard to role ambiguity and stress as well as service climate experienced' (Schneider 2004, p148).

What Schneider (2004, p148) advises, as a summary, is to:

1 Get marketing, HRM and operations management talking with each other.

2 Put in place measurement systems that focus on service quality indicators.

3 Do an analysis of the strategic focus accorded to all HRM practices, 'selection procedures (competencies sought), training programs (skills taught), promotion systems … performance management systems … and mentoring and career development initiatives …'.

4 At all costs avoid the 'coffee mugs and posters' approach to service quality – this approach has no lasting impact.

What Schneider does not offer in his article is an analysis of what happens if these elements are not put in place. In some respects it is a very unitarist approach to managing people for better performance. It does not take a pluralist perspective, taking into account the employee or other third-party views, such as unions.

Hope Hailey et al (2005) in their longitudinal study of a high street bank (1994 through to 1999) considered the organisation's performance and HR practices over a period of five years. The analysis of the study was conducted against Ulrich's earlier (1997) model of HR roles:

> … 'administrative expert', which is process oriented with a day-to-day, operational focus, based on the management of the firm infrastructure … the other process oriented role, 'strategic partner', which is future-focused, based on the strategic management of people and aligning HRM strategy with business strategy. The operationally focused, people-oriented role of 'employee champion', in which HR is responsible to employees, contrasts with the people-oriented strategic role of 'change agent', which is focused on managing organisational performance. (Hope Hailey et al 2005, p51)

Hope Hailey et al (2005) found that there was, in their case study, a conflict between the people-oriented role of 'employee champion', which was left to an ill-equipped line management to fulfil, and that of 'change agent' and 'strategic partner'. As a result of this conflict of role (role ambiguity), the employee lost its voice. The focus of the bank on purely bottom-line (monetary) performance measures and cost reduction as a strategic aim can lead over time to both firm economic decline and employee alienation. There needs to be incentives to encourage high-commitment strategies, with a focus on delivery of quality training and development, encouraging employee voice and so on.

The problem in essence, for HR, is how to balance the four roles of the 1997 Ulrich model (note: the Ulrich model was updated in 2005). It is clear though that if line management is to fulfil some of these roles, for example 'employee champion' and 'change agent', that they need appropriate training so that they [line managers] understand both what is required of them and the importance of the roles. And this has to be reflected in the metrics against which management is measured. In the case study it was found that line managers were geographically dispersed, their roles had been reduced and all this at a time when people problems were at their most serious. The measurement of their success was by measuring the financial performance of their units (sales targets), not by how they managed their people.

In their study, Hope Hailey et al (2005) found that although the HR department, over time, took a strategic perspective, it did not set the conditions nor encourage employee discretionary behaviour. In conclusion the following is offered in the context of HRM and performance:

- The conceptual model of employee linkage needs to be extended by '… bringing employee voice into the equation, observing the processes implemented for creating opportunities for two-way communication'.

- Although the best employee policies [on staff development] may be designed, in the case of the bank it was the introduction of open learning centres. But if these cannot be used, because of pressure of work, then their effectiveness is limited.

- High performance is not sustainable unless attention is given to developing innovative HRM policies that develop the firm's human capital.

Kaplan and Norton (1996) offer the 'balanced scorecard' as a means of, as its name implies, a 'balanced' way of setting metrics, which are both financial and non-financial, against which the business and the people within it can be measured. The emphasis on the balanced scorecard is that these measures of business performance '… emphasises that financial and nonfinancial measures must be part of the information system for employees at all levels of the organization'. The balanced scorecard can be both tactical and strategic in nature and consists of:

- **financial measures** – objectives, measures, targets, initiatives

- **internal business processes** – those processes that the organisation must excel at to deliver targets for shareholders (increase in return on capital invested by 100%, increase sales by 30%, introduce new products into service)

- **learning and growth** – this could be a focus on mentoring, coaching, employee development, education but, above all, there must be an effective delivery to relevant staff
- **customer** – how the customer should see the organisation (such as customer service, delivering on promises, dealing with customer queries, handling customer complaints, paying accurate salaries and allowances, handling wage queries and so on – in the latter cases it is the employee as the internal customer).

The above will only work if it is effectively communicated to staff at all levels and each level has a chance to air its views and have them recognised.

MANAGING THE RELATIONSHIP BETWEEN HR AND ITS INTERNAL CUSTOMERS

Regular face-to-face discussions with, for example, the IT department, with whom the HR business partner is providing a general resourcing, reward, leadership and development service, are of immense importance. However, it is useful to move the 'taken for granted service' into a more formal arena. It is at this stage that service level agreements (SLA) can be incorporated into HR practice. The SLA is, in effect, an internal contract for service without the legal binding nature of the formal contract. This sounds a contradiction but the worth of an SLA is in its intention and the transparency that it creates.

An SLA covers issues such as:

- Who will provide a particular service, for example the developing of a job description to be used as the basis of an advertisement for a position?
- Who will take responsibility for framing an advertisement for a position?
- Who will 'sign-off' on the content of the advertisement?
- Who will pay for its placement in a newspaper or professional journal?
- Who will physically do the first shortlist of candidates?
- Who will approve the first shortlist of candidates?

The SLA has many advantages. It forms the basis for discussion and in some cases causes discussion of and about issues, hopefully leading to clarity of provision. It does not necessarily systemise the provision of a service but rather states who is responsible for activities, who is accountable and thus, as mentioned above, signs off an activity, who needs to be aware of an activity and agreed timescales and budgetary responsibilities. In essence it gives a responsibility to act and an accountability for performance.

ACTIVITY 3.5

Service level agreement

Taking the role of an HR business partner, think of an activity (in recruitment, reward, learning and development and so on) for which you could provide a service to a line management function. Working with a colleague, who will take the role of a line manager, develop a draft service level agreement covering the areas mentioned above – and any more you can think of. How 'water-tight' (specific) do you think the SLA needs to be?

SUMMARISING HR AND CUSTOMER SERVICE

The above discussions show that time must be given to recruiting people who can add to the organisation and who have the appropriate skills and attitudes. There is also a need to consider how to engage with those employees, crucially ensuring that there is both upward as well as downward communication. It is essential that those on the receiving end of the upward communication actively listen to what is being said; failure to do this can have a detrimental effect upon the organisation's effectiveness.

Clearly 'management' of customer and staff expectations is not an easy process to co-ordinate. To use one-dimensional measures of performance, such as company share price, can lead to unintended outcomes: employee stress, disaffected employees and lack of commitment. Organisational success and organisational improvement are very important but it is also important to recognise the need to give employee voice, as mentioned, and to encourage other high-commitment practices for those employees who will eventually deliver the essential organisational outcomes.

SUMMARY

There is a wide variety of views about human resource management. The concept has been variously interpreted and the style with which its principles and practices are applied varies among academics, practitioners and indeed from one country to another. The history of management thought, which began in earnest in the early twentieth century, produced theories that contain allusions to what we now regard as HRM principles and practices (Taylor 1947; Burns and Stalker 1966), but they were not introduced into British organisations as a totally new management system until the 1980s.

Research shows that HRM has been *more* or *less* adopted by organisations (Beardwell and Claydon 2004, p26). British managers, however, have a record of reluctance to adopt new ideas in the comprehensive sense; they are very financially orientated and change, which is always a costly process, is usually carried out in a cautious and piecemeal fashion. Differences between the underlying philosophies and practices in 'personnel and industrial relations' and those of HRM have been postulated by Storey (1992), who clearly outlines 27 points of difference showing how those who have adopted HRM have shifted towards a more open and flexible approach.

Throughout the *classical* and mid-twentieth-century studies of management, the accepted managerial skills were described as *planning, organising, directing* and *controlling* – the four functions being linked together through co-ordination. By contrast, HRM engages the employee by changing the nature of the manager–worker relationship away from the *control* and *compliance* model towards a *colleague* relationship, meaning working *with*, rather than working *for*.

There are a variety of definitions of HRM, each stressing at least one main feature that differentiates it from other approaches to managing the personnel function. These main features range from 'integrating the management of personnel with core management activities', 'moving towards a more flexible organisation in order to achieve a competitive advantage' to 'a strategic and coherent approach to the management of an organisation's most valued assets, the people working there'.

Distinctions have been drawn between hard and soft HRM, in which *hard* HRM is typified by an emphasis on numbers of people, while little regard is paid to their needs. *Soft* HRM, on the other hand, is typified by a flexible workforce whose talents are nurtured and developed further to enable them to make contributions to the achievement of a competitive advantage.

Strategic human resource management integrates organisational strategy with operations, whereas previously they were regarded as separate entities. In this way employees' understanding of the strategy means that they can see how the nature of their work contributes to the success of the strategy. This, in turn, influences employees' attitudes to their jobs and encourages commitment to and involvement with the all-round success of the organisation.

Finally, this chapter deals with the notion of HR, as a function, in its role as a service provider and the idea of how HR can itself provide its customers with a service and how it can encourage staff to 'go beyond' their written contract of service. Customer service has to be considered in a multi-layered manner. Customers can be internal to as well as external to an organisation. Measuring organisation performance should not simply focus on one measure, such as share price or profitability, but recognise, as Kaplan and Norton (1996) propose, a balanced spread of measures. Schneider (2004) suggests that measures which focus on 'employee contribution' should take account of how employees engage with customers.

1   If you were asked, 'What is the difference between personnel management and human resource management?' what would be your interpretation?

2   What do you understand by the following terms:

    ● unitarist?

    ● pluralist?

3   How might the introduction of HRM into an organisation affect how the non-personnel functions are managed?

4   Why has British industry been slow to take up HRM?

5   It has been said that the adoption of HRM is not the only way to achieve a competitive advantage. To what does this statement refer?

6   What is meant by the terms 'hard' and 'soft' HRM?

7   What are the four main managerial skills associated with earlier theories of management?

8   What is the main reason why an organisation would take up HRM?

9   Why do you think organisations that have adopted HRM aim to reduce the size of the workforce? Which employees did they not keep?

10 What events brought about the rise of HRM?

11 Why does the 'best-fit school of strategic human resource management' measure the degree to which there is vertical integration?

12 Of the three SHRM resourcing strategies discussed within the chapter, which of the three – *best-fit*, *best practice* or *resource-based view* – is more likely to be present in British industry?

13 Read Anat Arkin's (2007) article in *People Management* listed in the references at the end of the book and discuss what you understand by, in the modified Ulrich model, the following roles: transactional HR, embedded HR, centres of expertise and corporate HR.

14 What is good practice when considering the link between HRM and customer service?

15 What is a service level agreement (SLA)? What are the advantages of using SLAs?

BOOKS

BANFIELD, P. and KAY, R. (2008) *Introduction to human resource management.* **Oxford: Oxford University Press.**

Banfield and Kay offer a mix of both an academic and professional perspective on human resource management and strategic human resource management. Their text is well supported by diagrams and is easy to follow.

PILBEAM, S. and CORBRIDGE, M. (2010) *People resourcing and talent planning: HRM in practice.* **Harlow: Pearson Education Ltd.**

Although a postgraduate text, Pilbeam and Corbridge's book is very accessible. Chapter 1 deals with the changing nature of the role of the HR professional and introduces the concept of HR strategy. Chapter 2 deals, in more depth, with the ideas around HR strategy and also offers some critique of the concepts.

WEB LINKS

QinetiQ: www.annualreport2009.qinetiq.com

CHAPTER 4

The Role of the HR Practitioner

LEARNING OBJECTIVES

After studying this chapter you should understand:

- the responsibilities of HR practitioners
- the distinction between operational and strategic HR activities
- the range and scope of the activities of the HR practitioner
- the structure and uses of HR information systems and records
- the performance standards that are expected of an HR professional
- the code of conduct to which the HR professional is expected to adhere.

INTRODUCTION

This chapter examines and discusses the functions and activities in which the HR practitioner is involved and the variety of roles they may undertake. The performance standards that are expected of the practitioner and the code of conduct to which they are expected to adhere are also discussed. Historically the role was primarily confined to looking after the welfare of employees, but has grown over the years, broadening out into a wide range of areas – from administration through to organisational strategy.

In the HR field, practitioners operate at several levels, with the tasks and responsibilities varying according to their level and status. For example, those in senior positions – HR managers – are involved in departmental management, corporate strategy and HR policy formulation, while those in the middle ranks may be specialists (for example employee relations or recruitment) with sectional responsibility. Lower down still, HR officers and administrators carry out tasks at operational level. The range and scope of HR activities is wide, and there are often options to become specialists in one of the main functions, or to operate as generalists and work in several of the functions.

How HR practitioners operate in this respect determines, to some extent, the structure of the HR department. If practitioners operate as 'specialists', then the department is divided into sections according to the main functions and activities, for example recruitment, health and safety, employee development and so on. Where practitioners are generalists, the structure may mean that each practitioner is responsible for all HR requirements in a particular department or area of the organisation. There are, however, wide variations in the ways that organisations structure their departments.

What HR people actually do depends on the needs and HR policies of the particular organisation in which they work, and of course on their own individual capabilities. Table 4.1 is an analysis of the levels at which HR practitioners normally operate and their duties and responsibilities.

 ACTIVITY 4.1

What is the structure of HR in your organisation? Are there specialists or generalists? Or both? What activities do they undertake?

Table 4.1 Example of an analysis of HR responsibilities

Level	Responsibility and specialism
Senior HR managers	Participation in corporate-level strategic decision-making Formulation of HR strategy and policies Advising other managers on the implementation of HR policies and procedures
Middle-level HR managers and specialists	Managing specialist sections including: • HR planning • recruitment and selection • employee development • performance and reward • employee relations • health and safety management and welfare/well-being
HR officers and administrators	Day-to-day administration of the HR department Updating and maintaining secure and confidential records Ensuring efficient organisation of events including: interviews, induction and training Liaising with colleges and universities Attending career conventions Producing data for such purposes Maintaining and updating HR systems and procedures, for example absence records

It has to be stressed that Table 4.1 is only an example, since organisations vary in how they deploy their HR staff. It does, however, give a broad indication of the kinds of responsibility and tasks that are carried out at each level.

PAUSE FOR THOUGHT

Of course, in reality, the divisions may not be so clear. Some HR staff will be involved in both strategic direction but also deal with day-to-day issues around the employment contract, for instance. In many organisations, employees are encouraged to be involved in strategy, although decision-making is generally undertaken at the top. See Chapter 3 for more on this.

THE RANGE AND SCOPE OF HR ACTIVITIES

It can be seen that many of the functions in which HR practitioners become involved are well known. Most people, when asked 'what does HR do?' will reply with 'recruitment and selection, dealing with pay, handling redundancies, discipline and grievance'. These areas require specialised knowledge and skills and, very often, knowledge of the law.

However, much of the actual management of human resources and employee relations is primarily the responsibility of line managers. It is line managers who – hopefully with the advice and assistance of HR specialists – recruit staff, manage and lead people, allocate their work, assess their performance, guide and counsel them in their jobs, make decisions about their training and development, and handle employee relations problems such as matters of grievance and discipline. Much of what a line manager does is HR!

 KEY CONCEPT: LINE MANAGER

A line manager is a senior employee who is responsible for ensuring that all of the tasks necessary for the achievement of the objectives of an operational department or section are carried out on time and to the required standard.

However, line managers often have little knowledge or expertise of HR issues and thus it is vital that HR is able to provide this to support them.

 ACTIVITY 4.2

Talk to some line managers and see what aspects of HR they undertake in their daily jobs. How much need do they have for HR guidance and support?

Redman and Wilkinson (2009) suggest the following list of functions that are performed by HR:

- job analysis
- human resource planning
- recruitment and selection
- training and development
- pay and conditions of service
- grievance and disciplinary procedures
- employee relations and communications
- administration of contracts of employment
- employee welfare and counselling
- equal opportunities policy and monitoring
- health and safety
- outplacement
- culture management
- knowledge management.

 ACTIVITY 4.3

How does this list compare with what HR does in your organisation? Are all of these activities covered?

Ulrich and Brockbank (2005) have identified the roles of HR specialists as falling into the following categories:

- employee advocate
- functional expert
- human capital developer
- strategic partner
- HR leader.

Employee advocate: This is closely linked with the historical role of the welfare officer, in which HR has its roots. This role focuses on understanding the needs of the employees but also communicating with and on behalf of them. It can include discipline and grievance as well as discrimination issues.

Functional expert: This is where the HR practitioner will use their expertise and knowledge to undertake specialist HR practices, for example recruitment and selection or performance and reward. This is often an administrative role or one where advice and guidance is given to line managers.

Human capital developer: This role is about training and developing staff to ensure they have the right skills, knowledge and attitudes to do their jobs. It can also encompass knowledge management – the need to develop knowledge, innovation and creativity within the business.

Strategic partner: This is a higher-level role, with involvement in organisational strategy. It is about ensuring that HR has an input into how the business runs and that HR policies and procedures are in line with where the business is going. Having an HR director on the company board who can advise on where HR can help the organisation to achieve its objectives can be important here.

HR leader: This involves leading the HR function, setting goals and working with all parts of the business on HR. This role is not just at the top of the organisation – *all* HR managers should be leaders.

A different model is put forward by Armstrong (2006). He outlines several roles provided by HR (below):

- **Providing services:** HR provide services such as recruitment and selection, training, health and safety, human resource planning, employee relations, reward and so on. It's about providing an efficient service to managers to help them run the business and may include issues such as counselling and welfare.

- **Advice and guidance:** This is about providing advice and guidance to managers – both at a strategic level and on a day-to-day basis.

Table 4.1 showed the ideal situation in which senior HR managers are involved at the top level. They formulate HR strategy and policies, have these integrated into the overall corporate strategy and offer guidance to other senior managers on the implementation of policy.

Top-level managers rely on the expertise of HR managers for guidance on such matters as the availability of particular knowledge and skills in the internal and external labour markets (see Chapter 5), since the employment of people with appropriate knowledge and skills is essential for the achievement of objectives.

Line managers turn to HR practitioners when they need guidance on such matters as policies and procedures in relation to pay, absenteeism, grievance and discipline, redundancy, bullying, and so on. Often this advice is in relation to legislation, for instance adhering to discrimination laws. Then there will be advice given to employees – on a variety of issues, such as career development, grievances, stress or personal problems.

- **Business partner:** As in the Ulrich model above, this is a role that focuses on how HR can help the business. It is about having the knowledge of the organisation and the commercial awareness of how HR can help to achieve business goals. It involves working with line managers to run an efficient and effective organisation.

- **The strategist role:** HR strategists should be looking at the long-term issues affecting the organisation. They should contribute to the formulation of business plans.

- **The innovation and change agent role:** HR specialists need to be innovators and also be able to manage change. They should use their expertise in communication, facilitation and championing change to provide effective people management.

- **The internal consultancy role:** This is where HR can diagnose problems and provide solutions. Again, HR works in conjunction with line managers in areas such as team-building, objective-setting and making recommendations for a more effective business.

- **The monitoring role:** Often seen as a 'policing' role, HR do have to audit policies and practices – for instance, equal opportunities – to ensure that legislation is being adhered to. Unfortunately, this is often seen by line managers as HR 'checking up' on them, but is all too often essential to ensure no laws are being broken, and that managers are abiding by company policies – for the benefit of all.

- **The guardian of values:** This is where HR act as the conscience of the management, ensuring that company values concerning people are upheld and checking that behaviour meets these values. This is a difficult role to perform.

(Adapted from Armstrong 2006)

ALIGNING HR TO CORPORATE STRATEGY

HR strategy should always fit with the corporate strategy – our goals and priorities in HR should be steered by the organisation's goals and aims. To provide a good service, HR needs access to a vast amount of information: absence records, labour turnover figures, recruitment data, pay structures – these are just a few areas where accurate data can impact on important decisions to be made by the organisation. If the organisation wishes to expand, data about effective recruitment will be vital. If cost-cutting is paramount, data on pay, staffing numbers and expenditure on training may all be key to achieving the organisation's goals.

While 'soft' HR approaches can help with improved productivity, motivation and discretionary behaviour, the 'hard' approach may be essential in achieving cost savings vital to the survival of the business. HR practitioners need to keep their eye on the ball with regard to finance – all too often the criticism is made that HR does not understand the financial side of the business – and today, that is just not acceptable. Whatever we do in HR must be financially viable. If we want to gain the support and 'buy-in' of line managers (and of senior managers), we need to show the value of our work. To be fully effective and add value to the organisation, HR must have influence at board level and be able to influence things at a strategic level. It is important that managers see the value of HR and how HR can help the business.

THE STRUCTURE AND USES OF HR INFORMATION SYSTEMS

CONFIDENTIALITY

The need for information has been steadily increasing over the past 20 years. With the advent of the Internet, the world's advanced economies have now entered the information age and the basis upon which management decisions are made has become more systematic, factual and information-based. Records on sickness absence, turnover, ages, race and gender of staff, number of those with disabilities are some of the information kept by organisations, either to inform them in making policy decisions or to fulfil government requirements. Inability to provide information at an employment tribunal can, for example, lead to the loss of a case, which might have seemed 'cut and dried'. The HR practitioner needs to have information at their fingertips. Legislation also demands information, and the amount of research carried out by educational and industrial organisations grows larger by the day. The amount of available information, therefore, has grown considerably. Much of this information is confidential and needs to be treated carefully.

MANUAL VERSUS COMPUTERISED SYSTEMS

Most organisations now have access to and use computer databases. There will still be paper-based items such as employees' original application forms, contracts of employment and any other documentation – letters, references, and so on – that relate to employment. Such records should be systematically filed for security purposes and ease of access to authorised users.

COMPUTERISED HR INFORMATION SYSTEMS

Taylor (2008, p36) cites Parry and Tyson's research (2007) on the use of IT in HRM, highlighting the growth of computerised information systems in recent years, which has enabled HR practitioners to improve their ability to monitor what goes on in the business. Not only can absence, turnover, pay and training be monitored easily, but specific programs on human resource planning, psychometric testing, employee development and appraisals can be used to help make relevant decisions. Databases containing employee details can be a real time-saver when it comes to working out pay awards, statistics on how many people have been trained, who is due for retirement and so on.

This means that an established, well-maintained, up-to-date and accurate computerised HR information system has many advantages. It:

- provides a reliable basis for strategic decision-making
- supports services to line managers
- can provide guidance and advice to line managers on HR matters
- gives immediate access to policy statements

- provides information when decisions need to be made about the future of an individual employee
- ensures that information required by law is readily available.

At the strategic and policy-making level, managers turn to the HR department when they need particular information, for example information about numbers and locations of staff, pay structures, or skills audits, which might be useful in a redundancy situation.

USING AND MAINTAINING HR RECORDS

One of the most important administrative duties of the HR practitioner is keeping records. Acas, the Advisory, Conciliation and Arbitration Service, suggests that all organisations, however large or small, need to keep records of their employees. Some records are kept to comply with the law and others are useful for internal administration. For example, keeping records of pay rates will help employers to check they are complying with the National Minimum Wage Act 1998 (www.acas.org.uk). From the records, the HR department can provide strategic planners and other managers with information that will enable them to make good-quality decisions about people. In fact, it is continuously necessary as a basis for decisions affecting major HR functions at an organisational level, such as human resource planning, recruitment and selection, performance management, succession planning and health and safety.

HR records should be seen as a useful tool of management, and maintaining them can be a full-time job. Well-maintained records are up to date, accurate and secure, yet easily accessed. If they are neglected, especially in terms of keeping them up to date, they do not become merely useless, they can become dangerous. Sending someone a letter about their 'long service award' when they died in service six months ago is something to be avoided! Clearly, poor decision-making will result from the use of out-of-date records as a source of information for matters of importance.

Information about the human resource is vital to the successful management of the whole organisation. If we don't have information about how high our staff turnover is, for instance, then how can we do anything about it? Such information can give an insight into problem areas in the organisation and point to where changes can be made for the better. A detailed examination of labour turnover may show high turnover in certain areas of the business that are costing the organisation very dearly. The 2009 CIPD Recruitment, Retention and Turnover survey report gives a figure of £6,125 replacement cost for every employee who leaves an organisation. Multiplied up, this can mean enormous costs for the business – so it is essential to know what our turnover figures are and then decide what can be done about it. A lack of such information can mean we are spending money unwisely or are wasting money – so HR information of this kind can be extremely important in increasing the profitability of the business.

WHAT THE RECORDS CONTAIN

The HR department keeps and maintains records that include the personal details of all employees and the events and activities in which they become involved during their period of employment. For example, a personal history is kept on every individual employee from when they first joined the organisation. The details that are held should include:

- the employee's original application form
- copy of the contractual arrangements
- job title on joining (updated with any changes) and, if possible, job description
- date on which employment commenced
- background and previous employment history
- department in which the employee works
- employee category (staff or hourly paid, etc)
- state of health on joining
- National Insurance number
- date of birth
- gender
- ethnic origin
- marital status
- salary/wage details and other rewards
- hours of work
- record of attendance and absences
- personal contact details
- academic achievements
- training and further education undertaken before and since joining
- performance assessments
- suitability for transfer and promotion
- career interviews with managers and HR staff
- pension contributions
- trade union membership
- disciplinary record.

 ACTIVITY 4.4

If you work in HR, have a look at the records and see the types of information that is held. Are they stored in a way that is easily retrievable – and useable?

USES OF INDIVIDUAL INFORMATION

It can be seen that when individual information is held on all employees, it represents an extremely useful data bank for management and for planning purposes when viewed collectively. But the individual records themselves are also valuable. If, for example, a case arises that concerns an individual's current employment or future position, their personal history will provide background information that will assist in managerial decision-making. Similarly, when people are being considered for further training and development, promotion or special assignment work, their personal records provide an ideal basis upon which good-quality decisions can be made, which would be to the benefit of the individual and the organisation.

STATISTICAL INFORMATION

Organisational statistics serve two very important functions:

- They provide essential information about main areas affecting the general state of the organisation at a particular time.
- They also indicate trends that need to be made apparent so that timely measures may be taken to improve conditions of work and performance.

HR-related statistics can be drawn from accumulated individual records that have been collated, such as those for attendance management, accident rates and wages and salaries. Statistical information may also be drawn from accumulated records relating to staff turnover, workforce stability, sickness absence, skills inventories, deployment, job analyses, recruitment trends and employment costs. Externally gathered data may also be added to provide information on the availability of labour, including special or rare skills, local, regional, national and international employment trends, and average earnings. Information of this type and quantity is indispensable to senior managers and HR strategists, especially in relation to aspects such as HR planning.

LEGAL ASPECTS OF RECORD-KEEPING

On the one hand, many managers are reluctant to allow employees access to the information about them that is on record, while on the other, most employees feel that they are entitled to have access, even if only to check that the information is correct. The Data Protection Act 1998 (DPA98) provides a legal entitlement for employees to access their own personal records and, indeed, any information about them. See Chapter 16 and Chapter 19 for more on data protection laws.

HR PROFESSION MAP

The CIPD HR Profession Map covers the *technical elements* of professional competence required in the HR profession as well as *behaviours* that an HR professional needs to carry out their activities. It describes what you need to do, what you need to know and how you need to do it within each professional area at four bands of professional competence. It is organised around areas of professional competence, not organisation structures, job levels or roles. The HR Profession Map replaces the CIPD's Professional Standards as the CIPD's new benchmark for the profession.

The Map is a comprehensive view of how HR adds the greatest sustained value to the organisations it operates in, now and in the future. It combines the highest standards of professional competence with the closest alignment to your organisational goals, to deliver sustained performance.

It captures what HR people do and deliver across every aspect and specialism of the profession and it looks at the underpinning skills, behaviour and knowledge that they need to be most successful. It also creates a clear and flexible framework for career progression, recognising both that HR roles and career progression vary.

The map covers ten areas:

- strategy, insights and solutions
- leading and managing the human resources function
- organisation design
- organisation development
- resourcing and talent planning
- learning and talent development
- performance and reward
- employee engagement
- employee relations
- service delivery and information.

There are four bands of professional competence that define the contribution that professionals make in the following key areas:

- the relationship that professionals have with clients, such as support, adviser, consultant or leader
- the focus of the activities performed by professionals, such as support, advising or leading
- where professionals spend their time, such as providing information, understanding issues, understanding the business or understanding organisational issues
- what services are provided to clients, such as information-handling issues, providing solutions or challenging hard issues
- how their contribution and success is measured.

Figure 4.1 Behaviours

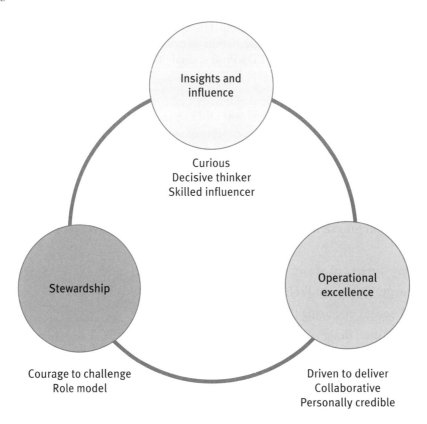

The behaviours are as follows:

- **Curious:** Shows an active interest in the internal and external environment and in the continuous development and improvement of self and others at both organisation and individual levels. Is open-minded with a bias and willingness to learn and enquire.

- **Decisive thinker:** Demonstrates the ability to analyse and understand data and information quickly. Is able to use information, insights and knowledge in a structured way, using judgement wisely to identify options and make robust and defendable decisions.

- **Skilled influencer:** Demonstrates the ability to influence across a complex environment to gain the necessary commitment, consensus and support from a wide range of diverse stakeholders in pursuit of organisation benefit.

- **Driven to deliver:** Demonstrates a consistent and strong bias to action, taking accountability for delivery of results both personally and/or with others. Actively plans, prioritises and monitors performance, holding others accountable for delivery.

- **Collaborative:** Works effectively and inclusively with colleagues, clients, stakeholders, customers, teams and individuals both within and outside of the organisation.

- **Personally credible:** Builds a track record of reliable and valued delivery using relevant technical expertise and experience and does so with integrity and in an objective manner.

- **Courage to challenge:** Shows courage and confidence to speak up, challenge others even when confronted with resistance or unfamiliar circumstances.

- **Role model:** Consistently leads by example. Acts with integrity, impartiality and independence, applying sound personal judgement in all interactions.

(Taken from the CIPD website at www.cipd.co.uk/hr-profession-map/)

The CIPD itself encourages its members to adopt continuing professional development (CPD) and to urge organisations to encourage their employees to engage in personal development planning. See Chapter 10 on human resource development for more on CPD.

 ACTIVITY 4.5

Do you keep a log of your activities and what you have learned from them? Do you have a plan outlining your future development? Why not start now? How do you go about doing it?

Next Generation HR is the CIPD's new flagship research project. Based on feedback from a variety of sources, including more than 80 one-on-one interviews across 14 separate organisations, the research aims to prompt the profession to start thinking about what it needs to look like in the future. The project focuses on testing three hypotheses: first, that HR's purpose needs to shift to being about sustainable organisational performance; second, that in order to do this it needs to focus on building a culture of authenticity, demonstrating a balanced approach to risk management and developing organisational agility; and last, that both of these hypotheses will, in turn, affect the type of HR leadership we will need in future.

Work to test these hypotheses took place in 2009 in a range of organisations including BT, Standard Chartered, Nationwide, Shell, Cambridgeshire County Council and Cancer Research.

CASE EXAMPLE

'Next Generation HR will influence our thinking, behaviour and actions well into the future.' (John Wrighthouse, Human Resources Director, Nationwide)

People Management 19 November 2009

Next Generation HR is one of the most compelling pieces of work undertaken by our professional body. If we get this right, it will influence our thinking, behaviour and actions well into the future. It is this order of magnitude that underlines why we all need to be engaged in determining the future of HR: what we do, how we do it and the legacy we gift to the organisations of which we are a part.

HR has always been about creating the environment, the platform, conditions and ingredients that we believe drive organisational performance and success. In recent times, we have perhaps forgotten these core ingredients in the rush for perceived instant results – in the good times, perhaps we are less vigorous about putting in place the conditions for future success. But HR isn't just for the good times! Our shareholders and stakeholders may have once valued short-term success, but they are increasingly focused upon the sustainability of such success. This applies to all sectors and organisations, and it is for this reason that we all need to be engaged in determining the role that we will have in Next Generation HR.

Being in HR means being brave and challenging the unquestioned by being curious. It means being authentic for yourself and for your organisation. To have the impact that is necessary to drive change and influence means being curious about your organisation, about your competitors and, significantly, about what makes your organisation work. The purpose of HR is changing, because the landscape has shifted. Make no mistake – this is the moment to mark: the expectations of HR have changed. The preoccupation of some about how HR should be organised and the internal view taken has been no more than a sideshow. Next Generation HR compels HR people to think about the role they have in their organisation: how to create sustainable competitive advantage for the future. The very best HR professionals of the future will be those who lead the business agenda through the organisation's people resource. Sustainable business performance is what it's about: the key drivers of this are a relentless focus on creating the conditions for organisational adaptability, flexibility and agility. Business is about sustainable performance. HR is about creating the conditions for such sustained performance.

Nationwide has strong business and customer values. It cannot 'live' to these values unless all our employees and workers are proud to be a part of the business and genuinely share our values. It is HR that 'connects' the business to our customers through our people. The function has a unique ability to be both the advocate of business values and also mirror back the reality. No other business function has this quality.

What do you think? Do you agree with John Wrighthouse? Where do you think the future of HR lies?

SUMMARY

In this chapter we have discussed the varied functions and roles of HR. We have seen that HR responsibilities can take on many forms, depending on what level we are at. Most practitioners are involved at the 'coal-face' – they deal with the everyday issues and problems of people management in organisations, such as grievance and disciplinaries, selection interviews and welfare activities. But according to Ulrich and Brockbank (2005), there are several roles to play: those of employee advocate, strategic partner and human capital developer, as well as HR leader and functional expert.

The activities within these roles are again wide and varied – carrying out job analysis, advertising vacancies, training staff, supporting the performance management process, monitoring absence, to name but a few. The average day of someone in HR is full of variety, from sorting out pay queries and making someone redundant, to delivering an induction programme and then handling a disciplinary interview. You never know what the day will hold in store – and that is part of what makes it exciting to work in HR. The level at which HR staff work may also be varied – dealing with an individual's flexible working claim one minute then writing a company-wide policy on bullying the next. Administration and record-keeping may be part of HR's work, but it is rarely dull and boring.

The HR Profession Map reflects this variety. It identifies the behaviours required in an HR professional, from being curious and possessing the ability to challenge, to acting as a role model and being personally credible. Being able to deliver is important, as is the need to work collaboratively. Being in HR means you will need knowledge as well as many skills and talents – hopefully reading this book will help you in developing some of them.

REVIEW QUESTIONS

1   What is the difference between an HR specialist and an HR generalist?

2   Who is responsible for managing, leading and developing people?

3   What roles can HR play in an organisation, according to Armstrong?

4   How can HR help to add value to the business?

5   What does the role of a human capital developer entail?

6   Why are good HR records important?

7   How can computerised HR records help the HR practitioner?

8   How is the HR Profession Map relevant to your career?

9   Name the ten areas covered by the HR Profession Map.

10 Using the HR Profession Map, what behaviours are HR professionals expected to display?

EXPLORE FURTHER

BOOKS

ARMSTRONG, M. (2009) *Handbook of human resource management practice*. **London: Kogan Page.** (This is a down-to-earth book that covers most aspects of HR.)

WEB LINKS

For anyone considering a career in HR, the CIPD Profession Map makes essential reading:

www.cipd.co.uk/hr-profession-map

The Advisory, Conciliation and Arbitration Service provides excellent HR information: www.acas.org.uk

CHAPTER 5

Human Resource Planning

LEARNING OBJECTIVES

After studying this chapter you should:

- understand the elements of human resource planning in the traditional and modern contexts
- understand how human resource planning relates to the overall business strategy
- be able to make meaningful contributions to the human resource plan
- be able to forecast HR supply and demand
- understand and be able to use the internal and external labour markets
- be able to carry out a job analysis and understand the various approaches to it.

INTRODUCTION

More than ever before, human resource planning plays an essential and integral role in the achievement of the overall business strategy. The purpose of this chapter is to explain and discuss the techniques that are applied to human resource planning (HRP) and to demonstrate how the HR plan relates to the organisation's overall business plan. First, there is a brief history of its background, including definitions of traditional and modern systems. Second, we detail the ideas and theoretical concepts that form the basis upon which traditional and modern HRP activities are founded. Third, we examine and discuss the activities in which you become involved when operating as an HR planner. Fourth, there is guidance on how the activities themselves may be carried out.

The chapter contains case studies and activities for you to work through and, to aid your understanding, there are examples based on organisational situations, some of which are hypothetical while others have been taken from real life.

A BRIEF HISTORY

From the very early days of industrial activity, organisations have tried to ensure that they would have people 'coming up through the ranks' or indeed recruited fresh into the organisation to succeed longer-serving skilled employees.

Apprenticeships, for example, in which, traditionally, young people learn the skills that will be needed in the future, date back to the 'cottage industries' that preceded the Industrial Revolution. It made sense for master craft workers to take on apprentices and train them in their crafts.

It is important to bear in mind that these arrangements for continuity of the crafts were made in the days when change was slow; the craft workers could rely on their skills remaining useful long into the foreseeable future, and they could safely pass their industrial genes down to the rising generation. With the Industrial Revolution came the development of factories and larger-scale industries, which created a demand for a more organisation-wide approach to planning of the future workforce. The craft guilds also provided a certain amount of 'job protection' for those lucky enough to be members.

THE GROWTH OF PLANNING FOR THE FUTURE WORKFORCE

By the twentieth century, apprenticeship was widespread across a broad range of skills and crafts. Modern Apprenticeships, which fall within the Government's vocational and education initiatives (refer to Chapter 10), are for those 16 years of age and over. Currently there are three levels of apprenticeship:

- **Apprenticeships** – the apprenticeship gives the equivalent to five GCSE passes. Apprentices work towards work-based learning qualifications such as an NVQ Level 2, Key Skills and, in most cases, a relevant knowledge-based qualification such as a BTEC.

- **Advanced apprenticeships** – the apprenticeship gives the equivalent of two A-level passes. Advanced apprentices work towards work-based learning qualifications such as an NVQ Level 3. Candidates are required to have five GCSEs at grade C or above.

- **Higher apprenticeships** – Higher apprentices work towards work-based learning qualifications such as an NVQ Level 4 or a Foundation Degree.

(National Apprenticeships website)

Key to the national apprenticeship is funding and at the moment funding is available from the National Apprenticeship Service. The size of the contribution varies and depends on the sector and the age of the candidate. If the apprentice is aged 16–18, then 100% of the cost of the training will be paid; for apprentices 19+, then the funding is reduced to 50%.

 ACTIVITY 5.1

Go on to the National Apprenticeship and the National Employer Apprenticeship websites and read about the different opportunities for apprenticeships. What is the key difference about the apprenticeship funding, as advertised by the National Apprenticeship website, compared with that advertised by the National Employer Apprenticeship website? The websites are given at the end of this chapter.

MANPOWER PLANNING

The *manpower planning* process first appeared in the 1960s. This was the first attempt to develop a systematic method of ensuring that the organisation would have a continuous supply of the people it needed now, and would need in the future, in order to carry out the tasks that led to the achievement of objectives.

 Aspire Housing

CASE EXAMPLE

The Aspire Housing Group is a non-profit-making social landlord, based in Newcastle-under-Lyme, which employs 420 people. The organisation manages the housing stock in the local area, of which they took ownership from the borough council in January 2000. They manage, maintain and improve the housing stock, renting and leasing properties.

As part of their social inclusion agenda, Aspire Housing has always employed apprentices, also valuing the business benefits of doing so. The apprenticeships they offer are closely aligned to the organisational needs identified through their workforce planning, enabling them to fulfil anticipated skill requirements. In 2008 they acquired PM Training, a social enterprise providing young people with the skills and training they require to obtain employment. Through this acquisition, Aspire Housing was able to further develop its apprenticeship scheme, targeting young people from disadvantaged backgrounds from the local area, particularly those with whom PM Training was already working.

Apprenticeships bring a wealth of benefits to the company. They ensure that our workforce have the skills and qualifications that Aspire needs now and in the future. Apprentices receive on-the-job training so are able to contribute to the business whilst learning. They are also highly motivated and committed to the business and therefore stay with us and often progress through the company. Since the training is specific to Aspire Housing they learn about

our business processes, can address skills gaps and fill vacancies which are difficult to recruit for. (Ele Morrissey, Head of Organisational Development)

Apprentices are recruited through external applications as well as via PM Training. Candidates are invited to meet with Aspire Housing for an informal discussion about the role, determining whether the applicant is suitable and whether they are keen to pursue employment. Rather than following a formal written application process, an informal discussion facilitates a two-way dialogue. Successful candidates are offered a four-week unpaid trial, which again benefits both parties. The apprentice gets to experience the job first-hand and Aspire Housing is able to further assess suitability. Line managers meet weekly with the apprentice during the trial to provide support and address any issues directly as they arise. Each apprentice has a mentor as well as a line manager. The mentoring system provides further support for the apprentice as well as allowing the mentor to develop managerial skills.

I've been an apprentice mentor for almost a year and it's been challenging at times, but extremely rewarding, to see a young person settle into work and grow. Supporting a young person with no skills is an extremely important role. There is a distinct difference between the role of a mentor and a line manager. The line manager's role is to create a plan of learning and development and to assign work, whereas my role is to oversee their development as an individual. (Sue Cawley, Payroll Manager)

Currently there are 15 apprentices, 11 in vocational trades and 4 within business administration. The apprenticeship schemes last for between two and three years and provide people with the opportunity to obtain knowledge and skills on the job at the same time as working towards a National Vocational Qualification (NVQ). The importance of providing continuous development opportunities is emphasised. For example, one employee has completed his apprenticeship and gone on to study for an HND, which Aspire Housing is encouraging and funding.

Looking forward, there are plans to develop the apprentice scheme further, enabling youngsters to develop generic trades. They are also trying to attract female applicants to construction-type vacancies, which have traditionally been male-dominated. Initiatives include providing work experience for local schoolgirls, holding career events and working with local schools and colleges.

Information provided by Ele Morrissey, Head of Organisational Development

Questions:

- How does Aspire Housing benefit from having its own apprentice scheme? Refer to the National Apprenticeship website for ideas.

- How does Aspire Housing ensure that the potential apprentices fit in with the culture of the organisation?

- What does and what can Aspire Housing do to retain its apprentices once they have qualified? Refer to Chapter 8 for ideas.

When manpower planning was first proposed, manufacturing represented 60% of jobs and the planners relied on the availability of traditional skills. The process was analytic, and it was comprehensive in the sense that it set out to provide the staffing needs of the whole organisation. This approach was fine for the purpose it served, since the demand was for traditional knowledge, skills and competence across the total spectrum of organisational activities. By today's standards, change was still relatively slow, large-scale change was rare, and innovation was limited to little more than the modification of current methods and techniques.

Few organisations, however, developed and maintained manpower plans. In the absence of computers the related tasks were found to be cumbersome and time-consuming, and many organisations thought of it as an unwarranted cost. It was a paper exercise in which the need to maintain and keep the plan up to date included a set of tasks that could be likened to painting the Forth Bridge.

 ACTIVITY 5.2

The following definition of human resource planning was defined by Department of Employment in 1974 as:

a strategy for the acquisition, utilisation, improvement and retention of an enterprise's human resources.

1 Do you think that this definition has maintained a currency over the passage of time, especially when enterprises have become smaller and times have become more uncertain?

2 What would you add to or subtract from the definition?

MANPOWER PLANNING AND HUMAN RESOURCE PLANNING (HRP)

The term *human resource planning* came into being in the 1980s, when human resource management (HRM) first appeared. Around the same time, political correctness was introduced and it was inevitable anyway that an alternative term to *manpower* planning would have to be found. Modern *human resource planning* is different from manpower planning. Attempts to define them show there are areas that are common to both, but they differ markedly in the strategic approach and purposes. Definitions of processes, however, say more than simply what a process is; they also indicate the thinking that underlies the approach to its implementation.

For example, the original thinking behind defining manpower planning was that it was a strategy that '*secured the enterprise's human resources*', which amounted to acquiring the right number of appropriately skilled people when they were needed. The central idea was to achieve a match between manpower demand and manpower supply. *Demand* means the organisation's current and future human resource requirements, while *supply* refers to the degree to which the demand may be met, from the current workforce and externally. Cost and statistical analysis was central to the whole process.

DEFINITIONS

Julie Beardwell and her colleagues define modern HRP as 'the process for identifying an organisation's current and future human resource requirements, developing and implementing plans to meet these requirements and monitoring their overall effectiveness' (Beardwell and Claydon 2007). According to Bulla and Scott (1994), it is the process for ensuring that the human resource requirements of an organisation are identified and plans are made for satisfying those requirements.

According to Armstrong (2006, p368), planning is to:

- attract and retain the number of people required with the appropriate skills, expertise and competencies;

- anticipate the problems of potential surpluses or deficits of people;

- develop a well-trained and flexible workforce, thus contributing to the organisation's ability to adapt to an uncertain and changing environment; reduces dependence on external recruitment when key skills are in short supply by formulating retention, as well as employee development strategies;

- improve the utilisation of people by introducing more flexible systems of work.

 KEY CONCEPT: HUMAN RESOURCE PLANNING

Human resource planning (HRP) is a strategic management function, the aim of which is to ensure that the organisation will have the human resources it needs currently and in the future in order to realise its strategy and achieve its business objectives.

THE NATURE OF PLANNING

Before giving in-depth consideration to such a specialised area of planning as HRP, it is essential for you to develop a clear understanding of what we mean by planning. All organisational processes are planned to serve the overall corporate strategy.

AN IMPRECISE PROCESS

Organisational planning is not a precise activity. Indeed, the question has been asked, 'If it is an imprecise process, then why do it?' Truly, the predictions and demands that form essential components of a plan are seldom precise, but having some information with which to work is better than having no information. The rigorous application of related skills can produce a plan that is manageable, and in terms of precision, one can actually come close. In fact, all of business planning is like that; after all, few strategists would try to predict the precise nature of the business environment of the medium- or long-term future.

This is not to say that the future is a complete mystery to the strategist, since the organisation itself, by developing and marketing new products and new and creative ways of serving its customers, does have an influence on what happens in the future. There are, however, many external factors that are beyond the organisation's control; competitors' activities and the vagaries of the economy are two examples of this.

PLANNING PERIODS

Plans are normally divided into short, medium and long terms. The period over which business plans extend varies from one organisation to another, depending on the type of organisation, the type and state of market it serves (see the following example), the rate of internal change and its financial situation. Since we cannot predict all of the future, long-term plans have to be fairly vague in their content and direction. Medium-term plans, on the other hand, are slightly easier to specify; clearly, we can forecast more accurately what will happen in the forthcoming, say, two to five years. Short-term plans, which might range from the present day to two years hence, need to be precise and crystal clear; they are plans that demand more or less immediate action.

 Factors influencing planning timescales

CASE EXAMPLE

Consider the following: Sugar is a *stable product*, a product for which the demand is steady and long term. There is no *product innovation* and there are few companies in the industry at a primary level. With such a dependable market, the companies can draw up marketing plans that stretch far into the future and invest in capital equipment, confident that since there will not be a significant reduction in demand, they will get a return on their investment.

Software, on the other hand, is an *unstable product*, the demand for which changes rapidly and continuously. Product innovation is the main route to survival, and there are many companies in the industry. Few such companies have a long-term plan. To them, the medium term might be 18 months and the short term is in real time, depending on the rate at which the specifications of their products change. Mobile telephones and computer products fall into this category.

THE PLANNING PROCESS

All types of planning have a set of features in common. For example, according to Maund (2001) there are five stages in the planning process:

1 identification of the goal

2 clarification of the present position

3 consideration of the range of strategies that could be used to achieve the set goal

4 choice of the most appropriate strategy

5 the breaking down of the chosen strategy into smaller, more manageable steps.

 A simple analogy: planning

CASE EXAMPLE

All five of these stages are interrelated, and in the simplest of terms, the process is no different from that of planning a journey. Suppose for example you wanted to drive from London to Exeter. Your goal (Stage 1) is to get to Exeter. You know that London is your starting position (Stage 2). Then you consider the variety of routes that would enable you to achieve your goal and arrive in Exeter (Stage 3). After that, you select the route that you think is best suited to your purpose (Stage 4). Clearly, there will be grounds upon which you selected the route; for example, the time you need to be at your destination will be an important factor in making this decision. Finally, if you break the route down into its natural geographic stages, allowing yourself times and places for rests, you will be able to manage the trip more easily (Stage 5).

Certainly, business planning is more complex than planning the journey, as described in this example, but the simplicity of the analogy is intended to clarify the nature and sequence of the stages in the process.

 The importance of planning

CASE EXAMPLE

Two weeks ago, Alan submitted an assignment report and was glad to have seen the end of it; he had found it particularly arduous. Now, he has been notified of the grade and it is much lower than he had anticipated. Reflecting upon how he went about this task, Alan concluded that his poor performance was due to his lack of planning:

1 He failed to clarify his true goal.

2 In terms of other commitments, he had not assessed his position in terms of time management before he had started.

3 He had launched himself in at the deep end without considering alternative methods of approach to the task.

4 He could not, therefore, select an appropriate method.

5 He carried out the work randomly, as and when he felt like it.

Task: Draw up a plan for carrying out your next assignment.

Reflection: What have you learned from Alan's experience? How will you approach your assignments in the future?

Plans are a very important part of business and have a number of uses:

- They give an opportunity for individuals to give serious thought to what they want and not be panicked into quick and sometimes irrational decisions. All factors are considered, such as resource requirements, for example financial demands, logistical and so on, and time periods.

- Goals are more likely to be achieved in full.

- Relevant people who may be able to 'throw more light' on to the subject can be involved.

- Planning saves time in the long run because many of the issues that may arise will have been tabled for discussion and decisions approved.

TRADITIONAL AND MODERN HRP

At this stage it is necessary to draw a distinction between what many writers refer to as *traditional* and *contemporary* (or *modern*) HRP. In Chapter 3 we drew a distinction between hard and soft HRM. The approach that is taken here is that traditional HRP largely follows the 'hard' approach, meaning numbers and skills, while contemporary HRP equates with the 'soft' approach, meaning attitudes, motivation and teamworking. Most writers would agree that the elements of manpower planning are indicative of hard HRP.

It is important to note that while modern HRP has found a firm foothold in British industry, one should not assume that it is widespread. Many HR planning specialists are still using traditional systems, largely because their organisations have not adopted the principles and techniques of HRM. In the rest of this chapter, therefore, it is necessary to explain and discuss traditional and modern approaches to HRP.

Beardwell and Claydon (2007) argue that for modern human resource planning (HRP), consideration should be given to both hard and soft factors of the HRP because it is not just the hard factors alone – numbers – that should be considered, but in a world where customer service is king (or queen), the soft issues of planning such as the behaviours and attitudes that staff exhibit, as mentioned above, should be at the forefront of the process.

HRP has grown in importance in recent years, and in well-run organisations it is firmly integrated with business planning. Advances in information technology (IT) have eased the tasks that industry used to complain about and added impetus to the formulation and maintenance of HR plans. Now, with the right software, the computer has eliminated the tedious pen-pushing element and turned HRP into a dynamic, interesting and, at times, exciting function.

 ## ACTIVITY 5.3

1   Think of three companies that you consider would plan for the very long term and three that would have to be short term. Write down a justification for your selection.

2   In 2009 British Airways planned to make significant job reductions. Do you think that this was a result of poor HR planning or were other factors at play?

HR PLANNING AS A COMPETENCE-CENTRED FUNCTION

In modern management terms the human resource is the most important resource in the organisation, which means that HRP is one of the most important processes. Human resource planning is a *competence-centred* activity, since its central purpose is to match the knowledge and skill *supply* to the organisation's knowledge and skill *demand*. To this end, HR specialists study and analyse business plans, consult the business's managers to obtain information about their HR needs, make decisions about the nature of the HR requirement in terms of competence, and identify the most appropriate sources of supply.

SHADOWING THE BUSINESS PLAN

The best HR plans are produced by those who understand how their particular organisations interact with their total business environment, since this enables them to understand the thinking that underlies the business plans. It is essential for the HR plan to complement the business plan. To meet the needs of an ever-changing business environment, business plans are continuously monitored and updated to ensure that the organisation competes effectively and continues to serve the needs of its customers and clients. This means that those who create, maintain and update the HR plan appreciate that both business and HR plans are interdependent living entities that are continuously changing. The business plan changes to continue to reflect and create external market demands, while the HR plan, in a classic sense, changes to complement the business plan. The HR planner therefore has to shadow and keep pace with the business plan to maintain this complementary relationship.

TRADITIONAL APPROACHES TO HRP

There are four main activities involved in the HRP process:

- forecasting HR demand
- identifying sources of HR supply
- producing the HR plan
- activating and maintaining the plan.

In 1975, John Bramham devised a model depicting the HRP process, which he modified in 1994. This was adapted by Pilbeam and Corbridge in 2006 (see Figure 5.1).

According to the model, the HRP process goes through four main stages:

1 analysis and investigation
2 forecasting
3 planning
4 implementation and control.

ANALYSIS AND INVESTIGATION

This first stage is concerned with analysing and investigating the condition of the internal and external labour markets and the current capability of the organisation in terms of knowledge, skills and competence. The corporate strategy also has to be scrutinised for details of any future changes that would affect the HR requirement. For example, in its simplest terms, if a product expansion is expected then clearly more staff would be required. The sooner this is known the better, because new employees would have to be recruited and trained to the required competency levels.

Figure 5.1 Stages in the process of human resource planning

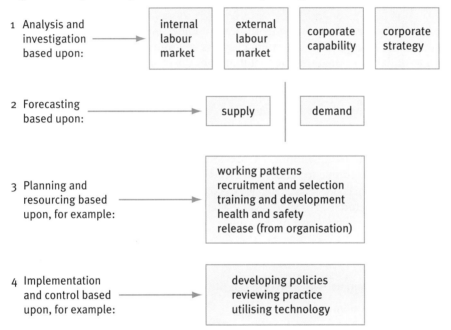

Adapted from Pilbeam and Corbridge (2006) and Bramham (1994) and reproduced with kind permission of the CIPD.

INTERNAL LABOUR MARKET

Qualitative and quantitative information has to be gathered about the current workforce in terms of the kind of work that is carried out by each individual: the qualifications, experience, skills and competence they need to do the job and the level at which they operate. When you assess the current workforce as a source of supply, you do so within the context of continuous movement and activity. It may be that a large proportion of the employees will remain in their present positions, but there are always people leaving and joining the organisation, being promoted, transferring, and so forth. From your HR records you should be able to assess:

- how many employees there are
- the nature of their skills and other qualities

- their level or status in the organisation
- the standards of their performance
- their attitudes and versatility
- their potential for promotion or other movement
- how many are likely to go sick, and when
- how many are likely to resign or be dismissed
- how many will retire, and when.

EXTERNAL LABOUR MARKET

Where the results of the HR demand analysis produces shortfalls in staff numbers and required competences, we gather and assess information about the external pool of potential future employees. The nature and levels of the jobs that are, or will be, affected by the shortfall means that the HR planner needs to search the labour markets at three levels: locally, nationally and internationally.

It also has to be borne in mind that other organisations will be searching at the same three levels and competing with your organisation for the same people. To compete effectively with other organisations, you must develop and keep up-to-date records of terms and conditions of employment that are offered at regional and industrial levels. This is often referred to as the *going rate*.

From a national perspective the Office for National Statistics (ONS) offers a range of useful statistics that can, in a *hard* sense, be incorporated into the organisation's macro planning activities. The set of statistics in Figure 5.2 were taken from the ONS website and depict the range of unemployment rates across Great Britain (Wales and Scotland are not regionalised).

Figure 5.2 Local unemployment rates by English regions and GB countries for April 2008 to March 2009

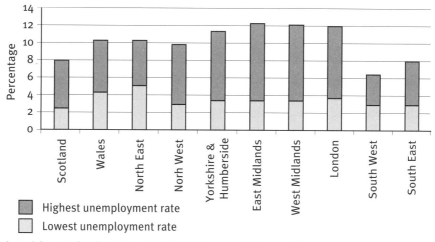

Adapted from Office for National Statistics (www.statistics.gov.uk)

The figures in Figure 5.2 have been sourced from data of those receiving 'Jobseeker's Allowances'. This type of information would be useful to companies who may be considering expansion activities and so would be searching for areas where there is a source of available labour, that is, where there is a *loose* labour market. Loose refers to the type of labour market where there are more people for jobs than there are jobs for people. A *tight* labour market would be one where there are more jobs than there are skilled people for those jobs. In Figure 5.2 the range of unemployment varies between 2.4% and 12.2%.

CORPORATE CAPABILITY

Information is gathered about the performance of the organisation, its structure, the technology it uses and intends to use in the future. You need to gather information about the organisation's strengths and weaknesses; the results of a recent SWOT analysis will provide much of this data (see Chapter 1).

CORPORATE STRATEGY

This is where the focus is on the organisation's future direction. Strategy is seldom a 'more of the same' process; in today's business environment strategic planning, for most organisations, spells change. The organisation's current capability, therefore, may not totally match up to the requirements that are laid down in the strategy and there is a requirement, therefore, to compare this with the predicted future capabilities.

 ## ACTIVITY 5.4

Obtain a copy of your organisation's annual report (or one of an organisation that you know) and compare what is said about the degree to which past objectives were achieved with what is said about how any problems with achieving future objectives might be overcome. Investigate how these predictions were developed.

FORECASTING HR DEMAND

Looking again at Figure 5.1, you will see that at the second stage, the planner studies the data gathered from the analysis and investigation to identify, and thereby forecast, the HR demand and supply.

Forecasting HR demand is a data-gathering process. It involves identifying the kinds of knowledge, understanding, skills and competences that will be required, where in the organisation the requirements exist, when they are needed, and in what quantities. The data must be gathered in an organised and systematic way.

According to Armstrong (2001) there are four basic demand forecasting methods for estimating the numbers of people required:

- managerial judgement

- ratio-trend analysis

- work study techniques

- modelling.

MANAGERIAL JUDGEMENT

This is a subjective technique and is not renowned for its accuracy. It is, however, the most commonly used. It is most effective in small organisations and those whose structure, technology and productivity remain relatively stable. What happens is that the organisation's managers estimate their future workloads and decide how many people they will need. The managers' decisions are based upon what they know about past trends and forthcoming changes. Managers sometimes do this under the guidance of their seniors who, in turn, are probably acting on the advice of specialists, such as those in the HR department. The information they are given may include:

- replacements for retirements, leavers, transfers and promotions

- possible improvements in productivity

- redeployment of existing staff

- planned changes in output levels

- planned reorganisation of work

- the impact of changes in employment law or collective agreements

- downsizing, which may cause a requirement for a redeployment of staff and therefore upskilling, for some individuals.

Armstrong (2001) refers to this *top–down* approach to HRP and suggests an alternative and additional *bottom–up* approach, in which the line managers submit staffing proposals for agreement by senior managers. He further suggests the use of both approaches in which, in addition to being given guidelines, line managers are encouraged to seek the help of the *HR (and in large organisations [authors' comments]), the organisation and methods (O&M)* or *work study* departments. Staffing targets are usually set and while the line managers are producing their departmental and functional forecasts, HR, work study and O&M get together to produce an organisation-wide HR forecast.

The use of this technique draws on the contents of the business plan in that guidelines are issued to the managers indicating which of the organisation's future activities will be most likely to affect their departments.

Both forecasts (the line managers' and the HR version) are then reviewed by an HRP committee consisting of functional heads. This committee reconciles with departmental managers any discrepancies between the two forecasts. The process introduces alternatives and provides checks and balances within the process.

RATIO-TREND ANALYSIS

The effectiveness of this technique is determined by the future stability of the relationship between the productivity volume and the number of employees. It would, however, be risky to assume that this relationship will remain constant. Few organisations would survive without at least some element of growth and enrichment, and the technique, therefore, does emphasise the need to allow for foreseeable changes. This implies that the efficiency with which the technique is managed relies upon the planner's ability to handle (juggle with) changing ratios, a task that is made somewhat easier when the changes are planned, or at least foreseen.

One could imagine that for a fruit-growing farmer in the south of England, he will require a workforce that reduces in winter to a level that is commensurate with the reduced needs of the business. The winter work would be about setting out new seed beds, maintenance work on existing poly-tunnels and other preparatory work getting ready to produce the summer crop, when larger numbers of people are required. In this relatively stable environment the farmer could trend his usage of labour over the seasons and so, in a timely manner, recruit and release staff.

Using ratio-trend methodology is appropriate so long as stable conditions prevail. A number of factors can trigger change and the kinds of change they bring about. If, for example, the organisation plans to introduce new technology into the picking process then the demand forecasts would have to be based upon knowledge of the new processing technique, probably reducing the demand for human resources or perhaps changing the skill requirements of the human resources employed. In essence, managerial judgement would have to be introduced into the planning process.

WORK STUDY TECHNIQUES

Work study techniques are used much less frequently than they were in the twentieth century, largely owing to the decline in manufacturing. They are used to measure work in terms of how long it takes for operators to carry out particular tasks and how many operators would be required to carry out a total work schedule. The work study approach is most effective when it is used to forecast requirements on the factory floor and in administrative sections where the tasks are repetitive.

MODELLING

This refers to mathematical modelling techniques in which spreadsheets are used in the preparation of demand and supply forecasts. Modelling can be a very powerful tool, especially in large organisations, such as manufacturing and process industries where productivity levels can be equated to head count. Factors such as retirement dates, wastage – in terms of staff turnover rates, reduction in head count caused by the introduction of new technology – can all be factored into and 'tweaked' within a spreadsheet. The timelines for which the model is operated can be both stretched and compressed *but* the output is only as good as the data inputted and the premises on which the model is run. This type of technique can be used to supplement other methods of planning to try to 'home in' on to a realistic solution that can stand scrutiny.

FORECASTING HR SUPPLY

Forecasting HR supply involves using information from the internal and external labour markets. HR planners keep a monitoring eye on the staff turnover and workforce stability indices. The staff turnover index informs you of the turnover that is likely even when we discount any major or minor planned changes. The stability index gives you an indication of the degree to which long-serving employees remain with the organisation. You need to be able to calculate both of these indices.

FORECASTING INTERNAL SUPPLY

Most of the employees who will be needed in the future are already in the workforce and many of them will stay in their current positions. Staff movements, however, have to be taken into account.

CALCULATING STAFF TURNOVER

Staff turnover refers to the rate at which people leave the organisation. The turnover index is expressed as a percentage and is calculated as follows:

$$\frac{\text{Number of leavers in a year}}{\text{Average number of employees}} \times 100 = Y \text{ \% turnover}$$

CASE EXAMPLE

If the organisation employs an average of 2,200 people, and about 88 leave during the year, then the staff turnover is:

$$\frac{88}{2200} \times 100 = 4\%$$

DEPARTMENTAL OR SECTIONAL DISTRIBUTION OF TURNOVER

The simple calculation in the example above is acceptable if we wish to compare the staff turnover with that of other organisations in the same industry, or against national trends. But the figure is of limited use to the HR planner in a medium-sized or large organisation. In such organisations the planner needs to identify the sectional distribution of staff turnover. To achieve this, they have to calculate the turnover for *every* department and function in the organisation.

Calculating the sectional distribution of staff turnover is vital if your projection of future HR needs is to be useful. That is to say, if, as in the example given in the box above, the past turnover trend of 4% is likely to continue, then you can be reasonably sure that the HR department will need to recruit at least 88 new employees in the forthcoming year. Furthermore, having completed the calculation in other departments and functions, you will know where the replacement staff will be needed and the kinds of skills and other qualities contained in the requirement. The results of this second calculation, however, have been known to unveil problems that are unrelated to the task in hand.

 One problem leads to another

CASE EXAMPLE

The organisation has a staff turnover problem. In Department A, turnover is 2%, in Department B it is 3% and in Department C it is 7%, producing an average of 5% across all three departments.

Clearly, however, there is a more significant staff turnover problem in Department C and rather than simply allowing for such a high figure when she was projecting HR requirements, Julie, the HR manager, decided to investigate the possibility of reducing it. She wanted to know why it compared so unfavourably with the figures for the other departments, not only because a high staff turnover is costly in recruitment terms, but because Julie suspected that there might be a deeper problem.

She assigned the task to Jack, who discovered that people were leaving because they were fed up with the communication style of the manager. This triggered further investigation, after which the manager agreed to receive counselling and development training in interpersonal and basic people management skills.

This is an example of how a problem in one area of HR can uncover an entirely different kind of problem. Rather than being a problem based in hard HRM terms it was one with its roots in soft HRM.

Staff turnover figures vary considerably between different kinds of organisation and between different industries. The type of organisation in which you work and the industry in which it operates will have national turnover averages.

In the case example above, the point is made that recruitment is costly and a staff turnover that is too high can cause financial problems. Equally, however, a staff turnover that is too low may also cause problems. An organisation needs to maintain objectivity when it is assessing the efficiency and effectiveness of its operations and new people coming in bring good ideas; they can see things more objectively than those who have been with the organisation for many years.

Long-serving people fall into work routines that they perform out of habit; the habits become *activity ruts* and they fail to notice areas in which improvements could be made. New people will bring in a fresh perspective influenced by different experiences in other organisations. If a too-high or a too-low staff turnover rate can be problematic, then the aim is to achieve a healthy balance of in-house experience and incoming fresh ideas

 ACTIVITY 5.5

From the 2009 CIPD Recruitment, Retention and Turnover annual survey report, the average figures for staff turnover for the years 2006, 2007, 2008 and 2009 were, respectively: 18.3%, 18.1%, 17.3% and 15.7%. Why do you think that the average figure dipped to an average of 15.7% in 2009?

Using the above survey find out the average rate of turnover for your kind of organisation and the same for the kind of industry in which it operates. How does your organisation compare?

CALCULATING THE WORKFORCE STABILITY INDEX

Just as important as staff turnover is the workforce stability index (WSI). This is also expressed as a percentage and is calculated as follows:

$$\frac{\text{Number of employees with more than one year's service}}{\text{Number of employees employed one year ago}} \times 100 = \text{Workforce stability \%}$$

Experience shows that people who are going to leave do so in their first year of employment, and that those who stay for a year will probably stay for much longer. The WSI, therefore, is useful in that it provides an indication of the percentage of people who will be unlikely to leave in the forthcoming year. In the above form, however, it does not take account of the number of people joining the organisation during the past year, nor does it account for exact length of service, although there are techniques that can be used to obtain such information.

COHORT ANALYSIS

The WSI can also be used in an innovative way to calculate information about identifiable and specific groups/cohorts of staff who join the organisation, for example, graduate recruits. Consider the following analysis that considers what happens to graduates, from all its departments, recruited by a large supermarket chain.

Recruitment:

Cohorts: 2005 (10 graduates); 2006 (15 graduates); 2007 (15 graduates); 2008 (10 graduates)

In 2010 the records for the previously recruited cohorts were analysed and the following was found:

Cohort leavers: 2005 (6); 2006 (6); 2007 (6); 2008 (2)

From the above information the retention ratio (stability index) for five, four, three and two years was calculated for each of the cohorts using the stability index method and the retention ratios were:

Retention ratio: 2005 (40%); 2006 (60%); 2007 (60%); 2008 (80%)

Clearly something is amiss with the retention of the graduate intake, with the exception of the 2008 intake; but of course these graduates have only been in the business for two years! Further analysis, probably by taking a year-on-year view of the graduate leavers as well as on a departmental basis, would need to be conducted.

ANALYSES OF LABOUR TURNOVER

As far back as 1955, Hill and Trist identified three phases in labour turnover, the *induction crisis, differential transit* and *settled connection*. We alluded to the induction crisis above by saying that people who are likely to leave do so in the first 12 months of employment. The reasoning that underlies Hill and Trist's analysis is discussed in greater depth in Chapter 8.

According to Julie Beardwell and her colleagues, 'the major drawback with all quantitative methods of turnover analysis is that they provide no information on the reasons why people are leaving. … Quantitative analyses can help to highlight problems, but they give those responsible for planning no indication about how these problems might be addressed' (Beardwell et al 2004).

EXIT INTERVIEWS

In addition to quantitative methods of calculating turnover and stability, data from qualitative methods may be gathered, for example, from exit interviews. These are most frequently carried out when the departing employee is leaving to join another employer. The main purpose of carrying out exit interviews is for the organisation to gather information about the reasons for leaving. For example, the pay and other entitlements may be more attractive elsewhere, or the prospects of training and promotion are better. The organisation may find the interviewee's responses valuable in the sense that it may consider using them to make improvements.

It should be remembered, however, that the responses to an exit questionnaire or a face-to-face interview may not be totally reliable, bearing in mind that the person leaving will be aware that their next employer might request a reference. The interviewee's responses may therefore be couched in terms designed to ensure that nothing is said that might diminish the value of the reference; or the chance of re-employment at some stage later. You cannot make an employee submit to an exit interview, but most leavers will agree, if only on the grounds that a refusal might negatively influence the reference.

ACTIVITY 5.6

Considering the practicalities of conducting exit interviews, who do you think is best positioned to conduct the interview in respect of obtaining the *real* reason why someone has decided to leave the company?

What other options does a company have to obtain this type of information from leavers?

 PLANNING

DEALING WITH DEFICITS AND SURPLUSES

The third stage involves the planner in identifying imbalances between demand and supply. While this would have implications for recruitment, in terms of the geographic scope of the search for talent, it would also trigger a *skills audit* of the current workforce, and consideration of whether there are people who are retrainable. The planner has to take numerous factors into account, including future developments, work patterns and the structure, and such policies and procedures as those for managing reward, diversity, training and development.

O—🔑 **KEY CONCEPT: SKILLS AUDIT**

This is a way of identifying the competence gap at departmental and sectional levels. The skills needed to carry out all of the tasks on time and at the required standard are listed and placed against the skills possessed by all of the members of the section or department. Where deficits are found, arrangements are made for the gaps to be filled.

This is a reconciliation process in which the solutions to problems may be hard or soft. Piercy (1989), writing about strategic planning in the general context, suggests a set of tools to help managers to work through the issues that may arise.

On the hard side, the feasibility of the plan may be focused on the supply forecast being less than the demand forecast. For example, the forecasts may have revealed a shortage of a particular skill in the internal and external labour markets, to the extent that it might be difficult to fulfil parts of the demand. Piercy recommends that you might:

- Alter the demand forecast by considering the effect of changes in the utilisation of employees, such as training and productivity deals, or high-performance teams.
- Alter the demand forecast by considering using different types of employees to meet the corporate objectives, such as employing a smaller number of staff with higher-level skills, or employing staff with insufficient skills and training them immediately.

- Change the company objectives, as lack of staff will prevent them from being achieved in any case. Realistic objectives may need to be based on the staff who are, and are forecast to be, available.

When the demand forecast is less than the internal supply forecast in some areas – for example, you have more staff than you need in a department – the possibilities are to:

- consider and calculate the costs of overemployment over various time spans
- consider the methods and cost of losing staff
- consider changes in utilisation: work out the feasibility and costs of retraining, redeployment and so on
- consider whether it is possible for the company objectives to be changed. Could the company diversify, move into new markets, and so on (Piercy 1989)? This has links to the resource-based view (RBV) of the firm (see Chapter 3 on human resource management).

It is worth a reminder at this stage that HRP is a continuous and circular process (Armstrong 2006). Staff movements and changes to other plans trigger amendments to the plan to keep it up to date. On the soft side, however, there are factors that need to be taken into account, such as the degree to which the changes are acceptable to the senior managers and other employees who have their sights set on the vision of the future for the organisation, managing its culture and keeping abreast of environmental trends. Sometimes you will find yourself 'selling' the plan within the organisation, and you need to understand the people and the factors that could facilitate or hinder implementation.

WHAT MAKES AN HR PLAN?

Students often ask, 'What does the HR plan actually look like?' The answer is that it is virtually impossible, and not really advisable, to draw up a grand plan containing all of the necessary features. With the demand and supply situations reconciled, and feasible solutions decided upon, specific action plans are designed to include all of the organisational areas and activities. Rather than a single HR plan, therefore, there are a number of action plans.

The following is adapted from Torrington and Hall (1998) and Torrington et al (2007):

1 **Human resource supply plans:** Plans may need to be made concerning the timing and approach to recruitment or downsizing. For example, it may have been decided that to recruit sufficient staff, a public relations campaign is needed to promote the company image. Internal movement plans would also be relevant here. Serious consideration should be given to succession planning.

2 **Organisation and structure plans:** These plans may concern departmental structure and the relationships between departments. They may also be concerned with the hierarchy within departments and the levels at which tasks are carried out. Changes to organisation and structure will usually result in changes in employee utilisation.

3 **Employee utilisation plans:** Any changes in utilisation that affect human resource demand will need to be planned. Some changes will result in a sudden difference in employees' tasks and the numbers needed. Managers need to work out the new tasks to be done and the old ones to be dropped. Other plans may involve the distribution of hours worked: for example, the use of annualised hours contracts or the use of functional flexibility, where employees develop and use a wider range of skills. All of the employees involved will need to be consulted about the changes and be prepared and trained for what will happen. A final consideration is: if fewer employees are needed, what criteria will be used to determine which jobs should be made redundant and who can be redeployed and retrained, and into which areas?

4 **Training and management development plans:** There will be training implications for both the HR supply and utilisation plans. The timing of the training can be a critical aspect. For example, training for specific new technology skills loses most of its impact unless it is carried out immediately before installation. The organisation may wish to promote other training and development arrangements to entice candidates.

5 **Performance plans:** These directly address performance issues: for example, the introduction of an objective-setting and performance management system, setting performance and quality standards, or culture change programmes aimed at encouraging specified behaviour and performance.

6 **Appraisal plans:** The organisation needs to make sure it is assessing the important things. For example, if customer service is paramount, employees need to be assessed on relevant aspects (of customer service). This reinforces the importance of customer service and provides a mechanism for improvement in this area, and perhaps rewarding this, where appraisal is to be linked to pay.

7 **Reward plans:** It is often said that what gets rewarded gets done, and it is key that the rewards reflect what the organisation sees as important.

8 **Employee relations plans:** These plans may involve unions, employee representatives or all employees. They include any matters that need to be negotiated or areas where there is the opportunity for employee involvement and participation.

9 **Communication plans:** The way that planned changes are communicated to employees is critical. Plans need to include methods for informing employees what is expected of them, and methods that enable employees to express their concerns and needs if implementation is to be successful. Means of eliciting employee commitment are also important: for example, communicating information about the progress of the organisation.

JOB ANALYSIS

As a practitioner, your effectiveness in carrying out HR planning procedures will be influenced by the degree to which you understand the jobs: for example, in terms of their content, the required competences, where in the organisation they are situated, the degree to which they are subject to change and many other details. This information is obtained through the process of job analysis.

WHAT IS JOB ANALYSIS?

Job analysis is an operational, data-gathering process that involves reducing every job to its constituent parts including the nature of the activities, the task-related responsibilities that the job entails, the knowledge and skills that are required to carry out the work, the reporting responsibilities and the level of the job. Work methods sometimes change, perhaps through the introduction of new technology and, when this occurs, parts of the job need to be updated, which means that the future job-holder might use different work methods to achieve the same or modified ends. If the tasks and the skills needed to carry them out in the future are integrated into the final analysis, the process is referred to as *job modelling*.

PURPOSE

On the grounds that the products of job analyses are job descriptions and person specifications, books on this subject often discuss job analysis in a chapter on recruitment and selection. Pilbeam and Corbridge (2006, p146) argue that, 'In addition to recruitment and selection, job analysis information is fundamental to many other HR management activities, including establishing the job requirements for appraising performance development needs; making reward comparisons between jobs; considering the implications of legislation relating to health and safety, … disciplinary matters or the negotiation of job changes.' It is worth noting that job analyses that have been competently carried out are prerequisites for many decisions and activities that have a crucial influence on the lives of employees, including:

- designing systems of payment
- designing work systems
- designing and remodelling the jobs themselves
- assessing the competences that are required to carry out the job effectively
- training and longer-term career development needs
- building health and safety policies and procedures, and auditing health and safety practices.

Although not always evident in practice, there is an important distinction between *job-oriented* and *worker-oriented* procedures. 'As the terms suggest, job-oriented procedures focus on the work itself, producing a description in terms of the equipment used, the end results or purposes of the jobs, resources and materials utilised, etc. By contrast, worker-oriented analyses concentrate on describing the psychological or behavioural requirements of a job, such as communicating, decision-making and reasoning' (Arnold et al 2005).

ACTIVITY 5.7

First, analyse your own job or a job that you have held in the past and arrange the tasks and responsibilities in order of importance; compare what you have done with the contents of your job description. Second, do the same with a colleague's job. How do they compare? What are the key differences?

JOB DESCRIPTIONS AND ROLE DEFINITIONS

According to Michael Armstrong (2006, p327), a job:

> ... can be regarded as a unit in an organisation structure that remains unchanged whoever is in the job. A job in this sense is a fixed entity, part of a machine that is 'designed' like any other part of a machine. Routine, or machine-controlled jobs do exist in most organisations but, increasingly, the work carried out by people is not mechanistic.

FLEXIBLE APPROACH

Many academics and managers take a flexible view of what a job actually involves. Some even regard the job description as redundant and *role profiles* should be used to replace the traditional job description. The *role profile* defines the outcomes of the job rather than the detailed content of the job. The reason for this is that the rate at which organisations are changing and developing is still increasing, and many line managers feel that job descriptions inhibit the flexibility that is needed to respond adequately to customer demands. The case they make is that:

> inflexible definitions of jobs place limitations on change and development because they do not allow for changes in deployment or for multi-skilling and a wide variety of other factors that describe the reality of the ways in which the talents of the human resource need to be maximised in today's organisations. (Currie 2006)

DEFINING THE 'ROLE'

One approach to resolving this dilemma is for the organisation to reach an agreement with the employee in which the role is loosely defined and there is mutual agreement that within the limits of the individual's capabilities – and trainability – the role may be flexible and subject to change. The role defines both outcomes and behaviours of the individual and so is quite *loose*, when compared with the idea of a *rigid* job description. Bratton and Gold (2007, p255) further discuss the introduction of *performance contracts*: 'These contain details of what the job-holder agrees to accomplish over a period of time, summarizing the purpose of a job, how the purpose will be met over the time specified and how the achievement of the objectives will be met.' These approaches (see also Chapter

6) have implications for the kinds of people the organisation prefers to recruit: those people who are sufficiently willing and motivated to accept the challenge of change. This also implies that the traditional approach to analysing jobs may, in some organisations, be inappropriate.

PAUSE FOR THOUGHT

Job versus role

Stop and think for a moment. Would you prefer to have a job, which is described by Armstrong as a 'fixed entity, part of a machine that is designed like any other part of a machine'; or would you prefer to have a role in the organisation, which means playing a flexible part in the changing organisation?

INFORMATION FROM A JOB ANALYSIS

The information that you obtain from a job analysis may be summarised as:

- **The overall purpose of the job:** what the job is for and how it contributes to the achievement of the organisation's objectives.
- **The type of job:** the nature of the tasks and responsibilities; the duties to be carried out and the expected outcomes.
- **Professional jobs:** does the job-holder need to be a member of a recognised professional institution such as those for law, accountancy, HR, and so on?
- **Exclusivity:** is the job the only one of its kind in the organisation, or are there other similar jobs or jobs to which this one is related?
- **The location of the job:** in which department or functional area does it exist?
- **The status of the job:** where does the job stand in the departmental structure?
- **Reporting responsibilities:** to whom does the job-holder report, such as to a line manager for their work performance and to an appropriate senior for specialised responsibilities such as IT, marketing or finance?
- **Motivation:** the degree to which motivational factors and/or demotivators are built into the job.
- **Movement:** is the current job-holder likely to move upwards or laterally in the organisation in the foreseeable future?

GATHERING THE INFORMATION: FOUR STEPS

You need to gather as much relevant information as you can and you need to ensure that the information is correct. To achieve this the following four steps are suggested:

- **Step 1:** Examine documents that provide information about the job. These include the existing job description. Relevant information about the job may also be obtained from training manuals and other job-related records.
- **Step 2:** Interview the job-holder. Here, you seek information about the activities that are involved in carrying out the job.
- **Step 3:** Talk to the manager to whom the job-holder reports about the purpose of the job and to confirm the information that was provided by the job-holder.
- **Step 4:** Observe employees while they are doing their jobs.

Using a range of techniques and collating information from multiple sources, as suggested above, is more likely to deliver a quality job description.

EXAMINING DOCUMENTS

The important features of the existing job description are the date on which it was last reviewed and why it was reviewed. You need the existing job description so that you can see how well it matches up with the data you collect from the job-holder. As previously mentioned, training manuals will contain information about the knowledge and skills required to carry out the job effectively. Individuals' records include data about their performance standards and the training to which they have been exposed; the task is detailed, laborious and time-consuming.

INTERVIEWING THE JOB-HOLDER

Depending on the scope and complexity of the job, it may be advisable, two or three weeks in advance, to ask the job-holder to keep a diary or activity record of the tasks that they perform. Since this is done on a daily and weekly basis – as the job is being carried out – it avoids problems associated with faulty memory and the current incumbent talking up their job (see 'Conducting the interview' below). Again this may be difficult at times and time-consuming.

As soon as you have decided to interview the job-holder you should, as a matter of courtesy, tell their line manager about your intentions. In addition, it is essential to tell the interviewee the exact purpose/reason for conducting the interview. If this is not done the employee may become uneasy, thinking perhaps that the job is going to be redesigned or, even worse, they might be made redundant.

PREPARING FOR THE INTERVIEW

It is advisable to prepare for the interview by drafting a questionnaire that includes not only the basic elements of the job, as described above, but also further supplementary questions. The questionnaire will act as a checklist and enable you to build a logical sequence into the interview (see Table 5.1). Good practice is to prepare a semi-structured interview, with some pre-prepared questions, yet leaving gaps for the job-holder to give their own personal slant to the interviewer and so perhaps offer some things that were not obvious to the unskilled eye.

The questions listed in Table 5.1 are not exhaustive. Studying them, you will see what type of things may be asked about any job. It is an obvious advantage if the job has been analysed previously. The information that was gathered then – the answers to the questions – should have been stored in the HR department. By comparing the previously gathered information with what you have gathered, you will be able to assess the degree to which the job has changed.

CONDUCTING THE INTERVIEW

While common sense tells us that the job-holder should be able to give a good account of the information referred to in Step 2 (above), caution needs to be exercised since it sometimes happens that information obtained in this way conflicts with that provided by the manager. For example, when a job is first created it is the organisation that prescribes its content in terms of the order of importance in which the tasks and accountabilities are arranged. Experience shows that after individuals have settled into their jobs they unconsciously alter the task priorities to suit their own liking and abilities, favouring some tasks above others. Job-holders have also been known to give an inflated account of the importance of what they do. Despite this, the job-holder can provide some information, but it is always advisable to check it with the line manager, whom you interview after you have seen the job-holder.

Interviewees are sometimes inclined to offer more information than you have asked for, and some of this may not be relevant. On the other hand, answers may be lacking in sufficient detail, especially when answering questions about items that the job-holder appears to be unsure about or perceives to be at the bottom of their priorities. In such a case you have to probe more deeply to get the information you need.

Table 5.1 Job analysis interview – questionnaire

Questions
What is your job title?
What is the job title of your manager?
What is the purpose of your job?
Does anyone in the organisation do a similar job and, if so, how many?
What do you actually do? (Here you ask the job-holder to list the job-related duties, tasks performed, measurements taken, recording of information, types and communication with others [verbal, electronic, written] and so on.)
Did you require training to enable you to do your job?
Would anyone require training regardless of their qualifications and experience?
What knowledge and skills are needed to do your job?

What qualifications and experience do you need to carry out your job?
Do you have people reporting to you and, if so, how many?
What are their job titles?
How would you describe your responsibilities?
Do you have authority to make decisions and, if so, what types of decision?
Do you have contact with others within the organisation and externally?
Does your job involve travelling and/or working unsocial hours on behalf of the organisation?
What problems do you encounter in your job?
What performance standards are required of you in your job?

 ACTIVITY 5.8

First, think of the ways in which the information from a job analysis may affect people's lives at work. Second, think about how any significant changes made as a result of the job analysis and incorporated into the job description might affect the status of the job itself.

INTERVIEWING THE LINE MANAGER

The interview with the line manager should cover two main areas for discussion. First, it is to discuss the answers given by their staff member. For example, the manager may help you to sift out any irrelevant material – such as responsibilities that may have been inflated – or help with the technical detail that was not fully explained by the staff member. Second, it is to discuss what the manager knows about the future of the job. For example, technological change might be on the horizon that may have implications for the design of the job, including changes in the necessary competences.

USING OBSERVATIONAL METHODS

For this, *structured observational techniques* (see below) are used and those being observed should be advised that you are observing them at work and why you are doing it. The fact that they are aware of why you are observing them may cause them to modify what they would do in a normal unobserved situation, but it is still possible to gather useful information in this way from, say, office or factory floor workers.

> ⚬━⚷ **KEY CONCEPT:** STRUCTURED AND PARTICIPANT OBSERVATION
>
> Observation may be *structured*, in which the observer simply watches and notes what the person does, or it may be *participant observation*, in which the observer works with the person and gathers *qualitative* rather than *quantitative* information. In both cases the person being observed must be told the purpose of the observation.

MODERN APPROACHES TO HUMAN RESOURCE PLANNING

This section of the chapter focuses on the principles of human resource planning in terms of the modern approaches that are taken by many organisations. It reflects how traditional HRP has been revised to produce differences in the aims of HRP and the thinking that underlies modern practices. Armstrong (2006, p368) outlines these aims as:

- to attract and retain the number of people required with the appropriate skills, expertise and competences

- to anticipate problems of potential surpluses or deficits of people

- to develop a well-trained and flexible workforce, thus contributing to the organisation's ability to adapt to an uncertain and changing environment

- to reduce dependence on external recruitment when key skills are in short supply by formulating retention and development strategies

- to improve the utilisation of people by introducing more flexible systems of work.

As you will see, the first two of these aims are similar to those of traditional HRP. Largely, however, they are aims that redirect the focus away from the practices of traditional manpower planning and towards an emphasis on internal workforce flexibility. Problems of deficits and surpluses in the HR demand and supply situations are dealt with first through the development and redevelopment of the internal workforce. Where recruitment is necessary, part-time workers are brought in and short-term contracts are offered to people whose skills are needed for limited periods (see also 'Core and peripheral workers' in Chapter 1).

The underlying thinking here is that a more flexible workforce with a broad repertoire of skills and competences, available when needed, is more likely to be able to respond appropriately to the volatile demands of today's global market.

IMPLEMENTATION AND CONTROL

Once the planning process has been completed and budgets developed then the HR department's staff start to put the well-developed plans into action. This could mean a variety of things:

- by promoting and training existing staff

- recruiting and training people from outside the business.

Clearly the above two solutions are based upon the fact that the job still exists and the work cannot be achieved in some other way by part-time working, overtime working, or reorganising the work.

However, assuming that new plans have been put into place then the planning process will be revisited after a period of time. The period of time could be as little as 12 months for a micro plan, where a department or section is concerned, but could, for a full-scale planning activity, be undertaken after two to three years. The frequency will depend upon the type of sector and market that the organisation operates within.

THE INFLUENCE OF BUSINESS STRATEGY

The degree to which an HR strategist can operate effectively is determined by the clarity of the business strategy. In a previous era business strategies worked because the market was more stable than it is today. Now, however, the objective is to achieve a competitive advantage, and the ability of business strategists to be precise about their requirements is governed by market forces that, in turn, govern the degree to which the HR strategists can be precise. Whittington (1993) points out that strategies may be deliberate or emergent.

> Deliberate strategies assume a rational evaluation of external and internal circumstances and an identification of the best way to achieve a competitive advantage. Emergent strategies, on the other hand, are the product of market forces. (Beardwell et al 2004)

> The most appropriate strategies … emerge as competitive processes that allow the comparatively better performers to survive while the weaker performers are squeezed out. (Legge 1995, p99)

An *emergent strategy* is one that, as its name implies, emerges as the business trades. For this to work senior managers must be scanning their business for signs of an emerging trend on which a strategy can start to be formed. Text messaging was designed as a by-product of mobile telecommunications; there was initially no expectation, and therefore no strategy, to build it into the multi-million pound business it is today.

 ## ACTIVITY 5.9

1　How does the content of the teaching on your course match up to the ideas that are expressed above? Is the teaching, for example, emergent and does it develop as the course progresses, with the lecturer taking advantage of opportunities for learning in the class? Or is it deliberate and focused on a prescribed plan and delivery process?

2　Is the HR strategy in your organisation deliberate and focused on prescribed business goals and prescribed business strategy or is it emergent in nature? Can you think of examples in the workplace when issues have arisen that have caused policy to be changed?

SUMMARY

Those involved in early industrial activity, even before the Industrial Revolution, tried to ensure that there would be people feeding through businesses to succeed longer-serving skilled employees. With the Industrial Revolution came the development of factories and larger-scale industries, which eventually demanded a more organisation-wide approach to planning the future workforce. By the twentieth century, apprenticeship schemes were widespread and the demand was for the continuation of traditional skills to serve the purposes of a largely manufacturing economy. Manpower planning, now referred to as HR planning (HRP), appeared in the 1960s, and a modified version of it is still practised. Information technology has eased the activities related to HR planning. In the 1980s HR planning was revised to enable organisations to meet the demands of a rapidly developing and fiercely competitive global market. Many of the traditional practices are still used for HRP purposes, but new HR resourcing strategies have been introduced.

Planning itself always was an imprecise process, but the rate of change that was necessary to sustain a competitive advantage shortened planning periods and altered strategic emphases. The degree to which HR planners can be precise in their forecasts is determined by the business strategy, which, in turn, is strongly influenced by market forces. The ideas underlying modern strategic developments in the management of employment and employee relations call for a workforce that is flexible and able to respond appropriately. Planning needs to access the *soft* as well as the *hard* dimensions of HRM.

Staff turnover is an issue for many organisations. Using analytical means to calculate staff turnover rates can lead to insights into why turnover may be high in certain parts of the organisation.

REVIEW QUESTIONS

1. What are the purposes of HR planning?

2. Why were organisations slow to adopt manpower planning when it was first introduced?

3. How would you define HR planning?

4. What is meant by *soft* and *hard* HR planning?

5. What factors influence the length of planning periods?

6. What are the five stages of the planning process?

7. Why is HRP said to be a 'competence-centred' function?

8. What are the four main elements in the process of HR planning?

9. What is meant by the terms 'top–down' and 'bottom–up' in terms of approaches to HRP?

10. Find out from your HR manager how frequently your organisation engages in a full-scale planning activity that covers the whole firm. How often do micro planning activities take place where departments or sections are reviewed?

11. How would you calculate staff turnover rates?

12 How would you calculate the organisation's workforce stability index?

13 What is 'cohort analysis'?

14 How might imbalances between HR demand and supply be reconciled?

15 What are the four steps you can take to gather information when carrying out a job analysis?

16 How would you distinguish between deliberate and emergent strategies?

17 Referring to Figure 5.1, discuss the limitations of the data provided. What (external type) statistics would be more meaningful for an HR planner working in a medium to large organisation?

18 Using information from the Offices for National Statistics website at (www.statistics.gov.uk/elmr) find out how many people are employed in the following occupations:

- agriculture and fisheries
- energy and water
- manufacturing
- construction
- distribution
- transport
- finance and business
- public sector.

EXPLORE FURTHER

BOOKS

BANFIELD, P. and KAY, R. (2008) *Introduction to human resource management.* Oxford: Oxford University Press.

Banfield and Kay deal with human resource planning in a very thorough manner, covering both the *soft* as well as the *hard* issues of planning the workforce. As well as dealing with the traditional elements of HR planning (HRP), Banfield and Kay offer advice on measuring the effectiveness of HRP.

BRATTON, J. and GOLD, J. (2007) *Human resource management: theory and practice* (4th ed.). Basingstoke: Palgrave Macmillan.

Bratton and Gold address the fundamentals and the historic trajectory of HRP and, as one would imagine, also deal with the metrics used to measure issues of absenteeism and turnover. They also consider specific and specialist issues of human capital management, diversity and the impact of 'e-HR' on the subject of human resource planning.

WEB LINKS

CIPD *Recruitment, Retention and Turnover* annual survey report:

www.cipd.co.uk/subjects/recruitmen/general/_recruitment_2009.htm

National Apprenticeship website: http://www.apprenticeships.org.uk

National Apprenticeship Service (part of National Employer Service):

http://nationalemployerservice.org.uk/resources/national-apprenticeship-service

National Employer Service: www.nationalemployerservice.org.uk

Office for National Statistics: www.statistics.gov.uk

Office for National Statistics (Economic and Labour Market Review):www.statistics.gov.uk/elmr

Welfare-to-work initiatives

Jobcentre Plus: www.jobcentreplus.gov.uk

Business Link: www.businesslink.gov.uk

Learning and Skills Council: www.lsc.gov.uk

Department for Work and Pensions: www.dwp.gov.uk

Recruitment

INTRODUCTION

The main objectives of this chapter are to explain the purposes and the processes of recruitment. First, however, there is a discussion that is concerned with the traditional and modern perceptions of recruitment. Since the inception of HRM in the 1980s, perceptions of recruitment and the design of its related systems have been subject to significant change; advancing technology has facilitated new ways of recruiting. A large number of organisations have updated their systems, although others still use traditional systems. In the light of this, the discussion focuses on the current overall situation. As seen from previous chapters, recruitment and selection are seen as one of the key areas of HR. In fact, in the 2007 CIPD survey report *The Changing HR Function*, recruitment and selection was rated as the highest priority (CIPD 2007d). Taylor and Collins (2000, p304, cited in Redman and Wilkinson 2009, p64) give recruitment as the most critical human resource function for organisational survival or success. With the growth of 'talent management', attracting the right people with the right blend of skills and abilities is becoming ever more important. Recruitment is a costly business – according to the 2009 CIPD *Recruitment, Retention and Turnover* survey report, the average recruitment cost of filling a vacancy per employee is £4,000, increasing to £6,125 when including the associated labour turnover costs.

DEFINITIONS

In one sense, recruitment and selection may be regarded as separate functions in that selection begins where recruitment ends. In this context, recruitment commences when a genuine vacancy has been identified and ends when a list of candidates has been built from the applications that have resulted from making a vacant position known. The selection process then takes over. The applications are examined and sifted until a shortlist of the most suitable candidates is produced, after which the final elements of the process are activated, including arrangements for assessing the candidates. The selection process ends when a suitable candidate has been given and has accepted an offer of employment and is often seen to include the induction process.

Beardwell and Claydon (2007, p190) define recruitment and selection as integrated activities in which 'the recruitment and selection process is concerned with identifying, attracting and choosing suitable people to meet an organisation's human resource requirements', which seems to bind the two functions together. Foot and Hook (2002, p143) define recruitment more simply as 'all activities directed towards locating potential employees', the main aim being to 'attract applications from suitable candidates'.

Different methods and techniques are used in carrying out each of these functions, and for teaching and writing purposes, they are easier to understand if they are treated separately. In practice, recruitment and selection are a continuous process – one cannot take place without the other – and the relevant HR practitioners need to be skilled in both.

THE CONTEXT OF RECRUITMENT

Bringing new people into the organisation is an important function, especially now, when the focus is on people as the organisation's main means of achieving competitive advantage. Whether in a recession (where survival of a firm may depend on having competent staff who perform to a high standard) or in a boom, where competitive advantage depends on having talented workers, attracting and appointing the right staff is crucial. Pfeffer (1998) suggests that selective hiring is one of the important areas of HR that can affect the success of the business.

Fierce competition in a global market has brought with it the need for a multi-skilled, talented and flexible workforce recruited to cope with a strengthened customer focus. There is a need to attract 'talent' to compete and gain a competitive edge. All of this has shifted the emphasis away from attracting people who are potentially capable of operating effectively within the confines of a clearly defined job, and towards adaptable people who are prepared to take on a flexible role. This may mean moving away from the traditional 'person–job match' to recruiting suitable people whose attitudes match the organisation's culture and then developing jobs around their skills and capabilities. Organisations such as

Google use this approach to attract the right kind of people to the organisation and then let them develop the role.

DIVERSITY AND FLEXIBILITY

Another factor that has influenced change since the 1970s with the advent of equal opportunity and discrimination legislation is the increased level of diversity in the make-up of today's external labour market, from which, of course, new employees are drawn. This should ideally be reflected in the make-up of the workforce and has emphasised the importance of fairness in selection decision-making and the need to attract diverse staff during the recruitment process. There are, therefore, legislative measures for example, on discrimination, that affect recruitment and that demand particular approaches. These are discussed later in this chapter.

THE LABOUR MARKETS

Recruitment processes are carried out within the context of the internal environment (recruitment or promotion of staff who already work for the organisation) as well as the external environments (which may include candidates from outside the organisation and even outside the UK), both of which offer constraints and opportunities.

Internal labour market

When a vacancy or a new position arises, should the internal labour market be the first port of call? This can be justified on the grounds that first, it offers opportunities to existing employees, especially those whose current positions have become vulnerable to redundancy, perhaps owing to technological change or a restructuring programme. To some employees a new position might be more interesting and/or more challenging, or it might be a more senior position enhancing their terms and conditions of employment and providing an opportunity to raise the level of their contribution. In fact, some organisations are well known for 'promoting from within'. Employees of the high street banks and all of the emergency services, where training is a long-established tradition, are promoted up through the organisation because they have shown proficiency in their jobs. In the Civil Service, for example, long service may also be a factor in achieving promotion.

Second, from the organisation's point of view, recruiting from the internal labour market is much cheaper (no advertising costs, for example); and third, it demonstrates to the workforce in general that internal promotion is encouraged and career progression is possible – thus increasing motivation and morale. This is important if we are to recognise and reward the talented employees already within our workforce. Conversely, a good case can be made for achieving a healthy balance in the use of both internal and external labour markets, since all organisations benefit from injections of 'fresh blood' and too much internal selection may prevent new ideas and innovation entering the organisation from elsewhere. External recruitment may be vital if we are seeking new talent who can add creative new ideas to our competitive edge.

External labour market

The external labour market can be viewed on four different levels: local, regional, national and international. The size and location of the area from which you need to recruit is determined first and foremost by the nature of the job in terms of its level in the organisation, its technical complexity and degree of specialism, the qualifications, competences and experience required. Further important considerations include the related costs compared with the potential benefits to the organisation of using particular markets, especially the international market.

Searching for talent

CASE EXAMPLE

Solent Toys Ltd is a new venture in the south of England that will manufacture four different categories of toy. The company will be made up of four divisions, each of which will be headed up by a project director who will also be a member of the board of directors:

1 *The Nursery Division*, making soft toys such as cloth dolls and teddy bears.

2 *The Educational Division*, making problem-solving toys in the form of games and puzzles.

3 *The Electronics Division*, making interactive toys, such as robots and 'talk-back' gadgets.

4 *The Musical Division*, making toy keyboards and other instruments.

The company already occupies a large site, an office block has been built and the total building programme will be completed in four months. The board of directors, including the project directors and the HR director, are already in their positions and, to begin with, the HR director will have a small staff of specialists. The company now needs to embark upon a large-scale recruitment programme.

For each of the divisions the recruiters will be searching for managers, creative designers, quality inspectors, machine operators and administrative staff.

Think about the variety of competences, qualifications and experience that will be required across all of the divisions. For example, the company will need people who are skilled and experienced in designing and making soft toys, designing and making educational problem-solving toys, electronics experts to make interactive toys and people who are skilled and experienced in designing and making toy musical instruments. Just imagine the breadth of the range of knowledge and competences required to staff the whole organisation.

Task

Write down two categories of employee for whom you would search in each of the four main areas of the external labour market; that is: two from the local, two from the regional, two from the national and two from the international markets.

FACTORS AFFECTING SUCCESS

There are a variety of factors that can inhibit or facilitate an organisation's recruitment success rate:

● **Unemployment:** Unemployment fluctuates with the state of the economy. While in the UK, the economy is relatively stable, we should not assume that is the case globally, nor indeed that employment is evenly distributed across the UK. While low unemployment is regarded as a positive factor in economic terms, it does limit the availability of the 'right' or 'talented' people. On the other hand, when unemployment is high, job applications abound and the selection process has to be handled with great care if the organisation is to employ the kind of people it needs.

- **Diversity:** The increase in immigration rates in recent years has had a positive effect on recruitment in that it has raised the level of the availability of required knowledge and skills. In a moderate way, this has helped to alleviate the skill shortage. Among the overseas applicants for UK residency there are doctors, nurses, dentists, engineers and all of the trades and crafts. The influx of eastern European workers made an impact as the European Union has extended its membership. There have however been issues relating to whether this is unfair – in a recession situation, should jobs go to non-UK workers?

- **Skill shortages:** Advancing technology has created a 'talent war' in the external market, in which organisations are competing with each other to 'capture' people who possess exceptional knowledge and rare competences.

RECRUITMENT PROCESSES

This section explains the systems of recruitment and offers guidance on the related skills. Once a genuine vacancy has been identified, the recruitment process can be activated.

SYSTEMATIC RECRUITMENT CYCLE

The stages of the recruitment process may be seen as the 'systematic recruitment cycle':

- Stage 1 – Identify genuine vacancy.
- Stage 2 – Obtain authority to recruit.
- Stage 3 – Carry out job analysis or check that previous analysis still holds good.
- Stage 4 – Write or revise job description and person specification.
- Stage 5 – Make the vacancy known (write the advert and decide on relevant media).
- Stage 6 – Place the advert in the appropriate media.

The first stage is to identify that the job exists: how has the vacancy arisen? Then, in most organisations, there is a need to get approval to fill the post. Next we need to find out about the job (job analysis), followed by ensuring that there is an up-to-date brief of what the job is about and what kind of person is sought (job description and person specification), then attracting the right kind of people to the job (making the position known by advertisement).

Identifying the vacancy

If someone has left the organisation or has retired, then a vacancy will have occurred. Or there may be a restructure, which means a new post has arisen.

Gaining authority to recruit

Often, once a line manager has identified a vacancy, they have to complete an authority to recruit form. The design of the form will oblige the line manager, and at least one senior manager, to review the situation and decide whether the post needs filling at all. In some organisations this may be an informal process, while in others there will be 'approval to fill a vacancy' forms that require justification: do we need the job? Does the job need to be filled on a full-time or part-time basis? Can the work be done by any other means (overtime, casual labour, the introduction of new technology or machinery)? In the public sector this may mean approval by a committee and the process may take some time.

Job analysis

The following factors are identified from a job analysis (see Chapter 5) and they are used to write up a job description or role definition (see Table 6.1) and a person specification:

- the nature of the tasks that make up the job
- how the job has changed (if it has) since it was last analysed
- the priorities of the job and the key tasks
- the knowledge, understanding, skills, competence and other personal qualities needed for the job.

In practice, these documents are usually stored on a computer, but it is recommended that the HR practitioner and the line manager get together to agree on their contents in case there have been any changes since the documents were last drafted.

The job description

Every opportunity should be taken to keep job descriptions up to date. The fact that a specific vacancy has been identified provides an opportunity for the HR practitioner to make a further update, in consultation with the relevant line manager, who will be aware of any changes to the job. In addition to their use in recruitment, job descriptions have a key role in other activities, such as identifying training needs, and introducing or reviewing a job evaluation scheme and other systems of payment.

Table 6.1 A typical job description

Organisation	Farmed Freshly Foods Ltd, Wheatsheaf Lane, Penyard, Wiltshire
Department	Accounts department
Job title	Financial Accounts Section Leader
Main duties: Report to the accounts manager	1 Keep the accounts of the company's largest customers, ensuring their accounts are kept up to date and that invoices and statements go out on time. 2 Monitor credit limits, ensuring they are not exceeded without special permission. 3 Arrange that all credit limits above £2,500 are insured. 4 Maintain liaison with credit reference agencies. 5 Allocate work to clerical staff. 6 Supervise the work of a team of eight accounts clerks, offering advice and guidance where necessary. 7 Monitor the performance standards of accounts staff. 8 Supervise the efficient and effective operation of the accounts office. 9 Maintain good customer relations when responding to their accounts queries.
Salary and other main terms and conditions	Salary £35,000 p.a. plus company car. Relocation allowance, well-appointed office, situated in pleasant rural area. Option to join pension scheme after two years. Must participate in formal appraisal scheme after expiry of a six-month probationary period.
Performance and career prospects	Possible promotion to assistant manager after two years. The critical performance standards relate to the maintenance of good customer relations and the degree to which invoice and statement deadlines are met.

The person specification

This document is alternatively referred to as a recruitment, or job, specification. Its purpose is to detail the particular qualities that match the profile of the ideal person for the job, and these may include education, qualifications, experience, competences, attitudes and any specific requirements that are exclusive to the job in question.

The expectation that the main duties and responsibilities that are detailed in the job description will be fulfilled at, or above the required performance standards, and the nature of the duties and responsibilities themselves, will provide indications of the knowledge and competences that will be required of the prospective job-holder. The person specification, therefore, may be regarded as a reflection of the main features of the job description in the form of personal qualities.

In the past, considerable time and ingenuity went into the development of person specification models. Each model presented a basic set of criteria, against which 'minimum/essential' and 'desirable' job requirements can be set. The contents of the job description (see Table 6.1) provide the basic criteria for the person specification.

Three models that have, in part, stood the test of time are:

- the seven-point plan (Rodger 1952)
- the fivefold grading system (Munro-Fraser 1966)
- the eight-point plan (Plumbley 1976).

Rodger's model is the most well known and most frequently used.

While the structure of Rodger's model still holds good, the contents in their original form are not recommended for use today. They reflect the values that were held at the time of publication, which was 20 years before discrimination laws came into being. For example, items such as 'physical make-up' and 'circumstances' are potentially discriminatory. The model, however, provided a structure or 'checklist' that can be useful in placing the requirements against the appropriate categories on the specification. The seven-point plan is laid out in Table 6.2 as an example of the content and form in which all three models were originally written.

Table 6.2 Structure for a person specification – Rodger's original seven-point plan

Quality	Description
1 Physical	This covers health, physique, age, appearance, hearing and speech. Physical attributes may be added or removed as necessary.
2 Attainments	Including academic attainments, training received, knowledge, skills and experience already developed.
3 Intelligence	The general intelligence, specific abilities and the methods for the assessment of these.
4 Special aptitudes	Any special aptitudes, such as mechanical, manual, verbal, numerical, creativity, and so on.
5 Interests	Personal interests as possible indicators of aptitudes, abilities or personality traits (for example intellectual, practical/constructional, physically active, social, artistic).
6 Disposition	Personality characteristics needed (for example equability, dependability, self-reliance, assertiveness, drive, energy, perseverance, initiative, motivation).
7 Circumstances	Personal and domestic circumstances (for example mobility, commitments, family circumstances and occupations).

The points used by the other two models are:

- **fivefold grading system (Munro-Fraser):**
  - brains and abilities
  - qualifications
  - impact on others
  - adjustment
  - motivation

- **eight-point plan (P. Plumbley):**
  - general intelligence
  - special aptitudes
  - attainments
  - physical make-up
  - disposition
  - circumstances
  - interests
  - type of person.

The dangers of using any of these models are that they can be seen as possible means of discrimination. We are no longer allowed to ask about age, for example.

Table 6.3 **A typical person specification**

Farmed Freshly Foods Ltd	Job title: Financial Accounts Section Leader	
Job requirements	**Essential**	**Desirable**
1 Qualifications	AAT and business studies.	ACCA or accountancy degree.
2 Knowledge	Good understanding of financial accountancy.	Understand all aspects of financial and management accountancy.
3 Skills	Ability to keep accounting systems. Able to handle accountancy IT packages.	Exceed minimum standard and maximise on use of IT software.
4 Experience	Experience of being a team leader or in a supervisory role.	Some experience of a relevant team leadership role. Accustomed to dealing with supermarkets' accounts departments.
5 Management	Accustomed to leading a team of accountants. Able to monitor and assess performance standards.	Ability to exceed minimum requirements. Able to raise performance standards.
6 Personal qualities	Polite manner. Good oral and written communicator.	Good leadership skills and accustomed to pressure.

Even qualities such as 'mature' or 'youthful' can be seen as age discrimination. Personal/domestic or family circumstances should not be pertinent to the job; and questions at an interview about such would be seen as possibly discriminatory. However, with care, the structures are still useful. Staying with the job of financial accounts section leader, Table 6.3 is a general adaptation of the structure that, in the light of current legislation and modern approaches to recruitment, might prove to be legitimate and useful.

 ACTIVITY 6.1

Draft a person specification for your own job, or one that you have held in the past, and another for a colleague's job that is different from yours.

MAKING THE VACANT POSITION KNOWN

Depending on the level of the position, advertising may not necessarily be the best option and can be expensive. The word 'advertise' comes from the Latin *advertere*, which means to make known, and the fact that a position is vacant may be made known in several ways. For example:

- **Advertise internally** on notice boards and in the company magazine, but check the frequency of the magazine, find out its closing date for the acceptance of advertisements and see how this matches up to the target date for filling the vacant position.

- **Search the HR records** for suitable internal candidates and scan the files on people who have previously sent in CVs on speculation. The internal advertisement should still appear, since everyone should have an equal opportunity to apply for the post.

- **Use general and specialist selection consultants:** Consultants are brought in when the organisation would benefit from their expertise in recruiting for positions in the higher levels of the organisation, and when vacancies occur in key specialisms, such as in certain aspects of engineering, IT, chemicals – whatever the organisation needs.

- **Use employment agencies:** People associate employment agencies with temporary and part-time staff, but most of them are extremely good at finding people for positions in other areas of the workforce. Their reputation is for finding administrative and clerical workers, but many specialise in particular kinds of function, such as finance, catering, the building trades, HR and IT.

- **Invite applications from 'work experience' students:** This can be quite a good source, especially since the managers have already met the candidate and seen something of their work.

- **Contact schools, colleges and universities,** support their career conventions and maintain good relations. These are opportunities to meet prospective employees and 'sell' the benefits of working in your organisation. Often organisations recruit their graduates from students who have done their placement year with them – and this can act as a good way of finding the right person who will fit in with the organisation.

- **Use Jobcentres:** People who register with Jobcentres are usually unemployed, and some employers may see this as a disadvantage, questioning why the person is unemployed. On a more positive note, Jobcentres can produce applicants very quickly and cheaply.

According to the CIPD's 2009 *Recruitment, Retention and Turnover* survey report, by far the most commonly used methods for attracting candidates are through an organisation's own corporate website (78%), recruitment agencies (76%) and local newspaper advertisements (70%). The use of new media such as social networking sites, for example Facebook, LinkedIn and MySpace, is currently low (7%), but will undoubtedly increase.

EXTERNAL ADVERTISING

The benefits of using an advertising agency cannot be overemphasised. An agency can provide expertise in copywriting, producing artwork and eye-catching captions and other forms of visual impact. It can advise on all aspects of advertising including the legal aspects (discrimination), media selection, placing the advertisements and working with you on response analysis. Agents can also provide anonymity, in which your advertisements appear under the name of the agency. The organisation may decide to do this when it is carrying out confidential marketing or developing a new product and does not wish the job titles in the advertisements to reveal the nature of its plans. All of this has a cost, of course, but the benefits usually outweigh it.

TYPES OF RECRUITMENT ADVERTISEMENT

The most commonly used media for recruitment advertisements are newspapers and magazines in which the advertisements may be:

- **Classified:** sometimes referred to as lineage or run-on, classified advertisements appear in single columns and are a typical feature of newspapers, especially the local and regional papers.

- **Classified semi-display:** which also appear in single columns among the classified advertisements. The idea is to make the advertisement stand out from the ordinary ones by using bold captions to head up the advertisement, perhaps narrowing the body of the text or placing the advertisement in a single column box.

- **Displayed advertisements:** these have borders and contain artwork that is designed to project the organisation's corporate image, usually including a logo. They are the most expensive type of advertisement but they do produce a greater impact than classified ads and are ideal for advertising the more senior technical and professional jobs. They also create an image with which readers will eventually become familiar.

PLACING AN ADVERTISEMENT

Handling classified and semi-displayed advertisements is a fairly simple process, since they can be placed by telephone, letter or email. There are, however, a few 'dos' and 'don'ts', given in Table 6.4.

Table 6.4 Dos and don'ts for placing advertisements

Do	Don't
Get the line manager to approve the advertisement.	Allow the tele-ads sales people to talk you into taking more space than you actually need.
Ensure that the copy you have written conforms to the provisions of the legislation on discrimination.	Place the advertisement by telephone.
Ensure that your written material includes the date the advertisement will be published.	Write too much without checking how much it will cost. Large adverts can be very costly!
Get written confirmation of the actual copy that will appear and the date when it will appear.	

Full display

Handling a full display advertisement is best left to the experts. Few individuals have the capacity to, first, produce good copy, second, produce artwork that will be indicative of, and reflect well on, the organisation, and third, lay out an advertisement that will compel the attention of a serious potential candidate. Most display advertisements are designed and placed by advertising agents.

WHAT THE ADVERTISEMENT SHOULD CONTAIN

The advertisement should contain a caption, and usually this is the job title. On the other hand there may be something about the job that is more likely to 'draw the eye', such as the salary, prospects or the location. 'Come and work in the Lake District', for example, would make an attractive caption. On the question of the job title, it should be remembered that people who scan the recruitment section of a newspaper are looking for something familiar, so 'playing' with job titles in an attempt to attract may lose you a candidate. From an ethical point of view, it is better to be honest about the job. The clearer you are in the advert, the more likely you will get a candidate who fits the job as they will be able to 'self-select'; only those who meet the criteria will apply and you will not waste time with dozens of applicants who don't stand a chance of getting the job. Salary should be included where possible, as again it is one of the things everyone looks for when scanning for jobs. Salary will give some indication of the level of the job and help people to self-select. If it's flexible, then you may want to say so, but a rough indication is helpful to those who want to know whether it's a waste of time applying because they are already on a higher salary.

Location is also important and will often be a 'deal-breaker', so if your vacancy involves travelling throughout the UK, or is based in London, then say so. It will stop anyone applying who doesn't want to move house, or dislikes being away from home, for example. You do not want to waste your time (or company money) on someone who really wants to stay in their current location and is not prepared to move. Better to say what is required and let people make their own decisions.

ACTIVITY 6.2

Look through some recent job advertisements in the national press. See what job titles are used. Do they actually describe what the job does? Which jobs would attract you? Do you think the jobs will actually be like they say they are in the advert?

Include also a brief synopsis of the job content, its requirements, reporting responsibilities and benefits. Say something about the organisation itself, its status in the industry, employment policy, promotion prospects, and so on. Obviously, advertising space is expensive and limited, so you cannot eulogise for too long! Finally, the advertisement should inform the reader how to apply for the job. This might be by submitting a letter of application, CV, by writing or telephoning for an application form. This last is seen by many organisations, especially those in the public sector, as an opportunity to send out 'further details' about the job, which may include a job description and person specification. Alternatively, many advertisements refer the reader to an application form on the organisation's website.

ACTIVITY 6.3

Draft the copy of an advertisement for your own job and one for the job of a colleague. What would attract you to apply for it?

OTHER MEDIA

Large organisations, such as the armed services, the National Health Service and government departments, use television, often as part of a campaign that includes displayed advertisements in newspapers and magazines. Television is the most expensive medium to use, and advertisements in spoken and written media are transitory and therefore have to be repeated, but the impact cannot be matched through any other medium.

RECRUITING ELECTRONICALLY

There has been a significant growth in making vacant positions known by electronic means, largely through the use of the Internet and the organisation's own intranet, with responses by email. It has been estimated that about 75% of employers now use some form of electronic recruitment, especially email responses and the acceptance of CVs via email (CIPD 2009j). Traditional and electronic activities can be combined at almost any stage. For example, a press advertisement may direct readers to a website providing further information, or a corporate website may require applicants to request an application form via email or telephone that will then be processed manually

Advantages and disadvantages of electronic recruitment

E-recruitment gives access to a large number of people at a very reasonable cost. Indeed if using the organisation's own website, the actual advertising cost is minimal, as the site exists anyway. Using a job vacancy site such as Monster (**www. monster.co.uk**) or Hays (**www.hays.com**) will incur a cost but is more likely to reach those who are actively in the job market seeking a position. The sites will advertise the job for you, but usually offer other services as well, such as shortlisting.

Using social networking sites can be useful in attracting applicants – especially graduates. However, in the 2008 CIPD *Recruitment, Retention and Turnover* survey report, employers were concerned about damaging remarks being made on such sites:

> From an employer branding perspective, they are concerned about damaging comments about the organisation being posted on social networking sites and blogs (62% agree/strongly agree).

PAUSE FOR THOUGHT

Graduate recruitment

For years, graduate recruiters had to fight among themselves over the young and educated elite. They ran expensive on-campus marketing campaigns and created flashy websites highlighting their corporate social responsibility efforts and work–life balance initiatives – all to attract good candidates well aware of their own worth. A feature of the boom years was that graduates more or less expected to walk into a top job of some kind with a reasonable lower second class honours degree, and to get into a big accountancy firm or the City 'with an upper second class honours degree', says John McGurk, CIPD Adviser, Learning and Talent development. 'It's been a big shock to graduates that vacancies have reduced by a quarter.' As the term 'recruitment shortfall' becomes defunct in big organisations, for now at least, so 'graduate recruitment' is a phrase that many smaller employers are beginning to use. Graduates are now more willing to search far and wide for employment, accepting lower salaries, reduced benefits and smaller companies.

Source: *People Management*, 10 September 2009. p24.

Use of social networking sites is currently not all that popular (only 7% of those employers in the 2009 CIPD survey said they used them) but an educated guess suggests that this will change as they develop and grow in future.

APPLICATION FORMS

The advantage of using application forms is that they set out the information you need in a standardised format. This speeds up the pace of manually sifting applications since, unlike CVs, which may take many forms, you know where on the form to look for each successive item of information. With online recruitment, forms can be scanned electronically at the shortlisting stage, which may speed up the process even further. See Chapter 7 for more on shortlisting.

RESPONSES TO ADVERTISEMENTS

It was said above that information about how prospective candidates may register their interest in the job is part of the advertisement content itself, which means that applications will soon be received. It is at this point that recruitment ends and selection commences.

CASE EXAMPLE

Talent puddles helping to feed the people capability needs at Nestlé

Nestlé is a large global food and beverage manufacturer. Its aim is to manufacture and market products in such a way as to create value that can be sustained over the long term for shareholders, employees, consumers and business partners. The business focus at the moment is very much on nutrition, health and wellness and coming up with new products to meet countrywide trends, while at the same time driving down costs. Nestlé employs 6,000 people in the UK and recruitment services are responsible for the resourcing issues relating to all of them.

In November 2001 the HR function within Nestlé UK moved from the HR generalist model to the 'three box' model of HR business partners, shared services and centres of expertise. The latter are: recruitment services, learning and development, the information and administration centre, and policy, remuneration and reward. Initially the recruitment team was made up of a mixture of new hires with recruitment backgrounds

and some generalist survivors from the HR restructuring. According to Fionna White, Head of Recruitment at Nestlé, 'Now, five years on it has transformed itself and is a group of true experts in their field operating as an in-house recruitment agency.'

People capability requirements

Nestlé's multi-channel talent pipeline aims to feed two broad capability requirements of the organisation. First, the core capability pool is populated with employees who make up the larger portion of the workforce and have the technical skills and capabilities that are essential to keep the organisation running. The second group of people is the high-potential pool. This comprises employees who make up the smaller portion of the workforce who are considered to have sufficient potential to become their high-performers and senior managers of the future. Each category is filled through a combination of existing employees and new recruits.

Introducing talent puddles

Recruitment services have worked with a number of functions to develop a multi-channel approach to filling their recruitment needs. Supported by the HR business partners, the function identifies its talent shortfalls and recruitment services subsequently devise an attraction strategy to fill the specific talent gap. The pool of talent Nestlé is seeking to tap into is from a candidate-driven market. The latest initiative to help overcome the shortage of skilled applicants is Nestlé's 'talent puddles'. This is a targeted pool of talent that is easier to access and manage than a broad generic talent database, which after time grows too unwieldy to identify the appropriate candidates.

Earlier efforts to implement talent pools failed owing to poor IT systems – recruiters were unable to find suitable people as the search facility was inadequate. However, the talent puddles are much smaller and contain potential talent for each function rather than the whole company. White describes them as 'the same as talent banks, just separated from a huge speculative pool'.

The first talent puddle was set up in September 2006 with a £5,000 budget. Creating micro-sites for jobs the department needed to recruit for was the initial step. This was followed by a targeted online campaign to generate candidates who were then interviewed and kept warm until an appropriate role arose. This candidate relationship management strategy allows the company to have candidates who are 'offer ready' and interested in Nestlé when a vacancy comes available. 'Essentially it was a selling job to drive more traffic to Nestlé's website. Persuading senior management wasn't difficult. Our business case highlighted a £56,000 cost of placing 13 people within the organisation via agencies versus the talent puddle and candidate relationship management concept, which generated 14 offers from just £700,' explained White.

The attraction strategy is designed to fill specific jobs and 'difficult-to-fill' roles. Because of this the company is up front with people that there are no jobs in existence. The motives for choosing the supply chain first was the interest they showed in the initiative and the fact that their career paths and succession planning were the most advanced. The supply chain talent puddle, which was launched at the end of last year [2006], now contains 120 shortlisted candidates and has placed eight people. Nestlé have also implemented it for finance and are about to launch it for the marketing and sales functions.

The recruiter's role

This new approach to resourcing has affected the recruiters' roles. A significant portion of their time is now spent calling people and sifting through CVs from the talent puddle. When people apply, recruiters look at the quality of the applications and assess what level/grade they are operating at, ranking and recording them accordingly. Candidates are met and interviewed by the recruitment team and line managers before being placed in the talent puddle.

Business benefits

Reducing the time to hire and fill vacancies and the cost of recruiting are just some of the business benefits. One vacancy filled via this method led to an offer being accepted in 24 hours. White points out that 'managers are beginning to think ahead, for instance the resourcing team were asked by one manager to start looking for someone to replace a member of staff who is to be promoted in future months'. White believes it has also encouraged the organisation to become better at its resource planning by turning line managers' conversations to focus on identifying talent gaps and what they are going to do to fill them proactively as opposed to reacting 'once the horse has bolted' as was done in the past.

With their candidate relationship management strategy, referral scheme and drive to increase the number of direct hires, the company has also reduced their agency dependency over the past five years from 80% to 29% (against an industry norm of 30%), saving the business £300,000 during 2006 in agency placement fees. 'This approach is just one part of the multi-channel approach we have to generating a talent pipeline to meet the business's needs,' says White.

Information provided by Fionna White, Head of Recruitment, Nestlé

Source: CIPD Recruitment, Retention and Turnover survey report 2007

SUMMARY

This chapter has looked at recruitment – one of the key areas of HR. Being able to resource talent is vital if we want to compete and succeed in the business world. The various stages of the systematic recruitment cycle are outlined as:

- Stage 1 – Identify genuine vacancy.
- Stage 2 – Obtain authority to recruit.
- Stage 3 – Carry out job analysis or check that previous analysis still holds good.
- Stage 4 – Write or revise job description and person specification.
- Stage 5 – Make the vacancy known (write the advert and decide on relevant media).
- Stage 6 – Place the advert in the appropriate media.

We have looked in more detail at job descriptions and person specifications and have seen the importance of these when recruiting. The growth of e-recruitment has also been discussed, together with the impact of this on the recruitment process.

Recruitment can be a costly process – so getting it right is one of the most important things HR can contribute in adding value to the organisation.

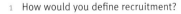

REVIEW QUESTIONS

1 How would you define recruitment?

2 What are the factors that have influenced change in approaches to recruitment advertising?

3 What societal factors have caused an increase in the importance of recruitment?

4 Why, when recruiting for a vacant position, might the internal labour market be your first choice?

5 Why, on the other hand, might the external labour market be your first choice?

6 Once a job vacancy exists, what is normally the first stage in the process?

7 What should be included on a job description?

8 What is the purpose of a person specification?

9 Why should we be careful if using Rodger's seven-point plan?

10 What are the main benefits of using an advertising agency?

11 When making a vacant position known, what are the alternatives to advertising jobs in newspapers and magazines?

12 What can be done to help candidates 'self-select'?

13 What are the benefits of using e-recruitment?

14 What might be the best way of recruiting graduates?

EXPLORE FURTHER

BOOKS

TAYLOR, S. (2008) *People resourcing*. 4th ed. London: Chartered Institute of Personnel and Development.

Taylor's text covers a range of resourcing-related issues in an easy-to-read style.

Most HR textbooks have a section on recruitment and selection.

WEB LINKS

The CIPD annual *Recruitment, Retention and Turnover* survey report is an essential read for the latest trends in recruitment and selection. The 2009 survey is available at: www.cipd.co.uk/subjects/recruitmen/general/_recruitment_summary.htm

CHAPTER 7

Selection

LEARNING OBJECTIVES

After studying this chapter you should:

- understand traditional and modern approaches to selection
- be able to organise a selection event
- understand and be able to participate in a variety of selection methods
- understand the legal aspects of selection.

INTRODUCTION

As we have seen in the previous chapter, attracting the right calibre of people is vital for the success of the business. The selection stage is where we make the decisions about who to appoint from those who have applied. Hopefully, if the recruitment stage went well, you will have a good pool of talent from which to choose.

Selection is one of the most important tasks of the HR practitioner, since it is vital to fill vacant positions with people who are not only suitably skilled for specific jobs, but are also flexible, and willing and able to cope with change.

Those involved in selection include both HR practitioners and line managers, in the sense that HR tend to actually organise the selection events and participate in them all the way through to the final selection decisions, offering advice to the line manager throughout the process. Senior managers formulate selection policies, draw up the procedures and facilitate training for those involved at the interface.

THE SEARCH FOR 'TALENT'

The search for talent is paramount in gaining the competitive edge and so it is important that the selection process is effective, reliable and also cost-effective. To achieve this, there is an increased emphasis on the use of complex selection techniques, such as assessment centres, which may include a variety of activities such as presentations and in-tray exercises as well as interviews. Selectors may also use occupational tests that are designed specifically to identify in candidates the necessary skills and competences that are required to carry out the work, and psychological tests that identify candidates' personality characteristics, intelligence, values and attitudes that are necessary for the appropriate adoption of the role.

The job interview, which was once the central feature of the selection process, still has an important part to play, but the use of more sophisticated techniques has moderated its significance. Research studies on the effectiveness of different selection methods in predicting a person who will be good in the job, such as those by Anderson and Shackleton (1993), found the techniques often used in assessment centres, for example ability tests and structured interviews, are more accurate in predicting future success in the job. Ideally we would like a selection technique that will definitely predict whether someone will fit into the job and do well. But unfortunately, such a test has yet to be devised! It is probably better to use a variety of methods because then it is far more likely that you have enough information on which to base a sound decision.

TRADITIONAL METHODS

All of this is not to say that traditional methods of selecting new employees have been completely abandoned. Organisations often use the 'classic trio' – application form, interview and references – as their means of recruiting and selecting staff. Most people would not wish to appoint someone they have not talked to at an interview at least – but nowadays there are such a wide variety of other methods; it would make sense to use some of these to make a better informed decision. Bearing in mind that the 2009 CIPD *Recruitment, Retention and Turnover* survey report states that it costs an average of £6,125 to replace a member of staff who leaves, it is crucial that selection is undertaken in a cost-effective and reliable manner. The last thing you want is to appoint someone and then have them leave fairly soon, thus meaning you have to start the whole process over again. Anyone in HR who has been through this situation will know the frustrations of this happening. And possibly even worse – appointing someone who stays in the job but who does not perform well. It becomes more and more vital that selection is done as carefully as possible in order to have a successful outcome. And what is better, in terms of job satisfaction for an HR practitioner, than to see someone you have selected doing well in the company and to think 'I appointed that person'! The use of complex and perhaps lengthy selection procedures can mean that line managers are unwilling to use them. Often the attitude is just to replace someone as quickly as possible, and while this is obviously a good thing to aim for, it should not be at the expense of appointing a good-quality candidate. The old phrase 'marry in haste, repent at leisure' could well be applied to selection! Better to spend time doing it properly and end up choosing the 'right' person – a talented and successful employee who will add value to the organisation.

SELECTION POLICY

This is part of the organisation's overall employment policy, and should state how the organisation intends to go about the selection of new staff. The policy statement should relate the selection systems directly to the achievement of the organisation's aim to achieve a competitive advantage. The actual procedures, therefore, should be designed specifically to bring in people with knowledge, skills, competences and attitudes that will enable them to make appropriate contributions towards the achievement of that aim. We have seen in the previous chapter how we can match the candidates to a person specification and get people whose attributes are exactly what we need in that job.

But sometimes we may see a candidate who is not right for the job we are filling, but who does have abilities and qualities that we think would be useful in the organisation. In these cases, should we appoint them anyway and let them develop a job around their skills? This idea of 'job sculpting' is an excellent way of developing staff and fits in with the adage of 'recruit for attitude, train for skill'. Unfortunately, not many companies have the luxury of being able to do this and usually we have a specific job in mind when we are selecting staff. This kind of approach works well when taking on graduates, for instance, when we have some leeway in the specific job we have in mind. Recruit them and see which area they do best in, before placing them into a final job.

EQUALITY AND DIVERSITY

The policy should also state the approach to selection in relation to ensuring equal opportunities. Organisations vary in their approaches to formulating ethical and legitimate strategies and policies on discrimination. This is an extremely important section of the policy statement and is dealt with at greater length in Chapter 15. The main thing to bear in mind is that all selection procedures must adhere to legislation and must be seen to be fair and equitable. It is a good idea to ask yourself throughout the process, 'Would this be acceptable if it went to an employment tribunal?' Phrasing of interview questions, use of tests, and so on, can all be seen as discriminatory if care is not taken. And this is where HR advice to line managers can be essential in averting disaster!

THE SELECTION PROCESS

As we have said earlier, selecting new employees is a critically important task. It is about predicting potential and in-job performance, and the final decisions should be based on data of the highest possible quality.

Successful recruitment will have produced applications from qualified and experienced people from whom the best person for the job can be selected. The next stage is to screen the applications, develop a shortlist of candidates, and organise and conduct interviews and other selection activities.

SELECTION STRATEGY

So, what selection strategy should you use? The strategy incorporates which methods should be used, how much should be spent on the process, who will be involved, and so on. The selection strategy should be flexible enough to accommodate the selector's needs in respect of the variety of jobs that exist in the organisation. For example, the strategy that might be adopted to select, say, a factory operative will be different from that for selecting a senior manager. It may be seen as worthwhile to have a lengthy (and costly) selection process for a management post, whereas not so important for the factory operative. Some organisations, however, such as Toyota, carry out assessment centre activities for all jobs – perhaps taking the view that all selection decisions are important.

SCREENING APPLICATIONS

In many organisations this is still carried out manually, but computerised systems are available for use when the response material has been designed for use with this method. Used mostly by recruitment agencies and where large numbers of application forms are received, the forms can be processed electronically using specific programs designed to select candidates with the required attributes. When screening is carried out systematically, all of the applicants are subject to exactly the same process and are therefore all treated equally. However, the danger of this is that some very good candidates may be missed because they have used different phrases to the ones programmed. For example, if the computer is looking for leadership qualities and therefore picks out any applications that mention the words 'leader' or leadership', it may miss someone who has written about their experience of being 'head of a group', just because they have used different terminology. The human mind will notice and pick up on different experiences and see their worthiness, whereas a computer will not.

PRODUCING THE 'LONG' SHORTLIST

After making a list of the basic details of all of the applicants (name and contact details), you should read through the applications, comparing their contents with the demands of the person specification and sort them into piles under the headings of rejections, possibles and probables. Possibles are those who could do the job perhaps with some training, while probables are those who meet most or all of the criteria and therefore are a close match with your requirements. A courteously worded letter should then be sent to the rejected applicants and the 'long' shortlist is made up of the remaining possibles and probables.

If, at the advertising stage, a large number of applications is anticipated, a line may be inserted in the advertisement saying that only those who reach the minimum standard will receive further correspondence, thus heading off the need to spend time and money on written replies. Or even better, to say that if candidates have not heard by a certain date, they can assume they have been unsuccessful. There is a dilemma here – should unsuccessful candidates be notified, as part of common courtesy, or is the cost saving justified? Remember that any recruitment exercise is an opportunity to expose the business to the public – and any unprofessional behaviour will reflect badly on the organisation.

EQUAL OPPORTUNITIES

A word of warning here: the whole selection process can be prone to claims of discrimination. You may wish to use equal opportunities monitoring forms as a means of reducing the risk of illegal discrimination. Some companies now use them as part of the application form and remove them before shortlisting. When producing a 'long list' the use of only numbers reduces even further the chances of discrimination based on foreign sounding names or of whether the candidate is male or female. Though this will obviously become apparent at interview stage!

SHORTLISTING

The next step is to re-screen the 'long' shortlist, and it is important to involve the line manager at this stage. They will have had a hand in the development of the person specification and will understand the purposes of the job, the meaning and importance of any technical aspects, and how the job might develop in the future.

The process begins by re-reading through the possibles, studying those that most closely match the demands of the person specification and deciding, with the line manager, if any of them could be moved into the probables file. With this task, it is best to err on the side of caution and the rule is: *if in doubt, retain.*

ORGANISING INTERVIEWS AND TESTS

The approach to this is determined by the selection strategy. In this context, the word 'interview', colloquially, can refer to all of the selection process, which may, of course – depending which strategy has been decided upon – include occupational tests and assessment centres, which can include job simulation/ work sampling and/or group selection methods. The interviews may be held in one-to-one or two-to-one situations, panel interviews, selection boards or a combination of these models.

SCREENING INTERVIEWS

Sometimes the competition for the job is particularly tight, making it difficult to distinguish clearly between the possibles and probables. One approach to this problem is to hold preliminary interviews to clarify specific points with the candidates, with the final interviews following at a later date. Those that are not rejected at that stage make up the shortlist. Rejection letters are then sent to all of the remaining applicants and interview invitations are sent to the applicants who have been shortlisted.

TELEPHONE INTERVIEWS

Screening interviews may be held by telephone – a cheap way of screening candidates. Those that are successful would then be invited in for second interviews and further selection procedures. A telephone interview may enable you to cut your list down from 'probables' to 'definites' for the rest of the selection procedure. The remaining applications are then studied and finally checked to ensure that they all meet with your selection criteria. There is the potential for individual prejudices and biases to creep in when only one person speaks to a potential employee, so try to be aware of this: having a structured set of questions to follow will help. Also give candidates plenty of warning so they have time to prepare themselves. Telephone interviews can be just as daunting as the real thing.

ADMINISTRATIVE PREPARATION

The arrangements, including the venues, timing and all who are to be involved, need to be carefully co-ordinated. The answers to the following questions make a reasonable administrative checklist:

- **Timing:** Have all relevant dates been set and agreed by everyone involved?
- **Venues:** Has all of the necessary accommodation been booked for:
  - waiting area?
  - interviewing?
  - selection testing?
- **Reception:** Have the staff on reception been given a list of the candidates, the title of the job, the times and dates of their arrival, where they are to wait?
- **Personnel:** Has everyone who will be involved in the process been briefed on the timing and sequence of events?
- **Testing:** If testing is included, will a qualified test administrator be available?
- **Candidates:** Have all shortlisted candidates been advised of the relevant times and dates, and has their availability been confirmed?
- **Special needs:** Have appropriate arrangements been made for candidates, and members of your own staff, who have special needs? This should include access to the premises, car parking and physical assistance where required. Did your invitation letter make it clear what assistance would be available?

ARRIVAL AND WAITING

When candidates arrive, they should be shown to the waiting area and told approximately how long they will be waiting, which should not be so long as to give the impression of a poorly organised event. This stage can be handled by the receptionist, but some organisations, especially for important jobs, have one of the selection team ready to go out, greet the candidate and make them comfortable.

Reasonably comfortable chairs, coffee tables, recent editions of the company magazine, a copy of the latest annual report and accounts and any other relevant literature may be placed in the waiting area. Candidates will be keen to learn as much as they can about the organisation before the interview process starts.

OCCUPATIONAL TESTS

Properly trained people are needed to carry out selection tests, and suitable accommodation has to be available. Large organisations are usually well provided for in this respect, although some tend to use local hotel accommodation. It can be quite costly to train a member of the HR staff to administer tests, but if you wish to use tests as part of your selection procedure, then it will be money well spent.

ASSESSMENT CENTRES

An assessment centre is usually a full day of selection tests and activities, designed specifically to test out the skills and abilities of the candidate in relation to the job. Assessment centres take a lot of planning. It is important to think of which skills and qualities are required (gathered from the person specification) and then to devise exercises that will test out those qualities. For a post of training officer, for example, where presentation skills, organisation and interpersonal skills are required, the day might involve doing a presentation, taking part in a group problem-solving discussion, undertaking some in-tray exercises and having a panel interview. Each exercise will relate to a specific skill needed for the job. Candidates are assessed by trained observers in each activity and scored accordingly. At the end of the day, a sound decision can be made by comparing the performances of each candidate.

Where assessment centres or group selection methods are used, more time has to be allowed and the process may last more than one day, in which case candidates should be given advance warning of this.

If we are to select the best talent available then assessment centres may be the best way of ensuring that we achieve this.

 ACTIVITY 7.1

Think of your job – what exercises would you include in an assessment centre that would test whether you have the ability and skills necessary to do your job?

INTERVIEWS

Depending on the interview strategy, sufficient time has to be allowed and the interviews have to be organised so that every candidate is allocated the same amount of time. It is important to plan what questions will be asked and who will cover which areas. One-to-one interviews, while perhaps more informal, may have problems in that if there is an accusation of discriminatory behaviour by the interviewer, it is difficult to refute, being only the word of the interviewer against the word of the interviewee. Panel interviews are generally safer for this reason. They also allow several members of the panel to discuss their decisions at the end and to justify their choice.

USE OF OCCUPATIONAL TESTS

Research by Anderson and Shackleton (1993) and Robertson and Smith (2001) suggests that the use of tests can add to the accuracy of the selection decision. There are a number of different tests that can be used.

If the candidate knows that the interviewer is in possession of the test results from the start of the interview, they may be more inclined to be frank about their strengths, weaknesses and any other qualities that the tests were designed to elicit.

PSYCHOMETRIC TESTING

 KEY CONCEPT: PSYCHOMETRICS

Psychometrics is the measurement of psychological attributes, including mental testing such as intelligence and personality, usually in the form of questionnaires. As the term implies, a psychometric test is one in which the outcome is analysed statistically.

Components of intelligence, such as verbal, spatial and numerical ability, are measured through cognitive tests. Personality tests are concerned with identifying a person's disposition to behave in certain ways in certain situations. Cognitive and personality tests are available commercially.

WHO DESIGNS OCCUPATIONAL TESTS?

Selection tests are not randomly designed by HR people, nor usually by anyone else in the organisation. Ideally, they will have been designed by psychologists employed by a firm of consultants who are experts in the field. The consultancies train their clients in test administration, which includes the use of psychometric techniques, through which the test performance of the candidate is elicited. Tests should be 'valid', which means that they measure what they purport to measure, and 'reliable', which means that they produce consistent results.

WHY USE SUCH METHODS?

There has been a steady growth in the use of occupational testing in recent years, partly because of the doubt that research evidence has thrown upon interviewing, and partly because the principles and practices of HRM have highlighted the importance of people as the means of achieving a competitive advantage. Such emphasis has caused selectors to use the best means available to achieve this. Also, the use of evidence from tests supports the organisation's drive for fairness and equal opportunities, since all applicants for any one particular job undergo exactly the same test, and it is not a test that has been devised by the selectors. Problems with bias and discrimination in interviews, for example, is minimised by using a test that is seen to be fair and equitable to all candidates.

The advantage of using psychometric testing techniques is that they produce corroborative and objective evidence, although an employment decision should never be made on the sole basis of test results. Some objective evidence, however, is better than none, especially if it supports what you subsequently learn about the candidate during the interview.

WHO CONDUCTS THE TESTS?

The British Psychological Society (BPS) now requires test users to be properly trained and certified. Any organisation considering the use of psychometric measures for selection purposes must ensure that properly trained personnel are available. For organisations that lack properly trained people, there are independent consultants who can provide the appropriate service.

CULTURAL DIFFERENCES

It is necessary to be careful with occupational tests as they may contain cultural bias. Those undertaking such tests also need to have a reasonable command of the English language. Inferences that are drawn from the results of tests through psychometric techniques may not pick up the fact that, for example, someone who has failed a test of 'leadership ability' did so because they did not know how to take the test; they might well have good leadership potential.

JOB SIMULATION

This is an exercise in which the candidate is required to deal with situations that typically represent the job for which they have applied. Often, in-tray exercises and role-plays are involved. For example, asking a lecturer or a training officer to give a short talk or presentation would be a valid means of testing out their abilities in this area. It is what they would be expected to do in their everyday job, if they were successful in being appointed. The candidate is observed throughout the process.

WORK SAMPLING

This involves placing the candidate in the role for a predetermined amount of time and assessing their performance.

FURTHER SOURCES OF INFORMATION

There are several additional sources of information about candidates:

- **Biodata**, in which the data about the candidate is collected from the application form and/or from a biographical questionnaire. The data relates to criteria such as qualifications and experience. Large organisations gather information (biodata) about their successful employees and form a profile of a 'good employee'; they then try to match the candidates' biodata to this. This may be seen as discriminatory, as information on a person's background (gender, age, race, and so on) might be used as part of the selection decision, rather than on their skills and abilities.

- **Peer assessment** is of little use in the assessment of external candidates. It can, however, have some predictive value when assessing internal candidates who are well known to their peers.

- **Graphology** is the study of a person's social profile through their handwriting. Its use in selection is based on the idea that handwriting reveals something about the individual's personality, which provides the basis for making a prediction about work behaviour. Used in Europe, especially France, more than in the UK. It is hardly better than flipping a coin in terms of predictive validity.

- **References** may be obtained from several sources including previous employers and academic tutors; also personal character references may be obtained from independent parties. The reliability of references is sometimes questionable; opinions about character and suitability are less reliable. If you write someone a bad reference, you may be in trouble if they then don't get the job. Can you justify the things you say about the person? Best to stick with the facts such as nature of previous job, time in employment, reason for leaving, salary and academic achievement. Robertson and Smith (2001) suggest that they are one of the least reliable means of selection. Many companies now will only provide the very briefest of references (based on confirming that the person did work for them), rather than be taken to court for defamation of character! The opposite may of course be true – would you write someone a good reference just to get rid of them? If you do use references, make sure you use them carefully and only as a small part of the whole selection process. References can be important in certain circumstances – in the context, for example, of the Soham murders, where references were not taken. If references had been taken, the school would have found that Huntley had not worked in the schools and places that he had said that he had worked in. It is part of the security checking and ties a person to a time and place. For a useful guide, see the Employment Records section of the 'Employment Practices Data Protection Code', available on the website of the Information Commissioner's Office at **www.ico.gov.uk**.

INTERVIEWING

Torrington et al (2007, p232) define the selection interview as 'a controlled conversation with a purpose' and note criticisms of interviews as being 'unreliable, invalid and subjective'. Research by Anderson and Shackleton (1993) tends to support this by casting doubt on the power of unstructured interviews to predict competence in the job. By their very nature, interviews are subjective, although the need to treat all candidates equally has encouraged selectors to structure interviews, which also goes a little way towards reducing subjectivity. Having said all that, the absence of the interview from the selection process would be regarded as unusual and it is still widely used as a selection method.

STRUCTURED AND UNSTRUCTURED INTERVIEWS

It was mentioned above that interviews may be structured or unstructured. Much of the criticism mentioned above is levelled at unstructured interviews, in which the interviewer enters into a free-flowing conversation with the interviewee. Truly, there are some experienced people who can derive a considerable amount of information about a candidate in this way, but where this method is used, it is unlikely that all candidates will be treated in exactly the same way.

Structured interviews should be standardised as much as possible, as is suggested by their name. This helps to avoid discrimination claims if all candidates are asked the same questions. This is where advanced preparation is important – decide with the other interviewers which areas will be covered and by whom. Use the job description and person specification as a basis for your questions, or a competency framework if you have one.

COMPETENCE-BASED INTERVIEWS

The questions in an interview should be closely related to the job, either by linking them to the job description and person specification as noted above, or by relating them to 'competencies' – 'a set of behaviours that individuals demonstrate when undertaking job-relevant tasks' (Whiddett and Hollyforde 2003). There may be 'core competencies' that apply to all employees whatever their job (for example teamworking) and 'job-specific competencies' (for example analytical ability) that are the specialised attributes necessary for the job in question. If you have a set of competencies for the job, then questions can be linked in to those, thus providing a valid structure to the questions asked. Answers are then scored and comparisons between candidates can easily be made. There is less likelihood of bias and justification of decisions is far more transparent.

The following case example provides a practical example of the differences between structured and unstructured interviews.

CASE EXAMPLE

Structured versus unstructured interviews

Jennifer, an HR officer at Solent Toys, and Tony Jackson, the manager of the electronics subsidiary company, have shortlisted ten candidates for the job of electronics engineer. Ideally, they would have preferred about six candidates, but in the second screening process there was little to choose between the final ten. They agreed that they would each interview all ten to create a final shortlist and then compare their choices.

Tony carried out his interviews sitting at his desk in his office with the candidate sitting opposite him. He established a rapport with the candidate by chatting generally, and at the same time, he was trying to gather an impression of what kind of person he had in front of him. Some of his questions were rhetorical, such as, 'You're probably OK at designing interactive toys, aren't you?' – to which, of course, the answer was 'yes.' Most of the questions were about the candidates: availability, what they enjoyed about their work, leisure pursuits, and so on.

Jennifer's approach was quite different. She began by showing all the candidates around the factory, so that they could see the work situations for themselves. She then used an interview room that had a few comfortable chairs and coffee tables. The atmosphere was relaxed and friendly but businesslike. Jennifer asked every candidate the same set of questions, which were mostly about the job. She asked open questions that began with phrases such as, 'Tell me about…' and 'Why did you decide…?', and so on. She had designed a form (see Figure 7.1)

on which she graded each candidate's interview performance, and as soon as each candidate left, she completed the form for that person.

When Tony and Jennifer compared their results, they found major differences in their choices. Only two of Tony's top six were in Jennifer's top six. Clearly, their strategy had not produced the results they were expecting, and when they discussed this, it emerged that Tony's choices were influenced by the 'types' of people he had interviewed. He attributed importance to their qualifications and the personal impression they gave. Jennifer, on the other hand, had focused on the candidates' knowledge, experience and competences, and her questions were largely about the job.

Discussion

Clearly, Tony used an unstructured approach to the interview. He focused on the person rather than the job, which meant that each of the ten candidates had a different interview experience with him. Jennifer, on the other hand, had prepared a structure, and had notes that she had made shortly after each interview, while the candidates' responses were still fresh in her mind. Since Jennifer centred her questions on the demands of the job, the data she had gathered about each candidate was more objective and enabled her to predict each candidate's likely performance in the job.

Figure 7.1 Candidate's interview performance form

Candidate name			Position			
Grade			Department			
Criteria	Poor	Fair	Adequate	Good	Excellent	Comments
Qualifications						
Experience						
Previous relevant training						
Education						
Knowledge and skills						
Appearance (where relevant)						
General rating						

If you prepare a separate form in respect of each candidate, you can record any new information that came to light during the interview, and jot something down that will enable you to remember which candidate is which – some distinctive feature or something they were wearing. When you have interviewed ten candidates in a row, it is difficult to recall who said what. Remember you are going to have a discussion with your interviewing colleagues afterwards, and you will want to make a sensible and meaningful contribution. Be careful about making personal comments, however. If there is a case that goes to an employment tribunal for, say, sex discrimination, all your notes, private or not, will be made public. So writing 'the candidate wore an awful yellow cardigan – no fashion sense!' will not add to your integrity when read out at the tribunal!

USING THE APPLICATION FORM

Some interviewers recommend basing the interview structure on the contents of the application form, so that the form acts as a kind of checklist. This is not always a good idea: the completed application form contains factual information, but it may also include information that the applicant wished to present to you. It is also important to identify gaps on the CV or application form – be prepared to ask questions on these to ensure you have the full story.

The main aim of the interview is to select the best person for the job, which is achieved through predicting the in-job performance of each candidate. To aid this objective, the interviewer uses the factual information on the application form in addition to information that was gathered from tests, other assessment methods and references (if they are available at that stage).

TYPES OF INTERVIEW

Interviews may be held as one-to-one, two-to-one or panel interviews. Where there are several interviewers, the person who takes the lead should be a good interpersonal communicator, have a sound knowledge of the job for which the selection is being made, and be capable of controlling the track of the interview and of establishing and maintaining a healthy rapport with the interviewee throughout. Plan the structure before the interview – who will ask what? And have the same set of questions for each candidate. Inevitably, you will want to perhaps follow up and ask probing questions that will differ slightly for each candidate, but the basic set should be the same for all, as this avoids claims of discrimination, as we saw earlier. A professional approach will leave the candidates feeling that they have been treated well, and even if they are not successful in getting the job, they will at least feel they have had a fair trial.

INITIAL EXCHANGES

At the outset, you will know more about the candidate than they know about you or the company, and it is a good idea to redress this imbalance right away. Your manner when you are doing this should help to put the candidate at ease. A nervous interviewee will give you less information about themselves than will one who is relaxed. From that point on, the interviewee should do most of the talking. Allowing them talk for 70% of the time, while you talk 30% is the recommended balance; the longer you talk, the more you will deprive the candidate of the opportunity to tell you things about themselves.

PROBLEMS WITH INTERVIEWING

Be aware of some of the dangers of interviewing. Bias towards a favoured candidate that you like the look of as soon as they enter the room (the 'halo effect') or against one whom you dislike (the 'horns effect') can affect your objectivity when making a rational decision. Make sure you listen to all that your candidate has to say throughout the interview and don't make snap decisions based on the answers to the first few questions.

There is also a danger of stereotyping (see below) and of choosing someone who is 'like me'; we tend to want to appoint people we will like and with whom we identify. But unless we want an organisation full of clones of ourselves, then it makes more sense to make our decision based on the person specification and the competences for the job, rather than on personal liking. Be aware of discrimination: remember that you should always be able to justify your decision and be able to confirm that you have appointed the 'best person for the job' – assessments of candidates should focus on their abilities in relation to the job.

QUESTIONING TECHNIQUES

How you ask a question is every bit as important as what you ask. Questions should be framed in a way that invites the candidate to reply in full. Questions may be closed or open. A closed question is one that invites a short but informative answer, often used to check and confirm facts: for example, 'How many years did you work there?', answer: '15'. Some writers advise against the use of closed questions, but they can be useful, especially at the beginning of an interview when trying to establish a rapport, the answers usually being easy and non-contentious. Open questions are those that begin with 'why …' or 'what do you think of …?' Such questions should not be too long or convoluted, and you should ensure that there is only one question in there. If you ask more than one question in a single statement, you will only get an answer to the last one. Here is an example of the difference between open and closed questions:

> *Open version*: **'Why do you enjoy working in business development?'**

> *Closed version*: **'So you enjoy working in business development?'**

The answer to the open version allows the candidate to explain the outcomes of the work and why it is enjoyable, while the answer to the closed version is 'yes.' The more relevant information you have about the candidates, the more able you will be to make a good-quality selection decision.

Be careful to avoid 'leading' questions too. Questions such as, 'So you agree that leadership is about controlling people?' are likely to make a candidate think this is what you are looking for and they will therefore go along with what you say. After all, the candidate is trying to appear to be the person you want – and this may inhibit them from giving their true feelings. If you ask instead, 'What do you feel are the main components of leadership?', then you are giving nothing away, and the candidate is more likely to say what they really think.

Questions such as 'Can you cope with pressure?' are also likely to elicit a response of 'yes'. Who would answer differently, if they want the job? A better way would be to ask, 'Tell me about a time when you have dealt with pressure,' which forces the candidate to rely on their past experience and actually say how they have dealt with it. If you ask questions that make candidates draw on their actual experience, you are more likely to get a truer response, rather than one they might make up.

Replace hypothetical questions such as, 'How would you deal with a difficult customer?', where they have to invent a scenario, with 'How have you dealt with difficult customers?', which should elicit a more realistic and reliable answer. As we saw earlier, basing your questions around the competences necessary for the job makes for a much more relevant interview, focused on the real attributes required.

ACTIVITY 7.2

Devise a set of questions that you might ask if you were advertising for a replacement for your own job. What are the key things you would want to find out about the person in terms of skills and experience?

QUESTIONING AND EQUAL OPPORTUNITIES

Be careful to avoid stereotyping – make sure you base your decisions on reality. Making assumptions about people based on their gender, age or ethnic origin, for instance, or about what a disabled person is capable of, without checking the reality of the situation, is a dangerous game. Always gather enough information to corroborate your decisions.

When questioning candidates always bear in mind that their domestic situation and personal circumstances have no bearing on the case for employment. If the recruitment process has been handled according to good practice, the shortlisted candidates will only have proceeded with their applications if they are sure they could meet the demands of the job. One approach is to ensure that all questions relate directly to the job, its technicalities, duties, responsibilities and the performance required. Again, a set of competences for the job will provide a useful format on which to base your questions, ensuring that they all relate specifically to the job.

CLOSING THE INTERVIEW

When you have got all the information you need, the interview is almost at its end. It is then that you should give interviewees the opportunity to make any points or ask questions. Candidates may have studied the job requirements and come to the interview hoping to put across several points that they feel are in their favour. During the course of the interview, they will have taken any opportunities that arose to express these points, but there may be something they wish to say that they feel would complete their case for being appointed.

MAKING THE DECISION

Selection decisions are seldom made by just one person sitting alone, and while HR people do contribute with information and legal guidance, they should make such decisions only if the position is in the HR department.

The objective is to select the best person for the job, and the decision has to be made fairly and legally. To achieve this, you have to be sure that all of the candidates received exactly the same treatment, that the selection process (including any selection tests) was structured in the same way for everyone, and that they all received an equal opportunity to make a case.

The whole process has to be fair, and be seen to be fair. A structured decision-making process that focuses upon how each of the candidates rated throughout the selection process, in which evidence from tests and interviews is seriously considered, has the hallmarks of a fair system. Notes can be compared and agreements reached about the performance of each individual. One suggestion is to develop a *candidate ranking form* (see Figure 7.2) on the basis of the person specification, on which each candidate may be graded according to their performance in the interview and on any tests that were carried out.

In Figure 7.2, the left-hand column indicates the seven most important criteria for selection. The criteria are taken from the person specification and entered on the form in their order of importance. During the interview, prearranged questions that relate to the criteria are asked and the interviewee is scored according to their responses. Obviously, the best performers would be candidates who scored well in the top right-hand area: that is to say, people who scored highly against the most important criteria.

Having borne in mind the demands of fairness, legality and the provision of equal opportunities, it is up to the decision-makers to select the candidate they think is the best person for the job. This is a difficult decision to make, not least because the very idea of selecting just one person makes the whole process discriminatory.

Figure 7.2 Candidate ranking form

Candidate name:			Interviewed for (job title):		
Criteria	**Assessment**				
	1	*2*	*3*	*4*	*5*
1 Most important	Low				High
2					
3					
4					
5					
6					
7 Least important					

MAKING AN OFFER OF EMPLOYMENT

An offer of employment is usually made 'subject to satisfactory references'. The candidate's permission to take up references should be obtained, especially since one will be from the current employer (if any). This may be problematic in that sometimes people do not want their employer to know that they have applied for another job, so do not want to ask for a reference before they have a firm offer. Of course, if you then receive a poor reference, will you rescind the job offer? As we discussed earlier, references may not offer any real insight into the candidate's suitability but do give important information about the candidate's employment history. However, most employers do use them, and it is worth making sure that you have followed correct procedures. If there is more than one possible choice of appointment, it is wise to wait until the offer has been accepted in writing before communicating the final decision to the rest of the candidates.

MEDICAL EXAMINATION

Most organisations will make some medical checks on prospective employees, e.g. completing a health questionnaire. Medical examinations should only be carried out where it is necessary to determine the potential employee's suitability for the post, e.g. whether they have sufficient strength to carry out the work.

OTHER CHECKS TO CARRY OUT

For certain posts you may need to carry out further checks. If you are recruiting to a post where the job involves dealing with vulnerable clients, for example in social services or in education, you may need to get Criminal Records Bureau (CRB) checks done before the offer is confirmed and the person can start work. These can be slow to process, so build this into your timing. These checks cannot be obtained by members of the public directly but are only available to organisations and only for those professions, offices, employments, work and occupations listed in the Exceptions Order to the Rehabilitation of Offenders Act 1974.

There are two types of check – standard and enhanced.

Standard CRB checks are for people entering certain professions, such as members of the legal and accountancy professions. Standard checks contain the following:

- convictions
- cautions
- reprimands
- warnings

held in England and Wales on the Police National Computer. Most the relevant convictions in Scotland and Northern Ireland may also be included.

Enhanced checks are for posts involving work in a regulated activity for a regulated activity provider with children or vulnerable adults. In general, the type of work will involve regularly caring for, supervising, training or being in sole charge of such people. Examples include a teacher, scout or guide leader. Enhanced checks are also issued for certain statutory purposes such as gaming and lottery licences (**www.crb.homeoffice.gov.uk/guidance/applicants_ guidance/levels_of_crb_check.aspx**).

With the influx of workers from abroad and the extension of the European Union, where foreign workers are entitled to work in the UK, it is important to check that your candidates have the right to work here. The Asylum and Immigration Act 1996 made it a criminal offence to employ those who do not have permission to live or work in the UK. This was updated by the Immigration, Asylum and Nationality Act 2006, which came into force on 29 February 2008. Basically employers should ask all EEA nationals to confirm their nationality by producing a specified document as laid out in the Border Agency guidance booklet. Legislation changes fairly frequently, so to make sure you are up to date; see the UK Border Agency website (**www.ind.homeoffice.gov.uk**) for more details.

MAKING APPOINTMENTS

Appointments should be handled sensitively, as there may be a number of internal candidates who did not get the job. Reasons for appointing the one candidate you have chosen must be sound – and *be seen to be* sound, if you wish to avoid staff being demoralised because they didn't get the job.

FINAL WORD

If the right selection procedures are used, then you should find that you can select talented workers in an effective and cost-efficient way that will help to convince line managers of the usefulness and value of HR. A professional approach will impact not only on the business internally, but also on those outside it who have contact with you in the selection process.

SUMMARY

In this chapter we have moved on from recruitment to selection and have considered a wide variety of selection techniques that can be used in the search for talent. These include traditional methods such as the classic trio of application form, interview and references, but also more modern techniques, such as assessment centres and psychological tests that identify candidates' personality characteristics, intelligence, values and attitudes.

The need to avoid discrimination is imperative – the whole selection procedure must be fair, ethical and equitable. The selection process reflects on the organisation, so it needs to be handled as professionally as possible, so that both employer and candidate are satisfied.

Interviews are an integral part of the selection process, with structured interviews being seen to be a better predictor of eventual performance in the job. Some hints and tips have been given on how to interview, with discussion of questioning techniques together with some of the pitfalls of interviewing, such as stereotyping. The competence-based interview is a modern approach that can help the interviewer to focus on the job and helps to alleviate some of the discrimination traps where candidates are asked about their private lives, which have nothing to do with the job in question.

This chapter has covered the entire selection process and has given practical advice on how to select candidates so that we can identify talented people who will be a credit to the organisation and who will perform well once appointed. A key part of HR, selection must be carried out professionally and efficiently – if you follow the advice in this chapter, you will be well versed in how to tackle this major HR activity.

REVIEW QUESTIONS

1   Name five different methods of selection.

2   Why is there an emphasis on the importance of selecting new employees?

3   How much does the CIPD say it costs to recruit someone every time an employee leaves?

4   What is the difference between an open and a closed question?

5   Why is it good practice to structure a selection interview?

6   What are the main disadvantages of carrying out unstructured interviews?

7   What do you think has caused the increase in the use of selection tests?

8   What activities might you include in an assessment centre?

9   Why are references an unreliable source of data on a candidate?

10   What checks should you do before confirming an offer of appointment?

EXPLORE FURTHER

BOOKS

TORRINGTON, D., HALL, L. and TAYLOR, S. (2008) *Human resource management.* **Harlow: Pearson Education.**

There are many textbooks on selection interviewing, but this is a sound textbook on HR that has a good section which focuses on selection interviewing skills.

WHIDDETT, S. and HOLLYFORDE, S. (2003) *A practical guide to competencies.* **London: Chartered Institute of Personnel and Development.**

This book has a chapter on using competencies in selection.

Web links

As advised in Chapter 6, the annual CIPD *Recruitment, Retention and Turnover* survey report makes essential reading. The 2009 survey is available at: www.cipd.co.uk/subjects/recruitmen/general/_recruitment_summary.htm

Criminal Records Bureau: www.crb.homeoffice.gov.uk/guidance/applicants_guidance/levels_of_crb_check.aspx

Home Office UK Border Agency: www.ind.homeoffice.gov.uk

Information Commissioner's Office: www.ico.gov.uk

CHAPTER 8

Induction and Retention

LEARNING OBJECTIVES

After studying this chapter you should understand:

- the purpose of induction and the variety of approaches that are used in today's organisations
- the concept of employer branding
- the typical causes of the induction crisis and the steps that may be taken to prevent it
- the importance of retaining key employees
- the measures that may be put into action to achieve effective retention and be able to contribute to the retention plan.

INTRODUCTION

The purpose of this chapter is to discuss, first, the systematic induction of new employees into the organisation after recruitment checks have been carried out and they have been appointed to their positions. Second, the notion of employee branding is discussed in the context of retention. And finally, retention issues are discussed and retention plans are designed to encourage people, especially employees, to remain with the organisation.

Induction activities start as soon as the new member of staff starts to apply for a position with the company and continue, in a more formal and active manner, once the person has started work. Retention activities start once the employee is embedded in their post. Without an effective induction programme the likelihood that an employee will leave a company within the first 12 months is increased.

INDUCTION

As stated above, induction starts before the first day at work (Pilbeam and Corbridge 2006). It is not about 'sheep dipping' new starters into the company with a two- or three-day programme of information, but rather a socialisation of the individual into the organisation.

The *Oxford Dictionary of Human Resource Management* defines induction as: '... the process through which newcomers become familiar with an organisation or workgroup, learn its norms and begin to share its values. There is usually a formal process of induction, whereby new employees are introduced to co-workers and managers, given a tour of the workplace, and told about rules and procedures.' This definition is limited in so much as it does not take into account how aware the potential employee is of the organisation's environment from the time they make their first tentative telephone call for an application form or, more than likely, fill in an online recruitment form. Impressions are formed by how the company responds to requests and queries from the new starter, the invitation for interview and the subsequent recruitment and selection process. The organisation's external publicity, as well as all of the events mentioned above, have an impact on the potential future employee.

 KEY CONCEPT: INDUCTION

Taylor (2002, p116) says the following about induction: 'Induction is used as a general term describing the whole process whereby new employees adjust or acclimatise to their jobs and working environment.'

THE PURPOSE OF INDUCTION

The purpose of induction is twofold. First, it is to help make new employees become effective in their job, and second, to socialise individuals into the organisation, that is, to help give them a better understanding of what the company expects from them and what it is prepared to offer in return. The second objective links strongly into the retention aspect of the induction process.

Michael Armstrong (2006, p471) proposes that induction serves four purposes:

- to smooth the preliminary stages when everything is strange and unfamiliar to the new starter
- to establish quickly a favourable attitude to the company in the mind of the new employee so that they are more likely to stay
- to obtain effective output from the employee in shortest possible time
- to reduce the likelihood of the employee leaving quickly.

Induction commences from the time an individual makes contact with an organisation, through the recruitment and selection phases until beyond the time the individual gains competence in their role.

The individual's best performance will not emerge, however, until they have attained a sense of direction and identity in the workplace and settled into their job. Correctly handled, the induction process will help the individual to become effective more quickly.

THE IMPORTANCE OF INDUCTION

Attitudes towards induction differ widely from one organisation to another. Not all organisations recognise its importance and simply leave the new starter to make their own way in the labyrinth of organisational complexity. Issues can range from the important aspects of knowing the name, status and reputation of the new employee's manager, what work will they will be involved in and payment arrangements. There are also the more trivial, but still important questions of, when to take a break and the location of the toilets. Good inductions help the new starter set their organisational compass so that they can start early to map out, in their mind, what makes the organisation 'tick' and what it stands for in terms of principles and values. How the organisation handles the process is determined by what emphasis it places on induction, the level of resources the organisation will commit and the expertise available to carry out the process.

It has to be borne in mind that when people first come to the organisation to work, they will be keen to gather as much information about the place as possible, to begin to build their internal map. They go through the process of socialisation (see below). Without a formal induction process the individual will learn about the organisation by default; their work colleagues will present their own interpretations of 'the way things are done around here', which may not match the facts nor the culture the organisation intends to create and maintain. Refer to Chapter 2 for a description of culture and its importance to the organisation,

Induction, at its extreme, is the first opportunity to introduce the individual into the company's culture, its norms, standards (values) and expected behaviours. This is particularly so with large corporate organisations where there are strong cultural identities. The intention here is to start the process whereby external expectations (of the company) are slowly internalised by the new employee (Poulter and Land 2008). How ethical this approach is would depend upon how far the indoctrination into the organisation's culture goes (enculturisation).

The Ritz-Carlton organisation in the United States even goes so far as having a training institute where they not only train their own staff in the fundamentals, general and specific requirement of customer service, but they also market their training to other organisations. It is worth reading Paul Hemp's (2002) article in the *Harvard Business Review*, where he, as senior editor for the *Harvard Business Review*, spent two days of induction and four days working in the Ritz-Carlton, Boston. The induction covers everything from the 'appropriate language' to use when addressing a guest to the uniform worn by a member of staff. The induction programme is key to carrying the culture into new employee generations.

EMPLOYER BRANDING

The idea of employer branding is twofold: to attract good candidates but also to create a culture that, if promises are kept, will retain those who have commenced employment. Employer branding is about defining the employer's totality of perspective on the employment relationship from how they intend to reward and develop and communicate with their staff. There are strong links to product and consumer brand identification.

Clearly for the large national or multinational organisation there are clear advantages in developing an employee brand, because there is already in existence a recognisable consumer brand, but for the smaller business this may present more of a challenge. However, there are paybacks in terms of recognition of the brand by local communities, which increases the likelihood of the probability of becoming an employer of choice with its links into people recruitment and employee retention.

Lucie Carrington (2007) describes the pitfalls of employer branding in terms of the difficulty of putting a value on the effectiveness of the branding process. Making the link between cause and effect between employer branding and its impact upon recruitment, quality and quantity is like trying to determine the effectiveness of HRM as a process; both pose problems for the researcher.

INDICATIONS OF A SUCCESSFUL INDUCTION PROCESS

- new employees taking little time to become effective in their jobs
- an increase in the rate at which employees adapt to their surroundings
- good interpersonal relations between new and longer-serving employees
- a reduction in staff turnover, thus reducing recruitment costs and disruption to workplace productivity
- a satisfactory staff retention rate and stability index.

Having made the case for a strong induction process, read the article by Lashley and Best (2002) entitled 'Employee induction in licensed retail organisations', in which they explore the extent and scope of induction in the licensed retail trade just to see how hit and miss the induction process can be, although they do indicate '... that some form of induction does take place in most firms' (Lashley and Best 2002, p8). They also argue that 'best practice suggests that induction should be an ongoing process starting before the employee joins and extending through a period of weeks and months' (p12).

KEY CONCEPT: SOCIALISATION

Socialisation is the process through which individuals become familiar with their environment and learn about the kind of behaviours that are expected of them. It is experienced in our early development years and what we learn then stays with us for the rest of our lives. When we enter an organisation, we go through it all again. This time it is kind of micro-socialisation, which involves learning a culture that is different from that of the outside world and different from that of any other organisation.

THE INDUCTION CRISIS

As the new employee begins to get to know the job and the organisation, there may be second thoughts about the original decision they made to join the organisation. Then they may decide to leave. The strength of these feelings depends upon the degree to which the job and the organisation match up to the employee's expectations and, in some cases, the employer's promises, as mentioned in our discussion on employer branding. Additionally, the decision to stay or leave may be determined by other factors, such as pay, working time and the possibility of finding another job.

If the strength of the crisis is not enough to justify leaving, the employee may decide to 'put up with it for now', and hope that things will improve. In this case a period of *accommodation* (see below) may follow, in which they begin to adjust. During this period personal perceptions may modify and expectations go through a process of rationalisation. Inside the first year there may be further minor crises and, if the person stays for more than a year, then they are likely to stay at least a further year.

 KEY CONCEPT: ACCOMMODATION

In the context of a new experience, accommodation is the process by which individuals alter their perception of a situation so that the original perception is replaced by the new one. People do this when they discover that things are not what they thought they would be. For example, if a job does not in fact match up to the job description and perhaps to what others have told them about it, the person taking the job has to re-establish a more realistic perception or 'personal reality'. Naturally this will alter the person's attitude towards the job.

INFLUENTIAL FACTORS

The new employee's co-workers can influence how they feel about the job, especially if they have negative feelings because, for example, they had built up a close rapport with the previous incumbent and the new person's behaviours differ significantly from what they had previously experienced *and* liked.

It may be that there is a discrepancy between what the new employee had been told to expect about the job and working atmosphere. This mismatch between expectation and reality can cause doubts in the mind of the individual as to whether they wish to stay with the organisation because they may feel let down and even that they have been lied to.

Recruiters are key culture carriers for the organisation and, if they have not fully understood the nature of the job and have passed on, inadvertently, false information, this may build unrealistic expectations in the new employee and so becomes a key area to be addressed – to prevent the problem from recurring in the future. At the recruitment stage all documentation and briefings should reflect, as accurately as possible, the reality of the job and working environment.

Van Dick et al (2004, p352) argue that the:

> … research suggests that social identification in organizational contexts is a powerful concept to explain individual's performance, well-being and turnover intentions. … Organizational identification contributes to levels of self-enhancement, … self continuity, and reductions of uncertainty. In addition, the more an employee identifies with an organization, the more this employee's self image incorporates the organization's characteristics. Thus the more I identify myself with my organization, the more I define myself in terms of this particular membership and the more is my own future determined by the organization's future.

APPROACHES TO INDUCTION

The differences in senior managers' attitude to induction determines the level of resources that are invested in the process; the quality and effectiveness of the induction will vary according to the time, effort and money devoted to it. Well-run organisations will have several different induction systems that are relevant to each type and level of employee. For inducting large numbers of employees it may be advantageous to have common elements – for example discussion of health, safety and welfare issues, pay and conditions of service and so on – and to run the induction process with participants from, for example, finance, marketing, sales and operations because it is both cost-effective and ensures that there will be an intermingling of staff that may bear fruit at a later time by generally improving communications within the organisation. However, there will be a need to have job- or role-specific elements conducted within specific departments, tailored for their new staff, or presented by department specialists.

The following gives some examples of induction. You may wish to reflect which type would be more effective for yourself:

- **In writing**, in which the new employee is presented with an *induction pack*. This may include a 'company handbook' that gives the main terms and conditions of service (salary, holiday entitlement, disciplinary and grievance procedures), a copy of the corporate structure, a brief history of the organisation and a site map of the building with the main facilities identified, and perhaps something about company plans for the future. For senior management the induction 'pack' may also include a copy of the annual report. In general, care should be exercised to ensure that the materials included should reflect the level of the job and new recruit.

- **Walk 'n talk**, in which the new employee is shown around the site and is given explanations about each work activity on the way around the facilities. Towards the end of the tour the department in which they will work is visited and more detailed explanations of what happens are given. This is a good time to introduce new employees to their new colleagues.

- **Induction training.** This is the most successful and effective form of induction and a large number of organisations have adopted this practice. The approach takes the form of a number of training sessions, each of which deals with a particular aspect of work and each is usually delivered by a specialist in that subject area. The duration of the induction is usually staggered over a period of days or even weeks, depending on the amount and complexity of the information to be delivered.

- **Coaching and mentoring** is also used in many organisations to help the new starter over the longer term. Once the initial flurry of induction activity has died down, the new employee will more than likely still require some form of support. It can be quite embarrassing to have to constantly ask one's colleagues for advice, so to have a mentor who can give advice and be trusted is helpful.

When inducting employees into the organisation it is important to be aware that new recruits may have special needs caused by a disability, for example sight or hearing impairment or learning difficulty. The induction process must, therefore, be structured to help these people to assimilate information and so to become part of the team.

 ## ACTIVITY 8.1

Think back to your first few days at work in your organisation. Try to recall what actually happened and how you were treated. Which of the approaches, listed above, most closely matched your experience? Did you find it:

- friendly and satisfactory?

- unfriendly and unsatisfactory?

- mystifying?

STAGES OF INDUCTION

People may be inducted at two main levels: corporate and department. At the corporate level people learn about the size and shape of the business, for example in which countries it operates, where the corporate head office is located, how many branches it has, its values and beliefs. Second, they will learn some information about their terms and conditions of employment and, third, they will want to see their place of work, meet their new work colleagues and learn about the job itself.

INITIAL BRIEFING

It is the HR practitioner who usually receives new employees and who will explain to the new starter the main points, which includes the kind of information that is in the 'induction pack', as previously discussed. Using the 'induction pack' and laboriously working through it is not an effective way of communicating the key points. The initial briefing should be short, keeping the information to the essential 'need to know' and 'interesting to know' materials. A detailed description is not appropriate at this stage and departmental managers can fill in the salient points of what happens at the workplace. The HR practitioner who greets the new starter should be prepared and ready to get on with the task, to create an appropriate atmosphere right from the first 'hello'.

Most of us when we start a new job feel nervous. Being fed with streams of information is likely to create information overload and we will not remember half of what has been said.

From the HR practitioner who has done the initial meet and greet and obtained the essential regulatory information, for example to load into the payroll system, the new starter will probably go on to meet the department manager, who will continue with the induction. Once again preparedness is important.

INDUCTION TRAINING

The simplest, but probably least effective way, is to load or overload people with information, sending them home at the end of their first day carrying an armful of documents – which they may get down to reading one day. Of course some of the information will be critical and it should not be left to chance that the new starter accesses and understands its content. A more effective approach to induction is through a dedicated training event or series of events, where the information is delivered in a more controlled manner. In this way the information will have a better chance to be internalised and 'stick'. A problem with this type of programme is that those who pass through it are, in effect, being 'sheep-dipped', the (training) process being automatic and not responsive to individual needs.

New starters who are key specialists, for example people who have been recruited into managerial positions, are usually inducted on a one-to-one basis and do not undergo an 'induction training course as such'. When numbers of people are recruited at the same time, a formal induction event is usually organised. The programme will normally be led by an experienced HRM or HRD practitioner, with some of the event being delivered by departmental or subject specialists.

The timing of the formal induction event is important. It should occur as soon as possible after the new person starts with the company. Leaving matters until a quorum of several people have arrived so that, for some, the event may occur several weeks after they have started with the company will nullify its effect for those people because they will have already 'learned the ropes' and, perhaps at the same time, some bad habits; in effect they are not new starters. Timely delivery of the induction materials is critical if the event is to have a positive effect on the new employee.

METHODS AND MEDIA

Some induction courses can be lengthy events that take place over a number of days. The training programme may consist of a number of discrete sessions livened with a variety of media presentations, PowerPoint, DVD, and other visual aids such as actual photographs used to illustrate, for example, bad or good practice in the workplace. In this way the main points of each subject can be delivered and emphasised.

A session or seminar with a senior manager, whose presence will emphasise the importance of the induction activity and at the same time convey a message about what the company sees as important, is vital to the effectiveness of the event. Managers, as well as HR, are key cultural carriers of the organisation and for one to take time out of their busy day sends a strong message about what is important to the company. Having a senior management team representative present to answer questions about the company – for example its approach to and philosophy of managing people and, of course, company values – significantly increases the weight and importance of the messages transmitted and received.

PURPOSE

The purpose of the induction process can be seen as twofold. It is about providing the inductee with a thorough understanding of the organisation, its mission, history, products, current situation and its plans for the future. For the larger organisation a complete corporate picture will include details of the organisation's main policies, its status in the industry, photographs and thumbnail biographies of the board and senior managers, along with charts of the organisation's structure. Second, the induction process starts the enculturisation of the individual as to what it sees as important in terms of work ethic and values – for example, how the organisation views work–life balance issues and how it views safety, does it pay lip-service or does it take safety issues very seriously?

For a smaller organisation the induction process will be of no less importance but the scope clearly will be reduced. The company history may be shorter but still relevant; the senior managers and their, possibly extended, roles and the company structure will be discussed. Introducing the new starter to a member or members of the management team, where they can either question them about issues raised in the formal process of induction or perhaps listen, firsthand, to a manager speaking of and about the organisation, is key to the socialisation process and as important as what may happen in larger businesses.

INDUCTING MINORITY GROUPS OR THOSE WITH SPECIAL NEEDS

Care needs to be taken when inducting employees who are new to this country or who have special needs, perhaps because of a disability or those who have special educational needs. The speed and type of delivery or even lack of understanding of the English language may seriously impair the effectiveness of the induction process. Think of the worst-case scenario where the programme is addressing health and safety matters and there is a clear requirement for the inductees to go away with a uniform vision of how company views health and safety in the workplace. Equally, inductees should understand the company's discipline and grievance procedures. A good induction process should address these issues.

 ACTIVITY 8.2

How would you structure the induction process to meet the needs of a:

- partially sighted person?
- a non-native English speaker?
- someone with special education requirements?

Minority groups, especially from overseas, will probably have come from a culture far removed from the UK culture and so will, on the one hand, be socialising themselves into the UK's societal culture and, on the other hand, be trying to come to terms with the company's organisation culture; they have a mountain to climb. They may have to settle into a job, learn or consolidate a new language, be socialised into the local community, and find schooling for their children, all concurrently and in strange surroundings.

 Positive action

CASE EXAMPLE

Michael Wynne is the HR manager of ClassKitchens Ltd (CKL), a medium-sized manufacturing company based in the north-west of England; the company employees 2,500 people. CKL regards itself as a manufacturer of top-quality products and every effort is made to impress potential purchasers with the classic image.

Michael has noticed that in recent years many of the new employees from minority groups, especially ethnic minorities, have failed to be selected for promotion, despite the fact that, from personal knowledge of some of the workers, they possessed the knowledge, personal and practical skills

required for the higher positions. Michael is very concerned since research within the company has revealed that the proportion of immigrants in middle and senior management positions falls short of the equivalent for non-minority groups.

Liz Forsythe, who leads the HR development function, has also noticed the trend, and she can see that if it continues, it is going to be very difficult to satisfy the HR demand for managers and supervisors in forthcoming years. She knows that the skills that are required do exist within the current workforce, and cannot understand why such a large number of promotion candidates have failed. Liz and Michael discussed the situation and decided to commission a study to find out where the problem lay.

The resulting report pinpointed the promotion selection policy as a problem area. For the past two years CKL has been using psychometric tests as part of the selection process, and James Willis, the consultant who produced the report, pointed out that the company had been

discriminating against new immigrants by placing them at a disadvantage. James went on to explain that the new immigrants do not know how to conduct themselves at, for example, assessment centres, nor do they know how to take the tests.

Question: What can CKL do to ensure that the supply of the right people with the required knowledge and skills successfully pass the selection process?

WHAT CAN ORGANISATIONS DO?

The Equality and Human Rights Commission says the following about positive discrimination:

> Where members of the relevant sex or racial group are under-represented, there are limited exceptions allowing discrimination in training, or encouragement to apply for particular work. These lawful exceptions are often referred to as positive action.

In the Acas *Delivering Equality and Diversity: A summary guide*, they suggest that within your organisation's 'equality action plan', statistics should be held on: gender, race, disability and age. They suggest that, when recruiting people into the organisation and, by implication, promoting people into positions, information on the numbers of applicants is recorded for the post, split by the above typologies together with the success rates, again split by the various categories of gender, race, disability and age.

The Acas guide proposes the following: that the action should be a simple list about what will be done, by when and by whom. In particular it sets dates on when you will do the things, such as:

• monitoring, reviewing procedures, and training

• expands on how these will be done and by whom [and] set your measures of success

• considers how you will evaluate them and how and when you will review the overall working of your policy.

(Acas, *Delivering Equality and Diversity: A summary guide*)

Further advice on discrimination management can be found on the Business Link website (see 'Explore Further' at the end of this chapter).

The Commission for Racial Equality (CRE), which was superseded by the Equality and Human Rights Commission, suggested the following ways to promote equality within the organisation:

- review recruitment, selection and training procedures regularly
- draw up clear and justifiable job criteria that are demonstrably objective and job-related
- offer pre-employment training, where appropriate, to prepare potential job applicants for selection tests and interviews
- consider positive action (see 'Key Concept' below) to help ethnic minority (one could also include those with special needs because of, for example, a disability) employees to apply for jobs in areas where they are under-represented.

 KEY CONCEPT: POSITIVE ACTION

This is a concept that should not be confused with *positive discrimination*, which means favouring members of a particular group at the point of selection for a job. Positive discrimination is unlawful for a job in the UK, although it has been 'talked about' in the context of recruiting, particularly people from ethnic minorities, into occupations where there are groups that are under-represented and where, over time, it has been difficult to recruit the necessary people to bring about a balance in terms of proportional representation, for example the Prison or Police Service.

Positive action means that it is lawful to take measures designed to encourage members of under-represented groups to *apply* for a job or promotion. In all cases the actual *selection* must be made on merit.

POSITIVE ACTION TRAINING

Where particular racial groups have been under-represented in particular work at any time in the past 12 months, the Race Relations Act 1976 (Part VI) allows positive action measures to be taken to:

- encourage applications for an under-represented group for vacancies in particular work
- provide training to help members of an under-represented group for the particular work.

Full details of the Act can be found on website of the Office of Public Sector Information.

DURATION OF INDUCTION PROGRAMMES

Induction programmes vary in their complexity and duration. There are programmes that last for no more than a day and yet are effective. Others may last several days, or even weeks, although a new employee would benefit from no more than one day during their first week. There is no set pattern or universal blueprint for an induction programme; the content and process of it is determined by the varying needs of the new employees and the complexities of different organisations.

It would be unusual for the duration and content of the induction programme to be the same for all new starters into the organisation because – other than perhaps for health and safety awareness and employment handbook generic-type issues that equally affect all employees, such as the discipline and grievance procedures and the presentation of the company structure and how it is organised – much of the other parts of the induction process are likely to be different and delivered to different depths.

However the induction programme is structured it should be revisited on a frequent basis to make sure that the material and structure has not become obsolete.

TERMS AND CONDITIONS OF EMPLOYMENT

The induction training environment is an ideal place in which to provide new employees with a copy of the particulars of their main terms and conditions of employment (service). It is advisable to make this a discrete event, rather than issue this type of information along with a sheaf of other documents, which may be filed away in the 'induction pack' never to be opened.

 KEY CONCEPT: TERMS AND CONDITIONS OF EMPLOYMENT

To serve as evidence that a contract exists between employer and employee, the Employment Rights Act (ERA96) requires an employer to issue a statement of terms and conditions to all employees who are employed for one month or more. This is an important document that should be issued as soon as possible after the person commences work and, in any case, within two months of the person's first day.

The minimum terms and conditions of employment, which the employer must specify, are together called the 'principal statement' and include (in brief): the employer's and employee's name; the date of commencement of employment; the date on which continuous service commences; the notice period; the rate of pay and the scales of pay; whether the individual is paid hourly, weekly, monthly; normal hours of work; job title; place or places of work; plus the items detailed in the company handbook.

THE COMPANY HANDBOOK

All organisations have rules of behaviour that are written down in the form of procedures and regulations. In many organisations these are presented in the *company handbook.* A small firm would normally issue a copy of the company handbook to the new starter or, for larger organisations or those who maximise web use, its whereabouts on the company intranet site is demonstrated as part of the induction process. The rules relate to general behaviour in the workplace. The company handbook will include the following type of information:

- the payment systems, including the frequency of payments and the deductions that are made, for example tax, National Insurance, pension deductions
- holiday entitlement
- holiday and sick pay arrangements
- sickness absence procedure
- promotion policy
- discrimination and equal opportunities policy
- health and safety policy
- disciplinary rules
- grievance procedures
- education and training policy
- provision for employees' well-being
- available benefits and facilities
- trade union and joint consultation arrangements
- special working arrangements overseas (if applicable).

 ACTIVITY 8.3

Does your employer issue a handbook? If so, read through it and see how its contents compare with the previous list. What type of circumstance in your organisation may cause you to read the handbook?

For further information on handbooks, go to the Acas website and access their advisory handbook, *Employing People: A handbook for small firms*.

DEPARTMENTAL INDUCTION

When all of the main points have been explained and questions answered in the companywide context, the new employees are moved on to the *departmental induction*, which is more directly concerned with the new employee's role in their immediate work area. The departmental induction, as well as forming a first and formal introduction to colleagues and supervisor, is also concerned with the technicalities and other details of the job itself. The new employee's expectations are founded upon the job description and person specification, and so it is at this time that expectation is turned into reality. The idea is to settle the new starter into their new place of work and to try to make them feel welcome.

A new entrant will be interested in the departmental environment, including: working relationships, what the supervisor and departmental manager are like (for example, are they approachable), where the wash facilities are, when breaks and meal times are taken, where their place of work is. It is normal to show the person around and to introduce everyone. As for information about the job, this will come from the department manager and, in somewhat more detail, the supervisor or team leader. It is important that the department manager be present at this time so as to be seen as an active colleague, rather than someone sat in an 'ivory tower'. As previously mentioned, the supervisors and managers are key culture carriers for the organisation. They should affirm and reaffirm what is expected of the new employee, in terms of behaviours, so as to commence the socialisation of the individual into the expected norms of the organisation.

Once the new employee becomes accustomed to the workplace, the job can be explained in terms of how it can contribute to the department's objectives. Clearly this should be done in a manner that arouses interest by explaining how the role played by the employee fits into the overall department task and, ultimately, the company. For example, an invoice clerk in the finance department has a role that is key to chasing late or unpaid invoices. This is a task that impacts upon company cash flow, which, in turn, is critical in reducing company borrowing. The level of involvement and enthusiasm of whoever is providing the information will be communicated verbally and non-verbally to the newcomer, and thus, depending upon how it is done can have either a motivating or demotivating effect. The information given should include details of performance standards and also training and career prospects.

At a department level it is an opportunity to start the process of building the psychological contract between supervisors, team leaders, managers and the new employee. As Armstrong explains (2006, p472), the psychological contract:

> … consists of implicit unwritten beliefs and assumptions about how employees are expected to behave and what responses they can expect from their employer. It is concerned with norms, values and attitudes. The psychological contract provides the basis for the employment relationship and the more this can be clarified at the outset the better.

INDUCTION INTERVIEWS

Induction interviews should be given to all employees taking up jobs for the first time, whether the person has been recruited from outside the organisation or promoted from within. When people start a new job they may feel insecure and anxious about the unknown future, especially if they have chosen to leave an organisation or perhaps move within the organisation, so moving outside of their comfort zone. During the preceding induction process they may have heard negative things about the department or organisation through rumour and speculation or may have not understood something said. The induction interview, held informally but with an agenda, is an ideal opportunity to answer these types of question or to allay fears. The interviews are a kind of 'wash-up' session after experiencing corporate and departmental components of the induction process, a chance to clarify, dispel and reinforce aspects presented and discussed, but above all a time for someone to listen to the new employee. This type of activity may be carried out by the line manager, the HR practitioner or perhaps the team leader.

Tyson and York (1996) indicate that the main purpose of the interview is to provide reassurance and to develop positive attitudes, confidence and motivation. Induction interviews should cover the following points:

- the job description and person specification so that the job-holder understands what is required of them
- how the job relates to the work and purposes of the group and the organisation as a whole
- all the attendant circumstances of the job, for example pay, conditions, welfare, and so on
- the performance appraisal system and what part the job-holder will be required to play
- an assessment of any training and development needs that require immediate action
- general plans for training and development
- career prospects.

(adapted from Tyson and York 1996)

BUDDY SYSTEMS AND MENTORS

When the new person starts work on the job itself, the section or team leader should introduce them to a 'buddy', someone who understands the organisation, can be trusted to carry out the role professionally, who will act as a kind of guide and to whom the new starter can relate.

In their article, Lau et al (2009) say that having a buddy system can offer significant advantages to a business. They argue (p27):

> The buddy can make the new employee feel welcome, answer questions and help the new person navigate the organization's culture. This leads the new employee to feel comfortable sooner and to achieve a sense of acceptance and belonging. For example, new hires may be uncomfortable asking questions for fear of appearing incompetent.

According to Lau et al (2009), the 'buddy' or mentor system should be focused on the needs of both the buddy and the new starter. There should be a clarity about '… the knowledge which should be imparted to increase productivity and performance' (Lau et al 2009, p27). Further, there should be empathy to and clear understanding about the needs of the new employee and some form of feedback system to check that the process is in fact delivering the intended outcomes. The overall aim is to bring about an assimilation of the new starter into the organisation as quickly as is practicable while building upon the psychological contract, which in turn should reduce the probability of the person leaving.

The mentor or buddy system should not be entered into lightly. As previously mentioned, the buddy or mentor should be professional and so they should fully understand their role, which implies a degree of personal development on their part, which, in turn, implies commitment to the development process by the company.

RETENTION, WORK AND WHY PEOPLE WORK

At the heart of why people work is motivation; one could consider the motivation to pay the bills at the end of the month or perhaps motivation to do an interesting job. Early theories and work on motivation focused on money as a motivator, as espoused by people such as Henry Ford and engineers such as F.W. Taylor (1911). There was, as Matthewman et al (2009) write, a focus on the instrumentality of work; purely and simply, work was means to an economic end, the bills were paid at the end of the month with some money left over for entertainment.

There are many and varied theories of work. Trist and Bamforth (1951) recognised in their studies that the social dimension of work cannot be alienated from the actual task itself, as F.W. Taylor attempted to do to prevent what he called *systematic soldiering* – in essence, working to a pace less than the individual or group was capable of working at (see Huczynski and Buchanan 2007, p412).

Money (pay) as a motivator has been, and still is, used to motivate. For example, performance-related pay (PRP) is still used extensively in the marketing sections of companies and by telephone sales organisations. As Arnold et al (2005) point out, pay and other material rewards often signal that a person is successful. So from this perspective pay *is* a motivator. Herzberg (2003), on the other hand, in his *two factor theory model*, considers that pay is a hygiene factor and would contribute to work dissatisfaction, while things such as growth, recognition, responsibility, work itself and achievement were motivators. As Herzberg suggests, to have fulfilment at work, things such as the nature of the work and how we are held responsible for the part of the work we do all contribute to the feeling of satisfaction. There are many factors to take into consideration when trying to understand why people work. For example, those who have a vocational calling will occupy positions in the church, nursing and perhaps overseas aid, despite the comparatively low rewards for doing so. This of course does not mean that all vocational callings are not well rewarded; one can cite as examples of well-rewarded occupations in the legal and medical practitioner sectors.

How people view work is a function of individual choice. As previously indicated, there are those who see work in instrumental terms. Others see work as being central to their social being, while there are those who see work as central to their life and enjoy practising their skills and employing their knowledge.

We have discussed the importance of work and motivation in the workplace, but what is work? Drenth et al (1998, cited in Matthewman et al 2009, p4) define work in the following terms: '[work] … concerns the individual's activities, thoughts and feeling and its design meaning and challenges. This includes job analysis, task characteristics, ergonomics, fatigue, design of work, and performance measurement.'

How effective are we at motivating people in the workplace? Critical to business success is how effective people are engaged with their work and would be inclined, for example, to recommend [where they work] to family and friends. Buckingham's (2001) research into workforce engagement suggests that 'more than 80 per cent of employees in the UK are not engaged at work'. Some are, of course, but the total only amounts to 17% of the British working population, with 63% productive but not engaged; the remaining 20% of the workforce are disengaged. This means that employers are losing out, with the estimated cost to industry of disengagement going into the tens of millions of pounds.

PAUSE FOR THOUGHT

Why do you go to work? If you are a student on a degree or professional course, why did you choose that particular subject? Are you drawn to it as an occupation that you think you are likely to enjoy? Do you have a vocational calling? And finally, how much serious research have you done into finding out what the subject professionals actually do?

RETAINING STAFF

In the light of what has been previously said, it is clear that success in bringing in and retaining the right people is determined not only by ensuring that they are indeed the 'right' people in terms of knowledge, skills and, additionally, by their attitudes to work. The time, money and other resources spent on recruiting, selecting and inducting the right people is only a worthwhile investment if they remain with the organisation in the medium to long term. An implication for retaining staff is that the recruitment and selection process should have a degree of sophistication and should use a range of selection processes (see Chapter 7).

Retention became an important issue when organisations recognised that human resources are just that – key resources – which, if managed effectively, can grow in value. Talent should be nurtured and developed; it is vital to the success of the business. Talent is hard to find and sometimes hard to keep. Manfred Kets de Vries (cited in Williams 2000, p28) states: 'Today's high performers are like frogs in a wheelbarrow: they can jump out at any time.' The message from this is clear: organisations that wish to retain their core staff should take positive steps to ensure that they do so.

According to Linda Maund (2001):

Many organisations are of the opinion that, once employed, individuals will remain with them, unquestioningly believing that a wage or salary secures their loyalty and long service. However, the strategy involved in recruiting new employees should be progressed into plans for their retention, and failure to do so is likely to result in demotivated staff and a high labour turnover. (p192)

RETENTION PLAN

An increasing number of organisations have heeded this message, or have learned by experience! Organisations that succeed in keeping their key staff have a retention plan that is based upon the results of staff turnover analysis. Retention measures can include some or all of the following (IDS 2000, CIPD *Recruitment, Retention and Turnover* survey report 2009):

- **Pay and benefits:** competitive rates of pay, deferred compensation – for example share option schemes, generous pension schemes [although these may not be final salary schemes – author comment] – retention bonuses, flexible benefits, a benefits package that improves with service.

- **Recruitment and selection:** set appropriate standards, match people to posts, provide an accurate picture of the job.

- **Training and development:** good induction processes, provision of development opportunities to meet the needs of the individual and the organisation, structured career paths.

- **Job design:** provision of interesting work, as much autonomy and teamworking as possible, opportunities for flexible working to meet the needs of the individual.

- **Management:** ensure managers and supervisors have the skills to manage and coach their staff effectively.

- **Make changes to improve work–life balance.**

- **Offer coaching, mentoring and buddying systems.**

In turbulent times the CIPD suggests that the approach should be no less rigorous; just because it is more difficult for staff to move when the jobs market becomes 'tight' in times of recession, it does not mean that less stringent efforts should be made to retain staff because employees, once times are better, will start to vote with their feet and leave the business. The employer cannot become complacent. The talent pools have not swelled in these more turbulent times, so employers still need to nurture and develop these staff. The top six reasons that staff left organisations, according to the 2009 CIPD survey, are presented below:

1 promotion outside the organisation

2 change of career

3 lack of development and career opportunity

4 redundancy

5 retirement

6 level of pay.

Item 4 may be a 'given' to the organisation in the hard economic environment encountered in 2008 and 2009 as companies shed staff. Some, certainly not all, organisations may be taking advantage of the downturn in business to release their poorer-performing staff within their redundancy programme. However, the remaining factors expressed can be impacted upon by positive company action (see James Brocket's article (2009), which discusses how employer branding can still make an impact on retention when economic pressures begin to challenge).

 ACTIVITY 8.4

Employee turnover

The 2009 CIPD *Recruitment, Retention and Turnover* survey report gives the average cost to replace an employee as £6,125, and for a manager this increases to £9,000. How would you go about costing employee turnover? What factors would you include?

How would you go about retaining key staff?

RETENTION AND HRM

While positive retention planning has become an integral part of HR strategy, the activities that are implied by typical retention plans in organisations that have adopted the principles and practices of HRM are aimed largely at key staff. Peripheral workers, by definition, are not treated so generously, although new legislation on agency workers will impact upon their salaries when they are doing similar work to company core staff. The underlying rationale here appears to be that 'there is a talent war going on out there and if we are lucky enough to get the high-fliers, then we should make every effort to keep them, we can pick up the rest whenever we need them'.

This is a pragmatic and practical view, and few would argue with the facts that all organisations need highly talented staff at the core, but it can create a visible class system between and among employees. However, the consequence of not identifying and nurturing talent is equally fraught with problems because not to identify potential, at an early stage, and develop these staff will stifle the aspirations of the future business leaders with a consequence that they may leave. The talented staff are exactly those who, in a 'tight jobs market' (when jobs are not easy to come by), can still move from one employer to another. Not to actively manage the career paths of the company's talented few is not an option for the smart employer.

A complete retention plan should include arrangements for ensuring the retention of peripheral staff, since high turnover anywhere in the organisation is costly and counterproductive (see Activity 8.4). It is costly in terms of replacing peripheral staff; if the accepted notion is that they are inferior, this is counterproductive because continuity is vital if productivity is to be maintained. Additionally, care needs to be taken to ensure that equality, fairness and compliance with employment legislation are maintained when benefits and facilities are on the retention agenda.

MANAGING CONTRACT ORGANISATIONS

In a wider context, if the organisation relies upon a significant number of contractor organisations for services, the quality of their staff can and does have a significant impact upon the level of service that your organisation can supply. High turnover and poor retention in the contractor become as much an issue for your organisation as it does for the contractor themselves. The quality of the HR processes that the contactor applies to its own staff can, to some degree, be controlled through the tender document, with clauses that sanction regular auditing by the contracting organisation. In this way a 'knitting vigilance' can be maintained over key contract operations so that timely interventions can be managed. How a contractor manages their staff directly impacts upon the overall service quality of the principal organisation.

RECORDING AND ANALYSING INFORMATION

It may sound obvious but there is a need to keep a variety of records on the staff employed by the organisation as well as staff who are potential recruits for positions in the organisation. In addition to the name, age, gender and ethnicity of the individual, which are normally asked for at the recruitment stage, information should be kept on staff turnover.

The CIPD recommends that staff turnover is calculated on an annual basis as follows:

$$\text{Turnover} = \frac{[(\text{number of staff left within 1 year})}{(\text{average number of staff within 1 year})]} \times 100\%$$

The staff turnover values can be calculated as an average for the whole organisation or by department. With the quality of HR information systems (HRIS) this calculation, once set up, becomes routine and figures for different departments and the organisation as a whole can be provided regularly. Data should also be kept for key groups of staff, graduates and managers; in essence those who have been identified as talented or key employees. However, keeping statistical information is no good unless it is accessed and analysed for 'hotspots', that is, where there are high turnover rates.

SUMMARY

INDUCTION

The purpose of induction is twofold:

- to make the new employee effective in the job as soon as possible
- to socialise the new employee to help prevent the individual prematurely leaving the organisation.

New employees are in a learning situation as soon as they join: they need to attain a sense of identity in their new place of work and a true perception of the role. They need to understand the organisational and departmental cultures and the expectations that others have of them. Some employees experience an 'induction crisis', which occurs shortly after joining, and happens as a result of the job failing to match up to expectations. A frank job description or role profile and honest depiction of the job at interview is important so that the picture (of the job) that the potential employee builds in their mind is not too far removed from reality.

An induction crisis may cause someone to decide to leave the organisation. An effective induction system is handled through training and contains corporate and departmental induction processes. Indications of a successful induction programme are:

- new employees quickly becoming effective in their jobs
- an increase in the rate at which employees adapt to their surroundings
- good interpersonal relations between new and longer-serving employees
- a reduction in staff turnover
- a satisfactory retention rate.

RETENTION

Retention became an issue when organisations realised that the success of the business depended on its ability to attract and retain people who were capable of making contributions that would give an organisation a competitive advantage. To achieve this, organisations formulate a *retention plan*, the components of which are designed to encourage people to remain with the organisation.

People are more likely to remain with an organisation if:

- they believe their manager shows interest and concern for them
- they know what is expected of them
- they are given roles that fit with their capabilities
- they receive regular positive feedback and recognition; 'people leave managers, not companies'.

Retention plans need to be aimed at all new employees, whether they are recognised as a high-potential graduate recruit or staff who have been recruited to fill routine roles. There is a cost to staff turnover for all grades of staff. The average cost of replacing a member of staff is over £6,000 (CIPD *Recruitment, Retention and Turnover* survey report 2009).

REVIEW QUESTIONS

1   What are the main purposes of induction?

2   When does induction begin?

3   What do socialisation and accommodation mean in the context of induction?

4   What is meant by the term 'induction crisis'?

5   How would you advise the organisation that wishes to reduce the prospect of having an induction crisis?

6   What are the main purposes of an induction interview?

7   What are the main elements that should make up an effective induction programme? Write up a brief description of each.

8   What are the two main levels at which employees are inducted?

9   Why may new immigrants or people with learning difficulties perform poorly when undertaking psychometric tests?

10 What is the difference between 'positive action' and 'positive discrimination'?

11 What elements would you expect to find in a company handbook?

12 How are induction and retention related?

13 What is the advantage of having a mentoring or buddy system working in the organisation? Can you afford to have all staff with mentors?

14 Why do people work?

15 What has caused staff retention to become more prominent in recent years?

16 Where can you find information on the cost of staff turnover?

17 How is the cost of staff turnover calculated? What factors are taken into consideration?

18 What factors form the basis of a retention plan?

19 Why should a retention plan include arrangements for ensuring the retention of peripheral as well as the recognised company 'talents'?

EXPLORE FURTHER

BOOKS

BANFIELD, P. and KAY, R. (2008) *Introduction to human resource management*. Oxford: Oxford University Press.

There are few texts that deal holistically with induction as a process. Banfield and Kay offer some insight into the process and the issues that arise if time and effort are not spent on getting the induction process correct.

WEB LINKS

Acas guidance *Recruitment and Induction*, designed to assist anyone dealing with, or who is affected by, the processes of recruitment and induction. Available as a PDF file at: www.acas.org.uk/index.aspx?articleid=744

CIPD factsheet on induction – gives introductory guidance dealing with the purpose, advantages and disadvantages of formal workplace induction programmes. It also considers the role of HR in the induction process and gives some practical advice in the form of a checklist. The factsheet can be found at: www.cipd.co.uk/subjects/recruitmen/induction/induction.htm

Business Link: www.businesslink.gov.uk

Office of Public Sector Information (Acts of Parliament): www.opsi.gov.uk/revisedstatutes

Information Commissioner's Office: www.ico.gov.uk

Home Office UK Border Agency: www.ind.homeoffice.gov.uk

Learning

INTRODUCTION

The purposes of this chapter are: first, to discuss the strategic importance of learning; second, to examine ways in which the organisation and the individual may benefit from learning; and third, to define and explain learning. This is followed by a discussion of the principles of learning and an examination of some early and more recent theories. Finally, we consider learning styles and explain how you can identify your own way of learning.

THE STRATEGIC IMPORTANCE OF LEARNING

Nobody would argue with the view that the need for organisations to stay ahead of the game in the midst of fierce global competition has brought the importance of learning and development to the forefront of strategic thinking. In times of recession, it becomes even more important to have highly skilled staff who will give you the competitive edge and help you survive the difficult times. The president of the Chartered Institute of Personnel and Development (CIPD) in the 2000 annual report said, 'People are our only source of differentiation and sustainable competitive advantage' (Beattie 2002). The director general of the CIPD maintained that: 'Staff management and development will become the primary weapon available to managers to generate success' (Rana 2000).

In the 2009 CIPD *Learning and Development* survey report, 70% of employers surveyed agreed that learning and development (L&D) continues to be a high priority in their organisation, and over three-quarters (76%) felt that it is seen as an important part of business improvement. Indeed, 65% anticipated that L&D activity will become more closely integrated with business strategy in the near future.

HUMAN CAPITAL AND KNOWLEDGE MANAGEMENT

Organisations today rely very much on 'human capital' – the knowledge and skills that their people possess, which will enable the organisation to function and be competitive.

 KEY CONCEPT: HUMAN CAPITAL

Human capital includes knowledge and competences that are required for particular jobs and that can be developed by learning to achieve higher performance. It includes the flexibility of individual employees that turns them into valuable assets when, through learning, they find themselves able to make high-performance contributions to the organisation.

If we can develop our human capital, then we can increase our competitiveness. We will have staff whose knowledge can be used to benefit the business. Today, many businesses rely on knowledge as the main means of staying ahead. Without knowledge, our competitors will gain advantage by having better ideas and better strategies, and will achieve better success. In a traditional economy, companies make money by converting raw materials into items: metal into cars, for example. However, in a knowledge economy, the added value comes from taking good ideas and developing them into services. 'Company value has come to be increasingly dependent on intangible assets, knowledge assets, intellectual capital and intellectual property. Back in 1996 94% of Microsoft's market value (US$119 billion) came from intangible assets' (Quintas 2001), which means its value comes from knowledge and ideas, not from machinery, buildings, factories or materials. Without innovative new ideas, Microsoft would not be the success that it is.

Think about the computer games industry. The successful companies are those who come up with the best ideas, not the ones who sell the cheapest games – it's about having staff who can be innovative, who can use their ideas and knowledge to keep the company ahead of its competitors. Google might be another example. Its success comes from providing a service, not from converting raw materials into goods. Without intelligent staff who develop ideas, Google would not exist. Sun Microsystems' Chief Technology Officer Eric Schmidt said that research and development are now measured in 'webweeks' and estimates that 20% of the knowledge generated inside his company becomes obsolete within less than a year (Rifkin 2000, p22).

ACTIVITY 9.1

What organisations can you think of that rely particularly on knowledge? Obvious ones might be law firms, architects, universities. What other businesses could not function without specialist knowledge?

In Activity 9.1, you might say that all organisations need and use knowledge – and you would, of course, be right. Garages, supermarkets, shops, for instance, all need to have knowledge of their customers, of products, of their competitors, and so on, so that they can stay ahead of the game. Knowledge is essential to all businesses to some extent. In today's world, knowledge is becoming more and more crucial if the business wants to survive.

 ACTIVITY 9.2

What knowledge is crucial to the survival of your own organisation? Are there specialists who add value to the business, just by possessing expert knowledge that helps to keep it competitive? If that knowledge became out of date, what would happen?

If a business wants to develop the knowledge of its staff, it may strive to be what Pedler et al describe as a 'learning organisation'. A learning organisation 'is an organisation that facilitates the learning of all its members and continuously transforms itself' (Pedler et al 1997).

 KEY CONCEPT: LEARNING ORGANISATION

A learning organisation is an organisation that learns and encourages learning among its people, promoting exchange of information between employees, hence creating a more knowledgeable workforce.

This produces a very flexible organisation where people will accept and adapt to new ideas and changes through a shared vision.

Peter Senge (1990) suggests that a learning organisation is one 'where people continually expand their capacity to create the results they truly desire, where new and expansive patterns of thinking are nurtured, where collective aspiration is set free, and where people are continually learning how to learn together'.

Learning organisations therefore believe that learning is a good thing for the business and that it should be continuous and never ending. It should be something that is on the conscious agenda of the organisation.

THE PRINCIPLES OF LEARNING

The purpose of this section is to define, explain and discuss learning. You may come across various terms, such as:

- **Education**: broadly based 'training for life' and society
- **Training**: particular to work, specific tasks
- **Development**: personal growth, as organisations and employees require a broader range of skills

However, distinctions have become blurred – for example GNVQs, education and vocational training. Now, perhaps, the focus is more a question of 'learning'.

 KEY CONCEPT: LEARNING

Learning takes place when an individual has understood and internalised new information and/ or has developed a new skill as a result of an experience. Evidence that learning has taken place may be inferred from a change in the individual's behaviour. Learning is an active process that may occur socially, systematically or experientially.

SELF-LEARNING

'All development is self-development' (Drucker 1977). In this context, Drucker was saying that people can teach, train and coach you, but nobody can learn for you. Learning is a 'do-it-yourself' activity. It is important here because it forms the basis for education, training and development. And now that 'jobs for life' no longer exist, learning, including self-learning, sustains the individual's employability. Information technology facilitates self-learning as never before, since it has broadened and deepened the available range of methods and media through which learning may take place.

At work today, the development of *competence* is a critical factor; your employability depends on it. You need to be aware that traditional ways of working are dying out while new ways are continually evolving, and these demand more than just competence: they require new knowledge and skills, creativity, flexibility and commitment on your part. From the above definition we can see that learning may take place socially, systematically or experientially, that is, learned through the normal course of work and life experiences.

SOCIAL LEARNING

We often learn from others. It is part of our natural development. We learn to conform to societal, group and family norms by observing and copying the behaviour of others and through a system of reward and punishment. If, for example, in the early stages of development, we behave in a way that invokes the disapproval of parents or teachers, they express that disapproval with more or less strength, depending on how seriously they regard the behaviour. On the other hand, they will reward behaviour that is in accordance with their expectations. As time goes by we develop patterns of behaviour based around the societal norms that we have learned, many of which we have internalised as habits, so that much of what we do is done without conscious thought.

SYSTEMATIC LEARNING

This is the learning that is experienced through formal education, or through training and instruction in the organisation or externally in a local college or university. Whereas social learning occurs naturally and teaches us the norms of our society, *systematic* or *organised learning* occurs when something specific is to be learned and is developed within you with instruction and guidance from others, usually through the processes of formal education, a training course, or coaching and counselling sessions.

THE FACTORS OF LEARNING

For education, training and development to be successful, learning must take place. Superficially, this seems obvious, but the circumstances in which learning is acquired have been the focus of academic interest for at least 100 years. Clearly, those responsible for teaching and training must be skilled in developing others and the learner has to know *how* to learn.

 ACTIVITY 9.3

Think about how you dress, how you speak and how you behave generally when you are out with your friends. Compare that with how you behave at work, in the classroom or at home with your family. What is it that determines the nature of your behaviour? *How do you know* how to behave in those very different situations? You were not born with such social skills and therefore you must have learned them.

PERSONAL CHARACTERISTICS

The motivation to learn plays a significant role. If the learner lacks interest in the subject and is therefore unwilling or reluctant to learn about it, learning will not take place. The trainee must be motivated to complete a course, for example, and must see some benefit from it (for example pay, promotion, and so on).

The learner also has to be *able* to learn. The learner, for example, may be highly motivated, but if their intelligence is such that they are unable fully to grasp the ideas or achieve the necessary performance standards, the likelihood is that *sufficient* learning will not take place.

THE TRAINER

To be effective, trainers have to possess several particular qualities. First, and rather obviously, they must be well versed in the subject matter of the training. Second, they must have the ability to transfer their knowledge and skills to others to the extent that those others become competent enough to meet, and preferably exceed, the required standards. Third, the trainer must have credibility. If, for example, you announced that you were going to deliver a talk on the finer points of football, you would be lucky if just two or three people turned up for the event. Conversely, if you announced that you had managed to get David Beckham to deliver such a talk, he would have a full house. Someone who is known to be an authority on a subject has credibility, especially if their expertise is apparent in the content and the style with which the material is delivered. Credibility may also be earned by a trainer through the obvious authority with which they deliver the material and generally conduct the training session.

KEY CONCEPT: KNOWLEDGE AND TRAINING — TWO SEPARATE SKILLS

The fact that someone is regarded as an expert in that they possess particular knowledge and skills does not carry with it the guarantee that they have the ability to *develop* those qualities within others. That is a separate skill.

THE LEARNING SITUATION

This refers to the physical environment in which the learning takes place, the ambience of the location and the shape and size of the training room. All of these factors have to be conducive to learning and appropriate and suitable in the light of the subject to be learned. Considerable time and ingenuity have been invested in the study and creation of effective learning situations. As we shall see later in this chapter, there are a variety of situations in which learning typically takes place.

EXPERIENTIAL LEARNING

In a sense, what has been described above as social learning is *experiential learning*. As a baby gradually becomes aware of the environment into which they have been born, they begin to attempt to make sense of it all.

PAUSE FOR THOUGHT

Transferable skills

Is it possible that your non-work learning could turn out to be useful in the workplace? If you reflect on this, you might conclude that what you learn from carrying out tasks such as maintaining your home and your car, and what you learn from others, becomes useful in all areas of life. Those who are involved in sports teams, voluntary groups or parent–teacher organisations, for example, may all gain skills that are transferable to the workplace. Fundraising, organising others and motivating group members are all skills that might be useful at work.

When the term 'experiential learning' is used in a professional context, it generally refers to learning from organisational situations. Sometimes such situations occur unexpectedly, as for example when there is an emergency and you have to find a way of dealing with it. By its nature, it may be something that you have never previously encountered, so you have to analyse the situation, diagnose the problem and find and implement a solution. When this happens to, say, a busy manager, they will handle it and then move on straightaway to the next task.

If the emergency was indeed something the manager had never previously encountered, two questions might be relevant. First, where and when did the person gather the knowledge and skills that enabled them to cope with the situation? Second, should the manager reflect upon what they learned from the experience, instead of dashing off to the next task? Maybe the pressure to move on did not allow for reflection, in which case the opportunity to reflect should be taken at the next convenient time. Otherwise, whatever learning was gathered might be forgotten.

 KEY CONCEPT: REFLECTION

Reflection is the active process of mentally summarising what you have learned from a particular experience. Its purpose is to increase your awareness of the knowledge and skills that you have added to your repertoire.

PLANNED EXPERIENCE

This may occur as part of a staff development programme in which employees are placed in situations from which they learn. A manager, for example, might assign a task to an employee, after which the employee reports back on what was learned from the experience. In most cases, however, when a manager delegates a task, they do so simply because it needs to be done. To a good manager, one of the most important aspects of allocating work is selecting the employee who is to do it.

For example, there are times when a task has to be completed quickly to meet a customer's delivery deadline. At such times, the manager will select an employee who is fully competent to do the job, with all the required knowledge and skills. There are also times when things are not so urgent, however, which is when the manager might select an employee who would have to learn something to complete the task successfully. This might be referred to as *developmental delegation*; it provides the employee with vital experience and concurrently gets a necessary job done.

EARLY THEORIES OF LEARNING

In this section, we examine the theories of learning that were proposed in the early part of the twentieth century. The early theorists were mostly interested in learning as a psychological process, while the later theorists took the psychological aspects into account, but tended to focus upon the practicality and effectiveness of deliberately created learning situations.

When you study the early theories of learning, therefore, you are trying to develop an understanding of the three main psychological divisions of learning theory, which include *classical conditioning*, *operant conditioning* and *cognitive learning*.

CLASSICAL CONDITIONING

The first theory of classical conditioning was propounded by the Russian physiologist Ivan Pavlov, who published his theory of 'conditioned reflexes' in 1927, although he carried out most of the research much earlier than that. He was interested in internal reactions to external stimuli, and he used dogs as the subjects of his experiments. He fed the dogs at the same time every day and as he gave them the food, he rang a bell. One day he rang the bell but did not feed the dogs, and he discovered that they were salivating, obviously not at the sight or the smell of food, but at the anticipation of it. They were reacting automatically to the sound of the bell, an indication that they associated it with the food. They had become 'conditioned' to salivating at the sound of the bell. It is important to note that in 'classical' conditioning, the subject of the experiment always has a passive role.

OPERANT CONDITIONING

The American psychologist E.L. Thorndike, a contemporary of Pavlov, was the founder of operant conditioning (sometimes referred to as *instrumental conditioning*). The subjects of his experiments were cats. Operant conditioning differs from classical conditioning in that the subject's response occurs before the reward is given.

In Thorndike's experiments (1913), a hungry animal was placed in a cage from which it needed to escape in order to get food. The animal therefore had to learn how to escape, usually by pulling on a wire or pressing a lever. This differs from Pavlov's experiments in that the animal played an active role. Thorndike maintained that when the required response is followed by the reward, the behaviour is more likely to occur again, provided the circumstances are similar; he called this the 'law of effect'.

Today, the researcher mainly associated with operant conditioning is the American B.F. Skinner, whose work (1953) is really an extension of the work of Thorndike. Experiments involving animals typified the work of both researchers, although Skinner, after researching mainly with rats and pigeons, went on to research into human learning, to produce what he called *stimulus–response psychology*, which is generally known for short as S–R psychology. The main idea here is that we react to a stimulus with a response. For example, the stimulus of hunger will prompt us to respond by seeking food.

BEHAVIOURISM

The works of Pavlov, Thorndike and Skinner classify them as *behaviourists*. This is an approach to the study of human behaviour that was first proposed by John B. Watson in 1913, and it is an approach that is not universally accepted by psychologists. Behaviourists work within limited parameters and their approach to the study of animal and human behaviour excludes factors that many psychologists regard as basic requirements (Watson and Rayner 1920).

COGNITIVE LEARNING

Cognitive theorists are mainly interested in changes in individuals' knowledge, since they regard this as more important than changes in what the learner does. Cognitive learning includes all of the elements of human consciousness that the behaviourists ignore: imagination, creativity, problem-solving, human intuition and perception. The cognitive approach has two components: *insight learning* and *latent learning*.

Insight learning

Having an understanding of what is being learned is an important feature of cognitive learning. To take a problem-solving exercise as an example, experience of working with children has shown that when a person is given a problem to solve, they sometimes study it, analyse and think about it and then, after a period of time, during which an onlooker might think that the person was stumped, the solution is suddenly produced. Wolfgang Koehler (1959) carried out experiments with chimpanzees after which he claimed that such insight was not exclusively human behaviour.

Latent learning

According to cognitive theorists, learning may also be latent. This means that something can be added to someone's knowledge and then used only as and when needed, that is, at a later time. An interesting feature of latent learning is that the learner does not always appreciate that they have gathered something new and added it to their knowledge. Trainees, for example, sometimes come away from a course complaining that they have learned nothing. It is not until a later time, perhaps at work, that they find that they can solve particular problems or carry out tasks that they could not do prior to the training about which they had complained – realisation that the training was useful after all.

MODERN THEORIES OF LEARNING

Most of the modern theories of learning have their roots in the theories explained above. Indeed, the psychological aspects of some of the older theories still exercise a degree of influence over current practice. Modern theorists, however, are not so keen on developing hard and fast rules of learning. They are more inclined to empower individuals over the means through which they are developed.

ACTION LEARNING

Reg Revans introduced the idea of 'action learning sets', which accepts that learning is participative – groups of learners meet together and discuss real problems that exist in the workplace. Revans used action learning sets as a means of developing managers. He got them to work together on issues to help them learn and develop new ideas and solutions (Revans 1982).

KOLB'S LEARNING CYCLE

The *experiential learning cycle*, developed by David Kolb in 1979, is probably the most well-known model in modern theory (Kolb 1985). If we study what happens in learning situations today, it is not difficult to challenge Kolb's perception of the approaches of teachers and trainers to developing people. He claimed that students and trainees in the classrooms were being processed under the *authority* of the teacher or trainer, while the learner played a passive role. This situation, he said, detaches the learner from reality. The implication here is that the learner is taught something, but does not actually have to demonstrate the ability to do it or that they know it. It is 'separated' learning and doing, as if they were different activities. In fact, this has not been the case, at least not in the UK, for several decades.

Kolb contrasted this 'teaching at people' type of learning with problem-solving, in which the responsibility for producing solutions rests with the learner. In other words, he distinguished between 'teacher-centred' and 'student-centred' learning. Kolb regarded the classroom situation as a necessary function, his main criticism being that insufficient attention was being paid to other forms of learning such as problem-solving. When developing his experiential learning cycle (Figure 9.1) he incorporated the features of both the classroom and problem-solving situations.

Kolb explained this cyclical process with the following analysis:

1   Concrete experience is the first point in Figure 9.1, in which the learner practises a skill for the first time, such as using a machine.

2   This is followed by a process of familiarisation, in which the learner makes observations and reflects on the experience.

3   From there, they begin to make sense of the structure of the machine. In other words, they formulate abstract concepts and generalisations, and begin to realise how the machine functions – what it is for.

4   The learner then returns to the machine. This produces a new situation because it includes prior learning, which is then tested in the new situation and includes using the machine, bringing the learner back to the first point in the cycle, in which the use of the machine provides a new experience.

Learning improves as the cycle continues. Kolb emphasises that this whole process is driven by the individual learner, thus empowering the individual to strive towards their own internally motivated needs and goals.

Figure 9.1 The Kolb experiential learning cycle

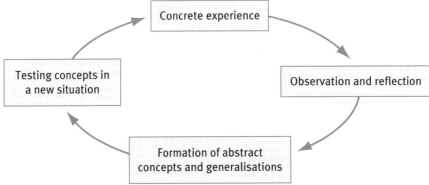

Learning is a psychological event and since individuals are all different from each other, they all learn differently. In other words, everyone has their own *learning style*. Some learn best from experience, while others prefer to study or hear about the subject and reflect upon what they have learned. Yet others are dependent on being shown or taught, requiring detailed coaching and real-time feedback, while others again prefer not to be coached but to be given time to learn alone.

In light of this, a good trainer will construct the course to reflect the learning styles of the trainees. Additionally, trainees benefit, first, from understanding their own learning style and, second, from knowing how to learn. With these factors in mind, several researchers have produced 'models' and 'inventories' designed to assist students, and in particular management trainees, to identify their own learning styles.

Alan Mumford states that the 'stimulus to my own thinking beyond "people learn differently" was provided when I first encountered the work of David Kolb. ... [He] would not, I think, claim his concept of the learning cycle was wholly new.' With Peter Honey, he took Kolb's original concepts and developed a questionnaire and improved processes for making use of the results (Mumford 1993) (see Figure 9.2).

The implication here is that an individual can be classified as having a particular learning style. They might, for example, be an *activist, reflector, theorist* or a *pragmatist*. Several learning styles inventories (questionnaires) have been produced, most of which were based on Kolb's (1985) experiential learning theory.

LEARNING STYLES

Figure 9.2 Honey and Mumford's learning cycle

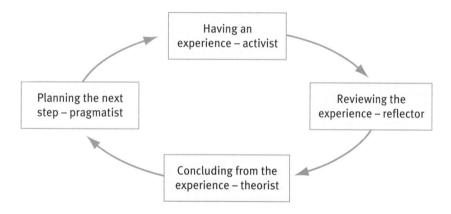

 ACTIVITY 9.4

What is your learning style?

Think of a skill you have learned recently. Perhaps it was how to operate a new mobile telephone, use new software, play a musical instrument or fix a broken window. Now consider how you went about learning the skill. The following questionnaire is based on Honey and Mumford's learning cycle and is designed to allow you to identify your own learning style; no one style is better or worse than another. As you complete the questionnaire, give a high rating to those words you think most closely characterise the way you learn, and a low rating to those words you think are least characteristic of the way you learn.

You may find it difficult to choose the words that best describe your learning style because there are no right or wrong answers. There are just different characteristics. The aim of the inventory is to discover your own personal learning style and not to evaluate your learning ability.

Now see if you recognise your own characteristics in the lists below.

Procedure

There are nine sets (the columns) of four words (the rows) listed below. Working on one row at a time from left to right, rank each set of four words 1–4, assigning 4 to the word that you think best and most closely characterises the way you think you learn, 3 to the next best, 2 to the third best and 1 to the word that you think least characterises the way you learn.

Table 9.1 Score sheet

Row	A	B	C	D
1	Discriminating ( )	Tentative ( )	Involved ( )	Practical ( )
2	Receptive ( )	Relevant ( )	Analytical ( )	Impartial ( )
3	Feeling ( )	Watching ( )	Thinking ( )	Doing ( )
4	Accepting ( )	Risk-taker ( )	Evaluative ( )	Aware ( )
5	Intuitive ( )	Productive ( )	Logical ( )	Questioning ( )
6	Abstract ( )	Open observer ( )	Concrete ( )	Active ( )
7	Present-orientated ( )	Reflecting ( )	Future-orientated ( )	Pragmatic ( )
8	Experience ( )	Secret observer ( )	Conceptualiser ( )	Experimenter ( )
9	Intense ( )	Reserved ( )	Rational ( )	Responsible ( )

Figure 9.3 Learning styles axes

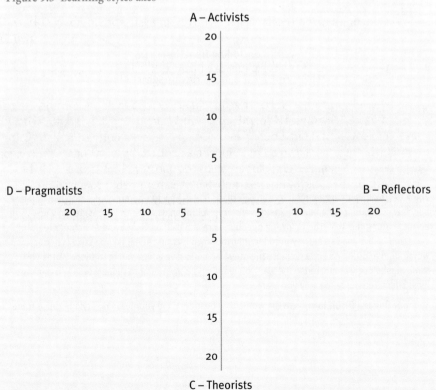

Important: be sure to assign a different number to each of the four words in a row. Do not rate any two words equally in a row. Taking the top row, for example: discriminating [2], tentative [1], involved [3], practical [4].

Scoring: Add the columns using only the scores for the row number shown in brackets, [A 234578] [B 367891] [C234589] [D136789]. Then plot the scores for each of the columns A, B, C and D on the learning axes below.

Conclusions

You will find that you have scored unequally on all four axes. In other words, there are elements of all four styles in all of us. The axis bearing your highest score represents your predominant learning style.

A: Activists value the opportunity to take an active part in their learning. They like high-profile activities, such as giving talks.

Strengths

- keen to try out new ideas
- open-minded
- flexible

Weaknesses

- act without thinking
- get bored with implementation
- take unnecessary risks

B: Reflectors are people who learn through watching things and thinking them over. They enjoy opportunities to mull over their ideas in an unhurried way and then produce carefully thought out conclusions. They learn little when they are forced into activities at short notice with inadequate information. They do not enjoy having to take shortcuts to a solution.

Strengths

- careful
- methodical
- thoughtful

Weaknesses

- slow to make up their minds
- not very forthcoming
- too cautious

C: Theorists like to understand the concepts underlying what they are learning and to explore the implications. They dislike unstructured situations where emotions run high.

Strengths

- disciplined approach
- objective
- rational

Weaknesses

- intolerant of anything subjective

D: Pragmatists learn best when they can link the content of their learning to a real problem. They dislike theoretical ideas but like ideas leading to practical outcomes.

Strengths

- businesslike
- realistic
- straight to the point
- practical

Weaknesses

- tend to reject that which does not have an obvious application
- down to earth
- not very interested in theory

Bear in mind that learning styles are not rigidly fixed – they may change over the space of time. You may dislike theoretical study in your youth, but find it more interesting as you grow older and enjoy learning about things in more depth. Alternatively you may be an activist who, with age and experience, becomes more reflective.

TRANSFER OF LEARNING

Where learning results from specific training, *learning transfer* is the most important aspect of training programmes. Bearing in mind the amount of money spent on training, it would be considered a waste if the knowledge and skills acquired are not successfully transferred back to the workplace.

Barriers to learning transfer may include participants who are afraid of change and are lacking in confidence; managers who do not provide support; and HRD practitioners who are suffering from work overload (Gilley et al 2002, cited in Mankin 2009, p269).

Much of this may be related to the organisational culture – if the organisation does not value training and realise its importance, then employees who attend training events will not be encouraged to put their newly found skills into practice when they return to the workplace.

CHOOSING A CAREER

While learning and development are critically important at work, they are also predominant in your mind when you are at the stage of choosing a career for yourself. Many students have made this choice before entering university and, obviously, it is a choice that has helped them to decide on the nature of the course they will take. Others, however, use the university course as a 'dip your toe in' exercise, to learn about particular subjects that, in turn, will help them to decide what they would like to do as a career.

PERSONALITY AND CAREER CHOICE

Above we alluded to the importance of learning and development, but research also shows that career choice is related to personality type. Holland (1985), for example, developed a theory of career choice rooted in personality. He maintains that people in each personality type (see Table 9.2) are drawn towards a small set of jobs. They are drawn in this way because they are seeking work that is compatible with their likes and dislikes. Holland's theory is based on six different personality types.

There is also research evidence that suggests that when people choose a career that suits their personality, they are more likely to be satisfied with their choice and less likely to change professions (Feldman and Arnold 1985). It is worth noting at this point that there are obvious implications here for personality testing as part of the recruitment process and for employee development and retention.

Theories such as Holland's, however, while compelling, do not take account of the fact that people change over time; they become wary of getting into a rut or career trap and, as a result, even after many years, might decide on a career change.

 ACTIVITY 9.5

Study Table 9.2 and try to find a set of personality characteristics that most closely matches your own. How does it relate to your career plan?

Table 9.2 **Personality types and career choice**

Personality type	Occupational choice
Realistic Outdoor type who enjoys, and is usually good at, physical activities requiring strength and/or co-ordination.	Farming; Sport-related; Carpentry; Architecture
Investigative Tends to get involved in observing, organising and understanding data. Good at abstract thought.	Mathematics; Engineering; Dentistry
Social Enjoys the company of others more than being engaged in intellectual or physical activity. Tends to be warm and caring and enjoys the process of informing, training and enlightening others.	Religion; Social work; Diplomatic service; Teaching
Conventional Likes rules, regulations, structure and order, and is prepared to subordinate personal needs to situations where personal or organisational power and status exist. Usually well organised but is not very imaginative.	Accounting; Finance; Military; Clerical work
Artistic Dislikes ordered and repetitive situations. Prefers to express feelings and ideas, and be imaginative. Enjoys drama, music and art.	Advertising; Interior design; Entertainment business
Enterprising Enjoys activity rather than observation and reflection. Likes to use verbal communication skills to persuade others and gain power and status.	Publishing; Employee relations; Sales management

Adapted from Holland (1985). Table reproduced with kind permission of Pearson Education Ltd.

Learning and career planning

Amandeep Kaur has just successfully completed the second year of a degree in general business studies. So far, she has studied many aspects of organisational behaviour, change and globalisation, and the influence of HRM. The business subjects she has taken include HR, finance, marketing and business planning.

At present she is unsure about the kind of career that she would enjoy and in which she would be successful. Above all, she wants to avoid making a wrong choice, but having had no business experience at all, how could she make the right choice? She found that the uncertainty was stressful and decided to seek advice from the university's career advisory service. The service was run by Gerry Macmillan, an experienced adviser of many years' standing.

Gerry told her that the first thing she had to do was to assess herself in terms of her strengths and weaknesses, preferences and prejudices, likes and dislikes. He also recommended that she write up a summary of her knowledge, skills and competences: not just the work-related aspects, but things that she had learned through hobbies, in social and domestic situations and things she had learned from friends.

Amandeep winced at the thought of the amount of time it would take her to do all this, but Gerry mentioned that the advisory service runs a 'self-awareness' course that is specifically designed for people experiencing the quandary in which she finds herself. He explained that when you 'know yourself', are aware of your strengths and weaknesses, and so on, you will know what you have to offer a potential employer.

He said that the course 'will help you to reflect upon your past experiences in a systematic way, the learning you have achieved within the university and outside of it, so that you can write up a complete and correct analysis of your past experiences'.

When Amandeep took the self-awareness course she was very surprised by what she discovered about herself; the volume of data was much greater than she had anticipated. Subsequently she was able to identify several areas of business that attracted her, and after looking into them more deeply, she realised that she would have to draw up a personal development plan, since there were gaps in her understanding that might be of concern to a potential employer.

Gerry was able to organise some work experience for her and that really opened her eyes to what she should expect as a full-time employee. She got on well with the people in the company, the managers noticed how keen she was to learn and to advance herself, and when she had finished her degree, she was offered a job for a probationary period.

SUMMARY

In this chapter we have looked at the strategic importance of learning and defined some important terms such as human capital, knowledge management and the concept of the learning organisation. We have discussed learning in detail, including early learning theories such as those of Skinner and Thorndike. We have also introduced Kolb's learning cycle, Honey and Mumford's learning styles and Revans' 'action learning sets'. There has been an opportunity to assess your own particular learning style and the chapter concludes with a look at career choice and personality types.

REVIEW QUESTIONS

1   Why is learning important in times of both recession and boom?

2   Who are the beneficiaries of training and how might they reap such benefits?

3   How would you define learning?

4   What is meant by 'human capital'?

5   What is the difference between a traditional economy and a knowledge economy?

6   What is meant by the term experiential learning? Describe a situation in which this might take place.

7   What are the four learning styles according to Honey and Mumford?

8   Why is the transfer of learning important?

9   People sometimes find that they have made the wrong choice of career. How might the risk of this have been reduced?

10 If you have read this entire chapter, you should have a fairly sound understanding of learning. How would this understanding help you to design a training course?

EXPLORE FURTHER

BOOKS

REID, M.A., BARRINGTON, H. and BROWN, M. (2004) *Human resource development: beyond training interventions*. London: Chartered Institute of Personnel and Development.

For a good, down-to-earth book, see Reid et al's text.

HARRISON, R. (2009) *Learning and development*. London: Chartered Institute of Personnel and Development.

For something a bit more in-depth and with more theory, interlaced with some good case studies, try Harrison's book.

MEGGINSON, D. and WHITAKER, V. (2007) *Continuing professional development*. 2nd ed. London: Chartered Institute of Personnel and Development.

This is a comprehensive text on CPD and has lots of practical ideas for your own continuing professional development

CHAPTER 10

Human Resource Development

LEARNING OBJECTIVES

After studying this chapter you should:

- be able to define human resource development (HRD)
- understand the current status and the strategic importance of HRD
- understand the role of government in education, learning and training
- be aware of the importance and uses of the Investors in People programme
- understand systematic training and development
- be able to organise and deliver a training course.

INTRODUCTION

The first aim of this chapter is to explain and discuss the current status of human resource development (HRD), particularly in terms of its importance to individuals, organisations and the country. Second, we examine and discuss the factors that comprise HRD: as we saw in Chapter 9, there are a number of terms that we may come across associated with this area: 'learning', 'education', 'training' and 'development'. Third, we explain the practical aspects of HRD.

THE STRATEGIC IMPORTANCE OF HRD

As early as 1970, Nadler discussed HRD and defined it as 'organised learning experiences provided by employers, within a specified period of time, to bring about the possibility of performance management and/or personal growth' (Nadler and Nadler, cited in Gold et al 2010, p14).

Suffice to say here that after the inception of HRM in the early 1980s, UK employers gradually began to recognise the factors that contributed to the success of their major global competitors. Prominent among these factors was HRD.

Other major contributing factors include, first, the organisational changes brought about by the implementation of HRM practices – through which knowledge and competence of the human resource are regarded as a valuable means of achieving a competitive advantage – and second, technology, particularly IT and the Internet, which allowed organisations to reach out to a worldwide audience. Purcell et al (2003), in their research on 'The People and Performance Link', list training and development as one of the 11 key HR factors in encouraging 'discretionary behaviour' that leads to higher productivity in the workplace.

 KEY CONCEPT: HUMAN RESOURCE DEVELOPMENT

Human resource development (HRD) encompasses a range of organisational practices that focus on learning: training, learning and development; workplace learning; career development and lifelong learning; organisation development; organisational knowledge and learning (Mankin 2009).

In practice, many people still refer to the term 'training' in the workplace and use it to encompass all manner of workplace learning. As we can see from the above definition, the term human resource development suggests a wider approach with a strategic viewpoint.

TRAINING AND DEVELOPMENT

Noe (2010) defines training as: a 'planned effort by a company to facilitate employees' learning of job-related competencies'. In short, this means that training is the means by which employees acquire the competences they need to carry out their work to the required standard.

Whereas training is needed in the shorter term to carry out tasks that are needed now, the term 'development' refers to the broader landscape. It relates to the future, to the longer-term development of people throughout their careers, providing them with the kind of confidence, maturity and stability that enables them to adopt greater responsibility. Training produces competence while development produces continuous *psychological growth*. It could be said, therefore, that training is for *now*, while development is for *the future*.

THE RELATIONSHIP WITH RECRUITMENT AND TALENT MANAGEMENT

If we remember the adage 'recruit for attitude, train for skill', then we can see the importance of training and development. It is vital for organisations to recruit and select the right kind of people to work for them, but once they are employees, it is just as important to ensure they are not only trained to do their *current job*, but also to develop their skills, to prepare them for *promotion* within the organisation. If we see talent management as being crucial for the success and survival of the business, then training, learning and development are key to this. We need to employ the best talent we can and to *develop* that talent to retain our competitive edge.

The term 'human capital' suggests that we are all valuable resources, which can be invested in and can grow in value. If we take on a new graduate, for example, they will have the potential to become a successful employee, but unless we train them and give them the opportunity to improve their skills and abilities, then they will become bored, demotivated and will eventually leave. We should, then, ensure that our staff are treated as valuable assets and allow them to develop and grow accordingly.

So, should we see our 'talent' as the top employees – those with special skills, who are our 'elite'? Or does the term 'talent' apply to everyone? We need *all* our employees to work to their full potential, so does it make sense to only develop 'the chosen few'? With the rising importance of flexibility and multi-skilling, the need to have well-trained workers becomes essential.

 ACTIVITY 10.1

Think of a time when you have been into a shop and wanted to buy something quite technical – a computer or a DVD, say. What was your experience like? Was the shop assistant well informed about the product? Or were you frustrated by their lack of knowledge and ability to answer questions? Does training in product knowledge – or lack of it – make a difference to whether you might buy the product?

'TIME TO TRAIN' LEGISLATION

New legislation in April 2010 gives employees working in organisations that employ 250 or more people the legal right to request time off for studying or training. This will then be extended to all organisations from 6 April 2011. It is only applicable to employees who have worked for their employer continuously for at least 26 weeks. As with a request to work flexibly, the employer must consider the request to train and can only turn it down if they have a good business reason for doing so, which may include the cost.

THE BENEFICIARIES OF HRD

'Who should pay for training and why?' Since there are three parties who benefit from training – the state, the employer and the individual – it can be argued, perhaps, that all three should be responsible for paying.

THE INDIVIDUAL

Individual employees benefit from training and development in several ways. First, if they understand how their tasks should be carried out, they are more motivated to do them well and thereby experience satisfaction from what they do. If they know they are good at what they do, they feel valued and respected. Training gives people skills, which in turn makes people competent, gives them confidence and feelings of security, and they feel that that their presence in the organisation is worthwhile.

Second, people who seek a career and plan their own future development will regard training sessions as important opportunities to extend their repertoire of knowledge and competence. This enhances their employability and their promotion prospects. Studying for CIPD qualifications can, for example, add to your employability and enhance your career prospects considerably in the professional field of human resource management. Many employees, with the support of their employers, have created their own personal development plans (PDP) in which the identification of their developmental needs forms an integral part of the performance management system.

PAUSE FOR THOUGHT

Continuing Professional Development (CPD)

Do you have a personal development plan? The CIPD defines CPD as a personal commitment to keeping your professional knowledge up to date and improving your capabilities throughout your working life. It is about knowing where you are today, where you want to be in the future, and making sure you get there. We return to CPD in Chapter 11.

THE ORGANISATION

The definition of HRD (above) says that it is a strategic approach to investing in human capital. The organisation benefits when the knowledge and competence of its employees, combined with their commitment and involvement, are specifically geared to the achievement of objectives, and thereby the realisation of strategy. Those who lead today's organisations have grown to understand the strength of the relationship between human performance and organisational success, which is why they now see HRD as a critical factor in the organisation's future.

THE STATE

The state benefits when organisations perform well in the home market and compete effectively with their overseas industrial counterparts. A knowledgeable and skilled workforce contributes enormously to the economy of the nation, creating wealth from which the whole of society benefits.

Advancing technology removes the requirement for traditional jobs and creates jobs that demand new knowledge and skills. An organisation that keeps pace with change by anticipating technological advances and preparing its workforce in good time will suffer least from the effects of a recession in the economy. For as long as technology continues to advance, organisations that fail to prepare their workforce will always experience the effects of the skills gap.

NATIONAL SKILLS STRATEGY

THE LEITCH REVIEW

The Government commissioned the Leitch report in 2004, which was a major review of skills in the UK. The report was published in 2006 and suggested that radical action was needed to ensure that the UK achieved status as a world leader in skills by 2020. The main recommendations were for the Government to provide funding for basic skills, and the aim is to achieve this via initiatives such as Train to Gain, the government flagship programme. The report also recommended that employers and individuals should contribute to paying towards achieving higher-level skills as they are the main ones to benefit. Targets include 95% of adults to have achieved the basic levels of functional literacy and numeracy by 2020, with 90% to reach at least a level 2 qualification (for example GCSE equivalent). A further target is for 40% of adults to be qualified to level 4 (degree-level equivalent) by 2020.

APPRENTICESHIPS

Under Leitch there is greater emphasis on apprenticeships, which provide work-based learning and experience tied in with gaining a qualification. The National Apprenticeship Service (NAS) has responsibility for apprenticeships in England and has been designed to increase the number of apprenticeship opportunities. It provides a dedicated, responsive service for both employers and learners.

TRAIN TO GAIN

Train to Gain is the national skills service meeting the needs of employers of all sizes and in all sectors to improve the skills of their employees as a route to improving their business performance. The service offers skills advice on everything from basic skills through to leadership and management training (www.traintogain.gov.uk). Over 1 million employees have benefited from training through the service as of March 2010 and the programme is due for even greater investment from the Government in 2011. Statistics on the success of this and other educational initiatives such as apprenticeships can be found at: www. thedataservice.org.uk/statistics/sfrdec09

DIPLOMAS

Recent developments in this area of education have led to the new diploma qualifications – which are equivalent to GCSEs and A levels, but have an employer input. The qualification is not just academic, but has a work experience component, is designed to be more practical and gives students a chance to see what work in that area is like. The pay-off for the employer is that new recruits, who possess the diploma, will have many of the skills that employers are looking for – a criticism of many of the other qualifications that are on offer.

INVESTORS IN PEOPLE (IIP)

Developed in 1990 by a partnership of leading businesses and national organisations, the Investors in People standard provides a practical framework for improving business performance and competitiveness through good practice in people. It is currently the UK's principal standard for business improvement through people. Responsibility for IiP lies with the UK Commission for Employment and Skills, which acts as a champion for the award with effect from April 2010.

IiP has been taken up by over 40,000 organisations across the UK (32% of employers) and covers 8 million employees (UKCES 2010). Generally these organisations report that achieving the required standards for recognition as an Investor in People is extremely beneficial.

IiP recognises that organisations use different means to achieve success through their people and does not, therefore, prescribe any one method for doing this. Instead, it provides a framework to help organisations to find the most suitable means for achieving success through their people. The main outcome of the review of the standard is the provision of a simplified structure to provide a better fit with how organisations operate. The focus is on helping employers to 'plan, do, and review' their business strategy.

 ACTIVITY 10.2

Your organisation, or an organisation with which you are familiar, would like to be recognised as an IiP organisation. Get a copy of the IiP standard and prepare a programme that should lead to this achievement.

SYSTEMATIC TRAINING

In corporate terms, the ultimate purpose of training is to improve the performance of employees, and thereby the whole organisation. Individuals, however, may regard training as one of the means by which they can improve themselves to enhance their career prospects. Viewed in this way, training may be driven by both the organisation and by its employees.

TRAINING POLICY

Since the advent of HRM in the 1980s, the importance of developing staff has grown markedly. Training was once regarded as a comparative luxury. Senior managers seldom regarded it as one of the organisation's top priorities and therefore were reluctant to allocate significant resources to it. That attitude has now changed somewhat and modern organisations realise that it is in their best interests to formulate a clear and cost-efficient statement of intent to provide resources for a training programme that is accessible to all areas of the enterprise. In the 2009 CIPD *Learning and Development* survey report, 76% of respondents agreed that learning and development in their organisation is 'seen as an important part of business improvement'. Eighty-one per cent of employers in the same survey stated that development of management and leadership skills is most important in meeting business objectives in the next two years.

It is the responsibility of the HR manager to develop a training policy that meets the needs of the business and to have it accepted at the top level. Additionally, they should have a training needs analysis (TNA) carried out that links the needs of the business and of individuals, the findings of which will determine the specification of the training programme. The HR manager may achieve this by setting up a training committee, with a membership drawn from all areas of the organisation. To be an effective player on such a stage, HR practitioners must equip themselves with the knowledge and skills that enable them to provide training at operational level.

DEVELOPING A TRAINING COURSE

Since the professional expertise in training resides in the HR department, the responsibility for its provision lies in that department, and in particular with the HR specialist – who may have the title 'training and development manager' or 'HRD manager' – assisted by HR practitioners or 'trainers'.

Developing a training course involves the practitioner in a well-known sequence of activities. The activities form a cyclical process that is generally referred to as the *systematic training cycle* (see Figure 10.1).

THE COMPONENTS OF THE SYSTEMATIC TRAINING CYCLE

From Figure 10.1, you will see that the *systematic training cycle*, sometimes referred to as the *systematic approach to training*, is made up of six

Figure 10.1 The systematic training cycle

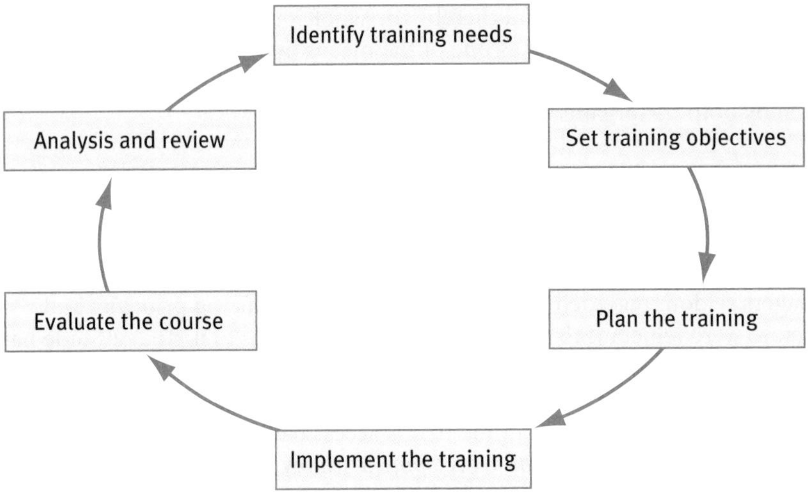

interdependent and interrelated components. It has been used successfully in industry and the public sector for many years and is regarded as a sound basis for cost-effective training.

STAGE 1: IDENTIFY TRAINING NEEDS

The most objective and effective approach to this task starts at job level. Carrying out a *job analysis* forms the basis for the production of job descriptions and specifications. The knowledge and competences that a job-holder needs to meet the required standards, and the standards themselves, are clarified in a completed job analysis. The next stage is to identify the *competence gap*. By performing a 'gap analysis' we should be able to determine the difference between what the job-holder *is* able to do and what they actually *should* be able to do. In behavioural terms this can be expressed as what the job-holder is *expected* to do and what they *actually* do. Where there is a gap between actual and required performance, it may be filled by training.

There can be a danger that training is seen as a panacea – the answer to all performance problems. This may not be the case; the employee may possess the ability, but the gap between actual and required performance may be caused by lack of motivation to perform. Training may be a possible answer, but there may be times when there is a need for disciplinary action, for example where an employee has the right skills but just does not perform well owing to their attitude. There may, of course, be other reasons why someone may not perform well – perhaps through being poorly managed or owing to lack of support from the rest of their team.

HOW TRAINING NEEDS ARE IDENTIFIED

There are several ways in which training needs may be identified:

- *Performance appraisal:* managers identify training needs in their day-to-day monitoring of staff performance and when they carry out formal performance appraisal sessions. For example, the manager identifies a training need when an employee's standard of performance needs to be raised.

- Individuals may notice their own lack of knowledge of techniques or systems, or they may identify gaps in their skills when asked to carry out particular tasks.

- Training needs may also be identified during the selection process. The 'best person for the job' hardly ever possesses every single item of knowledge, skills and competence that the job demands.

- A mentor or coach may identify a training need – especially in relation to the employee's personal development.

- *Assessment or development centres:* employees may go through tests and exercises that identify areas where they excel, are competent or where they require extra training.

TRAINING NEEDS ANALYSIS

The technique for identifying training needs at individual, group and corporate levels is known as a *training needs analysis* (TNA). This may be carried out through a formal training survey that is conducted across the whole organisation. Typically, this is needed when a company-wide change is taking place, such as when new technology is being introduced, or when restructuring occurs. In such cases, new competences need to be learned and tasks and responsibilities are redistributed. A company-wide training survey is a massive undertaking and its effectiveness will be maximised if it is started well in advance of the anticipated change.

STAGE 2: SET TRAINING OBJECTIVES

The next stage is to set the training objectives. In general, the objective of training is to develop in people the knowledge and understanding, skills and competence that they need to meet required performance standards. The training objectives, therefore, should be set out in behavioural terms, specifying what the trainee should know and be able to do as a result of the training. As an example, if you look at the box at the beginning of every chapter in this book, you will see how the learning objectives are set out.

SMART OBJECTIVES

The acronym SMART is often used as a mnemonic to aid those who regularly set objectives for others. SMART means that objectives should be: **S**pecific, **M**easurable, **A**chievable, **R**ealistic and **T**ime-related.

Specific means making a clear statement about the knowledge or skill that the trainee should be able to do and actually demonstrate at the end of the course. This includes the level of operation, such as, 'After the training, the trainee should be able to use the machine safely and efficiently to produce the product at the specified quality.'

Measurable means that the standard of the trainee's performance after the training can be measured in terms of, for example, quality and number of items in a specified period of time.

Achievable means that it should be possible for the trainee to achieve the objectives in the light of the situation, the practicability, and the intelligence and motivation of the trainee.

Realistic means that the objectives should be obviously useful and clearly related to the type of work that the trainee carries out.

Time-related means that the trainee should be able to develop understanding, attain concepts and demonstrate skills within a pre-specified period of time. For example, you might be able to type a letter perfectly if you took an hour to do it, but not if you only had five minutes. A skilled typist would be able to achieve the objective in the shorter time.

STAGE 3: PLAN THE TRAINING

Bearing in mind the nature of the subject matter in which the employee needs to be trained, decisions have to be made about how and where it is to be carried out. There are several choices. Most training, however, falls into one of two categories:

1 *On-the-job training*, which, as the term implies, takes place while the trainee is actually working. This can include:
   - E-learning (electronic learning), using the Internet or the organisation's own intranet – e-learning may also be done 'off the job'.
   - 'Sitting by Nelly', in which the trainee is taken through the steps of the job by a colleague – you may see this in supermarkets when new checkout operators are being trained, for example.
   - Use of instruction manuals – this may rely on the trainee teaching themselves the required skills by reading the manual.
   - Completing a project or assignment related to the job.
   - Coaching – usually performed by a line manager.

2 *Off-the-job training*, which may be external training, when, for example, an individual or a small group is sent out to a local college or training centre, or to a higher education institution to undertake a professional qualification. Off-the-job training may also include in-house training, for example when the trainee undertakes a short course (for example a health and safety course) or carries out an assignment supervised by the manager. This might include undertaking role-plays, discussing case studies, attending workshops, and so on.

TRAINING STRATEGIES

It is important to consider the best way of fulfilling the training need. Questions to think about include:

- Should the training be carried out in the organisation's own training facility by one of the managers or specialists, or by an external trainer? Cost may be a factor to consider here.

- Is it a subject that would be best handled externally, perhaps by a college or a private training establishment? Do you have experts in-house with the right knowledge to deliver the training?

- Is there a government training initiative that would serve the purpose?

- Could the employee's competence gap be filled by coaching, on-the-job training or counselling?

- Could the organisation sponsor the employee to undertake a course that bears a qualification?

- Could the manager give an assignment to the trainee who could then be coached by either the manager or another suitably qualified person? In this way, the employee may emerge from the assignment having learned enough from it to fill their competence gap.

- Could the training objectives be achieved through e-learning, in which the employee uses the Internet or the organisation's intranet to gather the knowledge, understanding and competences they need?

- How is the training to be funded?

The advantages and disadvantages of all of these options have to be weighed carefully, since training can involve considerable cost and commitment on all sides. While cost is an important factor, the nature of the training objectives is the key to the answer. Cheap training may not be the best – 'cost-effectiveness' would make a better criterion. The factors of learning that are outlined in Chapter 9 should also be considered, for example people's learning styles. They may provide a good starting point for making this decision.

STAGE 4: IMPLEMENT THE TRAINING

If it is decided that external training would be the most appropriate way forward, the HR practitioner becomes involved in administering the event: for example, securing the trainee's entry to the course, ensuring that the fee is paid and monitoring the trainee's progress. The trainee's manager, however, should be involved in a different way, as the following case example shows.

CASE EXAMPLE

Taking an interest

Arshad had worked for Harvey Plastics as a product designer for three years. He was excellent at his job and popular with his work colleagues. During a performance appraisal interview with his departmental manager, Anita Brown, she told him that she was pleased with his overall performance, and started to talk to him about his career.

During the conversation, she mentioned that there was a vacant position as a team leader in the department, and said she would like to put his name forward as a candidate for the job. Arshad pointed out that he had not had any supervisory experience, but Anita replied that she had noticed that his colleagues had become

accustomed to approaching him for advice. She also said that if he were to get the job, the company would sponsor him on a team leadership course at the local college.

Arshad applied and was selected for the position, which would become vacant owing to the present incumbent's retirement in eight weeks. The HR department provided Anita with a copy of the course curriculum and she and Arshad met to discuss it. It was a 12-week course and Arshad would have to attend on two evenings a week, so he would be well into the course by the time he took up the new position. The selection process had included a psychometric test and Anita had a copy of the test report. While they were discussing the course content Anita pointed out to Arshad several areas to which she wanted him to pay particular attention.

After Arshad started the course, they had further meetings during which they discussed the items she had highlighted for his attention, asking him what he had learned from them and how he thought they were relevant to his new position.

Arshad made excellent progress on the course – demonstrated by his high marks. He was performing well in the seminars and often emerged as the leader when they were carrying out group work. Finally, Anita said that if he wanted to discuss any part of the course with her, she would always make the time to see him.

Commentary

It has to be pointed out that not all managers take such an interest in the development of their staff, as in this case. This is evidenced by the fact that at enrolment in colleges for part-time and short courses, you will usually find that it was the student's, rather than their employer's, idea to take the course.

ACTIVITY 10.3

Think about a course you are on, or have been on. Where did the idea come from to attend the course? Was your manager supportive? Did they take an interest in what you learned? Were you able to put the learning from the classes into place back at work?

PAUSE FOR THOUGHT

Why should managers take an interest in what their staff learn? In what ways do you think this has broader implications for the organisation?

RUNNING AN IN-HOUSE COURSE

If it is thought that in-house training would be the best way forward, the HR practitioner becomes involved in organising and administering the course. This includes setting the date and organising the venue for the training, and ensuring that the prospective trainees and their managers receive sufficient notice of the times and dates of the training events. Where the subject matter is HR-related, such as training managers in a new system of appraisal or in selection interviewing, the HR practitioner is often expected to be able to deliver it. Otherwise, a trainer who is an expert in the subject should deliver the course, especially if it is a technical subject. For this purpose, it may be possible to enlist the services of a manager or specialist from within the organisation. If not, then you may have to buy in the services of a training consultant.

TRAINING CONSULTANTS

Some HR departments have a register of external specialists who come in to the organisation to deliver the training. When this happens, the HR practitioner will have made the consultant aware of the training objectives and the consultant will have developed an appropriate course that they will bring to the training area. It is necessary to be certain, however, that the course meets the needs of the trainees precisely, and this may involve meetings with the consultant.

It is important at such meetings not to allow the consultant to dominate the proceedings. With the appropriate managers, the HR practitioner will have set the training objectives, and it is only by these objectives that the training must be driven. While the views of an experienced consultant might be valuable, they cannot know the organisation and its training requirements as well as its staff do, so do not allow the training to be driven by what the consultant would like to deliver – make sure it is exactly what your organisation needs and that it fits the objectives.

COST-EFFECTIVENESS

Earlier we alluded to the cost of training, and while we almost instinctively relate cost to college fees, engaging external trainers, travel expenses and so on, it can still be costly to run an in-house course. Cost-effectiveness may also be related to the number of trainees on the course at any one time, since many organisations calculate the cost per head.

There is a balance to be achieved here in the sense that while the number of trainees has to justify the cost of the course, it also has an influence on the event. Too few trainees may not provide a suitable mix or allow for syndicate work, while too many may make it difficult for the trainer to deal with questions. A large number of trainees may also influence your decisions about the methods and media to be used (see below) and the duration of the course. If, for example, you decide to use syndicate work, you have to consider the amount of time it is fair to allocate to delegates when they return from their discussions to present their findings.

Costs do not just relate to paying for the course, but also the 'opportunity costs' of people not being at work and doing their job while they are attending the training course, which can be significant.

COURSE DEVELOPMENT

Let us now assume that the subject matter of the training is HR-related and that you are going to organise and deliver the training. First, the course objectives have to be studied carefully and you have to decide how they are going to be achieved. Second, therefore, you decide what the course should contain and what methods and media would be most likely to achieve the objectives.

Table 10.1 Training methods

Method	Usage
Lecture	Presenting information, particularly to a large number of people. Keep lectures as brief as possible as attention spans are short. Making lectures interactive by encouraging or asking questions throughout is a good tip.
Seminar	Ideal to discuss a topic or concept. The trainer may introduce the subject and run a group discussion on it. Trainees can present their views on which the trainer may comment.
Case study	These may describe hypothetical situations, while others are based on reality. They are a useful way of exposing trainees to organisational situations that are relevant to what the trainer wishes to communicate.
Role-play	This is a case study in which the trainees adopt the roles of the characters in the situation. Usually, it is a problem-solving situation related to the subject of the course. Ideal for exercising interpersonal skills and for training in recruitment and selection interviewing, for example. Where necessary, the trainer intervenes to offer guidance.
Syndicate work	Normally a problem-solving session in which the trainees are given a problem based on an organisational situation. The course members are divided into small groups and asked to occupy syndicate rooms (where they are available) and try to find a solution to the problem. When they return to the main training area, they present their findings to the group.
Exercises	These are suitable for trainees to learn and practise skills for the first time. This might be to complete a questionnaire or a quiz, to work out answers to problems, or to do a physical activity, such as playing a game.

TRAINING MEDIA

Information technology has extended the range of training media, especially in the area of visual aids. These include PowerPoint and DVDs. Other visual aids include overhead projectors (OHP, now rather old-fashioned), electronic whiteboards, flipcharts, videos and films. Handouts may also be used to get your message across.

There are occasions when the media you use are determined simply by what is available in the training facility, and sometimes therefore you just have to make do. Having said that, each of the media mentioned above lends themselves to particular subject matter. You should always make sure you have a back-up plan. If the electronic technology fails, you need to have written handouts perhaps, to work through, or to convey your points on a flipchart. A trainer should always be ready for things that may go wrong. Technology may be a wonderful thing, but you do not want to face a room of eager trainees and not be able to teach them just because the computer isn't working! Beware – this happens far more frequently than might be imagined.

Meanwhile, Table 10.2 lists the most commonly used media and the purposes for which they are suitable.

Table 10.2 Commonly used visual training aids

Medium	Usage
PowerPoint	Everything is prepared on the computer. It is usual to run off copies of the PowerPoint slides to hand out to the trainees as aide-memoires. With this medium you can use colour and animation. Be wary of getting carried away with fancy tricks, though – it is the content of your PowerPoint slides that counts, not whether your text flies in with a whooshing sound!
Smartboards	These are whiteboards on which you can play PowerPoint slides, write down points as you go along, or access Internet sites – all of which will enhance your presentation. You may for example be discussing Investors in People and then be able to click on a weblink that takes you straight to the IiP website.
Whiteboard and flipchart	Handy for summarising syndicates' findings, trainees' answers to your questions and for laying out the main points of a talk.
DVD, video, film, YouTube clips	There is an infinite selection of these. Some are made specifically for training purposes in which actors adopt roles in case studies and problem-solving situations. Others are well-known feature films in which there are leadership and motivation issues.

PREPARING THE COURSE

Thorough preparation is the key to delivering a successful course, and there are several factors to be considered. You need to:

- Assess the training venue and see what media hardware is available and in good working order (note the warnings above about the unreliability of technology!).

- Create the course structure – refer back to the course objectives. How will you achieve these in the time available?

- Decide what methods and media you are going to use.

- Draft your presentation notes.

- Develop the visual aids.

- Select the DVDs, videos, films, YouTube clips (if any) you intend to use.

- See what you can find out about the trainees.

ASSESSING THE VENUE

It is important to take the time to visit the training facility. You need to know:

- The size and layout of the place – will it accommodate your trainees comfortably? From which point in the room will you deliver the course? What visual and other training aids are available and are they all in working order?

- How many syndicate rooms are there (if any)?

- How does the place 'feel' in terms of its ambience? In other words, is it conducive to a pleasant and successful experience for the trainees? Is the room warm enough (but not too warm that they will be encouraged to sleep!)?

- What are the catering facilities like? Are you providing coffee, tea, biscuits, lunch? Are there any special dietary requirements? It's a good idea to have coffee at the start as it encourages people to mix and chat before the course starts and is thus good for helping to establish rapport.

CREATING THE COURSE STRUCTURE

Having decided on the duration of the course, you now have to decide how much of the time to allocate to each of its elements. Here, your priorities are governed partly by the importance of the elements in relation to each other, and partly by their detail and complexity, the latter implying that the trainees will need time to understand and internalise them. You also have to create a logical sequence in which they are to be delivered, allowing for reasonable breaks between each session.

METHODS AND MEDIA

These are listed in Tables 10.1 and 10.2, and bearing in mind the course objectives and the nature of the material you need to deliver, you have to select the methods and media that you regard as the most suitable in terms of purpose and clarity. Some subjects seem naturally to lend themselves to particular methods and media.

 Testing your learning

CASE EXAMPLE

Lee Chen, HR adviser at Harvey Plastics, had been involved in planning the company's new approach to performance appraisal, and was now designing a one-day course to train managers in how to implement the system. To explain the details of the course, he decided to deliver an illustrated talk using PowerPoint, to be followed by a question and answer (Q&A) session to clear up any points the managers raised. After the Q&A session, there would be a brief refreshment break at which the managers could chat to each other about the system. This would be followed by a role-play exercise in which the managers would conduct one-to-one interviews with each other on the basis of fictional performance records. Obviously, the roles would be 'appraiser' and 'appraisee'. He injected a little humour into the fictional performance records to ensure that the session was enjoyable as well as instructive.

WRITING YOUR TRAINING PLAN

This involves working out the detail of the training session and also drafting your notes of what you are going to say. Go through each element of the course carefully, draft a separate set of notes for each element and place them in a file in the order of delivery. On the right of each page, leave a margin that is wide enough to make 'reminder' notes, such as when a PowerPoint slide should be shown or when the trainees may need a slight pause while they absorb a particular point or concept. It is also useful to have the plan to hand, so that you can refer to it if you get lost – you may come to the end of a set of slides and then panic about what comes next. A quick glance at the plan will show you what exercise or activity you need to deliver. You need to get to know your plan so well that you hardly ever have to refer to it; just take it in as your security blanket!

DEVELOPING VISUAL AIDS

Some visual aids come ready-made, such as DVDs, videos and films. Others, such as PowerPoint presentations, you have to make yourself.

Flipchart

This is quite a versatile tool. One of its main advantages is its portability. You may have to run a session in an area that is not customised for training, and if it is off-site, the flipchart will fit into the back of your car. Alternatively, syndicate groups can make their presentations on a flipchart, having prepared them during the syndicate session. In this way, different people's conclusions and recommendations may be compared, contrasted and discussed in a subsequent plenary session. When using the flipchart yourself, as a trainer, try to develop the skill of writing and speaking while facing the audience as much as possible. Talking into the flipchart should be avoided where possible.

RUNNING A TRAINING SESSION

In advance of actually running a session, a good trainer will go through their notes thoroughly and learn them so well that they seldom need to refer to them. If you have never done it before, practise your delivery as if you are in the real situation. Performing in front of a mirror, or in front of a friend or colleague is a good idea, as they can give you feedback. Be careful to choose someone who will be constructive, though – someone who is destructively critical is not a good idea! (For this reason, avoid asking your partner/wife/husband to do this!)

To run a session effectively, you have to be skilled in the use of visual aids. You may be able to develop the skills if you are on an HR course. Many universities and colleges offer a short course in the use of media and training aids generally.

Establishing rapport

Before introducing the subject matter, you need to develop a friendly but businesslike atmosphere that is conducive to learning. If you have a class of students or trainees whom you have never previously met, you may wish to tell them something about yourself (although without sounding too self-important). Putting cards with their forenames on, in front of the trainees is a good idea, not only so that the trainer will know who they are, but in case they have never met each other.

Icebreakers

At this early stage, you can run a brief interactive session. The idea is to get the trainees talking to each other and to relax. People can be quite intimidated at courses, especially in front of a big group, so the more you can get them to relax and enjoy it, the more easily they will learn. Using the following as an icebreaker can be very entertaining. Lengthy introductions can become boring – so if the course is a short one, you don't need to spend too long on this. If you are running a longer course, perhaps where the trainees will be together for a number of sessions or weeks, then it is worth spending longer on letting them get to know each other.

CASE EXAMPLE

Icebreaker

Ask each of the trainees to tell the group one thing they have in their pockets or handbags that means something to them. They may have a photo of a child or partner, a memento from a parent or it may just be their credit card without which they can't function!

Introduction

It is vital for you to arouse the immediate interest of your audience with a good introduction of the subject. Without going into too much detail, tell them what you have planned for the session and the order in which each part of the course will be delivered. Then, just in case it was not understood by everyone, summarise it so that you are sure everyone knows what to expect.

Main sections

At this stage you start to deliver the first section of the course. Speak fairly slowly at first (without boring the audience) to make sure you are getting your points across. Use simple, everyday language and speak clearly. Never use jargon and avoid specialised terms, except when it is absolutely necessary. Round off one idea or concept, pause, and then introduce the next.

There is a limit to the amount of information you should express verbally; good visual support material is essential. Focus your attention on concepts rather than detail; you can always provide detail on handouts at the end of the session. If you have included citations or web links on your PowerPoint slides, leave them on show long enough for the trainees to jot down; otherwise include them on your handouts.

It helps to build and maintain rapport with the group if you can use people's names. It is also a good tip to refer back to any comments they have made during the course. For example, if you say, 'As Bernadette mentioned earlier, role-plays are an excellent method of training,' it shows that you have remembered what they said and reinforces that they made a worthwhile comment. This can make people feel valued – and helps to build up their confidence.

PAUSE FOR THOUGHT

If you are on a course, observe your lecturer; see how they deliver the material and, at the end of the session, think about the planning that must have gone into it. Well-delivered training should appear effortless – we should all be aware that it is not!

Handling questions

Keep a close eye on the clock! If you overrun you may not have time to answer questions. It is wise to lay the ground rules for questions from the beginning of the session. There are several ways of handling this. First, are you willing to take questions at any time? Second, would you prefer to take them at the end when you can see how much time you have left? (As your experience of training grows you will become adept at timing the sessions.) Third, you may decide to ask for questions at sectional points when, for example, you have just finished explaining a concept. There are advantages and disadvantages to all of these options.

If you allow the interruptions you may decide to turn these to your advantage. They may allow you to focus upon particular points of interest and engage your audience by encouraging them to participate with their thoughts and to change the pace and direction of your delivery. It is not unusual to be interrupted by someone who wishes to have a point clarified. This can be useful, since the understanding of what follows may depend on this. It may be that others in the group also feel they would like this point clarified but have not had the confidence to ask. It takes courage for people to speak out in front of a group, so if someone asks a question, it is better to give an answer, even if a brief one.

If you take questions at the end you can be sure of a free run throughout your delivery, which would allow you to focus exclusively on what you are doing, while avoiding any digressive discussions. The danger of this is that people do not feel able to question throughout – and this may mean that they stop concentrating because they have failed to understand a point. If trainers tell trainees to keep that question to the end, most times, the question will never get asked.

You may find that one person hijacks the session by asking too many questions about their own personal circumstances, for instance; it may be worth asking them to chat to you over the coffee break, where you can speak to them in more detail. You do not want to lose the interest of the group by concentrating on one particular issue. On the other hand, sharing that one person's experience may be invaluable to the rest and this opportunity should not be overlooked. If possible, it is best to give a quick answer at the time without getting too off track.

Always allow some time for questions, otherwise people may go home feeling they haven't really understood the session. Time management of the session is important here. Too many questions may mean you over-run, which is something to avoid. It is better to have a session's structure planned with time for questions, but with an optional activity available if the group does not ask questions and you are left with time to spare. As a trainer you will need to build in flexibility to allow for things such as this. If you invite questions intermittently this is an opportunity to engage the audience and give them a sense of participation. Also, it provides you with on-the-spot feedback: first, on how you are being received and, second, to check the trainees' understanding.

PAUSE FOR THOUGHT

Think of a time when you have attended a course and wanted to ask a question. How did the trainer handle it? If you were told to wait until the end, did you have the courage to ask it at the end? Or did the question get forgotten in the meantime? How do you feel about not having your question dealt with?

STAGE 5: EVALUATE THE COURSE

Running and participating in a training session – perhaps a one- or two-day course – should prove to be an interesting and exciting event for the trainer and the trainees. It is a socially interactive process after which the participants should feel confident that they have all learned from the experience. Additionally, it should also be effective in terms of achieving the training objectives; and it should be cost-effective.

PAUSE FOR THOUGHT

For developmental and financial reasons, evaluation is a vitally important process and yet most organisations pay little attention to it. They have ineffective systems of evaluation, or they ignore the need completely. Do you think that training without evaluation is a risky investment? Why?

Training evaluation is often criticised for only taking account of whether the trainees enjoyed the course and not whether they actually learned anything that they could apply back in the workplace. Since 1975 the most commonly espoused model of evaluation has tended to be that of Kirkpatrick, who developed a four-level framework consisting of:

- **Level 1, reaction:** This is where trainees state what they thought of the course, whether they enjoyed it and whether it was useful.

- **Level 2, learning:** Has the trainee actually learned anything? Have the learning objectives been achieved?

- **Level 3, behaviour or performance:** Has the training actually made any difference to the trainee at work? Can they do their job better as a result?

- **Level 4, results:** Has the training had any impact on the organisation? Have sales increased? Are things being run more efficiently? Are there fewer accidents? Is there less waste or fewer errors?

The higher the level, the more difficult it is to relate the results back to the training. For example, how do we know whether sales have increased due to the training, or whether it is as a result of our competitors closing down? Is the manager better because they attended a 12-month course, or because they now have an extra 12 months' experience of managing staff? Russ-Eft and Preskill (2005, p71) reviewed training evaluation practices worldwide and concluded that there was little formal evaluation of training, little rigour and evaluation did not focus on the organisational/corporate level. As employers are currently spending an average of around £220 per employee (CIPD *Learning and Development* survey report 2009g), it seems ridiculous that we do not monitor how well that money is spent!

HOW TO EVALUATE

So with this in mind, *how should* we evaluate? Let us take Kirkpatrick's four levels:

- **Level 1** is relatively easy. We can ask trainees to complete a questionnaire at the end of the course (a 'happy sheet') to see whether they enjoyed the course and felt it was worthwhile. It may be that they did indeed enjoy the training, that it was good fun, a day off work, and so on, but that they did not actually learn very much at all that would be useful.

- At **Level 2**, learning can be assessed by giving tests, assignments and projects, much like you will be used to as students on educational courses such as the Certificate in HR Practice, or even for a degree.

- **Level 3** evaluation looks at whether performance or behaviour has changed. So we could use performance appraisals to see whether there has been any marked difference in how the person does their job. Or we could observe the person both before the training and then again afterwards and see if there have been any changes in behaviour. Can the trainees deal with issues better than they did before?

- **Level 4** evaluation needs to use data relevant to the type of course: for example, figures such as accident rates in the case of health and safety training, customer complaints in the case of customer care training. But it can become difficult. If we run recruitment and selection training, we may need to look not only at retention levels (on the assumption that a good recruitment process will appoint people who will stay with the organisation), but also at things such as a drop in the number of discrimination cases taken as a result of better interviewing, or an improvement in the induction crisis. This data may be hard to come by and even then may not prove whether the training was actually the cause of the improvements.

STAGE 6: ANALYSIS AND REVIEW

It is rare for a training session that is being run for the first time to achieve every single aspect of every objective, and even more rare for it to fail completely. Analysis and review is the final stage of the systematic training cycle. The task is to review how the course was received and to examine its effectiveness. An analysis of the results of evaluation will reveal areas that need to be improved. Evaluation, analysis and review are components of a continuous process, so after a course has been run a second time, it is reviewed again and re-evaluated to achieve improvements. Are there things we need to change? Can we do things better, cheaper, faster?

SUMMARY

We have seen in this chapter how important human resource development can be. Whether we are in a recession or boom times, training can be used to add to an organisation's competitive edge. Developing people is not only beneficial for individuals in that it adds to their employability and furthers their career prospects, but it is essential for businesses today by helping to ensure an organisation's survival in a global economy. Appointing people with talent is important – *developing* that talent is essential if we want to retain good people in the organisation and achieve a competitive edge.

REVIEW QUESTIONS

1 What were the main factors that focused managers' attention on HRD?

2 How would you define HRD?

3 Who benefits from HRD and why?

4 What are the main outcomes of the Leitch review?

5 What are the advantages of being an Investor in People?

6 What are the components of the systematic training cycle?

7 How would a job analysis help you to identify training needs?

8 What is meant by the acronym SMART and how would you explain each of the elements?

9 What are Kirkpatrick's four levels of training evaluation?

10 How can we evaluate training courses?

EXPLORE FURTHER

BOOKS

HACKETT, P. (2003) *Training practice*. **London: Chartered Institute of Personnel and Development.**

This is an excellent book on the practicalities of training.

SIMMONDS, D. (2003) *Designing and delivering training*. **London: Chartered Institute of Personnel and Development.**

This book provides a solid introduction to the subject.

TRUELOVE, S. (2006) *Training in practice*. **London: Chartered Institute of Personnel and Development.**

All three books provide practical help on how to design and deliver training.

WEB LINKS

Apprenticeships: www.apprenticeships.org.uk

Statistics on educational initiatives: www.thedataservice.org.uk/statistics/sfrdec09

Investors in People: www.investorsinpeople.co.uk/Pages/Home.aspx

Train to Gain: www.traintogain.gov.uk

UK Commission for Employment and Skills: www.ukces.org.uk/

CHAPTER 11

Performance Management

LEARNING OBJECTIVES

After studying this chapter you should:

- be able to define performance, performance management and performance appraisal as separate concepts

- understand performance management as a process through which the organisation achieves its ultimate goals

- be able to explain how particular organisational factors may influence performance

- understand the factors that motivate individuals and the main theoretical concepts underlying work motivation

- understand modern performance assessment systems

- be able to create your own personal development plan.

INTRODUCTION

The aim of this chapter is to explain performance management and discuss it as a management function. To clarify your understanding of this, there are separate definitions and descriptions of *performance management*, *performance* and *performance appraisal*. The main body of the chapter explains and discusses the principles and processes of performance management and the traditional and modern approaches to assessing performance.

BACKGROUND

Organisations have always been interested in employee performance, but the term 'performance management' is relatively new. It has its foundations in the HRM belief that organisational success is determined by the performance of its employees and the most valuable assets of any business are its people. Systems of appraisal are still used to monitor performance in retrospect, whereas performance management is a carefully planned attempt to ensure a high future performance. This involves running programmes of employee development and encouraging employees to have their own personal development plans.

Performance management is an organisation-wide concept. That is to say, if an organisation realises its overall corporate strategy, then it must have performed according to plan, been successful in the pursuit of its goals and achieved its objectives through the efforts of the managers, teams and individuals. Viewed in this way, performance management can be seen as a concern of everyone in the organisation.

And in a recession, there is even more interest in focusing effort on the things that really matter for the business.

DEFINITIONS

Armstrong and Baron defined performance management in 1998 as:

> ... a process which contributes to the effective management of individuals and teams in order to achieve high levels of organisational performance. As such, it establishes shared understanding about what is to be achieved and an approach to leading and developing people which will ensure that it is achieved.

This still holds true today. Armstrong and Baron's later work in 2005 provides evidence for performance management as a means of integrating a number of activities relating to individual contribution, such as talent management, career planning, and learning and development.

The CIPD survey of 507 organisations, *Performance Management in Action* (2009h), found 'a surprising degree of agreement that performance appraisal, objective-setting, regular feedback, regular reviews and assessment of development needs are the cornerstones of performance management'. It found that:

> Appraisal, objective-setting and review and development still top the list of activities most commonly carried out under the banner of performance management. ... There is a trend of integrating performance management more firmly with other HR processes to manage talent, develop potential, plan careers or support individuals through coaching or mentoring.

It seems that performance management is indeed an important tool for managers today in increasing engagement, communicating with staff and in aligning individual effort and goals with business objectives.

 KEY CONCEPT: PERFORMANCE MANAGEMENT

Performance management is a systematic and strategic approach to ensuring that employees' performance, as individuals and team members, enables the organisation to achieve a competitive advantage by producing the level and quality of products and services that lead to customer satisfaction and, thereby, the achievement of objectives and the ultimate realisation of strategy.

PERFORMANCE MANAGEMENT THROUGH DEVELOPMENT

The main purpose of performance management is to improve the performance of all employees across the whole organisation; *employee development*, therefore, is a key issue. To improve performance it is necessary for the organisation to have a set of effective development programmes that are accessible to everyone. Improved performance is also achieved through encouraging individual employees to create their own personal development plans (PDPs) so that they can build on their repertoire of competences and monitor their own performance. In a 2005 CIPD survey, *Managing Performance: Performance management in action* (Armstrong and Baron 2005), 87% of organisations surveyed used a formal performance management process – for 83% of these, the focus was developmental.

To make this work, managers have to develop a personal communication style that informs and involves employees to the extent that they understand what is required of them in terms of standards and competence, and elicits their co-operation, commitment and involvement. Managers need the co-operation of employees to achieve the objectives of teams and departments, and it would be unreasonable for them to expect employees' co-operation unless they are told precisely the nature of what is required.

Managers should also listen to and think about what employees have to say and, where desirable and feasible, act upon their ideas.

We will return to the very important 'development' aspects of performance management later in the chapter.

 Achieving co-operation

CASE EXAMPLE

Just before the battle of El Alamein in the Second World War, Field Marshal Montgomery wanted to talk informally to his troops. He wanted to tell them about his plan for the battle and why he thought it was the best way forward. Instead of lining them up in formal ranks, he asked them to gather around him and he addressed them from the top of a bren carrier (a small armoured vehicle). He wanted their co-operation: after all, they too had an interest in achieving a victory. That was indicative of the style with which he led them into one of the most significant turning points in the war. It succeeded.

PRINCIPLES OF PERFORMANCE MANAGEMENT

The principles of performance management were summarised in 1996 by the IRS as follows and still hold good today:

- It translates corporate goals into individual, team, department and divisional goals.
- It helps to clarify corporate goals.

- It is a continuous and evolutionary process in which performance improves over time.

- It relies on consensus and co-operation, rather than control or coercion.

- It encourages self-management of individual performance.

- It requires a management style that is open and honest and encourages two-way communication between supervisors and subordinates.

- It requires continuous feedback.

- Feedback loops enable the experiences and knowledge gained on the job by individuals to modify corporate objectives.

- It measures and assesses all performance against jointly agreed goals.

- It should apply to all staff; and it is not primarily concerned with linking performance to financial reward.

 ACTIVITY 11.1

Think about what you have just read. Do you think you now know what performance management is? Could you paraphrase one of the definitions?

WHAT IS PERFORMANCE?

Before taking this discussion any further, it is as well to clarify what is meant by the word 'performance'. It is one of those words that one would think hardly needs to be defined since we all somehow think we know what it means. In organisational terms it seems to be difficult to define without mentioning *measurement*, which, of course, introduces the subject of *performance appraisal*.

PERFORMANCE AS BEHAVIOUR

In fact, performance is behaviour and it is not anything else, because when you perform – you are doing something – you are behaving. It may be the cause of an outcome, but it is not the outcome itself. In the organisational context, therefore, performance is about doing the job. Actors perform and, as in the workplace, some perform better than others, and some perform brilliantly in one role and not so brilliantly in another.

 KEY CONCEPT: THE PEOPLE AND PERFORMANCE LINK

Purcell et al (2003), in their study *Understanding the People and Performance Link: Unlocking the black box*, suggested that performance is a function of ability, motivation and opportunity. Discretionary behaviour (the willingness to 'go the extra mile') happens when capable people are motivated to work hard and are also given the opportunity to do so.

You can, therefore, talk about the level and the quality of performance, and clearly an individual can only do a job if they possess the necessary knowledge and skills. However, the fact that a person possesses knowledge and skills does not guarantee that they will use them to the organisation's advantage; people have to be motivated. People only ever do what they are motivated to do.

 The influence of motivation

CASE EXAMPLE

Two people are doing exactly similar work and both are equally competent, yet one of them is putting in a better performance than the other. Since you know that neither one is better than the other at doing the job, you have to ask yourself, what could be the cause of the difference in performance?

The only possible answer is a difference in their motivation. Perhaps the poorer performer is unwell or distracted by a personal problem, in which case they are motivated to focus on that rather than on the job. Alternatively, they might not like doing the job.

FACTORS INFLUENCING PERFORMANCE

Appointing the right people in the first place is important – remember: 'recruit for attitude, train for skill' – but once good staff have been appointed, we need to make sure that they are motivated to perform and that they have the opportunity and support they need to perform well.

Table 11.1 Organisational factors influencing motivation

Factor	Effect
Training and development	Raises morale and brings about feelings of competence, visible changes in the employee's behaviour and tangible benefits in terms of performance improvement. An important outcome of training is that it increases the versatility of the employee; multi-skilling and sharing complex tasks inspires confidence and mutual respect.
Employee relations	Sound and fair policies and procedures sustain an individual's motivation to work. Since the 1980s, an appreciation of the mutual interest that managers and employees have in the survival and enrichment of the organisation has had a motivating effect.
Reward	This plays a vital role in work motivation. Reward in the financial sense is seen by employees as a return on the investment of their time, skills and efforts. If, therefore, they see reward as fair and reasonable, they will continue to be motivated to work.
Leadership style	Many employees still see themselves as 'working for', rather than 'working with', their managers. The style with which managers communicate with their staff, therefore, has a significant effect on the effort that the employee is prepared to put in *for the manager!*

The motivation to perform, however, is influenced by many factors, some of which are organisational, while others are related to the individual's attitudes and other personality factors.

Organisational factors relate to the work environment, such as the state of the employee relationship, the leadership and communication style of the managers and the general organisational culture (see Table 11.1).

Table 11.1 shows the main organisational factors that influence motivation, and as one would expect, the same factors also influence morale. Morale, however, is a *group* phenomenon, whereas motivation is an *individual* phenomenon. Culture, for example, which is an organisational factor, may be benign or hostile and may raise or lower the morale of the employees as a group, whereas *personality factors* may relate to the individual's attitude to work, the job itself and the organisation.

All individuals are different from each other in terms of their attitudes towards things, their likes and dislikes and so forth. When you make an offer of a job to someone, you usually do so on the grounds that they closely match the requirements of the job as written up in the person specification. When they come into work, however, it is not just the qualities you want that turn up: it is the whole person, complete with hang-ups, preferences, prejudices, personal values, needs and expectations. Remember, however, that appropriate psychological testing will help to indicate these factors before the person is employed.

MOTIVATION

While there is no universal definition of motivation, it is generally accepted to be 'the willingness to apply one's efforts towards the achievement of a goal that satisfies an individual need'. It is a natural human response to a stimulus. The response involves action designed to satisfy a need or attain a particular goal.

Work motivation is 'the willingness to apply one's efforts towards the achievement of the organisation's goals, while concurrently an individual need is satisfied'.

The main interest of managers is to achieve their objectives by maximising their resources, including human resources. Their goal, therefore, is to elicit a performance from their staff that will lead to the achievement of their objectives. To reach that goal, managers often look for clues in motivation theories, on the grounds that 'a motivated workforce is a high-performing workforce'. As we saw above, Purcell et al's research (2003) might support this, as they suggest that performance is a function of ability, motivation and opportunity. The manager's aim, therefore, should be to change employees' motivations from what they are, to what the manager wishes them to be.

SCIENTIFIC MANAGEMENT

It is more than 100 years since academic interest in the human side of industry was stimulated by Frederick Winslow Taylor, a US steel engineer, when he worked in Chicago as a management consultant at the Bethlehem Steel Corporation (BSC). It was there that he carried out the work for which he is most well known. While he did not propose a formal theory of motivation, he did devise a practical way of improving the productivity of manual workers, using money as the incentive.

Taylor developed a set of principles that formed the core of a system that was later referred to as *scientific management* (Taylor 1911, 1947). His central principles were:

1 Apply scientific methods to management by using work measurement as a basis for accurate planning and production control.

2 Establish the best work methods: give each worker a clearly defined task.

3 Select, train and instruct subordinates scientifically.

4 Pay people fairly: high pay for successful completion of work.

5 Obtain co-operation between management and men and divide responsibility between them.

Taylor studied the jobs of tough manual labourers, who spent the day loading pig iron on to railway tenders. He studied the capabilities of the human body and the length of time it took to carry out particular tasks. In other words, he invented what we now call *work study*. He then tied the pay of the workers to their performance. Today this is referred to as *payment by results*, or PBR schemes, which are now far more sophisticated. Taylor's development of scientific management is one of the most well-known studies in the history of management thought. He was concerned that industry was afflicted with problems that were rooted mainly in a severe lack of knowledge. 'Management,' he declared, 'is ignorant of what men can produce … and they make no effort to find out or even define what a day's work is.' The workers took it for granted that there would be delays, 'down time' and other problems because they did not realise that there might be a better way of doing things; nor did they know how to improve their performance because they had not been shown.

Taylor's aim was to remove the guesswork from management and replace it with facts. He showed the men how to use their physiques to the best effect to increase their productivity, and he motivated them to do this by tying their pay to their performance.

PAUSE FOR THOUGHT

Reflect on your organisation, or one with which you are familiar. Do you think Taylor's principles apply today?

It was Taylor's belief that people worked to obtain financial rewards rather than because they were interested in what they were doing. His main objective was to increase productivity, and it seemed logical to him to simply show the workers how they might increase their rewards: 'The more you produce, the more you will earn.' The notion that the labourers with whom he dealt would benefit psychologically from job satisfaction and involvement probably did not occur to him. Taylor's philosophy was that money was the motivator.

PAUSE FOR THOUGHT

Is money a motivator? Consider your own situation. Would you still go to work if you were paid less? Does money actually make you work harder? What about voluntary work? What makes people work in that situation – where they are not paid?

THEORIES OF MOTIVATION

Two main approaches to motivation were proposed in the twentieth century. The first is based on *content theories*, in which people are said to have basic needs that provide the motive for their actions (that is, *what* actually motivates them). Second are *process theories*, which explain the cognitive (or mental) processes whereby people make decisions on how to act (that is, *how* people decide on what to do). This is based on our experience, which has taught us that certain behaviours produce particular outcomes and we will act in the expectation of achieving desired outcomes. In this way, motivation is generated through a mental process, rather than as a response to particular job factors.

CONTENT THEORIES OF MOTIVATION

By far the most well known of these theorists was Abraham Maslow (1954, 1972). He proposed a *theory of growth motivation*, in which he classified five human needs and said that we behave in ways that are designed to have those needs met in a particular order of priorities. The classification, which is referred to as a *hierarchy of needs*, is as follows:

1 **Physiological**: these are the basic biological needs that lead to our survival. Human beings are born with primitive emotions that are aroused when the body needs something and we respond by behaving in ways that are designed to reduce the emotions, thus:

Emotion	*Motivated behaviour*
• thirst	• drinking
• hunger	• eating
• fear	• escaping or confronting
• fatigue	• resting/sleeping
• sex	• ensure survival of species

2 **Safety and security**: the need for a danger-free, non-threatening and secure environment.

3 **Belongingness**: the need to feel part of humanity; attached to other individuals and groups.

4 **Love and esteem**: the need to know where we stand with our relationships with others; how we are seen in terms of respect, especially by those whom we ourselves value.

5 **Self-actualisation**: the need to be self-fulfilled by developing our capacities and expressing them through our behaviour.

Maslow maintained that we progress through the hierarchy so that when we are sure that our physiological needs are or will be met, we will move up and turn our attention to safety and security. Next we turn to love and esteem needs and so on until we reach self-actualisation. He further classified the first, second and third levels as *lower-order needs* and the fourth and fifth as *higher-order needs*.

Other motivation analysts have proposed content theories similar to that of Maslow: for example Clayton P. Alderfer, whose research and publications took place between the 1940s and 1980s.

ERG THEORY

Alderfer (1972) proposed three categories of need that were a kind of contraction of Maslow's classification. Essentially, what he did was to draw a parallel between Maslow's five categories and three categories of his own, which he referred to as *existence*, *relatedness* and *growth*.

Existence needs are concerned with physiological, safety and security needs and cover all needs of a material nature that are necessary for human survival. *Relatedness* needs mean those for love, esteem and belongingness, while *growth* needs are represented by achievement, recognition and the realisation of potential: what Maslow called self-actualisation.

MOTIVATION–HYGIENE THEORY: F.W. HERZBERG ET AL

Herzberg (Herzberg et al 1957) was principally interested in job satisfaction. He wanted to know which job factors created feelings of satisfaction within employees and which created dissatisfaction. The subjects of his research were asked to recall things that had happened at work that produced feelings of satisfaction and dissatisfaction. Herzberg labelled the factors that produced satisfaction as *motivators* and those that produced dissatisfaction as *hygiene factors*. He thought that even if the hygiene factors were satisfied, it wouldn't necessarily make people motivated – it would just reduce their dissatisfaction. If we want people to be motivated to work harder, then we need to ensure that the 'motivators' are in place.

The most frequently occurring *motivators* were:

- achievement
- recognition
- the work itself
- responsibility
- advancement.

The most frequently occurring *hygiene* factors were:

- company policy and administration
- supervision – the technical aspects
- salary
- interpersonal relations – supervision
- working conditions.

PAUSE FOR THOUGHT

Having thought earlier about whether money motivates you, think now about what else might motivate you at work. Do you identify with any of Herzberg's factors?

EXTRINSIC JOB FACTORS

Extrinsic job factors might be described as those things that are not a part of the job itself, but that do impact on the job. Extrinsic job factors might be listed as:

- company policy
- health and safety
- managerial style
- working time
- culture
- holiday entitlement
- peer relationships
- pension scheme.

Note that none of the above factors is a *central feature of the job itself.*

INTRINSIC JOB FACTORS

Intrinsic job factors relate to things that actually make up the job, for example the tasks, the responsibilities of the job. They are an integral part of the job.

Table 11.2 Intrinsic job factors

Authority	The right amount for what I do and for the position of the job in the organisation/department
Responsibility	For my own productivity and quality of my work
Autonomy	Freedom to be a 'self-starter'; to make decisions about how the job might be carried out
Variety	The opportunity to exercise a variety of skills, removing boredom from the job
Recognition	For the quality of my work and general performance standard

PAUSE FOR THOUGHT

Some organisations try to appoint good staff and then fit the job around the person, instead of matching the person to a specific job description. Do you think this would work in your organisation? How feasible do you think it might be?

Herzberg believed that it was important to improve the intrinsic job factors to motivate people. He suggested using job rotation and job enrichment to make the work more interesting and thus increase workers' motivation and performance.

THEORY X AND THEORY Y

McGregor (1960) claimed that managers may have a view of their staff that may affect how they treat them. Managers who have a *Theory X* viewpoint see the individual as having an inherent dislike of work, lazy and who will avoid work whenever possible. Continuous prodding, coercion and even threats are needed to get this kind of person to work. Managers who are authoritarian by nature tend to treat people in that way.

Managers who adopt a *Theory Y* view believe workers do not need to be coerced or threatened. They see workers as being self-motivated, willing to do their best and who can be trusted to work hard.

In other words, it is said that there are 'Theory X managers' and 'Theory Y managers'. A manager's attitude to their workers may thus influence how they treat them and this, of course, may impact on workers' motivation.

CRITICISMS OF NEED-BASED/CONTENT THEORIES

There are criticisms of these theories. In the case of Maslow, for example, the structured progression through the lower-order to higher-order needs seems not to occur for many people. Research has shown (Rauschenberger et al 1980) that a significant number are happy to accept the satisfactions provided by the lower-order needs. People need to fulfil themselves, yes, but in many cases that fulfilment is achieved by pursuing interests outside the workplace. There is also criticism that little evidence supports its strict hierarchy; people may find that social needs, for instance, are more important than physiological needs – especially in some cultures (Adler 1986, pp128–9). And often we don't address only one need at a time.

PAUSE FOR THOUGHT

What is your opinion of the theories mentioned above? Do you know managers who have a 'Theory X' viewpoint? What is your own view? Consider Maslow's theory – does your experience of workers' motivation fit in with this?

PROCESS THEORIES OF MOTIVATION: EXPECTANCY THEORY

This theory was first proposed by Vroom (1964) and is based on the idea that as we develop we come to understand that our behaviour has consequences. We do things because we believe they will lead to outcomes we want.

Expectancy theory has three components:

- expectancy
- instrumentality
- valence.

We therefore choose to take a course of action based on the 'expectancy' (what we think the outcome will be), the 'instrumentality' (whether we think our actions will *actually lead to* the outcome) and the 'valence' (how much we really *value* the results of the outcome). If there is no valence, you won't be motivated, because you are not interested in achieving the outcome – you have no desire for it (for example, if you were offered more money but you are already rich, you may not want to work more hours in overtime). If you think that whatever you do towards the goal, it won't actually help you to achieve it, then your efforts have no 'instrumentality' – your hard work is not instrumental in gaining the outcome.

PORTER AND LAWLER'S EXPECTANCY THEORY

Porter and Lawler (1968) further develop Vroom's ideas, indicating that it is in fact performance that produces satisfaction. They point out that effort alone is not enough to produce a good performance; the individual has to be equipped with the right knowledge and skills too – that their efforts will lead to the outcome and that the outcome is actually achievable and likely. They say that while there is a relationship between motivation, satisfaction and performance, all three are discrete variables, and that the *levels* of motivation, satisfaction and performance are determined by the individual's perception of the outcomes.

If you feel that you have put in a lot of effort at work, but you do not possess the right skills to do the job, then it is unlikely that you will achieve the outcome or required performance, that is, you may try really hard, but have not been trained to do the job properly – so you will not be able to perform well.

It may be that you *do* have the right skills to do the job, and you also put in the effort, but there may be other factors outside your control that stop you achieving the required performance (for example lack of management support, lack of help from other colleagues). In this situation the fact that you are working hard towards a desired outcome will not be instrumental in achieving the desired outcomes. This might then affect your motivation – however hard you work, you will still not achieve success – this can be a real demotivator.

EQUITY THEORY

This process theory (Adams 1961) is based on the concept of fairness or, more accurately, a *fair exchange*. We know that people expect certain outcomes from their behaviour, but what is their perception of those outcomes in terms of value? In the work situation, for example, how does the value of the worker's input compare with the value of the related outcome: for example, 'a fair day's work for a fair day's pay'? This is a question of *perceived* value. Individuals might ask themselves: is the reward worth the effort I put in, compared with that of others? This might arise when two people are doing what they perceive to be similar work but one gets paid less than the other. Of course, if this really was the case, and one person is male and the other female, there could be a case for an equal pay claim.

Adams' central theme is that it is the quest for perceived equity that motivates the work effort:

- Where reward values are perceived to exceed input values, the work effort will increase because of feelings of guilt or inadequacy. This may be the case where we feel that because we receive a very good salary, we should work harder (or, as is often the case, long hours!) to earn it.

- Where the input values are perceived to exceed the reward values, the work effort will decrease in an attempt to redress the balance. So, if we think we are working harder than our colleagues, but still being paid the same, then we might not work as hard in future.

It is likely, however, that the individual's perception of fairness, or a *fair exchange*, in the above respects will influence their *behaviour* rather than exclusively the work effort. An alternative to feelings of guilt or inadequacy, for example, could be fear – especially where the perceived value of the reward is considerably greater than the value of the worker's input. The worker may decide to look busy, as if they are overloaded with work, without actually putting in any extra effort.

Where the value of the work is perceived to be greater than the reward, rather than decrease the work effort, the individual might constantly feel aggrieved (perhaps that others are 'getting away with less work') and feel that they are a martyr.

CASE EXAMPLE

Relative values

Gerry Reed, a labourer, was working on one of two office blocks that were being erected by different contracting firms on opposite sides of a road in a new out-of-town business park. One day, Gerry had just started to have his lunch when he looked across the road and saw that his cousin Pete, also a builder's labourer and a near neighbour, was working on the building opposite, so Gerry went across to see him and they had their lunch together. After exchanging the normal greetings, the conversation turned to pay, and Gerry discovered that Pete was earning £1.50 an hour more than he was for doing similar work.

During the rest of the building programme, Gerry and Pete saw each other across the road and they smiled and waved to each other, but did not engage in conversation; nor did Gerry walk across to have lunch with Pete. Instead, Gerry preferred to stay on his site and have lunch with his workmates, all of whom were on the same pay as he was.

Question: Considering the ideas within the content and process theories discussed above, which theoretical ideas do you think most closely match Gerry's behaviour? What other actions do these theories suggest Gerry might take?

SUMMARY OF MOTIVATION THEORIES

Content theorists stress the importance of environmental and in-job factors and say that employees are more or less motivated by the presence or absence of desired factors. Process theorists, on the other hand, say that people *choose* to behave in particular ways because they expect to achieve desired outcomes. It is a *mental process* that motivates us towards a particular course of behaviour, and we speculate or predict the outcomes before we act. It is important for managers and HR practitioners to have a sound understanding of what motivates people to work. Motivation leads to performance, and the degree to which a knowledgeable and skilled individual will apply their best efforts to a task is determined by the degree to which they are motivated.

Despite the criticisms of content theories, there is no doubt that most employees are motivated by such extrinsic rewards as money, friendly relationships with workplace peers and a managerial attitude that offers recognition, respect and consideration. It is also true that when people are faced with a number of alternative courses of action that might lead to the achievement of their desired outcomes, they go through the mental process of choosing the most appropriate behaviour.

Additionally, it is important to bear in mind the element of individual differences. People have their own unique attitudes to work, the job and the organisation, and they are not all turned on by the same motivators or possible types of outcome.

PERFORMANCE ASSESSMENT SYSTEMS

First, this section discusses and critically reviews the traditional approaches to managing individual performance that are still widely used in the UK. Following that we shall move on to discuss modern approaches.

Performance management activities are designed to assess and improve employees' performance. How the activities are carried out has undergone considerable review since the 1980s, when HRM drew attention to the importance of performance as a means of achieving a competitive advantage. Some organisations, however, have either ignored or only partially adopted the principles and practices of HRM, and in UK industry today there are a variety of assessment systems.

REWARD AND POTENTIAL

Many organisations use systems that include mechanisms for calculating, on the basis of the person's performance, the amount of pay they should receive in future and the individual's suitability for promotion. Systems of this nature often involve the use of complex calculating mechanisms designed to culminate in 'grading' the appraisee. How they are treated thereafter in terms of pay and promotion prospects depends upon the level of the grading given. Clearly, such systems should be fair and assessment should be based on valid evidence.

APPRAISAL

Appraisals may or may not be linked to pay. If they are, then it is usual for performance to be rated and assessed against standards set previously. Has the person achieved the targets set, and can this be linked in to their incentive bonus, or salary rise?

But Armstrong and Baron's survey (2005) showed that many appraisals are carried out mainly with development in mind, rather than as a means for assessing past performance to pay a salary or bonus.

The results of performance appraisal may be used for a variety of purposes. In addition to those mentioned above, they may be any of the following:

- to reinforce performance standards
- to agree future standards
- to motivate the appraisee
- to identify training needs
- to address any problems the appraisee has encountered
- to assist in writing and progressing the individual's personal development plan.

ESTABLISHING ASSESSMENT CRITERIA

Regardless of the approach that is used, the criteria against which assessments are to be made have to be clear to the person carrying out the appraisal and to the appraisee. The key factors that are identified through job analysis are used as criteria, and the performance requirement in terms of standards is set when the job is first described.

The job tasks are analysed and rating scales set against each one. The factors on the list may include such job-related features as the knowledge and skill requirements, competences required for the job – for example leadership, teamwork, and so on – and perhaps several personal qualities such as initiative, intelligence, social skills, and so on, depending on the nature of the job and its requirements. Employees are then rated on the degree to which they possess these factors.

TRADITIONAL SYSTEMS

There are several approaches within the traditional models of performance appraisal, but the one that is familiar to most managers and employees involves the manager in an annual interview with each individual employee to carry out a review of the employee's performance. The stages involved in this model are as follows:

1 About two weeks prior to the interview, the employee is given a *self-assessment form* that is designed to give the employee a measured way of assessing the key points in the job. The underlying idea is that the questions on the form will focus the employee's attention on to the various features of the job, and cause them to try to make an objective assessment of their own performance.

2 The manager also has a form that they complete in advance of the interview. It is important that the manager assesses the employee in the light of valid and verifiable information. The manager will rate the employee against the criteria.

3 The two then get together to reach agreement over the degree to which the employee has met the required standards and targets.

RATING SCALES

There are a number of ways of rating people. We can use numbers: from 1 to 5, where 1 rates as 'poor' and 5 is 'excellent'. Or we can use words to rate them, such as 'poor', 'fair', 'good', 'very good', 'excellent'. Or even 'low', 'average', 'high'. Some may use a Likert scale, where statements are made, such as 'the employee works hard', to which the response is '1 – strongly agree', '2 – agree', '3 – neither agree nor disagree', '4 – disagree' or '5 – strongly disagree'. The drawback with ratings such as these is that it is very subjective. And not very scientific – what one person rates as 'very good', may be seen by someone else as merely 'good'. Bias can creep in too, where personality clashes can impact on the rating. If you and your manager don't see eye to eye, then this will have an effect on your rating.

If the appraisal rating is related to your salary increase or bonus, this can be of serious concern.

BEHAVIOURALLY ANCHORED RATING SCALES (BARS)

This is more recent than any of the other traditional models and it differs from them in that it attempts to measure performance in terms of behaviour. This is what the individual actually does, rather than the person's capabilities or other qualities, although personal qualities such as initiative are deduced from what the individual actually achieves. Scales for this model are devised after discussion, observation of behaviour and analysis, usually by managers, HR practitioners and sometimes external consultants. Job analysis is critical to this process, since the first objective is to identify the key categories of performance in each job or *job family*.

With BARS, it is usual to have statements relating to performance in the job. For example:

- deals with customers in an expert way, always going beyond the call of duty
- deals with customers in a satisfactory way, so that the customer receives good treatment
- deals with customers in a slapdash way, leaving them barely satisfied
- deals with customers badly, leading to complaints.

There may be a rating scale applied to each statement, in order to add up to a total for each area of work. This process can be quite costly and time-consuming, as statements need to be given for all of the relevant job tasks, and examples of good and poor behaviour found. This can be a tedious process. However, the BARS approach reduces the effect of bias through a consensus, since several people establish the performance criteria. It can be useful in achieving credibility in that specific behaviours are cited, which can be justified much more easily than just rating someone as 'good' or 'poor'.

Some appraisals will not necessarily rely on a rating system, but will assess the employee against whether they have met targets. So this might lead to a more fruitful discussion on performance, where employees do not feel they are being rated, but are merely discussing what they have (or have not) achieved. This can be less confrontational and therefore more productive.

CRITICISMS OF APPRAISAL SYSTEMS

It has to be borne in mind that all appraisal systems are susceptible to subjectivity on the part of the manager and the employee. As we saw above, when discussing rating scales, bias is often inherent in the appraisal system. It is very difficult to appraise someone totally objectively.

On the question of subjectivity, Ian Roberts (2001) says that 'the inherent subjectivity of the assessment process may lead to claims of favouritism, bias and arbitrariness'.

A further problem is indifference or lack of interest, in which the process becomes a kind of form-filling exercise: an annual ritual in which the manager and the employee meet primarily to complete the forms, which end up gathering dust in a cabinet in the 'HR office'. If nothing comes out of the appraisal then people soon lose interest in its credibility and pay no attention to it. If, during the appraisal, an employee asks for training in a new area, and it is agreed, but then this does not happen, the employee will become disillusioned with the whole process.

There is also the danger that managers underestimate the importance of the role of appraisals in motivating staff and thus improving their performance. They see it as too time-consuming, instead of acknowledging the benefits of talking to their staff about their jobs. Appraisal should be a tool of good management.

MORE RECENT APPROACHES

Since the 1980s the attitudes of many organisations to people management have changed. In organisations that have adopted the principles and practices of HRM, with its lean and flattened structures, the manager and the employee have a close working relationship. The old-fashioned 'boss–subordinate' relationship has been replaced by what is more like a working partnership.

PERFORMANCE AGREEMENT AND PERSONAL DEVELOPMENT PLANS

In the situation described above, it is easier for the manager and the employee to reach agreement over the performance requirements and the job's key result areas. This can be turned into a *performance agreement*. The agreement, therefore, is based on the assumption that the employee is clearly aware of what is expected in terms of performance and of how their performance will be assessed. This may then be linked in to the employee's personal development plan (PDP), which outlines what skills need to be developed and how this might be achieved. Training plans, time off and financial assistance for courses or qualifications, or acquiring a mentor, may all be part of the support the employee needs.

360-DEGREE FEEDBACK

This is a comparatively recent development that has grown in popularity and is used for development purposes as well as for performance appraisal. What happens is that the people with whom the individual has day-to-day contact provide measures of their performance by completing a questionnaire that includes a rating scale designed to measure competences. Their data is fed into the process to be collated.

These may include, for example, the person's immediate boss, peers such as team colleagues and individuals, internal and external customers and suppliers, other work colleagues and subordinates. Clearly, in advance of the formal assessment, the manager and the employee already possess much of the criteria-related information that will be used, but it is equally clear that the manager will not always be present when the employee encounters others in the course of the job.

Figure 11.1 A model of 360-degree feedback

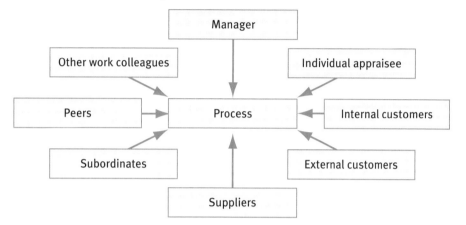

In Figure 11.1, you can see that all of the stakeholders feed their assessment data into the process. This shows the range of possibilities of who may be involved in the process.

Use of the outcomes

360-degree feedback is a versatile model, serving the purposes of the organisation and the individual. Organisations use it primarily for appraisal, but also for career management and resourcing purposes (Handy et al 1996). The outcomes are also used for decisions on promotion and pay.

However, the advantage is that there is less chance of bias and it is seen as being a fairer means of assessment. There could still be a danger of responses being untruthful – how do you choose who to ask to complete the appraisal? Would employees only choose those who are likely to give them a good rating?

It is quite a cumbersome process and is very time-consuming, which also means it is more costly.

THE PERFORMANCE APPRAISAL INTERVIEW

While in modern terms managers and employees work closely, a tradition has been established in which the normal practice is to hold an annual review of each employee's performance. Generally, the purposes are to:

- review the employee's performance over the past appraisal period

- identify training/counselling needs when discussing shortfalls in performance and future development
- motivate the individual and set and agree future objectives and performance standards
- agree arrangements for future development and, in particular, discuss and exchange ideas about the employee's personal development plan.

PAUSE FOR THOUGHT

How would you feel if, after taking so much trouble, you entered the interview room to find that the manager was short of time, rushing through the forms and – the most crushing factor – appears to be thinking about something else when you are talking? How can we make sure this doesn't happen – which all too often is the case?

Preparation

Particular attention should be paid to the venue. It should be held where both parties can be certain they will not be disturbed (for example, in a quiet room where there is no telephone or other distraction). The review itself should be planned well in advance, and an appropriate amount of time reserved for it. All of the relevant documentation and information should be studied, and any static information already entered on the forms. This heads off the need for copious notes to be made during the interview so that both parties can pay full attention to each other.

Outcomes to aim for

At the end of the interview, the employee should leave the room:

- believing that the manager is aware of their total job situation
- knowing exactly what lies ahead in terms of the standards and objectives to be achieved and that they are attainable
- being aware of any training that will be provided to help them achieve the objectives and to fill in any gaps in knowledge or skills
- with a general feeling that the perceptions, decisions and agreed action were fair and reasonable
- motivated to perform well.

Interviewing style

The interview has been defined as a conversation with a purpose. The purpose here is to exchange views and information about the employee's performance. Clearly, the manager is running the interview, but they should allow the employee equal participation. As we saw in the chapter on selection, interview technique is important and it is important to remain as unbiased and open as possible.

MANAGING POOR PERFORMANCE

It is important to see the benefits of appraisal as a means of encouraging better performance and as a tool for motivation. However, there may be times when the employee's performance is poor and the manager will need to have a conversation with them that addresses that performance: instruction should be given in very straightforward terms about how they must improve. This, of course, can be difficult – none of us like having to give negative feedback. It is much easier to be able to tell an employee that they are doing well and to give praise than to tell them that they are not doing as well as is expected.

In this case, it can be useful to ask the employee to say which areas they think they are not performing well in – often the employee will be aware of their own weaker areas and will voice their concerns. It is far easier to pursue this if the employee raises it first. Being told that they are not doing well can lead to the employee becoming defensive and can turn the whole appraisal process into a negative experience and one that can be a real demotivator. Be careful, however, not to turn the appraisal interview into a 'disciplinary interview'. If there are serious issues relating to performance (incapability, irresponsible behaviour, being late for work, and so on), these should be addressed at a separate disciplinary interview and not in the appraisal.

 ACTIVITY 11.2

It has been said that 'performance appraisal looks like a good idea on paper but seldom works well in practice'. Do you think there is any truth in this statement? If you do think so, why?

PERSONAL DEVELOPMENT PLAN (PDP)

As we saw earlier, one of the main focuses of performance management is development and part of the appraisal process is to elicit a personal development plan (PDP). Personal development planning (PDP) can be seen as an essential component of performance management, and the CIPD encourages its members to develop themselves and take responsibility for their own continuing professional development (CPD).

 PAUSE FOR THOUGHT

Does everyone need to be a high flyer? What do we do about those people who just want to come to work and do their job, without wishing to be developed or get promoted? Should we let them just do their job?

> ⚷ **KEY CONCEPT:** PERSONAL DEVELOPMENT
> PLANNING
>
> Personal development planning is a dynamic process. The plan itself is a draft describing how
> you propose to learn and develop yourself and your achievements to date. You need the active
> co-operation of your line manager or an HR practitioner to guide you through the process,
> although you are responsible for your own further development.

WHO BENEFITS FROM PDP?

There are two main considerations in PDP. First, the organisation needs you to develop yourself to enhance your performance. Second, there are your own needs in terms of career development. You develop transferable competences, increase your repertoire of knowledge and skills, and thereby enhance your flexibility and employability. These considerations are not mutually exclusive, since you may centre your planning on your current job. You can achieve these aims concurrently by:

- identifying your developmental needs and setting learning objectives
- costing and time-scaling your plan (most employers will underwrite this)
- using a wide range of developmental methods
- making yourself aware of your own learning style and using it to advantage
- identifying suitable sources of relevant information and practical support
- maintaining a comprehensive record of your current and future development.

A PDP is made up of your past, present and future learning. First, this involves reflecting upon your past and current experiences and writing down what you have learned from them. Second, clarify your current position by reviewing and recording the competences you now possess. Third, you can then identify the point at which your future planning commences and have some ideas about what things might be part of your future development. This might include attending a course, researching a particular subject, improving a skill or gaining a qualification. For example, at the end of a course such as the Certificate in HR Practice, you may decide you want to continue with further CIPD qualifications to enhance your career prospects – this could go into your plan for the future.

LEARNING ACTIVITIES

You cannot go through a day without learning something:

- all of your experiences of listening to what others have to say
- observing what they do and how they do it
- solving problems at work and at home or in your local community
- helping others to develop by coaching them
- reading good-quality material and watching TV documentaries.

Traditionally, many people initially turn to training courses to develop themselves and, undoubtedly, if you are motivated to learn and careful about your choice of course in terms of its relevance to your needs, your knowledge and competences will increase. There are, however, several additional learning sources:

- **E-learning (electronic learning)**: information technology makes it possible for you to learn sitting at the computer.

- **Project and assignment work**: this is learning from experience. Usually it involves problem-solving and training. You have to learn to complete the work satisfactorily.

- **Learning from others**: see how other people go about their work. You need to find those people who are generally regarded as being good at what they do. Talk to them and find out why they do things in the way they do.

- **Studying job descriptions and role definitions**: choose more senior-level jobs or jobs that you aspire to. Study them to identify the knowledge and competences that are required to do the work.

SELF-APPRAISAL

As you make progress, write down the details of your development and review your situation intermittently. This involves studying and updating your plan, noting your recent learning and deciding on the best way forward. A good time to do this is immediately after your appraisal interview at work, when you have all of your manager's comments to hand along with the suggestions they have made for your future development.

 ACTIVITY 11.3

In your organisation, or one with which you are familiar, analyse the performance appraisal system with a view to updating and improving it. Prepare yourself to answer questions on why your proposed changes would improve the system.

SUMMARY

We have looked at the differences between performance, performance management and performance appraisal.

Performance management is wide-ranging and can involve such things as managing absence or handling disciplinary issues, but from a more positive viewpoint it is about improving performance – most commonly by the use of appraisal interviews. This may mean looking at past performance or setting targets for the future. To improve performance, employees need to be motivated to work harder or more effectively and, with this in mind, the chapter has discussed a number of motivation theories.

The appraisal interview has its critics and, to be effective, it needs to be executed professionally and with care. If the appraisal uses a rating system, there is a danger that bias may creep in and the process may be discredited, leading to disenchanted and demoralised staff. Carried out correctly, performance appraisal can be a useful tool in motivating staff and improving the performance of individuals and, consequently, of the business. One way of reducing the effects of bias is to use 360-degree appraisals, though these are costly and time-consuming to do.

A major way of improving performance is to undertake training and development and this should be a key focus of appraisal. Appraisal should be about agreeing joint objectives, with support given to help an employee to develop their skills and abilities, to enable them to perform more effectively. One way of doing this is to write a personal development plan as a result of the appraisal, which summarises the learning required to achieve the objectives set.

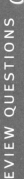

REVIEW QUESTIONS

1 How would you define performance management?

2 What is performance?

3 What factors influence performance?

4 How would you differentiate between *intrinsic* and *extrinsic* job factors?

5 Do you think McGregor's X–Y theory describes managers' attitudes that you know?

6 Why is it important to assess employees' performance?

7 How might the organisation use the outcomes of 360-degree feedback?

8 What criticism can be made of appraisals?

9 How would you define personal development planning?

10 Who benefits from personal development planning and in what ways?

EXPLORE FURTHER

BOOKS

ARMSTRONG, M. and BARON, A. (2004) *Managing performance: performance management in action*. London: Chartered Institute of Personnel and Development.

This is a major text on the subject.

ARMSTRONG. M. (2009) *Handbook of performance management: an evidence-based guide to delivering high performance*. London: Kogan Page.

This is a more recent text that covers the entire subject of performance management in some depth.

CHAPTER 12

Employee Reward

LEARNING OBJECTIVES

After studying this chapter you should:

- be able to describe the concept of employee reward
- understand how reward is managed, in terms of the organisation's reward policies, systems and procedures
- be able to explain what is meant by non-financial rewards
- be able to advise on suitable payment systems and make meaningful contributions to their development and implementation
- be able to identify key legislation that has impacted upon how people are rewarded.

INTRODUCTION

This chapter introduces the concept of reward, including payment and non-cash rewards. Payment is seen as a component of the 'exchange' element of a contract (consideration); here it is also seen as a motivator and as an indication of how employees are valued by the organisation in terms of their contribution to the achievement of objectives.

The concepts of *incentive* and *equity* systems of payment are explained, including job evaluation, payment by results, performance-related pay and non-cash rewards. Reward also has strong implications for equal treatment, and the discussion here explains this in legal and business terms.

The chapter includes explanations of the management philosophies, strategies and policies that lead to the choice and development of reward systems, and an examination of the factors that determine pay levels. The discussion also includes new and traditional systems of payment.

PERCEPTIONS OF REWARD

The terms *reward* and *reward management* are relative newcomers to the managerial vocabulary. Before the 1980s, references were made to 'money', 'pay' and 'systems of payment', and today the word 'reward' is often used to refer to payment.

DEFINING REWARD

It is not possible to define reward in a single statement because perceptions of it vary from one person to another and from one situation to another. A manager, for example, might define reward as 'the payment that an employee receives in accordance with the value of his or her work contribution to the organisation'. An employee, on the other hand, may say that it is 'the return that he or she receives on the investment of his or her time, knowledge, skills, loyalty and commitment'. Non-financial factors such as the benefits and facilities that the organisation offers to its employees are also regarded as reward, as are recognition, praise and career development.

In fact, reward literally means something that is given or received in return for a service or for merit, and it is often financial. Where we refer to reward, in the United States the word *compensation* is used, but that sounds more like the outcome of a lawsuit than payment for a valued performance. Truly, 'pay' or 'payment' in the forms of wages and salaries are what spring to mind first when one thinks of reward in the organisational context, but since 'reward' entails more than just money, that is the word we will use here as a description. When dealing with the detail, however, we shall call things what they are, such as *wages*, *salaries* and *payment*.

HRM AND REWARD

According to Pointon and Ryan (2004), 'reward management' has often been viewed as the 'poor relation' of HRM, concerned with 'systems, figures and procedures'. On the other hand, organisations that have adopted the principles and practices of HRM say that their reward philosophies are consistent with and act in support of other HRM principles; for example, that they reward a good performance because that adds value to the organisation. The organisation sees its employees as its most important resource, and therefore it invests in that resource through the development of knowledge and skills to enhance employees' performance and thus get a return on its investment (see Chapter 3).

THE NEW PAY

Since 1990, when E.E. Lawler coined the phrase *new pay*, there has been a great deal of activity in industry concerning the fitness of the older and more traditional pay systems to serve the needs of modern organisations.

The managers of such organisations rightly believe that the success of the organisation is ultimately determined by the performance of its employees. It follows, therefore, that it needs to recruit and retain people who are appropriately skilled, flexible in their outlook and who are prepared to become involved in and committed to the purposes of the organisation, and are at one with it in the belief that the achievement of objectives is a good thing, not only for the organisation, but for the employees too. This is the idea of the unitary approach and is rooted in the philosophies of HRM. From this, it follows that the reward systems must support the overall business strategy, indeed that they should flow from it, and that pay should be commensurate with such employees' contributions.

 KEY CONCEPT: THE 'NEW PAY'

The underlying philosophy that follows the principles of HRM brought a fresh strategic approach to reward management. In this approach, reward is firmly linked to actual performance. According to Heery (1996), new pay, which reflects a unitary approach, is often contrasted with 'old pay', which reflects a pluralistic approach in that it (old pay) uses job-evaluated grade structures, payment by time and seniority-based financial rewards and benefits.

New pay is focused on paying for contribution and not paying for time served in the role.

Schuster and Zingheim (1992), who further developed Lawler's concept of the new pay, state that:

> The new pay view provides that organizations effectively use all elements of pay – direct pay (cash compensation) and indirect pay (benefits) – to help them form a partnership between the organization and its employees. By means of this partnership, employees can understand the goals of the organization, know where they fit into those goals, become appropriately involved in decisions affecting them, and receive rewards to the extent they have assisted the organization to do so. New pay helps link the financial success of both the organization and its employees.

NON-FINANCIAL REWARDS

The total range of what might be classified as 'reward' is considerable and may reach beyond the workplace. Few firms provide the complete range, and others prefer to provide only the statutory rights, such as, for example, a healthy and safe work environment and the provision of maternity and paternity rights. There are, however, a range of benefits and facilities that are designed to demonstrate to employees that the organisation values them and is therefore prepared to enhance the quality of their life at work. The 'benefits package' is also provided to match those (benefits) offered by similar organisations and so the concept has strong links to employee retention. Typically a 'benefits package' might include:

- an attractive pension scheme (although in recent years the performance of company pension schemes has persuaded employees to make their own financial arrangements for a reasonable income in retirement). Many final salary pension schemes have been closed to new employees and some are currently being closed, because of financial cost reasons, to existing employees. Information about the prevalence of pension schemes can be found in the CIPD annual survey report on *Reward Management*, which is available from **www.cipd.co.uk/subjects/pay/_rewrdmansurv.htm**

- life insurance
- access to private medical care
- help with long-term sickness
- assistance with family matters, such as bereavement, crèche facilities, help with schooling and transport and supported housing for families who are moved around geographically
- counselling services
- access to occupational support schemes (OSS) and employee assistance programmes (EAP)
- staff restaurant and social and recreational facilities
- preparation for redundancy and retirement
- car parking
- advisory services for contemporary welfare issues, such as HIV/AIDS and sexual health generally; problems with drugs and alcohol and the formulation of policies on smoking in and around the workplace.

 ACTIVITY 12.1

How would you justify introducing a company pension scheme to the board of an organisation when so many 'final salary' schemes have come into disrepute with management because of the ongoing costs to business?

CAFETERIA, OR FLEXIBLE BENEFITS

Some organisations offer a range of benefits from which an employee may choose from a mixture of cash and benefits that are on offer. Organisations, through leverage of size, can get good deals against benefit costs, which they can either offer to employees at no cost or at a substantially reduced cost. In this way this allows employers to offer choices geared to their employees' lifestyle changes, such as marriage, the arrival of children and even divorce. Wherever an employee receives a benefit there can be a tax liability so employers need to consider this carefully before making promises that may be expensive to keep.

Flexible benefits are also associated with the employee value proposition (EVP), in terms of the type of person the organisation wishes to recruit. By getting the reward mix correct then the organisation is more likely to be able to recruit successfully the type of person it seeks. Hutchinson, in a CIPD (2007c) event report, states: 'Flexible benefits, as a concept, gives focus to investments and empowers employees to choose for themselves the benefits that best suit their needs.' As a suggestion the report (p16) advises that employees can '… buy and sell benefits to achieve personal aims'. 'Stand alone' benefits include:

- salary sacrifice schemes that buy enhanced pension benefits, childcare vouchers and so on
- holiday buying and selling plans
- voluntary contributions to buy higher levels of cover for certain benefits
- cycle purchase schemes.

THE TOP BENEFITS GIVEN TO STAFF

According to the 2009 CIPD annual survey report *Reward Management*, the benefits that all respondents to their survey offered their staff were as follows:

- pension plan
- training and development
- 25 days or more paid leave (note the statutory minimum holiday is 28 days, but this can include statutory holidays)
- tea/coffee/cold drinks
- Christmas lunch or party
- on-site car parking
- childcare vouchers
- life assurance
- eyecare vouchers
- enhanced maternity and paternity leave.

 ACTIVITY 12.2

Given the opportunity to start with a clean sheet, what would you include in a benefits system and why? What criteria would you use to guide you in your decision-making? You may find some help within the CIPD's factsheets on reward benefits.

REWARDS WITH FINANCIAL VALUE

People might receive special rewards, perhaps for performance, such as the successful outcome of a particular project, or for making a useful suggestion or delivering on targets set over the previous year. One of the most important aspects of such rewards, however, is the influence of the element on individual differences. Porter and Lawler (1968), for example, point out that it is just that type of performance that produces job satisfaction, and that where an expected reward stands in different individuals' value systems determines how much they value the expected outcome (reward). The level of values that people place upon rewards therefore differs from one individual to the next.

CASE EXAMPLE

The wrong vintage

Prithpal Chopra was the IT manager of Gray, Green and Blue (GGB), a large firm of solicitors with its head office in Bath and branches throughout the West Country. GGB employed 500 solicitors and some 1,600 managerial and administrative staff. In his spare time Prithpal was a keen collector and renovator of vintage cars, and he was very skilled at restoring them to their former glory. He often used his cars to travel to work, and the staff used to stop to admire them in the company car park; they regarded him as a 'perfectionist'. While he respected the technology that went into modern production-line cars, he did not like their design or the materials that were used in the interior.

The senior partners of GGB offered Prithpal the task of setting up a fully equipped

computerised information service for the managers and specialist solicitors, and they told him that there would be a 'significant reward' for a good job, but they did not tell him the exact nature or value of the reward.

It was clear to Prithpal that the new system was important to GGB and he relished the challenge. It was a long and painstaking job but when it was finally up and running, it was obvious that Prithpal had upheld his reputation as a perfectionist. A special presentation event was organised and took place in the spacious entrance hall of the head office. Imagine how Prithpal must have felt when the senior partners led him to the centre of the hall and proudly unveiled his reward, which was a modern 1800 cc 16-valve saloon car!

FACTORS THAT INFLUENCE REWARD

Reward systems are founded upon the organisation's strategies and policies for compensating employees for their performance, and the investment of their time, knowledge, skills and competence. The rewards employees receive are based on their perceived value of the individual to the organisation, what their skills are worth on the employment market, the nature of the industry and the financial health of the organisation.

The availability of labour rises and falls with the economy, and the intensity of competition for the appropriate staff to fill vacancies fluctuates accordingly. The new millennium brought with it a 'talent war', fuelled by the skill demands of ever-advancing technology and the fierceness of global competition. Obviously, the size and nature of the rewards that are being offered for those who possess the required skills will determine the organisation's ability to compete effectively for staff.

There is always a tension between market forces, the need to pay the 'going rate' for people with particular skills and maintaining internal consistencies in terms of, for example, paying a newcomer to the organisation more than those who are already in employment. Tensions clearly can arise so there is a requirement placed upon the remuneration specialist to maintain a watching brief over the changes that may occur in external remuneration practices. This can be achieved by either joining a 'jobs club' where local employers get together to benchmark jobs in terms of pay and benefits offered, or paying a commercial organisation, such as Towers Watson, to obtain access to their pay and benefits survey data.

The strategy adopted by the organisation should address its need to obtain, retain and motivate committed, competent, experienced and loyal employees.

DETERMINING REWARD STRATEGY

The organisation has to be *financially able* to provide the levels of reward that enable it to compete with other organisations for staff. When formulating reward strategy, therefore, decisions have to be made about how much of the financial resource can be allocated for reward. Such decisions are influenced by the current and expected future profitability of the organisation, the negotiating positions of the relevant parties and the percentage of overall costs that are represented by pay.

The organisation's freedom to formulate reward strategy and set salary and wage rates is constrained by internal and external influences and obligations. The main pressures may be summarised as follows:

- the organisation's values and pay stance
- the organisation's ability to sustain pay levels
- comparisons with what other organisations pay
- national and industry-wide trends
- trade unions'/employees' demands
- current and expected productivity levels
- legislation on pay, for example the minimum wage levels
- UK government and European policies on pay
- changes in technology, the economy and the labour market
- cost of living increases
- the availability of particular skills
- levels of knowledge and competences required
- the evaluation of employee performance
- the relative values of the jobs, as produced by job evaluation.

The reward strategy should support the business strategy. HR strategy is usually derived from the business strategy and the reward strategy flows from the HR strategy. The reward strategy can be very influential in the business because it can influence the ways people work and also whether or not individuals wish to remain with or even work for the organisation. Reward can affect:

- resourcing, attracting and retaining people
- development of employees by linking development to skill or competence-related pay
- the employee relations environment because how reward is seen to be developed and operated affects the climate of trust, fairness and involvement with employees; it is key to the notion of employer branding (Allen 2008)
- the effectiveness of the organisation.

One cannot consider the above in isolation but these factors must be considered within the framework of other HR strategies, policies and procedures.

Key to developing the reward strategy is consideration of the aims and objectives of reward. One could consider that reward is about: encouraging adoption of the organisation's values and required behaviours, ensuring that the workforce is skilled and competent to do its job, supporting the culture of the organisation and, of course, contributing to the competitiveness of the organisation.

 ACTIVITY 12.3

Read the article written by Rebecca Johnson in *People Management* entitled 'E.ON's ahead' (7 February 2008) and discuss what E.ON's HR director considers the aims and objectives of the company's reward strategy to be and how it is supporting the company's objectives.

REWARD SYSTEMS

It is necessary for you to develop an understanding of both traditional and modern reward systems since, at particular times in your career, you may be expected to work effectively with both the old and the new. Also, the point should be made here that although organisations with a modern outlook on reward have introduced 'new pay' systems, some still use traditional systems, and many organisations use both to reward different categories of employee appropriately.

The decline in manufacturing in the UK and the complementary increase in 'service' and sedentary types of work has reduced the demand for some of the traditional pay systems. Now, however, there is a demand for new and innovative pay systems, especially in the light of the need to attract, retain and motivate highly skilled staff, even in times of economic stress.

WAGES AND SALARIES

Before we go any further it is important for you to understand the difference between *wages* and *salaries*. Wages are paid weekly to employees who are paid on an hourly or weekly rate, while employees who are on an annual salary are paid less frequently, usually monthly. It will become clear to you that the older and more traditional pay systems were largely designed to motivate and reward factory-floor wage-earners in manufacturing companies. Basic pay can be paid hourly, weekly, monthly or annually (annualised hours), in other words it is a *time-rated* pay system, based upon a rate for the job. This type of salary reflects both internal and external relativities and may even involve trade unions in the negotiation, as is the case with teachers and university lecturers. The problem with this type of system is that it may not change over time and thus become outdated.

CONTINGENCY PAY

Contingency pay is additional to the basic pay of the employee. This part of the pay is called contingent because it is *at risk* pay and is therefore, in some way, dependent upon performance. It may consist of a mix of the following:

- performance-related pay (dealt with below)
- bonuses
- some form of incentive pay linked to targets
- commission
- service-related pay, which is pay dependent upon how long the individual has been with the organisation
- skill-based pay
- competence-related pay
- career-related pay, which is linked to increased responsibility
- allowances, perhaps for working in harsh conditions or shift-type working.

 KEY CONCEPTS

- *Total earnings* is the sum of basic pay plus additions from variable pay.
- *Total remuneration* includes the above plus benefits and indirect pay.
- *Incentives* aim to motivate – so are future oriented.
- *Rewards* are given for achievement – so are associated with past events.

The following section will deal with some of the elements listed above.

INCENTIVE AND EQUITY PAY SCHEMES

Systems of payment may be *incentive-based* or *equity-based*. Incentive-based schemes are designed to motivate a good performance in terms of the quantity and quality of what is produced. Equity systems, for example stock option-based pay schemes, tend to link reward with the importance and value of the job, as well as to the person actually doing it.

INCENTIVE SYSTEMS OF PAYMENT

It was in the early twentieth century that F.W. Taylor introduced a system of payment that was designed to motivate employees by rewarding their performance fairly. He devised what we now call *work study*, and after calculating how much work a human being could achieve in a particular amount of time, he linked employees' pay to their performance. Pay mechanisms such as these came to be referred to as *payment by results*, or PBR schemes. In organisations where they are now used, such schemes are more sophisticated than those of Taylor, but the basic principle remains the same.

Taylor's main objective was to increase productivity, and it seemed logical to him to simply show the workers how they might increase their rewards: 'the more you produce, the more you will earn'. He claimed that managers were ignorant of what men [sic] could produce, and criticised their lack of effort to find out. He believed that people worked to obtain financial rewards, rather than because they were interested in what they were doing. Clearly, they [the employee] needed a reason to work (in addition to keeping their jobs), and he devised a system of payment by results to provide an attractive incentive.

PAYMENT BY RESULTS SCHEMES

Payment by results schemes are those in which pay is tied to actual performance. The idea of pay being tied to actual performance is illustrated simply by *piecework*. This is where employees, whose job it is to produce a certain number of items daily or weekly, are paid in accordance with an agreed rate per item for the number of items produced. When this kind of system was introduced, almost 100 years ago, it worked in a totally direct fashion (see Figure 12.1).

Figure 12.1 Example of a piecework scheme

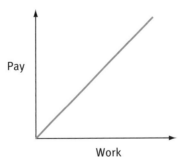

This indicates that if the employee produced very few items, perhaps through being unwell, or being absent through sickness, they would receive very little, or even no, pay. Where this system is still in use it has been modified to provide for a guaranteed basic wage, in which the worker receives at least the minimum wage. Beyond the guaranteed wage level, workers are given targets which, when exceeded, makes them eligible for a piece-rate bonus (see Figure 12.2).

Figure 12.2 Guaranteed wage plus piece-rate bonus

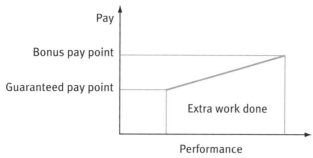

In Figure 12.2, note the angle of the curve beyond the 'guaranteed' point. Through the bargaining process, managers and workers negotiate what they call the steepness or flatness of the scheme. In a 'steep' scheme, as in Figure 12.1, fewer items may be produced to obtain a high bonus, whereas in a 'flat' scheme a greater number of items would have to be produced to achieve the same bonus.

Criticisms of piecework include the idea that it places the productivity effort in the hands of the workers, instead of the managers, and that the 'money-motivated' rush for quantity adversely affects the quality of the product. Also, workers tend, informally, to standardise productivity beyond the guaranteed point, and trouble may arise when the need for productivity reduces. Trouble may occur since in the medium to long term, employees become accustomed to receiving regular weekly piece-rate bonuses, and unconsciously they incorporate the extra cash into their perception of their 'income'. When they are asked to reduce productivity, therefore, the inevitable slimmer pay packet comes as a shock.

Obviously, workers who are paid in this way have an advantage over the support workers, such as clerks and administrators, who have less control over what is in their pay packets. This sometimes creates dissatisfaction among the support workers, and many companies have successfully minimised the discontent by introducing organisation-wide bonus schemes, in which all workers benefit from the profitability produced by their efforts, whether they are classed as 'direct' or 'support' employees.

FIXED INCREMENTAL PAY SCALES

Some organisations, particularly those in the public sector, have fixed incremental pay scales. Within each job there is a scale through which the job-holder may progress in an annual 'step-up' fashion (see Figure 12.3).

In most organisations that use this system, the regular and unquestioned 'step up' has been replaced, so that now managerial discretion, usually based on performance ratings, may be used to reduce or increase the value of each increment.

Figure 12.3 Example of a fixed incremental scale

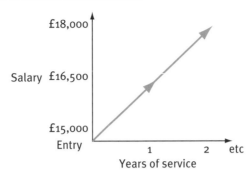

BONUS SCHEME

This is a company-wide scheme in which all employees are rewarded with an annual or biannual bonus on the basis of the organisation's productivity as a whole. The reward is usually a percentage of each person's annual pay. It is important to note that with this kind of scheme the productivity measure that is selected is one that genuinely reflects that the employees exceeded a previously agreed productivity standard over the relevant period. In this way, the amount of bonus paid is directly related to employee performance. The rationale for this kind of scheme is that employees will co-operate with each other and with the managers to achieve as high a bonus as possible.

MEASURED DAYWORK

It was noted above that PBR schemes have been criticised because they place the control of productivity in the hands of the employees. One approach to solving this problem was to introduce measured daywork schemes, which became popular in the 1950s and 1960s when there was a large number of mass production factories in the UK. Armstrong (2004) describes this as a system that fixes employees' pay 'on the understanding that they will maintain a specified level of performance, but pay does not fluctuate in the short term with their performance' (as it would with a piecework scheme). Measured daywork provides an incentive for the employee to perform at a required level. This puts the employee under an obligation to meet that level since the incentive is guaranteed in advance.

TEAM REWARD SCHEME

Reputedly, this is a simple concept but it can be extremely difficult to administer. The idea is that an incentive-based pay system that rewards teams by reinforcing desired behaviour should lead to effective teamwork. Armstrong (2004, p340) suggests that rewarding teams should be defined by a strategic intent and demonstrates three things: (i) that one of the organisation's core values is teamworking, (ii) by clarifying what teams are expected to achieve by relating rewards to the attainment of agreed targets, and (iii) to encourage group effort and co-operation.

For team remuneration systems to work, that is, all of the team members are to share the rewards equally, then the assumption must be that all team members put in an exactly equal contribution to the effort that earned the reward!

PAUSE FOR THOUGHT

Whenever a group or team is formed a leader appears. The leader may be one that is appointed by the organisation (a *formal leader*), or one that has emerged by mutual consent to represent the team (an *informal leader*). Leaders report to the people who put them where they are. A group, therefore, may have two leaders. The question that arises is: which leader decides on the amount of work effort that is *actually put in*, and thereby controls the value of the bonus?

JOB EVALUATION SCHEMES

Why conduct a job evaluation? According to Acas (2008, p4), job evaluation is '... a method of determining on a systematic basis the relative importance of a number of different jobs'. Job evaluation schemes are used as the basis for fair pay systems. With these types of scheme, jobs are compared with each other and then graded according to their values, yet while also trying to maintain some sort of process that allows for a competitive pay structure, which enables the organisation to recruit from the external market. While the grades do not constitute a payment system, they do provide the basis for one. Job evaluation allows for internal relativities of jobs to be determined. Job evaluation structures are developed/suggested by job evaluators and approved by a job evaluation committee or panel.

There are several approaches to job evaluation, some of which are 'non-analytical' and some 'analytical'. The non-analytical approach does not offer a defence against equal value claims. Sometimes, the greatest effectiveness is achieved by using different approaches in different parts of the organisation. Here, we shall discuss three approaches:

- job ranking
- job grading or job classification
- points rating.

JOB RANKING

This is a non-analytical process that simply compares whole jobs with each other without breaking them down into their component parts. The whole process centres on assessing the comparative worth of jobs. Evaluators, usually managers who know the jobs, identify the positions of jobs and rank them hierarchically in order of their size. Jobs that are perceived to be of equal value are placed into groups. A criticism of job ranking is that it is a subjective process in that there are no reputed standards for assessing the sizes of the jobs, although it can be argued that employees will regard it as fair when they see where their jobs are ranked (positively) in relation to other jobs. In a sense, however, job evaluation in general may be seen as a subjective process since, as we shall see, even analytical systems are ultimately based on the consensus of a panel of evaluators.

CASE EXAMPLE

Job ranking

In this example, four jobs have been selected and job descriptions written:

- administrative assistant
- accountant
- office supervisor
- middle manager.

We can see immediately that each of the jobs has a different value. Other office jobs are then ranked alongside the administrative assistant, slightly higher jobs alongside the accountant, and so on. It is a rather crude and basic form of job evaluation, and it is sometimes necessary to grade certain jobs individually, since not all jobs fit neatly, even into broad categories, on the hierarchy. Some jobs, as they say, 'stick out' as isolated entities.

As mentioned above, because the process is non-analytical, it does not offer a defence against equal pay challenges by employees.

JOB GRADING/CLASSIFICATION

Job grading, or job classification as it is often called, is another non-analytical approach. It is similar to job ranking except that the evaluators decide on the groupings or pay grades in advance, after which a general job description is produced for all of the jobs in each group. A typical individual job is then identified and used as a benchmark. Finally, each job is compared with the general job description and the benchmark job, then placed in an appropriate grade. This can be useful in times of change, since new or redesigned jobs can be assessed according to the criteria and placed at the appropriate level. On the other hand, modern thinking about organisational design tends to favour lean and flattened structures with a reduced number of levels, which can produce difficulties when categorising jobs in a scheme such as this.

Another approach to job grading is to categorise the jobs according to the criteria without considering their potential hierarchical position. In this way, criteria are related more directly to the actual work itself, so that the levels of knowledge, skills and competences required to do the work are taken into account, along with responsibilities and the importance of the decisions the job-holder takes.

The process reveals a similarity between the methods of job grading and those of job ranking, in that when the committee is making comparisons, it treats jobs as whole entities. The job evaluation committee makes its decisions by reaching a consensus, but it is also open to consider appeals from employees who feel that their jobs have been unfairly or inappropriately graded. In some organisations, appeals are considered by independent panels.

As mentioned above, because the process is non-analytical, it does not offer a defence against equal pay challenges by employees.

POINTS RATING METHOD

This is an analytical method and probably the most commonly used. The principal feature of points rating is that instead of comparing the value of whole jobs, as in non-analytical approaches, it analyses and compares jobs on the basis of such factors as: qualifications and competences required, degree of responsibility, customer contact, job complexity, physical requirements and working conditions. Each of these factors carries a number of points, and the amount apportioned to each job is determined by the degree to which the factors are present within it. A hierarchical structure is produced on the basis of the points rating of each job. Pay for a particular job is determined according to the number of points it carries.

Job analysis is an essential precursor to a points rating system. When the factors mentioned above have been identified, job descriptions and specifications need to be reviewed, revised and, where necessary, completely rewritten. The ultimate scheme has to be seen to be fair, and since the differences between jobs are measured in accordance with the degree to which the selected factors are present, great care must be taken over the analysis. In all systems the volume of work does not play a part in the value that is placed on a job. If the volume of work is large then more people are employed to do the work!

Deciding how many points to allocate to each factor is a well-known problem in points rating. The factors vary in their importance to each job, and the most complex or most important are allocated the greatest number of points. This is called the *weighting* of factors. The factors are placed in order of importance and complexity, and weighted according to a maximum number of points, bearing in mind the degree of importance that each factor has in a particular job. Each job is then graded according to the level at which the factors are present. See also the discussion below, which addresses equality and reward.

MANAGEMENT CONSULTANTS' SCHEMES

Several management consultancy firms can provide 'tailor-made' job evaluation schemes (which are usually analytical). Alternatively the organisation can commission the consultancy to custom-build a scheme for it.

As a 'do-it-yourself' exercise, the development of a job evaluation scheme can be costly and time-consuming, and it may ultimately be more cost-effective to engage a consultancy and to use a proprietary system of job evaluation, such as the Hay method.

Wright (2006, p55) offers the following comments about proprietary and tailor-made schemes:

The advantages of proprietary schemes are that they offer:

- expertise from consultants in setting up and using job evaluation
- access to quality pay information
- the possibility of using the same scheme as well-known companies.

The advantages of tailor-made schemes might be:

- control over development of the scheme in-house to suit highly specific organisational environments
- possibly cost-effective, depending on which staff might be involved in developing a new scheme and how their time is accounted for
- opportunity for internal HR staff and managers to gain detailed knowledge of the scheme – its drawbacks as well as its advantages.

JOB EVALUATION AND EQUAL VALUE

The Equality and Human Rights Commission (EHRC) says the following about equal pay for equal value of jobs:

> The equal pay legislation does not require an employer to use job evaluation. However, the concept of equal pay for work of equal value, whereby a woman can claim equal pay with a man doing a completely different job, means that an employer will have to apply techniques akin to those used in job evaluation, in order to assess the demands of the jobs being compared. Similar provisions are likely to apply in relation to ethnicity, disability and age.

> It therefore makes sense for employers to opt for job evaluation as a basis for a grading and pay structure. A job-evaluated system will also assist in providing a defence to an equal pay claim and greatly facilitate carrying out an equal pay audit.

According to the EHRC (*Job Evaluation Defence*) the Equal Pay Act 1970 gives job evaluation schemes two roles:

a. A woman can claim equal pay on the ground that a scheme has rated her job, although different, as equivalent to that of a man (this is known as a 'work rated as equivalent' claim).

b. An employer can defend a claim for equal pay for work of equal value if a non-discriminatory analytical job evaluation scheme rates the woman's job as lower in value than her male comparator's job. This is known as the job evaluation defence. In essence the implication of this is that a job evaluation scheme should be analytical.

A good job evaluation scheme should involve employee representatives and be thorough in its approach to finding out about the jobs to be evaluated and, once an approach to the evaluation has been agreed, then the methodology should be communicated to those involved because it is important that the system is not only managed in a transparent and logical and open manner but that the system is one that is 'felt fair' by all whom it impacts upon (adapted from Acas 2008).

When working through the dimensions of an analytical scheme the factors that are chosen must be done so that they cannot be construed to have any reference to discriminatory factors that are or can be construed to be sex-, age-, ethnicity-related, and so on, but should be solely on neutral grounds.

The job should be thoroughly researched to ensure that all relative factors are included, for example someone working in a crèche should have the caring nature of the role included. The weighting of factors should also be carefully assessed to ensure that inappropriate weighting is not given to those factors that are typical of a man's job. For example, the physical effort that a miner may be required to exert compared with the applied knowledge or skill with the use of medical instruments that a nurse may be required to have should not be overrated. The problem of weighting the factors used in an analytical scheme is recognised to be notoriously difficult.

Consider Table 12.1, which compares the relative merits of a professional gardener, educated to foundation degree level, who has several people reporting to them, to that of a primary school teacher. The maximum rating for each factor is variable and is given in Table 12.1.

Table 12.1 Factor analysis – primary teacher vs. professional gardener

Factor	Gardener	Primary school teacher	Rating maximum
Informing	20	30	35
Lifting	17	5	25
Application of specialist knowledge	15	20	30
Use of specialist equipment	20	25	30
Conditions of work (poor to good)	20	5	25
Liaison with public	17	10	20
Planning	15	15	30
Leading people	15	8	20
Co-ordinating	25	20	30
Specialist study	20	25	35
Skills updating requirements	10	15	20
Totals	**194**	**178**	**300**

In the above example the primary school teacher's job, predominantly a female role, would be rated at a lower value than that of the professional gardener. However, the fact that lifting has been used as a factor would immediately raise the question as to why mechanical devices are not being used to help the gardener perform their role. This factor, which is fraught with gender linkages, perhaps should be removed and could be replaced with an alternative, for example, 'offering specialist advice'. One might argue though that the gardener's role does require the expending of some energy so physical effort may be a criterion that could be included. Similarly the weighting given to conditions of work, although not gender-biased, may have been incorrectly assessed because, in poor weather conditions, the professional gardener can always retreat to their greenhouse or office. There is no provision for caring as an activity in the list of factors, which one might expect a primary school teacher to exhibit; in essence, the factors are incomplete. The weighting and totality of the different factors would need to be examined in more detail. Even with these minor challenges it can be seen that the relationship between the two roles changes.

In reality, the grade values would be reviewed in bands so the above two positions would be likely to be graded as equivalent as things stand above, that is, jobs banded between 170 and 200 would all fall into the same band. Removing 'lifting' from the equation may cause the gardening role to fall into a lower band.

ACTIVITY 12.4

In groups, draw up a comparative analytical job evaluation scheme for a nurse and an AA patrol technician. Which role would you rate as warranting the higher rate of pay? Go to the Hay website or the Unison union's website to see the factors they recommend when conducting job evaluations.

Unison: **www.unison.org.uk/acrobat/B1912.pdf**

Hay Group: **www.haygroup.com**

PERFORMANCE-RELATED PAY

The bases for performance-related pay (PRP) are fairness and equity. While the idea is to reward good performance, it is hard to resist the notion that once it is established in an organisation, it also provides an incentive to perform well. *Merit* pay was a similar performance-based idea originated in the early twentieth century, which was an attempt to provide satisfactory rewards for the exercise of ability and current performance. According to Tyson and York (1996), 'Merit increases are ... given to show recognition and to imply the kinds of actions and attitudes which the company wishes to reward.' The same principle applies with PRP, in which it is fair to reward various levels of performance differentially.

PRP has been through varying levels of popularity and unpopularity over the years. In the 1970s, for example, when inflation was running in double figures, the percentage increases that were awarded seemed of little financial value. In the 1980s, however, inflation began to fall. A survey carried out by the Institute of Personnel and Development (now the CIPD) in 1998 found that although there had been a growth in the use of performance-based schemes, only 43% of the responding organisations reported that they used performance pay for managerial and non-managerial staff. There are arguments about PRP as a motivator. As Perry et al (2009, p40) point out, PRP is based upon expectancy theory, which itself assumes that '... individuals will exert effort if they expect it will result in an outcome that they value'. We will not enter into the detail of these arguments here, but in broad terms surveys have indicated that while there is general support for the principle of PRP, most respondents did not believe that it had improved their motivation (Marsden and French 1998). Other research has suggested that PRP is actually demotivating staff, rather than encouraging them (Bevan and Thompson 1991).

INFLUENCE OF INDIVIDUAL DIFFERENCES IN RELATION TO PRP

Individually different perceptions of these schemes and of the purposes of reward in general have a strong influence on the results of such surveys. Some people, for example, adopt a particular profession because they feel naturally drawn to it, and while clearly they have to maintain a particular standard of living, it is the work itself that motivates them, rather than what they receive for carrying it out. Perry et al (2009, p45) pick up on this point when they argue that PRP has not, in the public sector (of the USA), delivered its intended outcomes:

> Although research has identified occasional performance pay successes, the programs typically have fallen short of intermediate and long-term expectations. We argue, however, that our findings are less cause for despair than for caution and more strategic thinking. The reasons for the persistent failure of performance-related pay are more likely its incompatibility with public institutional rules, proponents' inability or unwillingness to adapt it to these values, and its incompatibility with more powerful motivations that lead many people to pursue public service in the first place.

On the other hand, Taylor's assumption (1911, 1947) that people work exclusively for money was based on his perception of entirely different types of worker. According to Goldthorpe (1968), we have seen that the same types of manual worker are motivated almost entirely by 'extrinsic' rewards. In other words, they see it as the means by which they are able to sustain a particular living standard.

 ACTIVITY 12.5

1 In your organisation, or one with which you are familiar, identify three job-holders who you believe would be motivated mostly by financial reward and three who would be motivated mostly by the work itself.

2 Do you think that PRP has a place in a not-for-profit organisation such as a charity, for example the RSPCA or the RNLI? Read the article in *People Management* (Arkin 2002) entitled 'Tides of change'.

GUIDELINES TO ACHIEVE ACCEPTANCE

A set of guidelines for action designed to achieve a positive attitude towards a PRP scheme might include:

- integrative bargaining for the optimal scheme
- the selection or creation of a scheme in which all employees may participate
- the onus of responsibility to identify the level of an employee's performance in relation to the minimum standard being placed firmly on the manager
- managers who operate the scheme being trained to do so, and given a thorough understanding of the spirit as well as the letter of its regulations
- steps being taken to ensure that all employees are provided with an explanation of the scheme and access to further explanatory information and advice
- employees being given the right of reassessment by request.

Further in their article on PRP, Perry et al (2009, p43) cited a study by Greiner (1977) that indicated that schemes '… in which goals were clear, compensation was adequate, and a significant amount of support for merit pay plans existed, performance-related pay resulted in positive outcomes'.

HOW PERFORMANCE-RELATED PAY WORKS

The in-job performance of employees is appraised and there is a mechanism through which overall performance levels are identified. The gradings might be as follows:

- Level 1 – Excellent. Has exceeded all standards and objectives.
- Level 2 – Good. Has met standards and achieved objectives.
- Level 3 – Average. Has met most standards and achieved objectives.
- Level 4 – Poor or unsatisfactory. Has failed to meet standards or objectives.

The company must first of all agree what 'bonus pot' it will allocate to the annual exercise. This will of course be dependent upon the performance of the company and the organisation's current ability to pay and how it sees contingent pay supporting the overall organisation's strategy. One may decide to put further restrictions on management as to how they can award bonuses, for example only 10% of the workforce can be rated as Level 1, 30% as Level 2, 60% as Level 3 and of course one would hope that no one falls into the Level 4 banding. This type of *forced distribution* would have to then be fed into the appraisal process. The outcome of the exercise would then look something like Table 12.2.

Table 12.2 Bonus table

Level	Bonus as a percentage of salary
Level 1	10%
Level 2	7%
Level 3	3%
Level 4	0%

In the above example, an employee on £20,000 would receive a bonus based upon the organisation's performance and their own personal performance in the following way. Assume that the organisation has agreed an overall performance bonus plus a cost of living increase of 2.5% (of base salary) and the employee, as a level 2 performer, has a personal bonus of 7% (of base salary), then the overall bonus would be, for the year's work, 9.5% of £20,000 = £1,900.

The question then arises as to whether the above should be included as part of the new base, and therefore pensionable, salary or paid as a one-off lump sum. Paying the amount as part of the base salary is attractive for the employee but for the employer this is seen as 'salary creep' and as such continues to reward individuals, year on year, for past performance.

As with any system of payment, a PRP scheme must be handled with care and continuously monitored for its fairness and effectiveness. The attitudes of the managers and employees towards a particular scheme are of critical importance, and if the basis on which the scheme is founded is perceived as flawed, or the approach to assessment is regarded as biased, the scheme will fall into disrepute.

 ACTIVITY 12.6

Read the article entitled 'Mutiny of the bounty' by Jane Pickard in *People Management* (19 November 2009). Is this article and the corresponding advice to which it refers (from the CIPD's Reward Panel entitled 'CIPD issues executive pay guidelines that can be applied across the board', 2009c) supporting the media discussion about the excesses of bankers' pay? In groups consider whether you think that bankers should be paid significant and sometimes uncapped bonuses to retain their talent. What is the advice given in the CIPD's executive pay guidelines about how bonus arrangements for bankers should be structured?

OTHER FACTORS IMPACTING UPON REMUNERATION

LEGISLATION

All organisations have to bear in mind the provisions of the legislation on pay, for example the National Minimum Wage and discrimination laws. When developing and administering a payment scheme, therefore, the organisation has to conform to the minimum standards, which include the provisions of:

- the Equal Pay Act 1970
- the Equal Pay (Amendment) Regulations 1983
- the Employment Rights Act 1996
- the National Minimum Wage Act 1998.

TOTAL REWARD

Previous discussion has centred on monetary reward, the exchange between labour and pay for services rendered. However, this is not by any means the full picture, especially when one considers the totality of the factors that impact upon motivation in the workplace. When we consider all the factors that motivate people then it is important to include the non-monetary rewards such as praise and career development; the reward equation must include both tangible and intangible rewards. According to Armstrong (2006), total reward is made up of:

Financial reward + Non-financial rewards = Total reward

Table 12.3 Total reward (adapted from Armstrong 2006, p633)

Financial reward	Non-financial reward	
	Learning and development	
Base pay	Workplace learning	
Contingent pay: bonuses, PBR schemes, profit-sharing	Training	
	Educational development	
Long-term incentives: share incentive plans (SIPs), Save as You Earn (SAYE) schemes	Performance management	
	Career development	
Perquisites and benefits	**Work environment**	**Total reward**
Pension	Recognition	
Holiday	Core values of the organisation	
Health care	Leadership	
Personal insurance, crèche vouchers, and so on	Employee voice	
Other perquisites	Achievement	
Flexible benefits	Job design	
	Work–life balance	
	Talent management	

Armstrong suggests (2006, p633) that the rewards in Table 12.3 can be split and considered as a mix of *transactional* reward, that is, those which include the work, pay exchange, and others, which are *relational* in nature and thus depend upon how they, the employees, are engaged by the line manager and organisation in general. The mix and how the above factors are managed impact heavily upon the psychological contract.

For a fuller treatment of total reward, refer to Rumpel and Medcof (2006).

ACTIVITY 12.7

Discuss why you think that reward is one activity – perhaps the most significant and critical – within the HR armoury that impacts upon the relationship between the organisation and the individual employee. You may wish to read the *People Management* article by Perkins et al (2008).

CONTEMPORARY ISSUES

GREEN REWARD

Many employees and other stakeholders are concerned about both their own and the organisational carbon footprints. There is sufficient evidence to assert that if we do not do something about our carbon emissions then the world will gradually heat up with severe results for the planet's climate. Michael Rose, CIPD Vice-President, Reward, led a session at the CIPD's 2007 Reward, Research into Practice event, where green issues were debated. At a company-wide level the view was that (CIPD 2007c p15) company benefits which are on offer to employees could be restructured in the following way:

- mileage rates for polluting cars could be reduced
- petrol cards could be removed from company benefit schemes
- assistance with company transport costs could be provided
- provision of secure cycle storage
- advice on home energy usage
- gift incentives could include carbon credits
- pension funds should invest in environmentally friendly funds.

 ACTIVITY 12.8

What sort of benefits would you consider as being feasible (acceptable and affordable to your organisation) and which would reduce your organisation's carbon footprint or could be considered to be environmentally friendly?

What sort of barriers would you consider that there would be in the way of introducing such benefits?

EQUAL PAY REVIEWS

The Fawcett Society (2009) points out that the gender pay gap is still significant and currently (November 2009) stands at 17.1% for full-time employees, which, as their website quotes, '… is equivalent to men being paid all year round while women work for free after 30th October'. In its 2009 *Reward Management* annual survey report, the CIPD advises '… that overall, 52% of respondents have already carried out, or plan, an equal pay review (EPR)'.

Why is it good practice to carry out an EPR? The Equality and Human Rights Commission (EHRC n.d.[b]) argues that:

> Under the Equal Pay Act employees may claim equal pay with colleagues of the opposite sex where they are in the same employment and are doing equal work. Equal work can be:
>
> ● The same, or broadly similar (known as like work)
>
> ● Different, but which is already rated under the same job evaluation scheme as equivalent to hers (known as work rated as equivalent)
>
> ● Different, but which would be assessed as equal in value in terms of demands such as effort, skill and decision-making (known as work of equal value)
>
> … the same principles are likely to apply in equal pay cases in relation to race, disability, age and whether employees are full-time or part-time.

The EHRC recommends that all employers carry out an equal pay review but they stop short of making the review compulsory. The CIPD welcomed the fact, in a press release (Cotton, 16 March 2009), that the EHRC has not made the review compulsory because, as they say:

> We believe the greatest return will come from a tireless and concerted effort by government and other agencies to promote the business case for fair pay – in good times and bad. Change will only truly occur through sustained communications to alter entrenched attitudes and practices. Enforcing equal pay audits could easily end up creating a box-ticking exercise that does little to tackle the broad and deep seated causes of gender pay inequality.

It is worth going on to the Hay Group's (HR consultancy) website at **www. haygroup.com** to see their advice on equal pay audits.

 ACTIVITY 12.9

Using the advice given on the EHRC (n.d.[b]) website, explore how an equal pay audit should be conducted. Do you consider that there are jobs or groups of jobs within your organisation that would be shown to be under- or over-valued when compared with others that are staffed mainly by female employees?

NATIONAL MINIMUM WAGE (NMW)

Workers are entitled to be paid at least the level of the statutory National Minimum Wage (NMW) for every hour they work for an employer. The level of the wage is reviewed by the Low Pay Commission on an annual basis (for further information go to Chapter 16).

SUMMARY

As indicated earlier in this chapter, success of the organisation is ultimately determined by the performance of its employees. It follows, therefore, that the organisation needs to recruit and retain people who are appropriately skilled and flexible in their outlook. From this, it follows that the reward systems must support the overall business strategy, indeed that they should flow from it, and that pay should be commensurate with employees' contributions to the positive outcomes of the organisation.

The chapter discusses and explains what is meant by reward in its widest sense. Reward is a mix of financial and non-financial factors that, when managed in a holistic manner, are seen as contributing to how an individual is compensated for their efforts.

E.E. Lawler (1990) and Schuster and Zingheim (1992) were the first to put their names to the concept of 'new pay'. The focus of this concept is that reward should be linked to performance. Perry et al (2009, p45) argue, though, that PRP, especially in the public sector, has not delivered the intended outcomes; it has provided more rhetoric than reality. It does, however, have its roots in fairness and equality. In some cases, within the private sector, where the conditions have been appropriate and there has been care over communication of its aims, it has had some limited success.

How someone is remunerated is a mix of base pay, contingent pay, which is dependent upon some deliverable outcome, and benefits. Contingent pay can be based upon some form of incentive, that is, upon the successful delivery of a completed item, or alternatively the incentive could be based upon a measure of quality. Payment schemes, especially in manufacturing, have developed over the years and can be based upon rate per item completed or perhaps a base pay with bonuses paid for items completed over and above a threshold level. Schemes have also been designed that reward the achievement of competences.

Part of the package of reward is made up of benefits; the benefits package can be fixed so that all within the organisation receive the same, or it can be flexible, in which case employees can choose and even swap cash for benefits or even buy supplementary benefits. The benefits package, especially if it is tailored to the needs of the organisation, can be powerful in the retention of employees. The CIPD gives advice on the most common range of benefits offered by organisations.

Total reward is a concept that brings all elements of reward into the equation, including non-financial reward. Savvy organisations consider how they link, in a joined-up manner, base pay, contingent pay, benefits and non-financial rewards (recognition, leadership and so on – Herzberg's motivators) and how they wish to position themselves in context to the employees' perception of the organisation. Total reward has strong links to the notion of *employer branding* and the *employee value proposition* (EVP).

The chapter concludes with a review of two issues that are current and that are exercising the minds of HR professionals: green rewards and equal pay reviews. Both have a currency because there are moral and social imperatives to be addressed. We need to do something about our carbon footprint and, in the case of equal pay for equal work, too much time has elapsed since the 1970 Equal Pay Act; women's pay is still lagging behind that of their male counterparts by 17.1% (Fawcett Society 2009).

REVIEW QUESTIONS

1 How would you define 'reward'? Would you prefer to use the US expression 'compensation', or would you use simply 'payment'?

2 Why do you think E.E. Lawler proposed the 'new pay'?

3 What are non-financial rewards?

4 Why does an organisation offer particular benefits and facilities? What is in it for the organisation?

5 Define the following:

  - total earnings and total remuneration

  - incentives and rewards.

6 What are the constraints and obligations (or pressures) that influence the formulation of reward strategy? (You may wish to go onto the Towers Watson website at **www. towerswatson.com** to see what advice they offer on reward strategy.)

7 Incentive schemes are so called because they are designed to have a positive influence on future performance, but what does a PRP scheme reward?

8 Download the *Pay Gap Map* for 2008 from the Fawcett Society's website at **www.fawcettsociety.org.uk/ documents/pay%20gap%20map.pdf** and see if you can identify why the pay gap between men and women should be so varied around the countries of England and Wales.

9 Go to the website of the Low Pay Commission and see what they have to say about the levels of the National Minimum Wage. What are the current levels?

EXPLORE FURTHER

BOOKS

ARMSTRONG, M. (2010) *Armstrong's handbook of reward management practice: improving performance through reward.* **3rd ed. London: Kogan Page.**

Any suggested further reading list is not complete without mention of Michael Armstrong's text on reward management. Armstrong writes in an authoritative yet easy to understand style. His text covers all aspects of reward and is one of those books that an HR professional should have on their bookshelf ready for easy access should the need arise.

WRIGHT, A. (2006) *Reward management in context.* **London: Chartered Institute of Personnel and Development.**

Angela Wright deals with many aspects of reward, from pay systems to job evaluation. She writes fluently and in a style that is easily accessible. Her work is supported by many practical examples.

WEB LINKS

The CIPD offers a number of factsheets and surveys dealing with reward issues: Reward podcast, *Reward and Diversity*, *Reward Management* annual survey, *Reward Strategy*, *Rewarding Performance* and *Rewarding Work: The vital role of line managers [in the reward process]*. These factsheets can all be found at: www.cipd.co.uk/onlineinfodocuments/atozresources.htm

Acas: www.acas.org.uk

Business Link: www.businesslink.gov.uk

Department for Business, Innovation and Skills: www.bis.gov.uk/

Equality and Human Rights Commission: www.equalityhumanrights.com

Fawcett Society (charity): www.fawcettsociety.org.uk

Hay Group (consultants): www.haygroup.com

Low Pay Commission: www.lowpay.gov.uk

Office of Public Sector Information: www.opsi.gov.uk

Schuster-Zingheim and Associates (consultants): www.paypeopleright.com

Towers Watson (consultants): www.towerswatson.com

World at Work (consultants): www.worldatwork.org

Unison (union): www.unison.org.uk

CHAPTER 13

The Employment Relationship and Work–life Balance

LEARNING OBJECTIVES

After studying this chapter you should:

- be able to define the employment relationship and understand its legal framework
- understand the psychological contract
- understand how the multiple agencies and organisations impact upon the employment relationship
- understand the collective bargaining process
- be able to explain the processes of the internal justice system.

INTRODUCTION

The aim of this chapter is to provide an understanding of the employment relationship and the elements that shape its formal and informal structure. Rose (2008, p4) suggests, '... aspects of Employment Relations have certain appeal and often hit headlines when there are, for example, strikes, redundancies or discrimination cases'. It is important to understand that the term 'employment relations' not only applies to any collective agreements between unions and management but also includes the contractual and statutory rights and obligations of the employer and the employee; the importance of the psychological contract within the employee relationship; and the rules and procedures that are put in place to manage the employment relationship collectively and at individual level. Employment relations (ER) and, more specifically, industrial relations (IR) carry with them all sorts of negative connotations, such as what happens when there are industrial disputes with management that can have as their outcomes strikes and also downturns in business, which can lead to redundancies.

KEY CONCEPT: THE EMPLOYMENT RELATIONSHIP

Blyton and Turnbull (cited in Rose 2008, p7) define the employment relationship as being: '… the context within which intricate interactions between employees, who may be unionised or non-unionised, and employers are conducted, both collectively and individually'.

It can be argued that the 'interactions' are framed by the relationship between employer and employee. There is of course a contractual relationship but one where there is plenty of scope for filling in gaps with meaningful and constructive discussion and negotiation.

THE EMPLOYMENT RELATIONSHIP

In simple terms, this means exactly what it says: that there is a relationship between the employer and the employee. There are formal and informal aspects to the relationship and both parties have rights, obligations and expectations. The formal side is regulated through the provisions of the *contract of employment*, and in the UK legislation sets common standards for the conduct of the relationship. Some of the relevant legislation is explained and discussed later in this chapter. In very broad terms it can be said that the informal side of the relationship is governed by what is known as the *psychological contract*, which is also addressed later.

PAUSE FOR THOUGHT

Think of your own organisation or one that you have a frequent business contact with:

- List all types of people or organisations that may be involved with and impact upon the employment relationship.

- How many of these organisations or actors impact upon the day-to-day relationship, and which affect the relationship infrequently?

DIFFERENCES BETWEEN CONTRACTS

As is discussed in detail in Chapter 16, all employees have a contract of employment. The contract is based on what both parties have agreed to be a *fair exchange* (the employee's time and skill in exchange for a salary or wage), that is, the notion of wage/effort or pay/performance bargaining. However, as well as the formal contract of employment there is a relationship, hopefully positive, which has developed between the employer and the employee. This relationship, although not bound by a formal agreement, is of equal importance because it can influence how far the employee is prepared to exercise discretionary behaviour, sometimes called organisational citizenship behaviour, and work beyond the formal contract of employment. The way that line managers handle the relationship between themselves and their staff is key to how employees feel about and thus are prepared to engage in their work. As Kinnie et al (2005) write, '... employee attitudes are influenced not so much by the way these policies [meaning HR policies] are intended to operate as by the way they are actually implemented by line managers and team leaders on a day-to-day basis'.

 ACTIVITY 13.1

discretionary behaviour

Access the CIPD's factsheet, *How to … Unlock Discretionary Behaviour*, available from **www.peoplemanagement.co.uk/pm/articles/2006/10/howtounlock.htm**. Compare and contrast what is said in this article with the view on discretionary behaviour expressed by John Philpott in his *People Management* article 'By the book' (Philpott 2004, p26).

Is Philpott realistic in his view that a system should be developed to design out the requirement for an individual to exercise their discretionary behaviour?

THE EMPLOYMENT RELATIONSHIP

THE PSYCHOLOGICAL CONTRACT

This is a contract that is based upon the employee's subjective expectations of, and beliefs about, the relationship between themselves and the organisation. It is tacit, not negotiated, and includes subjective assumptions made by both sides.

> A major feature of psychological contracts is the concept of mutuality – that there is a common and agreed understanding of promises and obligations the respective parties have made to each other about work, pay, loyalty, commitment, flexibility, security and career advancement. (Pointon and Ryan 2004, p520)

With the exception of pay, all of these promises and obligations are items you would not find in the formal employment contract, but they are important determinants of behaviour.

It was Edgar Schein who first identified the concept and used the term 'psychological contract'. He said that 'the notion of a psychological contract implies that there is an unwritten set of expectations operating at all times between every member of an organisation and the various managers and others in that organisation' (Schein 1965). Even before that, respected academics (Vroom 1964; Katz and Kahn 1978) used the term 'behavioural expectations'.

It is within the reciprocal spirit of the psychological contract that people are motivated to work, gain satisfaction from what they do, develop feelings of job security, belongingness and commitment, and enjoy a culture of trust and mutual respect. All of this implies that the *exchange* aspect of the psychological contract is about mutual expectations and the satisfying of needs.

BREACHING THE PSYCHOLOGICAL CONTRACT

The psychological contract needs to be handled with care. As with any other kind of contract, it is capable of – and even susceptible to – being breached. Where it is breached by the organisation it seriously affects employee morale. Goodwill is one of the mainstays of a positive relationship between employer and employee. It leads to mutually advantageous informal employee behaviour, such as carrying out tasks that are not on the list of duties. Such behaviour should be fostered, since if everyone did exactly what was on their job descriptions and nothing else, you would never get everything done. Goodwill can take a long time to establish, yet it can be destroyed with a single thoughtless act.

PAUSE FOR THOUGHT

Do you feel as if you have a psychological contract with your employer? What do you expect from your employer that is not in your employment contract? What do you think your employer expects from you? Additionally, what about your tutors at the university or college you attend? Is there a psychological contract between you and them? What are the unwritten expectations of both parties?

PERSPECTIVES ON THE EMPLOYMENT RELATIONSHIP

In the previous section we learned about the psychological contract and the unwritten expectations associated with this concept. However, there are other perspectives on the relationship between management and their employees. The previous concept, the idea of building a positive psychological contract, leads to goodwill and positive employment relations, but there are other ways to view the employment relationship. Examples of these perspectives are the unitary and the pluralistic perspectives.

THE UNITARY PERSPECTIVE

Managers who take this view regard themselves as the only legitimate source of power and authority, which they value and protect. They see their role as one of controlling the activities of the workforce and assume that all employees share the common goals of the organisation, are loyal to the 'management team' and totally committed to the purposes of the organisation.

Reward for effort comes only if the organisation functions efficiently and effectively enough to achieve its economic and growth objectives. Where conflict occurs, its cause is attributed to communication failures or the foolish temperaments of those involved. Trade unions are unwelcome and the managers fiercely fend off their approaches for recognition. The philosophy of HRM, with its emphasis on commitment and mutuality, is based on the unitary perspective.

THE PLURALISTIC PERSPECTIVE

Here, managers may allow and actively foster freedom of expression and the development of groups, which establish their own norms and elect their own informal leaders. In this way, power and control arise in several areas of the organisation and loyalty is commanded by the leaders of the groups, which are often in competition with each other for resources. The managers achieve results by joining the groups, encouraging participation, motivating employees and co-ordinating their work efforts. It is also achieved by working with unions, engaging in the processes of negotiation and consultation and more recently seen in partnership working. Pluralism rests on managing by consent, rather than by right. This, it is said, represents good leadership, although sometimes it can be difficult to achieve the necessary balance, in which the interests of all stakeholders have to be taken into account. However, according to Rensis Likert, when employees become involved in solving work-related problems and making decisions, they become involved in what they are doing and committed to the achievement of successful outcomes (Likert 1961).

 ## ACTIVITY 13.2

Think about how your organisation (or one with which you are familiar) is managed. How do you think you are/were regarded by the managers? What does the managerial style indicate to you? In the light of what is said above, do you regard it as a unitary or a pluralistic organisation?

HRM AND PLURALISM

There are aspects of HRM, such as *individual* commitment and *mutuality of interest* in the success of the organisation, which seem to be in sympathy with the unitary concept, and therefore in conflict with a pluralistic philosophy. But can HRM incorporate any of the aspects of pluralism? According to Armstrong (2006, p13): 'The new model of HRM is composed of policies that promote mutuality – mutual goals, mutual influence, mutual respect, mutual rewards, mutual responsibility. The theory is that policies of mutuality will elicit commitment, which will in turn yield both better economic performance and greater human development.' There is a significant body of evidence which suggests that good HRM coexists with good union relations (see Guest 1995).

PARTIES IN THE EMPLOYMENT RELATIONSHIP

Taking a pluralist perspective of the employment relationship, if you are asked how many parties are involved most of us would probably answer that there are perhaps four: the employer, the employee, perhaps a trade union and maybe the Government; some may think of and add a further party, which would be the body that represents the interests of employers at a government level, the Confederation of British Industry (CBI).

 ACTIVITY 13.3

Before looking at Figure 13.1, see how many bodies you can think of that may play a role in the employment relationship. You need also to give some idea of what their role is or the purpose they achieve.

Figure 13.1 Some key players in the employment relationship

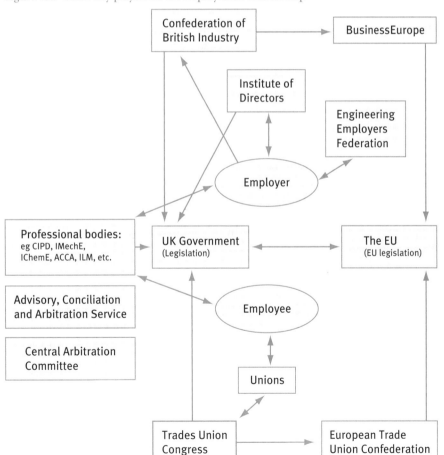

Note: Lines and arrows indicate where there is influence and/or lobbying.

As can be seen from Figure 13.1, there are a significant number of players in the employment relationship. The role of some of the key players is explained below.

CONFEDERATION OF BRITISH INDUSTRY (CBI)

The CBI are, as they say on their website, '... a lobbying organisation for UK business on national and international issues'. Their aim is to represent views of UK business and try to influence the UK Government and international legislators throughout the world. They have permanent offices in the UK, Brussels and Washington, DC (USA). They take a stance, on behalf of their business members, and then represent this view to government, whether this be in the UK or overseas. The CBI has close links with 'BusinessEurope'.

BUSINESSEUROPE – THE CONFEDERATION OF EUROPEAN BUSINESS

On behalf of its European members, of which the CBI is one, BusinessEurope deals with the following policy areas: economic and financial affairs; international relations; social affairs; industrial affairs; legal affairs; entrepreneurship and small and medium-sized enterprises (SMEs); and the internal market. BusinessEurope has a voice on the European Union's European Economic and Social Committee (EESC), which is itself 'an advisory body representing employers, trade unions, farmers, consumers and the other interest groups that collectively make up "organised civil society". As a member of the EESC, BusinessEurope presents views of its members and defends their interests in policy discussions with the (European) Commission, Council and the European Parliament' (European Union n.d.).

The EESC gives the citizens of the EU's countries a voice and is an integral part of the decision-making process. Groups such as the CBI, through Business-Europe, trades union representative bodies such as the European Trades Union Confederation (ETUC), consumers, and so on, all have a place at the European Union's table, where their voice can be heard and taken into consideration when policy and legislation is developed.

INSTITUTE OF DIRECTORS (IOD)

The role of the IOD is varied, ranging from the improvement of expertise, competence and professionalism on the boards of organisations to lobbying government and responding to government policy Green Papers (a Green Paper is a proposed policy document that is made available by the UK Government on which interested parties can comment and offer counter or supportive views).

The IOD has over 55,000 members and is non-political. As well as acting as a lobbying organisation on behalf of its members, it offers guidance and advice to directors to help them run their businesses.

ENGINEERING EMPLOYERS FEDERATION (EEF)

The EEF – as well as being a lobbying organisation that represents the manufacturing industries' perspective at government level – is an organisation that offers practical guidance to its members. It offers the opportunity to network through its seminars. It also offers guidance on employment law and other legal advice, pay review data, health and safety and training as well as consultancy programmes covering a variety of disciplines and activities.

PROFESSIONAL BODIES

The bodies mentioned in Figure 13.1 are just representative of a vast swathe of professional institutions. The ones given in the figure are:

- CIPD – Chartered Institute of Personnel and Development
- IMechE – Institution of Mechanical Engineers
- IChemE – Institution of Chemical Engineers
- ACCA – Association of Chartered Certified Accountants
- ILM – Institute of Leadership and Management.

Each of the professional bodies, within their unique domains, set standards of professional behaviour and competence. They offer training and, in some cases, set, mark and grade examination scripts for their professional programmes of education. As well as setting and policing their standards, professional institutions are involved with organisations and educational institutions (to encourage and inspire potential candidates). The professional bodies, on behalf of their members, will take a view on developing policy issues and present them to interested bodies, which could be government or government-related organisations. They also, through research and best practice models, seek to influence their members to adopt certain practices and thus, in turn, these practices will feed through into organisational standards of member groups. For example, the Institution of Mechanical Engineers (2010) says:

> In the UK, engineering has achieved great successes, but in a quiet way. We're looking to shout about the achievements of our members and the industry, taking a positive, inspiring message into schools and out into the media. By being independent of both government and business, and avoiding strategic relationships with single-issue bodies or pressure groups, we can deliver genuinely impartial advice in a passionately committed manner.

UNIONS AND THE ROLE OF UNIONS

 KEY CONCEPT: TRADE UNION

'A continuous association of wage-earners for the purpose of maintaining or improving the conditions of their working lives.' (Sidney and Web 1920, cited in Hollinshead et al 2003, p126)

Unions are, themselves, organised in different ways – occupational, craft-based, general, and so on – but there has been a recent trend towards mergers to create super unions, a development that, in itself, will shift the dynamics of the relationship.

The most common role that a trade union provides and that tends to be presented in the media is where the trade union represents its members in pay disputes or where conditions of service are being negotiated. Unions, for example, will support individual members when grievances or disciplinary proceedings have been raised.

Rose (2008, p15), citing the Trades Union Congress (TUC) in its evidence to the Royal Commission on Trade Unions and Employers' Associations (known as the Donovan Commission) 1968, identified the role of a union as to:

1 improve the terms of employment

2 improve the physical environment at work

3 achieve full employment and national prosperity

4 achieve security of employment and income

5 improve social security

6 achieve fair shares in national income and wealth

7 achieve industrial democracy

8 achieve a voice in government

9 improve public and social services

10 achieve public control and planning of industry.

 ACTIVITY 13.4

The role of the trade union

Point 10 above states that the role of the union '… is to achieve public control and planning of industry'. Is this a realistic aim? Do you think that it is an aim that is high on the agenda of unions?

According to the *Social Trends* report for 2008 (Self and Zealey 2008, p59):

> One of the aims of a trade union is to represent and assist people who feel they have been treated unfairly in the workplace. According to the First Fair Treatment at Work Survey, 1.6 million or 6.9 per cent of employees in Great Britain in 2005–06 said that they had personally been treated unfairly at work in the last two years. Those with a disability or long term illness were twice as likely as other employees to say they had personally experienced unfair treatment at work (15.1 per cent) as were employees whose sexual orientation was gay, lesbian or bisexual (13.8 per cent).

Self and Zealey (2008, p60), quoting from the 'The First Fair Treatment at Work Survey, 2007', show how people are discriminated against at work; this is fertile ground for union involvement and support to employees. Respondents to the survey were offered the categories listed in Table 13.1 and they were able to choose more than one of the options.

Table 13.1 Employees experiencing unfair treatment at work

Employees experiencing unfair treatment at work	Percentage
Age	12.1
Long-term illness	11.0
Accent or the way I speak	7.3
Race or ethnic group	6.2
Disability	5.9
Physical appearance	5.9
Gender	5.5
Nationality	5.1
The way I dress	5.1
Union membership	4.8
Religion	4.0
Colour of skin	4.0

Note: The data shows as a proportion of all employees who said that they had been treated unfairly at work. The employee could choose more than one category.

Hollinshead et al (2003, p126) argue that, 'Trade unions are "secondary" organisations, since, as Hymans puts it, "they are organisations of workers who are already 'organised' by those to whom they sell their labour power and whose actions they are designed to influence". ...' In essence a trade union recruits people who are already informed by the norms of the organisation for which they work and who have a vested interest in their workplace.

ACTIVITY 13.5

Labour disputes

Go to the *Social Trends* survey report (Self and Zealey 2008, p60) – available at: **www.statistics. gov.uk/downloads/theme_social/Social_Trends38/Social_Trends_38.pdf** – and identify the causes of labour disputes in 2006. From these [types of] figures it can be seen in what activities union time is absorbed.

The presence of a union in the workplace acts as a brake on possible management actions because of the collective power that union membership offers; remember how we have discussed the implications of the unitary as opposed to the pluralistic perspective on the relationship between management and their staff. However, the role of the union goes further than representation of rights, in terms of contractual pay and conditions. The presence of a union gives a voice to the workforce, a voice that has, through its privileged position, a right to be heard. Trained union members can be asked to accompany employees at disciplinary hearings and, for example, trade unions have to be included in the safety management of the organisation. Section 3 of the Safety Representatives and Safety Committees Regulations 1977 says the following: 'For the purposes of section 2(4) of the 1974 Act [Health and Safety at Work Act 1974], a recognised trade union may appoint safety representatives from amongst the employees in all cases where one or more employees are employed by an employer by whom it is recognised.' One can see therefore that unionism forms an integral part of the way an organisation operates; smart employers work with rather than against their trades union.

 ### PAUSE FOR THOUGHT

Are you a member of trade union or do you know someone who is? What factors would influence you to become a union member (or did influence the person you know)?

TRADE UNIONISM AND THE LAW

The law on trade unionism is quite broad. If one considers how unions are constrained by legislation across the European Union, the unions in the UK remain the most legally restricted. Essentially the following legislation controls the operation of and gives rights to trade unions and their members:

- Trade Union and Labour Relations (Consolidation) Act 1992 (c. 52)
- Trade Union Reform and Employment Rights Act 1993 (c. 19)

- Employment Rights Act 1996
- Employment Relations Act 1999.

There is, of course, a mass of other legislation but the above four Acts of Parliament cover some of the key themes associated with trade unions and trade union membership.

TRADE UNION REPRESENTATION

The membership of trade unions has declined over the years, overall, from a peak of membership of 13.21 million employees, represented by 453 unions in 1979, down to 7.63 million employees in 2006–07 (Barratt 2008, p11). Rose (2008, p157) points out that while union membership is falling, 58.8% of public sector workers were, in 2007, members of a trade union and unions were present in 86.8% of public sector workplaces. Some 47.1% of UK employees were in a workplace where a trade union operated. The implication of these facts is that, although union membership is declining, unions still have influence in the workplace.

Rose (2008, p159) points out that although union membership has fallen, it has not in terms of gender changed equally in a downward direction. 'During the 1970s a large proportion of the increase in membership was the increased unionisation of women. During the 1980s, however, there was a much faster decline in the unionisation of men compared to women, and this trend continued into the 1990s.' Barratt (2008, p42) points out that in 2008, '… females accounted for 52.8 per cent of union members and males accounted for 47.2 per cent. Public sector employees accounted for 59.7 per cent of union members. Overall, union membership is falling but increasing numbers of union members are women.'

The key issue is the extent to which employees have their terms and conditions determined by collective bargaining. The *Workplace Employment Relations Survey* (2004) tells us that this is sector-specific, with the public sector still overwhelmingly covered by collective bargaining.

 ACTIVITY 13.6

Unionisation of women

Can you explain why the union membership of women increased during the 1970s and decreased for men in the 1980s?

ACTIVITY 13.7

Trade union membership

Part 1

Go to the website 'Trade Union Membership 2008' (Barratt 2008) – available from **http://stats. berr.gov.uk/UKSA/tu/tum2008.pdf** – and determine the relative proportion of union as opposed to non-union membership. You will find useful information on Chart 6.2, page 42: 'Characteristics of union compared to non members, 2008'.

The narrative under Chart 6.2 (ibid) is of particular interest because it gives an idea of the spread and impact of union membership, by age, full- or part-time working, professional associations and so on.

Part 2

Using the same source as above, find Table 6.2, pp44–5, and review the split by percentage membership of trade unions by occupation. Which occupational group forms the backbone of union membership and which grouping of members forms the largest group by 'industry' sector? Can you argue why this should be the case?

THE TRADES UNION CONGRESS (TUC)

The TUC is *not* an organisation that unions in the UK must join; membership is voluntary. As its website indicates (TUC 2010a), the TUC, '… brings together Britain's unions to draw up common policies and lobbies Government to implement policies'. Its focus is on people in the workplace.

The remit of the TUC is broad in terms of its activities; the full rules and objectives of the TUC are available on its website (TUC 2010b). It currently represents 59 unions. As an organisation it carries out research on employment, helps to facilitate negotiations between unions and management and will help to avoid clashes between two unions. It also has links worldwide in its endeavour to promote unionism.

The TUC website is also worth accessing regarding information on employment rights.

ACTIVITY 13.8

Access the TUC website – available from **www.tuc.org.uk/index.cfm** – and determine the range of information they have on employee (worker) rights.

The TUC has an annual congress at which issues are discussed and motions carried. For example, one of the 'resolutions carried' at the TUC 2009 Congress was for the TUC Council to campaign (TUC 2010c) '… for a large-scale Government crackdown on employers who don't provide basic employment rights such as holiday pay, sick pay and redundancy pay for their work force'.

ACTIVITY 13.9

Campaign in action

How has the TUC sought to influence the Government to '… crackdown on employers who don't provide basic employment rights such as holiday pay, sick pay and redundancy pay for their work force'? You may find it useful to access the TUC website to see what it says.

THE TUC AND UNION LEARNING

The TUC has established an organisation called 'unionlearn', which has the following aims (unionlearn 2009):

- to help unions support 250,000 members a year to access and progress through lifelong learning based on quality standards, including 25,000 on Skills for Life courses
- to help unions to develop collective approaches and increase the quantity and quality of learning, as well as ensure a fairer distribution of opportunities
- to strengthen union capacity on learning by training and supporting 22,000 union learning representatives and embedding learning within core union activities and structures.

The objective is to provide effective union representation in the workplace by training union representatives and union professionals.

'unionlearn' offers training and education courses to national standards; it is approved by the Qualification Credit Framework (QCF), the Qualifications and Curriculum Authority (QCA) and the National Open College, and educational courses are quality assured by the Office for Standards in Education (Ofsted). The chairperson of 'unionlearn' and its council members are all members of the major unions that support the TUC.

Union learning centres are supported by local providers who, in partnership with the union, ensure that learning is delivered by qualified tutors. The range of learning opportunities vary, according to the needs of local union membership, but information and communication technology (ICT) and Skills for Life are part of the offer to union learners. 'unionlearn' is active in offering a broad range of skills and educational courses. For example, its educational courses range from Championing Disability at Work, Countering the Far Right, Health and Safety, Finding a Work–life Balance, Diplomas in Trade Unionism and Employment Law, to specific courses for the role of the union representative (Union Representative Stage 1, Stage 2) and so on.

Time off for learning, although it cannot be guaranteed to occur at specific times, is, however, a provision of legislation, particularly the Trades Union and Labour Relations (Consolidations) Act 1992 and the Safety Representatives and

Safety Committee Regulations 1977. This legislation gives trade union and safety representatives a legal right to reasonable time off, with pay, to attend courses that are approved by the TUC or a recognised union. The common-sense approach is that the 'reasonable time off' is negotiated with management; it cannot just be taken.

To encourage and support union members, 'unionlearn' has trained a significant number of union learning reps (ULRs), with a goal of training 22,000 by the end of 2010. The key functions undertaken by ULRs (unionlearn n.d., p19) are set out in the Employment Act 2002. ULR statutory functions are:

- identifying learning or training needs
- providing information and advice about learning or training
- arranging learning or training
- promoting the value of learning or training
- consulting the employer about carrying out such activities
- preparing to carry out any of the above activities.

In the past, many ULRs have had difficulty in obtaining time off from employers to carry out their duties and to train for them. That is why the TUC and its unions persuaded the Government to introduce statutory recognition that gives learning reps similar rights to union representatives as a whole.

The Employment Act 2002 gives rights to paid time off to ULRs provided they are in independent unions – such as those affiliated to the TUC – or they are in workplaces where unions are recognised by the employer for collective bargaining purposes.

All in all, the aspirations of unionlearn are extensive and carry on the long traditions of union activities.

THE EUROPEAN TRADES UNION CONFEDERATION (ETUC)

The ETUC has a very similar function to the industrial body that represents European business as a social partner at the European Union's European Economic and Social Committee (EESC) – BusinessEurope, the Confederation of European Business – but the ETUC works on behalf of European trade unionism.

The ETUC has the following aims (ETUC n.d.):

The ETUC exists to speak with a single voice, on behalf of the common interests of workers, at European level. Founded in 1973, it now represents 82 trade union organisations in 36 European countries, plus 12 industry-based federations.

The ETUC's prime objective is to promote the European Social Model and to work for the development of a united Europe of peace and stability where working people and their families can enjoy full human and civil rights and high living standards. The **European Social Model** embodies a society combining sustainable economic growth with ever-improving living and working standards, including full employment, social protection, equal opportunities, good quality jobs, social inclusion, and an open and democratic policy-making process that involves citizens fully in the decisions that affect them.

The ETUC believes that workers' consultation, collective bargaining, social dialogue and good working conditions are key to promoting innovation, productivity, competitiveness and growth in Europe.

As part of the ETUC dialogue with the EU's social partners, it has been instrumental in informing and moulding employment legislation, with its industrial and other social partners, for example:

- European Works Councils Directive (1994)
- Information and Consultation Directive (2002)

And, specifically, with the industrial partners, it helped to give form to the legislation on Directives on:

- parental leave (1996)
- part-time work (1997)
- fixed-term contracts (1999).

All this legislation, which emanated from the European Union, has found its way into the UK's legislative framework.

The ETUC is based in Brussels and brings together thinking from its partner organisations from around the EU, for example the UK's Trades Union Congress. Because of its geographic location and because it is formally recognised as one of the social partners that has an entitlement to have its voice heard at the European Commission and Council of Ministers, it, in part, reflects the social dimension to the European Union. The Council of the European Union represents the individual member states and the European Commission seeks to uphold the interests of the EU as a whole. The ETUC would automatically be included, and thus have a voice, on matters that relate to employment legislation, which of course would impact right across all the EU member countries.

PAUSE FOR THOUGHT

Reflect upon the advantages and disadvantages of the approach that the EU, as explained above, has on the effectiveness of developing employment legislation through engagement with a range of 'social partners'.

ADVISORY, CONCILIATION AND ARBITRATION SERVICE (ACAS)

Acas offers free advice to employers and employees on employment legislation and employment relations issues. It is largely funded by the Department for Business, Innovation and Skills (BIS) and has been operating, in its present form, since 1975 but has a history dating back to 1896 when the Government launched a voluntary conciliation and arbitration service, which also gave free advice to employers and unions on industrial relations and personnel problems (Acas n.d.). The advice and services it offers are impartial, neither favouring employers nor employees.

In particular, Acas (n.d.) offers the following range of services to those who seek its assistance: '... an independent and trusted service for dealing with disputes (collective conciliation) between groups of workers and their employers (collective disputes). We also deal with disputes where individuals claim their employer has denied them a legal right.' Over and above these services, Acas (n.d.) provides '... authoritative advice and guidance on employment and work policies to the Government and social partners (trade unions and employers or their representative organisations)'.

 KEY CONCEPT: ARBITRATION

'The hearing of and determination of a dispute, especially an industrial dispute, by an impartial referee selected or agreed upon by the parties concerned.' (Collins 1998)

In the context of industrial arbitration, then, the outcome of the dispute, if managed with the Trade Union and Labour Relations (Consolidation) Act 1992, becomes legally binding.

CENTRAL ARBITRATION COMMITTEE (CAC)

The role of the CAC (n.d.):

> ... is to promote fair and efficient arrangements in the workplace, by resolving collective disputes (in England, Scotland and Wales) either by voluntary agreement or, if necessary, through adjudication. The areas of dispute with which the CAC currently deals are:
>
> i.   applications for the statutory recognition and derecognition of trade unions;
>
> ii.   applications for the disclosure of information for collective bargaining;
>
> iii. applications and complaints under the Information and Consultation Regulations;
>
> iv.   disputes over the establishment and operation of European Works Councils;

v.   complaints under the employee involvement provisions of Regulations enacting legislation relating to European companies, cooperative societies and cross-border mergers.

As Rose (2008, p19) points out, '... CAC will arbitrate directly in an industrial dispute ... as well as receiving requests from Acas.'

The chairperson and the members of the CAC are appointed by the Secretary of State.

COLLECTIVE BARGAINING

Where trade unions or staff associations are recognised by organisations, collective bargaining is the means used to address conflicting issues between the organisation and its employees. Collective bargaining also takes place when there are disputes between managers and employees at national level, such as, for example, the Post Office dispute of 2009.

This section explains and discusses the roles of the various participants in collective bargaining at national and organisational levels. These include shop stewards and managers, union officials and employers' associations.

TYPES OF COLLECTIVE BARGAINING

There are two types of collecting bargaining, which may be referred to as distributive and integrative bargaining (Walton and McKersie 1965):

- **Distributive bargaining** is described as 'the complex system of activities instrumental to the attainment of one party's goals when they are in basic conflict with those of the other party'.

- **Integrative bargaining** is described as 'the system of activities which are not in fundamental conflict with those of the other party and which therefore can be integrated to some degree'. The objectives referred to are about 'an area of common concern, a purpose'.

To someone who has little experience of collective bargaining, the above definitions must seem to be something of a mystery. Nevertheless, it is important for you to attain a sound understanding of both definitions, and it is hoped that the following case example will be helpful. The case example is about job evaluation.

Distributive and integrative bargaining

P and E Components (PEC) is a company distributing plumbing and electrical components to the trade. PEC is owned and managed by Ritik Kapoor and Anil Roshan. PEC has four operating geographic divisions in which there are 60 stores and four warehouses; it employs some 1,500 people. Wages and salaries are individually negotiated at regional and local levels, depending on the seniority of the jobs. PEC recognises several trade unions, which represent 75% of the workforce, and there is a system of collective bargaining in place.

After reading a report by the HR manager, Ritik and Anil decided they would like to introduce a system of job evaluation, which they thought would be more equitable than the current arrangements. Their first step was to approach the chief shop stewards to put the idea to them. The stewards decided to have a separate meeting, after which they went back to Ritik and Anil to ask what kind of job evaluation scheme they had in mind.

Jointly, Ritik, Anil and the stewards decided to have a larger meeting at which the HR manager would be present. After a long negotiation, the shop stewards agreed to put the idea to their members and to recommend that they voted in favour of a points rating scheme. In this scheme, the job factors are each evaluated and awarded a number of points. The number of points awarded, therefore, determines the salary of the job-holder.

The trade union chiefs declared that after the scheme had been drawn up, they would wish to have further negotiations to try to agree the value of the points, and the managers agreed to this.

Discussion of the case example

The case example involves both integrative and distributive bargaining. Can you see which negotiations were 'integrative' and which were 'distributive'? The managers and shop stewards discussed the introduction of job evaluation, and when they agreed about that, they moved on to discuss the kind of scheme that would be most appropriate to their company. That was integrative bargaining.

Integrative bargaining occurs when both sides recognise that they have common problems, the solution to which is to everyone's benefit. In this case they both wanted job evaluation but between them, they had to decide on a particular scheme. In other words, they had to agree about the best way forward, or how they should go about doing things. What typifies this kind of integrative bargaining is that both sides adopt a joint problem-solving approach. They pool their knowledge and ideas to achieve something that meets the needs of both parties.

At the next session, however, when they were negotiating the value of the point, they were engaged in distributive bargaining. This occurs when the negotiators are in conflict over how something should be divided or distributed. The issues that divide them usually concern pay, time or power, which are all limited so that the main flavour of this kind of bargaining is a 'my loss is your gain' attitude. An obvious example is an employee's demand for a higher rate of pay. It is as if a cake is to be sliced in two and the question that arises is, 'How big a slice do I get and how much do you keep?' Other examples may include demands for increased holiday entitlements or a reduction in working hours.

It is worth noting that this is discussed in 'either–or' terms, while in fact there are many 'mixed' sessions in which distributive and integrative take place simultaneously.

PRODUCTS OF COLLECTIVE BARGAINING

It was noted above that pay, working time and holiday entitlements are typical issues that are resolved through distributive bargaining. These are generally referred to as substantive issues: the outcomes alter employees' terms and conditions of employment. Agreements that are reached in this way are referred to as *substantive agreements*.

The agreements that are reached through integrative bargaining are referred to as *procedural agreements*, because the parties are engaged in 'how we shall go about doing things'. Typical internal issues are related to health and safety procedures and procedures that form part of the *internal justice system*, such as those for handling grievances and dealing with matters of discipline.

THE INTERNAL JUSTICE SYSTEM

All organisations have an internal justice system (IJS), which on the one hand enables organisations to take action against individuals who misbehave and, on the other, enables the individual to seek a solution to perceived unfairness or ill treatment. In this way, both sides of the employee relationship have access to a system through which redress may be sought. The formal processes of the IJS are managed through a *disciplinary procedure* and a *grievance procedure* (see Chapter 16 for further discussion).

The use of these procedures tends to be psychologically negative, since the disciplinary rules, for example, define unacceptable items of behaviour, ranging from minor indiscretions to comparatively serious offences, which are referred to as 'gross misconduct'. Additionally, through the grievance procedure, employees seek solutions to negative situations. Circumstances in which one party or the other is not satisfied by the outcomes of the process may lead to recourse to internal mediation and perhaps external institutions, such as employment tribunals, Acas or the courts.

MANAGING A KEY EMPLOYMENT RELATIONS ISSUE

ABSENCE MANAGEMENT

This is one of the longest-running causes of serious concern to managers. Unapproved absence from work causes a multitude of problems to managers and involves the organisation in significant extra costs. According to Torrington et al (2008, p340, citing Bevan 2002):

> ... research from the Employment Studies Institute, suggests that there are virtually no robust data on direct and indirect costs of absence and that most employers underestimate the true costs of sickness absence, particularly in respect of long-term sickness. Costing currently does not distinguish between short-term and long-term sickness.

As well as employee wages, other costs must be included:

- line manager costs in finding a temporary replacement or rescheduling work
- the actual cost of the temporary employee
- costs related to showing a temporary employee what to do
- costs associated with a slower work rate or more errors from a temporary employee
- costs of contracts being completed on time.

 KEY CONCEPT: POLICY ON ABSENCE

Employees have the right, under the Employment Rights Act 1996, to be provided with information about 'any terms and conditions relating to incapacity for work due to sickness or injury, including any provisions for sick pay'.

MANAGING AND CONTROLLING ABSENCE

Considerable attention has been paid to the problems related to absenteeism, and this has resulted in the use of management control systems, some of which are linked to the disciplinary procedure. On the other hand, the objective in setting up an absence management system is to head off the need to use the disciplinary procedure. For an employee to be of use to the organisation they have to be present, no matter how competent or willing they may be. However, there is some good news because the CIPD's 2009 *Absence Management* annual survey report (p5) indicates that 'the average level of employee absence has fallen to 7.4 days per employee per year, working days lost, from 8.0 days per employee per year, based on a 228-day working year. ... lowest level of employee absence ever recorded by the CIPD's *Absence Management* survey'. The report indicates that the average cost of absence has risen from £666 per employee per year (2008) to £692 per employee per year (2009). These are the overall average costs, but if one views these figures by sector they differ; for example, for the public sector, the cost of absence increases to £754 per employee per year.

In an attempt to create a positive culture in the workplace that recognises the impact that absence has on both the business and those who are present and who have to cover work for absent colleagues, many organisations (CIPD 2009a, p16) '... have a target in place for reducing absence, with public sector organisations most likely to have a target (63%) and private services sector organisations least likely to (35%)'.

REASONS FOR ABSENCE

According to a CIPD survey report (2009a, p20) there are many reasons that people take time off work. Short-term absences can be categorised as, in order of frequency:

- minor illnesses, such as colds and flu
- musculoskeletal injuries
- home and family responsibilities
- back pain
- recurring medical conditions such as asthma, angina, and so on
- injuries and accidents not related to work.

One of the features of this list is that some of the reasons given are predictable, and therefore easier to manage since they can be planned ahead. On the other hand, unapproved absence is unpredictable and difficult to manage. Importantly, the former does not cause a reduction in productivity, whereas the latter does. Another cause of lost productivity is when an individual is on the premises but absent from their job without permission; this is a frequent occurrence that usually passes unnoticed.

 ACTIVITY 13.10

Long-term absence

Access the 2009 CIPD *Absence Management* annual survey report from **www.cipd.co.uk/ subjects/hrpract/absence/_absence_management_2009** and determine the reasons for long-term absence.

MEASURING ABSENCE

Managers know when there are absences from their daily contact with the staff, but only monitoring absence and measuring its frequency will reveal the true extent of the problem. If the problem is serious, then the task is to identify the causes and decide what to do about it. Persistent and widespread absence may be found in a particular department, in which case the departmental issue needs to be investigated to discover the cause. It might have been caused by unpopular changes in the work systems, the style with which the manager leads and communicates with the staff, or an increase in the workload.

On the other hand, absenteeism may be endemic across the whole organisation; it might be taken for granted that staff take unapproved time off, such as a 'duvet day'. In some cases, it is almost as if it is an entitlement.

THE BRADFORD FACTOR

There are several systems available for measuring absence. The Bradford factor is probably the most well known and is used by many organisations. The system is designed to identify persistent short-term absences by measuring the number of spells of absence. It is calculated according to the formula: S x S x D, where S =

the number of spells of absence by an individual in 52 weeks; and D = the total number of an individual's absence in 52 weeks.

CASE EXAMPLE

The Bradford factor

Ten one-day absences = 10 × 10 × 10 = 1,000

One ten-day absence = 1 × 1 × 10 = 10

Five two-day absences = 5 × 5 × 10 = 250

Two five-day absences = 2 × 2 × 10 = 40

It was noted above that when the causes have been identified, the next task is to decide what to do about it. The involvement of the line manager is key to the success of the steps that are taken to reduce absenteeism. First, the manager needs to keep a record of the frequency of the spells of absences and the number of days taken in each spell. The effectiveness of the action that they take is determined by their leadership skills, since only as a last resort should the disciplinary procedure be invoked.

RETURN-TO-WORK INTERVIEWS

These have proved to be an effective intervention on the part of the line manager. They give the line manager the opportunity to talk to staff about the underlying causes of absence. The use of disciplinary procedures for unacceptable absence may be used if the organisation wants to make it clear that unjustified absence will not be tolerated and that absence policies will be enforced (CIPD 2009a).

MANAGING ABSENCE: SOME CONCLUSIONS

Managing absence in the workplace is a key ER issue, an issue that is fraught and charged with emotion. The previous discussion offers, in a very clinical and managerialist way, a process to reduce absence. It is a process that has been adopted throughout private and public bodies and with success. However, everything is not always so clear-cut and in many respects this is what makes the role of line management and that of the HR specialist so interesting.

Problems occur in many forms and with many subtleties. Consider the person who has a long-term illness, who wants to work but every three or four months has to undergo treatment at hospital as an outpatient, which takes them away from their workplace for three or four days, maybe more, at a time. Their Bradford score goes sky high on an equally regular basis. How is this managed? What are the implications for management? Should they make a special case in respect of this person? Should the treatment of the individual be completely different and the person is taken out of the Bradford system for these episodes?

EMPLOYMENT RELATIONSHIP SUMMARY

Managing the employment relationship is governed by certain rules and regulations within many Acts of Parliament and also internal organisational protocols, such as the Bradford system for absence management, the introduction of which will have been negotiated at a local level to provide a mechanism for control and to bring about parity in the handling of absence. But the employment relationship is also about the interaction between management and their staff. The key question is what type of relationship does organisation A or organisation B wish to have with its employees? There are, as has been discussed, options. One may take a very managerialist and unitary perspective or one may opt to share the role with other partners; in some respects this exists in reality, whether it is or is not fostered by, or encouraged by, management. Figure 13.1 on page 279 gives some ideas of the parties who can potentially be involved and who can all play a part.

WORK–LIFE BALANCE

 KEY CONCEPT: WORK–LIFE BALANCE

In the Work Foundation's survey, Jones (2006, p4) says that 'work–life balance is meant to articulate the desire of all individuals – not just those with families or caring responsibilities – to achieve and maintain a "balance" between their paid work and their life outside work, whatever their "life" involves, from childcare and housework to leisure or self-development.'

THE MEANING OF WORK

The word 'work' can mean many things. For example, people do work at home, such as housework and DIY jobs. In another context, participating in sports may be regarded as work. In fact work is any physical or mental activity that expends energy. In the context of work–life balance, work refers to paid employment, which is usually a significant component of people's life structure. In the same context, the word 'life' refers to all of the non-work aspects of people's total lifestyle, while 'balance' refers to the reasonableness with which everything in their life fits together.

 PAUSE FOR THOUGHT

The fact that issues such as work, home and family, personal interests and leisure pursuits are being considered should tell you that work–life balance is a relative thing. In other words, there is no universally acceptable work–life balance. What is appropriate for one person might be inappropriate for another.

THE ROLE OF WORK

Work is a central feature in the lives of most people. To some, it is simply a means to an end in that it supports a desired standard of living. To others, it is the main life interest, the all-consuming top priority, a so-called 'vocational calling'. However, the old 'either–or' saying that 'some people work to live and others live to work' is not totally accurate. People's attitudes to work vary widely, ranging from the perception of it as a chore they have to bear to provide for themselves and others, to being the main reason for their existence.

When people ask about your work, they often say, 'What do you do for a living?' That well-worn phrase tells us about the traditional role that work has played since the beginning of the Industrial Revolution. For most people, work provides the central structure of their lives, while everything else is organised around it. It determines:

- where employees should be at particular times of the day and week
- the time of arrival at, and departure from, the workplace
- how much time they have to themselves
- their annual holiday entitlement
- their general standard of living (through finance).

In fact, work even tells them what time to get out of bed in the mornings!

ACHIEVING WORK–LIFE BALANCE

Although we have said that there is no universally accepted work–life balance, there are common factors that people need to think about when attempting to achieve a work–life balance that is satisfactory to them. Clutterbuck (2003), for example, says that achieving a work–life balance can arguably be boiled down to:

- being aware of different demands on your time and energy
- having the ability to make choices in the allocation of time and energy
- knowing what values you wish to apply to choices
- making (conscious) choices.

Achieving a satisfactory work–life balance is not simply a question of summarising everything one does and putting it all into some kind of order. In fact it is quite a complex task that involves time management, deciding what the priorities are in terms of work, paying due consideration to the needs of important others – such as a spouse/partner and children (if any) – and of course making time and provision for personal interests, such as hobbies and leisure pursuits.

TIME MANAGEMENT

While this section is not about time management *per se*, how people allocate their time and energy to their obligations, responsibilities and pleasures does play a significant role in their achieving a satisfactory work–life balance. Everyone, regardless of who they are or what they do for a living, is allocated exactly the same amount of time, and the question is, 'What do you do with yours?'

Consider the following four facts:

1 There are 120 hours in a five-day week.

2 According to the Working Time Regulations (WTR), employers can demand no more than 48 hours a week.

3 Let us assume that the average 'home to work and back' travel time is two hours daily.

4 Let us assume that many people sleep for between seven and a half and eight hours in a period of 24 hours.

What do these facts give us? If we add the time spent on the activities in 2, 3 and 4 and subtract the result from 120, we are left with 22 hours to ourselves in the working week, or 4.4 hours a day (within a five-day week). During this time we eat and maintain the social bonds between our family and our friends.

In the Work Foundation survey, Jones (2006, p6) finds that:

> Paid work – particularly full-time paid work – is also having an impact upon people's leisure activities and eating habits. ... Over a third (36%) of full-time and part-time workers in our sample agree that 'In the evenings I am so tired I just fall asleep on the sofa'. The fact that both full-time and part-time workers say this demonstrates that unpaid activities, such as housework and childcare, can be at least as exhausting as paid employment.

LONG-HOURS CULTURE

Many employees in the UK work longer hours than the Working Time Regulations (WTR) limit of 48 hours a week. This is a phenomenon that takes many forms:

- Even if employees have not signed the opt-out clause from the Working Time Directive, some simply continue working voluntarily beyond the contracted time. This practice is often called *presenteeism*, which is done because some people think that staying on implies commitment.

- Others work more than the contractual time by taking work home.

- Low-paid employees have to work overtime simply to earn a reasonable living.

- Further considerations include the time spent talking and thinking about work.

The practice of supplying employees with laptop computers and hand-held devices that can deal with mobile telephone and emails all adds up to further pressures on individuals to be working outside what we take to be normal office hours. Couple this with the ability of these devices to communicate on a global basis and it further adds to the pressure to 'just answer this email' and so further reducing the time available for 'self'.

ORGANISING WORK–LIFE BALANCE

It is unlikely that an individual will achieve a satisfactory work–life balance without the co-operation and assistance of others. The employer has a significant role to play in this. Gradually, employers are becoming more flexible and understanding of their employees' commitments, and there is also legislation that requires employers to assist in particular circumstances (see below). Ultimately, however, it is up to the individual to envisage a work–life balance that would be satisfactory.

THE BUSINESS CASE FOR WORK–LIFE BALANCE

The CIPD's 2007 guide on flexible working (p10) argues that their research shows that flexible working, with the object of improving work–life balance, has distinct advantages for the organisations:

- **Recruitment and retention:** Organisations believe that by offering flexible working they attract and keep people who would not otherwise be working for them.

- **Engagement:** Employees are grateful for the chance to achieve a better balance between home and work, and as a result show greater loyalty and commitment. And this is reflected in their performance.

- **Reduced stress:** Many of today's jobs are potentially stressful, but working flexibly makes it easier for many employees – particularly those with small children – to cope.

- **Reduced absence and employee turnover:** Flexible working means that staff are absent from work less frequently and are less likely to leave, with a corresponding reduction in recruitment, induction and training costs.

- **Reputation:** Flexible working helps build a positive image of the employer among customers and in the wider community

NOT A STRICT REGIME

When you start to consider your own situation in terms of how important each aspect of your life is to you and how all its component bits fit into your overall pattern of life, you will find that work–life balance is a fluid concept. That is to say, the time and attention that you give to different aspects of your life varies from one day to another, from one week to another. For example, emergencies might happen to those closest to you, such as your spouse/partner or your children. If a child falls ill or is having problems at school, they will claim your attention at the expense of the other aspects. A satisfactory work–life balance, therefore, cannot be achieved simply by allocating set amounts of time in accordance with their importance.

The point here is that the aspects of our lives, including work, create conflict in that they compete with each other for our time and attention. Individuals have to be prepared to decide which aspects they wish to attend to at any particular time, and which go on their waiting list; and difficult as it may be, there will be times when they have to say 'no'.

HAVING THE 'RIGHT' JOB

The likelihood that a person will achieve a satisfactory work–life balance depends, to a considerable extent, on their employer, and it is important to be able to distinguish between 'good' and 'bad' employers. Work–life balance involves more than juggling with time; it also includes people's health and happiness, which are best achieved by having a job they enjoy and in which they are treated fairly and with respect.

CHOOSING AN EMPLOYER

For many years, it was traditional for the job selection decision to be entirely in the hands of the employer. In the past, employers tended to give the job to a candidate, the implication being that it is a one-sided choice and that the candidate should somehow be grateful. Candidates too have played their parts in this; they enter the interview room eager to please and hoping to be selected, while in fact the decision should be mutual.

Before applying for a job, a person should find out as much as possible about the organisation. Does it have a good reputation for the way employees are treated? If the organisation is local, its reputation as a caring and fair employer should be easy to discover. A prospective candidate should seek information about:

- its employment policies and procedures
- the training, development and career opportunities
- its policies and practices on equal opportunities
- the normal terms and conditions of employment
- what it is like to work there.

If the information gathered from such enquiries turns out to be positive and leads to a decision to apply for the job, the written response from the organisation to the application, which usually includes the job description and material about the organisation, will provide further information about its style and culture. If then a prospective candidate who makes preliminary enquiries in this way, progresses to the selection stage, they will be in a good position to consider the organisation as a prospective employee.

CONSIDERING THE OFFER

A candidate who is offered employment will have been through the selection procedure, perhaps involving a tour around the workplace and meeting managers and employees, and might have come to regard the organisation as a 'good' employer. However, they still should consider whether they feel comfortable in terms of fitting into the culture and how working there is likely to affect the other aspects of their life.

This is a vitally important decision, because if an individual finds that they are working for a 'bad' employer who fails to recognise that employees are individually different, and does not consider their non-work needs, then the ability of that individual to achieve a satisfactory work–life balance will be severely inhibited.

SO WHAT CAN EMPLOYERS DO?

The employer has a significant role to play in work–life balance, and in fact the employer can make a contribution that will make an important difference. Here, we examine and discuss, first, what employers can do to assist, and second, what the law says they must do.

GETTING STARTED

According to Business Link (2005), employers should regard the achievement of work–life balance not as a 'one-off' exercise, but as a long-term commitment to operating the business in a way that respects their employees' responsibilities outside of work. The organisation needs to consider 'the policies that are designed to achieve this need to strike a balance between the needs of the business and those of the employees'.

Clearly, employers will know what they wish to achieve in terms of their core business requirements, but if they regard the long-term well-being of the employees as important, then the employees, along with their representatives (trade unions), need to be consulted about what they too wish to achieve. The employer should:

- take the lead in demonstrating a commitment to work–life balance
- explain any changes to employees and keep them abreast of regulatory changes, for example the right for parents to request flexible working (see Chapter 16).

David Clutterbuck says that employers should give employees the tools to create their own work–life balance. For example, employers may offer employees briefings or training in how to set about creating a better balance of work and non-work in their own lives. There are a number of issues that people might need help to tackle, including:

- what they actually want from each aspect of their lives – how important each aspect is to them now and how important they expect it to be in the future
- how they sort out conflicting demands on their time and physical and emotional energy
- how they achieve the self-discipline required to set boundaries and to say no when demands from others threaten to breach those boundaries

- how to recognise and manage the stress that comes from conflicting or excessive demands upon them. (Clutterbuck 2003)

Organisations that do not offer training/counselling on these issues have found that, increasingly, employees are consulting the organisation's *occupational support system* or the *employee assistance programme* over matters of work–life conflict.

Specifically, Jones (2006, pxiv), when investigating what companies offer to their employees in the context of well-being and flexible working initiatives, gives the example of PricewaterhouseCoopers, which has policies in place for:

- flexible benefits
- flexible working (for example part-time, job-share, annual days, homeworking)
- career breaks
- childcare vouchers
- enhanced maternity leave
- fully paid paternity leave
- flexible leave arrangements
- employee assistance programme
- lifestyle management support and training.

NO ONE BEST WAY

There is no universal prescription for a satisfactory work–life balance for individuals, and since all organisations are different from each other, the same

Table 13.2 Forms of flexible working offered by employers (%)

	Total	Available to some staff	Available to all staff
Working part-time	86	43	43
Term-time working	38	23	15
Job-sharing	63	34	29
Flexitime	55	34	21
Compressed hours (for example four-day week)	47	32	15
Annual hours	28	20	8
Working from home on a regular basis	55	48	7
Mobile working	27	24	3
Career breaks/sabbaticals	42	17	25
Secondment to another organisation	37	19	18
Time off to work in the community	22	7	15

applies to the achievement of a mutually satisfying pattern of working in terms of attendance.

The CIPD (2005) survey, *Flexible Working: Impact and implementation – an employer survey*, found that part-time working was the most common option of flexible working offered by organisations. Table 13.2, taken from that survey, details the popularity of other options.

THE LAW AFFECTING WORK–LIFE BALANCE

The HR practitioner is often the prime mover in designing and integrating the policies needed to achieve work–life balance, and in convincing the top managers that it is a worthwhile investment. It is essential, therefore, not only for them to be able to communicate effectively the voluntary arrangements that the organisation can offer to its employees and the benefits that accrue from making such offers, but also to understand and advise on the relevant law, of which, incidentally, there is quite a lot.

KEEPING TRACK OF THE LAW

HR practitioners are faced not only with understanding the law but also with keeping abreast of the changes and the rate at which those changes are made. The law that is explained and discussed in Chapter 16 (under 'Family-friendly rights') – much of which affects work–life balance – was up to date at the time of writing, but as an HR practitioner who is responsible for advising senior and line managers, you will need to keep a constant watch on the publication of new legislation and amendments to established laws.

HOW DOES THE LEGISLATION AFFECT WORK–LIFE BALANCE?

The CIPD (2009l) factsheet on work–life balance says the following:

- **Annual leave:** From 1 April 2009, all employees are entitled to a minimum of 28 days' paid annual holiday. Bank holidays can be counted towards this entitlement.

- **Working time:** The working week is limited to 48 hours, averaged over 17 weeks, for employees who have not 'opted out'. The Working Time Regulations also provide for minimum rest periods and make special provision for night work.

- **Parental leave:** There is a right to 13 weeks' unpaid parental leave for men and women at any time up to the child's fifth birthday. This must be taken in blocks or multiples of one week, with 21 days' notice given to the employer.

- **Time off for dependant care:** The right to take unpaid time off to deal with family emergencies (for example concerning an elderly parent, partner, child or other person living as part of the family).

- **Maternity leave:** All women are entitled to 26 weeks' maternity leave, plus an extra 26 weeks' additional maternity leave, making 52 weeks in total.

- **Paternity leave:** Fathers are entitled to two weeks' paid paternity leave, which can be taken as a single block of one or two weeks within the 56 days following the child's birth.

- **Adoption leave:** Employees adopting a child are entitled to 26 weeks' ordinary adoption leave and 26 weeks' additional adoption leave. Only one parent may take adoption leave: if they qualify, the other parent may take paternity leave.

- **Right to request flexible working:** Employees with children under the age of 17 (under age 18 if disabled) and those with caring responsibilities for adults including those with elderly or disabled relatives can request a change to their working arrangements, for example, in their hours, time or place of work. The employer can refuse such a request on specified business grounds but must follow a detailed procedure.

- **Part-time work:** Part-timers are entitled to the same hourly rate of pay and the same entitlements to annual leave and maternity/parental leave as full-timers but on a pro rata basis. Part-timers must also have the same entitlement to contractual sick pay and no less favourable treatment in access to training.

REQUESTS AND ENTITLEMENTS

When studying employee rights in these respects, it is important to distinguish between situations in which the employee has a 'right to request' and those in which there is a clear 'statutory right'. Every one of the rights listed above is related to attendance, and it has to be borne in mind that to survive, develop and attend to customer demands, organisations have business needs and priorities that, at times, may conflict with the needs of employees.

CONSULTATION

All organisations and all employees, however, have individually different needs, so there is little to be gained from looking over the fence. In any organisation, the strategy for work–life balance has to be specifically tailored to meet both business and individual needs. It involves more than simply conforming to the law; it means finding out directly from the employees about their personal needs and priorities, then considering how they can be met in ways that positively support business needs and priorities.

VOLUNTARY MEASURES

There are several benefits that an employer may offer above and beyond the legal standards that may help employees to achieve a satisfactory work–life balance. Some of these are beneficial to the organisation as well as the employee. They may include unpaid career breaks, paid sabbatical schemes and financing educational and training courses. Additionally, there are more informal benefits such as allowing the occasional paid or unpaid day off to attend to an important, but non-urgent matter at home or in the community. Furthermore, the minimum standards set down in legislation for maternity, paternity and other matters could be enhanced by offering higher pay and/or longer leave.

Such schemes not only give employees a great measure of control over how their working lives fit in with everything else they do, they also foster goodwill, loyalty, motivation and commitment.

WHY BOTHER?

Advancing technology has created the need for knowledgeable and highly skilled people who are deeply involved in the kind of work they do, and organisations are in competition for such staff. This so-called 'talent war' puts such employees in a position that enables them to be selective when it comes to choosing an employer. By implication, this means that organisations have to ensure they have sound retention plans. An attractive work–life balance policy, which has been constructed with the co-operation of, and contributions from, the staff will demonstrate the organisation's commitment to its employees' quality of life.

WHAT HR CAN DO

The HR contribution to the formulation of a feasible work–life balance policy is probably more significant than any other. The objective is to ensure that the organisation is one that encourages a healthy balance between work and non-work commitments among its employees. The task is eased if the top managers genuinely value their employees and are open to suggestions about a way forward. In the first instance, there are several steps that can be taken:

1 Organise a meeting with the employees and managers to tell them about your intentions and find out from them where they think improvements might be made.

2 Gather relevant information about the business needs and identify how the implementation of a policy will contribute to the achievement of business objectives.

3 Formulate a work–life strategy that will benefit both the business and the employees. The essence of the strategy is that the organisation and its employees are working in a mutually beneficial partnership.

4 Consider the arrangements that will be needed to cover for absence, to preserve goodwill with customers and between the employer and employees.

5 Draft a feasible and cost-effective action plan to accompany the strategy.

6 Take the package to the top managers and explain to them how and why the right work–life balance policy will benefit the organisation and its employees.

The package should include:

- policies that match operation needs
- reward and performance measures based on staff effectiveness in terms of results
- clear guidelines about the proposal, particularly for the line managers
- details of a meeting with staff to explain the new policies

- arrangements to have a joint meeting with staff to hear their views, discuss any ideas they may have for further improvement

- arrangements to have regular meetings with staff to advise them on any changes and listen to their ideas

- a monitoring system to check progress and identify and correct faults.

While it is the line manager who is in the best possible position to observe employees and identify those in need of assistance, it is primarily the role of HR to advise and assist in the development of a workplace culture that is supportive of employees striving to achieve a satisfactory work–life balance (WLB). Clutterbuck (2003, p4) maintains that:

> … only HR can make a convincing case for the business impact of investing time and money in promoting good work–life balance; only HR can craft and sell in to top management viable strategies for taking advantage of the competitive potential that a proactive approach to WLB brings; only HR can design and integrate the wide portfolio of policies needed; and only HR can develop and implement the processes for measuring progress against WLB goals.

It is important to involve staff in developing work–life balance policies rather than to decide for them in a paternalistic manner. Including discussion of work–life balance issues in the annual appraisal process is a way to elicit (to find out) on an individual basis the concerns of individuals that can be factored into future policy development or in fact form the basis of immediate action. Focus groups and staff surveys all form part of the process by which information about staff views on flexible working and work–life balance can be determined.

SUMMARY

Employment relations, in simple terms, means exactly what it says: that there is a relationship between the employer and the employee. There are formal and informal aspects to the relationship and both parties have rights, obligations and expectations. As well as the written contract of employment there is a relationship that is built between the employer and the employee, which is based upon the subjective expectations of, and beliefs about, the relationship between the employee and the organisation. Breaching this 'psychological contract' can be relatively easily achieved through promises made and not kept, but rebuilding it can be very difficult.

The chapter addresses the idea of the unitarist and pluralist perspectives on the employment relationship. Managers who take the unitarist view regard themselves as the only legitimate source of power and authority, which they value and protect. On the other hand, those who take the pluralist perspective allow and actively foster freedom of expression and the development of groups, which establish their own norms and elect their own informal leaders. In reality the management of people sits somewhere in the middle of the two extremes.

There are many parties in the employment relationship, ranging from line managers and the employees, who have daily contact between each other as well as with organisations such as unions and management organisations, for example the Confederation of British Industry. These types of organisation are indirectly involved in the worker–management interface yet can, from time to time and over time, influence the nature of the relationship; Figure 13.1 offers a view of the complexity of the pluralist nature of employee relations.

The chapter also addresses the role of the union and how it provides a formal negotiating body between management and employees during disputes or when an employee needs representation at a disciplinary hearing.

The TUC has established an organisation called 'unionlearn', which has the aim to help unions support 250,000 members a year to access and progress through lifelong learning.

The final section of the chapter deals with work–life balance, both from the perspective of an employee – that is, how they can seek to achieve a positive work–life balance and the downside of not achieving this status – and also from the perspective of management, who have targets to meet. Discussion also centres on the case for introducing policies that support staff in their aim of achieving a balance between home life and work as well as addressing some of the enabling legislation, much of which has emanated from the European Union.

REVIEW QUESTIONS

1 How would you define the employment relationship?

2 Why do you think it is said that the principles and practices of HRM have their roots in a unitary philosophy?

3 How would you distinguish *distributive bargaining* from *integrative bargaining*?

4 Using the CIPD annual *Absence Management* survey report, find out what organisations do to manage absence.

5 How would you define work–life balance?

6 What are the negative effects of working long hours?

7 Why is work–life balance a 'fluid' concept?

8 How would you go about choosing a job that would enable you to achieve a satisfactory work–life balance?

9 Why should an employer be concerned about employees' lifestyles?

10 What can HR do to help bring about work–life balance in the organisation?

BOOKS

HOLLINSHEAD, G., NICHOLLS, P. and TAILBY, S. (2003) *Employee relations.* **2nd ed. Harlow: Pearson Education Ltd.**

ROSE, E. (2008) *Employment relations.* **3rd ed. Harlow: Pearson Education Ltd.**

These two texts give a solid grounding in the arena of employment relations. Both offer a detailed analysis of the employment relations scene and are essential reading for students who have aspirations of furthering their careers in this field.

WEB LINKS

The CIPD also offers a podcast, and the results of its annual survey on employment relations can be found at: www.cipd.co.uk/onlineinfodocuments/atozresources.htm#e

Advisory, Conciliation and Arbitration Service: www.acas.org.uk

Central Arbitration Committee: www.cac.gov.uk

Confederation of British Industry (CBI): www.cbi.org.uk

Engineering Employers Federation (EEF): www.eef.org.uk

Find out about the EU: http://europa.eu/index_en.htm

Institute of Directors (IOD): www.iod.com

Institution of Chemical Engineers: www.icheme.org

Institution of Mechanical Engineers: www.imeche.org

unionlearn: www.unionlearn.org.uk

CHAPTER 14

Health, Safety and Well-being

INTRODUCTION

Whenever the conversation turns to health and safety at work people usually talk about the organisation's obligations under the law. Undoubtedly, conformity to the provisions of the law is of paramount importance, but there is also a strong business case for providing a healthy and safe working environment. After all, if the organisation is good at attracting the right people, it is more likely to retain them if it looks after their health and safety and takes whatever steps are necessary to ensure their well-being while they are at work.

Although *health, safety* and *well-being* are inextricably linked, in this chapter they are discussed separately, and the relationships between them are explained within the context of the discussions. First, however, the relevant legislation is examined, and since the HR practitioner has a significant administrative and advisory role, there is guidance on how the provisions of the law may be implemented.

HEALTH AND SAFETY LAW

Historically, the UK's long-term record for ensuring the health and safety of employees is poor. During the Industrial Revolution little was done to protect employees, visitors, local residents or passers-by from the hazards that arose from organisations' activities. Those most likely to be the victims of health and safety risks were the employees, and this is still the case. Several Factories and Shops Acts were passed in the early twentieth century but most employee protection was derived from the common law. Until 1949 there was no such thing as legal aid, and employees had to rely on the goodwill of their 'masters' to compensate them for injuries or health problems that were attributable to conditions in the workplace.

THE HEALTH AND SAFETY AT WORK ACT 1974

The Health and Safety at Work Act (HSWA) 1974 places an obligation on everyone involved in the organisation to maintain standards in the health, safety and well-being of people throughout the workplace, whether they be fellow employees, visitors or members of the general public passing by or living close to the premises. The responsibility includes protecting and securing people's safety and preventing environmental pollution of any kind.

THE HEALTH AND SAFETY EXECUTIVE (HSE)

The HSE is the primary delivery agent for the Department for Work and Pensions' (DWP) strategic objective of improving health and safety outcomes. The framework document between the DWP and the Health and Safety Executive states that (HSE n.d.[a], p2):

> The Secretary of State for Work and Pensions agreed that the HSE's aims should be to:
>
> i.   continue to deliver its mission of preventing death, injury and ill health to those at work and those affected by work activities; and
>
> ii. deliver any targets agreed for work-related health and safety.
>
> The HSE will also
>
> i.   protect the health and safety of workers and minimise risks from work to members of the public; and
>
> ii. ensure that the major hazard industries (such as nuclear, petrochemicals and offshore oil and gas) manage and control the risks around their work to a high standard which enhances assurance and allows these industries to operate with a high degree of public acceptance.

The framework document between the DWP and the HSE also sees the HSE as having an influencing role and an investigative role:

- to embrace high standards of health and safety;

- promote the benefits of employers and workers working together to manage health and safety sensibly;
- investigate incidents, enquire into citizens' complaints and enforce the law.

The full rights and responsibilities that the HSE has can be found by going to **www.hse.gov.uk/aboutus/howwework/management/dwphse.pdf**

HSE inspectors have the right to enter premises without notice and examine records. They can issue *enforcement notices* and prosecute serious and persistent offenders. The point should be made, however, that HSE inspectors have these powers in case they need them, rather than to fill the courts with minor and accidental offenders. HSE inspectors advise organisations on health and safety at work, and persuade them to behave responsibly.

WHAT ORGANISATIONS MUST DO

There are particular steps an organisation must take to conform to the law. One way to explain this is to imagine that you have just set up a new organisation. There are ten actions (steps) you must take to provide your organisation with a sound basis for health, safety and well-being, as listed below:

1. Write a *health and safety policy*. This means deciding how you are going to manage health and safety.

2. Set up a *risk assessment system*. Decide what could cause harm to people and how to take precautions. They must also keep records of the findings of the risk assessments.

3. Buy *employers' liability insurance* and display the insurance certificate in your workplace. If you employ anyone, you must do this.

4. Provide free health and safety training for your workers so they know what hazards and risks they may face and how to deal with them and provide them with personal protective equipment (PPE).

5. Engage *competent advice* to help you to meet your health and safety duties. Advisers can be your own workers, external consultants or a combination of these. If an organisation recognises a trade union in any part of the business then the Safety Representatives and Safety Committees Regulations 1977 (as amended) will apply. If the organisation does not recognise a trade union then the Health and Safety (Consultation with Employees) Regulations (as amended) will apply. Both of these regulations set out the duty of the employer in respect of how they must treat their safety representatives.

6. Provide toilets, washing facilities and drinking water for all of your employees, not forgetting those with disabilities. These are the basic health, safety and well-being needs.

7. Consult employees on health and safety matters. Most organisations have a *health and safety committee*.

8 Display the *health and safety law poster* or provide a leaflet containing similar information.

9 Report particular work-related accidents, diseases and dangerous events. You must also report if you are starting a construction project. RIDDOR is the Reporting of Injuries, Diseases and Dangerous Occurrences Regulations 1995; in the context of RIDDOR, the Health and Safety Executive requires organisations to report work-related illnesses and accidents to them.

10 Register with the HSE or your local authority, depending on the kind of business you are in.

HEALTH AND SAFETY POLICY

First, this is a statement of how the organisation intends to manage the health, safety and well-being of its employees, visitors and the general public. Second, it describes how health and safety will be organised and how the high standards that have been set will be achieved through the involvement of everyone, at all levels, throughout the organisation. Third, the statement includes details of how the policy will be implemented.

PAUSE FOR THOUGHT

Have you read your organisation's health and safety policy? Can you remember what it contains? Does it make you feel that the organisation is committed to providing a healthy and safe working environment?

What would you put into a health and safety policy? You will find help from the HSE (2008a), *An Introduction to Health and Safety*, available from **www.hse.gov.uk/ pubns/indg259.pdf**

RISK ASSESSMENT

This is about the identification of current and potential hazards, analysing the possible attendant risks and making recommendations for the removal or reduction of the risks. The HSE (2006) says that health and safety is about preventing people from being harmed or becoming ill through work; a *hazard* is anything that can cause harm or make people ill. *Risk* is the chance, high or low, that someone will be harmed by the hazard. The HSE (2006, p1) says:

> In many instances, straightforward measures can readily control risks, for example ensuring spillages are cleaned up promptly so people do not slip, or low filing cabinet drawers are kept closed to ensure people do not trip or the upper drawers are not overloaded so that the whole cabinet does not

over balance. For most, that means simple, cheap and effective measures to ensure your most valuable asset – your workforce – is protected.

STATUTORY REGULATIONS AND CODE OF PRACTICE

Risk assessment is regulated by the Management of Health and Safety at Work Regulations 1992 and the Code of Practice on Risk Assessment, which offers guidance on implementation. The regulations say that the employer must 'carry out a risk assessment of the workplace and make all necessary changes to bring property, practices and procedures up to the required standard'.

CARRYING OUT A RISK ASSESSMENT

If you employ five or more people, your risk assessments must be recorded. Clearly then, an employer who fails to carry out risk assessments is breaking the law, and the penalties can be severe. In the code of practice there is great emphasis on the identification of hazards, and the HSE, for example, points out various tasks and situations in which typically high-risk hazards are found:

- receipt of raw materials, for example lifting, carrying
- stacking and storage, for example falling materials
- movement of people and materials, for example falls, collisions
- processing of raw materials, for example exposure to toxic substances
- maintenance of buildings, for example roof work, gutter cleaning
- maintenance of plant and machinery, for example lifting tackle, installation of equipment
- using electricity, for example using hand tools, extension leads
- operating machines, for example operating without sufficient clearance or at an unsafe speed; not using safety devices
- failure to wear protective equipment, for example protective (hard) hats, boots, clothing
- dealing with emergencies, for example spillages, fires, explosions
- health hazards arising from the use of equipment or methods of working, for example VDUs, repetitive strain injuries from badly designed workstations or working practices.

FIVE STEPS TO RISK ASSESSMENT

The HSE (2006, p2) explains the risk assessment process in five steps:

- Identify the hazards.
- Decide who might be harmed and how.
- Evaluate the risks arising from the hazards and decide whether existing precautions are adequate or if more should be done.

- Record findings and implement them.
- Review the assessment periodically and update if necessary.

When carrying out the evaluation of risk, those involved should assess the level of risk in relation to each separate hazard. The severity of hazards may be classified on a short scale of, for example, 'slight risk', 'medium risk' and 'high risk'. Holt and Andrews (1993) proposed a severity rating scale as given in Table 14.1.

Table 14.1 Risk assessment: severity rating

1 Catastrophic	Imminent danger exists, hazard capable of causing death and illness on a wide scale
2 Critical	Hazard can result in serious illness, severe injury, property and equipment damage
3 Marginal	Hazard can cause illness, injury or equipment damage, but the result would not be expected to be serious
4 Negligible	Hazard will not result in serious injury or illness, remote possibility of damage beyond minor first aid case

Source: Holt and Andrews (1993)

The risk assessment process is not complete until action has been taken to eliminate any hazards found in the assessment and analytic process. Many organisations have staff members who are experts in the relevant fields, and the organisation's safety manager/officer will play a significant role in the whole process and in ensuring that appropriate action is taken. Where it is needed, however, specific advice is also obtainable from the HSE.

The reviews may be regularly undertaken, say annually or biannually, but special reviews may be necessary when change takes place, such as the introduction of new technology or a reallocation of jobs.

PAUSE FOR THOUGHT

When was a risk assessment last carried out in your area of work? Go on to the HSE (2006) website and download their guide to risk assessment, *Five Steps to Risk Assessment*, from **http://books.hse.gov.uk/hse/public/saleproduct. jsf?catalogueCode=INDG163REV2**

According to the HSE (2008b, p47), the factors that cause workplace risks are as follows:

- skin contact with irritant substances, leading to dermatitis, etc
- inhalation of respiratory sensitisers, triggering immune responses such as asthma

- badly designed workstations requiring awkward body postures or repetitive movements, resulting in upper limb disorders, repetitive strain injury and other musculoskeletal conditions

- noise levels that are too high, causing deafness and conditions such as tinnitus

- too much vibration, for example from hand-held tools leading to hand-arm vibration syndrome and circulatory problems

- exposure to ionising and non-ionising radiation including ultraviolet in the sun's rays, causing burns, sickness and skin cancer

- infections ranging from minor sickness to life-threatening conditions, caused by inhaling or being contaminated by micro-biological organisms

- stress causing mental and physical disorders.

ACCIDENTS AT WORK

References to accidents at work may invoke a variety of recollections ranging from those of our own individual experiences of witnessing or being personally involved in minor accidents or 'close shaves', to those major incidents that remain in our minds forever, such as large-scale factory fires, explosions in chemical plants, mining disasters and rail crashes – for example the Bhopal chemical factory explosion in India, the Kings Cross Station fire and the capsizing of the Herald of Free Enterprise. Even since the 1974 Act came into force, thousands of people have been killed or injured as a result of minor and major industrial accidents.

Discovering the causes of accidents, therefore, is an extremely important aspect of accident prevention. The causes identified through accident investigations may lead to appropriate preventive measures. Explanations for accidents are many and varied and attempts have been made to categorise them. These include: (i) environmental, (ii) behavioural and (iii) physiological (Molander and Winterton 1994).

It is important to regard the three sources of explanation as interrelated. For example, individuals' responses to the environment and the factors within it are both behavioural and physiological. Also, particular types of behaviour, such as alcohol or drug abuse, cause perceptive and physiological disorders that produce a negative and often dangerous psychological state.

ENVIRONMENTAL CAUSES

The working environment is extremely important, especially in industries that clearly are very hazardous, such as working on railways, at sea on ships and oil rigs, chemical factories, and building and mining operations. In such industries, however, both organisational and employee awareness of risk is high, and significant progress has been made in training and the provision of safety equipment.

While this high level of safety consciousness has resulted in fewer accidents, such industries are still regarded as high risk, although industries which clearly are less hazardous by their nature have a higher incidence of minor accidents. With many people, environmental causes of accidents are thought of as 'factory floor' phenomena, but the point has to be made that an office environment, with carelessley laid extension leads across the floor, faulty electrical fittings and insufficient working space, can also be a dangerous place.

Office workers often attempt to make minor repairs and adjustments to their electrical equipment, lighting and so forth, without switching off the power supply and without the right equipment to reach the area in which they think there is a fault. Thus we find people standing on chairs to reach ceiling fittings, bending under desks to fiddle with connection boxes and so forth. Often, even the chairs they sit on are unsafe in one way or another.

BEHAVIOURAL CAUSES

Particular aspects of social learning are responsible for accidents at work. This refers to learning that has not been developed through formal education or training, but picked up from copying the behaviour of others, conformity to 'norms' and through trial and error. A new employee, for example, may notice that to achieve particular productivity levels, which carry extra pay, that some workers breach health and safety regulations by removing machine guards or engaging in other unsafe practices that enable them to reach bonus figures.

Also, people experiencing stress undergo changes in behaviour. When they are worried about their marriage, home and family, job security and career prospects, they are thinking about those things when they should be concentrating on what they are doing. It has long been known that 'daydreaming' is a cause of accidents at work.

PHYSIOLOGICAL CAUSES

In addition to those referred to above, there are several specific physiological causes of accidents. Poor eyesight, colour blindness, poor hearing, a limited sense of smell and other physiological problems can cause slow reactions to situations and might turn a prospective 'near miss' into an accident. Not everyone is fit and healthy, and managers and supervisors should be aware of their staff's state of health and fitness in relation to the nature of the work that they assign to them. This especially applies to young people who may not be aware of safety procedures and may be easily influenced by others who have bad safety habits.

MANAGING HEALTH AND SAFETY IN THE WORKPLACE

According to the HSE, managing a safe working environment can be done by a four-pronged strategy based upon:

- policy
- organising
- planning
- measuring performance.

The HSE present their strategy in *Successful Health and Safety Management*, arguing that (HSE 2008b, p7):

> … effective health and safety *policies* set a clear direction for the organisation to follow. They contribute to all aspects of business performance as part of a demonstrable commitment to continuous improvement. … Stakeholders' expectations in the activity (whether they are shareholders, employees, or their representatives, customers or society at large) are satisfied. There are cost-effective approaches to preserving and developing physical and human resources, which reduce financial losses and liabilities.

In terms of *organising* there needs to be an effective management structure in place that is committed to safety through staff involvement and communication. In fact, the HSE uses the four 'Cs' of *control, co-operation, communication* and *competence*, which are necessary to deliver workplace safety. It can clearly be seen that management's role is to ensure that there is effective control over how work is done safely – that their beliefs are communicated, that they enlist the co-operation of their staff and treat them as equals in the context of safety. It is also important to recruit and develop competent staff who are capable of understanding the need for, and therefore who are able to deliver, a safe working environment for the good of all. They go on to say that (HSE 2008b, p7), '… Clearly management alone having an understanding of the policy is not effective.' It is management's vision, values and beliefs, in effect the culture that they, the management, wish to create and sustain, which has to be effectively communicated to their employees.

PLANNING

There needs to be a planned and systematic approach to implementing the health and safety policy through an effective health and safety management system. The aim is to minimise risks. Risk assessment methods are used to decide on priorities and to set objectives for eliminating hazards and reducing risks. Wherever possible, risks are eliminated through selection and design of facilities, equipment and processes. If risks cannot be eliminated, they are minimised by the use of physical controls, barriers, guards, and so on, or, as a last resort, through systems of work, meaning rules and regulations as to how things are done in the workplace, and the use of personal protective equipment (PPE). Performance standards are established and used for measuring achievement. Specific actions to promote a positive health and safety culture are identified. The *plan* is all about how, in a systematic way, the health and safety policy can be brought to life.

MEASURING SAFETY PERFORMANCE

Safety performance is measured against agreed standards to reveal when and where improvement is needed. *Active* self-monitoring reveals how effectively the health and safety management system is functioning. *Active* measurement systems review the planning of new equipment and plant that is to be installed into the workplace or the design of new ways of working. It is also about how effective safety systems are working and reviewing their operation against plan. *Reactive* measurement, on the other hand, monitors incidents, accidents and incidences of ill-health. Measuring how health and safety is operating in the workplace, which is the process of checking how effective safety systems are operating, is an opportunity to involve staff and so reinforce the safety culture of the organisation.

What the above means in practice could be having regular safety audits of parts of the organisation by senior management and safety representatives and also the conducting of staff surveys (HSE 2008b, p60).

NON-ACCIDENTAL HEALTH PROBLEMS

Not all health and safety problems are accident-related. When we think of accidents we think of events that cause physical injuries or even death. Serious damage to health, however, can be caused in the workplace by inhaling noxious gases or ingesting certain substances, perhaps caused by a failure to use safety equipment, or alternatively caused by carelessness, incorrect storage of materials or faults in production machinery and equipment. For example:

- Office workers may experience visual and musculoskeletal problems when using computer terminals.
- Repetitive strain injury (RSI) is the result of overuse of the same part of the body for too long a period, for example typing.
- Vibration 'white finger' is numbness in finger joints caused by continuous exposure to a vibration source such as a pneumatic road drill or a vibrator plate used for compacting hardcore.

Prevention of the above type of health problem is by regular communication to staff, use of 'toolbox talks', displaying posters and so on, and good-quality health and safety training.

HEALTHY WORKPLACE INITIATIVES

Healthy workplace initiatives began in 1992, when the national initiative *The Health of the Nation* was introduced in a white paper published by the Department of Health. The white paper recognised that the increasing concern of employers and their workforces over health issues provided opportunities to intensify health promotion in the workplace.

TASKFORCE SURVEY

A taskforce was appointed to examine and expand this activity. The taskforce carried out a nationwide survey and the results were set out in a report, *Health Promotion in the Workplace*, published by the Health Education Authority (HEA). The survey was designed to gather information about the nature and frequency of 'health at work' activities, in terms of track record, the present situation and future plans. In total, 1,344 organisations were examined.

Many aspects of workplace activity were covered by those questions, including:

- smoking and tobacco products
- alcohol and sensible drinking
- healthy eating
- weight control
- exercise/fitness/activity
- stress management and relaxation
- health screening
- cholesterol testing
- blood pressure control
- drugs/substance abuse
- back care
- HIV/AIDS
- heart health and heart disease
- breast screening
- cervical screening
- lifestyle assessment
- repetitive strain injury
- eyesight testing
- hearing
- women's health.

Not all organisations reported problems in every single area, so each of the 'healthy workplace' activities that were set up dealt with its own respective areas of concern. The initiative taken in the National Health Service, for example *Health at Work in the NHS*, was based on five main areas of concern: (i) occupational stress, (ii) sexual health (HIV/AIDS, etc), (iii) smoking, (iv) drug and alcohol abuse and (v) healthy lifestyle (eating habits, physical activity and so on).

HEALTH AND SAFETY AUDITS

Organisations should carry out health and safety audits, involving as many as possible of those directly concerned with health and safety issues. This may include health and safety officers and advisers, HR specialists, managers and trade union representatives. The purpose of such an audit is defined by Saunders (1992):

> A safety audit will examine the whole organisation in order to test whether it is meeting its safety aims and objectives. It will examine hierarchies, safety planning processes, decision-making, delegation, policy-making and implementation as well as all areas of safety programme planning.

The audit should include practical and quantitative issues, such as the adequacy and implementation of the organisation's health and safety policies and procedures, and safety practices such as the efficiency and effectiveness of risk assessments and accident investigations. Additionally it should cover attitudinal and qualitative issues such as commitment to all aspects of health and safety at work and the level of seriousness adopted by involved groups, such as the health and safety committee.

As with all audits, the purpose of a health and safety audit is to identify problems and areas for improvement, and ensure that appropriate action is taken to resolve problems and improve the relevant areas.

The law that applies to this is as follows:

- Management of Health and Safety at Work Regulations 1999 (risk assessment)
- Health and Safety (Consultation with Employees) Regulations 1996
- Safety Representatives and Safety Committees Regulations 1977.

 ACTIVITY 14.1

Next time you are walking through the workplace, university or college campus, keep an eye open for posters and other notices about health and safety. Count how many there are and note what they say.

STRESS-RELATED ILL-HEALTH

The word *well-being*, rather than *welfare*, is used in this chapter because it covers the services that one associates with welfare, but it also refers to individuals' physical and mental health, which implies that employees should be working in a physically safe and stress-free environment. Well-being is also concerned with employees' problems, such as their working hours, work overload, financial, home and marriage situations, susceptibility to stress and their general health and lifestyle.

WORKPLACE STRESS

The main emphases in this section are on the causes of stress, the nature and identification of the symptoms, and the steps that can be taken by the organisation and the individual concerned.

KEY CONCEPT: STRESS

It is sufficient for our purposes to say that stress occurs when an individual is pushed or pressurised beyond the limits of their normal coping capacity; when a person's perception of a situation induces tension and anxiety at a level that is beyond their normal experience.

THE SIZE OF THE STRESS PROBLEM

According to the HSE (2007):

- About one in seven people say that they find their work either very or extremely stressful.
- In 2005/06, just under half a million people in Great Britain reported experiencing work-related stress at a level they believed was making them ill.
- Depression and anxiety are the most common stress-related complaints seen by GPs, affecting 20% of the working population of the UK.
- When stress leads to absence, the average length of sick leave is 30.1 days (Labour Force Survey 2005/06).
- The above average is much higher than the average length of sick leave for work-related illness in general (21.2 days).
- A total of nearly 11 million working days were lost to stress, depression and anxiety in 2005/06.
- HSE research in 2003 into offshore work found approximately 70% of common work-related stressors are also potential root causes of accidents when they were caused by human error.

KEY CONCEPTS

(Taken from HSE 2009a, p24)

The **Labour Force Survey** (LFS) is a survey of 50,000 households each quarter which provides information on the UK labour market. The HSE's annual questions in the LFS are used to gain a view of work-related illness and workplace injury based on individuals' perceptions. The analysis and interpretation of these data are the sole responsibility of HSE. Further details about the LFS, and more specifically the HSE-commissioned questions, are available from www.hse.gov.uk/statistics/lfs/technicalnote.htm

Self-reported work-related illness (SWI): These are incidences of ill-health reported by people who have conditions which they think have been caused or made worse by their current or past work, as estimated from the LFS. The estimates of self-reported ill-health include long-standing as well as new cases; these 'incidences' comprise those who first became aware of their illness in the last 12 months. HSE has carried out SWI surveys, linked to the LFS, periodically since 1990 and have done, annually, since 2003/04.

THE LEGAL CASE: WHAT THE LAW REQUIRES

As described in more detail in Chapter 16, employers have duties:

- under the Management of Health and Safety at Work Regulations 1999: to assess the risk of stress-related ill-health arising from work activities
- under the Health and Safety at Work Act 1974: to take measures to control that risk.

The HSE expects organisations to carry out a suitable and sufficient risk assessment for stress and to take action to tackle any problems identified by that risk assessment.

SOURCES AND CAUSES OF STRESS

Sources of stress are those areas of life in which stressors are active. Research shows that there are six main areas of stress:

- the workplace
- personal finances
- marriage
- living accommodation
- home and family
- personal time and leisure.

STRESS AS A COMMUTER

The effects of stress that originates in one of the areas listed above stay with people as they commute from one area to the next. For example, people take their workplace stress home with them where its effects are communicated to the family. If there are additional pressures at home, perhaps over finances, the accommodation itself, or 'neighbours from hell', then they will be added to the load like a rolling snowball and carried to the other areas, including the workplace. In a severe case the load becomes too much to bear and ill-health follows.

STRESS AND PRODUCTIVITY

Stress adversely affects productivity. It has been estimated that around 100 million working days are lost annually through stress-related factors, such as sickness absence and reduced work performance. It is worth bearing in mind that these losses are 30 times greater than those associated with industrial relations problems, and an anomaly emerges when one compares the national and corporate investments that have gone into industrial peace with those dedicated to addressing stress problems.

THE HUMAN FUNCTION CURVE

This provides an explanation of what can happen when an individual is expected to cope with end-to-end emergencies, a continuously high workload or an excessive amount of time spent in the workplace. It is often said that 'a little stress is good for you' and that work performance increases as the pressure rises. 'It gets the adrenalin running,' they say, 'and you experience an energy boost.' The truth, however, is that such stress *actually reduces* one's ability to cope with the job, which in turn creates further stress (see Figure 14.1).

Figure 14.1 The human function curve

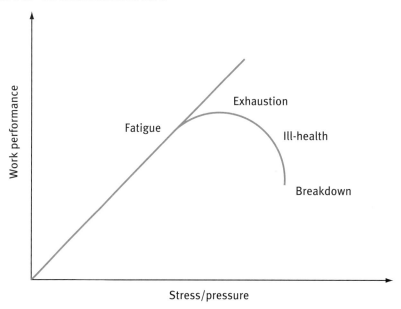

In Figure 14.1, the point at which *fatigue* appears on the curve will vary from one individual to the next, but the general principle is the same for everyone. *The curve of intended performance* provides an indication of the employee's unfulfilled intentions. In cases of severe stress, the employee is not always aware that their work performance is being affected in the way that is indicated in Figure 14.1.

DYNAMICS OF WORK STRESS

It was once thought that work-related stress was experienced mainly by company executives who claimed that time was their primary concern: always dashing about, attending breakfast meetings in the London boardroom and lunch meetings in Geneva. According to Smith et al (1978) and McLean (1979), stress-induced illnesses are not confined to either high- or low-status workers.

Regardless of how one job may compare with another in terms of stress, it is helpful to recognise that every job has potential stress agents (stressors). Additionally, it is helpful to note that an event or situation that one person may regard as stressful might be seen by another as an interesting challenge or even a route to success at something. Furthermore, stress affects different people in relatively different ways. Some people find it easy to cope with pressure, while others have great difficulty.

ORGANISATIONAL CAUSES

Researchers have identified a number of causes of work stress (Cooper et al 1988). Common to all jobs, these factors vary in the degree to which they are found to be causally linked to stress in each job and to the illnesses that may result from the experience of stress (see Figure 14.2 for a pictorial representation of how these factors are linked to the outcomes of stress).

Figure 14.2 Dynamics of work stress

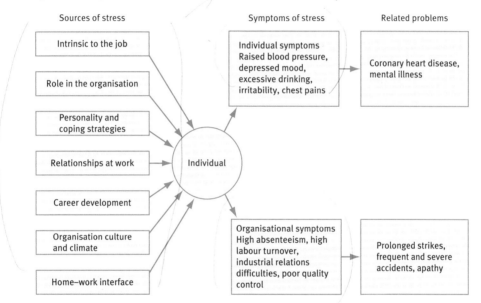

Adapted from Arnold et al (2005, p396)
Reprinted with kind permission of Pearson Education Limited (Copyright Pearson Education Limited 1991, 1995, 2005)

THE ROLE OF THE ORGANISATION

What can the organisation do to alleviate these problems? It was noted above that there are strong business reasons for the organisation to recognise the effects of stress and take action to alleviate it. In any case the organisation does have a social responsibility for the quality of life at work. Clearly, 'a little stress is good for you' is something that is not experienced by most people. Furthermore, it is clear that employees who work in a benign culture that provides a stress-free environment are enabled to concentrate exclusively on their work.

Stress has been classified as *transient, post-traumatic* and *chronic*, all of which are related to the timing of the events that caused them:

- **Transient stress:** occurs at the same time as the cause and is a short-term experience. For example, it may be experienced by emergency services workers when they are dealing with events such as public disorder, accidents, fires and a variety of other types of incident.

- **Post-traumatic stress disorders (PTSD):** occur after a shock caused by a critical life event, such as involvement in a serious traffic accident, sustaining severe personal injury or perhaps being mugged.

- **Chronic stress:** occurs as a result of continuous pressures being experienced by the individual for a period of time that is too long for the person to endure.

MANAGING STRESS

In this section, for the purposes of explanation, a distinction is drawn between *stress management* and *coping* with stress. Stress management consists of the arrangements that organisations, and others, make to minimise workplace stress, whereas coping with stress refers to the steps that an individual might take to moderate or eliminate their own personal stress.

Many organisations try to moderate the effects of stress by setting up an *occupational support service* (OSS), which is a section within the organisation through which employees may seek assistance when they experience the effects of stress. The scope of the service that may be offered by an OSS is determined by the number of employees and the kind of work in which the firm is engaged. A small to medium-sized organisation, for example, may arrange to access the skills of a nurse, an occupational psychologist and/or a stress counsellor, who can be called on as and when required. On the other hand, a large organisation might employ such experts and set up the OSS as a special department.

THE GOVERNMENT'S RESPONSE TO THE PROBLEM OF WORKPLACE STRESS

Because of the size of the problem of workplace stress the UK Government, through the HSE, has introduced *The Management Standards for Work Related Stress*. The standards consider and define the culture of how best to manage workplace stress. Particularly, as the website indicates (HSE n.d.[b]), the management standards for work-related stress help:

- identify the main risk factors for work-related stress

- employers focus on the underlying causes and their prevention

- provide a yardstick by which organisations can gauge their performance in tackling the key causes of stress.

The management standards for work-related stress cover six areas of work that are recognised to be stressors: The *demands* of the job, for example workload, the *control* of how much someone has over their work, the *support* by management that people receive, the quality of *relationships* in the workplace, the understanding of the work *role* and how might organisational *change* be affecting people.

The management standards (see HSE 2007) offer a tool with which to assess the state of the mental health of the organisation. The process that the HSE recommends is a five-step process:

1 Identify stress risk factors.

2 Decide who might be harmed and how.

3 Evaluate the severity of the risk.

4 Record the findings of the investigation.

5 Monitor and review progress.

As with many work-related issues, the process of risk assessment with respect to workplace stress can only be effective with the active support of senior management and engagement with and support of the employees and employee representatives.

 ## ACTIVITY 14.2

Go to the HSE's (HSE 2007) publication *Managing the Causes of Work-related Stress: A step-by-step approach using the Management Standards* and see how they suggest that a risk assessment on workplace stress should be conducted. You can access the publication from **www.hse.gov.uk/pubns/priced/hsg218.pdf**

The document is long but the key themes of how to go about a workplace stress-related risk assessment can quickly be determined. There is also a quick guide (HSE 2009b) called *How to Tackle Work-related Stress: A guide for employers on making the Management Standards work.* You can access this guide from **www.hse.gov.uk/pubns/indg430.pdf**

THE 'CARING' ORGANISATION

Some managers are reluctant to offer advice and assistance to employees on developing a healthy lifestyle. They regard lifestyle as a very personal issue and think that 'interference' by the organisation may be regarded as an unwarranted intrusion. Within the organisation, however, they have an opportunity to set an example by promoting a 'healthy workplace' by taking the following initiatives:

- **Smoke-free work areas**: It is now illegal to smoke in a confined public place. This also includes vehicles operated by an organisation. The onus is on management to police this piece of legislation.

- **Consulting the workforce** about the kinds of food that are served in the staff restaurant. This is best achieved by agreement and having a food policy.

- **Providing employees with information** about healthy living, including information on physical activity, healthy eating, generally looking after oneself.

Employees with health problems and disabled employees may need to consult a physician before adopting the advice.

- **Providing facilities**, where possible, for employees to engage in physical activity, and encouraging them to participate in sports.

- **Providing annual health checks**: There are 'well man' and 'well woman' schemes in which all occupational physicians are versed.

- **Creating and managing** a work environment that is physically safe and generally conducive to good health.

 Protecting the wrong people

CASE EXAMPLE

Phil Green had worked for seven years as a stock control computer operator in a large manufacturing company that supplied heavy machinery to industry. He was generally regarded as good at his job, reliable and always up to date. The shop floor was always busy so components were needed immediately on demand.

Phil was walking through the machine shop one day when he slipped on a patch of oil, lost his balance and fell to the floor, knocking his head on a machine on his way down. He was helped up and, after a brief rest, felt fine, and so he went on his way and thought no more about it. He did not report the accident for fear of getting someone into trouble. In the past week, however, Phil has felt that his ability to concentrate was failing him, he has frequent headaches and thought that his eyesight was not all it should be.

Eight days later Jack Hartnell, the section manager, came roaring into Phil's office and started shouting about a shortage of components. After telling Phil that he had had complaints about the shortages, he said, 'Your job is to make sure the stuff's there when it's needed. I've had enough of this, you'd better buck your ideas up if you want to keep this job – and you'd better take this as a warning.'

Three days after this Jack Hartnell started disciplinary proceedings against Phil. There was a hearing, which was chaired by Ian Cooper, the departmental manager, and

attended by Jack Hartnell and Tim Johnson from the HR department.

Jack Hartnell's evidence emphasised the problems that were caused by Phil's poor performance. The shortage of components meant that the assemblers could not do their jobs, and productivity was falling badly as a result. He concluded by saying that Phil should be given a formal warning. Ian invited Phil to explain the sudden reduction in his performance, but Phil said that he was unable to do so. From Ian's demeanour it was clear that he was reluctant to proceed with a written warning. Eventually, Tim asked Ian to bring the meeting to a close, saying that they needed time to decide what action should be taken and would let Phil have their decision as soon as possible. Ian agreed and the meeting closed.

The following day, Ian and Tim invited Phil to Tim's office 'for a chat'.

Questions about the case

1 Did Phil do anything wrong? If so, what was it?

2 What should Jack Hartnell have done when he spoke to Phil in his office?

3 What was missing from Jack Hartnell's evidence?

4 Why do you think Ian and Tim wanted to see Phil?

Discussion about the case

Obviously Phil could have been suffering from the effects of the accident, which of course, he should have reported, not only for his own sake, but for others who might also have had a fall. Action could have been taken to clean up the oil patch and then find out how the oil got there in the first place: one of the machines could have been leaking or it could have dripped from a fork-lift truck.

One of the first rules of management is that when something unexpected happens, the first response should always be to ask for an explanation and not jump to conclusions. Jack Hartnell failed in that respect. Clearly he was very annoyed, and it seemed that to him productivity was more important than his staff. His general manner did not represent good leadership. Because of that he missed an opportunity to have a chat with Phil to get at the real problem.

Knowing that Phil had a good long-term reputation, Ian and Tim had recognised Jack Hartnell's shortcomings in handling the situation and wanted to talk to Phil to find out why his performance was suffering in this 'out-of-character' way.

The situation says also a lot about the lack of a positive culture in the organisation. Not only should Phil have felt comfortable to report his accident, but there should have been a procedure to follow up the oil spillage because presumably others must have spotted that there was a hazard lurking on the shop floor.

This type of accident can also occur in offices where poor housekeeping results in trip hazards (bottom drawers of filing cabinets, waste paper bins left in walkways, and so on), causing unnecessary accidents. Safety audits should be conducted regularly in and around the work areas.

 ACTIVITY 14.3

Take a tour of your organisation, college or university campus and see how many hazards you can find that might put people's health and safety at risk.

You will find some help about how to conduct a risk assessment and how to meet minimum workplace health and safety standards by going to the Business Link website at: **www.businesslink.gov.uk/static/html/layer-222.html**

EMPLOYEE WELL-BEING

There are a range of approaches to achieving the holy grail of employee well-being. On the one hand there is a mix of encouragement and enforcement, which government offers; on the other hand there is the provision of family-friendly policies and employee assistance programmes adopted by organisations.

GOVERNMENT ENCOURAGEMENT

In 2005 the Government launched its health, work and well-being strategy (see the **www.workingforhealth.gov.uk/default.aspx** website). On 25 November 2008, Dame Carol Black, who heads up the government initiative, presented a review of the health of Britain's working age population (Black 2009). Her review was conducted against three principles (p9):

1 prevention of illness and promotion of health and well-being

2 early intervention for those who develop a health condition

3 an improvement in the health of those out of work, so that everyone with the potential to work has the opportunity they need to do so.

Dame Carol, in her review, justifies the Government's initiative by pointing out that 175 million working days were lost to illness in 2006 – this equates to over 5.7 days of work lost for each person employed per year. Further, she argues that on average the days lost to ill-health do not compare favourably with most other countries. This impacts negatively upon our ability as a country to compete in the global marketplace. The cost to the country of ill-health and worklessness amounts to over £100 billion annually (Black 2009, p10), which the review points out is equivalent to the total GDP of Portugal. Dame Carol gives the main causes of the problem (p10) in the following way: '... mental health problems and musculoskeletal disorders are major causes of sickness absence and worklessness due to ill-health'.

 ACTIVITY 14.4

Go to the Working for Health website at **www.workingforhealth.gov.uk/default.aspx** and explore the initiatives that the Government is encouraging organisations to become involved with around the UK. You may also wish to read the Government's response (Department of Health 2008) to Dame Carol's review at **www.workingforhealth.gov.uk/improving-health-and-work-changing-lives.pdf**

The Government (Department of Health 2008) is being proactive in response to Dame Carol's review by publishing its own response, entitled *Improving Health and Work: Changing lives*. It proposes (p25) four key initiatives:

1 **Electronic 'fit note'** – which will replace the current medical certificate, and GPs switch the focus of their advice to what people can do rather than what they cannot.

2 **A national education programme for GPs** – to improve their knowledge, skills and confidence when dealing with health and work issues and enable them to adopt the advice they give to help people stay in or return to work.

3 **Health, work and well-being co-ordinators** – The co-ordinators will stimulate action on health, work and well-being issues in their areas, offering advice and support to help local partnerships and engage with smaller businesses in particular.

4 **National Centre for Working-Age and Well-being** – The centre will form an independent and authoritative body providing a range of core functions related to the health and well-being of working people. These will include: gathering

and analysis of data; enabling the monitoring of trends; and helping to determine the impact of interventions and initiatives. The centre will identify evidence gaps and encourage research to close gaps.

THE GOVERNMENT AND WELL-BEING LEGISLATION

The organisation is responsible for the well-being of its employees while they are working on its behalf: the organisation is said to have a 'duty of care' for its employees. Today, it is becoming commonplace for employees, or ex-employees, to take legal action against their ex-employers for breaching their duty of care.

Increasingly, the kind of UK legislation that is related to employee well-being is the result of European directives that have been enacted in all of the member countries of the European Union, where the bases of the policies are: (i) equal treatment for all, (ii) fairness at work and (iii) family-friendliness. It is important to bear in mind that much of this legislation is directed at non-work areas, as well as the area of employment.

Although Chapter 16 deals with how employment legislation impacts upon the workplace, it would be remiss of us here if there were no mention of how legislation has sought to influence, through controlling measures, the link between work and a healthy workplace and healthy work environment, both physical and mental. The previous section sought to address how the Government, through the HSE, is seeking to influence behaviours in the workplace to encourage organisations to adopt healthy work practices, in the broadest sense. The Government explains this aptly (Department of Health 2008, p26) as, '... understanding of the importance of work for good health [by] enhancing education, training, and standards of care and service delivery ...'.

Legislation surrounding health and well-being has been included on the 'statute books' in the UK since the late 1990s. Specifically we refer to the Working Time Regulations, the Work and Families Act 2006 and the Health Act (England) 2006.

The Working Time Regulations address, as the name implies, among other things: the length of the working week, rest breaks and holiday entitlements. The focus of this piece of legislation is on the specification of the minimum standards with which all organisations must comply, in the context of the duration of work.

The Work and Families Act (WFA) seeks to remove some of the pressures that impact upon new parents. The law gives rights to parents to claim statutory maternity pay, take leave, upon the arrival of their new child, and also to request (not demand) flexible working. The right to request flexible working (see Chapter 16) offers the opportunity for certain groups of people, that is, those with children under six years of age (as of April 2009 the qualifying age has been increased to under 17 years), those with a disabled child under 18 years of age or those with caring responsibilities to apply for flexible working. 'According to Carersuk (**www.carersuk.org/Home**) there are six million carers in the UK of whom three million are working. Three in five people will be caring for someone at some point in their lives' (IDS 2006c). The stress associated with both caring for and finding the time to care for someone is immense. The right to request flexible working goes some way to mitigating the stress that this role causes employees and so may assist them to be able to remain in the workplace.

Finally, the Health Act (England) 2006 deals specifically with the health issues associated with smoking in the workplace. The driver for this Act of Parliament focuses on the right of employees to work in an unpolluted, smoke-free environment, '… given that the dangers of passive smoking are substantial, an employee who is exposed to smoke in the workplace, and whose employer does not respond to his or her concerns, could rely on this implied term [of employment]' (IDS 2007). This means that an employer would be breaking the implied terms of the employment contract, which is that they must provide a safe working environment – and clearly a smoke-laden environment would not be healthy!

It can be seen that the Government, through various Acts of Parliament, regulations and initiatives, is encouraging employees to adopt healthy lifestyles and employers to work towards creating healthy workplaces with a focus on both the healthy mind and the healthy body. The welfare system will have its focus on supporting people to work or enabling them to be able to work.

ORGANISATIONAL HEALTH AND WELL-BEING

The total cost to the country of ill-health and worklessness, as previously stated, is in excess of £100 billion annually; the actual cost to industry (2006), as estimated by the Confederation of British Industry (CBI), is £13.4 billion per annum; total costs include all causes (Asherson 2007). This level of loss cannot be ignored; the economic case for investing in the health of the working population is strong. In response to these high costs and the impact ill-health has upon organisations and those that work within them, Investors in People (IiP) have developed a health and well-being element for their existing standard, 'The Health and Well-being Framework', which is designed to help organisations address absenteeism (Department of Health 2008, p47).

The question of course for organisations is what to do? Some companies with available financial resources, such as Citigroup, invest heavily in the well-being of their workforce. They have invested in the building of a new health centre for their employees. Rob Green, Citigroup's EMEA Benefits Manager (cited in North 2008, p1) says, 'When it came to setting up the new centre we simply wanted to be the best in class. We wanted to lead the market with a clear focus on well-being and ultimately become an employer of choice.' Clearly Green is linking the benefits offered by the company in their 'health and well-being initiatives' to quality recruitment and selection. Citi's on-site health centre is estimated to have resulted in savings of over 20,358 working hours in 2007, simply eliminating the time it takes for an employee to travel to and from their previous health practitioner.

According to the CIPD's *Absence Management* survey (2008), 'a third of organisations now have an employee well-being strategy. This is down slightly from last year's figure of just over 40% but up from 26% recorded in the CIPD's 2006 survey.'

ACTIVITY 14.5

Access the CIPD's annual *Absence Management* survey for 2008 and examine the range of
initiatives and benefits that companies offer to their staff. How would you choose what to offer in
your organisation if you were asked to consider what well-being initiatives your company should
offer?

What to include in the well-being strategy is always a problem for employers,
especially the small to medium-sized organisation. The Government is coming to
the assistance of these sizes of organisation by piloting some projects under the
guidance of the NHS and under the banner of NHSPlus:

> The NHSPlus is a network of 115 occupational health providers across
> England (SALUS and OHSAS in Scotland) delivering services to the
> NHS employers and their staff. Through a £20 million capital fund, the
> Government is helping to establish eleven demonstration sites throughout
> the country, with the NHSPlus platform, to test out the most innovative
> ways of offering NHS occupational health services cost effectively to small
> and medium size enterprises (SMEs). (Department of Health 2008, p47)

EMPLOYEE ASSISTANCE PROGRAMMES

Larger organisations, as was described with Citigroup, may operate their own
occupational health schemes, but others, including some SMEs, may opt to buy
into *employee assistance programmes* (EAPs). An EAP is an external agency
commissioned by the organisation to manage employee well-being on its behalf.
The external agency is staffed by experts such as psychologists and counsellors,
and there is also access to other experts such as solicitors, accountants and
doctors, whose services might be required, depending upon the cause of stress
experienced by an employee. EAPs are seen as an alternative to occupational
support schemes. There are arguments for and against each kind of employee
service.

It is thought that employees have greater confidence in an EAP, since they may
be somewhat suspicious of the in-house *occupational support service* (OSS)
worker, who might be seen as a manager's informant. As an external agency, the
EAP has the added advantage of objectivity and, having no internal political axe
to grind, may be totally candid when it tells managers where there is room for
improvement in the way they handle staff.

It has been noticed that organisations that avail themselves of such external
services are well placed to demonstrate that they have a caring attitude towards
their employees, for example, if an ex-employee has taken legal action against
them on the grounds of a stress-related cause of illness and loss of employment.

In addition to the above, organisations may decide to offer a range of benefits,
from gym membership to yoga classes. Carolyn Boyd (2009, p1) has a word

of caution, quoting Keri Spooner from the University of Technology, Sydney, when she says, 'Staff who are healthier, both physically and psychologically, can grow productivity but free trips to the gym or massages at work will do little to make those suffering from illness or from dread of work refrain from taking sick leave.' Spooner sees a more 'productive' approach by, for example, having flu inoculations at work as being better targeted. To further muddy the waters, in the same article, Professor Don Iveson points out that Coors, the US beer company, has, through a cardiac rehabilitation scheme, got heart attack sufferers back to work earlier and worked with them to help them to a fuller life.

Making the right choice of what to do when introducing a well-being set of benefits or a full wellness programme, as an employer, is a crucial one. A knee-jerk reaction to introduce, for example, gym membership as a benefit, although administratively an 'easy' option, may not be the best overall approach to the problem for the company and its employees; and it may be perceived by the more cynical employee as tokenism. A better approach would be to involve those concerned and to ask their views.

SUMMARY

This chapter discusses the concept of health and safety at work and the importance it plays in the employment relationship. The Health and Safety Executive (HSE) is introduced as the overarching body that has been set up by the Government to deliver its mission of preventing death, injury and ill-health to those at work and those affected by work activities, and also, from a wider governmental perspective, to deliver targets agreed for work-related health and safety. The HSE is instrumental in developing and enforcing workplace legislation.

HR has a role to play in the health and safety of an organisation's employees because good health and safety practice is inextricably linked to behaviour in the workplace and is therefore a matter for the HR department. According to the HSE, managing a safe working environment can be done by a four-pronged strategy based upon:

- policy
- organising
- planning
- measuring performance.

Clearly, with the best will in the world there are those within the workplace who will either take shortcuts in work processes and expose themselves or others to dangers – for example driving a heavy articulated lorry above the speed limit in a built-up area – and so there needs to be legislation that acts both as a deterrent and as a punishment. This chapter therefore explores some, not all, of the legislation that applies in the workplace.

The word *well-being*, rather than *welfare*, is used in this chapter because it covers the services that one associates with welfare, but it is also refers to individuals' physical and mental health, which implies that employees should be working in a physically safe and stress-free environment. Well-being is also concerned with employees' problems, such as their working hours, work overload, financial, home and marriage situations, susceptibility to stress and their general health and lifestyle. A significant proportion of this chapter is devoted to stress in the workplace because it is one of the major causes of workplace ill-health. Stress is an invisible enemy but managers have no excuse if they do not recognise the signs exhibited by individuals or perhaps signs that may indicate that stress is being more widely experienced within the organisation.

The concept of employee well-being is discussed as well as how it has strong links to the bottom line; in 2006 there were 175 million work days lost to ill-health within the UK. The Government takes the prevention of work-related ill-health very seriously and in 2005 launched its health, work and well-being strategy. Dame Carol Black headed up the government initiative and she presented a review of the health of Britain's working age population. Her review considered: the prevention of illness and promotion of health and well-being; early intervention for those who develop a health condition; and an improvement in the health of those out of work, so that everyone with the potential to work has the opportunity they need to do so. The chapter concludes by discussing what measures organisations can take to improve the well-being of their employees.

REVIEW QUESTIONS

1 What should an organisation's health and safety policy contain? (You will find help by accessing the Health and Safety Executive's document, 'Successful Health and Safety Management' from **www.hse.gov.uk/pubns/hsg65**)

2 What are the main purposes of carrying out risk assessments? Where would you find information on how to carry out a risk assessment in the workplace?

3 How are the three main categories of accidents at work classified?

4 What is the purpose of a health and safety audit?

5 Why should the organisation offer support and assistance to employees with non-work-related problems?

6 How would you define stress? What is a stressor?

7 What types of worker are the most susceptible to stress?

8 What are the management standards for work-related stress?

9 What are the characteristics of a healthy workplace?

10 What can the HR department do in its role to promote a positive health and safety environment and culture?

11 In what circumstances might the Working Time Regulations be ineffective?

12 What are the negative effects of working long hours?

BOOKS

PILBEAM, S. and CORBRIDGE, M. (2010) *People resourcing and talent planning: HRM in practice.* **Harlow: Pearson Education Ltd.**

Pilbeam and Corbridge's text provides a very good introduction to the management of health and safety in the workplace.

WEB LINKS

Acas points out on its website that work can have a positive impact on the health and well-being of employees that impacts upon business performance. They have produced a booklet entitled *Advisory booklet: Health, work and wellbeing*, which deals with, as they say on their website: 'the relationships between line managers and employees, the importance of getting employees involved in job design, flexible working and the use of occupational health'. Their booklet can be downloaded from **www.acas.org.uk/index.aspx?articleid=693**

For practical advice on managing health and safety in the workplace, the Health and Safety Executive publish a series of books that are written in a very easy-to-understand style and deal in a practical way with the essentials of safety and health management in the workplace. Their book *Essentials of Health and Safety at Work* can be found at **http://books.hse.gov.uk/hse/public/saleproduct. jsf?catalogueCode=9780717661794**

Acas: www.acas.org.uk

Anxiety UK: www.anxietyuk.org.uk

Business Link: www.businesslink.gov.uk/static/html/layer-8.html

Carers UK: www.carersuk.org/Home

Charlie Waller Memorial Trust: www.cwmt.org

Department for Work and Pensions: www.dwp.gov.uk

Depression Alliance: www.depressionalliance.org

Government's health and work initiative: www.workingforhealth.gov.uk/default.aspx

Health and Safety Executive: www.hse.gov.uk

Health and Safety annual statistics: www.hse.gov.uk/statistics

Health and Safety Executive's role: www.hse.gov.uk/aboutus/howwework/management/dwphse.pdf

Institute of Directors guide 'Leading Health and Safety at Work': www.iod.com/intershoproot/eCS/Store/en/pdfs/hse_guide.pdf

International Stress Management Association: www.isma.org.uk

Managing the causes of work-related stress: A step-by-step approach using the Management Standards: www.hse.gov.uk/pubns/priced/hsg218.pdf

MIND (national association for mental health): www.mind.org.uk

Office of Public Sector Information (view Statutory Instruments ie Acts of Parliament): www.opsi.gov.uk

Rethink Severe Mental Illness: www.rethink.org

The American Institute of Stress: www.stress.org

The Samaritans: www.samaritans.org

The Work Foundation: www.theworkfoundation.com

EXPLORE FURTHER

CHAPTER 15

Diversity and Equality

LEARNING OBJECTIVES

After studying this chapter you should:

- understand what is meant by diversity and the implications it has for the organisation
- be able to define and describe discrimination in all of its forms
- understand the concept of fairness at work
- understand the law on discrimination and the provision of equal opportunity
- understand the role of the HR practitioner in the implementation of policies on equality and the management of diversity.

INTRODUCTION

The aims of this chapter are, first, to provide an understanding of diversity, including how it is managed in the organisation, its influence on the nature of social interaction and the general workplace culture. Second, the discussion includes how this aspect of organisational life is controlled by convention and to a considerable degree by an ever-growing list of complex legislative measures. Third, the chapter provides an understanding of the concept of fairness at work.

The view taken in this chapter is that while it is critically important to conform to the law in matters of discrimination, it is only possible to legislate against behaviour that is discriminatory. Prejudice, for example, which is the main root cause of discrimination, is a personality characteristic and is impossible to detect unless the person's behaviour allows it out, which is when it becomes harmful to people's feelings, and indeed to their rights. Legislation is therefore only part of the solution to discrimination, and additional solutions are suggested later in the chapter.

KEY CONCEPT: DIVERSITY, PREJUDICE AND DISCRIMINATION

Diversity, prejudice and discrimination are expressions that are used in an everyday context, but they have also been defined here for specific usage and to assist your understanding of this chapter.

Diversity
Diversity is present when, for whatever purpose, any number of individuals get together and interact. Generically the word *diversity* means variety. The term *organisational diversity* refers to the range of differences between the individuals and groups among employees.

Prejudice
In *generic* terms, prejudice means the holding of an unreasonable opinion or like or dislike of something. Heery and Noon (2001, p279) say that in the context of *workplace discrimination*, prejudice means holding negative attitudes towards a particular group, and viewing all members of that group in a negative light, irrespective of their individual qualities and attributes.

Discrimination
In very broad terms, we can say that discrimination occurs when, on grounds that are not relevant to a particular purpose, one person, or a group of people, is treated less favourably than others. Specific types of discrimination are defined separately by each of the relevant Acts of Parliament, and these are examined later in the chapter.

ORGANISATIONAL DIVERSITY

The general use of the word 'diversity' in relation to the make-up of an organisation's workforce is comparatively recent, but diversity itself is as old as humankind. The original concept is based upon individual differences, and since every individual is unique, organisations always have had diverse workforces. In modern terms, however, diversity also refers to differences between groups of different ethnic backgrounds, religious groups, sexual orientation, gender, marital status, disability and age.

INDIVIDUAL DIFFERENCES

All individuals are different from each other; they are different psychologically, physically and behaviourally. The chance of finding two people who are exactly alike is the same as that of finding two people who have matching fingerprints. Individuals have their own personal values, beliefs, feelings and attitudes that have developed from their long-term perceptions and interpretations of the world around them. Wherever people go, from one country to another, from one organisation to another, their unique personality characteristics travel with them.

Differences between people become apparent when you watch them work. Everyone has their own unique way of learning and of developing and using their knowledge, talents and skills. No two people work in exactly the same way. Even people who do the same job have their own peculiar way of doing it. All of this can be summarised in one word: *diversity*.

THE INFLUENCE OF DEMOGRAPHIC CHANGES

The demographic changes that have taken place in the UK population in recent years are reflected in organisations' workforces. Today's organisations employ people who hail from a range of national, religious, social, cultural and ethnic backgrounds. In addition, there are differences in age, gender and physical ability, including disability.

The demographic changes have broadened the diverse structure of the UK population, especially in terms of group types. In organisations, this has focused attention on the need to recognise diversity, learn how to manage it and how to eliminate discrimination. It is unlikely, however, that discrimination will ever be totally eliminated. The point was made above that discrimination is born of prejudice, which is a personality characteristic that causes particular individuals to discriminate against others simply on the grounds of their differences.

PAUSE FOR THOUGHT

How do people treat each other in your organisation or in your university or college? Do they all respect each other's beliefs and values? Or are there those whose prejudices show through now and again? Do you think it is important that people respect each other regardless of their background? Why?

WHAT ORGANISATIONAL DIVERSITY IS ABOUT

According to Daniels and MacDonald (2005), diversity is:

> … about recognising this range of differences in people and valuing people as individuals, respecting their differences and their different needs. It is also about accommodating differences wherever possible so that an individual can play a full part in the working environment.

The CIPD says that diversity is about 'valuing everyone as individuals, as employees, customers and clients' (CIPD 2010a). Bloisi (2007) says that diversity is about 'recognising that people are different and that these differences should be valued and used to enhance the workplace'.

PERSPECTIVES ON DIVERSITY

Since 1970 there has been a stream of legislation, codes of practice and regulations on many forms of discrimination. In 1970 there was the Equal Pay Act, then in 1975, the Sex Discrimination Act, followed by the Race Relations Act in 1976. The Disability Discrimination Act was a little later, in 1995, and then age discrimination legislation followed in 2006. The 2006 Equality Act brought much of this together by establishing the Equality and Human Rights Commission (EHRC) in 2007 to replace the Equal Opportunities Commission, the Commission for Racial Equality and the Disability Rights Commission to deal with all aspects of equality. In addition to sex, race and disability discrimination, the Equality Act covers discrimination on the grounds of religion or belief, sexual orientation, and imposes duties relating to sex discrimination on persons performing public functions. There is more on the law in Chapter 16.

Despite all of this activity, discrimination in the workplace still occurs. In terms of providing equal opportunities in the workplace, the rights of individuals have become well known, and yet there still are gaps in some employers' understanding of the moral, ethical and legal aspects of managing diversity and the provision of equal opportunities.

WHY BE CONCERNED WITH EQUALITY AND DIVERSITY?

There are two sets of arguments relating to why equality and diversity are important: 'the social justice case' and the 'business case'.

The social justice case

The social justice case relies on the premise that we have a 'moral obligation to treat employees with fairness and dignity' (Beardwell and Claydon 2007, p228). In fact, the fundamental objective of the EHRC as summarised in the Equality Act 2006 is to support the development of a society where:

- People's ability to achieve their potential is not limited by prejudice or discrimination.
- There is respect for and protection of each individual's human rights.
- There is respect for the dignity and worth of every individual.
- Every individual has an equal opportunity to participate in society.

There is mutual respect between groups based on understanding and valuing diversity and on shared respect for equality and human rights (Office for Public Sector Information 2006a).

The business case

Apart from treating people fairly being the 'right thing to do', there is the point of view that diversity and provision of equal opportunities make good business sense. Beardwell and Claydon (2007, p230) suggest four reasons to support this:

- better use of human resources
- leads to a wider customer base
- creates a wider pool for recruitment
- leads to a positive company image.

PAUSE FOR THOUGHT

Consider your own workplace – how diverse is the workforce? What difference does it make, do you think? Have you ever worked in an 'all-male' or 'all-female' team? Have you noticed any differences in the way they work together?

It is worth noting that organisations that demonstrate an interest in promoting social equality tend to attract good employees. If an organisation is seen as an equal opportunity employer, then it also sends the message that they care about their employees and thus are a 'good' employer. As we know, attracting the right kind of employees is vital in achieving a competitive edge, so being attractive to prospective employees is a definite plus point. All too often, equal opportunities and diversity is considered from a legislative point of view – 'we must ensure we don't break the law', but the business case for diversity is equally important.

EQUAL OPPORTUNITY AS A LEGAL OBLIGATION

The degree to which organisations are successful in the way they manage diversity is determined not only by the related policies and procedures but also by the collective attitudes of their managers: attitudes that lead to a particular approach. In broad terms, there are two types of approach. The first is to perceive equal opportunities as purely a legal obligation, something that has been imposed on the organisation from the outside, which implies that as long as the organisation conforms to the law and has acceptable policies and procedures in place, it will be regarded as a respectable employer in legal and ethical terms. The problem with this approach is that it reduces the concept of equal opportunity to little more than an administrative matter.

RECOGNISING DIVERSITY – THE ADVANTAGES TO BUSINESS

The second approach bears in mind that the primary purposes of an organisation are to survive and develop so that it can continue to provide the best possible service for its public, or to provide the highest possible return to its shareholders. To achieve those ends, the organisation needs a knowledgeable and competent workforce. A diverse workforce can mean that you have access to a wide range of people, with a variety of views, abilities and outlooks – all of which can enhance your business, by bringing different ideas and attitudes that may add to your competitive advantage.

Employing 'clones' will lead to less challenging attitudes and 'more of the same'. Having a diverse workforce brings variety, which may lead to creativity and innovative ways of working. This attitude is one that recognises the potential benefits that diversity can bring to the organisation. Your customers are likely to be a diverse group – it makes sense for your employees to reflect this diversity too. The more diverse the range of people and ideas in the organisation, the more likely that the organisation will accommodate changes and survive in a recession or compete in boom times. Diversity in the workforce encourages flexibility and adaptability – which are important to any successful business that wishes to stay ahead of its competitors.

PREJUDICE

It is evident from the definitions given earlier that prejudicial attitudes are towards groups, because they are different, and towards individuals, because they are members of those groups.

The factors that arouse prejudice against groups are often based on appearance. According to Heery and Noon (2001), for example:

> We typically think of prejudice as being against a particular group based on gender, race/ethnicity, religion, disability, age and sexual orientation. However, prejudice extends much further, and is frequently directed at other groups based on features such as accents, height, weight, hair colour, beards, body piercings, tattoos and clothes. It is extremely rare to find a person who is not prejudiced against any group – although most of us are reluctant to admit our prejudice.

STEREOTYPING

It was noted above that prejudicial attitudes are against groups and against individuals because they are members of particular groups.

 KEY CONCEPT: STEREOTYPING

The act of judging people according to our assumptions about the group to which they belong. It is based on the belief that people from a specific group share similar traits and behave in a similar manner (Beardwell and Claydon 2007).

Such biased perceptions occur when people rely on the stereotyped image and ignore factual information concerning individuals. For example, an elderly person will have outdated ideas; young drivers are reckless; men cannot multi-task and women are not good drivers. A glance at the facts, however, will tell you that none of these assumptions is true of all members of those groups. However, not all stereotyping results in creating negative images: the preconception can also be positive. For example, it might be believed all Welsh and Italian people are good singers.

ACTIVITY 15.1

Think of groups of people you know, for example students, British people on holiday, teenagers. What stereotypes come to mind? Do the people you know in these groups fit the stereotype? If you are a member of one of these groups (for example student), how does it feel to be viewed in this way?

It would be rare to find a person who does not attribute particular characteristics to members of diverse groups. Problems of discrimination arise when we base our impressions of people on stereotype alone.

PAUSE FOR THOUGHT

How do you think you would you react if you were presented with new information about an individual that contradicts your stereotyped image of him or her? Would the information cause you to alter your attitude towards that person? Or would you ignore the new information in order to maintain your original view? How dangerous is it to view people via stereotypes?

LEGISLATION ON DISCRIMINATION

Discrimination is a subjective term when used in normal daily life. When people make choices about what food or clothes to buy, they *discriminate* in favour of some things and against others. Such decisions reflect people's tastes and opinions. In such contexts discrimination is perfectly legitimate. In some other contexts, however, discrimination has been made unlawful – that is, where we discriminate on grounds that are not fair, for example if we base our decision on whether to appoint someone, on their race or their gender, rather than on their ability to do the job.

The law on discrimination is complex and extensive. For the purposes of this chapter, the emphasis is on employment law, although many of the legislative measures that are examined here also apply to circumstances outside of employment situations (see also Chapter 16).

At present some of the relevant legislation includes:

- **Equal Pay Act 1970** – purpose: pay and contracts must be the same for men and women doing like work.

- **Sex Discrimination Act 1975** – purpose: makes it unlawful to treat less favourably on grounds of sex, gender reassignment or marital status.

- **Race Relations Act 1976** – purpose: makes it unlawful to treat less favourably on grounds of colour, race, ethnic origin or nationality.

- **Trade Union and Labour Relations (Consolidation) Act 1992** – purpose: makes it unlawful to discriminate on the grounds of trade union membership.

- **Disability Discrimination Act 1995** – purpose: makes it unlawful to discriminate against disabled people in their terms of employment, promotion opportunities, by dismissing them or by subjecting them to any other detriment.

- **Part-Time Workers (Prevention of Less Favourable Treatment) Regulations 2000** – purpose: provides part-time workers, who are on the same type of contract as full-time workers, with equal treatment.

- **Fixed-Term Employees (Prevention of Less Favourable Treatment) Regulations 2000** – purpose: provides fixed-term employees with the right to treatment that is equal to that of equivalent permanent employees.

- **Employment Equality (Sexual Orientation) Regulations 2003** – purpose: protects people against discrimination on grounds of sexual orientation of any kind.

- **Employment Equality (Religion or Belief) Regulations 2003** – purpose: makes it unlawful to discriminate on grounds of religion or belief.

- **Employment Equality (Age) Regulations 2006** – purpose: prohibits unjustified age discrimination in employment and vocational training.

- **Equality Act 2006** – purpose: established Commission for Equality and Human Rights, responsible for enforcing anti-discrimination rules in the areas of sex, race, disability, sexual orientation, religion or belief. It has general responsibility for promotion of human rights.

DISCRIMINATION

Workplace discrimination has been illegal since 1970, when the provisions of the Equal Pay Act became law. Since then, increases in the amount and complexity of legislation and case law decisions have provided managers with the daunting task of keeping the organisation within the law and struggling to control discriminatory behaviour, not only in the implementation and interpretation of policy, but also on the part of employees.

INDIVIDUAL DISCRIMINATION

This occurs when, for example, in employment selection assessment and decision-making, selectors allow their prejudices to influence their decisions. Also, when in employment, members of minority groups are often denied the opportunity to be trained and developed, or to gain opportunities for promotion.

GROUP DISCRIMINATION

Group discrimination occurs on national and organisation-wide bases. For example, on a national basis, statistical information shows that in April 2009 hourly rates for men working full-time were £12.97, compared with only £11.39 for women (Office for National Statistics Nov. 2009). There is a gender pay gap (as measured by the median hourly pay excluding overtime) of around 12.2% for full-time employees.

ACTIVITY 15.2

In your own organisation, how many women managers are there? Do women reach their full potential? What is your experience of discrimination – have you ever felt that you were unfairly treated?

INSTITUTIONAL DISCRIMINATION

Discrimination against groups may become institutionalised. Sometimes the way the organisation operates is fundamentally discriminatory. Discriminatory behaviour becomes part of the culture. This kind of culture might be demonstrated by staff making jokes about certain racial groups or about disabled people, for example, and that becomes an accepted way of behaving. If it does become part of the culture, it may not be reported, since the employees may feel that their complaints, particularly of sex and race discrimination, will not be investigated thoroughly. Organisations such as the police have made great efforts to avoid institutionalised racism, for example, by changing their procedures and their culture and by training staff.

PAUSE FOR THOUGHT

When making a selection decision for, say, employment, promotion or to carry out a special project, selectors have to discriminate in favour of one candidate and against the others. However, the grounds on which such selection decisions are made are clearly prescribed by law. What approach do you think the selectors might adopt to ensure that such decisions are made without prejudice?

In Activity 15.2, disproportionate results might be attributable to employment selection and internal promotion procedures. Written policy statements usually demonstrate good intentions in legal and ethical terms, but implementation through the related procedures does not always reflect those good intentions. Interviewers may not ask overtly discriminatory questions, but may still harbour prejudice and discriminatory attitudes.

CATEGORIES OF DISCRIMINATION

Discriminatory decisions and behaviour may occur on the grounds of sex, marital status, sexual orientation, race, religion, disability and age. Such decisions and behaviour may be categorised as direct discrimination, indirect discrimination and victimisation.

 KEY CONCEPT: DIRECT DISCRIMINATION

Where a person is treated less favourably than another on the grounds of sex, marital status, sexual orientation, race, religion or belief, disability or age.

It is possible to place various interpretations on the term 'less favourably'. For example, a person who is treated differently from others might regard that treatment as less favourable than the treatment the others received. It might be, however, that the complainant's employment circumstances were just different from those of the other employees; different treatment is not always less favourable treatment.

 Direct sex discrimination

CASE EXAMPLE

A woman pilot working for British Airways made a flexible working request to enable her to work part-time; her request was refused. Supported by her union, she won her employment tribunal claim for sex discrimination. British Airways appealed twice to the Employment Appeals Tribunal (EAT) but the appeal was rejected (EAT/0306/05, 21 July 2005).

If there are a lot less of one type of group in your workforce (for example women, disabled people, and so on) then that group might be considered to be 'disadvantaged'. If there are very few ethnic minorities in the workplace, for example, they may be classed as a 'disadvantaged group'.

 KEY CONCEPT: INDIRECT DISCRIMINATION

Indirect discrimination occurs when a requirement or condition is applied universally and appears to therefore be non-discriminatory but *does* actually apply to more members of disadvantaged groups compared with other groups.

Indirect sex discrimination

CASE EXAMPLE

In the case of *Price* v *The Civil Service Commission*, indirect sex discrimination was demonstrated when a maximum age limit of 28 years was imposed on entry to the 'executive officer' grade. It was argued that under this ruling, women were considerably disadvantaged since they were often raising a family at that age, and that the imposed limit constituted indirect discrimination. This was not regarded as discrimination on grounds of age; the ruling given was that the imposed age limit constituted indirect discrimination (EOC Sex Discrimination Decisions no. 9).

ACTIVITY 15.3

Examine the definition of indirect discrimination (above), then study the case example. The person who brought the legal action was a woman, so she was a member of the disadvantaged group.

VICTIMISATION

This occurs when an employer treats an employee less favourably than other employees would be treated on the grounds that they have been, intend to be, or are suspected of being involved in legal proceedings against the employer to seek redress for discrimination on one of the prohibited grounds (for example sex, race, disability and so on).

SEX DISCRIMINATION

The Equal Pay Act 1970 (EPA) prohibits unjustified differences in pay and contracts: that is, the terms and conditions of employment, which must be the same for men and women doing like work. The Sex Discrimination Act 1975 (SDA) makes it unlawful to treat individuals less favourably on the grounds of sex or marital status. The initial purpose of both the EPA and the SDA was to provide women with protection from discrimination. However, it is important to note that under these Acts, men and women have equal rights to protection, although the number of legal actions brought by women is far greater than those brought by men.

GENUINE OCCUPATIONAL REQUIREMENT

Employers may be exempt from observing the provisions of the SDA for jobs that have particular requirements, which are known as *genuine occupational requirements*, or GORs. The purpose of this is to maintain public decency and/

or to meet certain expectations. For example, it is lawful to employ a person of one specific sex in jobs such as actor, model, changing room attendant and toilet attendant.

IMPLICATIONS FOR EMPLOYERS

These two major pieces of legislation carry widespread implications for employers. The areas that are most affected are:

- **Recruitment and selection**, in which every stage and action, from drafting a job requisition through to making the selection decision, is subject to the law.

- **Employment contracts**, including the terms and conditions of employment.

- **Training and development**, in which both sexes must be given equal opportunities to undertake courses, not forgetting longer-term courses financially sponsored by the organisation and involving attendance at a local college or university.

- **Promotion**, in which, again, equal opportunities must be given.

- **Benefits, facilities and services** such as pension schemes, medical care, help with long-term sickness and counselling services, in which equal access must be available to both sexes in all circumstances.

- **Severance**, including terms and conditions for share options, selection for redundancy and redundancy payments, in which the criteria must apply equally to both sexes.

GENDER REASSIGNMENT

It has been estimated that there are about 2,500 transsexuals in the UK (Gender Identity Research and Education Society 2010) and the likelihood of an individual HR professional encountering a discrimination case on these grounds is small. The purpose here is to cover the main points relating to discrimination on grounds of gender reassignment. More detail can be found by visiting the Gender Identity Research and Education Society website.

The Sex Discrimination (Gender Reassignment) Regulations 1999 amended the SDA75. The regulations are a measure to prevent discrimination against transsexual people on the grounds of sex in pay, vocational training and treatment in employment.

 KEY CONCEPT: REGULATORY LEGISLATION

It is important to note that the Sex Discrimination (Gender Reassignment) Regulations 1999 amend the SDA, and they become part of the Act itself. Thus, for the purposes of employment and vocational training, discrimination on grounds of gender reassignment constitutes discrimination on grounds of sex, which is a breach of the SDA. This means that any reference in the SDA to discrimination against men or women may be read as applying similarly to gender reassignment.

DISCRIMINATION: GENDER REASSIGNMENT

Since the medical procedure that achieves gender reassignment is in two main stages, discrimination is unlawful at either or both of those stages, or after the reassignment procedure has been completed. The definition of gender reassignment discrimination, therefore, is that it is unlawful to discriminate against a person for the purpose of employment or vocational training on the ground that the person (i) intends to undergo gender reassignment; (ii) is undergoing gender reassignment; (iii) has at some time in the past undergone gender reassignment.

In such a case, 'unfavourable treatment' means treating a person less favourably on gender reassignment grounds than you treat, or would treat, a person for whom no gender reassignment grounds exist. This category of discrimination also applies to recruitment, unless a GOR exists.

SEXUAL ORIENTATION

The relevant legislation for this is the Employment Equality (Sexual Orientation) Regulations 2003. The regulations make discrimination by employers and trade unions on the grounds of sexual orientation unlawful, and are intended to encourage tolerance and to protect the dignity of people in the workplace. Daniels and MacDonald (2005, p72) point out that numerous attempts have been made to assert that the Sex Discrimination Act 1975 should be interpreted so as to encompass discrimination on grounds of sexual orientation, but these arguments consistently failed both in the UK courts and at the ECJ. The word 'sex' in the Sex Discrimination Act 1975 clearly means gender and not 'sexual orientation' or 'sexual preference'.

The regulations cover direct and indirect discrimination, victimisation and harassment. The regulations define sexual orientation as 'a sexual orientation towards':

- persons of the same sex, for example gay men or lesbian women

- persons of the opposite sex, for example heterosexual men and women

- persons of the same sex and the opposite sex, for example bisexual people.

The regulations do not protect people whose sexual orientation leads them to become involved in such criminal activities as paedophilia and sado-masochism.

Sexual orientation

The first successful claim for this kind of discrimination was heard at Stratford Employment Tribunal in January 2005. The discriminatory acts against the claimant included senior colleagues nicknaming him 'Sebastian' after a camp character in BBC Television's *Little Britain* show, presenting him with a t-shirt with pink lettering before a conference of 60 colleagues, calling him a queer, queen and someone who liked poofy drinks (kir royale) and handbags. He was deeply offended and humiliated. His claims were for harassment, direct discrimination and constructive unfair dismissal. The tribunal awarded him £35,000 compensation.

LEGAL POINT

If a person wishes to show that they have been discriminated against, they must also show that the treatment received was different from that offered to other employees in a similar situation. A lesbian woman, for example, would have to show that she was treated differently than a heterosexual man would have been treated in a similar situation.

RACIAL DISCRIMINATION

The legislation that prohibits racial discrimination in the UK is the Race Relations Act 1976 (RRA). Under this Act discrimination is prohibited on grounds of colour, race, nationality, ethnic origins and national origins.

GENUINE OCCUPATIONAL REQUIREMENT

As with sex discrimination laws, discrimination is permitted for recruitment, selection, training or promotion on the grounds of GORs for certain types of work, for example to work in a Chinese restaurant for the sake of authenticity. However, discriminatory treatment in the terms and conditions of employment is not permitted.

DISABILITY

The initial legislative attempts to provide disabled people with protection from discrimination were the Disabled Persons (Employment) Acts of 1944 and 1958. These original Acts were aimed at helping those who were disabled during the Second World War and introduced a 3% quota of disabled employees for employers of over 20 staff. The protection provided by these Acts was generally regarded as inadequate, and those representing disabled people actively campaigned for improvements. Their efforts eventually paid off when the

Disability Discrimination Act 1995 (DDA95) was passed. The DDA95 came into force in 1996 and provided disabled people with discrimination law in line with sex and race discrimination and abolished the 3% quota.

 KEY CONCEPT: DISABILITY

Disability is defined as: 'a physical or mental impairment which has a substantial and long-term adverse effect on a person's ability to carry out normal day-to-day activities' (Disability Discrimination Act 1995). Examples include cancer, diabetes, multiple sclerosis and heart conditions; hearing or sight impairments, or a significant mobility difficulty; and mental health conditions or learning difficulties.

People who have a disability, and those who have had a disability but no longer have one, are covered by the Act. For practical reasons it is important to understand the meanings of two of the expressions used in the definition:

1 'Long-term' is defined as 12 months or more. The definition covers not only those who have been disabled for 12 months or more, but also those whose disability can be reasonably expected to last for at least 12 months.

2 'Normal day-to-day activities' does not refer specifically to the day-to-day activities that are involved in the individual's job. It refers to the activities that most people carry out as normal parts of their lives.

MAIN PROVISIONS OF THE ACT

There are two main provisions of the DDA95 that apply to employers:

1 It is unlawful to discriminate against potential or current employees for a reason that relates to an individual's disability, unless the discriminatory action can be justified. Employers therefore should not treat a disabled person less favourably than they treat or would treat others to whom the given reason does not or would not apply.

2 Employers must make reasonable adjustments to the workplace and to the employment arrangements to accommodate the individual needs of disabled individuals.

REASONABLE ADJUSTMENTS

This includes making changes to premises – for example wheelchair access, adjusting, modifying or repositioning equipment – and making changes to working hours and the nature of supervision. Recruitment and selection procedures may be changed to make it possible for a disabled person to apply for a job in the first place. This may include modifying the design of documents, for example large print, and a willingness to accept job applications on a CD, by email or other suitable media. It is worth mentioning at this point that telecommuting may be ideal for people with certain types of disability.

RELIGION AND BELIEF

Discrimination in employment and vocational training on grounds of religion was made unlawful by the Employment Equality (Religion or Belief) Regulations 2003. 'Religion or belief' is defined as 'any religion, religious belief, or similar philosophical belief'. Genuine occupational requirements apply here too, as with sex and race: an example might be a hospital or school chaplain or, in the Islamic faith, a halal butcher must be Muslim.

BELIEFS

Care needs to be taken over the interpretation of the word 'belief', since the beliefs that some people hold may not be religious. Many people believe in particular causes and they confer virtue upon what those causes are designed to achieve. Some such beliefs are political, while others may be environmental.

It is important to appreciate that diversity in religious belief is not a static concept. There are changes over time in the ways in which religions expect their adherents to behave. Within individual religions, different groups and individuals also have different standards of orthodoxy and devoutness, and may consider themselves to be bound by their religion to observe different forms or standards of behaviour.

 KEY CONCEPT: PREDOMINANT FORCES

The UK is a secular country and the most powerful influences over the way we live come from secular institutions, including industry. Christianity is the established religion in the UK, although different denominations predominate in different areas and among different sectors of the population. However, there are many non-Christian religious minorities, some of them very sizeable, such as Muslims and Jews. The law requires organisations in the UK to respect the customs of adherents to all accepted religions, and not just to Christianity.

IMPLICATIONS FOR THE ORGANISATION

The criteria for religious and belief discrimination are virtually the same as those for discrimination on grounds of race. While it is essential for employers, and particularly HR practitioners, to develop an understanding of the law in these respects, sound employment policies and practices are the real answer to ensuring the effectiveness of a diverse workforce. The degree of success in this respect is attributable to the culture of the organisation and how culture is managed.

Contrary to common assumption, the variety of religions and beliefs in the community has only slightly increased. The more obvious effect is the raising of the profile of particular religions and beliefs through a marked increase in their membership. This, of course, is reflected in workforces across the UK.

Employers must make sure that prejudice and stereotyping on the basis of people's ethnic origins and religious beliefs do not result in unfair decisions about jobs and training. Failure to do this could lead to legal costs, lost productivity and damaged reputation when the law is broken. (CIPD 2009i)

AGE DISCRIMINATION

The Employment Equality (Age) Regulations 2006 make it unlawful to discriminate against employees, job-seekers and trainees because of their age. This includes direct and indirect discrimination, harassment and victimisation. The regulations also:

- remove upper age limits on unfair dismissal and redundancy

- introduce a national default retirement age of 65, making compulsory retirement below 65 unlawful unless objectively justified

- give all employees the right to request to work beyond 65 or any other retirement age set by the company (Acas 2010a).

HARASSMENT AND BULLYING

Harassment and bullying at work may take many forms and be motivated by a variety of causes. Both can have a serious effect on the health and well-being of individuals, who can become stressed and fretful, demotivated and unproductive. It also has a damaging effect on groups whose members become demoralised; they close ranks and become detached from their colleagues in other groups. This can have a deleterious effect on the organisation in terms of absenteeism, lost productivity, an increase in staff turnover, and ultimately failure to achieve objectives.

 KEY CONCEPT: BULLYING

'Bullying may be characterised as offensive, intimidating, malicious or insulting behaviour, an abuse or misuse of power through means intended to undermine, humiliate, denigrate or injure the recipient.' (Acas, *Bullying and Harassment at Work: Guide for managers and employers*)

 KEY CONCEPT: HARASSMENT

According to Acas (2010a), harassment is defined as: 'unwanted conduct affecting the dignity of men and women in the workplace. It may be related to age, sex, race, disability, religion, sexual orientation, nationality or any personal characteristic of the individual, and may be persistent or an isolated incident. The key is that the actions or comments are viewed as demeaning and unacceptable to the recipient.'

Sexual harassment is one of the most common forms of harassment and is specifically outlawed by the Sex Discrimination Act (as amended October 2005).

PAUSE FOR THOUGHT

Have you ever heard someone spreading malicious gossip about another person, or seen someone being ridiculed by others at work? Did it occur to you that this might be constituted as bullying or harassment? Often this kind of behaviour is ignored or seen as 'usual'. People may fail to do anything about it because they may be thought of as over-reacting.

Facts do not cease to exist just because they are ignored or brushed aside, but it is possible for the top managers of the organisation not to be aware of what is going on at middle and junior levels. The following case example highlights what can happen if senior managers fail to keep themselves informed of what is happening in the organisation at other levels.

CASE EXAMPLE

How not to manage

In a nationally known large plc, a supervisor was subjected to a continuous stream of harassment by his manager. The supervisor became seriously stressed and had a heart attack. After a period of sickness absence he returned to work; the harassment continued and he had another heart attack. Fortunately, he survived the second attack, and was recovering at home when his manager sent him a memo saying that if he did not report for work within a week he would be disciplined. As a result of his reaction to this threat, he was taken back into hospital.

After he was discharged from hospital, he took the memo to his solicitor. Legal action was taken against the company, and that was the first indication of these events that the board of directors had received. Out-of-court settlements often result from this kind of action and this case was no exception. Eventually the company agreed to pay compensation in the sum of £250,000.

Discussion of the case

As you can see, the compensation was quite substantial, but that was not the total cost to the organisation. It had legal fees to pay, which were considerable, and further costs were involved in finding a replacement for the supervisor, who had been advised by his doctors that he should not return to work in the foreseeable future. The manager, who had admitted his behaviour towards the supervisor, resigned and a replacement had to be found for him.

Prospective litigants should be warned that when someone becomes ill and seeks compensation through legal channels, the individual must show that there is a definite causal link between what happened in the workplace and the illness. The task of establishing a causal link is eased considerably if the case is one of physical injury, but it can be more difficult if it is the kind of illness that someone might suffer as the result of harassment in the organisation.

THE LAW ON HARASSMENT

Harassment is not always linked to discrimination, but it can be based on one (or more) of the prohibited grounds for discrimination, and this possibility is specifically mentioned in the legislation. It is not always possible to bring a case to an employment tribunal directly on the grounds of bullying, but it needs to be linked to one of the laws on discrimination mentioned above, for example the Race Relations Act, the Employment Equality (Sexual Orientation) Regulations 2003, Disability Discrimination Act, and so on.

 KEY CONCEPT: THE ROLE OF CRIMINAL LAW

Individuals are also protected against harassment by some laws that make forms of harassment a criminal offence: for example, the Criminal Justice and Public Order Act 1994 and the Protection from Harassment Act 1997. Under the Criminal Justice and Public Order Act, it can be a criminal offence for an individual to deliberately harass another person.

WHAT SHOULD EMPLOYERS DO ABOUT BULLYING AND HARASSMENT?

Acas suggest that a formal policy is important. This shows that there is serious commitment from management about not tolerating this kind of behaviour in the organisation. The policy should be linked in to discipline and grievance procedures so that people understand the importance of bullying behaviour and how to act in the case of a complaint. It should also include examples so that people know what constitutes bullying – as we saw earlier, bullying behaviour may be seen as acceptable or even normal, perhaps a joke, but may not be perceived like that by the person receiving the bullying.

As with many issues relating to people management, it is also important to train managers to deal with these areas and make sure that they have the skills to deal with them. Any investigations must be done promptly and objectively. As a result of the investigation, it may mean that counselling needs to be provided for the person being bullied – and possibly for the accused as well as the complainant. Another useful option is to bring in an independent mediator who can help to resolve the situation.

 ACTIVITY 15.4

Find out if your organisation or university has a policy on harassment and a procedure for dealing with it. If it does, ask if you may read the relevant documents. What do the documents contain? Do they cover training for managers and HR specialists in dealing with harassment? Does the organisation provide access to counselling in cases of severe distress caused by harassment or bullying?

PERPETRATORS BEWARE!

It should be noted that when harassment is alleged, complaints handled inside the organisation might not bring an end to the matter. Those who harass their colleagues and subordinates could be committing a criminal offence, as was noted above. This is not an 'either–or' situation, since regardless of the action that is taken inside the organisation, the victim could also press criminal charges. The perpetrator could find themselves personally liable and be ordered to pay compensation, in addition to any payment the organisation agrees to make, or is ordered to make by a court of law or an employment tribunal.

SEXUAL HARASSMENT

Sexual harassment is unwelcome physical, verbal or non-verbal conduct of a sexual nature. It includes:

- demeaning comments about a person's appearance
- indecent remarks
- questions about a person's sex life
- sexual demands by a member of the same sex or opposite sex
- name-calling using demeaning terminology that is gender-specific
- unwelcome physical contact and other conduct of a sexual nature that creates an intimidating, hostile or humiliating working environment.

It is important to note that it is possible for two people to develop a relationship at work that is warm and friendly, without being sexual. If the relationship does develop further and it is welcome on both sides, that is acceptable. However, it might lead to sexual harassment if only one of the parties to the relationship persists in trying to take the relationship further, while to the other, such advances are clearly unwelcome.

SUMMARY

We have seen the enormous raft of legislation covering discrimination in the UK. There is more to come, with the current Equality Act which gained Royal Assent on 8 April 2010 and is likely to come into force in October 2010. The Bill is the most significant piece of equality legislation for many years and will simplify, streamline and strengthen the law on employment, equal pay and services. It will give individuals greater protection from unfair discrimination and will make it easier for employers and companies to understand their responsibilities. It will also set a new standard for those who provide public services to treat everyone with dignity and respect.

REVIEW QUESTIONS

1 How would you define the basic concept of unlawful discrimination?

2 What do people mean when they talk or write about diversity in the organisation?

3 How would you distinguish between the 'business case' and the 'social justice' case for recognising and respecting diversity?

4 What factors in an individual or group might arouse a person's prejudices?

5 Name the main Acts that legislate against unfair discrimination in the UK.

6 Under the Disability Discrimination Act, what do you understand by the term 'reasonable adjustment'?

7 It has been suggested that we should examine to what extent our impressions of others are based upon stereotyping. What are the dangers of doing this?

8 How do we distinguish 'direct' from 'indirect' discrimination?

9 What might constitute a 'genuine occupational requirement'?

10 What should a policy on bullying and harassment include?

EXPLORE FURTHER

BOOKS

DANIELS, K. and MACDONALD, L. (2005) *Equality, diversity and discrimination.* **London: Chartered Institute of Personnel and Development.**

This text is recommended for those who wish to take a special and detailed interest in this subject.

WEB LINKS

Acas (age discrimination): www.acas.org.uk/index.aspx?articleid=1841

Acas (bullying and harassment): www.acas.org.uk/index.aspx?articleid=797

Directgov (disabled people, employment rights): www.direct.gov.uk/en/DisabledPeople/index.htm

Equality and Human Rights: www.equalityhumanrights.com/

Gender Identity Research and Education Society: www.gires.org.uk/grp.php

CHAPTER 16

Understanding Employment Law

LEARNING OBJECTIVES

After studying this chapter you should:

- be able to find legislation using the Office of Public Sector Information website
- be able to define the employment relationship and understand its legal framework
- understand the contract of employment and the main statutory provisions that contribute to the regulation of the employment relationship
- understand employees' contractual and statutory rights
- understand the origins of: equal pay, family-friendly, disciplinary and grievance, and health and safety legislation
- be able to define the role of the Information Commissioner in the context of the Data Protection Act 1998
- understand the extent and the requirements that the Data Protection Act 1998 has on the organisation.

INTRODUCTION

The aim of this chapter is to provide an understanding of the employment relationship and the elements that shape its formal and informal structure. This includes the contractual and statutory rights and obligations of the employer and the employee.

THE EMPLOYMENT RELATIONSHIP AND LEGISLATION

The UK's employment legislation sets the formal framework within which the employer and an employee conduct their business. Employment legislation sets responsibilities for both the employer and the employee and also gives rights to the employee in the context of the employment relationship.

DIFFERENCES BETWEEN CONTRACTS

As previously mentioned in Chapter 13, there is a contract of employment between the employee and employer. The employment contract can be of defined duration or be continuous. Whether it is defined or continuous, the employer and employee are still governed by the legal statutes, regulations and directives that are in force.

All employees have a contract of employment. While it is based on what both parties have agreed to be a *fair exchange* (the employee's time and skill in exchange for a salary or wage), it is different from a commercial contract such as, for example, the sale and purchase of a car or house. Such contracts have completion dates and terms and conditions that are an integral part of the agreement. The employment contract, on the other hand, is continuous in that both parties intend that it should go on until one side or the other wishes to terminate the relationship.

THE COMPONENTS OF A CONTRACT

A contract contains four main elements:

- an offer
- an acceptance
- consideration
- the intention to form a legal relationship.

DIFFERENT TYPES OF EMPLOYMENT CONTRACT

As you are probably aware, there are people who work in or for the organisation who do not have a permanent and continuous employment contract such as that discussed above. There are a variety of ways in which agreement may be reached when, for example, an employer needs to access particular skills and the people who possess those skills are willing to trade them. The skills may be needed for a fixed period of time, during which perhaps one specific project needs to be carried out. Alternatively, there may be tasks that need to be carried out intermittently but on a regular basis. To cover various knowledge and skill needs, organisations offer several types of contract.

Temporary contract

This type of contract may have a specified termination date, or alternatively, the contract may not include a predetermined finishing date on the mutual understanding that the job is not permanent. In either case, the worker may not make a claim for unfair dismissal, nor are they entitled to redundancy payment. A temporary contract may be made permanent, in which case the person is offered an open-ended, continuous contract and officially becomes an employee of the organisation with all of the rights of a permanent employee.

Fixed-term contract

This kind of contract always has a clearly specified duration, spelling out the start and finishing dates. People are engaged on a fixed-term contract when they have come into the organisation to carry out a specific project or, for example, to stand in for a permanent employee who is away on maternity/paternity leave, absent because of a long-term illness or on an external secondment. Even though the term is fixed and cannot be changed, the worker enjoys some of the rights of a permanent employee, such as equal pay and pension provision. Additionally, the employer is not allowed to require or request the worker to waive their right to protection against unfair dismissal or redundancy (Employment Relations Act 1999).

 ACTIVITY 16.1

Finding employment legislation

The Government has, conveniently, placed all its legislation in an easily accessible website, the Office of Public Sector Information (OPSI). Go to the OPSI website at **www.statutelaw.gov.uk** and enter into the 'Title' and 'Year' fields 'employment relations' and '1999'. Press the 'Go' button with your mouse and you should be offered *Employment Relations Act 1999* as the first choice on the retrieved list of legislation. Click on the Act and see what the legislation has to say about being accompanied at a discipline hearing, Section 10, 'Right to be accompanied'.

Zero hours contract

With this kind of contract the worker is not guaranteed any paid work at all. The worker must be available, however, to be called upon when there is a need. While it may not appeal to many workers, a retired teacher or nurse may find it attractive since it provides an opportunity to earn a little extra cash. For example, they might be called upon to cover for a sick employee. Zero hours contracts are also offered to shop assistants to do casual work at busy periods such as Christmas and the January sales. Other organisations, such as theme parks, seaside shops and stalls, offer so-called 'seasonal' contracts which are, in effect, zero hours contracts. Supply teachers, who are employed by an agency and who 'fill in' when a permanent school teacher is unavailable for work, are also, in effect, on zero hours contracts.

 PAUSE FOR THOUGHT

Study what is said above about different types of contract, identify your own type of contract of employment and find out if it is different from those of your friends, co-workers and student colleagues. What types of contract do they have?

Buying a car

Have you ever bought a second-hand car? What happened? The car was for sale, you liked it and started to negotiate a price. Eventually, you made an *offer* for it. Your offer may have been a sum that was less than the original asking price but the person selling the car *accepted* your offer. They accepted it in *consideration* of your offer, as an agreed purchase price. A contract is drawn up and you both sign it. You hand over the money and the seller hands over the car and the legal documents are completed. The car is now yours; end of *legal relationship*; end of contract.

Unlike the type of contract described in the above example, in which the terms and conditions were agreed on a once-and-for-all basis, the terms and conditions related to the employment contract are subject to continuous renegotiation and change.

TERMS AND CONDITIONS OF THE EMPLOYMENT CONTRACT

These fall into three categories:

1 **Express terms and conditions**: This is the list of the terms and conditions that govern and specify the details of the contract, which is given to the employee in writing usually shortly after joining the organisation. The expressed terms may be incorporated in a collective agreement, that is, with trade unions who are recognised by the employer or with the whole workforce. The CIPD factsheet on contracts of employment (2009d) states that these could, in many cases, be terms that meet minimum standards required by law, in areas such as:

  - the right to paid holidays

  - the right to receive at least the National Minimum Wage

  - the right to receive statutory notice of termination

  - the right to daily and weekly rest breaks.

2 **Implied terms and conditions**: These are integral parts of the contract, although they are not usually given in writing. It is assumed, for example, that the employer will be fair and reasonable and provide a healthy work environment.

3 **Statutory terms and conditions**: The employer should abide by the provisions of employment legislation which, for example, lays down standards for health and safety, working time, data protection, discrimination and statutory notice periods when terminating one's employment.

EMPLOYEES' STATUTORY RIGHTS

While employees have rights under the terms of the employment contract they have with the organisation, they also have rights that are created by legislation in the form of Acts of Parliament, such as those for equal pay, data protection and discrimination. A large proportion of this legislation has its roots in European Union directives and regulations.

The UK legislation covering employee rights is the Employment Rights Act 1996 (ERA96). Before this Act, employees' rights were provided by employment protection legislation, most of which was enacted in the 1970s and 1980s. The ERA96 consolidates the provisions of the earlier legislation and includes additions. The ERA96 is a very powerful piece of 'employment law' legislation and bestows on UK citizens many rights of employment. It should be borne in mind that the legislation relating to employee rights lays down minimum standards and that many organisations enhance those standards, for example with a view to retaining valued staff. Alternatively, agreement over enhancing certain rights may be reached through collective bargaining. In this book, space limitations prevent the coverage of all statutory rights; those explained below are the main rights. In the context of the Act the meaning of a contract is given on the Office of Public Sector Information website (OPSI 1996, ch3, s230): '"contract of employment" means a contract of service or apprenticeship, whether express or implied, and (if it is express) whether oral or in writing'.

STATEMENT OF TERMS AND CONDITIONS

One of the most important rights of an employee is to receive a statement of the terms and conditions of employment within two months of joining the organisation. The details that the Act (ERA96) requires to be included in the statement are:

- the names of the parties to the contract (the employer and employee)
- date of commencement of period of continuous employment
- hours of work
- location of the workplace and an indication if there could be a requirement to work elsewhere

- details of pay: the rates of pay, how it is calculated and frequency of payment, for example weekly, monthly
- job title or a brief description of the duties and responsibilities
- holiday entitlements
- arrangements about sick pay and sick leave
- details of the pension scheme
- entitlement to receive notice of termination of employment and obligation to give notice
- date of termination if it is a fixed-term contract
- any terms of a collective agreement that affects working conditions
- the contract must specify any disciplinary rules
- the person with whom the employee can seek redress of any grievance procedure.

There are also specialist terms that will not be covered here but would apply if the employee were to be asked to work outside the UK for a period of time exceeding one month.

 ACTIVITY 16.2

Go to the Employment Rights Act 1996, which is available from **www.opsi.gov.uk/acts/acts1996/ukpga_19960018_en_1** and see what the Act has to say about discipline and grievance in the workplace and the protection the Act gives employees should they raise health and safety concerns.

CHANGING TERMS AND CONDITIONS OF EMPLOYMENT

The ERA96 also deals with changes to terms and conditions of contract. Employers may change terms and conditions of employment but employees have certain rights if the changes are made. For example, a sudden reduction in pay rates that is made without consultation and an agreement represents a serious breach of the contract. Similarly, the contract would be breached if unilateral changes (changes made without any consultation) were made to other terms and conditions of employment, such as the hours required of the employee to work, the times required to work and holiday entitlements and company pension contributions.

The essence of the ERA96, as its name implies and as previously mentioned, is to give rights to employees. Although other legislation may enable employees, for example, to request flexible working (the original regulations were the Flexible Working (Eligibility Complaints and Remedies) Regulations 2002 SI 2002/3236), it is the Employment Rights Act 1996 (s80F) that gives a statutory right to employees to actually make the request as a change in terms and conditions in respect of working hours, working time or place of work. Thus the ERA96 would be the legislation that enables any agreement between the employer and employee on the change of working time because of a request made under the Flexible Working Regulations 2002 or subsequent legislation on this subject.

COMPANY HANDBOOK

Most medium-sized and large organisations issue a copy of the company handbook to all employees on joining. Most of the items listed above are included in the handbook, as are copies of the disciplinary and grievance procedures. The company handbook may or may not form part of the main contract of employment. Much depends upon the detail and preciseness that the handbook deals with employment relations and employment rights issues.

RIGHTS TO TIME OFF

There is a long list of rights to time off, some of which are given below as examples and all of which are rights that are given in the ERA96:

- Employees with at least one year's service are entitled to 13 weeks' unpaid parental leave in respect of each child born or adopted.

- Time off for public duties – Employees who hold certain public positions are entitled to reasonable time off – which is paid – to perform the duties associated with them. For example, someone who is a member of: a local authority, a statutory tribunal, a police authority, a board of prison visitors or a prison visiting committee, a relevant health body, a relevant education body, or the Environment Agency or the Scottish Environment Protection Agency.

- An employee who is an official of an independent trade union must be allowed reasonable time off with pay to carry out those duties.

- Employees with more than two years' service who have been given notice of redundancy are allowed paid time off to seek alternative employment and to arrange training.

- An employee is entitled to be permitted by their employer (ERA96 Section 57a) to take a reasonable amount of time off during the employee's working hours to take action that is necessary:
  - to provide assistance on an occasion when a dependant falls ill, gives birth or is injured or assaulted
  - to make arrangements for the provision of care for a dependant who is ill or injured
  - in consequence of the death of a dependant (note: the term 'dependant' is clearly defined in the ERA96)
  - because of the unexpected disruption or termination of arrangements for the care of a dependant
  - to deal with an incident that involves a child of the employee and that occurs unexpectedly in a period during which an educational establishment that the child attends is responsible for them.

TERMINATION OF EMPLOYMENT

This refers to the amount of notice of termination given by both the employer and the employee.

KEY CONCEPT: TERMINATION OF CONTRACT BY THE EMPLOYER

Once again it is the Employment Rights Act 1996 (OPSI 1996a, s86), which specifies the minimum requirement for notice:

1 'The notice required to be given by an *employer* to terminate the contract of employment of a person who has been continuously employed for one month or more –

   a is not less than one week's notice if his period of continuous employment is less than two years,

   b is not less than one week's notice for each year of continuous employment if his period of continuous employment is two years or more but less than twelve years, and

   c is not less than twelve weeks' notice if his period of continuous employment is twelve years or more.

2 The notice required to be given by an *employee* who has been continuously employed for one month or more to terminate his contract of employment is not less than one week.

3 ... but this section does not prevent either party from waiving his right to notice on any occasion or from accepting a payment in lieu of notice.'

Termination of employment, as a subject, is discussed in detail in Chapter 17.

FAMILY-FRIENDLY RIGHTS

MATERNITY RIGHTS

It is the ERA96 that gives the right for maternity or adoption leave, but subsequent legislation – in particular the Work and Families Act 2006, which gained Royal Assent on 21 June 2006 – extended further the rights of employees in relation to maternity and adoption leave and pay, flexible working and paternity leave and pay.

In terms of ante-natal care the right is for pregnant employees to be granted reasonable time off work to attend medical appointments connected with a pregnancy, without loss of pay. Section 55 of the ERA96 states: 'An employee who is permitted to take time off under section 55 is entitled to be paid remuneration by her employer for the period of absence at the appropriate hourly rate.'

All pregnant employees are entitled to a period of 26 weeks' maternity leave regardless of length of service. Women are now entitled, irrespective of length of service, to an additional 26-week leave, termed additional maternity leave (AML), giving her 52 weeks in total. The changes in terms of the removal of the qualifying period for AML were introduced as a result of the Work and Families Act 2006 (WFA).

The Maternity and Parental Leave Regulations (1999) state that an employee '... is entitled, during the period of leave, to the benefit of all of the terms and conditions of employment which would have applied if she had not been absent ...'. These terms and conditions also apply to additional maternity leave and additional paternity leave as were amended in the 'Maternity and Parental Leave etc. and the Paternity and Adoption Leave (Amendment) 2008.'

Those who qualify for adoption leave also are entitled to similar rights as those entitled to maternity leave. All women who qualify for maternity leave must take two weeks' compulsory maternity leave (CML) for the two weeks after giving birth. An employee qualifies for ordinary maternity leave if she notifies her employer, at least 21 days before the date on which she intends her ordinary maternity leave period to start, of the following information:

- that she is pregnant
- the expected week of childbirth – she must also provide a medical certificate that confirms this if the employer requests it
- of the date she intends to start her ordinary maternity leave.

During the 26 weeks' leave she is entitled to benefit from all of her normal terms and conditions of employment except for pay; this is termed ordinary maternity leave (OML). At the end of it she has the right to return to her original job. If the job no longer exists, the employer must offer her a suitable alternative, but if this is not possible, she may be entitled to redundancy pay.

 ACTIVITY 16.3

Use your web browser to access the Work and Families Act 2006 (OPSI 2006b), available from **www.opsi.gov.uk/acts/acts2006/ukpga_20060018_en_1** and see what the Act has to say about:

- the length of time an employee during maternity or adoption leave is entitled to statutory maternity pay.

RIGHTS UNDER THE WORKING TIME REGULATIONS 1998

Regulations to implement the European Working Time Directive came into force in October 1998. The regulations apply to all workers, including most agency and freelance workers. The regulations place limits on working hours and provide certain entitlements such as rest breaks and annual leave. The Working Time Regulations are available from OPSI (1998b).

The Working Time Regulations specify a range of rights, in terms of length of the working week, hours of work and regulated minimum breaks to which each and every employee is entitled. For example, the maximum working week, aggregated over seven days, is limited to 48 hours.

The daily rest that employees are entitled to enjoy is not less than 11 consecutive hours in each 24-hour period during which we work for their employer. Currently, as a result of the Working Time (Amendment) Regulations 2007 there is an entitlement to, since 1 April 2009, 5.6 weeks' annual leave (28 days), which can include the nationally nominated bank holidays (8 days). Where a worker's working time is more than six hours, they are entitled to a rest break of not less than 20 minutes.

There are usually special requirements for young workers, and the Working Time Regulations entitle young people to take a 30-minute rest away from their workstation after 4.5 hours' work.

Clearly, as well as having impact under the heading of 'family-friendly regulations', the Working Time Regulations have an impact in the field of health and safety because they restrict practices that encourage employees to overwork, become tired and so more likely to make mistakes and have accidents.

 ACTIVITY 16.4

Access the Working Time Regulations 1998 (Statutory Instrument (SI) 1833), available from **www. opsi.gov.uk/si/si1998/19981833.htm** and identify how the Government 'specifies' a young person. You will find the definition in Part 1 General, Section 2 (Interpretation) of the Statutory Instrument.

Why do you think the authorities go to so much effort to be specific about definitions?

RIGHTS TO FLEXIBLE WORKING

Since April 2003, the right to request flexible working has been available to qualifying employees who care for a child or children under the age of six or, in the case of a disabled child, under 18. However, these regulations have since been updated:

- 'Options for extending the scope of the right to request flexible working were explored in the Government's consultation exercise, "Work and Families: Choice and Flexibility" (2005), in which the right was extended to a wider category of employees. Consequently, one of the key provisions contained in the Work and Families Act (WFA) is the extension of the right to request flexible working to employees with caring responsibilities for adults.' (IDS 2006c)

- As from 6 April 2009, parents can request flexible working if they have children under the age of 17. See the Flexible Working (Eligibility, Complaints and Remedies) (Amendment) Regulations 2009 [SI 2009/595] (OPSI 2009).

These rights were initially introduced following the Work and Parents Taskforce's report 'About Time: Flexible Working', and form part of the Government's campaign to support a family-friendly culture in business and to enable employees to balance family responsibilities and work.

The statutory provisions relating to the right to request flexible working are set out in section 47 of the Employment Act 2002 (OPSI 2002). This legislation became effective from April 2003.

Changes in work practices relate to:

- the hours they are required to work
- the times when they are required to work
- where, as between their home and a place of business of their employer, they are required to work.

PAUSE FOR THOUGHT

'Many employers argue that such measures (as the right to request flexible working) would add substantially to their costs and make them less competitive internationally. There is also evidence of discontent about such measures from employees who do not have families, and a fear that too much legislation rather than helping women's employment prospects is acting as a "disincentive to hiring women of prime child bearing age"' (Lea, cited in Torrington et al 2008, pp766–7).

Do you consider that the Government has gone too far with this kind of legislation and is making the UK a nanny state rather than a competitive state?

EQUALITY AND EQUAL PAY LEGISLATION

All organisations have to bear in mind the provisions of the legislation on pay, for example the National Minimum Wage and discrimination laws. When developing and administering a payment scheme, therefore, the organisation has to conform to the minimum standards, which include the provisions of:

- the Equal Pay Act 1970
- the Equal Pay (Amendment) Regulations 1983
- the Employment Rights Act 1996
- the National Minimum Wage Act 1998.

EQUAL PAY ACT 1970

The aim of the Equal Pay Act (EPA) is to ensure that employees who are doing like work, which is work that is the same or broadly similar regardless of their sex, must receive the same rate of pay or be paid on the same salary scale. Organisations that pay such employees differentially are breaking the law. Similarly, men and women whose jobs may be different in character, but have been assessed similarly under a job evaluation scheme, must receive the same rate of pay.

EQUAL PAY (AMENDMENT) REGULATIONS 1983

These regulations supplemented the EPA with a clause that provides for equal pay for men and women when the jobs they do are of equal value, regardless of their type or how they have been classified under a job evaluation scheme. Equal value is measured according to the job's requirements in terms of competence, responsibility and level of decision-making. Refer to Chapter 12 for a discussion of job evaluation, the technique that is used to compare jobs for equal value.

PART-TIME WORKERS AND EQUAL RIGHTS

In 2000, another milestone in terms of pay equality entered the statute books when the Part-time Workers (Prevention of Less Favourable Treatment) Regulations 2000 (SI 20001551) came into force (OPSI 2000b). These regulations give rights to part-time workers to receive equal treatment in respect of their contract of employment when compared with full-time workers. Subsequent regulations, amending the 2000 Regulations, do not make differences as to whether the part-time worker is on a fixed-term contract or one of enduring length. In practice this means that part-time workers' pay should be pro rata for hours worked when compared with full-time workers and that they should be entitled, for example, to join a company pension scheme if full-time workers enjoy these benefits.

PAUSE FOR THOUGHT

Think of the contract of employment that you are employed under. What benefits, other than pro rata pay, would part-time workers who work for your organisation be eligible to enjoy?

EQUALITY LEGISLATION

SEX DISCRIMINATION ACT 1975

Part I, sections 1 and 2 of the Act refer to discrimination against both women and men, simply because of their sex; sections 2A and 3 deal with discriminatory practices because of gender reassignment and marriage.

In essence the Act says in the case of women that discrimination occurs if:

- on the ground of her sex an employer treats her less favourably than he treats or would treat a man, or
- a condition is applied to a woman or would apply equally to a man but which is such that the proportion of women who can comply with it is considerably smaller than the proportion of men who can comply with it, and which cannot

be shown to be justifiable irrespective of the sex of the person to whom it is applied, and which is to the detriment of that person because she cannot comply with it (as taken from the Sex Discrimination Act, 1975, Part I, sections 1, 2 and 2A [OPSI 1975]).

The above conditions equally apply to men, people who have had their gender reassigned and to married people.

The first bullet point above describes 'direct' discrimination and the second bullet point describes indirect discrimination.

RACE RELATIONS ACT 1976

Section 4 of the above Act refers to applicants for positions as well as employees.

It is unlawful for a person, in relation to employment by him or her at an establishment in Great Britain, to discriminate against a person on racial grounds in the context of:

- offering employment
- the terms of employment offered
- refusing or deliberately omitting to offer a person employment
- refusing access to opportunities for promotion, transfer or training, or to any other benefits, facilities or services
- dismissing the person from employment on racial grounds
- subjecting any person employed or who has applied for employment to harassment.

 KEY CONCEPT: RACIAL HARASSMENT

Where a person on grounds of race or ethnic or national origins, engages in unwanted conduct which has the purpose or effect of violating that other person's dignity, or creating an intimidating, hostile, degrading, humiliating or offensive environment for that person (as taken from the Race Relations Act, section 3A [OPSI 1976]).

SUMMARY OF ANTI-DISCRIMINATORY LEGISLATION

The law on discrimination is complex and extensive. Much of the legislation discussed also applies to circumstances outside of employment situations. At present the legislation, some of which has been discussed in detail, may be listed as follows:

- **Equal Pay Act 1970** – purpose: pay and contracts must be the same for men and women doing like work.
- **Sex Discrimination Act 1975** – purpose: makes it unlawful to treat less favourably on grounds of sex, gender reassignment or marital status.

- **Race Relations Act 1976** – purpose: makes it unlawful to treat less favourably on grounds of colour, race, ethnic origin or nationality.

- **Trade Union and Labour Relations (Consolidation) Act 1992** – purpose: makes it unlawful to discriminate on the grounds of trade union membership.

- **Disability Discrimination Act 1995** – purpose: makes it unlawful to discriminate against disabled people in their terms of employment, promotion opportunities, by dismissing them or by subjecting them to any other detriment.

- **Part-Time Workers (Prevention of Less Favourable Treatment) Regulations 2000** – purpose: provides part-time workers, who are on the same type of contract as full-time workers, with equal treatment.

- **Fixed-Term Employees (Prevention of Less Favourable Treatment) Regulations 2000** – purpose: provides fixed-term employees with the right to treatment that is equal to that of equivalent permanent employees.

- **Employment Equality (Sexual Orientation) Regulations 2003** – purpose: protects people against discrimination on grounds of sexual orientation of any kind.

- **Employment Equality (Religion or Belief) Regulations 2003** – purpose: makes it unlawful to discriminate on grounds of religion or belief.

- **Employment Equality (Age) Regulations 2006** – purpose: prohibits unjustified age discrimination in employment and vocational training.

POLICING DISCRIMINATION

In 2006 the Equality Act 2006, which set up Equality and Human Rights Commission (EHRC), was given Royal Assent. The commission effectively became established in October 2007. Prior to this time the policing of discrimination was handled by a number of commissions, each dealing with their own specific area of discrimination, for example: the Commission for Racial Equality (CRE), the Disability Rights Commission (DRC) and the Equal Opportunities Commission (EOC).

The duties of the new EHRC are five-fold (IDS 2006b):

> [The] Commission shall exercise its functions … with a view to encouraging and supporting the development of a society in which:
>
> a. people's ability to achieve their potential is not limited by prejudice or discrimination,
>
> b. there is respect for and protection of each individual's human rights,
>
> c. there is respect for the dignity and worth of each individual,
>
> d. each individual has an equal opportunity to participate in society, and
>
> e. there is mutual respect between groups based on understanding and valuing of diversity and on shared respect for equality and human rights.

EMPLOYMENT AND PAY

EMPLOYMENT RIGHTS ACT 1996

As mentioned above, this legislation consolidates employees' statutory rights in a single Act of Parliament. It affects employees' pay in that it prescribes (lays down rules about) unwarranted deductions from pay unless such deductions are made in particular circumstances. The Act therefore legitimises deductions if any of the following circumstances apply:

- when deductions are authorised by law, such as income tax, National Insurance contributions or court orders, such as for payment of maintenance to an ex-spouse

- when there is a statement in the employee's written contract which specifies that certain deductions may be made from wages and when the employee has already given written consent, for example when agreed deductions are made as a result of poor performance or rule-breaking, such as unacceptable attendance times

- accidental overpayment of wages, or of expenses, even though this is likely to be the fault of the employer

- when the employee has been absent because they are taking industrial action

- in retail companies, to make good any cash deficiency in a till or a shortfall in the stock (though certain conditions apply, e.g. not exceeding 10% of the gross wages on any pay day).

NATIONAL MINIMUM WAGE ACT (NMWA) 1998

Workers are entitled to be paid at least the level of the statutory National Minimum Wage (NMW) for every hour they work for an employer. 'Workers' are entitled to be paid the NMW provided they have reached school-leaving age and work, or ordinarily work, in the United Kingdom. Employers are required to keep records of all those to whom they pay the NMW and employees on the NMW have the right to view these records.

The National Minimum Wage Act is available at **www.opsi.gov.uk/acts/acts1998/ ukpga_19980039_en_1**

The National Minimum Wage is not static and tends to be reviewed on an annual basis, in October, by the Low Pay Commission. Should an organisation fail to pay the NMW then in the most serious cases of non-compliance they will be tried in a crown court, which will have the power to impose, effectively, an unlimited penalty.

ACTIVITY 16.5

Access the Low Pay Commission website at **www.lowpay.gov.uk** and determine the following National Minimum Wage rates:

- adult rate (aged 22+)
- development rate (ages 18–21)
- 16–17-year-old rates.

You can also find out information about the NMW by accessing the Directgov website at: **www. direct.gov.uk/en/Employment/Employees/TheNationalMinimumWage/index.htm**

Can an employee agree to accept a wage that is less than the NMW? (Hint: you will find information about this question by accessing the Directgov website.) Is a foreign worker from outside the UK, someone *legally* working in the UK, entitled to the NMW?

GRIEVANCE PROCEDURES

The grievance process is based, as specified by the Employment Act 2008, on the Acas code of practice that came into force on 6 April 2009.

The formal grievance procedure provides a channel through which employees can have their grievances heard by managers. Most grievances take the form of dissatisfactions and complaints. The procedure has a structure that comprises, in effect, a number of stages, so that if an aggrieved employee does not obtain satisfaction at one stage, the process can move on to the next. In the event of repeated dissatisfaction, or if the issue is beyond the manager's control or authority, the grievance is heard at successively higher levels, ranging from the supervisor to a board member, such as the managing director or HR director. Each stage takes the form of an interview between the manager and the employee, who may be accompanied by a trade union representative or colleague.

Note: from 'Structure of a grievance procedure' below, it is clear that the HR department does not get involved at the initial stage. Experience shows that most grievances are resolved at supervisory or line manager level. Speed and fairness to all concerned are said to be the most essential ingredients of a good procedure. At any time during the process the issue may be resolved by introducing a third party who can mediate in the situation and help the two sides involved reach a conclusion. The mediator's job is not to find the solution but to help facilitate the two groups to reach a workable resolution to the problem.

If, at the close of the final stage, the matter still remains unresolved, a solution is sought through the organisation's disputes procedure, in which conciliation and arbitrative approaches are used. If the relevant trade union representatives feel strongly enough about the issue, they may take a vote for industrial action, although this is normally delayed until all possible avenues have been exhausted.

STRUCTURE OF A GRIEVANCE PROCEDURE

Preamble: This is an informal stage in which the employee airs the grievance to their immediate manager/supervisor and an attempt is made to resolve the issue informally.

Initial stage: This takes place if the issue was not resolved at the preamble and usually involves a more senior manager. The grievance, at this stage, must be made in writing. The employee states the grievance and an attempt is made to resolve it. At this more formal stage there is a right to be accompanied.

Mediation: This can be introduced at any stage.

 KEY CONCEPT: GRIEVANCE HEARING

For the purpose of this chapter a grievance hearing is a meeting at which an employer deals with a complaint about a duty owed by them to a worker, whether the duty arises from statute or common law (for example contractual commitments) (Acas 2009b, p47).

However, good practice suggests that the employee should be allowed to be accompanied at the hearing by a colleague or a suitably qualified union representative. The employee must make a 'reasonable request' to exercise this right. The Acas guidance (2009b, p51) suggests that once the grievance has been heard the meeting should be adjourned to allow reflection before a judgment is made. The decision should be communicated in writing.

The appeal: This takes place if the issue was not resolved at the previous stage and involves a more senior line manager and perhaps the HR manager. The grievance receives a full hearing and an attempt is made to resolve it.

A final appeal: In normal circumstances the grievance is resolved at this stage but there may be a final appeals process in a large organisation, for example. If the employee is allowed a second appeal, the grievance remaining unresolved, a meeting is held involving the employee, a senior director and, where appropriate, an area/regional union officer.

Few grievances reach the *final appeal* stage. Most are resolved at stage 1 and many at stage 2. In extreme circumstances, however, special panels may be set up, including the involvement of experienced external conciliators or arbitrators where appropriate, in attempts to resolve serious or complex grievances.

THE INITIAL GRIEVANCE INTERVIEW

Individuals may feel aggrieved for a variety of reasons. Grievances vary in their complexity and so, therefore, do the interviews. The initial interview has two purposes: first, for the employee to state the grievance, and second, for the manager to analyse what is being said, identify the cause and, where possible, eliminate it.

PREPARING FOR THE INTERVIEW

Employees are usually well prepared for such events and the manager should also prepare. They must state their grievance in writing; this helps to clarify what the real reason is behind the grievance. Before the interview, the manager should obtain an understanding of the problem at the root of the grievance. In a small organisation, the employee is probably well known to the manager and, indeed, may be known to be an inveterate griper. In large organisations, however, where it is not possible to get to know everyone personally, it is a good idea to check such matters with associates and take a look at the employee's record while maintaining an open mind.

Making enquiries will provide the manager with several perceptions of the individual and of the circumstances, so that when the employee's version of the grievance is expressed at the interview, the manager can put it into some kind of context, taking care not to jump to conclusions and only basing decisions on fact.

CONDUCTING THE INTERVIEW

At the interview, the manager should listen attentively and allow the person to speak freely. There is no better way of getting the employee's perception of the situation. After the manager has heard the grievance and established mutual agreement with the employee over its nature, both parties can adopt a joint problem-solving approach in which the employee is encouraged to suggest solutions to the problem. Some suggestions may be impracticable, or outside the limitations of the organisation's policy, but the manager can offer the employee guidance about the possibilities. It may be that the meeting is adjourned for the manager to investigate matters by speaking to relevant people. If agreement is reached over the solution to the problem, it is important for the manager to follow this up and ensure that any agreed action is taken.

Those who draft procedures try to write them in language that makes them watertight, so that the possibility of misinterpretation is reduced to a bare minimum. On the other hand, every case is different, and where a grievance has been shown to be justified, it is often possible for the manager to apply discretion to be fair to the employee and any others who may be involved.

DISCIPLINARY RULES

Standards of behaviour in organisations are regulated by systems of rules, codes of practice and procedures. The rules classify and define offences of which the organisation disapproves. While they vary from one kind of organisation to another, they may, for example, refer to:

- **general conduct**, such as violence, threatening/abusive behaviour and fooling around, such as horseplay

- **punctuality**, including arriving at and leaving the workplace at the agreed working times, being on time for meetings

- **personal appearance** – this is particularly important where the employee is in a customer-facing role; however, most organisations have minimum standards of dress code. The standards, of course should be clearly communicated to employees in their induction and be written down in the employee handbook

- **absenteeism**, including regular attendance – this refers not only to arriving and being in the workplace, but to the employee's actual workstation

- **health and safety** – this covers use of safety equipment on every occasion that the task demands and handling the equipment in a responsible manner so that no one is placed at risk

- **drug and alcohol abuse** – being on the premises while under the influence of drugs and/or alcohol

- **stealing**, including the removal of any of the company's property from the place it normally occupies, unless written permission has been given

- **bringing the organisation into disrepute** – this includes behaviour within and outside the organisation that throws a negative light on the reputation of the employer

- **discriminatory behaviour** – this includes behaviour that indicates dislike or hatred of members of the opposite sex or people of a particular colour or ethnic background.

Offences may be classified and action taken according to their seriousness as follows:

- **minor offence**, such as arriving slightly late for work on several occasions, for which the employee may receive a reprimand or an oral warning

- **serious offence**, such as neglecting or misusing health and safety equipment, for which the employee may be given a written warning

- **gross misconduct**, such as violence or stealing, for which the penalty is usually instant dismissal without compensation.

The aim of the above section is to provide examples of disciplinary rules, show how they are classified and the typical actions that are taken when the disciplinary procedure is invoked.

DISCIPLINARY PROCEDURES

Disciplinary procedures are usually compiled by the HR department, approved by the senior managers and agreed with the trade unions, where a union is recognised. The organisation should have a separate procedure for dealing with matters of capability, which includes poor performance and cases of ill-health. The Advisory, Conciliation and Arbitration Service (Acas) published a code of practice in April 2009 entitled *Code of Practice 1: Disciplinary and grievance procedures* (Acas 2009a). This is a set of guidelines on the content and process of these procedures.

Acas also published a more detailed guide called *Discipline and Grievance at Work: The Acas guide* (2009b), which advises on the practical aspects of implementing the disciplinary procedure. Both documents have been written specifically for employers.

WHAT THE DISCIPLINARY PROCEDURE SHOULD DO

The Acas code outlines the structure and content of a disciplinary procedure as follows, saying that it should:

- be in writing
- specify to whom it applies
- be non-discriminatory
- provide for matters to be dealt with without undue delay
- provide for proceedings, witness statements and records to be kept confidential
- indicate the disciplinary actions that may be taken
- specify the levels of management that have the authority to take the various forms of disciplinary action
- provide for workers to be informed, in writing, of the complaints against them and, where possible, all relevant evidence before any hearing, including witness statements
- provide workers with an opportunity to state their case before decisions are reached
- provide workers with the right to be accompanied
- ensure that, except for gross misconduct, no worker is dismissed for a first breach of discipline
- ensure that disciplinary action is not taken until the case has been carefully investigated
- ensure that workers are given an explanation for any penalty imposed
- provide a right of appeal – normally to a more senior manager – and specify the procedure to be followed.

HANDLING THE DISCIPLINARY PROCEDURE

The aims of a disciplinary procedure are to handle the process fairly and speedily. Because of its ultimate implications, a disciplinary procedure has to be seen to be fair to all who are involved. Fairness and justice should prevail and the approach, rules and practice surrounding the procedure should reflect this.

The Act of Parliament that provides for the individual rights of employees is the Employment Rights Act 1996 (ERA96). This Act states that employees have the right not to be unfairly dismissed, provided that they have at least one year's continuous service with the organisation, regardless of the number of hours worked.

Disciplinary procedures generally have been formulated with the law on unfair dismissal in mind. The structure that will be familiar to most practitioners provides for repeated offences and has a number of stages. The next section outlines a suggested structure for use when conducting a disciplinary process. Good practice would be to involve employees – in a unionised environment involve the union representative – in developing the company's procedure.

STRUCTURE OF A DISCIPLINARY PROCEDURE

1   An employee may be given an informal warning for committing a minor offence. The warning may be delivered orally or in writing; usually it is given orally. However it is given, it must advise the employee of the nature of the offence they have committed and of the possible consequences of repeating the offence.

2   If the employee continues with their misconduct or poor performance or commits a more serious offence, then the process must become more formal. The individual should be advised, *in writing*, of the nature of the problem and the facts surrounding the issue should be thoroughly investigated without delay.

   - The individual should then be called to a meeting, where they can be supported by a colleague or a qualified union representative. This should be done in writing, as mentioned above. Employers should include copies of any written evidence and inform the employee of their right to be accompanied at the hearing.

   - The manager conducting the process should listen to the employee's side of the argument and be prepared to call on any witnesses that the employee has indicated they may wish to use to present evidence in support of their case. If the employee is found to have committed the misdemeanour, then they can be issued with a warning, which should always be given in writing, stating the time, date, place and nature of the offence. Again, the possible consequences of repeating the misdemeanour should be pointed out and, in particular circumstances, the employee may be referred for counselling. Of course the employee has a right to appeal the result of the disciplinary findings.

   - The sanction, for example a written warning, may also be supplemented with counselling or perhaps training, all with a view of trying to help prevent further occurrences of the problem.

   - If an employee does not attend a disciplinary meeting after being called a number of times – without good cause – the employer can make a decision in their absence on the evidence available to them.

3   Further poor conduct, within the period of the initial warnings, could put the employee in danger of receiving a severe penalty and this should be made very clear by the manager. But once again the process should be repeated as in section 2, with an investigation, a hearing – where the accused may, if they

wish, be accompanied – and, if the case is proven, once again appeal against the decision.

- The removal of privileges, suspension or even dismissal could result from a repeated offence after a final written warning.

4 *If again the individual repeats the offence or commits a more serious misdemeanour, then* the form of hearing would probably be by a panel of senior managers, including the HR manager or director, but only after the case has been thoroughly investigated – process is very important. After the hearing, decisions are made about the culpability of the employee and, where appropriate, the penalty to be applied. Most often at this stage the penalty is dismissal.

If the cause of the problem is very serious and would be classed as gross misconduct then it is possible that the process would start at the final stage, where dismissal is a distinct possibility. One could imagine that this could be as result of the flouting of safety regulations, for example smoking in a restricted area while working in a petroleum refinery or, perhaps, vandalising company property.

 ACTIVITY 16.6

1 How long would:

   a. a first written warning remain on an employee's record?

   b. final written warning remain on an employee's record?

2 Subject to provisions in the contract of employment, what sanctions, other than dismissal, can an employer use if a disciplinary case against an employee is proven?

You will find some guidance on answering these questions by looking at Acas (2009b).

RECORD-KEEPING

The foreword to the code of practice (Acas 2009b) advises employers to keep a written record of any disciplinary or grievance cases they deal with:

Records should include:

- the complaint against the employee
- the employee's defence
- findings made and actions taken
- the reason for actions taken
- whether an appeal was lodged
- the outcome of the appeal
- any grievances raised during the disciplinary procedure

- subsequent developments
- notes of any formal meetings.

 At the betting shop

CASE EXAMPLE

Jane is 26, is a technician and has been working for her employer for four years. Her employer has a company that has an appliance installation and repair contract with a number of electrical retail stores in the area; they employ 15 technicians. Her job is to call at customers' homes once a new electrical or gas appliance has been delivered and to connect the appliance to the domestic services. She is a very competent technician and has previously been awarded the 'Technician of the Year' prize. Six months ago she returned from maternity leave, her partner opting to stay at home to take care of their child.

However, over the past six weeks, it has been noticeable that a pattern has been forming. Jane has not followed on with her final task of the day, opting to leave the day's last customer until the first job the following morning. This has caused a number of complaints to the stores that sell the appliances, which, in turn, has caused complaints to be received by Jane's employer. Clearly customer service is being affected. Rumours have been around the workshop that Jane likes to bet on the horses and has been finishing work to visit a betting shop.

The number of complaints has increased and clearly something has to be done; the majority of complaints can be traced to those jobs tasked to Jane and most of them are associated with late installations.

What issues does this case example raise? How would you handle the problem?

THE STRUCTURE OF THE DISCIPLINARY MEETING

The Acas guide (2009b, p20) offers the following advice when conducting disciplinary meetings and points out that the meetings may not proceed in neat, orderly stages but it is good practice to:

- introduce those present to the employee and explain why they are there
- introduce and explain the role of the accompanying person if present
- explain that the purpose of the meeting is to consider whether disciplinary action should be taken in accordance with the organisation's disciplinary procedure
- explain how the meeting will be conducted.

It is important that the events are seen to be transparent. It is usually advisable to keep matters formal and ensure that due process is followed, ensuring that the employee has the opportunity to clarify points, discuss issues with the person accompanying them and that the process is conducted in a logical and transparent manner, with care that a factual record of events is made.

HR'S ROLE IN THE DISCIPLINE PROCESS

The role of the HR practitioner in disciplinary matters varies from one organisation to another, but usually it is to ensure that corporate policy and procedures are followed and that employment legislation is strictly adhered to. In cases where a dismissal looks possible, the matter should be referred to a senior manager to gain approval for the proposed action. Normally managers and supervisors have some authority in disciplinary matters, but in the absence of a senior manager, it is recommended that HR practitioners do not dismiss the person, even in cases of gross misconduct. The procedure should allow for an employee to be accompanied by a trade union representative or colleague when the formal warning is issued, and the manager too is advised to issue them in the presence of another manager or an appropriate HR specialist.

It is important that a thorough inquiry is carried out at every stage of the procedure, and all of the facts are collected, witnesses interviewed and the evidence recorded, along with details of what happened, as detailed in 'Record-keeping' above. If the dismissal of an employee results in an employment tribunal, one of the first questions from the bench is to check whether a thorough and fair investigation has been carried out.

INVOKING THE DISCIPLINARY PROCEDURE

Managers and supervisors should not be too quick to invoke the procedure. Often, a manager under pressure, making a superficial assessment of the situation, does not get the whole story. For example, being late for work is an

 Late again, Price!

CASE EXAMPLE

Joe Price was a section leader in the IT department. He had been with the organisation for six years, his performance was good and he was normally reliable and punctual. Makpal Dospanbetova, the IT manager, noticed that on several days in the past two weeks Joe had been arriving late, sometimes by as much as 45 minutes, so she called him into her office to ask for an explanation.

It turned out that Joe's wife had left him. He now had his two children to look after, which included getting them ready in the mornings and taking them to school. His mother sometimes did this for him, but she was unable to do it every day and those were the days on which he was late. After school, a reliable neighbour picked up the children and looked after them until Joe got home.

Makpal's solution was to alter Joe's hours so that he started and finished work an hour later and that solved the problem. It was to be a temporary solution until Joe got himself sorted out. The idea of taking disciplinary action did not occur to Makpal.

Except in cases where flagrant breaches of the rules occur, disciplinary processes should begin with a *preamble*, in which the manager and the employee get together to discuss the reasons why a rule has been broken. This gives the manager an opportunity to discover any problems, assess the employee's attitude towards their behaviour and to decide what action might be taken.

offence in most organisations, but if an employee who has a good record for punctuality suddenly starts arriving late, the manager should investigate the cause, rather than go straight for the rule book.

Good workers are hard to find, and if a manager can counsel an employee, or guide them towards the solution to, say, a personal problem, a good worker can be turned into an even better, more loyal and motivated worker. The manager's first step, therefore, should be to ask for an explanation.

USING MEDIATION

Current practice suggests that it may be helpful to consider mediation at any stage of a dispute, whether the dispute may be a disciplinary case or a grievance issue. An independent third party or mediator can sometimes help resolve disciplinary or grievance issues.

 KEY CONCEPT: MEDIATION

'Mediation is a voluntary process where the mediator helps two or more people in dispute to attempt to reach an agreement. Any agreement comes from those in dispute, not from the mediator. The mediator is not there to judge, to say one person is right and the other wrong, or to tell those involved in the mediation what they should do. The mediator is in charge of the process of seeking to resolve the problem but not the outcome. Mediators may be employees trained and accredited by an external mediation service who act as internal mediators in addition to their day jobs. Or they may be from an external mediation provider.' (Acas 2009b, p7)

HEALTH AND SAFETY LEGISLATION

The law that applies to this is as follows:

- Health and Safety at Work Act 1974
- Employment Rights Act 1996
- Health and Safety (Consultation with Employees) Regulations 1996
- Management of Health and Safety at Work Regulations 1999 (risk assessment)
- Corporate Manslaughter and Homicide Act 2007.

Health and safety legislation, in the form we know it today, came to life with the Health and Safety at Work Act 1974 (HSWA). Prior to 1974 the limited health and safety legislation was focused on standards in the workplace, that is, sanitation and protecting people from hurting themselves on machinery. However, the introduction of the HSWA heralded a move from the focus on hardware to a focus that also brought into view people and improving their behaviours.

The HSWA gave general duties to employers to '... ensure, so far is reasonably practicable, the health and safety and welfare at work of all his employees ...' (HSWA, s2). The Act also made reference to maintenance of plant (equipment and machines) but in broad terms; as well as giving reference to safe handling and storage of goods. Key also to improving the workplace safety environment, specific mention was made of the requirement for training and supervision of the workforce. An important step was to require the employer to make a written policy statement with respect to health and safety in the workplace (s3). Recognising that all those who go to a place of work are involved in its safe operation, the Act introduced a mandatory requirement to involve recognised workplace trade unions in the safety process with a demand that management recognise a union-nominated safety representative. The Act gave true voice, through the union, to workers in the context of health and safety. The Act, crucially (s10), set up the Health and Safety Commission and the Executive in 1974; both bodies, since 2009, have merged into the Health and Safety Executive.

 ACTIVITY 16.7

Access the HSWA; it is available by going to **www.statutelaws.gov.uk/** and inputting 'Health and Safety' in the 'title' box and '1974' in the 'year' box. Once the title banner on the Act appears, click on this to view the Act.

What does the Act have to say about:

- the duties of employees (s7)?

- the duties of others involved in the workplace (s4)?

- the powers of inspectors (s20)?

The Employment Rights Act 1996 (OPSI 1996a) is important because it protects, for example, safety representatives from unlawfully being penalised in any way for involving themselves in safety matters. For example, to dismiss someone because they have raised an issue that their employer would rather 'brush under the carpet' because it causes real difficulties and may be an expense for the employer would be classed, automatically, as unfair dismissal.

In the context of the Health and Safety (Consultation with Employees) Regulations 1996 (No. 1513) (OPSI 1996b), the employer is required to consult employees, making sure the workforce knows who their safety representatives are and:

- in good time on matters relating to their health and safety at work and, in particular, with regard to – the introduction of any measure at the workplace that may substantially affect the health and safety of those employees

- about the introduction, including the planning, of new technologies into the workplace.

If there is not a recognised union, employees should be consulted directly or a representative should be nominated by the workforce. The regulations (s4), when discussing persons to be consulted, say the following: '... in respect of any group of employees, one or more persons in that group who were elected, by the employees in that group at the time of the election, to represent that group for the purposes of such consultation (and any such persons are in these Regulations referred to as "representatives of employee safety")'.

ACTIVITY 16.8

The TUC and health and safety

To find out what the Trades Union Congress (TUC) has to say about consulting with safety representatives, go to **www.tuc.org.uk/extras/brownbook.pdf** and download the TUC *Brown Book on Safety Representatives and Safety Committees*. (You will also find similar information about safety representatives by consulting the Unison union website at **www.unison.org.uk/acrobat/11191.pdf**)

● After reading the literature, how serious do you think the Trades Union Congress is about the appointment of a safety representative?

● How comprehensive is the literature they have produced on the above?

● Could you take on the role without specialist training?

● What criteria could be used to determine how many safety representatives would be needed within an organisation?

The Health and Safety Executive gives further information about this legislation at **www.hse.gov.uk/involvement/1977.htm#**

The regulations specifically require the health and safety representatives to raise issues about health and safety of the premises and equipment, on behalf of the employees. This puts an onus on the employee representative, as well as management, to respond to such concerns (under HSWA). The Act also gives a right to employee representatives to time off with pay for consultation and training purposes. In essence, the whole focus of the Health and Safety Executive is on dialogue, *shared rights and responsibilities* and worker involvement.

The Management of Health and Safety at Work Regulations 1999 (risk assessment) (OPSI 1999) introduce the requirement for an organisation to introduce risk assessments and employee health surveillance where risks have been identified. This could be, for example, where an organisation has to use chemicals that may be, if not contained properly, hazardous to health.

The regulations (OPSI 1999) also identify special categories of people, such as employees employed under a fixed-term contract, expectant mothers and young employees. Some of these groups, because of their ignorance of the work and required safe working practices, may be exposed to potential dangers. These categories of people should not be exposed to potentially harmful environments or complex machinery without having had appropriate training or perhaps being under close supervision – we all have to learn! In the case of temporary contract workers, they have to be informed of any special qualifications required for the work they are to be engaged to carry out. Expectant mothers are singled out as a priority case because of the obvious need to protect not only the mother but also her unborn baby. In essence the employer needs to carry out a risk assessment; the regulations state the following: '… [if] the work is of a kind which could involve risk, by reason of her condition, to the health and safety of a new or expectant mother, or to that of her baby, from any processes or working conditions, or physical, biological or chemical agents, … on the introduction of measures to encourage improvements in the safety and health at work of pregnant workers and workers who have recently given birth or are breastfeeding' (OPSI 1999, s16).

The Health and Safety Executive, in developing the legislation, also went further and recognised that, in many cases, two or more employers share a workplace. In these cases the employers must work together on safety matters that cross over and affect the shared premises, in terms of the various activities that occur in and around the shared area. For example, this could apply to the sharing of information about potentially harmful chemicals stored on part of the premises; it could also apply to the planning of fire drills together.

The Corporate Manslaughter and Homicide Act 2007 came on to the statute books in April 2008. The IDS Brief (IDS 2005, p1) says the following when discussing the difficulties that arose when trying to pin the blame for disasters when it is clear that it is a company's faulty culture that is wrong:

> The perceived problem with the [then] existing law on manslaughter is that, to secure a conviction, the Crown must identify and prosecute an individual who acted as the 'directing' or 'controlling mind' of the defendant organisation. In respect of large companies or other bodies, identifying one person who directs or controls the organisation is a near-impossible task, and this is one of the factors that has caused many of the attempts to prosecute companies following high-profile transport disasters to end in failure. The only successful convictions have involved small companies.

With this in mind the Government developed the Corporate Manslaughter and Homicide Act 2007.

The *Professional Engineering* magazine has the following to say about the offence (Sampson 2009, p20):

> Corporate manslaughter has to prove the failure of an organisation rather than an individual, and the failure must be by senior management. It carries an unlimited fine, the starting point for which is expected to be 5% of a company's turnover. Companies could also find themselves on the receiving end of a 'publicity order'.

PAUSE FOR THOUGHT

Think of your own organisation or an organisation you have worked in.

- Do you know who is on your safety committee and when and where it meets?
- Have you seen or been involved in a risk assessment in your office or in the factory where you work or have worked?
- What sort of considerations should be taken into account when conducting a risk assessment around the workspace and environment of a pregnant worker?

LEGAL ASPECTS OF RECORD-KEEPING

On the one hand, many managers are reluctant to allow employees access to the information about them that is on record, while on the other, most employees feel that they are entitled to have access, even if only to check that the information is correct. The Data Protection Act 1998 (DPA98) provides a legal entitlement for employees to access their own personal records and, indeed, any information about them.

 KEY CONCEPT: RIGHT OF ACCESS TO PERSONAL INFORMATION

The Data Protection Act 1984 (DPA84) provided people with the right to examine information about them that was stored electronically. The DPA98 extends this by providing right of access regardless of how it is stored.

Data protection is a critical aspect of record-keeping and this is discussed later in this chapter.

CONFIDENTIALITY

Confidentiality is a two-way issue. Most people would object to their personal information being disclosed to others unless it was clear that it was needed for legitimate purposes. However, there can be little harm in communicating collective and anonymous data in statistical form to internal and external third parties who, for example, are generally looking for information, such as absence or accident rates, which is normally acceptable. The really sensitive area is in passing on information from which people can be identified.

As a broad rule, therefore, the release of blocks of statistical data is normally acceptable, while the release of personal information about individual employees is not; at least not without the express permission of the employee concerned.

AUTHORISED ACCESS TO INFORMATION

With properly run computerised systems it is difficult for an unauthorised person to access information to which they are not entitled, although illegally 'hacking in' to systems – a process whereby unauthorised users gain access – obviously is always possible. There are a variety of ways in which systems may be made secure from 'intruders'. The most frequently used of these is the 'password' system, in which authorised employees are given a personal password, which is unknown to others and which will provide them with access to the information to which they are entitled.

 KEY CONCEPT: RELEASING INFORMATION

The release of personal information without the express permission of the employee concerned is actionable in law. HR records are confidential and should be kept under very tight control. A 'safety first' maxim in this respect is: 'if in doubt, hold back'.

Legislation provides for the protection of individuals and usually relates to information rather than the keeping of records, but if the data is kept in secure systems, maintained and updated regularly, the information that results is more likely to be lawful, accurate, useful and reliable. It can be accessed speedily and presented clearly and attractively.

LEGISLATIVE REQUIREMENTS

In addition to the above details, legislation demands that particular records are kept. For example, under health and safety law, there is a requirement to keep records of accidents, injuries sustained by employees, the training they have received to enable them to use equipment safely, and a host of other measures. Other legislative measures that demand record-keeping include the following:

- Race Relations Act 1976 (RRA76)
- Sex Discrimination Act 1975 (SDA75)
- Employment Rights Act 1996 (ERA96)
- Working Time Regulations 1998 (WTR98)
- National Minimum Wage Act 1998 (NMWA98)
- Health and Safety at Work Act 1974 (HSWA)
- Data Protection Act 1998 (DPA98)
- Equal Pay Act 1970.

Bearing in mind the provisions of the legislation listed above, organisations feel the need to protect themselves by keeping records that include accounts of relevant incidents and events that might lead to complaints of:

- race or sex discrimination

- unfair dismissal
- imposing unreasonable working hours on employees
- offering wages and salaries that are below the legal minimum limit
- breaching health and safety regulations
- refusing to allow justifiable access to individual records
- failing to provide equality data on the issue of employment contracts.

HR records contain information that may be used in evidence if an employee's claim leads to an employment tribunal or other legal proceedings. Employers try to avoid such circumstances, not only because of the cost but also because the organisation's reputation as an employer may be at stake.

DATA PROTECTION

This part of the chapter is largely about the law on data protection. Data protection is a legal issue that has been under close scrutiny, not only in employing organisations, but in many areas of our lives, for at least two decades and certainly since the period before 1984, when the DPA84 came into effect.

The DPA98 – which has its origins in the European Union Data Protection Directive – came into effect in March 2000, replacing the DPA84. The DPA98 has many provisions in common with the DPA84, but there are also significant differences. Space prevents us from going into the greater detail of the DPA98, but there are points of which the HR practitioner should be aware, especially since this is an area of the law that is having an important impact on how organisations are managed, although data protection is yet to become an issue at the management/trade union negotiating table.

Those who are familiar with the vocabulary of the DPA84 will need to understand two minor points on which the new Act differs from the old one:

1 The DPA98 changed the Data Protection Registrar's title to Data Protection Commissioner and in January 2001 the name was further changed to the Information Commissioner's Office and the 'Commissioner' was given the added responsibility of the Freedom of Information Act 2000.

2 The *registration* system under the DPA84 is replaced under the DPA98 by the *notification* system.

INDIVIDUAL RIGHTS

In the DPA98, the person about whom the information is held is referred to as the *data subject*. This Act defines data and refers to a *relevant filing system*.

KEY CONCEPT: RELEVANT FILING SYSTEM

Any 'set' of information relating to individuals to the extent that the set is structured by reference to individuals or by reference to criteria relating to individuals in such a way that specific information relating to a particular individual is readily accessible.

Any information falling into the category of a relevant filing system constitutes data. The new Act also distinguishes between *personal data* and *sensitive data*.

 KEY CONCEPT: PERSONAL DATA

Information about a living person who can be identified from that information.

PERSONAL DATA

Any individual employee is entitled to:

- receive a copy of any data – including manually stored data – processed by reference to them
- know what data is being processed
- know why the data is being processed
- know who might receive the data
- be told the source of the data – except in limited circumstances
- where data is processed automatically, and is likely to form the sole basis for any decision significantly affecting the individual, the right to know the logic involved in that decision-making and not to have significant decisions based on results of automatic processing
- prevent processing likely to cause damage and distress.

 KEY CONCEPT: SENSITIVE DATA

In this context, the HR practitioner is the 'guardian' of this kind of information, which the DPA98 defines as:

- racial or ethnic origin
- political opinions
- religious or similar beliefs
- membership of trade unions
- physical or mental health
- the person's sexual life
- commission or alleged commission of offences
- data relating to criminal offences, ongoing proceedings, or the decision of courts in respect of proceedings.

SENSITIVE DATA

There are other types of data that it is inadvisable (although not illegal) to process. For example, results of occupational or psychological tests may be misinterpreted if accessed by someone who is not an expert in testing and does not understand how and why particular inferences are drawn from test results. Most employers provide the test subjects with hard copies of their results.

Incidentally, a word of caution to all aspiring HR practitioners who may believe that the records they hold in the department are the only records that refer to employees: they are not.

KEY CONCEPT: PROCESSING OF DATA

Under the DPA98, the processing of sensitive data is forbidden unless:

- The 'data subject' provides explicit consent.
- It is necessary for the exercise or performance of a right or legal obligation in connection with employment. This could be in the processing of a payroll.
- It is necessary in connection with any legal proceedings or for obtaining legal advice.
- It is necessary for the administration of justice, or for the exercise of functions conferred by statute.
- It is in the data subject's vital interests.
- It is done for medical reasons by a health professional.
- It is processing of data on racial or ethnic origin needed to monitor equal opportunity.

Many line managers keep private notes about their staff, some of which are very personal. One manager, for example, was found to have information – which would be classified as 'sensitive data' – about his staff stored in his new electronic diary, which he was showing off to a colleague!

Know what you are doing

CASE EXAMPLE

Along with two of his colleagues, Ahmed, an employee in a Birmingham company, was being considered for an important promotion. As part of the selection process, they were all subject to a psychological test, which was conducted by properly trained and qualified people. The test results were stored electronically.

The general manager of the company, a very authoritarian person who had no training or background in psychological testing, accessed the results, after which he told Ahmed that, rather than being promoted, he should be dismissed. Obviously this caused Ahmed great concern and he feared for his future with the company. Despite this, Ahmed appeared before the selection panel and got the job. On hearing this, the general manager took the matter to the managing director, who had chaired the selection panel, and demanded an explanation for 'this very unwise promotion'.

On hearing what the general manager had to say, the managing director held a meeting with the HR manager, the general manager and the people who had conducted the tests. It became clear that the general manager had completely misinterpreted the test results and that Ahmed's appointment was fully justified.

Task: You have been asked to ensure that this kind of misunderstanding does not occur again. Write a brief paper outlining the action that you would take.

EMPLOYERS' OBLIGATIONS

Employers are obliged to notify the Information Commissioner (www.ico.gov.uk) if they process personal data. The individual must give consent for the personal data to be *processed*, unless it is necessary for certain specified circumstances.

 ACTIVITY 16.9

The role of the Information Commissioner

Access the Information Commissioner's website at **www.ico.gov.uk** and find out what the role encompasses. You will find that the Information Commissioner has much more responsibility than looking after data protection issues.

 KEY CONCEPT: PROCESSING DATA

Processing is defined as: organising, adapting, altering, retrieving, using, disclosing, combining, blocking or erasing data and calling up data on a computer screen.

There is a list of eight criminal offences relating to data protection, which are:

- processing without notification
- failure to notify the Commissioner of changes to notification register entry
- failure to comply with an enforcement or information notice
- making a false statement in response to an information notice
- obstructing or failing to assist with the execution of a search warrant
- obtaining or disclosing personal data without permission from the data controller
- selling or offering to sell unlawfully obtained data
- making a person supply a copy of their personal data, unless required or authorised by law or in the public interest.

 ACTIVITY 16.10

You work as an HR administrator and have been approached by a supervisor in the marketing department's administrative section. He has asked for information concerning one of the employees. How would you deal with his request?

DATA PROTECTION POLICY

Managers are advised to formulate and actively implement clear policies and procedures that will ensure that all employees understand the organisation's approach to compliance with the data protection laws. Employers, in their efforts to conform to the data protection laws, should, as a minimum, adopt the following eight data protection principles, which are recommended in the Data Protection Act (1998). Data should be:

- processed fairly and lawfully and shall not be processed unless certain conditions are met
- obtained only for specified and lawful purposes
- adequate, relevant and not excessive in relation to the purposes for which it is processed
- accurate and up to date
- kept for no longer than is necessary
- processed in accordance with the rights granted under the DPA98
- kept securely
- not transferred to a country without adequate data protection. [Authors' comment: The Information Commissioner's Office requires that individuals should be informed if processing of information is to be done outside the European Economic Area.]

This might necessitate programmes of training for particular employees, such as personnel practitioners, middle managers and team leaders. Also, there should be a system for monitoring the effectiveness of the procedures, which will be designed to ensure that the data protection principles are followed.

PAUSE FOR THOUGHT

The Information Commissioner has teeth!

Under provisions enacted by the Criminal Justice and Immigration Act 2008, the Information Commissioner is now empowered to serve a 'monetary penalty notice' on a data controller if satisfied that the latter has committed a serious contravention of the data protection principles in circumstances where the contravention was either deliberate or such that the data controller knew or ought to have known that the contravention would be likely to cause substantial damage or substantial distress (IDS 2008).

WHAT STEPS MIGHT ORGANISATIONS TAKE?

The CIPD has developed an extensive factsheet on data protection (CIPD 2009e), which includes a list of statutes that are concerned with the privacy of the individual, and access to and disclosure of information in the public interest that employers need to consider. All those collecting data have to ask themselves why it is being collected, how it is going to be used and who will have access to it. The statutes include:

- Public Interest Disclosure Act 1998
- Human Rights Act 1998
- Telecommunications (Lawful Business Practice) Regulations 2000.

The factsheet also contains an action plan that suggests ten steps organisations might take to ensure compliance:

- Organisations should consider the appointment of a person to be in charge of all aspects of information, including the Freedom of Information Act.
- Audit information system – find out who holds what data, and why.
- Consider why information is collected and how it is used. Issue guidelines for managers about how to gather, store and retrieve data.
- Ensure that all information collected now complies with the Data Protection Act 1998.
- Check the security of all information stored.
- Check the transfer of data outside the European Economic Area.
- Check the organisation's use of automated decision-making.
- Review policy and practice in respect of references.
- Review or introduce a policy for the private use of telephones, email and post.
- Review or introduce a procedure for reporting under the Public Interest Disclosure Act.

SUMMARY

This chapter has introduced you to a basic overview of the legislation relating to employment. As more and more legislation appears, the HR practitioner needs to be aware of the implications of the changes in the law as it affects the business and its employees. You may not be an employment law expert, but this chapter should have alerted you to the key pieces of legislation that impact on our day-to-day lives at work.

We have looked at the employment contract and employees' statutory rights, together with family-friendly legislation: maternity rights, Working Time Regulations and the right to flexible working. A major raft of legislation is related to equality and diversity, and we have discussed some of the relevant Acts briefly.

In addition to the various Acts of Parliament, we have also looked at discipline and grievance, based on the Acas codes of practice, and given advice on the processes involved that should help you as a practitioner to stay within the law.

The final part of the chapter discusses the legal aspects of record-keeping. One of the roles of HR is to keep employment records, and indeed the law requires HR to keep a large amount of data on such things as health and safety, accident records, training and so on. HR is responsible for holding personal information and this is covered by the Data Protection Act – there are rules on how and where data is held and processed.

The chapter is not intended to be an in-depth tome nor a definitive guide to the law, but it should give you a flavour of what to be aware of – and also where to go for more information should you need it. Any textbook is quickly out of date when it comes to the law, so do make sure you access websites that will keep you informed of changes.

REVIEW QUESTIONS

1   When can an individual legitimately claim time off work? Which piece of legislation gives these rights?

2   Explain the differences between compulsory maternity leave (CML), ordinary maternity leave (OML) and additional maternity leave (AML).

3   What are the main purposes of the Employment Rights Act 1996 (ERA96)?

4   Under what circumstances is it legitimate for an employer to make deductions from an employee's pay?

5   What considerations should an employee write about and address to their employer when they are requesting flexible working? You will find some guidance by referring to section 80F of the Employment Act 2002, available from **www.opsi.gov.uk/acts/acts2002/ukpga_20020022_en_1**

6   For what category of person can an employee request flexible working? What changes to employment could flexible working entail?

7   What are the three categories of the National Minimum Wage (NMW)? To whom should complaints about the NMW be made?

8   When conducting a formal disciplinary or grievance procedure, what type of record of events should be kept?

9   Who can accompany an employee, who is accused of a misdemeanour, to a discipline or grievance hearing? What is the role of the person who accompanies the employee to such a meeting? Can they speak for the accused employee? When would it be appropriate to suspend someone, with pay, during a disciplinary investigation?

10 What would constitute gross misconduct?

    (You will find guidance on these questions by accessing *Discipline and Grievance at Work: The Acas guide* (Acas 2009b).)

11 What is the role of a mediator in a disciplinary or grievance case? Who can take on the role of the mediator?

12 What steps might the organisation take to ensure compliance with the data protection principles?

13 What is the role of the Data Controller in an organisation?

EXPLORE FURTHER

BOOKS

DANIELS, K. (2008) *Employment law: an introduction for HR and business students*. 2nd ed. **London: Chartered Institute of Personnel and Development.**

There are numerous books on employment law, but Daniels' book an ideal one for HR practitioners.

LEWIS, D. and SERGEANT, M. (2009) *Essentials of employment law*. **London: Chartered Institute of Personnel and Development.**

This is another book suitable for those studying and practising HR.

WEB LINKS

For discipline and grievance don't forget to visit the Acas website. It is well worth browsing for sound advice on all kinds of HR issues: www.acas.org

BusinessLink: www.businesslink.gov.uk

Equality and Human Rights Commission: www.equalityhumanrights.com

Information Commissioner: www.ico.gov.uk

Low Pay Commission: www.lowpay.gov.uk

OPSI statute database: www.statutelaw.gov.uk

Pay and working rights: http://payandworkrightscampaign.direct.gov.uk/index.html

The HSE and safety representatives: www.hse.gov.uk/involvement/1977.htm#

Trades Union Congress (safety representatives): www.tuc.org.uk/extras/brownbook.pdf

TUC website: www.tuc.org.uk

Unite union: www.unitetheunion.org.uk

Worksmart (from the TUC): www.worksmart.org.uk/rights/viewsection.php?

CHAPTER 17

Ending the Employment Relationship

LEARNING OBJECTIVES

After studying this chapter you should:

- be able to describe the different ways in which the employment relationship might end
- understand the meaning of fair and unfair dismissal
- be aware of the legislative implications of redundancy
- be able to manage survivors of the redundancy process
- understand retirement as a fair form of dismissal.

INTRODUCTION

Ultimately the employment contract comes to an end, and there are a variety of circumstances in which this might happen. The most common reasons fall into two categories: first, the employer may terminate the contract and, second, the employee may terminate it.

In this chapter we will also be looking at the management of redundancy and retirement as fair forms of dismissal. Currently we are in difficult economic times, where redundancies are used as a form of cutting overheads. However, even in more buoyant times, organisations may need to restructure and re-form to maintain their competitive advantage in a global economy, thus possibly giving rise to redundancies. As we will see, the role of HR in handling redundancies is key – both in communicating to staff and in ensuring that the legal due processes are followed.

This chapter will also consider the legislation that impacts upon retirement.

TERMINATION OF CONTRACT

TERMINATION BY THE EMPLOYEE

There is a wide range of reasons why an employee may decide to terminate the relationship with their employer. Largely, these are either personal or career-related, and several typical examples of each are listed below.

Personal reasons:

- to take care of a sick relative
- to move to another area or country
- to escape from a hostile culture or unfriendly co-workers.

Career-related reasons:

- resigning to take up a post with another employer
- to undertake a full-time course
- the desire for a career change.

It is important to find out reasons for the termination, especially if there is high labour turnover. Part of HR's role would be to investigate reasons for leaving; this might be done by the use of exit interviews.

 KEY CONCEPT: EXIT INTERVIEWS

Exit interviews may be used with several purposes in mind. The data that is gathered from them is useful to those who manage the employment relationship and to HR planners. The objective of the exit interview is to try to find out the reasons for leaving. This may be difficult, as leavers may not always be truthful about their real reasons for leaving the organisation. For instance, they may not admit to having had difficulties with their manager because they may want a future reference, or even to return to work for the organisation at a later date.

 ACTIVITY 17.1

Conducting exit interviews

Considering the issues raised in the above Key Concept (exit interviews), who do you think should carry out exit interviews? How can we find out the true reasons for leaving? Are exit interviews the best way of finding this out?

There are a number of reasons why an employer might terminate the contract:

- **Disciplinary dismissal**: Employees who persistently break the rules or fail to meet requirements risk being dismissed, subject to the outcome of a disciplinary hearing and depending on the severity and frequency of the offence. The dismissed employee may have grounds for appeal to an employment tribunal for unfair dismissal.

- **Lack of capability**: It is legitimate for the organisation to dismiss an employee on the grounds that the person has shown themselves to be grossly unsuitable for the job; this may relate to attitude or aptitude. Admittedly the organisation will have had the opportunity to test an individual's knowledge, competence and personality prior to engagement, but the law recognises that errors can occur.

- **Redundancy**: This occurs when the organisation no longer requires a job, or set of jobs, to be carried out. With this kind of severance, the employee has a statutory entitlement to compensation. The employee may have grounds for an appeal to an employment tribunal for *unfair selection for redundancy*.

- **Retirement**: This is triggered by the organisation when the employee has reached the statutory 'retirement age'.

DISMISSAL

The repeal of the statutory dispute resolution procedures on 6 April 2009 means that an employer's procedural failures in carrying out a dismissal no longer result in the dismissal being deemed automatically unfair. From now on, most dismissal procedures will be subject to the new Acas *Code of Practice on Discipline and Grievance* – but the code does not apply to redundancies.

UNFAIR DISMISSAL

This is when an employer terminates an employee's contract unfairly. *Automatically unfair* reasons include (Acas 2010b; refer also to the Employment Rights Act 1996):

- **pregnancy:** including all reasons relating to maternity
- **family reasons:** including parental leave, paternity leave (birth and adoption), adoption leave or time off for dependants
- **representation:** including acting as an employee representative and trade union membership grounds and union recognition
- **part-time and fixed-term employees** [Authors' comment: *this applies to dismissal on the grounds that the person was part-time or on a fixed term contract. It does not mean that causes such as coming to the end of a contract or redundancy would not be considered as 'fair' dismissal*]

- **discrimination:** including protection against discrimination on the grounds of age, sex, race, disability, sexual orientation and religion or belief
- **pay and working hours:** including the Working Time Regulations, annual leave and the National Minimum Wage.

If an employee feels that they have been unfairly dismissed they can take their case to an employment tribunal. This has to be done within three months of the effective date of termination of employment. In most circumstances an employee must have at least one year's continuous service before they can make a complaint to an employment tribunal. However, there is no length of service requirement in relation to 'automatically unfair grounds'.

In 2008–09 there were 52,711 claims for unfair dismissal (Tribunals Service 2008–09).

If, after investigation at an employment tribunal, a dismissal is found to be unfair, then there are three options that the tribunal may recommend:

- reinstatement
- re-engagement
- compensation.

 ACTIVITY 17.2

Employment tribunals

Have a look at the following website: **www.employmenttribunals.gov.uk** Find the latest statistics relating to employment tribunals. How many tribunals does your organisation have to attend a year? How much do you think this might cost in terms of compensation, time for the investigation and other administrative costs? If we could reduce the number of tribunals the organisation has to attend, we could save a significant amount of money!

How much does it cost an organisation to go to a tribunal? (Think of all the costs that attending a tribunal incurs, from loss of wages of the staff who have to attend to the costs of the solicitor who will represent your case.)

FAIR REASONS FOR DISMISSAL

There can be many reasons for fair dismissal. These can include: poor performance, misconduct, redundancy, the ending of a fixed-term contract and, of course, retirement. A dismissal is fair if the employer had reason for the dismissal and acted reasonably in doing so.

Cases of 'gross misconduct', such as theft, downloading Internet pornography, serious insubordination, breach of confidence (for example 'rubbishing' the company on Facebook!), could be considered as fair dismissal, which could result in immediate termination of the contract without notice.

In a case where an employee has been dismissed, they may still have to work a period of notice or receive 'payment in lieu of notice'.

CONSTRUCTIVE DISMISSAL

If you resign from your job because of your employer's behaviour, it may be considered to be constructive dismissal. You would need to show that:

- Your employer has committed a serious breach of contract
- You felt forced to leave because of that breach
- You have not done anything to suggest that you have accepted their breach or a change in employment conditions. (Directgov 2009)

Examples of constructive dismissal might be where an employee has been psychologically bullied by a co-worker or their boss, or their conditions of work have been changed unacceptably, for example putting the employee on to shift work without consultation and agreement.

 ACTIVITY 17.3

Constructive dismissal

Can you think of any other reasons for constructive dismissal? Carry out some research, for example using the Directgov or Business Link websites, and interrogate the site about constructive dismissal.

REDUNDANCY

There are a number of Acts that relate to the detail of the management of redundancy, including:

- sections 188–198 of the Trade Union and Labour Relations (Consolidation) Act 1992 as amended by section 34 of the Trade Union Reform and Employment Rights Act 1993
- the Collective Redundancies and Transfer of Undertakings (protection of Employment) (Amendment) Regulations 1995 (SI 1995 No 2587) and 1999 (SI 1999 No 1925)
- Employment Rights Act 1996.

The Employment Rights Act 1996 simply defines redundancy in the following manner, where:

- an employer ceases to carry on the business
- an employer ceases to carry on the business *in the place where the employee was employed*
- the requirements of the business for employees to *carry out work of a particular*

kind have ceased or diminished and where the employee is employed to carry out that work (OPSI 1996a, s139).

HANDLING OF REDUNDANCY

Employers normally deal with redundancies in one of the following three ways:

- **an ad hoc approach** whereby there are no formally established arrangements, with the practice varying according to the circumstances of each redundancy

- **a formal policy** setting out the approach to be adopted by management when faced with making redundancies. In such cases the agreement of trade union or employee representatives with the contents of the policy will not have been obtained

- **a formal agreement** setting out the procedure to be followed when redundancies have to be considered. The contents of such a procedure will be the result of negotiation and agreement between management and trade union or employee representatives (Acas 2009c).

It is advisable to have a formal policy or procedure on redundancy. How redundancy is handled will depend on the numbers involved. If there are 20 or more to be made redundant, then there is a requirement to consult with the relevant unions or workforce representatives within a given timeframe and to notify the projected redundancies to the Department for Business, Innovation and Skills.

The timeframe for notification is as follows:

- 90 days (for 100 employees or more over a period of 90 days or less)
- 30 days (for 20–99 employees over a period of 90 days or less).

Common sense suggests that consultation should be as soon as possible in any case. Consultation must be completed before any notices of dismissal are issued to employees. Details of the consultation arrangements with any trade union or employee representatives should be made available. This might include details of any relocation expenses, details of the appeals procedures and information on the selection criteria to be used where redundancy is unavoidable, together with details of the severance terms.

Employees will be concerned about job losses so the policy should also give reassurances about maintaining job security wherever possible and particularly any measures for minimising or avoiding compulsory redundancies. The policy should also include details on the support the business is prepared to give to redundant employees to help them to obtain training or search for alternative work.

If there are fewer than 20 job losses then the process is different. Until 6 April 2009 the process for handling redundancies of this number was described in the Employment Act 2002 and required the employer to follow a fixed procedure. Failure to do so would make the dismissal automatically unfair. However, this process was repealed by the Employment Act 2008. (Whether the reasons for a redundancy are fair, though, is still set out in the Employment Rights Act 1996.)

The management of redundancies of fewer than 20 people is now defined by case law, known as the *Polkey* decision. IDS (2009b) describes the case of Polkey, a van driver who appealed against his redundancy when his employer reduced the number of vans required in his business from four to three. The appeal against redundancy went to the House of Lords after going through the employment tribunal and appeal stages. The House of Lords were clear in that he had been fairly dismissed and, although recognising that a normal procedure had not been followed, the fact that the procedure was missing did not make the redundancy unfair. However, the Law Lords went on to say, '... that dispensing with consultation would be "exceptional" ...'. This therefore implies that consultation is sensible and good practice, however many people are made redundant. Of course, if consultation is expected, the question is, 'what type of consultation should take place?' In essence the employer should consult and communicate fully with the employee on the following:

- warning should be given about impending redundancy (job loss)
- an idea of how selection for redundancy will be carried out
- the employee must have an opportunity to communicate their feelings and concerns
- consideration of alternatives (redeployment?).

One may of course finally say that the individual may challenge the need for any redundancy at all (IDS 2009b).

DISCLOSURE OF INFORMATION

Acas (2009c, p27) suggests that the following information is given in the course of the consultation:

- the reasons for the proposals
- the numbers and descriptions of employees it is proposed to dismiss as redundant
- the total number of employees of any such description employed at the establishment in question
- the way in which employees will be selected for redundancy
- how the dismissals are to be carried out, including the period over which the dismissals are to take effect
- the method of calculating the amount of redundancy payments to be made to those who are dismissed.

The Information and Consultation of Employees Regulations 2004 (IDS 2004, s20) give employees the right to be informed about the business's economic situation and also to be informed and consulted about employment prospects and about decisions that may lead to substantial changes in work organisation or contractual relations, including redundancies and transfers. Since 2008 these regulations apply to organisations that employ 50 or more staff.

REDUNDANCY PAY

Redundant employees are entitled to redundancy pay as compensation for loss of their job, security and career prospects. The redundancy payment due to each employee under the statutory redundancy payment scheme depends on their age and length of service (up to 20 years). This determines the number of weeks' pay due, which is then subject to a limit on weekly pay (see the Department for Business, Innovation and Skills website):

> To calculate the number of weeks pay due, you should use the following amounts –
>
> - 0.5 week's pay for each full year of service where age during year is less than 22
>
> - 1.0 week's pay for each full year of service where age during year is 22 or above, but less than 41
>
> - 1.5 weeks' pay for each full year of service where age during year is 41+.

There are circumstances where employees may not be entitled to compensation – for instance, if the employer has made a 'suitable' offer of alternative employment and the employee has unreasonably rejected it. There is a maximum statutory limit relating to a week's pay (£380 in October 2009). The BIS website offers a calculator for the statutory amounts of redundancy pay: **www.berr.gov.uk/ cgi-bin/er_feb07_reconner.pl**

ACTIVITY 17.4

Using the above ready-reckoner, calculate the statutory redundancy payment for your own job or a job of someone you know. Alternatively, calculate the redundancy payment for a 30-year-old employee with 12 years' service, currently earning £15,000 per annum.

VOLUNTARY SEVERANCE

The above payments are the statutory minimum that every employee is entitled to receive if they have two or more years of continuous service. However, many employers choose to encourage staff to leave the organisation voluntarily by offering an enhanced severance package. The individual makes the choice to leave and so does not have to go through a traumatic exercise of selection (for redundancy).

SELECTION FOR REDUNDANCY

The selection procedure must be, and be seen to be, fair and non-discriminatory. Criteria used should be designed to retain the best employees who will take the organisation forward in a competitive world. This might mean looking at skills and knowledge required by the organisation and past work performance (possibly from appraisal records). It may also mean looking at discipline and absence records. Care should be taken not to use any criteria that could be construed as being discriminatory, for example years' service. In the past, organisations have used 'last in, first out' (LIFO) as a means of selection, but this is now considered discriminatory in the light of age discrimination legislation. However, the case of *Rolls Royce v Unite the Union* at the Court of Appeal (*Rolls Royce plc v Unite the Union*, Court of Appeal, 2009 EWCA Civ 387) suggests that length of service, particularly *when coupled with other selection criteria* does *not* constitute discrimination because it '… was proportionate to achieving the legitimate aim of rewarding loyalty and creating a stable workforce in the context of a fai**r** redundancy' (IDS 2009a, 883).

CASE EXAMPLE

An offshore oil company needs to downsize its operation because it is closing down one of its onshore logistics bases. As a result of the downsizing it is necessary to make over 55 staff redundant. Clearly the company is required to notify the Department for Business, Innovation and Skills that there are over 20 possible redundancies. All employees who are 'at risk' need to be informed 30 days before any notice of termination. A consultation period with the representatives from the trade unions is planned.

HR needs to consider a range of options to deal with the impact of these redundancies.

These might include:

- Meet with affected management staff.

- Meet with the trade unions and/or employee representatives to inform them of the reasons for the redundancies and numbers involved, followed by further meetings on the terms and conditions of the redundancies.

- Meet with the workforce initially to present to them the nature and extent of the planned changes. This would include informing the rest of the workforce of the situation, initially through the works council and then through a series of briefings, to allay any fears. A series of questions and answers is to be placed on the company intranet to assist in this communication.

- Arrange meetings with individuals and management to discuss personal issues and concerns.

It is important to consider the needs of the employees because the company takes the view that people are important and are a valued asset. This is a message that the company wishes to give to the remaining employees in other sections of the business – so it is important to treat those facing redundancy well and with respectful care.

To these ends, HR is planning to put the following processes in place:

- Contract a counselling consultant to provide 24-hour telephone counselling for those who are finding the whole issue hard to cope with.

- Contract an outplacement provider who will help with CVs, skills analysis, advice on retraining and interview skills. Facilities for email, fax, printing and telephone communication are to be provided to help the employees in their job search.

- Time off for employees to seek other jobs – for interviews, for instance.

- Support employees with opportunities for retraining and redeployment into other areas of the business. Employees with suitable skills will be guaranteed an interview for any relevant vacancies within the company.

- Agree to release staff who gain new

employment without them having to work their contractual notice.

- Advice on financial issues to be provided by an independent financial adviser.

DEALING WITH SURVIVORS

Those employees who remain with the organisation after a compulsory redundancy exercise are likely to feel a range of emotions: shock, fear (of what may yet happen), anger and guilt. Alternatively, they may feel elation – that they have kept their jobs!

The effects of redundancy may also mean that there is more work to be undertaken by those who remain. This could have a negative effect on morale, counteracting the positive feelings of having escaped being made redundant.

Redman and Wilkinson (2009, p394) emphasise the above when they write, '... employees are more likely to have low morale and increased stress levels, be less productive and less loyal, with increased quit levels. Sennett describes survivors as behaving as though "they lived on borrowed time, feeling they had survived for no good reason". ...'

There is a need to communicate with employees about what has happened. The impact of any traumatic event on those involved means that there is a need to counsel both those who are directly affected by redundancy (that is, having lost their jobs) and also those employees who are impacted indirectly by the whole exercise. Line managers and HR both have a role to play in ensuring that the impact is minimised and the organisation continues to function efficiently. This would mean that the message needs to be communicated that redundancy was a last resort and that all alternatives were (and would be in the future) exhausted before relying on job cuts as a means of reducing costs. This is of course based on the premise that organisations take a 'best practice' approach to HRM.

Having gone through a careful selection process, designed to identify and keep the best staff, the last thing the business wants is to then lose them, possibly to a competitor. It is important to ensure that the business does not lose valuable staff who have the skills and knowledge that are essential to the future of the enterprise. Honest communication is therefore vital. There is no point in giving empty hope, but expressing the truth of the economic situation is more likely to inspire confidence and trust, at a time when rumours will be rife.

In addition to communication, HR can support the situation by focusing on learning and development activities for the survivors, which will improve employee engagement and help them to feel valued, thus reducing uncertainty.

In medium- to large-scale redundancies, there will probably be a need to reorganise the work; this should be seen as an opportunity to involve all those impacted and so be part of the confidence-rebuilding process.

Jobs can be restructured to use skills to best advantage. It would make sense to undertake a skills audit and training needs analysis to enable effective utilisation of staff. If survivors can see that they have an opportunity for training and development, they will be more likely to become engaged and committed, and therefore motivated to move the organisation forward.

WAYS TO AVOID REDUNDANCY

We should, of course, try to reduce or avoid redundancies as far as possible. This might be achieved by forward thinking and undertaking human resource planning (see Chapter 5).

If it is not possible to avoid redundancies altogether, we should at least try to protect the core workforce. So one step may be to release temporary staff. There should be a freeze on recruitment, and it is common sense to retrain and redeploy affected staff as vacancies occur throughout the business. Further steps would be to reduce overtime and, perhaps more drastically, move to short-time working and even pay cuts.

One option used by some employers during a recession is to use the spare work time for training, rather than lay people off or make them redundant.

RETIREMENT AS A LEGAL FORM OF DISMISSAL

It is the Employment Equality (Age) Regulations 2006 which allow for a default retirement age of 65 years. This will be reviewed in 2011. The employer, though, must follow a prescribed process to fairly dismiss an employee at age 65. A retirement age below 65 can be used but the onus is on the employer to justify this, and of course it would be open to challenge.

According to the Department for Trade and Industry in 2006 the default retirement age is useful to organisations because it allows them to plan their workforce. Cynically, one might ask, does it allow organisations to release older and more expensive workers from their payroll?

For a dismissal to be fair under the above legislation the employer must advise the employee between six and 12 months before the date of dismissal that they may request *not* to retire at the default retirement age of 65. It is, however, how the employer manages this process that determines whether or not the dismissal is fair (IDS 2006a).

SUMMARY

This chapter has covered the various ways of ending an employment contract: for example redundancy, retirement and dismissal. We have also discussed exit interviews and seen how important they can be in ascertaining why people leave.

We have looked at both fair and unfair dismissal and the reasons why these happen.

The issue of redundancy has been addressed in some detail (something commonplace in times of recession), giving an outline of how to manage the redundancy process fairly and effectively. Selection for redundancy, pay and consultation have all been discussed. The idea of managing survivors of a redundancy situation is also key – we must make sure that those who remain in the organisation are not demotivated and will continue to give their best, so that when times improve, the business is set up to compete and succeed.

Ending the contract can be messy and difficult, which is why dealing with it fairly and equitably is paramount. HR must handle the issues sensitively and with great care. There are a great many employment tribunal cases around redundancy issues and unfair dismissal. Many of these could have been avoided if they had been dealt with professionally, using correct procedures. The need to follow a logical process is vital – many a tribunal case has been lost because the process was not carried out properly. By reading and understanding this chapter, you should now have a basic knowledge about how to choose people for redundancy in a professional and fair manner.

Finally in this chapter we have considered retirement – and the impact of the Employment Equality (Age) Regulations 2006 on the default retirement age.

REVIEW QUESTIONS

1 What is the purpose of an exit interview?

2 What is meant by fair dismissal?

3 What constitutes 'automatically unfair' dismissal?

4 What are the conditions under which you can take a case of unfair dismissal to an employment tribunal?

5 What do you understand by 'constructive dismissal'?

6 How much notice has to be given if you are making 120 employees redundant?

7 What criteria can be used to select people for redundancy?

8 How can an organisation improve morale for the survivors of a redundancy exercise?

9 What are the options for avoiding or reducing redundancies?

10 What legislation has impacted on the UK retirement age?

EXPLORE FURTHER

BOOKS

REDMAN, T. and WILKINSON, A. (2009) *Contemporary human resource management: text and cases.* **3rd ed. Harlow: Pearson.**

This book includes a comprehensive chapter on downsizing and redundancy.

WEB LINKS

Acas (on redundancy): www.acas.org.uk/index.aspx?articleid=1411

Age discrimination (retirement information): www.dwp.gov.uk/docs/legislation-20-facts.pdf

Business Link: www.businesslink.gov.uk

Department for Business, Innovation and Skills: www.berr.gov.uk

Directgov (public services all in one place): www.direct.gov.uk/en/index.htm

Employment tribunals: www.employmenttribunals.gov.uk

CHAPTER 18

Change Management

After studying this chapter you should:

- understand the concept of the drivers and triggers of change
- understand and describe how the planned approach to change is designed to work
- understand and describe the emergent approach to change
- be able to describe Lewin's three-stage model of change
- be able to explain the role of the change consultant
- be able to identify and explain how some of the techniques of the change consultant are used.

INTRODUCTION

Lecturing at Manchester in 1832, Ralph Waldo Emerson said, 'The willingness to change is the most essential ingredient to success in any walk of life.' We create original concepts that bring about change, but we also adapt to changes that others have created. Emerson was referring to the latter when he made his famous comment at Manchester and, many years later, he included it in his paper *Conduct of Life*, which was published in 1860. In fact he was talking and writing about the conduct of individuals, but the principle is equally relevant to organisations today.

TRIGGERS (DRIVERS) FOR CHANGE

Burnes (2004) suggests that organisations should not become involved in planned change unless the change is significant. He argues that change should not be considered unless:

- The company's vision/strategy highlights the need for change or improved performance.
- Current performance or operation indicates that severe problems or concerns exist.

- Suggestions or opportunities arise (either from the area concerned or elsewhere) that potentially offer significant benefits to the organisation.

If one or more of the above circumstances arises, then this should trigger the organisations to assess the case for change. (Burnes 2004, p468)

THE NEED FOR CHANGE

The need for change often arises from changes in the external environment, especially market demands and the activities of competitors. Sometimes changes are needed urgently, induced perhaps by a crisis, and they have to be implemented as quickly as possible, but there is a limit to what can be done in the short term. Experience shows that the most effective and enduring changes take place when they have been carefully planned and introduced in gradual, incremental stages. To develop a culture that is conducive to the achievement of objectives, the envisioned culture and the organisation's future plans should be considered concurrently, from the beginning of the change process.

CHANGE FACTORS

Three of the major factors that have influenced and will continue to influence change, particularly as they affect HR, are:

- new and amended laws that affect employment, many of which, to a significant degree, have their origins in European directives
- the continuous advances in technology, especially in information technology
- human resource management (HRM), as a system that influences how the whole organisation is run, especially in terms of the internal structure, culture, development, human performance and the general working climate within organisations.

EVOLUTION AND REVOLUTION

The three change factors that are mentioned above are probably the most visible to those who manage organisations, but change has several perspectives. Charles Handy, for example, talks about two types of change: *continuous* and *discontinuous*. In an analogy that describes continuous change, he says:

If you put a frog in cold water and gradually turn up the heat, the frog will eventually let itself be boiled to death. Similarly, if we don't actively respond to the radical way the world is currently changing we will not survive. (Handy 1989)

The CIPD suggests in its factsheet on change management (May 2009b) that: 'The impact of failures to introduce effective change can also be high: loss of market position, removal of senior management, loss of stakeholder credibility, loss of key employees.'

⦿ ACTIVITY 18.1

How long have you been with your current employer? Look back to when you first joined and reflect upon what it was like to work there then. Now compare that with the way things are now. Try to identify exactly what has changed.

What Handy describes as *discontinuous* change is more revolutionary than evolutionary. This type of change imposes sudden, large-scale changes, such as the implementation of a major new policy, a merger with another organisation or the privatisation of a public authority, or the changes brought about by the banking collapse of 2008, which reduced the money supply to organisations across the world; but there are yet other evolutionary changes. Champy and Nohria (1996) claim that three major drivers are stirring organisational change faster than ever before:

- **technology**: particularly IT, which is transforming businesses in dramatic ways

- **government**: rethinking its role in business, with all governments on a worldwide basis initiating deregulation, privatisation and increasing free trade

- **globalisation**: where companies from all parts of the globe are competing to deliver the same product or service, any time, anywhere, at increasingly competitive prices, which is causing organisations and companies to organise themselves in radically different ways.

If we consider the introduction of new technology as an example, this can have both positive and negative outcomes.

On the positive side, it enables the organisation to:

- enhance the productivity rate and the quality of its goods and services, for example by the introduction of computer-aided design and robotic manufacturing systems

- broaden and deepen its range of goods and services

- increase the efficiency and effectiveness of administration and the speed at which administrative tasks are carried out

- communicate internally and externally almost instantaneously

- carry out some of its functions more cost-effectively by transferring them to overseas locations, for example call centres.

On the negative side:

- The initial capital outlay for new technology can be prohibitively high.

- The rate at which technology is developing means that further advances are made before the organisation has had a full return on its capital outlay.

- Advances in technology affect the types of knowledge and skill requirements, and often require costly, wide-ranging training and retraining programmes.

- Its installation may cause the organisation temporarily to lose its day-to-day effectiveness.
- Employees may be negatively affected by the 'threat' of technological change and concerned over job losses.

The above forces for change, as described by Champy and Nohria, are largely external forces to the organisation. However, other forces can bring about change, which are largely factors of the internal organisation.

But there are alternative views.

Hughes (2007, p40) suggests typical forces for change might include:

- competition
- government changes
- new senior management
- IT development.

Huczynski and Buchanan (2007, p589) offer the following as internal triggers for change:

- new product and service design innovations;
- low performance and morale, high stress and staff turnover;

PAUSE FOR THOUGHT

The headline from the *Daily Telegraph* on 4 June 2009 was: 'British Airways won't rule out pension closure'. Osborne and Dunkley (2009) wrote that 'BA estimated at the time of its full-year results last month that, on an accounting basis, its two final salary schemes – the Airways Pension Scheme and the New Airways Pension Scheme – had a £2.9bn deficit, up £1.2bn from previous estimates.' If the pension deficit is taken in context of a downturn in the transatlantic 'business flyer' market, which is key to BA's business model, then it is not surprising that British Airways was in negotiations with its staff to develop new ways of working.

Here we can see that two triggers for change, both significant, have come together to cause BA to consider how it should operate its business.

At the time of writing this chapter, one path the company had embarked upon was to negotiate with its staff on conditions of service and staffing of long-haul flights. Millward (2009), in the *Daily Telegraph* on 18 June 2009, wrote, 'A deal agreed by BA and the British Airline Pilots Association (Balpa) will also see 78 jobs go under a voluntary redundancy package. The agreement would see 3,200 pilots accept a 2.61 per cent cut in their basic pay from October. They will also take a 20 per cent reduction in the additional money pilots are paid while flying the aircraft itself.'

A second and significant change to how BA goes about its business is its plan to merge with Iberia, the Spanish carrier, during the first quarter of 2010.

- appointment of a new senior manager or top management team;
- inadequate skills and knowledge base, triggering training programmes;
- office and factory relocation, closer to suppliers and markets;
- recognition of problems triggering reallocation of responsibilities;
- innovation in the manufacturing process;
- new ideas about how to deliver services to customers.

ACTIVITY 18.2

All change at school

Think about how your college or university works. What factors external to the organisation and what changes internal to the organisation could cause it to change what it does, for example in the provision of undergraduate or postgraduate courses? (Hint: you could consider doing a PESTLE (STEEPLE) analysis.)

RESISTANCE TO CHANGE

The chief preoccupations of managers when they are planning and implementing change are usually related to the cost and technical aspects of the change process. This can be a complex and testing set of disciplines to handle. Mistakes can be costly, but the key factor and certainly the most essential ingredient to a successful change process is the way in which the employees are taken through it. It is hard to imagine a more stringent test of managers' leadership skills.

When, for example, technological innovation triggers change, many of the long-serving employees fear it. Their skills have served them well in terms of their performance and earning capacity, but they feel abandoned and redundant when their previously valued abilities are no longer needed by the organisation. They might resist change for several reasons, since to them it might mean:

- a threat to their stability and may make their jobs redundant
- a change of routines, which can be frustrating
- being moved into jobs they fear they may not understand
- a change in status
- a change in pay structure and other rewards
- having to work in a new area with previously unknown colleagues
- having to work for a new and unknown boss
- having to work for a boss who is known, but is generally not liked
- a change in working hours
- changing to a job that is insufficiently challenging.

As Hughes (2007, p11) says, 'Organisational change and transformations involve the redistribution of power, information, resources, status, authority, and influence. Therefore, individuals' rights, dignity and privileges can be at risk.'

Change is happening all the time and so employees must change and learn to cope with the changes that are, in many cases, forced upon them. It is not easy to cope with change, especially if, as Hughes (2007) indicates, it affects the individual in the organisation. The fact that change is forced or is in some way inevitable may cause the individual to resist the changes. Not all employees respond in the same way to change. Individual differences have a profound effect on how employees perceive change. Intelligence and motivational factors may frustrate retraining, and age differences may inhibit more mature employees when it comes to disrupting their routines and separating them from their long-term work colleagues. For these reasons, therefore, change may raise the staff turnover rate and lead to redundancy and recruitment programmes. Change therefore has significant implications for the HR role.

DEALING WITH RESISTANCE

Encountering resistance may be used as an opportunity to examine how the change proposal is being handled. If the nature of the change has not been fully explained to employees, the prophets of doom, from the ranks of the employee body, will step forward and rumours, especially negative ones, about the proposed change will become widespread. Resistance, however, can be turned around and made constructive if it causes managers to interact more frequently with their staff, for example when they explain the nature of the proposed change in detail.

The proposed change should be explained to employees from the very outset. If it is not, it will create uncertainty among employees about what their future holds, which may lead to personal feelings of insecurity on the part of individuals. The approach to delivering news of change to employees should be a consultative one, in which the managers elicit employees' feelings and opinions. This kind of approach has been known to cause managers to explore alternative ways of meeting the desired objective. It may be that the alternatives proposed by the employees represent an improvement on the original proposal. If the employees are asked to think about the change, they will get to know more about it, which will serve three possible ends: first, to allay any rumours; second, to produce an improved proposal; and third, to reduce or even eliminate the resistance. A positive outcome to a consultative approach may confer upon employees feelings of 'ownership' of the change process, which naturally leads to their commitment to it.

In order to involve employees and ensure that they engage with the change process, it may be worth considering the work of Tannenbaum and Schmidt (1958, cited in Mullins 2007, pp372–4), who suggest that there is a continuum of leadership and involvement, ranging from telling, selling, consulting and joining. There is a danger that if the management make all the decisions and simply 'tell' the employees about the change, there will be no buy-in from staff.

Alternatively, at the other end of the continuum, if managers involve employees in the decision-making process, that is, 'join' with them, there is more likely to be commitment and engagement to the change from staff. Often managers settle for the mid-way approach of 'selling' the benefits of the change or maybe going as far as 'consulting' staff. The optimum situation for gaining commitment from employees is, of course, to 'join' with them, thus allowing the employees to exercise 'employee voice' and to be fully involved with the change activity and embrace the changes positively.

USING A FORCE FIELD ANALYSIS TO OVERCOME RESISTANCE TO CHANGE

One method of trying to manage a change process in the context of overcoming the resistance to change is to perform a force field analysis (Lewin 1951). This examines the key drivers and key resistive forces to a particular change situation. One can imagine a change problem to be like a large and unwieldy block of material on rollers that has forces trying to push it forward and resistive forces trying to prevent it from moving (Figure 18.1).

Figure 18.1 Forces for and against change

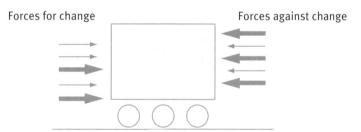

It can be seen that not all the forces are of the same magnitude; the width of the arrows gives some indication of this. Also, there may not necessarily be the same number of forces for the change as there are against the change. The art is in trying to identify all the relevant forces and then finding ways of increasing the strength of the forces for change and reducing the forces that are resisting change so that the heavy block on rollers, which represents the change process, moves to the right.

The work on the force field analysis was first conducted in the 1950s and is still relevant today. The following seven steps, developed by Senior (2002, p254) – who, in turn, drew on the work of Carnall (1995) and Huczynski and Buchanan (2001) – can be used when conducting a force field analysis:

- **Step 1:** The problem is defined in its present situation, with its strengths and weaknesses, and then the situation that the organisation would like to achieve is defined.

- **Step 2:** The forces for and against the situation are listed. These can be associated with people (who may be in positions of authority and so can impact upon the change positively or negatively), finances (and other resources), time factors, internal and external political factors, technical issues, competitor positions, what is the status quo with accepted and rigid ways of doing things – in fact, a mini PESTLE (STEEPLE) analysis can be conducted on the situation.

- **Step 3:** The forces are rated against a scale of 1 to 5; say, a force of 1 being weak and a 5 being strong.

- **Step 4:** A diagram is drawn, as in Figure 18.1, which has all relevant forces indicated.

- **Step 5:** Analyse each of the forces in turn, especially the strong forces, and think of ways that the forces 'for' can be improved and strengthened and the forces 'against' weakened.

- **Step 6:** After identifying the forces and the relative strengths, an action plan has to be agreed. It may be that if it is a person who is causing significant resistance to change, they can be 'turned' to work for the change by explaining to them issues and possible consequences of which perhaps they were not aware. Alternatively, as a final resort, they can be moved to another section or department of the organisation.

- **Step 7:** Identify the resources that will be needed to bring about the changes. Usually for large-scale changes a member of the senior management team (SMT) is identified as a change champion. This person will have the necessary authority to approve actions, budgets, make decisions and so on, to enable change to be effected.

Gold Line baby pushchairs

CASE EXAMPLE

Gold Line Baby Prams has manufactured a 'high end' quality pushchair for the past 20 years. Its design has not changed much; manufacturing is still done in a small factory that employs 50 people, mainly skilled. The workforce consists of 'expensive mechanical technicians', who assemble the parts of the pushchair, plus a number of machinists, who have to use lathes and similar machines to finish a number of parts that come from a foundry, where components are still cast in metal.

Narinderpal, who is a senior engineering manager and who has recently been recruited from a competitor business, is keen to modernise the equipment and move to 'Autocad' design of components. He believes the existing product design staff are capable of making the transfer from manual drawing to using computer design systems. The local college offers suitable courses using the type of equipment he would envisage the company would need to buy. Moving to automated design of the component parts of the pushchair would also enable essential machining of parts to be done automatically using automated metal-cutting machinery.

Narinderpal also suggests that there is a need to move away from foundry-produced components to ones that are manufactured using hot metal die-casting equipment. Components would be produced quicker and they would require little if any further finishing work. All in all, the entire product would be produced quicker without the loss of quality. What Narinderpal also suggests is that some production could be placed offshore to an organisation he has worked with in China, if they get heavy demands for a future product. This would be easy because the design and machining instructions could be transmitted electronically from the new desktop computer design equipment to the overseas manufacturer. For him, it is a 'no brainer', a win–win situation all round.

Tim, Narinderpal's boss and engineering director, does not see the sense in moving forward in the manner suggested because he feels that the company produces a limited number of styles of pushchair for a limited and exclusive market. He has been with the company since its inception and does not see a requirement to change the way things are done. He knows everyone who works for Gold Line and believes that changes in the way the product is manufactured will lead to redundancies in the technical workforce because the pushchairs will be able to be assembled by unskilled labour. Tim also believes that Narinderpal's ideas may lead the company to stop manufacturing locally and move it overseas.

The marketing director, Gurpreet, sees a common sense in Narinderpal's suggestion because, after discussion with him, she sees that the new manufacturing methods could allow product changes to happen quicker, when the demand for a particular type of pushchair increases at the detriment of another line; it would also allow the organisation to offer a wider range of products and enable quick design changes as consumer preferences change and so penetrate a wider market.

Mary, the chief executive officer (CEO), is very interested in Narinderpal's proposal. She realises that the changes would be significant and that she would have to borrow money to finance the purchase of new equipment and pay for the update training of the design staff.

Task

Using a force field analysis technique, how would you, as the CEO, go about bringing effective change? Draw the relevant force fields, with forces for and against, and develop an action plan of how you would go about moving to the new system as envisioned by Narinderpal.

CHANGING THE CULTURE

As we have previously seen, the foundations of the culture of any organisation are in its history. The traditions that have built up over time, including its methods of operating, tend to remain evident for as long as the organisation continues to succeed. What is done and how it is done are reinforced by success, and an 'if it ain't broke, don't fix it' attitude emerges. The fact has to be faced, however, that things do change. Competition becomes more fierce, market demands change as technological innovation continues to progress, people (customers) have become more discerning and price-conscious, and living standards are raised continually – at least, that is the case in the more advanced countries. Sometimes, however, the more senior members of the organisation may be inclined to place a high value on tradition, as the following case example shows.

Mitsubishi motors

In contrast to its main competitors, Honda and Daimler-Chrysler, Mitsubishi Motors experienced severe problems around the turn of the millennium. Unable to respond to the high demand for minivans and sport utility vehicles, it lost US$846 million in one year. The culprit was identified as the deeply rooted Mitsubishi culture, which was based on the traditions of the 1970s market conditions. The company appointed a new president – Katsuhiko Kawasoe – to try to change the culture.

Other Japanese firms had broken from the country's long-held beliefs in the importance of tradition and history, but Mitsubishi had continued to move at its own pace. While other Japanese companies had abandoned such notions as the 'job-for-life' tradition, which was no longer realistic in a highly competitive world marketplace, Mitsubishi continued to do things in its own way. When the chairman of Mitsubishi Heavy Industries was asked about laying off people, he replied, 'Employment is more important than profits! We are not concerned with return on equity ... if foreign investors don't see merit in our stock, they can sell it' – which of course they did!

A consultant who worked with Mitsubishi said the company was being held back by the lack of incentives and nobody holding management accountable. When something goes wrong, managers would say, 'It would be un-Japanese to fire anyone or close plants.' New recruits were not lectured on the importance of competition or profits. Instead, company executives continued to talk about Mitsubishi's 'special place in history and duty to the country'.

Discussion of the case

It is not difficult to identify past organisations in the West whose demise was largely caused by their attempts to survive on their historical traditions. What should Mitsubishi have done? The firm relied for its sales on the world markets but its deep-rooted culture was its main liability. In the 1980s, when global competition became a reality, and when speedy and sensitive responses to customer demands became the norm, deeply entrenched, old-fashioned cultures should have become redundant.

This was realised even as far back as 1966 by Burns and Stalker: 'Where customer demands are ever-changing, the organisation's speed of, and sensitivity to, response becomes the essence of success.' These writers were describing the kind of organisation that was most likely to succeed in a fast-moving and highly competitive market (what they referred to as *organic organisations*). This is still true over 40 years later.

MAKING THE CHANGE: CAN IT BE DONE?

In Chapter 2 references are made to the work of several eminent writers on culture, and from these you will have seen that culture is made up of relatively stable characteristics. From reading the first part of the following discussion, you will see that changing an organisation's culture appears to be an extremely difficult task. We hope, however, the evidence from the second part of the discussion will indicate to you that cultures can be changed.

PART 1: DON'T ROCK THE BOAT

The long-held beliefs and deeply rooted values to which the employees of an organisation are strongly committed motivate them to maintain the culture. In mechanistic organisations (highly structured organisations with centralised policies, rigid hierarchical ranks, a strong emphasis on administration), those typically servicing a stable market (see Chapter 1 for a fuller explanation), there are forces that combine to reinforce the importance of adhering to the cultural norms. These include written policies, mission statements and philosophies that emanate from the top, the infrastructural design, the buildings, the hardware, the structure, the style of leadership, the general climate of the place, the policies on recruitment, selection, training and promotion, the rituals and historic myths about the organisation and its key people.

Historically, mechanistic organisations have always attracted employees who seek stable and structured positions. Senior managers are selected on the grounds that they are the most likely people to perpetuate 'the way things are'. We saw that when Mitsubishi put a new president in place; it seems that rather than change the culture, the culture changed him!

PART 2: CATALYSTS OF CULTURE CHANGE

If, in the organisation-wide sense, the culture matches the values and philosophies of those at the top, there is an overall cohesiveness that makes for a strong culture, which is the most difficult type of culture to change. In any organisational scenario, the culture change process presents a daunting prospect, but research and experience shows that it can be done.

In particular circumstances, organisations are vulnerable to culture change when a severe crisis arises, such as when a competitor suddenly and unpredictably launches a new major product on the market, or there is a critical financial downturn such as that suffered by MG-Rover in 2004 or the banking collapse of 2008. In such cases, organisations usually bring in a new chief executive; sadly for MG-Rover, it was too late to do that. On a more positive note, change becomes necessary when the predicted sales of a new product are exceeded dramatically and the organisation has to move quickly to fulfil the demand.

When a long-established and successful organisation sets up a new major division or a subsidiary company in order to fulfil a major contract, the new organisation is ripe for the development of a culture that is conducive to success. In such a case, the top managers may instil new values, demonstrate new rituals and generally make the employees aware of the kind of behaviour that is expected of them.

In those circumstances, however, sometimes the managers and specialists needed for the new organisation are drawn from the main company, and if the new set-up is put together as a matrix, it will need to draw upon the expert and administrative services of the main company. In other words, the new employees' contacts will be those who espouse the old culture.

The new organisation will be more likely to succeed in shifting along the *mechanistic–organic* dimension (see Chapter 1) if new managers develop a culture that is appropriate for the central task. It is important to note that if nothing is done about the development of a fresh culture, then one will evolve anyway.

IDENTIFYING THE CULTURE GAP

In an organisation that has been established for several years, the managers may feel that the current culture is inappropriate for the achievement of corporate objectives. In such a case, the managers' first task is to envision the kind of culture that would be most appropriate for the foreseeable future. Second, they have to analyse and identify the true make-up of the current culture (see above), which will enable them to compare the two in order to identify the culture gap, at which stage they can develop a culture-change strategy; in other words, they have to fill the culture gap.

According to Armstrong (1999), culture change programmes can focus on particular aspects of the culture. The examples he cites include performance, commitment, quality, customer service, teamwork and organisational learning. All of these aspects have underpinning values that need to be defined. It would be necessary to prioritise by deciding which of them needs the most urgent attention.

ORGANISATION DEVELOPMENT

Organisation development (OD) is the term used to describe a process through which, using the principles and practices of behavioural science, a change programme is applied in the organisation, often on an organisation-wide basis. OD is driven by the ultimate purpose of creating an effective organisation by altering the structure and changing employees' attitudes, beliefs and values. It is concerned not with *what* is done but with the *way* things are done, and with creating a new culture of cohesiveness, interdependence and mutual trust.

KEY CONCEPT: ORGANISATION DEVELOPMENT

French and Bell (1990) defined OD as: 'a planned systematic process in which applied behavioural science principles and practices are introduced into an ongoing organisation towards the goals of effecting organisational improvement, greater organisational competence, and greater organisational effectiveness.'

The focus is on organisations and their improvement, or to put it another way, *total systems change*. The orientation is on action – achieving desired results as a result of planned activities. Once the areas and aspects that require change have been identified, the next step is to introduce the ideas to the employees. Employees vary in their attitudes to significant change. In general terms, the longer-serving employees, who have a need for job security, may fear that they will lose their jobs, and therefore they tend to resist it more than the younger employees, who may see it as an interesting challenge. The earlier part of this chapter deals with this problem and it will be helpful if you study the sections on 'Resistance to change' and 'Dealing with resistance'.

LEWIN'S THREE-PHASE MODEL OF CHANGE

Lewin's (1951) three-phase model consists of:

- unfreezing
- moving or changing
- refreezing.

UNFREEZING

Unfreezing the current behaviour is about getting employees to think about changing what they do, rather than being frozen in traditional ways. This is the period of time when the current circumstances are explained to those involved with the change. The situation is made difficult because the picture of the future is less secure and uncertain. It could be that a vision of competitor penetration into the market, in which an organisation has been operating almost as a single source (monopolistic), and all is about to change – because there is a need to change. The competitor is known to be entrepreneurial and is likely to change pricing, the nature of the product and is ready to market their goods. Management make it clear that 'things have to change'; if not then the company is likely to have to downsize and perhaps even go out of business. The idea is to try to create the mood among staff such that they will more readily be open to ideas that will bring about efficiencies, changes to ways in working, and so on.

Consulting employees

It is at this time that engagement with employees starts with a view to soliciting ideas of what type of change could occur and how they can contribute to the overall process. While the total change process is introduced and driven by the managers, employee groups should be consulted about specific changes that affect their areas of work. Management-led group discussions will help to clarify the nature of and the reasons for the changes, and should be carried out in a way that confers a significant degree of ownership on the employees. This is achieved by seeking employees' opinions, particularly about how the change process should be handled. Their advice should be considered seriously and their experience will be valuable, since they are the people at the work interface. The bonus from this is that when ownership of the change is felt by employees, they are less likely to resist and more likely to ensure that it succeeds.

The key to success is employee involvement. One way of eliciting employee involvement is through workshops where those involved are asked to consider the facts about the need to change and then to depict the change in the form of a cartoon or cartoons. The forces resisting the change being shown as crocodiles or monsters, each suitably labelled, while the forces and effects allowing/enabling the change being depicted as other more benevolent animals or symbols.

Communication is important at all levels, from team talks through to senior management. Typical communication processes are open forums, podcasts and use of the company intranet to answer frequently asked questions.

MOVING OR CHANGING

At this stage the ideas of what can happen and what management has approved to happen all start to occur. New sections are created, new equipment is installed, new work practices start to be introduced and old practices are discarded. Where jobs are to be reduced it is at this stage that people are redeployed and perhaps, as a final change, some people may be made redundant. The Lewin process does not necessarily require redundancies to happen but in today's cost-efficient and cost-effective world, either voluntary or compulsory redundancies are usually 'on the cards'. Voluntary redundancy is of course a preferred way of losing people because this has both a minimum effect on those that go – they have chosen to go – and also it is easier to manage the survivors: those that remain.

It is at this stage that the change champion may also have to become involved; as previously described, this is likely to be a senior director who has the muscle, the authority, to approve problematic changes and to make things happen. It may be their financial authority that is required to approve an expense or it could be the approval needed to make the changes to how a department is structured, even perhaps the number of jobs in a department. This of course may trigger work for the HR department in starting the process of redundancies or changing the terms and conditions of employment of staff. For example, if the change requires shift working to start, where before the operation was nine to five, then this will involve significant changes to how people work and therefore a change in the contract of employment, which will have to be negotiated.

Change levers

Some of the change levers described by Armstrong (2006, p316) include:

- **performance:** performance-related or competence-related pay schemes, performance management processes, leadership training, skills development
- **commitment**: communication, participation and involvement programmes, developing a climate of co-operation and trust; clarifying the psychological contract
- **customer service:** customer-care programmes
- **teamwork:** team-building, team performance management, team rewards
- **organisational learning:** taking steps to enhance intellectual capital and the organisation's resource-based capability by developing a learning organisation

- **values:** gaining understanding, acceptance and commitment through involvement in defining values, performance management programmes and employee development interventions.

REFREEZING

In this part of the process it is necessary to fix the changes to make sure that the old ways of working are not reintroduced. In its simplest form this could be the removal from staff computers of an old software program that staff could revert to using, as they get over the teething problems of introducing a new software system. In terms of how people work, getting them to accept and embed new practices may be difficult because they are comfortable with and know the issues and foibles of the old ways of working. The new strategies and structure (lines of reporting) within the organisation should, to some extent, prevent old habits from reappearing (Senior 2002, p309). HR processes such as recruitment, selection and development through promotion can be used to reinforce the essential changes. Moving section managers who are seen not to have embraced the new ideas or ways of working and introducing new ones, from other sections, all have an impact upon how people think and the messages that are embodied by those who are involved. Promoting people who have clearly embraced the new concepts and ideologies sends a strong message about what people need to do to 'get on' in the organisation.

In essence, while working on these change levers, the positive aspects of the old culture should be emphasised and reaffirmed, while the new values should be stated clearly and frequently. Employee behaviour that is conducive to the success of the change programme should be rewarded.

Schein (1985) listed five mechanisms for embedding and reinforcing the culture:

- what leaders pay attention to, measure and control
- leaders' reactions to critical incidents and crises
- deliberate role-modelling, teaching and coaching by leaders
- criteria for allocation of rewards and status
- criteria for recruitment, selection, promotion and commitment.

THE OD CHANGE MODEL

The OD model of change is a process-driven model and is logical in its working. The fact that it is process driven is also given as a criticism of the OD model, because change does not always happen in a logical and systematic manner. Change may, for example, because of a financial crisis, have to happen quickly without planning, discussion, negotiation, implementation and review.

As can be seen from Figure 18.2, the OD model of change is very systematic in its operation. In fact this is a criticism of the model because it can be argued that change, because of its nature, means the organisation, or that part of the organisation which is in change, is moving and in flux and therefore cannot be controlled in a systematic way. However, using the OD process as a model, one can see how change can be brought about. It gives us certain 'anchors' on which we can base our thoughts and actions.

The process starts by defining the current status of how the organisation or part of the organisation is operating, identifying the advantages of how it works as well as the disadvantages. The outcome of the deliberations is that the management team should have a clear vision of what the future should hold and what the organisation should be. There is a requirement to consider how internal and external forces may cause the organisation to change and how much

Figure 18.2 The OD model of change

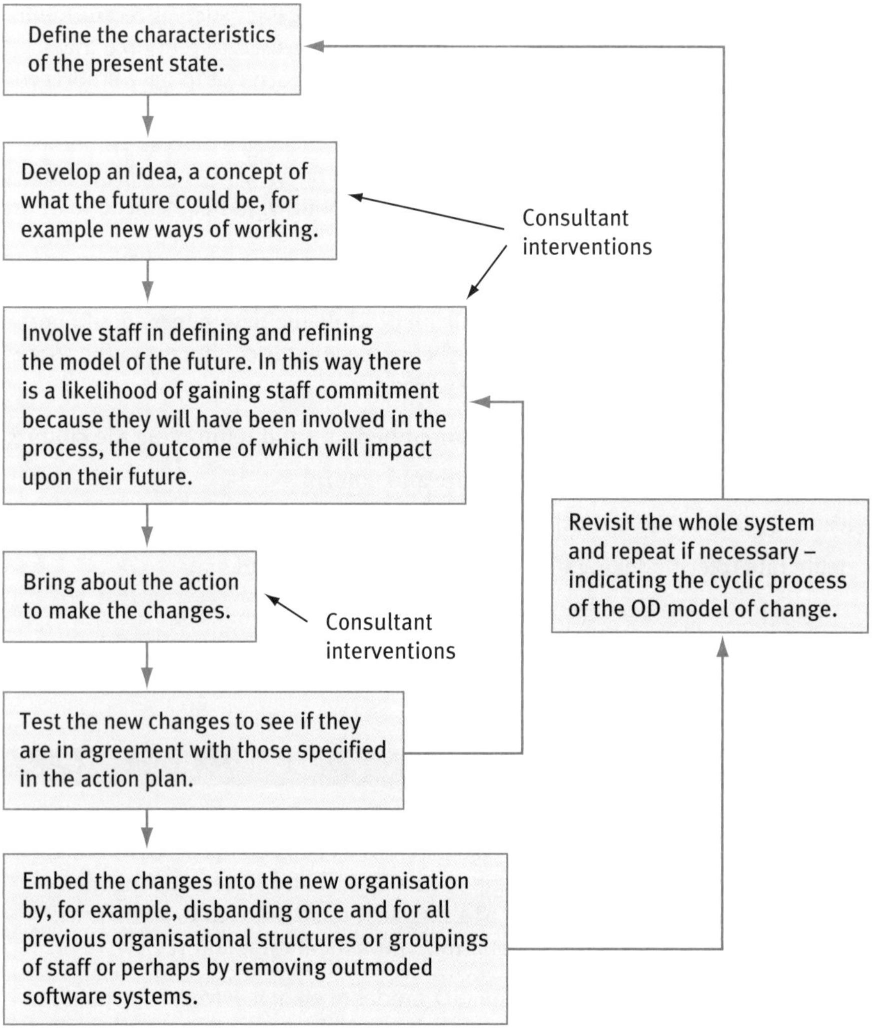

Adapted from Senior (2002)

it should change. As Senior (2002, p313) states, it is at this stage that there is a '... need for a more detailed examination of such things as:

- Individuals' motivation and commitment to their work organisation
- Recruitment practices, career paths and opportunities
- Prevailing leadership styles
- Employee training and development provision
- Intra- and inter-group relationships
- Organisation structure and culture.'

The next step is to develop an idea, a concept, of how the business could operate, perhaps by introducing new structures to reflect how the competition operates their organisation, or part of their organisation, and also how the structure may need to be improved to fit better with how new technology operates and how new customer interfaces are envisaged. At this stage employees should be intimately involved in how the new structures could be shaped and how perhaps new ways of working could better influence the shape and structure of the business. It is a time of honesty; because, if the new structures and new ways of working may lead to job losses, this should be stated 'up front'. However, this should not deter from the overall focus of the OD process, which is on staff involvement, with the objective of developing staff commitment to the changes. There needs to be an iterative process at this stage to check back with the original concepts and reasons for changing as the ideas developing are becoming more concrete in nature. This checking back and refining is called an iterative process: getting things better bit by bit.

Once the ideas and model of the future become more concrete, changes have to be made. Once again, as the changes are made there should be a process of checking back to the 'blueprint' to see if the changes are in line with the original proposals.

Finally, as all the new parts of the jigsaw start to fit into place, they need to be embedded to prevent the whole new organisation slipping back into its previous state. This could mean removing software systems from employee computers to prevent them from using old systems; the new systems, because of unfamiliarity, are perhaps perceived to be difficult to use. More significant changes have to be embedded by making sure that old organisational structures and groupings of employees are disbanded or those who have resisted areas of change are perhaps moved to new locations, where they have no historical context.

THE ROLE OF THE CHANGE CONSULTANT

A characteristic of the OD model of change is the intervention within the process of change by an internal or externally recruited consultant, sometimes called a change agent. In this context we are defining the change consultant or change agent as being different from the change leader.

The change leader is someone who has the responsibility to bring about the change in the organisation, probably a senior manager who is very close to the day-to-day operations and so will have difficulty standing back and not getting involved with issues because of personal preferences and alliances.

The change consultant can be from within the organisation or recruited from outside. There are disadvantages and advantages for taking either route. Using someone from within the company, preferably someone respected as being able to take a logical stance on issues, has the advantage of knowing the culture, people, processes and structures. However, no matter how they may try not to be partisan when issues arise and require resolving, they may be seen to be part of a particular camp. On the other hand, resourcing someone from outside the organisation has the advantage that they have no baggage with which to be burdened but they neither know the culture nor the people and processes; this of course can be perceived as an advantage.

The change consultant or change agent can act in a number ways. Ideally they should have no particular allegiance in the context of what the outcome of the change may be but should be an 'honest broker' in terms of reviewing ideas and perhaps offering suggestions for a way forward, not necessarily solutions because the solutions should come from those who are and will be working with the new systems and in the new structures. The change consultant should try to facilitate those involved with the process to get to the most appropriate solutions. They can also act as a mediator between competing groups in which negotiations and discussion have led to an impasse with progress stifled. They may offer different ways to view problems and thus energise staff to overcome issues.

Paton and McCalman (cited in Senior 2002, p320), offer the following as the skills of an effective change agent:

i.   To help the organisation define the problem by asking for a definition of what it is.

ii.   To help the organisation examine what causes the problem and diagnose how this can be overcome.

iii. To assist in getting the organisation to offer alternative solutions.

iv.   To provide direction in the implementation of alternative solutions.

v.   To transmit the learning process that allows the client to deal with change on an ongoing basis by itself in the future.

THE TOOLS OF THE CHANGE CONSULTANT

Huczynski and Buchanan (2007) and Senior (2002) offer a number of tools that the change agent can deploy when working with groups on a change process:

- **Survey feedback:** Consultants can use surveys to determine opinions and attitudes of groups of staff, to form a benchmark of 'where we are now' so that similar surveys can be conducted in the future to determine what changes, if any, have taken place. Surveys also give some idea of the temperature of parts of the organisation and where there are issues and thus problems to be resolved.

- **Organisational mirroring:** Using this technique, groups are defined, with one group becoming the host or home group. Other groups that interface with their operations and systems, which they 'own', are invited to comment. The idea is that the host group is not there to defend how they work but to learn how their way of working, in the context of relationships, impacts upon others. The consultant's skills can sometimes be sorely tested trying to prevent open hostility! There has to be clear ground rules and the consultant has to be very competent and professional when engaging with what could be very emotive issues – especially when the host group is listening to criticisms of the way they have been perceived to interact! Once one group has been the focus of the other groups in the process, places are exchanged.

- **Inter-group development:** Inter-group development is about addressing the functional boundaries that exist between groups. It may be that systems of operation cause clashes; for example, engineers need to spend money quickly to resolve technical problems, whereas accountants need authorisation before they can release money. In this case it is the different criteria for control and success that cause the conflict or disharmony between the groups. Inter-group development, as its name implies, is all about finding out about the barriers between groups that cause the business to falter and work in an inefficient manner. This activity is sometimes called inter-group confrontation.

- **Role negotiation:** Role negotiation is similar to organisational mirroring in terms of its intentions. The focus is on the relationships between individuals and why they are, as a small team or an interfacing part of the business, dysfunctional. The idea is to allow one person to air their perceptions of the other person, then to reverse the role, and thus, from the learning gained, some mutual understanding is arrived at with a view to improving the relationship and ways of working.

- **Quick wins:** Success breeds success and so if one can publish quick wins, where one part of a change programme has been successfully implemented, then the hope is that the advantages seen, by publicising the outcomes of a successful component part of the overall change process, will encourage and give hope to others to work through their part of the change initiative (Kotter 1996).

- **Team-building:** As the change progresses and new structures and groupings appear, there is a need to build internal morale. Especially where colleagues may have left under redundancy circumstances there is a need to support those who are left through group activities that are designed to improve that all-important morale. The most common form that many of us have experienced or have seen on television are the outward bound activities that cause people to work together to overcome obstacles that are placed in their (their team's) path. The objective is to create situations where people become reliant on their peers; it is also about building, in a 'forced manner', relationships that otherwise may take months or years to develop.

THE EMERGENT APPROACH TO CHANGE

In organisations today, minor day-to-day changes take place that are made as a result of 'on the hoof' decisions by managers and others. These changes go unnoticed at the time, such as a minor modification to a work system or a gradual change in the style of communication. This is evolutionary change in which organisations change gradually and evolve in ways that enable them to continue to meet the needs of the internal and external environments. It is also one of the ways in which organisations respond to the factors that are brought to light by a SWOT or PESTLE (STEEPLE) analysis.

In this case change is not a discrete, one-off activity. For those who are the proponents of the emergent approach to change, they consider change to be happening all the time in some part of an organisation as a response to emerging threats and changes in how work is done and people interact.

Burnes (2009, p368), using Weick's words, explains that:

> Emergent change consists of ongoing accommodations, adaptations, and alternations that produce fundamental change without a priori intention to do so. Emergent change occurs when people reaccomplish routines and when they deal with contingencies, breakdowns, and opportunities in everyday work. Much of the change goes unnoticed, because small alternations are lumped together as noise in otherwise uneventful inertia. ...

 ACTIVITY 18.3

All change

Think of some of the things that have changed in your workplace, college or university. Have the changes been planned or has something happened that has caused an activity or work to be done differently?

As Burnes (2009) suggests, change is not driven by recipes, but the essence of change is that work exists because of interactions between people, whether these be groups or individuals. By considering change as emergent and having a political dimension, the concept of change as an activity becomes more real if one compares this to the planned approach to change, which does not take into account '... the political nature of change into the more traditional [planned approach] and more prescriptive literature on change. ...' In essence, what emergent change recognises is that there are power and political dimensions to an organisation that must be managed.

There are a number of factors that can influence how people act and react when change opportunities occur. Burnes (2009) suggests that the nature and type of:

- organisational structure

- organisational learning
- managerial behaviour
- power and politics (within an organisation)

can all impact upon the readiness and ability of people, at all levels within the organisation, to become involved with change.

 ACTIVITY 18.4

Factors that impact on change

Can you explain how the factors cited above – organisational structure, organisational learning, managerial behaviour, power and politics – impact upon the ability of an organisation to engage with change?

ROLE OF HR IN SUPPORTING THE MANAGEMENT OF CHANGE

CIPD research, summarised in its factsheet on change management (CIPD 2009b), has also identified that HR's involvement in various aspects of change can make the difference between successful and less successful projects by, for example:

- involvement at the initial stage in the project team
- advising project leaders on skills available within the organisation – identifying any skills gaps, training needs, new posts, new working practices, and so on
- balancing out the narrow/short-term goals with broader strategic needs
- assessing the impact of change in one area/department/site on another part of the organisation
- being used to negotiating and engaging across various stakeholders
- understanding stakeholder concerns to anticipate problems
- understanding the appropriate medium of communication to reach various groups
- helping people cope with change, performance management and motivation.

CHANGE AND EMPLOYEE BEHAVIOUR

Each and every employee of an organisation will not necessarily respond the same, both in terms of their emotions and reactions, to the change process. There will be some who will see their world being turned upside down and be threatened by the change. They may see their territories, their status and zone of comfort all being threatened. They, potentially, could be some of those who could threaten the change from happening. It is with these people that time and effort will need to be spent communicating the need for the change and consequences of *not* changing. It may be, though, that they will never accept the need for the change. This has consequences for those who are managing change. One of the problems with change is that the outcome cannot be predicted accurately in all its facets; there will always be some uncertainty until the major part of the process is complete (is change ever complete?).

On the other hand, there will be those in the organisation who have been restricted in their work because of archaic and old-fashioned practices and processes and who will be extremely enthusiastic about the opportunities that new changes may bring. These will be the people who can be used as ambassadors for change, especially in their part of the organisation, and so help the process of change progress positively. They can be used to demonstrate and to advertise where the change process has resulted in beneficial outcomes.

It is important that communication with employees is frequent and honest. If the change process is likely to result in job and therefore people losses, through gains in efficiency, then this should be communicated early and thought given to how potential redundancies (see more on this in Chapter 17) are handled, perhaps in the first instance through voluntary severance or redeployment.

Where change happens on a frequent basis, employees may tire of the whole repetitive process. Even those who have previously embraced change in a positive way may find the experience draining and will not wish to engage.

SUMMARY

Change can have a severe impact upon people, both in a positive and negative sense. Hughes (2007, p11), citing Weiss, says that there are '... potential ethical dilemmas of change management. Organisational changes and transformations involve the redistribution of power, information, resources, status, authority, and influence. Therefore, individuals' rights, dignity and privileges can be at risk.'

However change is managed, it is incumbent upon those who do the managing to consider the sensibilities of those who are impacted by the change and the survivors of the change process.

REVIEW QUESTIONS

1 What are the possible consequences of allowing an out-of-date culture to persist at a time of significant external change?

2 What are the main drivers for change in an organisation?

3 What are the main forces that cause resistance to change?

4 Give some advantages and disadvantages of technology as a driver for change.

5 What is the role of:

- the change leader
- the change consultant or change agent?

6 What do you understand by:

- organisational mirroring
- survey feedback
- team-building?

7 What is meant by the emergent approach to change? How does the concept of 'emergent change' differ from the 'planned approach to change'?

8 What are the major criticisms of the planned approach to change?

9 What is the role of HR in supporting change?

EXPLORE FURTHER

BOOKS

SENIOR, B. and SWAILES, S. (2010) *Organizational change*. Harlow: Pearson Education Ltd.

Senior and Swailes' text covers a broad spectrum of change issues. The book addresses the nature of organisational change and how structure, culture and leadership impact upon change as well as the politics of change in the context of organisations. They also offer strategies for managing change. It is a solid, well-written text on change and the material is accessible to the student who is meeting the theory of change management for the first time.

HUGHES, M. (2006) *Change management: a critical perspective*. London: Chartered Institute of Personnel and Development.

Mark Hughes' text on change management takes the notion of change management and pursues its understanding from a number of different perspectives. It explores the idea of change as a concept, organisational change, individual change and change management as a process. The text takes a critical perspective and challenges some of the concepts and processes introduced in the course of the book. A new edition is due for publication in 2010.

WEB LINKS

Also worth a read is the CIPD's factsheet on change management. The CIPD looks at why organisations change and change strategies, and considers HR's role in change and how change can be managed more effectively. The factsheet can be found at: www.cipd.co.uk/subjects/corpstrtgy/changemmt/chngmgmt.htm

CHAPTER 19

Handling and Managing Information

LEARNING OBJECTIVES

After studying this chapter the student will be able to:

- understand the difference between the needs for strategic, tactical and operational information
- define what is meant by information in the context of human resource management
- identify the differences between types and usage of HR information systems (HRIS)
- analyse, make and prepare comparative types of data information
- understand information in bar chart and pie chart formats
- understand the operation of the Data Protection Act 1998 and Freedom of Information Act 2000.

INFORMATION COLLECTION

Appropriate identification of types of information and storage is a valuable tool for the HR practitioner. The majority of people reading this text will not have to decide upon what information to collect but will, from time to time, have to manipulate information.

Information can be classified, in terms of its usage, into three broad areas:

- strategic
- tactical
- operational.

STRATEGIC INFORMATION

In this case the information should be provided in broad or summarised terms, for consumption by the board of directors of the organisation. They need information to make strategic decisions that can inform the direction the company will take on issues. It may also include the results of monitoring of how policies are enacted within the organisation.

TACTICAL INFORMATION

Information of a tactical nature is for use by middle management. Consider the needs of the HR manager in a business. Tactical information will be required for them to able to determine the level of budget they need to demand in order to be able to operate their part of the business. The HR manager, for example, will need to know the recruitment and training and development activity, the number of the staff, and so on, to be in a position to request and therefore to manage that part of their departmental budgets.

OPERATIONAL INFORMATION

Operational activities occur at the level of the business. For example, the training manager will need a monthly update of the training budget expenditure so that they can monitor the budget, so ensuring that they do not agree to training or development that will push the organisation over an agreed budget.

CASE EXAMPLE

EPRO Oil and Gas is an international company that has its UK headquarters in Aberdeen, Scotland. It employs a total of 3,000 people in its onshore offices and gas plants and offshore platforms and drilling rigs. It both explores for oil and gas in the North Sea, as well as building fixed platforms from which it produces the oil and gas to pump to onshore refineries and gas plants where the oil and gas is converted in petrol, diesel, tars and 'consumer gas' to pump into the national grid to warm and provide heat for cooking in UK homes.

The company takes pride in its people management practices. HR business partners are responsible for its internal staff planning process as well as for providing a generalist HR service: recruitment, advice on development and training of staff, taking care of dismissals and activities such as advising on discipline and grievance cases, as well as handling personnel issues that flow into tribunal cases. There is a small corporate HR team which offers guidance on policy and other corporate issues; corporate HR also manages the payroll for the company.

The HR business partners also manage the staff planning side of the business, linking the business plan to staffing requirements, which involves the traditional areas of recruitment and selection and development.

A current area of concern for a number of the business partners is the relatively high turnover of staff. The senior management of the organisation have asked for an analysis of the figures.

Consider Table 19.1. It shows the key departments and the respective staff numbers, staff turnover (raw numbers) and percentage turnover numbers (see Chapter 5 for an explanation of how these numbers are calculated) on a year-by-year basis from 2005 to 2010. Clearly from one year to the next we can see that there has been some recruitment activity to maintain overall numbers in each department.

Strategic information management

From a **strategic perspective**, management can see, from the percentage turnover figures, that there has been little increase, over the years, with the turnover in the Production and Maintenance Department, but there has been a growing increase in the turnover in the Project Engineering and the Finance Departments.

The above information was collated by the HR business partners and given to the HR director, who presented the data to

Table 19.1 EPRO staff statistics 2005–2010

EPRO staff numbers	2005	2006	2007	2008	2009	2010
Production & Maintenance	1725	1715	1740	1755	1759	1760
Project Engineering	525	500	495	490	530	480
Logistics	495	500	470	495	503	492
Finance	169	170	175	175	175	175
HR	33	31	30	28	27	27
Law	10	12	11	11	12	12
Public Relations	5	5	5	5	5	5
Totals	**2962**	**2933**	**2926**	**2959**	**3011**	**2951**

EPRO turnover numbers	2005	2006	2007	2008	2009	2010
Production & Maintenance	208	205	200	204	206	204
Project Engineering	52	52	72	84	93	102
Logistics	32	42	36	29	24	27
Finance	5	9	14	16	19	24
HR	2	1	1	1	2	1
Law	1	0	1	0	0	0
Public Relations	1	0	0	0	0	0

EPRO % turnover	2005	2006	2007	2008	2009	2010
Production & Maintenance	12.1%	12.0%	11.5%	11.6%	11.7%	11.6%
Project Engineering	9.9%	10.4%	14.5%	17.1%	17.5%	21.3%
Logistics	6.5%	8.4%	7.7%	5.9%	4.8%	5.5%
Finance	3.0%	5.3%	8.0%	9.1%	10.9%	13.7%
HR	6.1%	3.2%	3.3%	3.6%	7.4%	3.7%
Law	10.0%	0.0%	9.1%	0.0%	0.0%	0.0%
Public Relations	20.0%	0.0%	0.0%	0.0%	0.0%	0.0%
Overall % turnover	**10.2%**	**10.5%**	**11.1%**	**11.3%**	**11.4%**	**12.1%**

the EPRO Oil and Gas management team. Although the turnover on the Maintenance and Production has not increased, the absolute value of the turnover is a concern. Clearly the *increase* in turnover in the Project Engineering and Finance Departments is a worry.

As a result of the above analysis and the meeting with the company's management team, a strategic decision was made to:

1 Start an in-house apprentice scheme, linked to a local college, for the Production and Maintenance Department, which in them comprises technicians. This was justified, initially, on the basis of the high staff turnover figures for 2005 to 2010, but compounded when the figures for recruitment for the years 1990 to 2010 were unearthed and calculations were made showing that £25.3 million was wasted on recruitment activities for the Production and Maintenance Department between 1991 and 2010. (This was based upon the cost of recruitment of 4,134 persons over the 20-year period, with cost data taken from the CIPD *Recruitment, Retention and Turnover* survey figures for 2009, which gives an average cost of £6,125 per employee recruited.)

2 Introduce a professional engineering development scheme for project engineers, for recently qualified graduates, linked to universities within and around the Aberdeen area.

3 Consider the introduction of a mentoring system for new employees into the organisation.

Tactical information management

We have seen from the data in Table 19.1 that, over the preceding three years to 2010, the turnover percentage of staff in the Finance Department increased from a figure of 5.3% for 2006 to 13.7% for 2010. Clearly something has happened that has caused this unacceptable increase in turnover. Turnover has increased during a period of time when the economy was going through troubled times and jobs, particularly outside the petroleum sector, were generally at risk; and still people were leaving EPRO Oil and Gas! From a tactical perspective a decision was taken jointly by the finance, engineering and HR directors to investigate the cause of the increase in turnover.

From a tactical perspective, three considerations came to mind.

1 Had there been some change in the management of the Finance and Engineering Departments?

2 Review the effectiveness of the induction programme to determine whether or not it is still fit for purpose.

3 Review the effectiveness of the exit interview process. The data obtained from recent exit interviews conducted by line staff was of limited use. It was thought that the methodology – that is, how the system operates, who conducts the interviews, when they are conducted, how and if the information from the interviews is (if at all) fed back into the review process and so on – needs to be reappraised.

Operational information management

There had been no change in the management of either the Finance or Engineering Departments.

From an operational perspective the information in Table 19.1 is not of much use. What is more important at an operational level would be access, for example, to the personnel files of staff who have recently joined the organisation to see if they have attended an induction course. Operational data would include information on individuals such as:

- department currently working in
- location of their workplace
- courses attended, for example if the employee has attended induction, first

aid training, or perhaps a management and leadership training course

- qualification attained – for example these may range from academic, NVQ-type qualifications to being recognised and recorded as being competent as a fork-lift truck driver or whether staff had passed the safety (survival) courses to be able to fly offshore in a helicopter

- current study – this is relevant if the employee is following a course of study: open learning, or perhaps at a local college or university

- level of skill – the employee may be rated as competent to train people on the job they do in the organisation

- specialist skills – the employee may have training and mentoring skills that can be used to mentor newly recruited people into the organisation

- preferred options for career development

- personal development plans (PDPs)

- required training, which may include mandatory health and safety training

- absence management information.

 ACTIVITY 19.1

Consider your own organisation, or an organisation you know, and list the type of information about an employee you would wish to have access to for operational or legal purposes. Do not simply list information, but rather think how you would make use of the information once you have access to it.

THE RANGE AND EXTENT OF HR INFORMATION HELD WITHIN AN HRIS (H.R. INFORMATION SYSTEM)

The above list of information (operational level) is focused on the employee. However, some information useful to HR and the company is not about one individual but may be about meeting targets or information about groups of people, which may have to be presented to management, for decision or simply for briefing purposes.

Management will certainly be interested in budgets and whether they have been under- or overspent; they will also be interested in such diverse matters as ethnicity monitoring within the organisation and the outcomes of staff satisfaction surveys and recruitment campaigns. Some of this information will be aggregated from individual records, for example data on ethnicity and absence, but data on staff satisfaction surveys will have to be inputted once they have occurred. Some data may have to be inputted manually but wherever possible data should be handled (in totality if at all possible) by electronic transfer for items such as staff satisfaction surveys; much depends on whether or not the data collection can be done online.

As mentioned above, one can think of information as being 'personal information', that is, about people, age, sex, date of birth, gender, home contact information, next of kin, contractual arrangements, learning and development, induction and general training records, and so on. However, to use an HRIS and all its computing power simply to store this type of information is to underuse the system. An HRIS can be incorporated into and form a key element of the knowledge management processes of the organisation.

Information gleaned from focus groups, client interviews, projects with (internal as well as external) client groups, the extent to which service-level agreements have or have not been maintained, and the learning gained from the experience of success or failure of a project all contribute to the wealth of knowledge that can be shared with others who will access the systems in future.

TYPES OF HR SYSTEM

Many HR information systems (HRIS) are still simply used as data banks and, as Ball (cited in Torrington et al 2007, p809) found, '… HRISs were still being used primarily for administrative rather than analytical ends and exploitation remains painfully slow and patchy. One of the key attractions for technology for the HR function is that it can reduce time on administrative chores to free up this time for strategic activities.' In a similar way Bandarouk and Ruel (2009, p504) argue that, 'as one of the early IT adopters in 1980s, HR functions used to employ IT for administrative processes, primarily payroll processing, with little attention being paid to so-called transformational HR practices. …'.

 KEY CONCEPT: HR INFORMATION SYSTEMS AND E-HRM

Haines and Petit (1997, cited in Bandarouk and Ruel 2009, p506) 'considered HRIS as a system used to acquire, store, manipulate, analyze, retrieve, and distribute pertinent information about an organization's human resources'.

Bandarouk and Ruel (2009, p507) define '… e-HRM as: an umbrella term covering all possible integration mechanisms and contents between HRM and Information Technologies aiming at creating value within and across organizations for targeted employees and management. …'.

The second definition expands on the first definition because its outlook is broader, recognising that all 'e' type channels of information can feed into and out of a system, thus enabling scope for manipulating data sets from different sources.

HRISs can be used to store and manipulate HR management data, the type previously described in this chapter. This is extremely useful as data is at one's fingertips; the key is making use of it, as per the example on the strategic use of data. According to Reddington (cited in Torrington et al 2007), the primary drivers for using HR information systems are 'operational', 'rational' and 'transformational'. The operational drivers of HRISs are along the lines discussed, the rational is associated with the demand of line managers and employees to have ready access to HR management data, and the transformational one may argue the availability and use of data that can be used in a strategic sense, as described in the previous case example on turnover.

There has been a growth in HRIS that allows employees to store and share information that aids personal development and career planning. This type of system may be used as a general data-sharing medium, similar to YouTube; it may have parts 'sectioned off' that are used as specialist areas where wikis (What Is Known Is) are set up to allow staff, perhaps working from diverse geographical locations, to share information on their specialist subject through the organisation's intranet. One can imagine the different functions in the business having these sites where essential information, gleaned from working for and with clients, is held and thus forms a critical means of knowledge management, which both supports current employees working with clients and also can be used when preparing bids for future business.

This type of HRIS is also very useful when employees are working towards in-house qualifications. Tutors in remote locations can monitor the progress of their 'students' because they (the students) can upload work within their own work-area site and from where tutors can access and assess the information, grade it and return it with comments. Within this type of system areas can also be allocated to groups for blogging about their work; once again this is all focused around knowledge and human capital (people) management and development.

The move is to enterprise resource planning (ERP) systems where, as Bandarouk and Ruel (2009, p504) write, 'for example, e-HRM applications are no longer "stand-alone" tools but mostly a part of more complicated ERP systems, where e-HR modules are integrated with financial or other modules'. In this way data from the HRIS can be integrated with financial data, manipulated and used by cross-functional teams for decision-making purposes. Bandarouk and Ruel point out, though, that there is not much evidence to suggest that organisations have become more strategic in their use of the information that an HRIS offers. In fact they argue that e-HRM was primarily used in support of routine administrative HR tasks. As well as the obvious advantages of a professional HRIS (ready access to various data sources, distributed access to data by different classes of user, management as well as employees), the fact that the majority of HRISs are not bespoke causes a convergence in their use, that is, if organisations have the same access to similar technology then there is nothing, in 'innovative technological terms', to harness to make any distinguishable difference between organisations and how they can operate. In short, there is nothing to give one organisation the competitive edge over the other.

 ACTIVITY 19.2

Access the websites for the following HRISs:

- PebblePad: www.pebblepad.co.uk/default.asp
- ORACLE – PeopleSoft Enterprise Human Capital Management: www.oracle.com/applications/peoplesoft/hcm/ent/index.html

Browse through the applications to view the range of activities that each of the systems offer.

ACTIVITY 19.3

Using your own organisation or one that you are familiar with, discuss which information, as held on the HRIS, is:

- (password) protected yet freely accessible to staff

- maintained on the system by employees themselves and which is maintained by HR staff.

USING INFORMATION TO BEST ADVANTAGE

Consider Table 19.2, which shows the recruitment activity for the Production and Maintenance Department. It is useful to analyse the data to get some idea of the extent (volume) of work, for example in recruitment, that the HR department has to manage on a regular basis.

Table 19.2 Recruitment of Production & Maintenance staff 1991–2010

EPRO recruitment	1991	1992	1993	1994	1995	1996	1997	1998	1999	2000
Prod. & Maint. Dept	202	198	200	214	215	216	208	203	204	202
	2001	2002	2003	2004	2005	2006	2007	2008	2009	2010
	198	208	199	205	198	230	215	208	207	204

Information can be analysed in many different ways. However, there are advantages if information is analysed in standard ways; this helps us make comparisons. Consider how the mode, median and average (mean) are used:

- **Mode** – this is the most frequently occurring value. In the case of Table 19.2 there are 2 modes: 198 and 208, which both occur three times.

- **Average** or **mean** (of people recruited per year) – this is the total number of people recruited divided by the number of years = 4134/20 = 207 – rounded up from 206.7 people recruited each year.

- **Median** – this is the value half-way along the data set. In our case this would be 204.5. For an even data set, you take the value, half way between the two middle values.

All of the above functions are available in Microsoft Excel.

RECRUITMENT AND TURNOVER AT EPRO OIL AND GAS PRODUCTION DEPARTMENT

Perhaps of greater use is if information is presented in a graphical fashion. Consider Figure 19.1, which presents in diagram format the data in Table 19.2

(extended back in time to 1991), which has been obtained using Microsoft Excel. Using a bar chart immediately presents the data in a way that is easily understandable and, perhaps of some importance, can be used in a PowerPoint presentation to highlight issues in a very visible manner.

Figure 19.1 Production & Maintenance recruitment 1991–2010

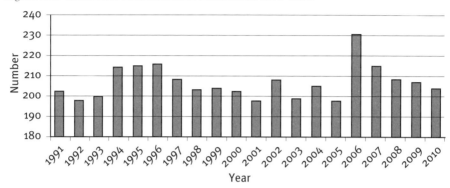

The type of presentation in Figure 19.2 clearly shows that recruitment has largely remained constant and below, or just peaking above, 216 per annum from 1991 to 2005; with some fluctuations around the average of 207 people per year recruited. The planned population of the Production and Maintenance Department from 1991 through to 2006 was 1,740 staff. We can see that there is a spike in the recruitment in 2006 of 230 staff. What could be the explanation of this deviation? It is clear, therefore, that to make sense of the above type of graph in its fullest sense, there is need for a narrative that can help explain changes in the profile of the graph.

The deviation (the recruitment spike) is because, from 2007, the workforce plan for the Production and Maintenance Department has changed. The original staffing plan requires a staff presence of 1,740 people; however, there is a change in the planned target population to 1,770 staff from 2007, the extra recruitment occurring in 2006. The change is as a result of increasing the size of one of the onshore gas plants to accommodate extra natural gas production supplied from natural gas tankers that bring the liquefied natural gas products from overseas and offload their cargo into the company's gas storage tanks at the coastal gas plant – for treatment and then injection into the UK's distribution gas pipe network for household consumption. Once this localised peak in recruitment has occurred we can see, from 2007 onwards, that the recruitment activity settles down to levels similar level to that between 1991 and 2005, that is, to cope with staff turnover requirements.

In fact, analysis of staff turnover (Figure 19.2) shows that turnover has *not* significantly changed between the years of 1991 and 2010. The question, of course, is why had there been no initiatives between 1991and 2010 to try to reduce the waste of time, energy and money in the recruitment of staff simply to cope with the average turnover rate of 11.9%.

Figure 19.2 Production & Maintenance turnover 1991–2010

TURNOVER IN THE EPRO OIL AND GAS FINANCE DEPARTMENT

Figure 19.3 shows the turnover of staff in EPRO's Finance Department. If the profile of the graph of this department is compared with the turnover graph (Figure 19.2) of the Production and Maintenance Department, it is starkly different. Where the graph of the turnover for the Production and Maintenance Department hovers around the average of 205 staff per year, the turnover in the Finance Department changes from a figure of around five per year and starts to 'ramp up' to a turnover, in 2010, of 24 per year. Clearly something is amiss and, whatever has happened, has changed since 2006. The HR Director, together with the Head of Finance need to investigate this phenomenon.

Figure 19.3 Finance Department turnover 1991–2010

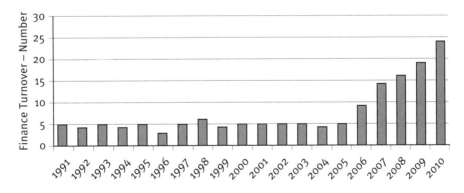

ACTIVITY 19.4

In groups discuss how the causes of the increase in turnover in the Finance Department can be investigated and perhaps explained. As the HR director, would you immediately approach the Finance Director with your findings?

RECRUITMENT AND TURNOVER AT THE EPRO OIL AND GAS PRODUCTION DEPARTMENT

The raw data figures for the training budget (current year) spend for EPRO Oil and Gas Production are presented in Table 19.3.

Table 19.3 Annual training budgets for EPRO departments

Department	Training budget spend
Production & Maintenance	£5,780,000
Project Engineering	£1,400,000
Logistics	£983,500
Finance	£67,000
HR	£54,125
Law	£64,800
Public Relations	£11,750
Total training budget	**£8,361,175**

The information is of course useful but it gives us no comparative measures. It is by making comparisons that judgements can be made. It may be useful to express the training budget expenditure as a percentage of operating expenditure or as a percentage of the department's annual salary budget. The annual salary budget for the EPRO departments is given in Table 19.4.

Table 19.4 Annual salary budgets for EPRO departments

Department	Salary budget
Production & Maintenance	£79,200,000
Project Engineering	£21,600,000
Logistics	£19,680,000
Finance	£7,875,000
HR	£1,215,000
Law	£720,000
Public Relations	£200,000
Totals	**£130,490,000**

Using the figures from Tables 19.3 and 19.4, the amount of the annual departmental training budget, as a percentage of the annual departmental salary budget, can be calculated:

[(Annual Training Budget) / (Annual Department Salary Budget)] × 100%

This information is presented in Table 19.5.

Table 19.5 Annual training budget expressed as percentage of annual salary budget

Department	Training budget as percentage of department salary budget
Production & Maintenance	7.3%
Project Engineering	6.5%
Logistics	5.0%
Finance	0.9%
HR	4.5%
Law	9.0%
Public Relations	5.9%
Total training budget	**6.4%**

Table 19.5 is very illuminating because it shows that the total training budget, expressed as a percentage of the annual salary budget, is 6.4% and, with the exception of the Law and Finance Departments, all other departments' annual training spend for the current year hovers around this value, give one or two percentage points. However, the Law Department has exceeded this value considerably, whereas the Finance Department has significantly underspent. This information can usefully, for presentation purposes, be displayed as a pie diagram (see Figure 19.4).

Figure 19.4 Training budget presented as a percentage of department salary budget

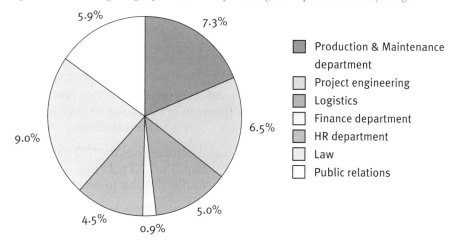

It can be clearly seen from Figure 19.4 that, as previously mentioned, the Finance Department has not been spending on training compared with other departments. There may of course be very good reasons for this parsimonious

behaviour on behalf of the Finance Department managers but, on the other hand, whatever the reason, this could be contributory to staff deciding to leave the organisation – because of lack of development or skills training.

Other than keeping records of training expenditure as a percentage of the department's and EPRO's salary budget, information can be used for comparison purposes and formulated in different ways, for example:

- training days per annum per employee (by department and by the organisation as a whole)

- training expenditure as a percentage of company operating expenditure (OPEX). It would not be meaningful to keep a figure for training expenditure as a percentage of department operating expenditure – because some departments have larger operating budgets than others.

The reason why EPRO Oil and Gas keeps its training expenditure as a percentage of salary budget is so that the international group of companies, to which EPRO belongs, can compare one company with another to determine how each of its operating companies manages its training expenditure. It gives some comparative view as to how companies are developing their staff.

THE LAW AND THE PROCESSING AND FILING OF INFORMATION

DATA PROTECTION ACT 1998 (DPA)

All public and private organisations are legally obliged to protect any personal information they hold, and may be required to notify the Information Commissioner's Office (ICO) of the information they are processing. They also are required to advise the ICO of the name of their data controller (there is a fee to register this information with the ICO). Public authorities are also obliged to provide public access to official information.

The Information Commissioner's website (ICO n.d.[a]), under 'Notification under the Data Protection Act 1998', states that:

> Notification is a statutory requirement and every organisation that processes personal information must notify the Information Commissioner's Office (ICO), unless they are exempt. Failure to notify is a criminal offence.

> Notification is the process by which a data controller gives the ICO details about their processing of personal information. The ICO publishes certain details in the register of data controllers, which is available to the public for inspection.

The penalties for non-compliance with the ICO can lead to penalties not exceeding £500,000.

Data controllers are persons who are nominated by organisations and whose details are kept on a list in the Information Commissioner's Office.

WHAT IS DATA?

The Data Protection Act 1998 (OPSI 1998a) refers to information that is being processed or filed by equipment that is operating automatically or is recorded by some form of filing system. Personal data is that which belongs to a living individual who can be identified either from the data or from other information that the data controller may have access to.

Data should not be kept any longer than is required for the purpose that it was originally sought. Sensitive data includes such information about people as their:

- race or ethnic origins
- political opinions
- religious beliefs
- membership of a trade union
- physical or mental health
- sexual life
- commission or alleged commission of an offence.

The Act applies within the UK and the European Economic Area.

INDIVIDUAL RIGHTS

Individuals have the right to be informed by the organisation's data controller about:

- their personal data that is held by the organisation
- the purpose for that the data is being processed
- the recipients of the data.

The organisation's data controller should give this information in a manner that the person who has requested it can readily understand. The data controller is not obliged to supply the information but must do so if they receive a written request for information about personal data.

It is problematic if the personal data requested impacts upon other people, that is, to release information about someone would also mean giving information about another person. In this case the data controller will have to ask permission from others implicated in the request. If they refuse to have their information divulged to a third party then the data controller can refuse to give the information requested.

PAUSE FOR THOUGHT

The Information Commissioner offers the following advice (ICO n.d.[b]) when organisations are considering processing or filing information. Think of how information is manipulated or stored within your organisation, or within an organisation that you know, and discuss whether you think that it complies with the following guidelines:

- Do I really need this information about an individual? Do I know what I'm going to use it for?

- Do the people whose information I hold know that I've got it, and are they likely to understand what it will be used for?

- If I'm asked to pass on personal information, would the people about whom I hold information expect me to do this?

- Am I satisfied the information is being held securely, whether it's on paper or on computer? And what about my website? Is it secure?

- Is access to personal information limited to those with a strict need to know?

- Am I sure the personal information is accurate and up to date?

- Do I delete or destroy personal information as soon as I have no more need for it?

- Have I trained my staff in their duties and responsibilities under the Data Protection Act, and are they putting them into practice?

- Do I need to notify the Information Commissioner and, if so, is my notification up to date?

EXEMPTIONS FROM THE ACT

There are some exemptions from the Data Protection Act. These exemptions occur in the spheres of national security, crime or work associated with the collection of taxes by government bodies or the work of government or voluntary organisations associated with health, education or social work.

Also the Act does not refer to organisations that process personal data only for:

- staff administration (including payroll)
- advertising, marketing and public relations (in connection with their own business activity)
- accounts and records
- organisations that process personal data only for maintaining a public register
- organisations that do not process personal information on computer.

ENFORCEMENT

The Information Commissioner can serve 'enforcement notices' on a data controller if the Information Commissioner considers that the data controller of an organisation, or more realistically people in their organisation, have been improperly processing or filing data. An enforcement notice usually requires the data controller to block, erase or destroy data. It is an offence not to comply with the demands of the Information Commissioner.

DATA PROTECTION PRINCIPLES

The Information Commissioner has defined eight principles of data protection (ICO n.d. [c]):

1 Personal data shall be processed fairly and lawfully and, in particular, shall not be processed unless –

   a. at least one of the conditions in Schedule 2 is met [see D.P.A, 1998], and

   b. in the case of sensitive personal data, at least one of the conditions in Schedule 3 [see D.P.A, 1998] is also met.

2 Personal data shall be obtained only for one or more specified and lawful purposes, and shall not be further processed in any manner incompatible with that purpose or those purposes.

3 Personal data shall be adequate, relevant and not excessive in relation to the purpose or purposes for which they are processed.

4 Personal data shall be accurate and, where necessary, kept up to date.

5 Personal data processed for any purpose or purposes shall not be kept for longer than is necessary for that purpose or those purposes.

6 Personal data shall be processed in accordance with the rights of data subjects under this Act.

7 Appropriate technical and organisational measures shall be taken against unauthorised or unlawful processing of personal data and against accidental loss or destruction of, or damage to, personal data.

8 Personal data shall not be transferred to a country or territory outside the European Economic Area unless that country or territory ensures an adequate level of protection for the rights and freedoms of data subjects in relation to the processing of personal data.

 ACTIVITY 19.5

Go to the Information Commissioner's website at **www.ico.gov.uk/for_organisations/data_protection_guide/exemptions.aspx** and see what is said about:

● guidelines for data protection

● the role of the Information Commissioner

● the amount of personal data that an organisation may hold

● the accuracy of personal data.

A common requirement for an organisation is to provide a reference for an employee. What should the referee say in the reference? The CIPD (2010b) says the following in its factsheet on references:

> If a reference is provided by an employee, the main legal risk lies in the law of negligence. An employer will be liable if loss results from the employer's failure to exercise reasonable care in the preparation of a reference. The leading case is *Spring v Guardian Assurance plc* [1994] IRLR 460, which demonstrates that the author of a reference owes a duty of care both:
>
> - to the person about whom it is written, and
>
> - to the recipient of the reference if the reference was carelessly favourable.
>
> The reference must not give an unfair or misleading impression overall, even if its discrete components are factually correct.
>
> There may also be a 'contractual duty' to provide a reference where:
>
> a. it is 'natural practice' to require a reference from a previous employer before offering that type of employment, and
>
> b. the employee could not expect to enter that type of employment without a reference.

Defamation

If a reference contains a false or unsubstantiated statement that damages the reputation of a former employee, he or she may be able to claim some damages for defamation. But the risk is slight, since there is no liability for libel if the employer believes the information in the reference is correct and given without malice.

Disclosure of convictions

Under The Rehabilitation of Offenders Act 1974 (ROA) an applicant is not obliged to give information regarding any previous convictions ('spent' or otherwise). Similarly, a referee is not required to disclose a 'spent' conviction. However, if an employer asks a direct question such as 'do you have any criminal convictions?' an incorrect response could amount to 'negligence'. A number of professions are excluded from ROA, including the medical, legal and accounting professions. For further information see the CIPD factsheet on employing ex-offenders.

THE FREEDOM OF INFORMATION ACT 2000

Operating hand in glove with the operation of the Data Protection Act 1998 is the Freedom of Information Act 2000. The Freedom of Information Act 2000 offers the following to those who require information from a *public body* (OPSI 2000a):

Any person making a request for information to a public authority is entitled—

a. to be informed in writing by the public authority whether it holds information of the description specified in the request, and

b. if that is the case, to have that information communicated to him/her.

The request for information must include the name of the person requiring the information and the address for correspondence.

The Information Commissioner offers the following advice as to which bodies are covered by the Freedom of Information Act (ICO n.d.[d]):

- government departments (this includes non-departmental government bodies)
- Parliament, the Northern Ireland Assembly and the National Assembly for Wales
- the armed forces (but not Special Forces or units working with Government Communications Headquarters)
- local authorities
- NHS bodies
- the Police
- other bodies and offices such as regulators and advisory committees
- wholly owned companies, and
- some bodies are only covered for certain sorts of information, such as the BBC and Channel 4.

There is no fixed fee for requesting the information. The government body from whom the information has been requested can refuse to supply the information if the cost to research the data is (currently) above £600 for government departments and £450 for public authorities. The only charges that can be passed on to the person requesting the information are those incurred for providing the information, which would include photocopying and postage.

SUMMARY

In this chapter we have considered that there are three types of information, which are differentiated by how they are used:

- strategic information
- tactical information
- operational information.

We have also addressed the issue of the effectiveness of HRISs in terms of how they can be used to maximum effect and how the future of HRISs will be to link with other IT-based systems, such as the organisation's finance department to form what is known as ERP (enterprise resource planning). The future HRIS, once it is integrated with other company-wide systems, will enable data to be manipulated to improve the quality and accuracy of decision-making.

The chapter has also given some examples of the use of information and how it can be used to interpret – using the EPRO Oil and Gas case example – and solve problems that arise (staff turnover). We have also seen how, by using some simple arithmetic measures such as mode, median and average (mean), we can, when used together with graphical analysis, interpret and make sense of information. Wherever we are presented with information pictorially, graphically or in a tabular format, there is usually a place for a narrative to qualify and explain what is happening.

This chapter has also addressed the law and data protection and requests for information (this is also addressed in Chapter 16); an example of the law in practice was given in the case of how references should be viewed.

REVIEW QUESTIONS

1 What is meant by the following three terms in the context of information management:

- strategic information?
- tactical information?
- operational information?

2 How would you define an HRIS?

3 What is a wiki?

4 Define the following three terms:

- mode
- median
- average (mean).

5 What is meant by 'personal or sensitive data'?

6 For how long should personal or sensitive data be held?

7 What type of information processing is exempt from the DPA?

8 What is meant by the data protection principles?

9 To what bodies does the Freedom of Information Act apply?

EXPLORE FURTHER

BOOKS

TAYLOR, S. (2007) *Business statistics for non-mathematicians.* **Basingstoke: Palgrave Macmillan.**

For further information on how to handle data, Sonia Taylor's book is a very good text to read and to experiment with the examples of practice she offers. The topic of data management is dealt with from the perspective of the complete beginner, with many examples of how data is manipulated.

WEB LINKS

The CIPD produces a factsheet on data protection. The factsheet introduces the law associated with data protection and privacy, provides an action plan for employers and also includes the CIPD viewpoint. The factsheet can be found at: www.cipd.co.uk/onlineinfodocuments/atozresources.htm#e

The Information Commissioner's Office: www.ico.gov.uk

References

ACAS. (n.d.) *What we do [online]*. London: ACAS. Available at: http://www.acas.org.uk/index.aspx?articleid=1410 [Accessed 21 January 2010].

ACAS. (2008) *Job evaluation: considerations and risks [online]*. London: ACAS. Available at: http://www.acas.org.uk/CHttpHandler.ashx?id=922&p=0 [Accessed 21 November 2009].

ACAS. (2009a) *Code of practice 1: disciplinary and grievance procedures [online]*. Norwich: The Stationery Office. Available at: http://www.acas.org.uk/dgcode2009 [Accessed 28 December 2009].

ACAS. (2009b) *Discipline and grievance at work: the ACAS guide [online]*. Norwich: The Stationery Office. Available at: http://www.acas.org.uk/CHttpHandler.ashx?id=1043&p=0 [Accessed 29 December 2009].

ACAS. (2009c) *Redundancy handling [online]*. London: ACAS. Available at: http://www.acas.org.uk/CHttpHandler.ashx?id=877&p=0 [Accessed 8 January 2010].

ACAS. (2010a) *Age discrimination [online]*. London: ACAS. Available at: http://www.acas.org.uk/index.aspx?articleid=1842 [Accessed 19 March 2010].

ACAS. (2010b) *Dismissal [online]*. London: ACAS. Available at: http://www.acas.org.uk/index.aspx?articleid=1797 [Accessed 8 January 2010].

ADAMS, J.S. (1961) *Towards an understanding of inequity.* In: LIKERT, R. (ed.). *New patterns of management.* Maidenhead: McGraw-Hill.

ADLER, N.J. (1986) *International dimensions of organizational behaviour.* Boston, MA: Kent Publishing Company.

ADLER, N.J. (1997) *International dimensions of organizational behaviour.* 3rd ed. Cincinnati: Southwestern.

ALDERFER, C.P. (1972) *Existence, relatedness and growth: human needs in organisational settings.* New York: Free Press.

ALLEN, D. (2008) Brand aid. *People Management.* 13 November.

ANDERSON, N. and SHACKLETON, V. (1993) *Successful selection interviewing.* Oxford: Blackwell.

ANSOFF, H.I. (1987) *Corporate strategy.* London: Penguin.

ARKIN, A. (2002) Tides of change. *People Management.* 7 February.

ARKIN, A. (2007) Street smart. *People Management.* Vol 13, No 7. pp24–28.

ARMSTRONG, M. (1987) Human resource management: a case of the emperor's new clothes. *Personnel Management.* August. pp30–35.

ARMSTRONG, M. (1999) *A handbook of HR management practice.* 7th ed. London: Kogan Page.

ARMSTRONG, M. (2001) *A handbook of HR management practice.* 8th ed. London: Kogan Page.

ARMSTRONG, M. (2004) *Reward management: a handbook of remuneration practice and strategy.* London: Kogan Page.

ARMSTRONG, M. (2006) *A handbook of HR management practice.* 10th ed. London: Kogan Page.

ARMSTRONG, M. and BARON, A. (1998) *Performance management: the new realities.* London: Institute of Personnel and Development.

ARMSTRONG, M. and BARON, A. (2005) *Managing performance: performance management in action.* London: Chartered Institute of Personnel and Development.

ARNOLD, J. with SILVESTER, J., PATTERSON, F., ROBERTSON, I., COOPER, C. and BURNES, B. (2005) *Work psychology: understanding human behaviour in the workplace.* 4th ed. Harlow: Pearson Education Limited.

ASHERSON, J.L. (2007) *CBI response to Dame Carol Black review of the health of the UK workforce [online].* London: Confederation of British Industry. Available at: http://www.cbi.org.uk/ndbs/PositionDoc.nsf/88676202a2a63e1e802573d300 540d6f/f710f9523357413b802573dd0039ee63/$FILE/blackreviewhsresp1107.pdf [Accessed 1 February 2010].

ATKINSON, J. (1984) Manpower strategies for flexible organisations. *Personnel Management.* August. pp28–31.

BANDAROUK, T.V. and RUEL, H.J.M. (2009) Electronic human resource management: challenges in the digital era. *International Journal of Human Resource Management.* Vol 20, No 3. pp504–514.

BARNEY, J. (1991) Firm resource and sustained competitive advantage. *Journal of Management.* Vol 17, No 1. pp99–120.

BARRATT, C. (2008) *Trade union membership 2008 [online].* London: Department for Business, Enterprise and Regulatory Reform. Available at: http://stats.berr.gov.uk/UKSA/tu/tum2008.pdf [Accessed 17 January 2010].

BEARDWELL, I. and CLAYDON, T. (2007) *Human resource management: a contemporary approach.* 5th ed. Harlow: FT Prentice Hall.

BEARDWELL, I., HOLDEN, L. and CLAYDON, T. (2004) *Human resource management: a contemporary approach.* Harlow: Pearson Education.

BEARDWELL, J. and WRIGHT, M. (2004) *in* BEARDWELL, I., HOLDEN, L. and CLAYDON, T. (eds). *Human resource management: a contemporary approach.* Harlow: Pearson Education.

BEATTIE, D. (2002) President's message. *Annual Report 2002.* London: Chartered Institute of Personnel and Development.

BEVAN, S. and THOMPSON, M. (1991) Performance management at the crossroads. *Personnel Management.* November. pp36–39.

BIS. (n.d.) *Redundancy payments [online].* London: Department for Business, Innovation and Skills. Available at: http://www.berr.gov.uk/whatwedo/ employment/employment-legislation/employment-guidance/page33683.html [Accessed 8 January 2010].

BLACK, C. (2008) *Working for a healthier tomorrow [online].* London: The Stationery Office. Available at: http://www.workingforhealth.gov.uk/documents/ working-for-a-healthier-tomorrow-tagged.pdf [Accessed 18 December 2009].

BLAU, P.M. and SCOTT, W.R. (1966) *Formal organisations.* London: Routledge.

BLOISI, W. (2007) *An introduction to human resource management.* Maidenhead: McGraw-Hill.

BOYD, C. (2009) Not all there. *People Management.* 29 April.

BRAMHAM, J. (1994) *Human resource planning.* London: Institute of Personnel and Development.

BRATTON, J. and GOLD, J. (2007) *Human resource management: theory and practice.* 4th ed. Basingstoke: Palgrave Macmillan.

BRECH, E.F.L. (1965) *Prejudice: its social psychology.* Oxford: Blackwell.

BROCKETT, J. (2009) Employer branding still makes its mark. *People Management.* Vol 15, No 6. pp12–13.

BROOKS, I. (2009) *Organisational behaviour: individuals, groups and organisations.* Harlow: Pearson Education Ltd.

BUCKINGHAM, M. (2000) Same indifference. *People Management.* Vol 6, No 4. pp44–46.

BUCKINGHAM, M. (2001) What a waste. *People Management.* Vol 7, No 20. pp36–40.

BULLA, D.N. and SCOTT, P.M. (1994) Manpower requirements forecasting: a case example. In: WARD, D., BECHET, T. P. and TRIPP, R. (eds). *Human resource forecasting and modelling.* New York: Human Resource Planning Society.

BURNES, B. (2004) *Managing change.* 4th ed. Harlow: Pearson Education Ltd.

BURNES, B. (2009) *Managing change.* 5th ed. Harlow: Pearson Education Ltd.

BURNS, T. and STALKER, G.M. (1966) *The management of innovation.* London: Tavistock.

BUSINESS LINK. (2005) *Meet the need for work–life balance: practical advice for business.* A guide developed with the Department of Trade and Industry. Available at: http://www.business link.gov.uk/bdotg/action/detail [Accessed 14 December 2005].

CARNALL, C. (1995) *Managing change in organizations.* 2nd ed. London: Prentice Hall.

CARRINGTON, L. (2007) Designs on the dotted line. *People Management.* Vol 13, No 21. pp36–39.

CENTRAL ARBITRATION COMMITTEE. (n.d.) *About us [online].* London: CAC. Available at: http://www.cac.gov.uk [Accessed 21 January 2010].

CHAMPY, J. and NOHRIA, N. (eds) (1996) *Fast forward: the best ideas on managing business change.* Boston, MA: Harvard Business School Press.

CHILD, J. (1988) *Organisation: a guide to problem and practice.* 2nd ed. London: Paul Chapman.

CIPD. (2005) *Flexible working: impact and implementation – an employer survey [online].* London: Chartered Institute of Personnel and Development. Available at: http://www.cipd.co.uk/subjects/hrpract/flexibleworkingpractices/flexworksurvey [Accessed 9 June 2010].

CIPD. (2007a) *Flexible working – good business: how small firms are doing it [online].* London: Chartered Institute of Personnel and Development. Available at: http://www.cipd.co.uk/onlineinfodocuments/atozresources.htm [Accessed 18 February 2010].

CIPD. (2007b) *Recruitment, retention and turnover [online].* Annual survey report. London: Chartered Institute of Personnel and Development. Available at: http://www.cipd.co.uk/NR/rdonlyres/746F1183-3941-4E6A-9EF6-135C29AE22C9/0/recruitretntsurv07.pdf [Accessed 22 April 2010].

CIPD. (2007c) *Reward: summary of the research into practice event [online].* Event report. London: Chartered Institute of Personnel and Development. Available at: http://www.cipd.co.uk/subjects/pay/general/_rwrdres07.htm?IsSrchRes=1 [Accessed 23 November 2009].

CIPD. (2007d) *The changing HR function [online].* Survey report. London: Chartered Institute of Personnel and Development. Available at: http://www.cipd.co.uk/NR/rdonlyres/9FC78BA5-B992-40B8-85ED-8FA5C3F9FACC/0/chnghrfunc.pdf [Accessed 22 April 2010].

CIPD. (2008) *Recruitment, retention and turnover [online].* Annual survey report. London: Chartered Institute of Personnel and Development. Available at: http://www.cipd.co.uk/NR/rdonlyres/746F1183-3941-4E6A-9EF6-135C29AE22C9/0/recruitretntsurv07.pdf [Accessed 22 April 2010].

CIPD. (2009a) *Absence management [online],* Annual survey report. London: Chartered Institute of Personnel and Development. Available at: http://www.cipd.co.uk/subjects/hrpract/absence/_absence_management_2009 [Accessed 21 January 2010].

CIPD. (2009b) *Change management [online].* Factsheet. London: Chartered Institute of Personnel and Development. Available at: http://www.cipd.co.uk/

subjects/corpstrtgy/changemmt/chngmgmt.htm?IsSrchRes=1 [Accessed 19 February 2010].

CIPD. (2009c) *CIPD issues executive pay guidelines that can be applied across the board [online]*. London: Chartered Institute of Personnel and Development. Available at: http://www.cipd.co.uk/pressoffice/_articles/090909CIPDexecpayguid elines.htm?IsSrchRes=1 [Accessed 22 November 2009].

CIPD. (2009d) *Contracts of employment [online]*. Factsheet. London: Chartered Institute of Personnel and Development. Available at: http://www.cipd.co.uk/ EmploymentLaw/empgdprc.htm [Accessed 22 December 2009].

CIPD. (2009e) *Data protection [online]*. Factsheet. London: Chartered Institute of Personnel and Development. Available at: http://www.cipd.co.uk/subjects/ emplaw/dataprot/dataprotec.htm [Accessed 25 March 2010].

CIPD. (2009f) *HR profession map [online]*. London: Chartered Institute of Personnel and Development. Available at: http://www.cipd.co.uk/ hr-profession-map/ [Accessed 22 April 2010].

CIPD. (2009g) *Learning and development [online]*. Annual survey report. London: Chartered Institute of Personnel and Development. Available at: http://www.cipd. co.uk/subjects/lrnanddev/general/_learning_and_development_09 [Accessed 24 February 2009].

CIPD. (2009h) *Performance management in action [online]*. Hot topic. London: Chartered Institute of Personnel and Development. Available at: http://www. cipd.co.uk/NR/rdonlyres/AC5B3F1D-CA83-4CB2-AD97-9B2333411133/0/ Performance_management_in_action.pdf [Accessed 11 June 2010].

CIPD. (2009i) *Race, religion and employment [online]*. Factsheet. London: Chartered Institute of Personnel and Development. Available at: http://www. cipd.co.uk/subjects/dvsequl/relgdisc/Racereligemplmnt.htm [Accessed 18 March 2010].

CIPD. (2009j) *Recruitment, retention and turnover [online]*. Annual survey report. London: Chartered Institute of Personnel and Development. Available at: http:// www.cipd.co.uk/NR/rdonlyres/41225039-A846-4D2D-9057-E02CDB6BFC0B/0/ recruitment_retention_turnover_annual_survey_2009.pdf [Accessed 22 April 2010].

CIPD. (2009k) *Reward management [online]*. Annual survey report. London: Chartered Institute of Personnel and Development. Available at: http://www.cipd. co.uk/subjects/pay/general/_rwdsmry09.htm [Accessed 24 November 2009].

CIPD. (2009l) *Work–life balance [online]*.Factsheet. London: Chartered Institute of Personnel and Development. Available at: http://www.cipd.co.uk/subjects/health/ worklifebalance/worklifeba.htm?IsSrchRes=1 [Accessed 9 November 2009].

CIPD. (2010a) *Diversity [online]*. Factsheet. London: Chartered Institute of Personnel and Development. Available at: http://www.cipd.co.uk/subjects/ dvsequl/general/divover.htm [Accessed 18 March 2010].

CIPD. (2010b) *References [online]*. Factsheet. London: Chartered Institute of Personnel and Development. Available at: http://www.cipd.co.uk/subjects/ recruitmen/selectn/references.htm [Accessed 22 March 2010].

CLAYDON, T. (2004) Human resource management and the labour market. In: BEARDWELL, I., HOLDEN, L. and CLAYDON, T. (eds). *Human resource management: a contemporary approach*. 4th ed. Harlow: Pearson Education.

CLEGG, S., KORNBERGER, M. and PITSIS, T. (2008) *Managing and organizations: an introduction to theory and practice*. London: Sage.

CLUTTERBUCK, D. (2003) *Managing work–life balance*. London: Chartered Institute of Personnel and Development.

COLLINS. (1998) *Collins English Dictionary*. Glasgow: HarperCollins.

COOPER, C.L., COOPER, R.D. and EAKER, L.H. (1988) *Living with stress*. Harmondsworth: Penguin.

COTTON, C. (2009) *CIPD welcomes 'pragmatic' line on equal pay audits from the EHRC [online]*. Press release. London: Chartered Institute of Personnel and Development. Available at: http://www.cipd.co.uk/pressoffice/_articles/160309Res ponsetoequalpayaudits.htm?IsSrchRes=1 [Accessed 24 November 2009].

CULLY, M., WOODLAND, S., O'REILLY, A. and DIX, G. (1998) *Britain at work: as depicted by 1998 Workplace Employee Relations Survey*. London: Routledge.

CURRAN, J. and STANWORTH, J. (1988) The small firm: a neglected area of management. In: GOWLING, A.G., STANWORTH, M.J.K., BENNET, R.D., CURRAN, J. and LYONS, P. (eds). *Behavioural sciences for managers*. 2nd ed. London: Edward Arnold.

CURRIE, D. (2006) *Introduction to human resource management: a guide to personnel in practice*. London: Chartered Institute of Personnel and Development.

DANIELS, K. and MACDONALD, L. (2005) *Equality, diversity and discrimination*. London: Chartered Institute of Personnel and Development.

DEPARTMENT OF HEALTH. (2008) *Improving health and work: changing lives [online]*. Richmond: OPSI. Available at: http://www.workingforhealth.gov.uk/ improving-health-and-work-changing lives.pdf [Accessed 18 December 2009].

DIRECTGOV. (2009) *Constructive dismissal [online]*. London: Directgov. Available at: http://www.direct.gov.uk/en/Employment/ RedundancyAndLeavingYourJob/Dismissal/DG_10026696 [Accessed 27 January 2010].

DRUCKER, P. (1977) *People and performance: the best of Peter Drucker on management*. London: Heinemann.

EHRC. (n.d.[a]) *Job evaluation defence [online]*. London: EHRC. Available at: http://www.equalityhumanrights.com/advice-and-guidance/ information-for-employers/equal-pay-resources-and-audit-toolkit/

step-2-additional-information/2.1-job-evaluation-check-job-evaluation-schemes-free-of-bias [Accessed 21 November 2009].

EHRC. (n.d.[b]) *Work of equal value [online]* London: EHRC. Available at: http://www.equalityhumanrights.com/advice-and-guidance/information-for-employers/equal-pay-resources-and-audit-toolkit/checklists-equal-pay-in-practice/3.-work-of-equal-value/ [Accessed 24 November 2009].

ETUC. (n.d.) *Our aims [online]*. Brussels: European Trade Union Confederation. Available at: http://www.etuc.org/r/2 [Accessed 20 January 2010].

EUROPEAN UNION. (n.d.) *European Economic and Social Committee [online]*. Brussels: European Union. Available at: http://europa.eu/institutions/consultative/eesc/index_en.htm [Accessed 15 January 2010].

FAWCETT SOCIETY. (2008) *Pay gap map 2008 [online]*. London: Fawcett Society. Available at: http://www.fawcettsociety.org.uk/documents/pay%20gap%20map.pdf [Accessed 3 January 2010].

FAWCETT SOCIETY. (2009) *Equal pay day 2009 [online]*. London: Fawcett Society. Available at: http://www.fawcettsociety.org.uk/index.asp?PageID=728 [Accessed 3 January 2010].

FAYOL, H. (1949) *General and industrial management.* London: Pitman.

FELDMAN, D.C. and ARNOLD, H.J. (1985) Personality types and career patterns: some empirical evidence on Holland's model. *Canadian Journal of Administrative Sciences*. June. pp192–210.

FEVRE, R., NICHOLS, T., PRIOR, G. and RUTHERFORD, I. (2009) *Fair treatment at work report: findings from the 2008 survey [online]*. London: Department for Business, Innovation and Skills. Available at: http://www.berr.gov.uk/files/file52809.pdf [Accessed 17 January 2010].

FIELDER, R. (2006) How to… unlock discretionary effort. *People Management*. Vol 12, No 20. pp44–45.

FOOT, M. and HOOK, C. (2002) *Introducing human resource management.* Harlow: Financial Times/Prentice Hall.

FOWLER, A. (1987) When chief executives discover human resource management. *Personnel Management*. January. p3.

FOX, A. (1966) *Industrial sociology and industrial relations.* Royal Commission on Trade Unions and Employers Associations. Research paper No. 3. London: HMSO.

FRANCIS, H. and KEEGAN, A. (2006) The changing face of HRM: in search of balance. *Human Resource Management Journal*. Vol 16, No 3. pp231–249.

FRENCH, W.L. and BELL, C.H (1990) *Organization development.* Englewood Cliffs, NJ: Prentice-Hall.

FURNHAM, A. and GUNTER, B. (1993) Corporate culture: diagnosis and change. In: COOPER, C.L. and ROBERTSON, I.T. (eds). *International review of industrial and organisational psychology*. Chichester: Wiley.

GENDER IDENTITY RESEARCH AND EDUCATION SOCIETY. (2010) Available at: http://www.gires.org.uk/grp.php [Accessed 19 March 2010].

GIDDENS, A. (1989) *Sociology*. Oxford: Polity Press.

GILL, A. (2009) Employee engagement in a change environment. *Strategic HR Review*. Vol 8, No 2. pp19–24.

GOLD, J., STEWART, J., ILES, P., HOLDEN, R. and BEARDWELL, J. (2010) *Human resource development theory and practice*. Basingstoke: Palgrave Macmillan.

GOLDING, N. (2004) Strategic human resource management. In: BEARDWELL, I., HOLDEN, T. and CLAYDON, T. (eds). *Human resource management; a contemporary approach*. 4th ed. Harlow: Pearson Education.

GOLDTHORPE, J.H. (1968) *The affluent worker: industrial attitudes and behaviour*. Cambridge: Cambridge University Press.

GOSS, D. (1996) *Principles of human resource management*. London: Routledge.

GRAHAM, P. (ed.) (1995) *Mary Parker Follett: prophet of management. A celebration of writings from the 1920s*. Boston, MA: Harvard Business School Press.

GUEST, D. (1989) Human resource management and industrial relations. In: STOREY, J. (ed.). *New perspectives in human resource management*. London: Routledge.

GUEST, D. (1995) Trade unions and industrial relations. In: STOREY, J. (ed.). *Human resource management: a critical text*. London: Routledge.

HALL, E.T. (1973) *The silent language*. New York: Doubleday.

HAMPDEN-TURNER, C. (1990) *Corporate cultures: from vicious to virtuous circles*. London: Random Century.

HANDY, C.B. (1976) *Understanding organisations*. Harmondsworth: Penguin.

HANDY, C.B. (1989) *The age of unreason*. London: Business Books.

HANDY, L., DEVINE, M. and HEATH (1996) *360 degree feedback: unguided missile or powerful weapon?* Berkhamstead: Ashridge Management Group.

HARALAMBOS, M. (1986) *Sociology: themes and perspectives*. London: Bell and Hyman.

HEERY, E. (1996) *Risk representation and the new pay*. Paper presented to the Buira/Eben Conference. Ethical Issues in Contemporary Human Resource Management. Imperial College, London, 3 April.

HEERY, E. and NOON, M. (2001) *Dictionary of Human Resource Management [online]*. Oxford: Oxford University Press.

HEMP, P. (2002) My week as a room service waiter at the Ritz. *Harvard Business Review*. Vol 80, No 6. pp50–60.

HENNESSY, J. and MCCARTNEY, C. (2008) The value of HR in times of change. *Strategic HR Review*. Vol 7, No 6. pp16–22.

HENRI, C. (2008) How to… lend HR expertise to mergers. *People Management*. Vol 14, No 4. pp42–43.

HERSKOVITS, M.J. (1948) *Man and his works*. New York: Knopf.

HERZBERG, F. (2003) One more time: How do you motivate employees? *Harvard Business Review*. Vol 81, No 1. pp86–97.

HERZBERG, F.W., MAUSNER, B. and SNYDERMAN, B. (1957) *The motivation to work*. New York: Wiley.

HILL, J. and TRIST, E. (1955) Changes in accidents and other absences with length of service. *Human Relations*.

HOLLAND, J.L. (1985) *Making vocational choices*. 2nd ed. New York: Prentice-Hall.

HOLLINSHEAD, G., NICHOLLS, P. and TAILBY, S. (2003) *Employee relations*. 2nd ed. Harlow: Pearson Education Ltd.

HOLT, A. and ANDREWS, H. (1993) *Principles of health and safety at work*. London: IOSH Publishing.

HOPE HAILEY, V., FARNDALE, E. and TRUSS, C. (2005) The HR department's role in organisational performance. *Human Resource Management Journal*. Vol 15, No 3. pp 49–66.

HSE. (n.d.[a]) *DWP/HSE framework document [online]*. Available at: http://www.hse.gov.uk/aboutus/howwework/management/dwphse.pdf [Accessed 12 December 2009].

HSE. (n.d.[b]) *What are the management standards for work related stress? [online]*. Available at: http://www.hse.gov.uk/stress/standards/ [Accessed 12 December 2009].

HSE. (2006) *Five steps to risk assessment [online]*. Available at: http://www.hse.gov.uk/pubns/indg163.pdf [Accessed 29 November 2009].

HSE. (2007) *Managing the causes of work-related stress: a step-by-step approach using the management standards [online]*. 2nd ed. Available at: http://www.hse.gov.uk/pubns/priced/hsg218.pdf [Accessed 12 December 2009].

HSE. (2008a) *An introduction to health and safety [online]*. Available at: http://www.hse.gov.uk/pubns/indg259.pdf [Accessed 12 December 2009].

HSE. (2008b) *Successful health and safety management [online]*. Available at: http://www.hse.gov.uk/pubns/priced/hsg65.pdf [Accessed 29 November 2009].

HSE. (2009a) *Health and safety – statistics 2008/09 [online]*. Available at: http://www.hse.gov.uk/statistics/overall/hssh0809.pdf [Accessed 12 December 2009].

HSE. (2009b) *How to tackle work-related stress: a guide for employers on making the Management Standards work [online]*. Available at: http://www.hse.gov.uk/pubns/indg430.pdf [Accessed 12 December 2009].

HUCZYNSKI, A. and BUCHANAN, D. (2001) *Organizational behaviour: an introductory text*. Harlow: Pearson Education Ltd.

HUCZYNSKI, A.A. and BUCHANAN, D. (2007) *Organizational behaviour*. 6th ed. Harlow: Pearson Education Ltd.

HUGHES, M. (2007) *Change management: a critical perspective*. London: Chartered Institute of Personnel and Development.

HUSSEY, D. (1996) *Business-driven human resource management*. Chichester: Wiley.

IDS. (2000) *Improving staff retention*. IDS study 616. London: IDS.

IDS. (2004) The Information and Consultation of Employees Regulations 2004. *IDS Employment Law Brief [online]*. Available at: http://www.idsbrief.com [Accessed 8 January 2010].

IDS. (2005) Corporate manslaughter. *IDS Employment Law Brief [online]*. Vol 788. Available at: http://www.idsbrief.com [Accessed 31 December 2009].

IDS. (2006a) *Age discrimination-3 [online]*. Vol 807. London: IDS. Available at: http://www.idsbrief.com [Accessed 20 January 2010].

IDS. (2006b) Guide to the Equality Act 2006. *IDS Employment Law Brief [online]*. Vol 818. Available at: http://www.idsbrief.com [Accessed 10 January 2010].

IDS. (2006c) Work and Families Act 2006. *IDS Employment Law Brief [online]*. Vol 816. pp12–18. Available at: http://www.idsbrief.com [Accessed 18 December 2009].

IDS. (2007) Smoking – the employment law implications. *IDS Employment Law Brief [online]*. Vol 829. pp12–18. Available at: http://www.idsbrief.com [Accessed 18 December 2009].

IDS. (2008) House of Lords throws light on meaning of personal and sensitive data. *IDS Employment Law Brief [online]*. 14 July. Available at: http://www.idsbrief.com [Accessed 9 January 2010].

IDS. (2009a) Length of service criterion in redundancy selection is lawful. *IDS Employment Law Brief 883 [online]*. Available at: www.idsbrief.com [Accessed 8 January 2010].

IDS. (2009b) Redundancy dismissal procedures after 6 April. *IDS Employment Law Brief 875 [online].* Available at: www.idsbrief.com [Accessed 8 January 2010].

INFORMATION COMMISSIONER'S OFFICE. (n.d.[a]) *Notification under the data protection act 1998 [online].* Wilmslow, Cheshire: ICO. Available at: http://www.ico.gov.uk/what_we_cover/data_protection/notification.aspx [Accessed 21 March 2010].

INFORMATION COMMISSIONER'S OFFICE. (n.d.[b]) *Notification under the data protection act 1998 [online].* Wilmslow, Cheshire: ICO. Available at: http://www.ico.gov.uk/what_we_cover/data_protection/your_legal_obligations.aspx [Accessed 21 March 2010].

INFORMATION COMMISSIONER'S OFFICE. (n.d.[c]) *List of data protection principles [online].* Wilmslow, Cheshire: ICO. Available at: http://www.ico.gov.uk/for_organisations/data_protection_guide/list_of_the_data_protection_principles.aspx [Accessed 22 March 2010].

INFORMATION COMMISSIONER'S OFFICE. (n.d.[d]) *Freedom of Information, FAQs – For the public [online].* Wilmslow, Cheshire: ICO. Available at: http://www.ico.gov.uk/Global/faqs/freedom_of_information_act_for_the_public.aspx#fA4236BFE-176B-4C39-8500-BC73EB7EE199 [Accessed 21 March 2010].

INSTITUTION OF MECHANICAL ENGINEERS. (2010) *About the Institution of Mechanical Engineers [online].* London: Institution of Mechanical Engineers. Available at: http://www.imeche.org/about [Accessed 15 January 2010].

IRS. (1996) Performance management. *Management Review.* Vol 1, No 1. London: Industrial Relations Service.

JOHNSON, J. and SCHOLES, K. (2002) *Exploring corporate strategy: test and cases.* Harlow: Pearson Educational.

JOHNSON, R. (2008) E.ON's ahead. *People Management.* 7 February.

JONES, A. (2006) *About time for change [online].* London: Work Foundation. Available at: http://www.theworkfoundation.com/assets/docs/publications/177_About%20time%20for%20change.pdf [Accessed 18 February 2010].

KAPLAN, R.S. and NORTON, D.P. (1996) *Translating strategy into action: the balanced scorecard.* Boston, MA: Harvard Business School Press.

KATZ, D. and KHAN, R.l. (1978) *The psychology of organisations.* 2nd ed. New York: Wiley.

KEW, J. and STREDWICK, J. (2005) *Business environment: managing in a strategic context.* London: Chartered Institute of Personnel and Development.

KEW, J. and STREDWICK, J. (2008) *Business environment: managing in a strategic context.* 2nd ed. London: Chartered Institute of Personnel and Development.

KINNIE, N., HUTCHINSON, S., PURCELL, J., RAYTON, B. and SWART, J.

(2005) Satisfaction with HR practices and commitment to the organisation: why one size does not fit all. *Human Resource Management Journal.* Vol 15, No 4. pp9–29.

KIRKPATRICK, D. (1975) *Evaluating training programs.* Madison, WI: American Society for Training and Development.

KOEHLER, W. (1959) *The mentality of apes.* New York: Vintage.

KOLB, D.A. (1985) *Experiential learning: experience as the source of learning and development.* London: Prentice-Hall.

KOTTER, J.P. (1996) *Leading change.* Boston, MA: Harvard Business School Press.

KOTTER, J.P. and SCHLESINGER, L.A. (2008) Choosing strategies for change. *Harvard Business Review.* Vol 86, No 7/8. July/August. pp130, 132–139.

KRULIS-RANDA, J. (1990) Strategic human resource management in Europe after 1992. *International Journal of Human Resource Management.* Vol 1, No 2. pp131–139.

LASHLEY, C. and BEST, W. (2002) Employee induction in licensed retail organisations. *International Journal of Contemporary Hospitality.* Vol 14, No 1. pp6–13.

LAU, S., NEAL, V. and MAINGAULT, V. (2009) Economic trends, buddy systems, receiving criticism. *HRM Magazine.* Vol 54, No 3. pp26–27.

LAWLER, E.E. (1990) *Strategic pay.* San Francisco, CA: Jossey-Bass.

LEGGE, K. (1995) *Human resource management: rhetoric or realities.* London: Macmillan.

LEWIN, K. (1951) *Field theory in social science.* New York: Harper and Row.

LIKERT, R.A. (ed.) (1961) *New patterns of management.* Maidenhead: McGraw-Hill.

LINTON, R. (1945) Present world conditions in cultural perspective. In: LINTON, R. (ed.). *The science of man in world crisis.* New York: Columbia University Press.

MANKIN, D. (2009) *Human resource development.* Oxford: Oxford University Press.

MARCHINGTON, M. and GRUGULIS, I. (2000) *International Journal of Human Resource Management.* Vol 11, No 6. pp1104–1124.

MARSDEN, D. and FRENCH, S. (1998) *What a performance: performance-related pay in the public services.* London: Centre for Economic Performance.

MASLOW, A.H. (1954) *Motivation and personality.* 1st ed. New York: Harper and Row.

MASLOW, A.H. (1972). *Motivation and personality.* New York: Harper and Row.

MATTHEWMAN, L., ROSE, A. and HETHERINGTON, A. (2009) *Work psychology.* New York: Oxford University Press.

MAUND, L. (2001) *An introduction to human resource management: theory and practice.* Basingstoke: Palgrave.

MAYO, E. (1933) *The human side of an industrial civilization.* New York: Macmillan.

MCGREGOR, D. (1960) *The human side of enterprise.* New York: McGraw-Hill.

MCKENNA, E. (1994) *Business psychology and organisational behaviour.* Hove: Lawrence Erlbaum.

MCLEAN, A. (1979) *Work stress.* Reading, MA.: Addison-Wesley.

MEANEY, M. and WILSON, S. (2009) Change in recession. *People Management.* 7 May. p62.

MILLWARD, D. (2009) BA pilots' union agrees pay cut. *Daily Telegraph.* 18 June.

MOLANDER, C. and WINTERTON, J. (1994) *Managing human resources.* London: Routledge.

MOORHEAD, G. and GRIFFIN, R.W. (1992) *Organizational behavior.* 3rd ed. Boston, MA: Houghton Mifflin.

MULLINS, L.J. (2007) *Management and organisational behaviour.* 8th ed. Harlow: Pearson Education Limited.

MUMFORD, A. (1993) *Management development: strategies for action.* London: Institute of Personnel Management (now CIPD).

MUNRO-FRASER, J. (1966) *Employment interviewing.* Plymouth: Macdonald and Evans.

NAROLL, R. (1970) The culture-bearing unit in cross-cultural surveys. In: NAROLL, R. and COHEN, R. (eds). *Handbook of methods in cultural anthropology.* New York: Columbia University.

NMWA. (1998) *The National Minimum Wage Act [online].* London: Office of Public Sector Information. Available at: http://www.opsi.gov.uk/acts/acts1998/ukpga_19980039_en_1 [Accessed 28 December 2009].

NOE, R. (2010) *Employee training and development.* New York: McGraw-Hill.

NORTH, S.J. (2008) Health starts on the inside. *People Management.* 26 June. pp24–27.

OPSI. (n.d.) *Statute law database [online].* London: Office of Public Sector Information. Available at: http://www.statutelaw.gov.uk [Accessed 2 January 2010].

OPSI. (1975) *Sex Discrimination Act 1975 [online].* London: Office of Public Sector Information. Available at: http://www.opsi.gov.uk/RevisedStatutes/Acts/ukpga/1975/cukpga_19750065_en_1 [Accessed 10 January 2010].

OPSI. (1976) *Race Relations Act 1976 [online].* London: Office of Public Sector Information. Available at: http://www.opsi.gov.uk/RevisedStatutes/Acts/ukpga/1976/cukpga_19760074_en_1 [Accessed 10 January 2010].

OPSI. (1996a) *Employment Rights Act 1996 [online].* London: Office of Public Sector Information. Available at: http://www.opsi.gov.uk/acts/acts1996/ukpga_19960018_en_1 [Accessed 23 December 2009].

OPSI. (1996b) *Health and Safety (Consultation with Employees) Regulations 1996 [online].* London: Office of Public Sector Information. Available at: http://www.opsi.gov.uk/si/si1996/Uksi_19961513_en_1.htm [Accessed 30 December 2009].

OPSI. (1998a) *Data Protection Act 1998 [online].* London: Office of Public Sector Information. Available at: http://www.statutelaw.gov.uk/content.aspx? [Accessed 21 March 2010].

OPSI. (1998b) *Working Time Regulations [online].* London: Office of Public Sector Information. Available at: http://www.opsi.gov.uk/si/si1998/19981833.htm [Accessed 22 December 2009].

OPSI. (1999) *Management of Health and Safety at Work Regulations 1999 (risk assessment) [online].* London: Office of Public Sector Information. Available at: http://www.opsi.gov.uk/si/si1999/19993242.htm [Accessed 31 December 2009].

OPSI. (2000a) *Freedom of Information Act 2000 [online].* London: Office of Public Sector Information. Available at: http://www.statutelaw.gov.uk/content.aspx? [Accessed 22 March 2010].

OPSI. (2000b) *Part-time Workers (Prevention of Less Favourable Treatment) Regulations 2000 [online].* London: Office of Public Sector Information. Available at: http://www.opsi.gov.uk/si/si2000/20001551.htm#5 [Accessed 27 December 2009].

OPSI. (2002) *The Employment Act 2002 [online].* London: Office of Public Sector Information. Available at: http://www.opsi.gov.uk/acts/acts2002/ukpga_20020022_en_1 [Accessed 23 December 2009].

OPSI. (2006a) *Equality Act 2006 [online].* London: Office of Public Sector Information. Available at: http://www.opsi.gov.uk/acts/acts2006/ukpga_20060003_en_2 [Accessed 19 March 2010].

OPSI. (2006b) *Work and Families Act [online].* London: Office of Public Sector Information. Available at: http://www.opsi.gov.uk/acts/acts2006/ukpga_20060018_en_1 [Accessed 23 December 2009].

OPSI. (2007) *The Corporate Manslaughter and Homicide Act 2007 [online].* London: Office of Public Sector Information. Available at: http://www.opsi.gov.

uk/acts/acts2007/en/ukpgaen_20070019_en_1#cpb5-l1g13_IDABX52B [Accessed 30 December 2009].

OPSI. (2009) *The Flexible Working (Eligibility, Complaints and Remedies) (Amendment) Regulations 2009 [online]*. London: Office of Public Sector Information. Available at: http://www.opsi.gov.uk/si/si2009/em/uksiem_20090595_en.pdf [Accessed 27 December 2009].

OSBORNE, A. and DUNKLEY, J. (2009) British Airways won't rule out pension closure. *Daily Telegraph*. 4 June.

PAVLOV, I.P. (1927) *Conditioned reflexes*. Oxford: Oxford University Press.

PEDLER, M., BURGOYNE, J. and BOYDELL, T. (1997) *The learning company: a strategy for sustainable development*. 2nd ed. London: McGraw-Hill.

PERKINS, S., WHITE, G. and COTTON, C. (2008) A ripping yarn. *People Management*. 30 October. pp28–30.

PERRY, J.L., ENGBERS, T.A. and JUN, S.Y. (2009) Back to the future? Performance-related pay, empirical research, and the perils of persistence. *Public Administration Review*. Vol 69, No 1. pp39–51.

PFEFFER, J. (1998) *The human equation: building profits by putting people first*. Boston, MA: Harvard Business Review.

PFEFFER, J. and SUTTON, R.I. (2006) Evidenced-based management. *Harvard Business Review*. Vol 84, No 1. pp62–74.

PHILPOTT, J. (2004) By the book. *People Management*. Vol 10, No 21. p26.

PICKARD, J. (2009) Mutiny of the bounty. *People Management*. 19 November.

PIERCY, N. (1989) Diagnosing and solving implementation problems in strategic planning. *Journal of General Management*. Vol 15, No 1. pp19–38.

PILBEAM, S. and CORBRIDGE, M. (2006) *People resourcing: contemporary HRM in practice*. Harlow: Pearson Education Ltd.

PLUMBLEY, P.R. (1976) *Recruitment and selection*. London: Institute of Personnel Management (now CIPD).

POINTON, J. and RYAN, A.J. (2004) Reward and performance management. In: BEARDWELL, I., HOLDEN, L. and CLAYDON, T. (eds). *Human resource management: a contemporary approach*. 4th ed. Harlow: Pearson Education.

PORTER, L.W. and LAWLER, E.E. (1968) *Managerial attitudes and performance*. Homewood, IL: Irwin-Dorsey.

POULTER, D. and LAND, C. (2008) Preparing to work: dramaturgy, cynicism and normative 'remote' control in the socialization of graduate recruits in management consulting. *Culture and Organisation*. Vol 14, No 1. pp65–78.

PRICE, A.J. (1997) *Human resource management in business context.* London: International Thomson Business Press.

PURCELL, J., HUTCHINSON, S., KINNIE, N., SWART, J. and RAYTON, B. (2004) *Vision and values: organisational culture and values as a source of competitive advantage.* Executive briefing. London: Chartered Institute of Personnel and Development.

PURCELL, J., KINNIE, N., HUTCHINSON, S., RAYTON, B. and SWART, J. (2003) *Understanding the people and performance link: unlocking the black box.* London: Chartered Institute of Personnel and Development.

QUINTAS, P. (2001) Managing knowledge in a new century. In: LITTLE, S., QUINTAS, P. and RAY, T. (eds). *Managing knowledge: an essential reader.* London: Sage Publications Ltd.

RANA, E. (2000) Predictions: enter the people dimension. *People Management.* Vol 6, No 1. 6 January. pp16–17.

RAUSCHENBERGER, J., SCHMITT, N. and HUNTER, J.E. (1980) A test of the need hierarchy concept by a Markov model of change in need strength. *Administrative Science Quarterly.* No 25. pp654–670.

REDMAN, T. and WILKINSON, A. (2009) *Contemporary human resource management: text and cases.* 3rd ed. Harlow: Pearson.

REVANS, R. (1982) *The origins and growth of action learning.* Bromley: Chartwell-Bratt.

RIFKIN, J. (2000) *The age of access: how the shift from ownership to access is transforming modern life.* London: Penguin Books.

ROBBINS, S.P. (2001) *Organisational behavior.* Upper Saddle River, NJ: Pearson Prentice Hall.

ROBBINS, S.P. and JUDGE, T.A. (2005) *Organisational behavior.* 11th ed. Upper Saddle River, NJ: Pearson Prentice Hall.

ROBBINS, S.P. and JUDGE, T.A. (2009) *Organizational behavior.* 13th ed. Upper Saddle River, NJ: Pearson Prentice Hall.

ROBERTS, I. (2001) Reward and performance management. In: BEARDWELL, I., HOLDEN, L. and CLAYDON, T. (eds). *Human resource management: a contemporary approach.* 4th ed. Harlow: Pearson Education.

ROBERTSON, I. and SMITH, M. (2001) Personnel selection. *Journal of Occupational and Organisational Psychology.* Vol 74, No 4. pp441–472.

RODGER, A. (1952) *The seven point plan.* London: National Institute of Industrial Psychology.

ROLLINSON, D. (2008) *Organisational behaviour and analysis: an integrated approach.* 4th ed. Harlow: Pearson Educational.

ROSE, E. (2008) *Employment relations*. 3rd ed. Harlow: Pearson Education Ltd.

RUMPEL, S. and MEDCOF, J.W. (2006) Total rewards: good fit for tech workers. *Research Technology Management*. Vol 49, No 5. pp27–35.

RUSS-EFT, D. and PRESKILL, H. (2005) In search of the Holy Grail: return on investment evaluation in human resource development. *Advances in Developing Human Resources*. Vol 7, No 1. pp71–85.

SAMPSON, B. (2009) Protect yourself. *Professional Engineering*. London: IMechE.

SAUNDERS, R. (1992) *The safety audit*. London: Pitman.

SCHEIN, E. (1965) *Organisational psychology*. Englewood Cliffs, NJ: Prentice Hall.

SCHEIN, E.H. (1980) *Organisational psychology*. 3rd ed. Englewood Cliffs, NJ: Prentice Hall.

SCHEIN, E. (1985) *Organisational culture and leadership*. New York: Jossey Bass.

SCHNEIDER, B. (2004) Welcome to the world of service management. *Academy of Management Executive*. Vol 18, No 2. pp144–150.

SCHUSTER, J.R. and ZINGHEIM, P.K. (1992) *The new pay*. New York: Lexington Books.

SCOTT, A. (2008) Clashes mar mergers and acquisitions. *People Management*. 1 October.

SELF, A. and ZEALEY, L. (2008) *Social trends [online]*. Vol 38. Basingstoke: Palgrave Macmillan. Available at: http://www.statistics.gov.uk/downloads/theme_social/Social_Trends38/Social_Trends_38.pdf [Accessed 17 January 2010].

SENGE, P. (1990) *The fifth discipline: the art and practice of the learning organisation*. London: Century Business.

SENIOR, B. (2002) *Organisational change*. Harlow: Prentice Hall.

SISSON, K. (1995) Human resource management and the personnel function. In: STOREY, J. (ed.). *Human resource management: a critical text*. London: Routledge.

SISSON, K. (2001) Human resource management and the personnel function: a case of partial impact? In: STOREY, J. (ed.). *Human resource management: a critical text*. 2nd ed. London: Thomson Learning.

SKINNER, B.F. (1953) *Science and human behaviour*. New York: Macmillan.

SMITH, M., COLLIGAN, M., SKJEI, E. and POLLY, S. (1978) *Occupational comparison of stress-related disease incidence*. Cincinnati, OH: National Institute for Occupational Safety and Health.

STOREY, J. (1992) *Development in the management of human resources: an analytical review.* London: Blackwell.

STOREY, J. (1995) *Human resource management: a critical text.* London: Routledge.

TAYLOR, F.W. (1911) *The principles of scientific management.* New York: Harper Bros.

TAYLOR, F.W. (1947) *Scientific management.* New York: Harper and Row.

TAYLOR, S. (2002) *People resourcing.* 2nd rev. ed. London: Chartered Institute of Personnel and Development.

TAYLOR, S. (2008) *People resourcing.* 4th ed. London: Chartered Institute of Personnel and Development.

THORNDIKE, E.L. (1913) *The psychology of learning.* Columbia University: Teachers College Press.

TORRINGTON, D. and HALL, L. (1998) *Human resource management.* 4th ed. Hemel Hempstead: Prentice Hall.

TORRINGTON, D., HALL, L. and TAYLOR, S. (2007) *Human resource management.* 7th ed. Harlow: Pearson Education.

TRIANDIS, H.C. (1990) Theoretical concepts that are applicable to the analysis of ethnocentrism. In: BRISLIN, R.W. (ed.). *Applied cross-cultural psychology.* Chicago: Sage.

TRIANDIS, H.C., VASSILIOU, V., VASSILIOU, G., TANAKA, Y. and SHANMUGAM, A.V. (1972) *The analysis of subjective culture.* New York: Wiley.

TRIBUNALS SERVICE. (2008–09) *Employment Tribunal and EAT Statistics (GB) 1 April 2008 to 31 March 2009 [online].* London: Tribunals Service. Available at: http://www.employmenttribunals.gov.uk/Documents/Publications/ET_EAT_Stats_0809_FINAL.pdf [Accessed 27 January 2010].

TRICE, H.M. and BEYER, J.M. (1984) Studying organisational cultures through rites and rituals. *Academy of Management Review.* No 9. pp653–669.

TRIST, E.L. and BAMFORTH, K.W. (1951) Social and psychological consequences of the long wall coal-getting. *Relations.* Vol 4. pp1–38.

TRIST, E.L., HIGGIN, G., POLLOCK, H.E. and MURRAY, H.A. (1963) *Organisational choice.* London: Tavistock.

TUC. (2010a) *About the TUC [online].* London: Trades Union Congress. Available at: http://www.tuc.org.uk/the_tuc/index.cfm [Accessed 20 January 2010].

TUC. (2010b) *TUC rules and standing orders [online].* London: Trades Union Congress. Available at: http://www.tuc.org.uk/congress/index.cfm?mins=294 [Accessed 20 January 2010].

TUC. (2010c) *Congress [online]* London: Trades Union Congress. Available at: http://www.tuc.org.uk/congress/index.cfm [Accessed 20 January 2010].

TYLOR, E.B. (1871) *Primitive culture.* London: Murray.

TYSON, S. and YORK, A. (1996) *Human resource management.* Oxford: Butterworth-Heinemann.

UK COMMISSION FOR EMPLOYMENT AND SKILLS. (2010) http://www.ukces.org.uk/a-new-home-for-investors-in-people [Accessed 12 March 2010].

ULRICH, D. (1997) *Human resource champions.* Boston, MA: Harvard University Press.

ULRICH, D. and BROCKBANK, W. (2005) Role call. *People Management.* Vol 11, No 12. pp24–28.

UNIONLEARN. (n.d.) *Section 3: functions and rights [online].* London: unionlearn. Available at: http://www.unionlearn.org.uk/ulr/learn-2110-f0.pdf [Accessed 30 January 2010].

UNIONLEARN. (2009) *Unionlearn annual report 2009 [online].* London: unionlearn. Available at: http://www.unionlearn.org.uk/files/publications/documents/152.pdf [Accessed 30 January 2010].

VAN DICK, R., CHRIST, O., STELLMACHER, J. et al. (2004) Should I stay or should I go? Explaining turnover intentions with organizational identification and job satisfaction. *British Journal of Management.* Vol 15. pp351–360.

VROOM, V.H. (1964) *Work and motivation.* New York: Wiley.

WALTON, R.E. and MCKERSIE, R.B. (1965) *Behavioural theory of labour negotiations.* New York: McGraw-Hill.

WATSON, J.B. and RAYNER, R. (1920) Conditioned emotional reactions. *Journal of Experimental Psychology.* Vol 3. pp1–14.

WEBER, M. (1964) *The theory of social and economic organisation.* London: Macmillan.

WHIDDETT, S. and HOLLYFORDE, S. (2003) *A practical guide to competencies.* London: Chartered Institute of Personnel and Development.

WHITTINGTON, R. (1993) *What is strategy and does it matter?* London: Routledge.

WHYTE, W.F. (1955) *The organization man.* Harmondsworth: Penguin.

WIGGINS, L. (2008/2009) Managing the ups and downs of change communication. *Strategic Communication Management.* Vol 13, No 1. December/January. pp20–23.

WILLIAMS, M. (2000) Transfixed assets. *People Management.* 3 August. pp28–33.

WOODWARD, J. (1980) *Industrial organisation: theory and practice.* 2nd ed. Oxford: Oxford University Press.

WRIGHT, A. (2006) *Reward management in context.* London: Chartered Institute of Personnel and Development.

WRIGHT, P., MCMAHAN, G. and MCWILLIAMS, A. (1994) Human resources and sustained competitive advantage: a resource-based perspective. *International Journal of Human Resource Management.* Vol 5, No 2. pp 301–326.

Index

360-degree feedback
  performance management, 240–241
Absence
  Bradford factor, 295–296
  conclusions, 296–297
  controls, 294
  management, 293–294
  measurement, 295–297
  policy, 294
  reasons, 294–295
  return-to-work interviews, 296
  summary, 297
ACAS
  employment relationship, and, 290
Accidents at work
  behavioural causes, 317
  environmental causes, 316–317
  introduction, 316
  physiological causes, 317
Action learning
  learning, 191
Adoption leave
  generally, 366
  work-life balance, 305
Advanced apprenticeships
  human resource planning, 88
Advertising job vacancies
  content, 130–131
  electronically, 132
  external, 129
  generally, 128–129
  internal, 128
  other media, 131
  placement, 130
  responses, 133
  types, 129
Advice
  employment relationship, and,
    312
Age discrimination
  generally, 353
Annual leave
  work-life balance, 304
Ante-natal care
  employment law, 365
Application forms
  recruitment, 133

Appraisal
  generally, 237
  human resource development, 207
  human resource planning, 107
  interview, 241–243
Apprenticeships
  human resource development, 204
  human resource planning, 88
Assessment centres
  human resource development, 207
  selection, 143
Audits
  employment relationship, and, 321
Authority to recruit
  recruitment, 124

Behaviour
  performance management,
    226–227
Behaviourally anchored rating scales
  performance management, 239
Behaviourism
  learning, and, 190
Belongingness
  motivation, 231
Biodata
  selection, 146
Bonus schemes
  employee reward, 258
Buddy systems
  induction, 173–174
Bullying
  employers' obligations, 355–356
  generally, 353–354
  legal framework, 355
  meaning, 353
Bureaucracy
  human resource management, 47
Business concerns
  classification of organisations, 4
BusinessEurope
  employment relationship, and, 280
Business strategy
  human resource planning, 115

'Cafeteria' benefits
  employee reward, 250–251

Candidate ranking form
selection, 153
Career planning
learning, and, 196–198
Central Arbitration Committee
employment relationship, and, 290–291
Change management
change consultants, and
general role, 425–426
tools and methods, 426–428
cultural change
catalysts, 419–420
generally, 417–419
identifying the culture gap, 420
emergent approach, 428–429
employee behaviour, 429–430
evolution and revolution, 410–413
inter-group development, 427
introduction, 409
Lewin's three-phase model
consultation with employees,
421–422
introduction, 421
levers of change, 422–423
moving or changing, 422–423
refreezing, 423
unfreezing, 421–422
mirroring, 427
need for change, 410
OD change model, 423–425
organisational development, 420–421
'quick wins', 427
resistance to change
dealing with, 414–415
force field analysis, 415–417
generally, 413–414
role negotiation, 427
role of HR in support, 429
survey feedback, 426–427
summary, 430
team-building, 427
triggers and drivers, 409–413
Charities
classification of organisations, 4
CIPD Profession Map
generally, 81–83
Classical conditioning
learning, and, 189
Classified advertising
recruitment, 129
Coaching
induction, 164

Cognitive learning
learning, and, 190–191
Cohort analysis
human resource planning, 103–104
Collective bargaining
distributive bargaining, 291–292
generally, 291
integrative bargaining, 291–292
procedural agreements, 293
substantive agreements, 293
types, 291
Commonweal organisations
classification of organisations, 4
Communications
human resource planning, 107
organisational culture, 36
Company handbook
contracts of employment, 364
induction, 170–171
Company practices
organisational culture, 36
Competitive advantage
best-fit model of SHRM, 57–58
best practice model of SHRM, 59–60
resource-based view of organisation, 60
restructuring the organisation, 62–63
role of HR professional, 61–62
structuring human resources in the
organisation, 61
Confederation of British Industry
employment relationship, and, 280
Confidentiality
information systems, and, 77
Constructive dismissal
employment law, 400
Consultation
employment relationship, and, 312
Contingency pay
bonus schemes, 258
equity pay schemes, 255
fixed incremental pay schemes, 257–258
generally, 255
incentive pay schemes, 255–256
measured daywork, 258
payment by results schemes, 256–257
team reward scheme, 258–259
Contracts of employment
adoption leave, 366
ante-natal care, 365
company handbook, 364
data protection
employers' obligations, 391

generally, 388
individual rights, 388
personal data, 389
policy, 392
processing data, 391
relevant filing system, 389
sensitive data, 389–391
disciplinary procedures
contents, 377
disciplinary meeting, 380
generally, 376–377
handling, 377–378
invoking, 381–382
mediation, and, 382
record-keeping, 379–380
role of HR, 381
rules, 375–376
structure, 378–379
discrimination
Equality and Human Rights
Commission, 371–372
legislative framework, 370–371
race discrimination, 370
sex discrimination, 369–370
employees' rights
company handbook, 364
introduction, 362
statement of terms and conditions,
362–363
termination of employment, 365
time off, 364
variation of terms and conditions,
363–364
equal pay, 368–369
equality
equal pay, 368–369
part-time workers, 369
race discrimination, 370
sex discrimination, 369–370
Equality and Human Rights Commission,
371–372
express terms, 361
family-friendly rights
adoption leave, 366
ante-natal care, 365
flexible working, 367–368
maternity leave, 365
working time, 366–367
fixed-term contracts, 360
flexible working, 367–368
formation, 359
grievance procedures

conduct of interview, 375
generally, 373–374
initial interview, 374
preparation for interview, 375
health and safety, 382–386
implied terms, 361
introduction, 358–359
maternity leave, 365
national minimum wage, 372–373
part-time workers, 369
pay, 372
race discrimination, 370
record-keeping
authorised access to information,
387–388
confidentiality, 386
data protection, 388–393
introduction, 386
legislative requirements, 387–388
sex discrimination, 369–370
summary, 393–394
temporary contracts, 359
termination of employment
constructive dismissal, 400
dismissal, 398–400
employee, by, 397
employer, by, 398–406
exit interviews, 397
introduction, 396
overview, 365
redundancy, 400–406
retirement, 406
summary, 406–407
unfair dismissal, 398–399
terms and conditions
company handbook, 364
generally, 361–362
statement, 362–363
variation, 363–364
time off, 364
types, 359–361
wages and salary, 372
working time, 366–367
zero hours contract, 360–361
Control and compliance
human resource management, 50
Core workers
organisational structures, 17–19
Corporate capability
human resource planning, 98
Corporate strategy
alignment of HR, 76

human resource planning, 98
organisations, 7
Cost-effectiveness
human resource development, 212
Course development
human resource development, 212–214
Course evaluation
human resource development
generally, 219–220
method, 220–221
Course preparation
human resource development, 214–219
CRB checks
selection, 154–155
Cultural differences
selection, 145
Culture of organisations
achievement culture, 35
boundaries, 27–28
change, 40
classification of thought, 31–32
communications, 36
company practices, 36
cultural fit, 38
cultural shift, 38–39
definitions, 24–25
differences, 27
dissection, 40–41
'enculturalisation', 39–40
ethnocentrism, 25–26
identification
generally, 33–36
introduction, 25
public sector, in, 36–37
importance of place, 37–39
individual differences, 33
'in-groups', 25–26
induction of new members, 39–40
industrial culture, 29–31
integration of diverse elements, 39
introduction, 22
language, 36
location, 26
meaning, 22–25
norms
generally, 23
power of, 23–24
organisational values, 33
person culture, 34
physical culture, 25
power culture, 34–35
purpose of study, 32–33

role culture, 34–35
societal culture, 28–31
subcultures, 31
subjective culture, 25
summary, 41–42
support culture, 35
task culture, 34
values and norms
generally, 23
power of, 23–24
Customer service
human resource management
generally, 63–67
relationship management, 67–68
summary, 68

Data protection
data, 445
defamation, 448
disclosure of convictions, 448
employment law, and
employers' obligations, 391
generally, 388
individual rights, 388
personal data, 389
policy, 392
processing data, 391
relevant filing system, 389
sensitive data, 389–391
enforcement, 446–447
exemptions, 446
generally, 444
individual rights
employment law, 388
generally, 445–446
law in practice, 448
personal data, 389
principles, 447
policy, 392
processing data, 391
relevant filing system, 389
sensitive data, 389–391
Decision-making
selection, 152–153
Defamation
data protection, and, 448
Deficits and surpluses of staff
human resource planning, 105–106
Demographic changes
diversity and equality, 339
Departmental distribution of turnover
human resource planning, 102–103

Dependant care
  work-life balance, 304
Development centres
  human resource development, 207
Diplomas
  human resource development, 204
Direct discrimination
  generally, 346
Disability discrimination
  generally, 350–351
  reasonable adjustments, 351
Disciplinary procedures
  contents, 377
  disciplinary meeting, 380
  employment relationship, and, 293
  generally, 376–377
  handling, 377–378
  invoking, 381–382
  mediation, and, 382
  record-keeping, 379–380
  role of HR, 381
  rules, 375–376
  structure, 378–379
Discrimination
  age discrimination, 353
  bullying
    employers' obligations, 355–356
    generally, 353–354
    legal framework, 355
    meaning, 353
  categories, 346–347
  direct discrimination, 346
  disability discrimination
    generally, 350–351
    reasonable adjustments, 351
  employment law, and
    Equality and Human Rights
      Commission, 371–372
    legislative framework, 370–371
    race discrimination, 370
    sex discrimination, 369–370
  gender reassignment, 348–349
  genuine occupational requirement
    racial discrimination, 350
    sex discrimination, 347–348
  group discrimination, 344–345
  harassment
    employers' obligations, 355–356
    generally, 353–354
    legal framework, 355
    meaning, 353
    sexual, 356

  indirect discrimination, 346–347
  individual discrimination, 344
  institutional discrimination, 345
  introduction, 338
  legislative framework, 343–344
  religion and belief, 352–353
  sex discrimination
    generally, 347
    genuine occupational requirement,
      347–348
    implications, 348
  sexual harassment, 356
  sexual orientation, 349–350
  victimisation, 347
Dismissal
  constructive, 400
  fair reasons for, 399–400
  introduction, 398
  unfair, 398–399
Display of information
  employment relationship, and, 313
Displayed advertising
  recruitment, 129
Diversity
  advantages to business, 341–342
  age discrimination, 353
  bullying
    employers' obligations, 355–356
    generally, 353–354
    legal framework, 355
    meaning, 353
  demographic changes, 339
  direct discrimination, 346
  disability discrimination
    generally, 350–351
    reasonable adjustments, 351
  discrimination
    age discrimination, 353
    bullying, 353–356
    categories, 346–347
    direct discrimination, 346
    disability discrimination, 350–351
    gender reassignment, 348–349
    generally, 344
    group discrimination, 344–345
    harassment, 353–356
    indirect discrimination, 346–347
    individual discrimination, 344
    institutional discrimination, 345
    introduction, 338
    legislative framework, 343–344
    racial discrimination, 350

religion and belief, 352–353
  sex discrimination, 347–348
  sexual orientation, 349–350
  victimisation, 347
equal opportunity, 341
gender reassignment, 348–349
genuine occupational requirement
  racial discrimination, 350
  sex discrimination, 347–348
group discrimination, 344–345
harassment
  employers' obligations, 355–356
  generally, 353–354
  legal framework, 355
  meaning, 353
  sexual, 356
importance
  business case, 340–341
  social justice case, 340
indirect discrimination, 346–347
individual differences, 338–339
individual discrimination, 344
institutional discrimination, 345
introduction, 337
organisational
  demographic changes, 339
  individual differences, 338–339
  introduction, 338
  nature, 339
perspectives, 339–340
prejudice
  generally, 342
  introduction, 338
  stereotyping, 342–343
recruitment
  context, 121
  success factors, 123
religion and belief, 352–353
selection, 139
sex discrimination
  generally, 347
  genuine occupational requirement,
    347–348
  implications, 348
sexual harassment, 356
sexual orientation, 349–350
social justice, 340
stereotyping, 342–343
summary, 356
victimisation, 347

Electronic fit notes

employment relationship, and, 330
Electronic recruitment
  advantages, 132–133
  disadvantages, 132–133
  introduction, 132
Employee relations
  human resource planning, 107
Employee reward
  bonus schemes, 258
  'cafeteria' benefits, 250–251
  contingency pay
    bonus schemes, 258
    equity pay schemes, 255
    fixed incremental pay schemes, 257–258
    generally, 255
    incentive pay schemes, 255–256
    measured daywork, 258
    payment by results schemes, 256–257
    team reward scheme, 258–259
  definition, 248
  equal pay reviews, 269–270
  equal value, and, 262–264
  equity pay schemes, 255
  financial value, with, 251–252
  fixed incremental pay schemes, 257–258
  flexible benefits, 250–251
  'green' reward, 269
  human resource development, 248–249
  human resource planning, 107
  incentive pay schemes, 255–256
  influencing factors, 252–254
  introduction, 247
  job evaluation schemes
    equal value, and, 262–264
    introduction, 259
    job grading/classification, 260–261
    job ranking, 259–260
    management consultants' schemes,
      261–262
    points rating, 261
  job grading/classification, 260–261
  job ranking, 259–260
  legislative impacts, 267–268
  management consultants' schemes,
    261–262
  measured daywork, 258
  national minimum wage
    generally, 270–271
    introduction, 267
  'new pay' concept, 248–249
  non-financial rewards, 249–250
  payment by results schemes, 256–257

perceptions, 248
performance management, 237
performance-related pay
   generally, 264–265
   guidelines, 266
   influence of individual differences, 265
   operation, 266–267
points rating, 261
strategy, 253–254
summary, 271–272
systems, 254
team reward scheme, 258–259
total reward, 268
wages and salaries, 254–255
Employee utilisation
human resource planning, 107
Employee well-being
See also **Health and safety**
co-ordinators, 330
education programme for GPs, 330
employee assistance programmes, 333–334
fit notes, 330
government encouragement, 329–331
introduction, 329
legislative framework, 331–332
National Centre, 330–331
role of organisations, 332–333
Employer branding
induction, 161
Employers' liability insurance
employment relationship, and, 312
Employment agencies
recruitment, 128
Employment law
adoption leave, 366
ante-natal care, 365
company handbook, 364
data protection
   employers' obligations, 391
   generally, 388
   individual rights, 388
   personal data, 389
   policy, 392
   processing data, 391
   relevant filing system, 389
   sensitive data, 389–391
disciplinary procedures
   contents, 377
   disciplinary meeting, 380
   generally, 376–377
   handling, 377–378
   invoking, 381–382

   mediation, and, 382
   record-keeping, 379–380
   role of HR, 381
   rules, 375–376
   structure, 378–379
discrimination
   Equality and Human Rights
      Commission, 371–372
   legislative framework, 370–371
   race discrimination, 370
   sex discrimination, 369–370
employees' rights
   company handbook, 364
   introduction, 362
   statement of terms and conditions,
      362–363
   termination of employment, 365
   time off, 364
   variation of terms and conditions,
      363–364
equal pay, 368–369
equality
   equal pay, 368–369
   part-time workers, 369
   race discrimination, 370
   sex discrimination, 369–370
Equality and Human Rights Commission,
   371–372
express terms, 361
family-friendly rights
   adoption leave, 366
   ante-natal care, 365
   flexible working, 367–368
   maternity leave, 365
   working time, 366–367
fixed-term contracts, 360
flexible working, 367–368
formation, 359
grievance procedures
   conduct of interview, 375
   generally, 373–374
   initial interview, 374
   preparation for interview, 375
health and safety, 382–386
implied terms, 361
introduction, 358–359
maternity leave, 365
national minimum wage, 372–373
part-time workers, 369
pay, 372
race discrimination, 370
record-keeping

authorised access to information,
387–388
confidentiality, 386
data protection, 388–393
introduction, 386
legislative requirements, 387–388
sex discrimination, 369–370
summary, 393–394
temporary contracts, 359
termination of employment
constructive dismissal, 400
dismissal, 398–400
employee, by, 397
employer, by, 398–406
exit interviews, 397
introduction, 396
overview, 365
redundancy, 400–406
retirement, 406
summary, 406–407
unfair dismissal, 398–399
terms and conditions
company handbook, 364
generally, 361–362
statement, 362–363
variation, 363–364
time off, 364
types, 359–361
wages and salary, 372
working time, 366–367
zero hours contract, 360–36
Employment relationship
absence
Bradford factor, 295–296
conclusions, 296–297
controls, 294
management, 293–294
measurement, 295–297
policy, 294
reasons, 294–295
return-to-work interviews, 296
summary, 297
ACAS, 290
BusinessEurope, 280
Central Arbitration Committee, 290–291
collective bargaining
distributive bargaining, 291–292
generally, 291
integrative bargaining, 291–292
procedural agreements, 293
substantive agreements, 293
types, 291

Confederation of British Industry, 280
differences between contracts, 275–276
disciplinary procedures, 293
Engineering Employers Federation, 281
European Trades Union Confederation,
288–289
Institute of Directors, 280
internal justice system, 293
introduction, 274–275
meaning, 275
parties
BusinessEurope, 280
CBI, 280
EEF, 281
Institute of Directors, 280
introduction, 279–280
professional bodies, 281
trade unions, 282–291
perspectives
introduction, 277
pluralistic, 278
unitary, 277–278
professional bodies, 281
psychological contract, as
breach, 277
generally, 276–277
recruitment, and, 300
retention, and, 300
return-to-work interviews, 296
summary, 307–308
Trades Union Congress
generally, 286–288
learning, and, 287–288
trade unions
ACAS, 290
CAC, 290–291
ETUC, 288–289
generally, 282–284
learning, and, 287–288
legal framework, 284–285
membership, 286
representation, 285
role, 282
TUC, 286–288
unitary perspective, 277–278
work-life balance
achieving, 298
business case, 300
choice of employer, 301
consideration of offer, 301–302
consultation, 305
employers' role, 302–307

legislative framework, 304–305
long-hours culture, 299–300
meaning of 'work', 297
organisation, 300
requests and entitlement, 305
role of 'work', 298
strictness of regime, 300–301
time management, 299
voluntary measures, 305–306
'Enculturalisation'
organisational culture, 39–40
Engineering Employers Federation
employment relationship, and, 281
Equal opportunity
diversity and equality, 341
selection
generally, 141
interviews, 152
Equal pay
employee reward, 269–270
employment law, 368–369
Equal value
employee reward, 262–264
Equality
equal pay, 368–369
part-time workers, 369
race discrimination, 370
selection, 139
sex discrimination, 369–370
Equality and Human Rights Commission
generally, 371–372
Equity pay schemes
employee reward, 255
Equity theory
motivation, 235–236
ERG Theory
motivation, 231
Ethnocentrism
organisational culture, 25–26
European Trades Union Confederation
employment relationship, and, 288–289
Exit interviews
human resource planning, 104
termination of employment, 397
Expectancy theory
motivation, 234–235
Experiential learning
learning, and, 187–188
Express terms
contracts of employment, 361
External labour market
human resource planning, 97–98

recruitment, 122
Extrinsic job factors
motivation, 232

Family-friendly rights
adoption leave, 366
ante-natal care, 365
flexible working, 367–368
maternity leave, 365
working time, 366–367
Financial value
employee reward, 251–252
Fit notes
employment relationship, and, 330
Fixed incremental pay schemes
employee reward, 257–258
Fixed-term contracts
employment law, 360
Flexibility of organisations
core workers, 17–19
flexible working, 17
generally, 17
numerical flexibility, 18
peripheral workers, 17–19
recruitment, 121
virtual organisation, 19
Flexible benefits
employee reward, 250–251
Flexible working
employment law, 367–368
work-life balance, 305
Flipcharts
human resource development, 216
Forecasting HR demand
introduction, 98–99
managerial judgment, 99
modelling, 100–101
ratio-trend analysis, 100
work study techniques, 100
Forecasting HR supply
dealing with deficits and surpluses,
105–106
internal supply, 101
introduction, 101
staff turnover, 101–104

Gender reassignment
generally, 348–349
Genuine occupational requirement
racial discrimination, 350
sex discrimination, 347–348
Graphology

selection, 146
'Green' reward
    employee reward, 269
Grievance procedures
    conduct of interview, 375
    generally, 373–374
    initial interview, 374
    preparation for interview, 375
Group discrimination
    generally, 344–345

Handbook
    induction, 170–171
Harassment
    employers' obligations, 355–356
    generally, 353–354
    legal framework, 355
    meaning, 353
    sexual, 356
'Hard' human resource management
    generally, 54
Health and safety
    accidents at work
        behavioural causes, 317
        environmental causes, 316–317
        introduction, 316
        physiological causes, 317
    advice, 312
    audits, 321
    consultation, 312
    display of information, 313
    electronic fit notes, 330
    employee well-being, and
        co-ordinators, 330
        education programme for GPs, 330
        employee assistance programmes,
            333–334
        fit notes, 330
        government encouragement, 329–331
        introduction, 329
        legislative framework, 331–332
        National Centre, 330–331
        role of organisations, 332–333
    employers' liability insurance, 312
    employment law, 382–386
    fit notes, 330
    generally, 311
    Health and Safety at Work Act 1974, 311
    Health and Safety Executive, 311–312
    healthy-workplace initiatives, 319–320
    introduction, 310
    legislative framework, 311–313

    management in the workplace
        generally, 318
        measurement of safety performance, 319
        planning, 318–319
    measurement of safety performance, 319
    National Centre for Working-Age and
        Well-Being, 330–331
    non-accidental health problems
        generally, 319
        healthy-workplace initiatives, 319–320
        taskforce survey, 320
    obligations of organisations, 312–313
    planning, 318–319
    policy, 313
    registration, 313
    reporting accidents, diseases and events,
        313
    risk assessment
        code of practice, 314
        generally, 313–314
        procedure, 314–316
        severity rating, 315
        statutory regulation, 314
    stress-related ill-health
        activity facilities, 328
        'caring' organisation, 327–329
        case example, 328–329
        chronic stress, 326
        commuting, 323
        consultation, 327
        duties of employer, 323
        dynamics, 324–325
        extent of problem, 322
        generally, 321–322
        government's response, 326–327
        health checks, 328
        human function curve, 324
        legal requirements, 323
        management, 326
        organisational causes, 325
        post-traumatic stress disorder, 326
        productivity, 323–324
        provision of information to employees,
            327–328
        role of organisation, 325–326
        smoke-free work areas, 327
        sources of stress, 323
        transient stress, 326
    summary, 334–335
    toilet facilities, 312
    training, 312
    washing facilities, 312

Health checks
occupational stress, and, 328
Healthy-workplace initiatives
employment relationship, and, 319–320
'Hierarchy of needs'
motivation, 230–231
Higher apprenticeships
human resource planning, 88
HR professional's role
alignment of HR to corporate strategy, 76
CIPD Profession Map, 81--83
competitive advantage, and, 61–62
information systems
computerised, 77–78
confidentiality, 77
contents of records, 79
legal aspects of record keeping, 80
statistical information, 80
use and maintenance of records, 78
use of individual information, 80
introduction, 71–73
Next Generation HR, 83–84
responsibilities, 72
scope of activities, 73–76
summary, 84–85
Human capital
learning, 183–184
Human resource development
analysis and review, 221
apprenticeships, 204
assessment centres, 207
beneficiaries
individuals, 202–203
introduction, 202
the organisation, 203
the state, 203
development centres, 207
diplomas, 204
employee reward, 248–249
evaluate the course
generally, 219–220
method, 220–221
identification of training needs
generally, 207
methods, 207
needs analysis, 208
implement the training
cost-effectiveness, 212
course development, 212–214
course preparation, 214–219
flipcharts, 216
in-house courses, 211

introduction, 210–211
methods and media, 215
running the session, 216–219
structure of course, 215
training consultants, 212
training media, 213–214
training plan, 215–216
venue, 214–215
visual aids, 216
Investors in People, 205
introduction, 200
Leitch review, 204
national skills strategy
apprenticeships, 204
background, 204
diplomas, 204
Investors in People, 205
'train to gain', 204
needs analysis, 208
off-the-job training, 209
on-the-job training, 209
performance appraisal, 207
plan the training
generally, 209
strategies, 209–210
recruitment, and, 201–202
set training objectives
generally, 208
SMART, 208–209
strategic importance, 201–203
summary, 221
systematic training
components of cycle, 206–221
developing training courses, 206
introduction, 205
policy, 205–206
systematic training cycle
analysis and review, 221
evaluate the course, 219–221
identification of training needs, 207–208
implement the training, 210–219
introduction, 206–207
plan the training, 209–210
set training objectives, 208–209
talent management, and, 201–202
'time to train' legislation, 202
'train to gain', 204
training, and, 201
training needs analysis, 208
Human resource management (HRM)
bureaucracy, 47
competitive advantage

best-fit model of SHRM, 57–58
best practice model of SHRM, 59–60
resource-based view of organisation, 60
restructuring the organisation, 62–63
role of HR professional, 61–62
structuring human resources in the
    organisation, 61
control and compliance, 50
customer service
    generally, 63–67
    relationship management, 67–68
    summary, 68
development of approach, 51–54
'hard' HRM, 54
introduction, 44
meaning, 45–57
operations, 56
organisation type, 45–47
resource-based view of organisation, 60
restructuring the organisation, 62–63
retention, and, 177–178
role of HR professional, 61–62
service level agreement, 68
socio-technical system, 50–51
'soft' HRM, 55–56
Storey's '27 points of difference'
    generally, 46
    table, 48–50
strategic HRM
    best-fit model, 57–58
    best practice model, 59–60
    generally, 56–57
strategy, 56
structuring human resources in the
    organisation, 61
summary, 68–69
theories and theorists, 49
traditional management, and, 47
Human resource planning (HRP)
analysis and investigation
    corporate capability, 98
    corporate strategy, 98
    external labour market, 97–98
    internal labour market, 96–97
    introduction, 96
appraisal, 107
apprenticeships, 88
business strategy, 115
cohort analysis, 103–104
communication, 107
competence-centred function, as, 95
content of plan, 106–107

corporate capability, 98
corporate strategy, 98
deficits and surpluses of staff, 105–106
definitions, 91
departmental distribution of turnover,
    102–103
employee relations, 107
employee utilisation, 107
exit interviews, 104
external labour market, 97–98
forecasting demand
    introduction, 98–99
    managerial judgment, 99
    modelling, 100–101
    ratio-trend analysis, 100
    work study techniques, 100
forecasting supply
    dealing with deficits and surpluses,
        105–106
    internal supply, 101
    introduction, 101
    staff turnover, 101–104
form of plan, 106–107
growth, 88
historical background, 87–88
implementation of plan, 114–115
importance, 93
internal labour market, 96–97
introduction, 87
job analysis
    examination of documents, 111
    information gathering, 110–114
    introduction, 107–108
    job-holder interviews, 111–113
    line manager interviews, 113
    meaning, 108
    observational techniques, 113
    purpose, 108
    relevant information, 110
job descriptions
    flexible approach, 109
    introduction, 109
    role definition, 109–110
job-holder interviews
    conduct, 112
    generally, 111
    preparation, 111–112
    questionnaire, 112–113
line manager interviews, 113
management development, 107
manpower planning, 89–91
modelling, 100–101

modern approach
   generally, 114
   introduction, 94–95
nature, 92–94
organisation, 106
performance, 107
planning periods, 92
plans, 106–107
process, 93–94
ratio-trend analysis, 100
retention of staff, and, 176–177
reward, 107
shadowing the business plan, and, 95
staff turnover
   analyses, 104
   calculation, 101
   cohort analysis, 103–104
   departmental distribution of turnover,
      102–103
   exit interviews, 104
   workforce stability index, 103
structure, 106
summary, 116
supply, 106
traditional approach, 94–95
training development, 107
work study techniques, 100
workforce stability index, 103

Identification of training needs
   generally, 207
   methods, 207
   needs analysis, 208
Implied terms
   employment law, 361
Incentive pay schemes
   employee reward, 255–256
Indirect discrimination
   generally, 346–347
Induction
   accommodation, 162
   approaches, 163–164
   buddy systems, 173–174
   coaching, 164
   company handbook, 170–171
   department, by, 171--172
   duration, 169–170
   employer branding, 161
   generally, 158–159
   importance, 160
   induction pack, 163–164
   influential factors, 162–163

initial briefing, 165
interviews, 172--173
introduction, 158
media, 166
mentoring
   generally, 173–174
   introduction, 164
minority groups, and, 167–168
organisational culture, and, 39–40
positive action
   case example, 167–168
   introduction, 167
   meaning, 169
   options available, 168–169
   training, 169
purpose, 159
socialisation, 162
special needs, and, 167
stages
   initial briefing, 165
   introduction, 164
   media, 166
   purpose, 166
   training, 165–166
success indicators, 161–163
terms and conditions of employment, 170
training
   generally, 165–166
   introduction, 164
'walk'n'talk', 164
Information handling and management
classification
   introduction, 432
   operational information, 433
   strategic information, 432
   tactical information, 433
collection
   case example, 433
   introduction, 432
   operational information, 433
   strategic information, 432
   tactical information, 433
computerised, 77–78
confidentiality, 77
data protection
   data, 445
   defamation, 448
   disclosure of convictions, 448
   enforcement, 446–447
   exemptions, 446
   generally, 444
   individual rights, 445–446

law in practice, 448
principles, 447
defamation, 448
disclosure of convictions, 448
freedom of information, 448
HR information systems
    range and extent of information held,
        436–437
    structure and use, 77–80
    types, 436–439
operational information, 433
record keeping, 80
statistical information, 80
strategic information, 432
structure and use of information systems
    computerised, 77–78
    confidentiality, 77
    contents of records, 79
    legal aspects of record keeping, 80
    statistical information, 80
    use and maintenance of records, 78
    use of individual information, 80
summary, 449–450
tactical information, 433
use and maintenance of records, 78
use to best advantage, 439–444
use of individual information, 80
'In-groups'
organisational culture, 25–26
In-house courses
human resource development, 211
Initial briefing
induction, 165
Insight learning
learning, and, 190
Institute of Directors
employment relationship, and, 280
Institutional discrimination
generally, 345
Internal justice system
employment relationship, and, 293
Internal labour market
human resource planning, 96–97
recruitment, 121
Interviews
administrative preparation, 142
arrival of candidates, 142–143
closure, 152
competence-based, 147–149
conduct, 143–144
equal opportunities, 152
format, 147–152

induction, and, 172–173
initial exchanges, 150
open questions, 151
organisation, 141
performance form, 149
problem areas, 150–151
questioning techniques, 151–152
screening, 141
structured, 147–148
telephone, by, 142
types, 150
unstructured, 147–148
use of application form, 149–150
waiting by candidates, 142–143
Intrinsic job factors
motivation, 232–233
Investors in People
human resource development, 205

Job analysis
examination of documents, 111
information gathering, 110–114
introduction, 107–108
job-holder interviews
    conduct, 112
    generally, 111
    preparation, 111–112
    questionnaire, 112–113
line manager interviews, 113
meaning, 108
observational techniques, 113
purpose, 108
recruitment, and, 124
relevant information, 110
Job classification
employee reward, 260–261
Job descriptions
flexible approach, 109
introduction, 109
recruitment, and, 124–125
role definition, 109–110
Job evaluation schemes
equal value, and, 262–264
introduction, 259
job grading/classification, 260–261
job ranking, 259–260
management consultants' schemes,
    261–262
points rating, 261
Job grading
employee reward, 260–261
Job-holder interviews

conduct, 112
generally, 111
preparation, 111–112
questionnaire, 112–113
Job ranking
employee reward, 259–260
Job simulation
selection, 145
Jobcentres
recruitment, 129

Knowledge management
learning, 183–184
Kolb's learning cycle
learning, 191–193

Labour markets
recruitment, 121–122
Language
organisational culture, 36
Large commercial enterprises
size of organisations, 6
Latent learning
learning, and, 191
Learning
career planning, and, 196–198
early theories
behaviourism, 190
classical conditioning, 189
cognitive learning, 190–191
insight learning, 190
introduction, 189
latent learning, 191
operant conditioning, 189–190
factors
experiential learning, 187–188
introduction, 186
learning situation, 187
personal characteristics, 186
planned experience, 188–189
trainer's qualities, 187
human capital, 183–184
introduction, 183
knowledge management, 183–184
modern theories
action learning, 191
introduction, 191
Kolb's learning cycle, 191–193
learning styles, 193–195
principles, 185
self-learning, 185
social learning, 185–186

strategic importance, 182–183
summary, 198
systematic learning, 186
transfer, 196
Leitch review
human resource development, 204
Lewin's three-phase model
consultation with employees, 421–422
introduction, 421
levers of change, 422–423
moving or changing, 422–423
refreezing, 423
unfreezing, 421–422
Line manager interviews
human resource planning, 113
'Long' shortlist
selection, 140–141
Love and esteem
motivation, 231

Management consultants' schemes
employee reward, 261–262
Manpower planning
human resource planning, 89–91
Maternity leave
employment law, 365
work-life balance, 304
Matrix organisations
organisational structures, 15–17
Measured daywork
employee reward, 258
Mechanistic organisations
classification of organisations, 5
Medical examination
selection, 154
Mentoring
generally, 173–174
introduction, 164
Minimum wage
employment law, 372–373
generally, 270–271
introduction, 267
Minority groups
induction, 167–168
Modelling
human resource planning, 100–101
Motivation
belongingness, 231
content theories, 230–234
equity theory, 235–236
ERG Theory, 231
expectancy theory, 234–235

extrinsic job factors, 232
generally, 228
'hierarchy of needs', 230–231
intrinsic job factors, 232–233
love and esteem, 231
motivation-hygiene theory, 231–232
physiological needs, 230
Porter and Lawler's theory, 234–235
process theories, 234–236
safety and security, 231
scientific management,. 229–230
self-actualisation, 231
theories
    content, 230–234
    introduction, 230
    process, 234–236
    summary, 236
Theory X and Theory Y, 233
Mutual benefit organisations
classification of organisations, 4

National Centre for Working-Age and Well-Being
employment relationship, and, 330–331
National minimum wage
employment law, 372–373
generally, 270–271
introduction, 267
National skills strategy
apprenticeships, 204
background, 204
diplomas, 204
Investors in People, 205
'train to gain', 204
Nationalised industries
classification of organisations, 5
Needs analysis
human resource development, 208
Next Generation HR
generally, 83–84
Norms
generally, 23
power of, 23–24
Numerical flexibility
organisational structures, 18

Occupational stress
activity facilities, 328
'caring' organisation, 327–329
case example, 328–329
chronic stress, 326
commuting, 323
consultation, 327
duties of employer, 323
dynamics, 324–325
extent of problem, 322
generally, 321–322
government's response, 326–327
health checks, 328
human function curve, 324
legal requirements, 323
management, 326
organisational causes, 325
post-traumatic stress disorder, 326
productivity, 323–324
provision of information to employees, 327–328
role of organisation, 325–326
smoke-free work areas, 327
sources of stress, 323
transient stress, 326
Occupational tests
conduct, 145
cultural differences, 145
design, 144
generally, 143
job simulation, 145
psychometric testing, 144
purpose, 144
use, 144–145
work sampling, 145
Off-the-job training
human resource development, 209
On-the-job training
human resource development, 209
Operant conditioning
learning, and, 189–190
Offer of employment
CRB checks, 154–155
introduction, 154
medical examination, 154
other checks, 154–155
Organic organisations
classification of organisations, 5–6
Organisational culture
achievement culture, 35
boundaries, 27–28
change, 40
classification of thought, 31–32
communications, 36
company practices, 36
cultural fit, 38
cultural shift, 38–39
definitions, 24–25

differences, 27
dissection, 40–41
'enculturalisation', 39–40
ethnocentrism, 25–26
identification
    generally, 33–36
    introduction, 25
    public sector, in, 36–37
importance of place, 37–39
individual differences, 33
'in-groups', 25–26
induction of new members, 39–40
industrial culture, 29–31
integration of diverse elements, 39
introduction, 22
language, 36
location, 26
meaning, 22–25
norms
    generally, 23
    power of, 23–24
organisational values, 33
person culture, 34
physical culture, 25
power culture, 34–35
purpose of study, 32–33
role culture, 34–35
societal culture, 28–31
subcultures, 31
subjective culture, 25
summary, 41–42
support culture, 35
task culture, 34
values and norms
    generally, 23
    power of, 23–24
Organisations
classification, 4–5
core workers, 17–19
corporate strategy, 7
culture
    See also Organisational culture
    boundaries, 27–28
    change, 40
    classification of thought, 31–32
    definitions, 24–25
    differences, 27
    dissection, 40–41
    'enculturalisation', 39–40
    ethnocentrism, 25–26
    identification, 33–37
    importance of place, 37–39

individual differences, 33
'in-groups', 25–26
industrial culture, 29–31
introduction, 22
location, 26
meaning, 22–25
organisational values, 33
purpose of study, 32–33
societal culture, 28–31
subcultures, 31
summary, 41–42
values and norms, 23–24
definitions, 3–5
development, 8
flexibility
    core workers, 17–19
    flexible working, 17
    generally, 17
    numerical flexibility, 18
    peripheral workers, 17–19
    virtual organisation, 19
introduction, 1
justification, 2
matrix organisations, 15–17
mechanistic organisations, 5
numerical flexibility, 18
objectives, 7–8
organic organisations, 5–6
peripheral workers, 17–19
PESTLE analysis
    generally, 9–11
    use, 11
policies, 7–8
private sector, in, 3
public sector, in, 2
purpose, 7
size, 6–7
span of control, 14–15
STEEPLE analysis
    generally, 9–11
    use, 11
strategic planning techniques
    generally, 8–9
    PESTLE analysis, 9–11
    STEEPLE analysis, 9–11
    SWOT analysis, 9
    use, 11
structures
    design, 13–14
    flexibility, 17–19
    generally, 12–13
    matrix organisations, 15–17

span of control, 14–15
summary, 19–20
SWOT analysis
  generally, 9
  use, 11
survival, 8
types, 2–3
virtual organisation, 19

Parental leave
work-life balance, 304
Part-time workers
employment law, 369
work-life balance, 305
Paternity leave
work-life balance, 305
Pay
employment law, 372
Payment by results schemes
employee reward, 256–257
Peer assessment
selection, 146
Performance agreements
generally, 240
Performance appraisal
generally, 237
human resource development, 207
human resource planning, 107
interview, 241–243
Personal development plans
beneficiaries, 24
generally, 243–244
introduction, 240
learning activities, 244–245
self-appraisal, 245
Performance management
358-degree feedback, 240–241
appraisal
  generally, 237
  interview, 241–243
assessment systems
  appraisal, 237
  establishing criteria, 238
  introduction, 237
  potential, 237
  reward, 237
background, 223–224
behaviour, as, 226–227
definitions, 224
development, through, 225
influencing factors
  generally, 227–228

motivation, 228
organisational, 228
table, 227
introduction, 223
meaning, 226–227
motivation
  belongingness, 231
  content theories, 230–234
  equity theory, 235–236
  ERG Theory, 231
  expectancy theory, 234–235
  extrinsic job factors, 232
  generally, 228
  'hierarchy of needs', 230–231
  intrinsic job factors, 232–233
  love and esteem, 231
  motivation-hygiene theory, 231–232
  physiological needs, 230
  Porter and Lawler's theory, 234–235
  process theories, 234–236
  safety and security, 231
  scientific management,. 229–230
  self-actualisation, 231
  summary of theories, 236
  theories, 230–236
  Theory X and Theory Y, 233
organisational factors, 227–228
performance agreements, 240
personal development plans
  beneficiaries, 24
  generally, 243–244
  introduction, 240
  learning activities, 244–245
  self-appraisal, 245
poor performance management, 243
potential, 237
principles, 225–226
rating scales
  behaviourally anchored, 239
  generally, 238–239
reward, 237
subjectivity, and, 239–240
summary, 245–246
traditional systems, 238–240
Performance-related pay
generally, 264–265
guidelines, 266
influence of individual differences, 265
operation, 266–267
Peripheral workers
organisational structures, 17–19
Person specification

example, 127–128
generally, 125–126
structure, 126–127
Personal characteristics
learning, 186
PESTLE analysis
generally, 9–11
use, 11
Physiological needs
motivation, 230
Planning periods
human resource planning, 92
Points rating
employee reward, 261
Policies
employment relationship, 313
organisations, 7–8
selection, 139
Porter and Lawler's theory
motivation, 234–235
Positive action
case example, 167–168
introduction, 167
meaning, 169
options available, 168–169
training, 169
Post-traumatic stress disorder
occupational stress, and, 326
Prejudice
generally, 342
introduction, 338
stereotyping, 342–343
Private companies
classification of organisations, 5
Private sector organisations
generally, 3
Process theories
motivation, 234–236
Professional bodies
employment relationship, and, 281
Psychometric testing
selection, 144
Public interest companies
classification of organisations, 5
Public PLCs
classification of organisations, 5
Public sector organisations
generally, 2
size of organisations, and, 6
Public-private partnerships
classification of organisations, 5

Race discrimination
employment law, 370
Rating scales
behaviourally anchored, 239
generally, 238–239
Ratio-trend analysis
human resource planning, 100
Record-keeping
computerised information systems, 77–78
confidentiality, 77
contents of records, 79
employment law, and
authorised access to information,
387–388
confidentiality, 386
data protection, 388–393
introduction, 386
legislative requirements, 387–388
legal aspects, 80
statistical information, 80
use and maintenance of records, 78
use of individual information, 80
Recruitment
advertising
content, 130–131
electronically, 132
external, 129
generally, 128–129
internal, 128
other media, 131
placement, 130
responses, 133
types, 129
application forms, 133
authority to recruit, 124
case example, 133–135
classified advertising, 129
context
diversity, 121
flexibility, 121
generally, 120
labour markets, 121–122
success factors, 122–123
definitions, 120
displayed advertising, 129
diversity
context, 121
success factors, 123
electronic recruitment
advantages, 132–133
disadvantages, 132–133
introduction, 132

employment agencies, 128

employment relationship, and, 300

external labour market, 122

flexibility, 121

identification of vacancy, 124

internal labour market, 121

introduction, 119

job analysis, 124

job description, 124–125

Jobcentres, 129

labour markets, 121–122

person specification

    example, 127–128

    generally, 125–126

    structure, 126–127

process

    authority to recruit, 124

    identification of vacancy, 124

    introduction, 123

    job analysis, 124

    job description, 124–125

    person specification, 125–128

    stages, 123

selection consultants, 128

skill shortages, 123

success factors, 122–123

summary, 135

systematic recruitment cycle, 123–128

unemployment, and, 122–123

'work experience' students, 128

Redundancy

avoiding, 406

dealing with survivors, 405–406

disclosure of information, 402--403

generally, 400–401

handling, 401–402

pay, 403

selection, 403–405

voluntary severance, 403

References

selection, 146

Regulated private companies

classification of organisations, 5

Religion and belief discrimination

generally, 352–353

Reporting accidents, diseases and events

employment relationship, and, 313

Restructuring the organisation

human resource management, 62–63

Retention

contractor organisations, and, 178

employment relationship, and, 300

generally, 175–176

human resource management, and,
    177–178

introduction, 174–175

plan, 176–177

recording information, 178

summary, 179–180

Retirement

termination of employment, 406

Return-to-work interviews

absences, and, 296

Reward

bonus schemes, 258

'cafeteria' benefits, 250–251

contingency pay

    bonus schemes, 258

    equity pay schemes, 255

    fixed incremental pay schemes, 257–258

    generally, 255

    incentive pay schemes, 255–256

    measured daywork, 258

    payment by results schemes, 256–257

    team reward scheme, 258–259

definition, 248

equal pay reviews, 269–270

equal value, and, 262–264

equity pay schemes, 255

financial value, with, 251–252

fixed incremental pay schemes, 257–258

flexible benefits, 250–251

'green' reward, 269

human resource development, 248–249

human resource planning, 107

incentive pay schemes, 255–256

influencing factors, 252–254

introduction, 247

job evaluation schemes

    equal value, and, 262–264

    introduction, 259

    job grading/classification, 260–261

    job ranking, 259–260

    management consultants' schemes,
        261–262

    points rating, 261

job grading/classification, 260–261

job ranking, 259–260

legislative impacts, 267–268

management consultants' schemes,
    261–262

measured daywork, 258

national minimum wage

    generally, 270–271

introduction, 267
'new pay' concept, 248–249
non-financial rewards, 249–250
payment by results schemes, 256–257
perceptions, 248
performance management, 237
performance-related pay
  generally, 264–265
  guidelines, 266
  influence of individual differences, 265
  operation, 266–267
points rating, 261
strategy, 253–254
summary, 271–272
systems, 254
team reward scheme, 258–259
total reward, 268
wages and salaries, 254–255
Risk assessment
code of practice, 314
generally, 313–314
procedure, 314–316
severity rating, 315
statutory regulation, 314
Role of HR professionals
alignment of HR to corporate strategy, 76
CIPD Profession Map, 81--83
competitive advantage, and, 61–62
information systems
  computerised, 77–78
  confidentiality, 77
  contents of records, 79
  legal aspects of record keeping, 80
  statistical information, 80
  use and maintenance of records, 78
  use of individual information, 80
introduction, 71–73
Next Generation HR, 83–84
responsibilities, 72
scope of activities, 73–76
summary, 84–85

Safety and security
motivation, 231
Scientific management
motivation,. 229–230
Selection
assessment centres, 143
biodata, 146
candidate ranking form, 153
CRB checks, 154–155
cultural differences, 145

decision-making, 152–153
diversity, 139
equal opportunities
  generally, 141
  interviews, 152
equality, 139
graphology, 146
interviews
  administrative preparation, 142
  arrival of candidates, 142–143
  closure, 152
  competence-based, 147–149
  conduct, 143–144
  equal opportunities, 152
  format, 147–152
  initial exchanges, 150
  open questions, 151
  organisation, 141
  performance form, 149
  problem areas, 150–151
  questioning techniques, 151–152
  screening, 141
  structured, 147–148
  telephone, by, 142
  types, 150
  unstructured, 147–148
  use of application form, 149–150
  waiting by candidates, 142–143
introduction, 137
job simulation, 145
'long' shortlist, 140–141
medical examination, 154
occupational tests
  conduct, 145
  cultural differences, 145
  design, 144
  generally, 143
  job simulation, 145
  psychometric testing, 144
  purpose, 144
  use, 144–145
  work sampling, 145
offer of employment
  CRB checks, 154–155
  introduction, 154
  medical examination, 154
  other checks, 154–155
peer assessment, 146
policy, 139
process
  assessment centres, 143
  equal opportunities, 141

interviews, 141–144
introduction, 139
job simulation, 145
'long' shortlist, 140–141
occupational tests, 143–144
psychometric testing, 144
screening applications, 140
shortlisting, 141
strategy, 140
tests, 141
work sampling, 145
psychometric testing, 144
references, 146
screening applications, 140
search for 'talent', 137–139
shortlisting, 141
sources of information, 146
strategy, 140
summary, 155–156
telephone interviews, 142
tests
   occupational, 143–144
   introduction, 141
   psychometric, 144
traditional methods, 138
work sampling, 145
Selection consultants
recruitment, 128
Self-actualisation
motivation, 231
Self-learning
learning, and, 185
Service level agreement
human resource management, 68
Service organisations
classification of organisations, 4
Sex discrimination
employment law, 369–370
generally, 347
genuine occupational requirement,
   347–348
implications, 348
Sexual harassment
generally, 356
Sexual orientation discrimination
generally, 349–350
Shortlisting
selection, 141
Skill shortages
recruitment, 123**1**
Small to medium-sized enterprises
   (SMEs)

size of organisations, and, 6
SMART
human resource development, 208–209
Smoke-free work areas
occupational stress, and, 327
Social justice
diversity and equality, 340
Social learning
learning, and, 185–186
Socialisation
induction, 162
Special needs employees
induction, 167
Socio-technical system
human resource management, 50–51
'Soft' human resource management
generally, 55–56
Span of control
organisational structures, 14–15
Staff turnover
analyses, 104
calculation, 101
cohort analysis, 103–104
departmental distribution of turnover,
   102–103
exit interviews, 104
workforce stability index, 103
Statistical information
information systems, and, 80
STEEPLE analysis
generally, 9–11
use, 11
Stereotyping
diversity and equality, 342–343
Storey's '27 points of difference'
human resource management
generally, 46
table, 48–50
Strategic human resource management
best-fit model, 57–58
best practice model, 59–60
generally, 56–57
Strategic planning techniques
generally, 8–9
PESTLE analysis, 9–11
STEEPLE analysis, 9–11
SWOT analysis, 9
use, 11
Stress-related ill-health
activity facilities, 328
'caring' organisation, 327–329
case example, 328–329

chronic stress, 326
commuting, 323
consultation, 327
duties of employer, 323
dynamics, 324–325
extent of problem, 322
generally, 321–322
government's response, 326–327
health checks, 328
human function curve, 324
legal requirements, 323
management, 326
organisational causes, 325
post-traumatic stress disorder, 326
productivity, 323–324
provision of information to employees,
    327–328
role of organisation, 325–326
smoke-free work areas, 327
sources of stress, 323
transient stress, 326
Subcultures
organisational culture, 31
Subjectivity
performance management, and, 239–240
SWOT analysis
generally, 9
use, 11
Systematic learning
learning, and, 186
Systematic training cycle
analysis and review, 221
evaluate the course
    generally, 219–220
    method, 220–221
identification of training needs
    generally, 207
    methods, 207
    needs analysis, 208
implement the training
    cost-effectiveness, 212
    course development, 212–214
    course preparation, 214–219
    flipcharts, 216
    in-house courses, 211
    introduction, 210–211
    methods and media, 215
    running the session, 216–219
    structure of course, 215
    training consultants, 212
    training media, 213–214
    training plan, 215–216
    venue, 214–215
    visual aids, 216
introduction, 206–207
plan the training
    generally, 209
    strategies, 209–210
set training objectives
    generally, 208
    SMART, 208–209

Team reward scheme
employee reward, 258–259
Telephone interviews
selection, 142
Temporary contracts
employment law, 359
Termination of employment
constructive dismissal, 400
dismissal
    constructive, 400
    fair reasons for, 399–400
    introduction, 398
    unfair, 398–399
employee, by, 397
employer, by, 398–406
exit interviews, 397
introduction, 396
lack of capability, 398
overview, 365
redundancy
    avoiding, 406
    dealing with survivors, 405–406
    disclosure of information,
        402–403
    generally, 400–401
    handling, 401–402
    pay, 403
    selection, 403–405
    voluntary severance, 403
retirement, 406
summary, 406–407
unfair dismissal, 398–399
Terms and conditions of employment
company handbook, 364
generally, 361–362
induction, and, 170
statement, 362–363
variation, 363–364
Theory X and Theory Y
motivation, 233
Time off
employment law, 364

'Time to train' legislation
  human resource development, 202
Toilet facilities
  employment relationship, and, 312
Total reward
  employee reward, 268
Trades Union Congress
  generally, 286–288
  learning, and, 287–288
Trade unions
  ACAS, 290
  CAC, 290–291
  ETUC, 288–289
  generally, 282–284
  learning, and, 287–288
  legal framework, 284–285
  membership, 286
  representation, 285
  role, 282
  TUC, 286–288
Training
  analysis and review, 221
  apprenticeships, 204
  assessment centres, 207
  beneficiaries
    individuals, 202–203
    introduction, 202
    the organisation, 203
    the state, 203
  development centres, 207
  diplomas, 204
  employment relationship, and, 312
  evaluate the course
    generally, 219–220
    method, 220–221
  identification of training needs
    generally, 207
    methods, 207
    needs analysis, 208
  implement the training
    cost-effectiveness, 212
    course development, 212–214
    course preparation, 214–219
    flipcharts, 216
    in-house courses, 211
    introduction, 210–211
    methods and media, 215
    running the session, 216–219
    structure of course, 215
    training consultants, 212
    training media, 213–214
    training plan, 215–216

    venue, 214–215
    visual aids, 216
  induction, and
    generally, 165–166
    introduction, 164
  Investors in People, 205
  introduction, 200
  Leitch review, 204
  national skills strategy
    apprenticeships, 204
    background, 204
    diplomas, 204
    Investors in People, 205
    'train to gain', 204
  needs analysis, 208
  off-the-job training, 209
  on-the-job training, 209
  performance appraisal, 207
  plan the training
    generally, 209
    strategies, 209–210
  recruitment, and, 201–202
  set training objectives
    generally, 208
    SMART, 208–209
  strategic importance, 201–203
  summary, 221
  systematic training
    components of cycle, 206–221
    developing training courses, 206
    introduction, 205
    policy, 205–206
  systematic training cycle
    analysis and review, 221
    evaluate the course, 219–221
    identification of training needs,
      207–208
    implement the training, 210–219
    introduction, 206–207
    plan the training, 209–210
    set training objectives, 208–209
  talent management, and, 201–202
  'time to train' legislation, 202
  'train to gain', 204
  training, and, 201
  training needs analysis, 208
Training consultants
  human resource development, 212
Training development
  human resource planning, 107
Training media
  human resource development, 213–214

Training plan
human resource development, 215–216

Unemployment
recruitment, 122–123
Unfair dismissal
termination of employment, 398–399

Values and norms
generally, 23
power of, 23–24
Victimisation
diversity and equality, 347
Virtual organisation
organisational structures, 19
Visual aids
human resource development, 216

Wages and salaries
employee reward, 254–255
employment law, 372
'Walk'n'talk'
induction, 164
Washing facilities
employment relationship, and, 312
'Work experience' students
recruitment, 128
Work sampling
selection, 145
Work study techniques
human resource planning, 100
Workforce stability index
human resource planning, 103
Working time
employment law, 366–367
work-life balance, 304
Work-life balance
achieving, 298
business case, 300
choice of employer, 301

consideration of offer, 301–302
consultation, 305
employers' role, 302–307
legislative framework, 304–305
long-hours culture, 299–300
meaning of 'work', 297
organisation, 300
requests and entitlement, 305
role of 'work', 298
strictness of regime, 300–301
time management, 299
voluntary measures, 305–306
Work-related stress
activity facilities, 328
'caring' organisation, 327–329
case example, 328–329
chronic stress, 326
commuting, 323
consultation, 327
duties of employer, 323
dynamics, 324–325
extent of problem, 322
generally, 321–322
government's response, 326–327
health checks, 328
human function curve, 324
legal requirements, 323
management, 326
organisational causes, 325
post-traumatic stress disorder, 326
productivity, 323–324
provision of information to employees,
327–328
role of organisation, 325–326
smoke-free work areas, 327
sources of stress, 323
transient stress, 326

Zero hours contract
employment law, 360–361